D1606305

Your Military Family Network

Copyright © 2008 by The Military Family Network

All rights reserved. No part of this book may be reproduced or utilized in any form or by any means, electronic or mechanical, including photocopying, recording, or by any information storage and retrieval system, without permission in writing from the publisher. Inquiries should be addressed to:

Capital Books, Inc.
P.O. Box 605
Herndon, Virginia 20172-0605

ISBN: 978-1-933102-35-1   (alk. paper)

Library of Congress Cataloging-in-Publication Data
Your military family network : your connection to military friendly
resources, benefits, information, businesses and advice / the Military
Family Network.
    p. cm. -- (A military family network book)
  ISBN 978-1-933102-35-1 (alk. paper)
 1. Families of military personnel--United States. 2. United States--Armed
Forces--Military life. 3. Military spouses--United States. I. Title. II
Series.

  UB403.Y78 2007
  355.1'20973--dc22

                              2007019977

Printed in the United States of America on acid-free paper that meets the American National Standards Institute Z39-48 Standard.

First Edition

10 9 8 7 6 5 4

The Military Family Network is not affiliated with the Department of Defense (DoD) or any branch of the Armed Services (Army, Navy, Air Force, Marines, or Coast Guard) and their inclusion in this book does not reflect endorsement by the DoD, any local government or their agencies. In matters pertaining to legal, financial, military, or medical concerns, please consult with your professional advisor or your military command. Although The Military Family Network believes that the information contained in this book is reliable and current at time of print, you are always advised to engage in due diligence before making financial contributions or donations.

Your Military Family Network

Your Connection to Military Friendly Resources, Benefits, Information, Businesses and Advice

The Military Family Network

CAPITAL
BOOKS, INC.
Sterling, Virginia

Dedication

For our active duty service members, our wounded, our veterans, our National Guard and Reserve, our fallen heroes, our military families, parents and children, and those who love them;

For all those answering the call to serve and those who have served and for the sacrifices they make and have made in the performance of that service for our nation;

For the heroes who live in the hearts of our communities around the world and for those who work everyday in support of them,

We humbly thank you and hope you find this resource and our Network helpful.

Contents

Acknowledgments

Your Military Family Network has been a labor of love for me. It has not only granted me the opportunity to provide a much needed resource for the military community, but it has given me the privilege to work closely with a variety of talented and dedicated individuals and organizations who have taken the time and effort to contribute their experience and knowledge to this book.

There are no words that can describe the beauty that occurs when passion, creativity, and mission align not simply with another but with many. It is an honor to know such people; and it is a testimony to our humanity that there are so many of us that care about our military service members, our veterans, their families, our neighbors and our communities.

As I stand back and survey the wealth of information and knowledge contained within these pages, recognizing that great individuals—all experts in their fields—created this resource, I am awed and humbled. It is more than I ever dreamed possible. When my colleagues and I began this project, who knew that we would gain from this experience as much as we gave? After all, our initial focus was to ease the burdens of daily life for those who carry the greater burden of defending our nation and protecting our freedom. To them, I am forever grateful. And to our contributors, I am sincerely indebted and offer my warmest appreciation. Caroline and Darrell, your hearts are worth their weight in gold and this is what makes The Military Family Network special. I am proud to call you friends, family and colleagues.

And to my husband, Luis, who worked selflessly and tirelessly, to keep me on point and to create an environment where I could work and prosper, I truly thank you. Your artistry always adds an element of beauty to everything you touch. I don't know where this book or I would be without your encouragement, support, and constant infusions of boundless energy. I am grateful to know you and fortunate to love you. Te amo con todo mi corazon.

—Megan Turak

When creating a project as important and impressive as this book, many people become involved and I would like to thank them. My biggest kudo goes to my best friend and wife, Megan Turak, who spent months and months making sure all materials submitted became relevant. Without her total commitment this book would not have become a reality. Megan, with all my love I say to you, Thank you.

—Luis Trevino

I must start by thanking my parents: my mom inspired me to dream, my dad instilled a moral compass and a sense of patriotism, and together they have shown me the very model of what a loving relationship is. A big tip of the hat goes to a high school teacher named Sara Auten, who helped me to believe in myself, and to Drill Sgt. Marlin, who showed a certain rebellious 19-year- old that discipline was not necessarily a bad thing. Tremendous thanks go also to my children: to my late son Jason, who taught me about hope in the face of overwhelming odds; to my son Jeremy, whose service in Iraq has helped me understand the perspective of a military family member; to my wonderful daughter Kelsey, who has sacrificed much herself so that this project may be completed. And finally, my MFN partners, Caroline, Megan, and Luis, deserve a wealth of gratitude: both for their tireless efforts on this project, and for their encouragement to me during my occasional less than enthusiastic moments. My sincerest thanks go to all of you, as well as to the countless others not named here.

—Darrell Shue

Foreword

U.S. Senator
John McCain

It is the company we keep, more than anything else, which forms our character. Twenty-two years of my life were spent in military service. I served with great men, many of whom paid a much higher price for their patriotism than was asked of me. I was blessed with the company of heroes, and it has made all the difference in the world.

During the Vietnam War, a group of students in Los Angeles started a campaign to show their support for prisoners of war. To this day, I continue to receive their POW bracelets, usually engraved with my name or that of a friend, which citizens wore during our imprisonment as a gesture of solidarity. In 1971, the Vietnamese dramatically altered the way they treated their prisoners of war. They had finally begun to realize that Americans cared about what happened to us. I believe this change can be attributed, in part, to the POW bracelet publicity campaign and the similar efforts of community-based programs.

In the years after my military career, I have been privileged to serve in elective office. One political duty that weighs heavily on my mind is the care and support of the servicemen and women who have, in the past and now, put themselves in harm's way to protect American lives and freedoms. Community and homegrown support are essential to the strength of our military forces.

The Military Family Network seeks to raise awareness of such military-friendly programs all over the world. Military families often lack adequate support as they move constantly, leaving behind friends and familiar associations and resources. As an information company owned by military spouses and veterans, The Military Family Network is uniquely qualified to facilitate these transitions.

The guidebook Your Military Family Network is a lifeline for veterans, military families, and anyone uprooted in the name of duty. It lists resources offered in each state and businesses that offer military discounts and military-friendly employment are also featured. Everyday my office receives letters from military families seeking guidance to these very resources. The Military

Family Network encourages families to recommend companies that demonstrate a capacity for military- and family-friendly service to the "Neighbor of Choice" business network. This is a valuable frame of reference for nomadic families that encourages them to build community relationships quickly.

Your Military Family Network then builds upon this database of community knowledge with insights from military members and spouses, as well as from leaders in their specific fields. Such topics range from an expert's definition and suggestions for treatment of Post Traumatic Stress Disorder, to helpful chapters provided by the Commissary Agency and the Military Exchange services on how best to use their benefits.

Military personnel are not the only ones to gain from Your Military Family Network. As a business catalyst, The Military Family Network has already proven itself with increased participation in the programs and special events it advertises. The City of Hampton, the Virginia Board of Elections, and the Armed Forces Job Fair Committee are among several community and installation boards that have all sought advice from the Military Family Network for successful interaction with the military community. Local businesses and events win when awareness is spread through the network.

With military branches seeing a swell in recruitment and the War on Terror calling many to see action, the demand for this network and the services it advertises will rise. As we see a higher number of servicemen return home requiring special services and physical therapy, I believe Your Military Family Network will quickly become a necessary guide for them and their families. It is important for America to demonstrate the pride we have for those good men and women serving our nation everyday at great personal cost. The continued show of grassroots support for them and their efforts not only boosts morale but also serves a greater common good.

—John McCain
United States Senator

How to Use this Book

Have you ever gone to a party where you were the friend of the friend who knew the person hosting the party? You were the outsider; you didn't know anybody and you felt out of place and the whole thing didn't seem like it was going to be much fun? Then, as the party wore on, you loosened up, began talking with others and before you knew it, you were having a great time. Well, this book is a little like that experience. Like that party, this book is so much more than it seems. If you simply sum it up to be another book for your bookshelf, than you have just missed out on a great party, because through these pages you will interact and engage with not only The Military Family Network but also many supporting organizations. You have friendships just waiting to be made. So while we want you to read this book, we also want you to become actively involved. Now we understand if you need to rush off and jump to another section of the book to uncover a certain mystery of military living, just remember to come back soon. Why? Because, how often are we reminded, "that when we signed the dotted line, we married the military?" Sometimes military folks can feel like followers, and this chapter will teach you how to turn that "follower" attitude into a "master of your own destiny" You'll become a follower with a plan! Sound like a paradox? Well, it's not and let's see why.

To become a "master of your own destiny," you must become informed. You need knowledge and information. You need to know. You need awareness about available resources to increase the range of options open to you. You need choice to ensure success and well-being. And, because of the nature of the military lifestyle, especially in regards to its mobility, we would venture to suggest that military families probably need to know a lot more than most families because they must integrate and conquer the scope of two communities, both military and civilian. So from communication and security to money and moving, from fitness and travel to employment and health, Your Military Family Network aims to get you connected.

We want to be your best friend—the friend that takes you to the party. You know, the friend that accompanies you everywhere; the friend you consult for advice and the friend that you trust most. We really want to be your *hand*book—we want to be on hand for you any time you need us. We are not strangers to you or your experience. We are members of the collective military family just like you.

Numerous members of this extended military community—each an expert in his or her field or profession—designed Your Military Family Network to guide you in your life with our nation's military. This book, while a tremendous resource fully capable of standing on its own merit, is best perceived as a "gateway" to a more comprehensive world discovered through the Internet. It is your invitation to take the contents of each chapter and pursue your journey through The Military Family Network at www.emilitary.org, where you can visit MFN's community partners or review a thorough listing of resources available about each chapter's topic.

The chapters are organized to present the subject matter and topics in an easy-to-follow format. Select what you need when you need it. Each section opens with an essay written by an expert from the field providing a general overview and an introduction to the subject matter, its jargon and definitions. Then, it will explore the topic's relevancy to your military lifestyle and guide you to additional information.

After the essay, you will find "Frequently Asked Questions" providing comprehensive responses to the most common inquiries about the topic. These questions will get to the core of the matter and direct you toward your next actionable steps.

The "Need To Know" section boils down the subject matter to its most essential facts. Find definitions, worksheets, bulleted to-do and/or how-to lists, descriptions of necessary documents, a series of questions to ask yourself or a professional; and other tools to help you get started.

Finally, and perhaps most importantly, as a part of our online network, we provide an ever-growing comprehensive list of references and resources to guide you in further discovery in an organized, efficient, reliable, accurate and thorough way. You will find these by visiting us online at www.eMilitary. org/yourMFN.html.

The second half of this book is dedicated to the community, military, business and state resources available to you as a member of the military community. We are proud to introduce you, for the first time in print, to a road map of resources our nation has created to celebrate and honor your service and sacrifice. You deserve the best and we are committed to ensuring you are connected to what you need.

Best wishes to you as you progress in your military life. We hope to hear from you often at www.emilitary.org/yourMFN.html

—Megan Turak

Part 1

Military Life Didn't Come with Instructions, Now What?

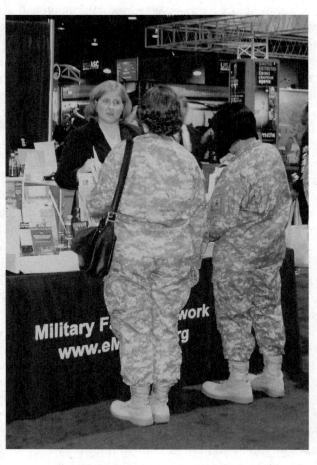

Photo: Luis Trevino

Connecting military and community

Introduction

Who can forget those memorable moments in movies like An Officer and a Gentleman, Top Gun, or Stealth where military service is sexy and full of honor and glory? Who can blame our recruits and our loved ones for embracing the mythic attraction to the uniform, the call to duty, the life of adventure and travel, the security of regular employment and lifetime pension? No one. Our country has been made great by the noble idealism that leads our young men and women to serve their nation.

When the recruiting is over, however, our new service members and families face a reality for which they are not well prepared. Basic training helps equip them for war, but not for the sociological demands of managing military life. Our spouses, especially those with little to no experience with the demands of the military lifestyle, may not know how to access the support available to them or have not prepared enough to be empowered during times of need. Parents, boy and girl friends and other loved ones have no one to turn to because of their lack of "official" status.

Our National Guard families face an extra challenge. They are geographically separated from traditional installations and do not have the benefit of the majority of support activities or trainings. Civilian organizations that they normally interact with and depend on confront similar difficulties because they have minimal, if any, knowledge of military life.

Disconnected

There is a critical disconnect in military family and community support. Although there are many contributing factors, the most serious challenge for us, as the military community, is gaining the networking experience necessary to access the information we need, when we need it.

Local community marketing of military programs and benefits is minimal. The traditional military communication model for reaching families is not inclusive of community resources. With most families residing off base, or geographically separated from one, as in the case of our National Guard and Reserve families, the significance of this omission becomes readily apparent.

The result, in many cases, is an under use of military and community programs and an unnecessary duplication of effort that negatively impacts both the military family and community organizations serving them. As a family readiness leader and volunteer trainer, I once brought these concerns to my installation Commander and his spouse during a social function. The Commander responded: "I can get the information out to my soldiers anytime—I have all their emails and I can order my leadership to pass out the fliers before they get to their cars and 'boom,' it's a done deal."

"Sir," I replied, "I know your soldiers follow your command and take their fliers home with them in their cars. I learn a lot every time I clean out my husband's SAAB."

My reply received applause from his spouse.

The Commander took my joke in good humor. The point is that many of our military service members work long hours, often on weekends or irregular tours. They may receive information, but may not see us (their spouses) when they get home. When they do see us, the first thing on their mind is not a flier with a financial readiness activity scheduled for a Saturday on the installation where they just spent their week. The bottom line is that it is simply not realistic to depend on the service members to get and "sell" the support resource to their families.

The truth is that there is a "wall" separating the military and the civilian community. Our families have limited access to information about installation or military resources when they live in the community, and the same is true for families on the installation with regard to civilian resources. There is little traditional communication that reaches us and we are not trained to get the information we need.

The Answer Is Out There

The great news is that there is an answer to bridging this gap. It just takes patience, a little training and connecting the dots.

How do we normally take care of each other? We tell each other things— we share. Sharing information on how to build a personal community network is critical. We direct people to the good and steer them away from the bad. We share our experiences so our friends, family, and those we care about can follow in our path.

Think about how geese travel south for the winter flying along in the "V" formation. You might be interested in knowing what science has discovered about why they fly that way. As each bird flaps its wings, it creates uplift for the bird immediately following. By flying in a "V" formation, the whole flock adds at least 71 percent greater flying range than if each bird flew on its own. Our military community can be viewed as the same kind of team, sharing a common direction. We have the ability to get where we are going more quickly and easily, if we choose to travel on the trust of one another.

Whenever a goose falls out of formation, it suddenly feels the drag and resistance of trying to go it alone and quickly gets back into formation to take advantage of the power of the flock. If we have as much sense as a goose, we will share information with those who are headed the same way we are going. When the lead goose gets tired, he rotates back in the wing and another goose takes over. It pays to share leadership and take turns doing hard jobs. Our military families can depend on each other, learn from their community experiences, and take turns leading the way.

The geese honk from behind to encourage those up front to keep their speed.

Words of support and inspiration help energize those on the frontline, helping them to keep pace in spite of the day-to-day pressures and fatigue. Military families, leaders, and community members can all work together to inform, share, and inspire so no one is left alone.

Finally, when a goose gets sick or is wounded by a gunshot and falls out, two geese fall out of the formation and follow the injured one down to help and protect him. They stay with him until he is either able to fly or until he is dead, and then they launch out with another formation to catch up with their group.

We can learn from our feathered friends. Military families lead stressful lives. Like geese, we have cycles of strength and weakness. When we stand together, we are stronger. This is an inspiring comparison and most military families, including myself, have experienced the loyalty and relied upon the friendship of one another to get through tough times. However, we can come together more, begin to build a library of community knowledge, and help network with each other.

The key is finding out what works.

The Military Family Network

Since military life did not come with instructions, The Military Family Network was founded to provide the tools our military community can use to learn about existing resources, to establish and grow our own personal community networks, how to maximize our connections, our knowledge and our opportunity to make our military life a successful and less stressful adventure.

"Give a man a fish, he can feed his family for a day; teach a man to fish, he can feed his family all his life." This principle speaks to the difference between simply providing information versus empowering ourselves with the knowledge of how to find resources and to build the relationships and the personal connections that ensure our success.

A little networking goes a long way

Located at www.emilitary.org, The Military Family Network is a community where our families find resources, have easy access to them, and learn how to connect directly to what we need. Our military family network reaches millions of military families and community members every year. We designed the Community Connections Program to give our families and the organizations that care a chance to connect and build supportive relationships and to have fun while learning about each other.

These are anxious times. Our military families face a lot of unknowns. Community doesn't have to be one of them.

Every organization, business and community group wish that we know more about them, what they are doing, where and who they are. The Military Family Network gives them the opportunity to talk about their programs and services in the best and most reliable place to get the word out.

Our network is a Google news provider and serves communities and military families across the world by ensuring that information about local, regional, and national programs and activities reaches us so we can use them and appreciate them.

Not Having to Learn the Hard Way—Again

Now, take a moment and ask yourself these questions:
- Did you ever buy a house in a neighborhood, only to find out later that it was not a good fit for your family?
- How long did it take you to find quality activities for your family? Did you ever wish you knew about a festival, event or family friendly location sooner?
- Do you want to know about businesses that offer discounts, special deals, or have a history of supporting military programs? Have you ever been taken advantage of because you did not know about good businesses in your new assignment community?

The Military Family Network is designed to provide families with core community and business information, but also acts as a living history of the community, helping families share the information they learn while stationed in the area. It's how you have fun now with your neighbors and your friends. It's where you go when you've had it with the shoe polish and the unexpected extra duty. It's where you go to find childcare when your husband is deployed. It's where you go when you have trouble sleeping at night . . . and need to connect with someone who knows what you are going through. Finally, it's where you go to get the discount that makes that restaurant trip suddenly fall within your budget.

The Military Family Network provides the forum. The only questions that remain are: "Will you take five minutes to be a neighbor?" "Will you help 'Make the World a Home for Military Families?'"

This book is your personal portal for building your network. Every chapter offers "From the Field" advice and guidance on topics you care about most—from people who have experienced military life. There are toolkits and connections to what you need to build relationships with the best people and resources in our nation. But don't stop there. Accept our invitation to join us online to continue your journey.

This is "Your Military Family Network." Read on and make the connection.

— Caroline Peabody, The Military Family Network

1 Staying Inspired in Your Military Life

From the Field with Patti Correa

Patti Correa *is an active duty Army spouse, mother of a service member and author of* From a Pebble to a Rock. *She hosts an online forum for military spouses on the Military Family Network at www.eMilitary.org/forums.*

"How do you do it?" is the question often asked not only of military spouses but also of the entire military family. There is never a single answer to this question. Each and every family's circumstances are diverse and dealt with in an entirely different way. We always hear about what war and deployment does to a soldier, but less is heard or written about the military family and how a deployment affects them.

Over the past sixty years there is one thing that has remained constant and that is the roller coaster of emotions experienced by military spouses whose soldier is deployed overseas or at war. There is no training manual for a spouse. We learn mainly by experience. Sometimes we find help from other spouses. Or, occasionally we discover resources that assist us in understanding the military way of life. Resources, like those we connect with on The Military Family Network (www.eMilitary.org), are important because they help us connect with each other and what we need.

In times of war or separation, life at home must still go on. Despite our pain of loneliness, heavier responsibilities, and the uncertainty that comes with separation, we still have children to care for and bills to pay.

As I reflect back on my first experiences as a military spouse, I realize I knew nothing about the military way of life. My road began nineteen years ago with uncertainty and fear. I felt helpless. Attending military functions was intimidating. I remember hearing seasoned spouses talking the military lingo and telling me I would learn it and to get used to it. Hearing those words was harsh, but very true. I needed to get involved if I was going to survive as a military spouse. I realized that it was up to me to make my situation harder or easier.

Despite the many challenges military families face, there are also immense opportunities and rewards. The unspoken camaraderie between spouses, and the appreciation you gain for the liberties and freedoms our country has to offer are two of the most important benefits available. Gaining knowledge of other cultures by experiencing travels to different countries, meeting people and making friends from all over the world is another. Also, once you get connected and develop a healthy and dependable support system, you realize that you are a part of a really big family: the military family – and the military takes care of its own. Learning that you have an abundance of friends and resources available to rely on to help you and your family is a big relief.

> **"I needed to get involved if I was going to survive as a military spouse."**

Understanding and making sacrifices are a big part of being a military spouse. In the beginning, as a spouse, it was hard to be second to the military. There was always that stigma that if the military wanted a soldier to have a wife, they would have issued you one. In today's world, the role of a military spouse is much different . . . they are the "rock," the support and refuge on the home front. I began the military life as a pebble, but now I am the rock behind my soldier. I am a warrior on the home front striving for the same cause . . . a peaceful world.

As military spouses we need to encourage and strengthen each other, be sensitive to each other's needs, influence each other with our smiles and acts of kindness, give of ourselves to our community, and face each day with courage and hope.

 **FAQs**

Q. How does a military family find resources that will help them during times of separation?

A. *Seek out resources from the service member's unit and attend Family Support Group meetings. Go to your installation family support center. Finally, remember to become a part of The Military Family Network. Registering with the* *network and participating in the forums (www.eMilitary.org/forums) will connect you with other spouses and help you understand that you are not alone.*

Q. How do I get through the rough days?

A. *Talk to friends, neighbors, or join a support group. Find the local MFN forum where you can meet up with others going through the same thing as you are. No one knows what you are feeling unless you reach out. Keeping a journal also helps to unload your feelings.*

Q. How do I deal with the challenges of homecoming?

A. *Relax and allow your service member to reconnect with the life that they left. Don't be too anxious to get back to everyday life. Put your needs aside for now. Your service member may not be the same person they were when they left. They may have experienced combat in a way we could not even imagine. Allow time for re-adjustment. Spend quality time together and as a family. Talk to each other openly.*

 Need to Know

You are not alone. There are other military families experiencing the same emotions, challenges and joys that you are.

- *Cry when you need to.*
- *Pamper yourself once in awhile.*
- *Volunteer in your community. It keeps your spirits up and makes time go by. When you focus on others, you will think less about yourself and what you are going through. Check out the Community Connections Portal (www. eMilitary.org/cchome.html) for other volunteer opportunities.*
- *Don't dwell on things you cannot change. Make new friends. Seek out ways you can help others.*
- *Ask for help. It is not a sign of weakness, but a way of gaining strength.*
- *If your service member is deployed, keep the packages, letters, and e-mails going.*

2 Communicate from the Heart on the Homefront

From the Field with Peggy Mertz

Peggy Mertz *is a military spouse and mother, an active volunteer with The Military Family Network; advisor to local governments on military spouse concerns and is the Remote and Waiting Spouses Group Leader for the Hampton Roads, Virginia military community.*

The most important word here is COMMUNICATE. It is vital to keep the lines of communication open. Don't keep secrets or give your deployed spouse surprises. They HATE surprises no matter how small or well meaning.

Just remember you are communicating with someone many, many miles away. You cannot gauge their reaction over a letter, e-mail, or even a phone call. So be very careful what you say and, in what tone you say it. Remember you can never take back anything you say or do. So pick your words carefully.

> **"Holding back is a bad thing... [Deployed] spouses know you are not going to have a perfect day, everyday."**

This does not mean that your conversation should always be positive. Holding back is a bad thing. Let's face it; our deployed spouses know you are not going to have a perfect day, every day. Be aware that there is a lot going on in their world, too. That is why it is so important to talk to someone about your feelings before you tell your spouse.

Tips on Finding Your Comfort Zone for Communicating On-line and with Others

When you e-mail your spouse, it's important to have as much privacy as possible. Try not to use a computer in a public place if you can. Even though it is e-mail, this is still an intimate moment between you and your spouse. Having a private place to e-mail also helps you to think of what you want to say.

If you don't have a computer at your house, you may wish to visit your local library or look into organizations that will gladly provide you with a computer. If you have a digital camera, take advantage of it. If you have a way to download pictures on your camera to your computer, by all means click away as much as you feel like. The sky can be the limit. There might be times that you think the picture you took was "silly," because at the time maybe it was; but later on that same picture may end up being a "treasured memory." Some places on the Internet let you create your own personal and secure web page. Try The Military Family Network at www.emilitary.org if you want to create a blog or private forum or if you want to create a secure web page for your spouse, friends and family. This may make it a lot easier for your spouse to view your pictures since graphics tend to be larger files and emailing them may take a long time to download – something your spouse may not have if they are sharing computer time with others. If you would like to make hard copies (prints of your pictures) there are several places around your area including Wal-Mart, Ritz Camera, Eckerd's, and Walgreen, just to name a few. Through Wal-Mart's website, you can order your prints right on your computer. I am sure if you call any of these businesses they would be willing to help you. I have even found fellow customers at these stores who were willing to help. You just have to ask.

To me, one of the best sources of support, information, help, and tips on coping is in a "support group"—whether it is your church, your spouses' unit, bowling league, women's group, or base/post support group. You may even find a friend online – check The Military Family Network's Community Connection forums at www.emilitary. org/forums. Find the support that fits you and with which you feel most comfortable. Please don't be under the impression that you can do this "alone" because even the strongest person needs a little help. And, some day you might be able to help someone else. Helping other people is very rewarding in itself.

> **"…even the strongest person needs a little help"**

Caring for Your Smallest Homefront Heroes

I know you think this is a really hard time on you, but just think about what your children are going through. On one hand, their parent (the one deployed or remote) is gone, out of reach, missing and out of the picture. The other parent is here, but not here. You may be physically here, but may not be mentally available. It is the responsibility of the parent left behind to shoulder the whole burden of the household. You are the giver of love and the giver of punishment. You are both Mom and Dad.

A lot of times, children resent the stay-behind parent and are hesitant about sharing their feelings with them, "good" or "bad." For some reason, they want to be with the parent who is gone (even if they did not have a good relationship before)—more than the parent who is there.

Children often feel awkward talking about their feelings to classmates, peers, or even their best friends, because they don't want to look weak or abnormal. So, they keep it bottled up inside of them until it comes out as an outburst of rage and anger. Adults around them don't recognize this release. As a result, they see this as disrespectful, not realizing that children do not have the same tools available as adults to cope with deployment. There is a much bigger support system out there for adults than for children. They don't have as many people or places to reach out to.

This is another reason for getting involved in groups. The remaining parent needs to help children to reach out, and there is no better way to do this than by example.

 **FAQs**

Q. Will this get easier each time we go through this?

A. *No, it doesn't get any easier being separated from your spouse and having your family pulled miles apart, but it does get easier to find ways to work it out. Don't ever get discouraged and think you are a bad spouse because you feel miserable. Just take it one day at a time and see where it takes you. Talking to other spouses that have been through this really does help. Try to stay as positive as possible.*

Q. Does my spouse miss me as much as I miss them or are they just saying that?

A. *I know that it may not seem that they miss you, but they do. Remember they have a job to do and are trying not to think of what they are missing at home. They are trying to cope with separation as much as you are. They just may be saying it differently.*

Q. Will my spouse be the same person as before they left? And if they change, will this be permanent?

A. *Every one is different. It is hard to say what they will be like when they come back. Some change, some don't. Don't try to pick out the changes. Focus on what you share in common. Both of you need to work it out. And you will.*

Q. Is it normal to feel anger toward my spouse?

A. *Oh yes! Most spouses I talk to have this feeling. But, before they come home, you need to find a way to get that anger out. I know that it will not be easy, to work through your feelings, but believe me when I say that they don't want to be deployed or separated any more than you do. Remember that this is your spouse's duty. You knew that this was a part of their career. Don't waste your time holding onto anger. Find a good way to channel that feeling into another emotion. Talk to someone who understands you and can help you with what you are going through.*

Q. What should I tell my children about the dangers of my spouse's job?

A. *Only you know your child. If you think they are not ready for that information, then by all means keep it from them. As a parent, one of your jobs is to protect your children. That means mentally, spiritually as well as physically. But give credit to teenagers; they are worldlier than we know. It is probably better to have things come from you than it would be to have them hear it from someone else. They will all have questions. Make sure you give them the best answers possible and that you take the time to explain things in an age appropriate way that they can understand. Give them the assurance that you and your spouse love them no matter what.*

Q. How do I make the time of separation go more quickly?

A. *Take up a hobby, volunteer, get a job (but not one that wears you out mentally and physically). Go to support group meetings, get to know someone else in your situation. Read that book you have always wanted to read. Don't be so busy that you don't have time for yourself. And remember, someday you will look back at this time, and you will be proud of yourself for getting through it.*

 Need to Know

Here are some tips to help you communicate from your heart on the homefront:
- Keep a little notepad and pen with you at all times. This is so if there is something you want to tell your spouse, you can jot it down. It may be something that happened recently or that one question you just keep forgetting to ask when you send e-mail or when they call. I always kept my

notepad by the phone when I knew my spouse was going to call me. You can also use it to write down topics of conversations. Because, believe it or not, sometimes I would run out of things to talk about, especially if I was only able to talk to my spouse once a week. Don't let things get stale where you don't have things to talk about or news to share. Make sure that your conversation is upbeat, fresh and not boring.

- Start your conversation by asking how they are doing. Don't begin with, "You would not believe what happened to me today." Mix up your good and bad news. Give your spouse the opportunity to start a topic, maybe there was something going on in their week and they want to share that with you; and, they may not feel like they want to tell you their news if you get bogged down with all your stuff in the conversation. Always make sure you tell them that you love them. Even if you think you tell them too much, it is never enough. Sometimes that is all they want to hear from us. And sometimes that might be the most important three words they have heard all week.

- Never end your e-mail or phone conversations with angry words or threats. My philosophy is: never go to bed angry or have the last words you ever say to your loved ones be mean or angry. Because, let's face it, that email will be the last impression they have of you until you e-mail or speak to them again. And what if you have angry words with each other and are unable to communicate for an entire month? Even a week is a long time to think someone is angry or mad at you. So always think ahead before you end your conversation. It is better to let the anger go, because most of the time the anger is not directed at them, but at the situation.

- Before your spouse leaves, make sure that you take a shirt or t-shirt that your spouse has recently worn and put it next to you in bed while they are gone. If you prefer, you can place it on a nice size teddy bear or stuffed animal, but simply laying it out next to you on the bed works, too. This way you don't feel so alone, and there is actually something next to you; and guess what? It smells like your spouse! What a simple and comforting thing to do to help you through the long days and nights while they are away.

Here are a few tips I found that help kids:

- Make sure to include children in everyday discussions and family decisions. For example, decide together what to make for dinner, which movie to see, what trips to go on and most importantly, what they want to put in the care package you send to your loved one. Let them know that you will help them make cards, artwork, and special gifts to include in the care packages.

- Help them with e-mails or letters, if they want to send them.

- Find out if there is something they would like to do, or someplace special they would like to go with "just" you. If you have more than one child, give each one of them their "special day" with you.
- Never substitute your anger toward your spouse with your child.
- Take turns.
- Have them read to you or you read them.
- Before your spouse leaves, if they have time, have them record your child's favorite story. This will give them (especially the little ones) a chance to hear the voice of someone familiar – the one they are missing.
- Try to make a bad day better by fixing their favorite food or make home baked cookies. They don't have to be from scratch. There are some great cut and bake cookies out there. You would be surprised how much the smell of fresh baked cookies will mean to someone. On occasion, I've even baked a few cookies for myself; and, on some days, that did the trick and I felt a lot better.

Make the Connection on MFN!
www.eMilitary.org/YourMFN.html

Sign on to the address shown above and Make the Connection to more resources on this topic!

- Assure your children that they can come to you any time, or any day, and that you are always there for them. If they are old enough, tell them how you feel. Say, for example, "I am sorry I am in a bad mood today. It was a bad day at work." Sometimes if they know what to expect, it may make it easier for them to cope.
- If there is a favorite movie that makes then laugh, play it as much as possible without making them hate it.
- If your child is young enough, hugs are a great way to put smiles on their faces. And, it will put a smile on your face, too.

3 Online Security- from the Homefront to the Frontline

From the Field with Darrell Shue

Darrell Shue *is a Vietnam era veteran, the Vice President of Web Administration and co-owner of The Military Family Network, founder and business owner of the Scribe Digital Design and has over twenty-years experience as a computer programming professional and "guru" for local and national organizations. He resides in Savannah, Georgia with his daughter.*

With advances in industry and technology, improvements in communication have increased the amount of information available to us with even greater speed and timeliness. The Internet is one of the latest innovations that have made this possible. Before you sign online and travel the information highway, make sure you know the rules of the road.

Today, most military families are able to communicate with their loved ones in the field on a regular basis. However, with this increased opportunity also comes increased responsibility. The Internet has had a dramatic impact on how we communicate. This chapter reviews the history of those changes and will give you the guidance and know-how so that you are empowered to use this powerful communications tool responsibly.

When the transcontinental telegraph was completed in October of 1861, communications in the United States underwent a revolution. No longer did citizens have to rely on newspapers that were weeks out of date by the time they were delivered, or on couriers that could take months to get a message from one coast to the other.

On October 10, 1869, when the golden spike was driven into the rails connecting the Union Pacific and Central Pacific rail lines, the new transcontinental railroad became another milestone in connectivity. Alexander Graham

Bell's invention of the telephone in 1876 began another communications revolution; and by the end of the century, the telephone was in widespread use.

The most recent communications revolution began in 1968 when the Advanced Research Projects Agency (ARPA) developed what became known as ARPANet, the forerunner of the modern Internet. This humble beginning—there were only four machines connected, at a blazing speed of 50kbps, slower than most of today's dialup lines—has become perhaps the most influential development of modern times. Initially developed for military communications, this network was used primarily by scholars in various universities and research labs. New developments followed, such as the first e-mail program in 1972, and the introduction of the TCP/IP protocol in 1973 (which allowed diverse computers to share information across this common network.) In 1992, with the introduction of the World Wide Web (www) the Internet became truly accessible to non-technical users, and the revolution went into overdrive.

Today, there are over one billion Internet users worldwide, taking advantage of quick communications and global access to a tremendous wealth of information. The Internet is a miraculous way to almost instantly communicate with your deployed military service member. But it can also expose you to a variety of annoyances, scams, high tech crimes, and information overload. Using the Internet unwisely can even place your deployed service member in harm's way. Terms such as viruses, spam, spyware, and phishing are common in today's language. However, various tools and your own common sense can minimize these risks.

> **"...various tools and your own common sense can minimize these risks."**

Potential Problems

Viruses, Worms, and Trojans, Oh My! Computer viruses are small, generally simple pieces of software that "sneak" into a computer system (piggybacked on another program or file) and perform undesirable functions—from minor annoyances such as displaying a silly message on your screen, to major problems like erasing or corrupting valuable data. E-mail viruses can infect your computer's e-mail program and mail itself to everyone in your address book. Computer viruses rely on other programs to run, and require the user to take an action, such as running the infected program to work

A worm is a small piece of software that replicates itself and spreads to other networked machines, taking advantage of security holes that often exist even in the most sophisticated software programs. This replication and spreading of the worm can cause tremendous strain on the computers and the network itself, leading to slow-downs and even complete crashes.

Trojans, or Trojan horses, are simply computer programs that claim to do one thing, but actually do another. For example, it may claim to be a game or a screensaver, but in reality, it may damage your data or crash your computer.

Spam. Spam is the junk mail of the high tech world. In other words, spam is unsolicited e-mail sent to large numbers of users. Experts estimate that spam makes up between 35 and 50 percent of all e-mail traffic! Though often just an annoyance, spam can also carry viruses, can decrease individual productivity, and can cause major network problems by overloading e-mail servers due to the sheer volume of mail. Spam may be used to advertise products or services, to recruit traffic to a website, or to spread viruses and other malicious software.

Spyware and Adware. Adware, as the name implies, is a program that generates advertising, usually in the form of popup windows or banners, on a user's computer. This is often the price of "free" software—you may play the game for free, but you are bombarded with advertisements during the process. These programs often also contain what is termed "spyware," which is software that tracks things such as your web surfing habits and reports this back to a central server using your Internet connection. This allows companies to target their advertising to you in a more specific manner, as well as to share it with third parties. Some spyware even tracks and sends sensitive personal information without your knowledge or permission.

Phishing. While not a brand new phenomenon, phishing is a threat that many users are not even aware of. Phishing is the practice of tricking users into revealing sensitive personal information such as credit card numbers, Social Security numbers, or passwords. "Phishers" pretend to be a legitimate business or organization, such as banks, online payment services (Paypal, for example,) or Internet Service Providers. You may receive an e-mail saying that "your account has been compromised," telling you to go to a specific website or follow a link where you must enter your information to confirm your account. These fraudsters are often very sophisticated, and the website may look legitimate, so users are fooled into revealing information that is then used by these criminal elements for nefarious purposes.

So, What Are We To Do?
The preceding information is not meant to scare you away from using the Internet. Just be aware of the need to protect yourself. Below are some tips to help you do just that.

Anti-virus Software. There are several popular and effective programs available to help protect you from viruses. McAfee and Norton are just two of the companies producing popular and effective anti-virus programs; and there are many others, including some that are available free. These programs scan your computer, your incoming e-mail and files, looking for known viruses. When a virus is found, the software alerts you to its presence, and allows you to clean or delete the offending file.

> **"...be aware of the need to protect yourself."**

Anti-virus software is one of the most basic things that EVERY computer user should employ. Of course, for the software to be effective, it must be running at all times! It does no good to install an anti-virus program, and then disable it from running; but you'd be surprised how often this is done. Also, since there are new viruses being created all the time, the software MUST be kept up to date. Most programs have an automated update service to keep it current without requiring any user interaction. This is usually included in the price of the software for the first year, and then requires a subscription after that. It is well worth the price!

Spam Blocking Software. If you have an e-mail address, you will eventually be a victim of spam. Several companies produce software that filters your e-mail looking for known spammers and/or patterns used by spammers. These employ a variety of methods to do this, generally by sorting your e-mail into predetermined legitimate versus spam e-mail. This can be a great timesaver, as the questionable mail is sorted to separate folders for later review. Many of these programs also use heuristic methods to "learn" as they are used, and become more accurate over time. They often also use "whitelists," that is, lists of legitimate mailers that are always considered "good" e-mails. For example, a program may whitelist everyone in your address book.

Firewalls. A firewall is a software application that filters traffic coming through your computer's Internet connection. This protects you from a variety of issues such as remote logins (where an outside source literally takes control of your computer,) backdoors (special features in some software that permit remote access,) and other types of outside attacks. Many operating systems, such as Windows XP, have a built-in firewall. There are also several types of software and hardware firewalls available.

Privacy Software. Privacy software offers an additional layer of protection by preventing personal information, such as financial data, from being accessed on your computer, either directly or remotely. Privacy software can further protect by deleting browser histories and cookies or overwriting deleted data to prevent it from being retrieved.

Anti-spyware Software. There are several good free resources to help keep your computer clean of spyware/adware. Like anti-virus software, these scan your computer for known spyware programs and give you the ability to remove them. These also must be kept updated on a regular basis. See the resources list at the end of this article for more information.

Anti-phishing Toolbars. Several companies now offer toolbars, which work in conjunction with your web browser to alert you to potential scam websites. At the time of this printing, Microsoft's newest Internet Explorer (version 7) includes an anti-phishing toolbar as a standard feature. Additionally, all browsers use the padlock in the bottom right corner of the browser to indicate that SSL (secure sockets layer) security is in place on the site you are browsing, and all have the address bar at the top which shows the web address (if you clicked a link in an e-mail, for example.) Be sure the site you think you are on is actually that site.

> **"Think before you click!"**

Operating System Updates. Although Microsoft Windows is the most widely used computer operating system, its past record of less than adequate security, makes it the most often exploited system out there. In the past couple of years, Microsoft has begun to approach security more seriously. They release security updates/patches on a regular basis, and you should certainly take advantage of this. It seems that nearly every week, there is a new security hole found in Windows, and a corresponding patch to fix it. If you are using Windows, your best bet is to use the Automatic Updates feature to stay current without requiring your interaction.

Common Sense. Perhaps the most valuable, and underutilized, tool in any user's arsenal is good old common sense! Think before you click! For example:

- NEVER open a file you receive via e-mail from someone you don't know. This is the easiest way to get a virus.
- Always use a virus scan program.
- Read the fine print! Many adware/spyware programs state somewhere in the license agreement that you are giving your permission to install such software along with that really cute fish screensaver.
- If you sign up for a lot of mailing lists, be aware that you may end up on a lot of spammers' lists also. Read the privacy policy before signing up. Beware of the "and our partners" phrase; that often means lots of spam.

- Be vigilant about phishing scams. If you receive an e-mail from "Fifth Third Bank" (a popular scam currently,) and you know you don't have an account with Fifth Third Bank, then DON'T click the website link and fill in personal information!
- Be aware that phishing scams often use legitimate business names, like Paypal or EBay. These legitimate sites will NEVER ask for passwords or other personal information via e-mail.
- NEVER send personal and/or financial information via e-mail.
- NEVER use a site that does not incorporate SSL security (look for the lock in the browser status bar) to make online purchases.
- UPDATE, UPDATE, UPDATE! Out of date virus scanners and operating systems are an open invitation for trouble.

These are but a few common sense tips that will help keep you secure online. This is an ever-changing landscape, and requires a little effort on each user's part to stay abreast, but using common sense and a little research will help ensure that your Internet experience is a pleasant one.

Operations Security (OPSEC)

Of special importance to military members, their families, and government employees and contractors is Operations Security. As defined by the 1st Information Operations Command (Land), Vulnerability Assessment Division, OPSEC Section: "Operations Security, or OPSEC, is keeping potential adversaries from discovering our critical information." Critical information does not necessarily mean secret information. Our enemies are always trying to collect information about us and our capabilities, and in the wrong hands, this information can be very dangerous. This is not simply paranoid thinking; it is a fact! Clichés become clichés because they contain a germ of truth, and the old adage "Loose lips sink ships" has never been truer than it is today in our Internet connected world.

> "...the old adage 'Loose lips sink ships' has never been truer than it is today in our Internet connected world."

As a military family member, you may use chat rooms, blogs, or message boards to keep in touch with your military member, and these can be a terrific resource. Some, like The Military Family Network, even offer the advantage of password protected forums and blogs, but you must remember that in today's world, nothing is 100% safe. However, you must be aware that our enemies monitor these same resources. Even if you are on a government or military sponsored site, you cannot assume that the information you post is secure from prying eyes. Military leadership reports a dramatic increase in monitoring of blogs and message boards by our enemies, hoping to collect information that may be used against our troops and us.

Even a seemingly innocuous post on a message board or in a chat room, such as, "My husband said his company is arriving in Fallujah in the morning, and that they are all exhausted," can tip off our enemies, often with deadly consequences.

 **FAQs**

Q. What is a cookie?

A. *A cookie is a small text file that many websites store on a user's hard drive. They simply allow the website to store information and retrieve it later. They are NOT programs, and they DO NOT collect or retrieve any information from you. These are used to enhance your experience by saving preferences, etc. For example, on the Military Family Network site, we use cookies to allow you to stay logged in to the forums.*

You can use your browser's 'Preferences Options' to disallow cookies if you want, but cookies are not dangerous and can enhance your browsing experience. Some privacy advocates complain about the use of cookies because they can be read across multiple sites to target banner ads. If you are not comfortable with this idea, you may disable cookies entirely, or ask your browser to inform you when a cookie is being used, and disallow it at that time.

Q. How can I get a virus from a website if I don't download any files?

A. *Malicious websites can run scripts that execute without you even knowing it! Files may be loaded onto your computer without your knowledge or consent (often called a "drive-by download".) This can even occur with HTML formatted e-mails. Your best protection against this is an up-to-date anti-virus program.*

Q. If I follow the guidelines above, am I completely secure?

A. *Unfortunately, no. There is no magic bullet for Internet security. The guidelines above will certainly help in that regard, but as previously mentioned, the*

Internet is an ever-changing landscape. In order to maintain your security online, you should periodically seek out new information on the latest threats, and review the steps to prevent them.

Q. Aren't there laws against spam?

A. *Yes, there are, but these are often not enforceable. The CAN-SPAM act of 2003 basically says that unsolicited e-mail must be clearly identified as such, and must include an opt-out provision so you can halt further e-mails from that particular organization. Unfortunately, spammers are often a somewhat disreputable bunch that has no interest in following the laws, and use various means to get around this. They may use false e-mail addresses and headers (info contained in e-mails that point to the origin, etc.) as well as using the opt-out link to their advantage. By clicking the link, you are sometimes merely confirming that your e-mail address is valid, and it is then put on spam lists that are sold by these disreputable entities.*

Q. Isn't Operational Security (OPSEC) the job of the military?

A. *OPSEC is EVERYONE'S job! As a military family member, you are often privy to information that is not available to the general public. You need to help protect that information, and keep it out of the hands of our enemies. The best way to do this is to simply be aware of OPSEC at all times, and be careful what you say, online and otherwise.*

"OPSEC is EVERYONE's Job!"

 Need to Know

You need to be thinking OPSEC at all times, and be very careful what you say. Basically stated, the points of OPSEC include:

- Don't discuss current or future destinations or ports of call.
- Don't discuss current or future operations or missions.
- Don't discuss current or future dates and times when military members will be in port or conducting exercises.
- Don't discuss readiness issues and numbers.

- Don't discuss specific training equipment.
- Don't discuss people's names and billets in conjunction with operations.
- Don't speculate about current or future operations.
- Don't spread rumors about current, future, or past operations or movements.
- Don't assume the enemy is not trying to collect information on you; they are.

Additionally, you should never post any information about troop movements or deployments, dates and locations of these deployments, job duties related to these, etc. Also, never post:

- Your military member's last name
- Any other military member's last name
- Your phone number, address or e-mail
- Your military member's phone number, address or e-mail
- Service member's personal identification numbers, social security numbers or any other personal identifying data.

As a military family member, you play a vital role in OPSEC. Your awareness and adherence to these guidelines are a vital part of the mission, and help to keep your military members safe and secure, and to ensure our nation's success.

Make the Connection on MFN!
www.eMilitary.org/YourMFN.html

Sign on to the address shown above and Make the Connection to more resources on this topic!

4 Building a Personal Support Network

From the Field with Caroline Peabody

Caroline Peabody *is the daughter of a disabled Vietnam era Marine, military spouse, former president of The Military Family Network, lifetime volunteer, and distinguished speaker and lecturer on military life. She holds a B.S. in sociology and M.A. in organizational management with extensive research on communication systems as they relate to military well being and community capacity-building. She is a published writer and columnist on matters relating to military families, military learning models, and military relations..*

A social support network is not the same as a family support group or family readiness group, which are designed primarily to be information-sharing environments. These groups are governed by regulations; and fall within the oversight of the military commander.

A social support network is the web of relationships that you establish in both formal and informal support systems. It is your own "customized" support network of family, friends, colleagues, and other acquaintances you can turn to—whether in times of crisis or simply for fun and entertainment.

What Is the Difference?
Many times, especially during times of deployment, family members are reluctant to attend meetings held on a military installation where they have to face the reality of the separation from their loved ones. Some military family members find listening to the stories of other families comforting, but some find it depressing—the last thing they want to deal with during their time of stress.

If you create your social support network from only one source—say a Family Support Group—and if that group is not able to meet your needs, you may be left without resources, at a time when you really need them.

When you are in the midst of a stressful period, building or expanding your personal social support network is almost an impossible challenge. The key to staying connected is preparation. The Key is finding and identifying relationships and environments that interest and nurture you and your family before you need to rely on them.

Benefits of Building Your Own Network

Simply meeting with a friend at a bookstore to share a funky coffee drink and chocolate treat, attending a class, or going to a church outing is good for your well-being. Having a personal social support network increases your sense of belonging, purpose and self-worth, promoting a positive outlook. These things nurture optimism and hope— two things critical to the overall success of military family health. A personal social support network can help you get through a deployment, or help you cope with life changes such as a relocation, a divorce, a job transition, loss, the death of a loved one, or the addition of a child to your family.

> **"The Key is finding and identifying relationships and environments that interest and nurture you and your family before you need to rely on them."**

Some people benefit from building a large and diverse personal support network, while others prefer a smaller circle of traditional relationships. The important thing is to develop an understanding of your family's unique needs for social support, and then work to create the relationships so they are available to you and members of your family when you need them.

 **FAQs**

Q. I just moved to a new town, how do I go about building my personal support network?

A. *As a transitional family, you have the opportunity not only to build, but also to expand your personal support*

> **See Chapter 5: Making the Connection Online and Off for more information on how to get started!**

network. While you may not be able to retain every relationship that you have established in a previous assignment, there are some that you can keep up at a distance. These ties are important to maintain especially during the first six to twelve months in a new town.

Growing your network from there begins with an assessment of your past and where you want to go in the future. You need to ask yourself some questions. For example, have faith-based communities been important to you in the past, or do you want them to play a more important role in your life now? If so, churches and other faith-based environments are an excellent place to begin establishing your personal support network. Start by finding a faith-based community that you identify with from your past, or from a friend's referral. Location may be important to you. Consider how far you want to drive to attend services or meetings. From my experience, it is the atmosphere of the community that is most important.

Other questions to consider:
• Do you want to go back to school?
• Do you want to work?
• Do you want to volunteer?
• Do you see yourself taking up a new hobby?
• What activities are your children in now?
• What activities do you think they might belong to in the future?

The answers to these questions and your participation in local organizations and events will bring you into contact with a diverse number of potential friends and community members on whom you can depend during times of stress.

Q. As a military family member who is always moving, I don't know if I have the energy to "make new friends and keep the old." What's wrong with just waiting out my service member's enlistment and staying away from all the complicated drama of relationships?

A. *All too often, the personal support network of military families is small––limited only to the military support group and one or two close friends. The risk of limiting a personal support network to two or three sources is that the relationships may suffer undue demands during times of need; and, (if everyone in the support network experiences the same degree of stress,) the network may not have the resiliency to handle the need. Compassion fatigue, conflict, and dysfunction may result when the demands on each other exceed the natural ability of the individuals to meet the need.*

However, if you have a more diverse support network (things to do, people to see, places to go), any stress you may endure need not have as great an impact upon you. There will be more sources of support to call upon in times of need.

In the end, people must make the choice to live as a part of the community or to live isolated from the world. Isolation may seem easier, —but it is not. Humans are social creatures. We need to belong, to feel appreciated, supported, and accepted. Most people choose isolation out of fear of being hurt or because they think it will require too much emotional energy. Moving and leaving friends and loved ones over and over is wrenching, to be sure. However, we must not forget those relationships and the years of nurturing, personal growth and support they provided to our hearts and souls while they lasted.

> **"Isolation may seem easier, —but it is not. [Military families] need to belong, feel appreciated, supported and accepted."**

Military living is difficult, and without a social support network of caring friends and nurturing places, it is nearly impossible. The risks of putting on a false bravado, living alone and handling it all far outweigh the perceived benefit. The results of this road are clearly seen in the rising divorce and depression rates for military families.

Q. I always do my best to get involved, but I just cannot stand the "whiney wifeys" at the support group meetings. How can I do what I need to do and avoid the complaining crowd?

A. *Making relationships that are healthy to your well-being involves give and take. Sometimes you're the one giving support and other times, you're on the receiving end. It is important to appreciate the people and organizations that mean the most to you. Letting family and friends know you love and appreciate them during regular times will help ensure that their support remains strong when you need it.*

However, lets not forget the airplane rule: "Always place the oxygen on your face first, then help those around you with theirs." It is important to understand that we all have bad days, but it could be that some of your relationships may be more harmful than beneficial. If your friends or the people you are with are constantly stressed, you may suffer with them—instead of gaining the support you need.

Many military spouses and parents have "caretaker" personalities. If you need help, however, and the people in your support network do not have the resources, time or energy to help you because of their own demands, you will find yourself frustrated. You will also not have the ability to take care of them, and you may experience guilt over this.

Beware of "energy vampires."

Beware of "energy vampires." If you are always feeling obligated to others because another person is keeping an emotional scorecard or makes you uncomfortable about expressing your feelings, values, or opinions—then carefully consider the price you (and your family) are paying to keep that relationship. Sometimes the healthiest thing to do is to limit contact with individuals who are too demanding of your personal resources. It's okay to be selective in your relationships.

Need to Know

Seeding that Support Network

If you want to expand your social support network, The Military Family Network is a great place to start. The Community Connection Forums at www.emilitary.org/forums will help you connect with other military families who have lived or are living in your community and have taken the time to share their information. After connecting with MFN, once you arrive in town—here are some things you can do:

- Work out. Seek out the local Morale Well-being Recreation (MWR) gym or YMCA (they may have free childcare), or start walking -studies show fitness is healthy for both the body and the spirit.
- Do lunch. Invite a new neighbor or someone you met at work or church to join you for breakfast, lunch or dinner. Volunteer. Help MFN with its Community Connection program or connect with location organizations like hospitals, places of worship, museums, community centers, libraries, and others. Many organizations need volunteers. You may meet some really interesting people!
- Get a hobby or go back to school. Find a nearby group with similar interests or take a college or community education course to meet people with similar interests.

Taking Good Care!

The military lifestyle is a challenging one. It is full of stressors above and beyond those of "normal" daily life. Whether you are a single person in the military or have a huge family, it takes a lot of work to keep healthy under the demands of military service.

- Simplify your life. As a military member or family member, your life already means that your in box is full, you plate is overflowing and your candle is burning at both ends.
- Learn to say "NO" and be sure to establish realistic goals and expectations for yourself.
- Take time to write down what you "absolutely must do" each day; know that it is okay to let the things go when you are not up to completing tasks. Forgive yourself, reschedule if necessary, and pat yourself on the back! I like to keep a notebook- like those black and white composition notebooks the kids use for school. I limit myself to five Must-dos a day, the rest are optional!
- Don't worry about making everyone happy. It will never happen anyway. From our collective experience here at The Military Family Network, we know that there are plenty of individuals out there who have opinions on what is best for you. Take some time, mental time, to think about what you know is best, then give yourself permission to do it. Do not feel bad about not living up to someone else's expectations. Remember that they do not wake up in your shoes, so they are not the expert on your life. You are!
- Understand and anticipate bad days. They are going to happen. We know that they do. Remember it is only that day. Simplify your goals and move on to the next day.
- Get to bed early. Get plenty of sleep. Rest does wonders!
- Depression happens. Paranoia and wild imaginative behaviors can and do occur. How many days have passed since you have heard from your spouse? Where are they? What are they doing? We have all been there. Separation is hard; it is hard to be alone (for you and your military member!). The best thing to do is to keep yourself busy with things that renew your spirit and refresh your soul. This might be in the church community (do you like the choir?) or reading some really good books! Whatever it is, know that you will have your moments. The goal is to make as few of them as possible and to limit their potential stress.
- Allow some time for yourself. For the suddenly single parent, nothing, absolutely nothing, replaces having time to just be YOU! Volunteering, when the organization pays for childcare, to give yourself a break or simply to help out the community, is recommended. Or, finding a babysitter for the ultimate treat is a must! Do not underestimate the benefits of having time away from the responsibility of child rear-

Make the Connection on MFN!
www.eMilitary.org/YourMFN.html

Sign on to the address shown above and Make the Connection to more resources on this topic!

ing. This is especially important if you have a bout where the kids have been sick, you have been sick, it has been a long deployment . . . it's called respite (I call it REST-a-BIT) care and you deserve it! Do not feel guilty.

Toolkit

Grab a piece of paper and answer these questions to help you get started on your personal support network:

Friends or family members I can call and talk about anything- the people to help me if I am bored, scared or need some advice. (Check the ones you can call at any time—or make a notation if you can't call after a certain time.):

_____

_____

Friends or family members I can count on if I need sudden or short term financial help:

_____

_____

Faith based community preference (Location: 5 miles, 10 miles, 20 miles, does not matter):

_____

_____

_____

My hobbies or things I am interested in learning more about:

_____

_____

_____

Hobbies of my kids (groups they have joined in the past or may join in the future):

_____

_____

_____

Activities or events that interest me:

_____

_____

_____

Organizations I have joined in the past or would like to join in the future:

_____

_____

_____

Personal fitness (what exercise program have I enjoyed or would like to try):

_____

_____

_____

Local places I can go to get away:

_____

_____

_____

Schools in the area or classes I want to take:

_____

_____

_____

Childcare resources:

_____

_____

_____

5   Making the Connection Online and Off

From the Field with Megan Turak

Megan Turak *is the daughter of a WWII Army veteran and spouse of a Vietnam era Marine, Executive Vice President and co-owner of The Military Family Network, former Medical Records Manager with the Department of Veteran Affairs, a published writer of informative topics positively impacting the well-being of military families and has over twenty combined years of experience in executive leadership in the financial management and communications industries.*

You may be wondering how to go about finding the resources and community groups you need to create your new personal network. Fortunately for you, there are multiple ways that you can do this and it is recommended that you use several of them in your approach. This allows you to broaden your search and greatly increases the success that you will find resources that you like and that will work for you. In addition, the more support services you have, the more useful your personal network will be. You will be better prepared and better equipped to deal with whatever life throws your way.

First, look to existing groups, organizations and services in your community. These come disguised as government services or agencies, non-profit or faith based organizations, civic or professional groups, local businesses or associations and even as your neighbors! Now that you know these entities exist, how do you learn about them? On the ground, you can expect to find helpful information by visiting your military family support center, local libraries, and places of worship, chamber of commerce, colleges and universities as well as government offices – to name a few. Once there, look for information tables, pick up flyers and brochures, read bulletin boards and talk to people! Ask questions and ask for help. Tell people why you are there and what you are looking for. You will be pleasantly surprised at how helpful people are and what they know. Keep your mind open and make sure you have a pen and note pad. You will learn about a lot of people, groups and places. Be prepared to write it down along with their contact information so you can review it later. Try to remember to withhold judgment at this stage. Something that doesn't sound interesting may just end up being exactly what you need.

Next, take your search to the web! This is another valuable place to conduct your search, because you can do research on the contacts you learned about during your adventure into the community and you can introduce yourself to other sources not yet known. This allows you to expand the reach of your personal network. Keep in mind that you are looking not only for support but also for support you feel comfortable with and will be likely to call upon if you have a need. In addition, different elements of support offer differ-

Check out some of our national military friendly organizations in our appendices!

ent advantages. It's not a 'one size fits all' solution, which is why you are taking the time to develop your own, personal network.

Begin with The Military Family Network, at www.emilitary.org. At MFN, you will find a community of support built exclusively for military service members, veterans and their families already in place. We have engaged the local and military communities, built relationships, amassed information and anchored it all to our website as a resource available for you. MFN puts you in the driver's seat by providing you with choice. You will discover new information, easier ways to find old information, tools to help you navigate your military life, awareness of community happenings, military and community benefits and services, friendships, shared experiences, support and much, much, more!

After your visit with The Military Family Network, you will want to branch out even farther, and with the availability and convenience of the Internet, it's easy to do. Using this powerful tool is like bringing all the biggest and best libraries from around the world right there in your home and more. As great as this sounds, the shear volume of information it locates for you can make searching for what you want to know a slow and tedious process.

Fortunately, you have two reliable resources to help you with this problem: librarians and Internet search engines. Your library's reference desk librarian (who I might add is one of the most important and yet most under recognized and often underutilized individuals on the planet) is a great place to start. Without the librarian's assistance in answering questions, refining topics and subject searches, providing instruction for locating information, and pointing out relevant reference materials, searching for information on the World Wide Web (or anywhere) can be both time consuming and frustrating. In fact, many public libraries offer free courses on using the Internet and you may want to avail yourself of this service.

Once you are ready to find information on the web, there are a number of "search engines" to facilitate your goal. Google, Alta Vista, Dogpile, Yahoo!, Ask Jeeves, MSN, and AOL are a few of the best places to start. Although these search engines are extremely useful, and some do certain tasks a little better than others, there is still more art to the overall search process than science. So, keep reading to learn how to use these tools to get the information and answers you need, perform the best search that you can in the shortest time possible.

 **FAQs**

Q. I don't always have available transportation to get around town. Is there another way that I can tap into some of those community resources that you discussed?

A. *Absolutely! Use your telephone. Call your military family support service to see what they may be able to share with you. Locate the organizations that interest you either by using the Internet search tools we talked about or pick up your local newspaper or telephone book. If you use your local newspaper, often the community or local section will have organizations listed and you can call them directly and this is normally a better approach then the phone book for these types of services, because you are likely to see a small description of them as well. If you use the telephone book, the government services are usually in the blue section. Make sure to call your librarian! You will be able to get information on the local chamber of commerce and a number of other organizations fitting your needs. It would also be advisable to contact local veterans organizations.*

Q. I don't have a computer or Internet service. How can I get connected to all of those online resources? I want to build a personal network, too.

A. *If you live near an installation, family support services may have computers available for you to use. Most certainly, however, libraries do. Contact your local library to learn about their online policies and hours of operation. You can even set up a free email account. In addition, depending where you* *live, there are organizations that provide computers to military service members especially those who are deployed. Ask around.*

Q. What kind of community tools does The Military Family Network offer? And, how do I use them to get connected and to build my own support network?

A. *The Military Family Network has a fully interactive platform where you can find information about local community organizations, where they are and what they have to offer your family. Military families are diverse and have diverse needs and interests. You may wish to simply look around our website for information on your own, or perhaps you just have a question about a community topic. Our social network platform and our forums (www.emilitary.org/forums) allow you to post your question and have other military family members share with you their experiences and information. We also have powerful search and navigation tools at your disposal in all areas of our website so that you can find the information you need and any topic of interest.*

Q. I finally got off the couch, took your suggestions and now, I have a great personal network of my own. I look forward to talking and going out with my new friends – I'm having fun! I have learned so much about the people, places and things in my community and it has helped me so much that I want to share this knowledge with other military families. How can I do this so that they know all this great stuff is out here for them?

A. *Our Community Connections Program (located at www.eMilitary.org/cchome.html) operates as a centralized communication and information portal for military families to receive information from and to communicate with each other and organizations and program providers that serve them.*

Think about the hundreds of thousands of military families who have been stationed in your community in the past. Now think about what you know about your community. Wouldn't this information, if you share it help someone in some way or another? Isn't this really what being a neighbor is all about? And wouldn't you agree that a strong community is a community that has participation from all of its members?

If you go online with our network, spend five minutes, sharing one thing you have learned or enjoyed about your community, a military program, a business or event—there would be a gigantic library of network data for everyone to learn from. And this resource would be a tremendous aid to our military families by getting us the information that we need when we need it. Think about your own experiences: Wouldn't this have helped you?

This is why The Military Family Network has community forums online for every military community. Families ask questions, post information, record their experiences and share their knowledge actively building "virtual neighborhoods" in these forums.

You are the most important part of the network.

 Need to Know

Here are some helpful hints for searching:

Start with a good quality "key word" for the search you want to conduct and expand upon it to include similar terms or word choices. If you use the tilde character (~) in front of the word, the search will include all synonyms as well as your initial keyword selection.

- If you want to narrow your search to exclude certain items that you know are irrelevant to your expected outcome, then go ahead and remove them from the results. Here's how: Just use the hyphen (-) after your keyword and add the word you would like to exclude. If you wish, you can also add the tilde character (~)to remove all synonyms for the excluded word as well. That would look like this: -~(selected word).

- If you are searching for a part of something that you have forgotten, like words to a song or a line in a famous poem, you can type what you recall and substitute an asterisk enclosed in parentheses (*).

- If you use Google, and you want to locate archived information, just visit the "cache option" provided by this leading search engine. Locate a link for it in the bottom line of most search results.

- If you need a telephone number, just type "phonebook" and the name and city or state of the individual you wish to find.

- If you already have a phone number, but no name, then just type in the number with no spaces, parentheses or hyphens.

- If you need the definition of a word or want to find a synonym to help you with your key word search, just type the word "define:" in the search line before your keyword.

- If you are interested in a particular individual working with a particular outfit, you may wish to scale back your search by typing what you know about the individual, like a title, and then add the organization or company website domain. It will look something like this: "president:whitehouse.gov".

- If you are looking for pictures, graphics or news, search engines like Google have that, too. Just type in the kind of picture you need in the search line and then click on the word "images" from the search engine tool bar. You can do the same for news; just click on "news" from the toolbar instead. (By the way, if there are certain news topics that you are always interested in, Google, in particular, allows you to subscribe to their news service to receive "news alerts" or notifications about that subject matter, directly to your e-mail for free.)
- Most search engines, like Google, also offer the opportunity for you to include their search bar into your browser. This puts many search features right in front of you for your use.

If you incorporate the above tips into your next Internet search, you should find your efforts rewarded handsomely. If, on the other hand, you find yourself still struggling with the results of your own work, a reference librarian is only a local library and phone call away.

(Some tips reference: Google.com and Peter Grad, "Trouble finding answers," The Record. December, 2005)

Make the Connection on MFN!
www.eMilitary.org/YourMFN.html

Sign on to the address shown above and Make the Connection to more resources on this topic!

Part 2
Military Family Money

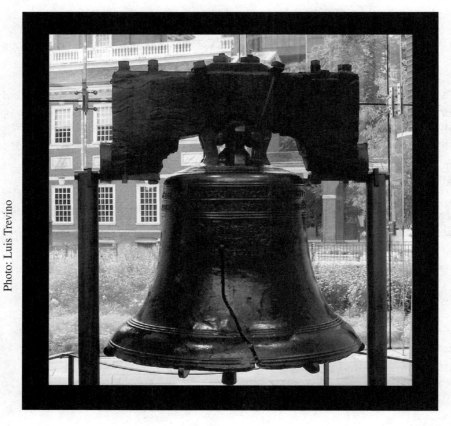

Liberty Bell

Introduction

This section presents the building blocks for getting a handle on your finances and taking control of your life. This doesn't always mean that you will always get everything you want, but it will greatly increase the chances that you will get what you need and in many cases, even what you want. These next pages will help you to understand that with sound personal planning, discovering "the good life" is not just learning about what money can buy. It is also about making decisions, reaching goals and feeling good about leading your life. When was the last time that happened for you?

We have all had the experience where money has made the decision for us. Maybe you saw a car you would have liked to own, but drove off the lot in a cheaper model. Maybe you were invited out of town to get some needed R&R, but couldn't afford the travel expense. Maybe you wanted to help a friend out of a jam, and couldn't because you had your own electric bill to pay. Maybe you wanted to send a larger care package overseas, but were afraid that the postage would cost too much. In all of these instances, financial decisions are being made. If you are not managing your money, than money is managing you. Each of these examples alone may not be a big deal. Add them together, and you have to ask, "Who is running my life? Me or my money?"

The following chapters build from budgeting and shopping on the Internet to financial planning, and using your military benefits. In fact, using your education benefit is one of the best deals available because it can increase both your standard of living and the quality of the life you lead. The best part about this is that you don't have to invent the rules yourself! You just have to teach yourself to follow the ones that already exist. This section of Your Military Family Network will help you to get a jump-start on learning how to manage your money and will direct you to other areas where you will find help.

6   Your Money, Your Life

From the Field with Megan Turak

Megan Turak *is the daughter of a WWII Army veteran and spouse of a Vietnam era Marine, Executive Vice President and co-owner of The Military Family Network, former Medical Records Manager with the Department of Veteran Affairs, a published writer of informative topics positively impacting the well-being of military families and has over twenty combined years of experience in executive leadership in the financial management and communications industries.*

Recently, an acquaintance suggested to me that if he were lucky enough to win the lottery, he'd simply hold on to a few dollars and give the rest of his winnings to a charity. At first I was a bit stunned by this revelation, since I had never really considered this acquaintance as a Mother Theresa type. Although providing for those less fortunate should be reason enough, I continued asking my acquaintance questions to try to understand if he really meant what he'd said. What I learned astonished me. While he certainly cared about those in need, and we both agreed that acts of charity should be a part of everyone's prosperity, it appeared that his primary concern had more to do with his belief that money is the root of all evil and that these winnings would ruin his life.

What he didn't say was more important to me than what he did say. His remarks clearly suggested to me that he possessed a modest understanding of finance and he was not confident about his money management skills.

How like so many of us! We are afraid of what we don't understand and so we respond with emotion instead of reason. When someone talks to us about money, we become overwhelmed. We think it's too complicated and that we won't understand. We refuse to take action and continue on in a state of denial.

Years ago, a friend married a successful and talented businessman and felt that she didn't need to concern herself with the family finances. When some of her husband's business decisions significantly jeopardized their family's well being, my friend suddenly became actively involved, and vowed never to be uninformed and passive again. What

> **"What we don't understand CAN hurt us."**

she learned is that what we don't understand can hurt us. It is not true that "ignorance is bliss."

Money managers like to say that managing your finances is a way for you to take back control of your life. It's true. Those who understand money understand discipline, restraint, and sacrifice; they understand the delicate balance between desire and need and between now and later. Most importantly, they understand that everything costs something, somewhere, some time; and the keys to succeeding are found though knowledge, self-awareness, practice, and planning. They also know all too well that these tools give you a greater chance of getting what you need and what you want—on your terms!

By mastering the rules of sound money management, you will increase the number of choices available to you so that, unlike my acquaintance's hypothetical response to winning the lottery, you will become more confident, and your financial decisions will become more thoughtful, deliberate, purposeful, and rewarding.

 **FAQs**

Q. So, the big question: If I win the lottery, should I take a lump sum or the annuity payments?

A. *No, the real question is: Why are you buying lottery tickets when the chances of winning are so dismal? You would be much better served investing your money into the stock market. But anyway, let's say that you received this lucky ticket as a birthday present. Should you take the lump sum or the annuity? This is a tricky question and certainly requires the input from a tax and financial advisor. It may also require the expertise of an attorney as well. This is because the answer depends on a number of factors including your life style, your income (both present and future) your age, your money management skills, what you expect to happen in the future (regarding taxes, economy, value of money), the type of winnings you will receive (there are different types of lotteries and annuities used by different states), etc. In general, it has been argued that taking a lump sum allows you to earn a potentially better rate of return than you would if you took the annuity; take the cash when you know the current financial circumstances like interest and tax rates; control your own lifestyle and estate planning, etc. Those who advocate the annuity typically do* *so after performing calculations to see if the rate of return is a better rate than offered in the market place and evaluating criteria about your life and how you will use your money. Regardless of the payout choice, there is a consensus that this once in a lifetime happening that should be treated carefully to receive its fullest value and benefit to your life.*

Q. Some months, it seems that I can barely meet my own needs – those bills keep coming and coming. With my head scarcely above water, how can I think about making charitable gifts?

A. *This is a tough situation that certainly requires a delicate touch that only you can provide. It's hard to think of others when you're struggling yourself. It's simply human nature. But there are several compelling reasons why you should give it a try anyway. You've heard the expressions "what goes around, come around" and "in giving you receive" and they speak volumes of truth. The difficulty that most people experience is that they expect to receive from the same place in which they gave. When this doesn't always happen, people feel as if these expressions are not true. This is not the case; the expressions are true, it's just that our expectations are askew. Do good deeds in your life without worrying where it will come back to you, and you will experience wonderful results. You will find yourself paying attention to even the smallest advantages wondering if that is goodwill being returned to you. It can be a lot of fun approaching your life in this manner. It removes your focus from the strain and struggle to the things that are going well in your life.*

See Part 8 on Volunteering and other opportunities

But there are more reasons for being charitable. It makes you feel good. In helping others, we feel good about ourselves. And if we can lend aid to others, then our situations are better than we imagined. They seem manageable. Keep in mind that you don't have to give dollars away to be charitable. You can give some of your time or talents. Maybe you have items like a lawn mower that you can lend out to a neighbor or you are a terrific cook who makes a mean bean soup that you can give to a member of your church going through a difficult time. There are all sorts of ways to get involved.

There are other advantages, too. Maybe you are looking for new employment or some help with childcare. Maybe someone you come in contact with while in the act of helping (remember it doesn't have to be the person you are actively helping) has a business lead for you. All sorts of unexpected opportunities arise when you interact with others. Volunteering opens doors to a multitude of benefits.

Q. I don't know a lot about managing money and frankly, I am confused and overwhelmed about how best to handle my finances. In fact, many times, I just don't do anything, because I don't want to make a mistake.

A. *First of all, realize that at some time or another, you are going to make a mistake. We are human and mistakes are going to happen. Your mission is not to avoid making a mistake (because that's just unrealistic), but to avoid making a big mistake or several mistakes. The best way to do this – and to manage your finances effectively – is to become informed. Educate yourself. Read, read, read. You can find resources to help you everywhere from your military installation to your local bank or library. Go online. Visit the financial resources assembled for you by The Military Family Network at www.eMilitary.org/yourMFN.html. Most financial institutions now have online resource and customer education sections. You just need to begin. Start with something really easy. Next time you are in your bank waiting for the teller, pick up one of the bank's brochures. They often offer brief yet easy to digest explanations and definitions. Schedule an appointment with a financial service advisor on base. Or ask a friend if they have a trusted professional you can talk to. Review the different chapters in this section. The DoD takes your financial well-being very seriously. They've launched the Department of Defense's Financial Readiness Campaign and are working hard to bring many educational programs to you. Look for them online at both .mil and .gov websites and within your branch of service. Also, beware of any programs or financial advice that offer returns too good to be true or fast, easy money. Acquiring wealth is typically a steady process of implementing sound financial principles. There is a lot of good information out there and most of it is free. Don't use your hard earned money paying upfront for help or "programs guaranteed to make you rich". By reading and learning more about your money, you should be able to spot legitimate offers from bogus ones. By the way, want to know one of the biggest secrets? Learn the banking jargon. You will find that you already know what the industry is talking about – they just call it by another name.*

Q. My friends and I make about the same amount of money, but their money seems to go so much farther than

my own. For instance, they all drive better cars than I
do and have nicer things. I confess that I have a budget
and I'm a saver and put money aside each month for
emergencies and retirement, but when I look at my bank
statements, it doesn't seem that I've saved all that much.
It certainly couldn't buy the lifestyle that they are living.
What's wrong here?

A. *There's nothing "wrong" here except your urge to compare yourself
with your friends. No two situations are alike. There are a lot of reasons
that their lifestyle may look different than yours. For instance, maybe they
are in debt over their ears; maybe they have another source of money that
they draw from; or, maybe they aren't saving anything for the future like you
are. You can't simply assess what is going on by the outward appearance of
things. However, from the information that you have provided, it seems like
you are responsibly managing your money. Perhaps, you just need to reward
yourself for doing a good job and loosen your budget just a bit so you don't
feel so left out. You might be trying to do too much too quickly. But it does
seem like you have a good sense of now and later. If the above approach
doesn't help you to stop making comparisons than try this one: Envision how
comfortable you will be in your retirement years while your friends are all
working and living on social security. Now that's a vision that should keep
all of us motivated!*

 Need to Know

Please remember one very important thing: Many people who receive advice
on financial affairs object to implementing the advice they receive. It's not
that they don't understand the rules of prudent money management or their
benefits. It's not that they believe in being unreasonable.

It's simply human nature. You must change your habits and change
your lifestyle. This is what makes money management so challenging.
Many of us simply don't want to make these changes in our life, because it
means that sometimes we might have to tell ourselves "No".

But I assure you, you have one of two choices: You can either choose the
manner in which you would like to make changes in your lifestyle, or your
finances will choose these changes for you. I guarantee you; most of us will
not like the choices that are made for us.

Toolkit

To help you begin to understand the meaning of choices, try the following exercise before you proceed. Take a pen and paper in hand. Think about yourself and your relationship to money and answer these questions:

1. What does money mean to you in 25 words or less?

    _____

    _____

2. Are you a collector? Do you just like having it? Saving it?

    _____

3. Are you a spender? Do you enjoy the things that money can buy?

    _____

4. Does it represent security? Or a world of possibilities?

    _____

5. Did you have what you needed as a child? Did you get what you wanted?

    _____

6. Is money about your independence? Or, is it a way for you to have power over your situation or others?

    _____

7. If you had all the money you wanted, what would that feel like to you? Is it relief? Or something else? Why?

    _____

    _____

8. If the opposite were true and you didn't have enough money, how would that feel?

    _____

    _____

9. How much money is "enough money" to you?

_____

_____

You get the idea. Think about your feelings. Write these ideas down for yourself; and, if you have a spouse or significant other, invite them to do the same. You might even want to have the kids take a crack at it.

If you have done the above work, you'll understand a lot more about your relationship to money and its motivation in your life. This self-discovery will lead to self-awareness about your spending and saving habits. It will also help you understand how other members of your family feel about money.

Make the Connection on MFN!
www.eMilitary.org/YourMFN.html

Sign on to the address
shown above and
Make the Connection
to more resources
on this topic!

This will be a vital source of information as you go through the money management process by helping you to communicate and establish goals, prepare a plan, and identify areas where you can find compromises or make changes that you and the whole family can live with.

7 Make the Most of What You Have

From the Field with Melissa Tosetti & Kevin Gibbons

Melissa Tosetti is the editor and publisher of Budget Savvy. *She is passionate about showing women how to enjoy life with the money they are making right now. She has appeared on* Pocket the Difference *on the Fine Living Network. She is often quoted in the* Miami Herald *and the* Chicago Tribune *among other publications.*

Kevin Gibbons is the managing editor of Budget Savvy. *A scientist by training, Kevin approaches budgeting as a challenging puzzle to be solved. Kevin brings an analytical viewpoint to Budget Savvy that helps set it apart from other women's lifestyle magazines. Previously, Kevin was the co-publisher of the newsletter,* Improvisations.

Do you think you make enough money right now? How much money would you have to make for it to be "enough?" The fact is most of us will never make "enough" money. We will always want just a little bit more. It is in our nature and advertisers, fashion magazines, and television reinforce that wish.

So, what can you do? Like everyone else, you can play the game of trying to increase your spending power by juggling credit cards, tapping into your home equity, even playing the lottery and hoping to strike it rich. Or, you can learn to enjoy life with the money you make right now.

The Four Steps to Enjoying Life with the Money You are Making Right Now

There is nothing wrong with having ambition and wanting to increase your wealth. We should all desire to prosper. What trips most people up is that they increase their cost of living long before they have the means to support that lifestyle. While it may sound daunting, learning to enjoy life while on the path to greater wealth is key to a successful journey. There are four simple steps to get started on the road to enjoying life with the money you are making right now.

Rule #1–Abide by the Golden Rule: Spend Less Than You Make

Did you know that the average American spends $1.22 for every $1.00 they make? With a $50,000 annual income, you will spend $61,000 that same year. That's $11,000 you have to borrow and pay back, and that does not include interest. In short, instead of having any disposable income, all your money is used to pay debts. That's why **Rule #1 is: SPEND LESS THAN YOU MAKE**

> **Golden Rule: Spend Less Than You Make**

Rule #2–Get Your Finances in Order

- **Balance your checkbook regularly.** Balancing your checkbook is the only way to know where you stand financially.
- **Pay your bills on time.** Late fees and bounced checks not only ruin your credit rating and drain you of your money, they provide you with no benefit.
- **Pay into a savings account.** Set up automatic payments into a savings account and decline ATM access. Make it as inconvenient to tap as possible, and give your money an opportunity to grow.
- **Start a spending account.** Just like a savings account, a spending account is disposable income you specifically set aside to spend as you please.

Rule #3–Spend Money on the Things You Want

If the Golden Rule and getting your finances in order are the keys to financial success; then learning to spend money on the things you want is the key to financial happiness.

Stop spending money on the things you don't want, so you can afford to spend money on the things you do want. The hardest part of controlling your spending is deciding what you truly want and having the discipline and the focus to get it. To make this happen, you need to:

- Define your goals
- Post your goals where you can see them

Suppose you really want to take a vacation to Italy—tape a note with the word ITALY on your ATM card, your checkbook, and your computer. The next time you go to buy something on impulse, and you see the word ITALY, ask yourself: Does this purchase get me any closer to my goal? If the answer is no, then walk away. By the way, there is no shame in putting an item back or telling the clerk you changed your mind— that's empowering.

Rule #4–Know When to Invest and When to Bargain

One of the most powerful financial tools you have at your disposal is knowing when to invest in an item and when to bargain hunt. This is largely a matter of personal taste. Common sense leads you to invest in those things that are important to you and bargain hunt for the necessities or luxuries that are less significant.

A general guideline is to invest in durable, important items and bargain on disposable, everyday purchases. For example, you might decide to invest in wardrobe basics, furniture, and vacations; but find bargains on trendy clothes, groceries, books, and movies. Now you are armed with the four steps it takes to put you on the path to enjoying life with the money you are making right now.

1. Abide by the Golden Rule—Spend less than you make.
2. Get Your Finances in Order—Just do it.
3. Spend Money on Things You Want—Decide what you want and buy it.
4. Know When to Invest and When to Bargain.

Be excited that you are making conscious decisions to obtain the things that are most important to you.

 **FAQs**

Q. Being Budget Savvy sounds great, but I just can't save any money. I ALWAYS come up short every month. What do I do?

A. *First of all, don't beat yourself up. This is a problem many people have. You have taken the first step of recognizing that what you are doing now isn't working and that you need to do something different. At some point in your pay period you are overspending. You need to figure out where you are overspending. To make you conscious of where your money is going, for the next week, keep track of every penny you spend, whether it's on a candy bar or a new couch. Once you recognize where your money is slipping away to, you can make changes in your spending habits to get it under control.*

This may require some drastic action, but you have to get to the point where you are spending less than you are making. First, look at where you can reduce your spending, and then look at how you can increase your earnings (it's usually easier to spend less than it is to make more.).

Do your best to continue your spending diary habit. Being conscious of your spending is the number one way to stay on track. It may not be entertaining or glamorous, but it works!

Q. Being on a budget is no fun. It's just like a diet. I can't stick with it for more than a month.

A. *Being in debt and never having money to spend is no fun either. A budget is not a straightjacket. It's simply a tool that allows you to spend within your means.*

It is possible that you are trying to be too strict with your finances. If you can afford to do so, adjust your budget and give yourself just a little more spending money, even if it means you are saving a little less. Budget sacrilege you think? Actually, no. If giving yourself just $20 or $50 more to splurge per pay period makes you stay on your budget and not blow it —then in the long run, you will save so much more!

Just like most diets that restrict you to 2,000 calories per day don't work––a budget that imposes a daily spending limit is unreasonable. What matters is how your finances look at the end of your pay period, not each day. You have the freedom to "income average," but you have to be sure to balance at the end of your pay period.

Q. It seems that everyone around me can afford new clothes, a new car, and dinner out several times a week. I can hardly pay my rent. Help!

A. *With the average American spending $1.22 for every $1.00 they make, I'd be itching to take a look at their credit card bills to see if they can really afford their ongoing luxuries. That aside, the most dangerous financial habit you can get into is comparing yourself to those around you. Perhaps they are deeply in debt for their purchases. Perhaps they have an inheritance that you don't know about. Perhaps they are savvy shoppers who pick up great clothes at rock bottom prices.*

You have to decide what is most important to you and focus on it, and you. Are you ready to replace your car? If so, then start researching what you can afford and start saving. The more money you put down up front, the more manageable your car payment.

Want to give your wardrobe an infusion? Go to every store that has a website and sign up for their email newsletters—it's a great way to find out about sales. Take your time and increase your wardrobe by one piece per pay period. Purchase only pieces you love and at the best prices possible.

As for dinner out—is that what is most important to you? If so, then pick and choose the restaurants you want to go to. If you can only afford to eat out once a week, go to a restaurant that you truly enjoy and make it worth your money.

 Need to Know

Financial Rules to Live by

There are so many rules, thoughts, and guidelines for managing your finances. It can get overwhelming. We have pulled together our favorite money mantras and offer them to you in bite size pieces.

1. Spend less than you make.
2. Balance your checkbook on a regular basis. Know where you stand financially.
3. Use the power of compound interest. The more you save, the more it grows. Conversely the quicker you pay off debts, the less money you pay in interest.
4. Don't let money rule your life. Money shouldn't get in the way of the things that are most important in life—family and friends.
5. Pay all of your bills on payday. Then you know how much disposable income you have for that pay period.
6. Even if you can't save 10 percent of your wages, save something. Just get into or stay in the habit of spending less than you make. Again, save something!
7. Put your savings where they are accessible in an emergency, but a little hard to get. If they are not linked to your ATM card, you are less likely to raid them.
8. Set financial goals. How are you going to get where you want to be if you haven't defined where you want to be?
9. Know when to invest and when to bargain shop. Before picking up the least expensive item, think about what you need it for and how long you want it to last. It may be worth investing in the pricier item for the long haul.

10. Spend money on the things you want. Before checking out at the register, scan your basket and make sure the items in there are the things you intended on purchasing in the first place and that you really want.

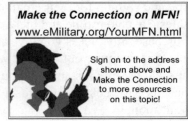

Make the Connection on MFN!
www.eMilitary.org/YourMFN.html

Sign on to the address shown above and Make the Connection to more resources on this topic!

11. Bonus Rule: Attitude is everything. A positive attitude about your financial situation can get you through the toughest times.

8 Financial Checklist For Deployment . . . Or Anytime!

From the Field with Carl Surran

Carl Surran is editor of Military Money Magazine *(www.militarymoney. com), published by InCharge® Education Foundation, a national non-profit organization that specializes in personal finance education and research. As members of the Department of Defense's Financial Readiness Campaign, In-Charge developed Military Money with the support of the Office of the Under Secretary of Defense for Military Community and Family Policy, and the National Military Family Association.*

In the military, it pays to expect the unexpected. The most successful military families know the need to plan ahead, since deployment or a PCS move can happen at any time. This is Military Money's five-step plan for dealing with deployment—or to use at almost any time.

The first step is to avoid a crisis later by sitting down now with your spouse to create a deployment action plan for your finances. It all starts with understanding your family's financial situation, including monthly bills, how much debt you owe, and how much you have for emergencies. Most people, military or civilian, do not realize that even one late payment on a credit card or utility bill can negatively affect your credit report. To make sure all bills get paid on time, take advantage of online banking services or automatic payment plans.

Second, review your life, auto, and homeowners or renters insurance policies to find out if they are up-to-date or need to be changed. The military offers low-cost life insurance—Service members Group Life Insurance (SGLI)— a mere 7 cents per $1,000 of coverage, or $29 per month for the maximum coverage of $400,000 (includes $1 per month for Traumatic Injury Protection coverage). Any family that's not taking advantage of the maximum coverage at such a low rate should do so. Spouse coverage up to $100,000 also is available at very reasonable rates.

Third, when the service member is away on a deployment, the spouse (the wife about 93 percent of the time) maintains control of the household and must have access to the deployed spouse's financial accounts, assets, and belongings. Make sure both spouses are listed as joint account holders on all accounts, such as credit card or checking accounts, so the spouse left behind during a deployment is authorized to make changes and get information. Contact your JAG office to create or update a will and a durable power of attorney.

Fourth, take advantage of the Service members Civil Relief Act, which provides several safeguards for deployed military members. Among these benefits are a 6 percent cap on consumer and mortgage interest rate debt if military duty has reduced the family's income, payment deferral for federal taxes, protection from foreclosure and eviction, and a stay on civil proceedings such as divorce and bankruptcy. To invoke your rights, notify creditors, landlords, etc., of your military status by sending a letter asking for relief under the Act along with a copy of current military orders.

The final step is to create and maintain a plan for saving. If your credit card debt is under control, begin saving for an emergency fund - typically six months of living expenses—in a savings or money market account. Start contributing to a retirement savings plan, such as an Individual Retirement Account (IRA) or the government-sponsored Thrift Savings Plan (TSP), and set up automatic withdrawals from each paycheck to make saving easier. Also, the military's Savings Deposit Program allows service members in a combat zone to contribute all or part of their pay up to $10,000 in a special savings account that earns a guaranteed 10 percent annual interest rate.

> "The final step is to create and maintain a plan for saving."

Finally, as long as you remain a military family, another deployment or move is likely to occur in the future. After the deployment has concluded, discuss what went smoothly and what could have been handled better. By updating your deployment plan while the experience is still fresh on your mind, you and your spouse can avoid making the same mistakes twice.

 **FAQs**

Q. Is it correct that everyone is now entitled to get their credit scores free from the major credit bureaus?

A. *No, all Americans are now entitled to free annual copies of their credit reports, but credit scores are not included in the deal. To obtain your free reports, you can use a website set up by the three major credit bureaus: www. annualcreditreport.com. Be careful to type in the address correctly, because there are many look-alike and bogus sites trying to cash in unfairly. Or you can call toll free 877-322-8228.*

All three credit bureaus will sell scores to consumers, but Equifax is the only bureau offering the same FICO score that lenders use. (The other two, Experian and Trans Union, sell "consumer education scores" which typically are not used by lenders.) To get your scores for all three bureaus, you can visit www.myfico.com.

Q. Why is renters insurance so important for anyone who lives in rental housing?

A. *Almost two-thirds of the approximately 80 million people living in rental units don't have rental insurance. That's astonishing when you consider that the average cost to replace all personal property in a two-bedroom apartment is about $25,000 and the annual cost for the insurance coverage is a tiny fraction of that value.*

Q. Do you have $25,000 saved to replace your possessions if they're all lost in a fire or a hurricane?

A. *Renters insurance is relatively cheap compared to the amount of property that could be lost in a disaster. The average cost is just $12 a month for about $30,000 of property coverage and $100,000 of liability coverage, according to the Independent Insurance Agents and Brokers of America. And most renter policies are easily transferable from state to state—a great benefit for military families who frequently relocate.*

Q. Why is it critical to have a will and a power of attorney?

A. *Everyone, whether military or civilian, should have a will and power of attorney. For the service member, the will takes care of your estate if you don't come home, and the power of attorney designates someone to handle your affairs while you're away.*

It's important to have an up-to-date will because it guarantees that all of your property would go to those relatives, friends, and organizations you care about most. Without a will, the state decides for you what happens to your possessions.

The person to whom you grant power of attorney has the legal right to act on your behalf even without your consent. So make certain that you completely trust this person, such as your spouse or a parent. It's wise to limit the power of attorney to a specific period of time and to spell out exactly what the holder is authorized to do, such as payment of specific bills.

> **Check out Part 9: Military Family Law & Legislation for more information on wills.**

Q. What laws are on the books specifically to protect the civil rights of service members and veterans?

A. *Three major laws have been written specifically to help safeguard the financial security, civilian employment rights, and voting rights of service members and veterans:*

- **The Service members Civil Relief Act (SCRA)** *provides civil protections for military personnel while on active duty. (For more details, please read the section "Need To Know: Federal Law Helps Family Finances, But You Must Ask.")*
- **The Uniformed Services and Re-employment Rights Act (USERRA)** *prohibits employers from discriminating or retaliating against an employee or applicant because of past, present, or future military obligation.*
- **The Uniformed and Overseas Citizens Absentee Voting Act (UOCAVA)** *requires that states allow certain groups of citizens, including service members and their families, to register and vote absentee in a timely manner in elections for federal offices.*

> **Check out Chapter 45: Protecting Your Civilian Career.**

An online partnership between the U.S. Justice Department and other federal agencies that oversees these rights and protections, www.Service members.gov, has been launched to provide more information. The website also provides directions to file complaints with the Justice Department and other agencies that investigate and prosecute possible violations.

Q. How can I invest through the Thrift Savings Plan in a way that provides the highest possible rate of return for the amount of risk taken?

A. *The federal government's Thrift Savings Plan (TSP) began offering "lifecycle" —or "L"—funds in 2005 as a choice for those interested in saving for retirement. These funds make investment mixes, or allocations, based on your projected retirement date—such as 2020, 2030, etc.*

If your retirement target date is a long time from now, the lifecycle fund will be more heavily weighted toward stocks or stock mutual funds. As the date approaches when you will need your money, the investment mix will become weighted more heavily toward fixed-income or stable value investments, including bonds or bond funds and U.S. Treasury securities. This gradual shift to more conservative investments is designed to reduce your risk as you approach retirement.

 Need to Know

Federal Law Helps Family Finances, But You Must Ask

Some lenders, debt collectors, landlords, lawyers, and judges are unaware of a federal law that protects families of deployed service members (including mobilized National Guard and Reserves) from foreclosures, evictions and other financial consequences of military service.

Since the start of the Iraq war, The New York Times and other media outlets have published reports of lenders repossessing cars and foreclosing on homes owned by military members deployed overseas—despite federal law prohibiting these actions. Although most companies understand the law and try to follow it, others, such as smaller banks and car-loan companies, are not as informed.

The Service members Civil Relief Act (SCRA), signed by President Bush in 2003 as an expansion of a 1940 federal law, provides several safeguards for all deployed troops: protection from foreclosure and eviction, payment deferral for federal taxes, a 6 percent cap on consumer and mortgage interest-rate debt if military duty has reduced the family's income, and a stay on civil proceedings such as divorce and bankruptcy.

But military families need to understand that help is not automatic—you must ask for it. To invoke your rights, you must notify your creditor or landlord of your military status by sending a letter asking for relief under the Act along with a copy of current military orders.

Make the Connection on MFN!

www.eMilitary.org/YourMFN.html

Sign on to the address shown above and Make the Connection to more resources on this topic!

Active-duty military members may contact their local military legal assistance offices to assist them in understanding and enforcing their rights under the Act. The legal assistance attorneys can draft letters or make phone calls, if necessary, to help solve the problem.

9 Healthy Habits for Sound Money Management

From the Field with Megan Turak

Megan Turak *is the daughter of a WWII Army veteran and spouse of a Vietnam era Marine, Executive Vice President and co-owner of The Military Family Network, former Medical Records Manager with the Department of Veteran Affairs, a published writer of informative topics positively impacting the well-being of military families and has over twenty combined years of experience in executive leadership in the financial management and communications industries.*

Have you ever walked by a penny lying on the ground? Sure, many of us have. Would you have walked by a ten-dollar bill? Probably not! What was the difference between these two fortunate events? They're both legal tender—money—after all. Have you ever stopped to consider why you chose to pick up money in one situation and not pick up money in the other? Do you think, perhaps, it had something to do with how you perceive money in your life? Granted, a penny does not have the same value as ten dollars; and, as a result, you don't believe that it can affect your life in a meaningful way?

Well, you'd be right in one sense: ten dollars is more money than one penny. But this isn't the entire story; and if you stop there, you're losing out. Period. If you begin to think about that penny in terms of purchasing power, then the story begins to unfold with a little more clarity.

My grandfather once told me that a penny is very powerful. Of course, I doubted him and challenged his assertion. At that, my grandfather asked me to consider a hypothetical situation: If I wanted something at the store and it cost a dollar, but I only had ninety-nine cents, could I still get what I wanted? At that, my eyes grew wide. "You have just experienced the power of a penny," he told me.

Now you might argue that, these days, a store clerk will throw in that penny for you, and she just might. But have you ever stopped to think about all of the corporations that continually deal in pennies? On Wall Street, earnings are announced in terms of pennies; your calling card sells you calling minutes in pennies; a home contractor bases his or her estimate for work to be done on your

> **"You have just experienced the power of a penny."**

home in terms of pennies per square foot; when you dump all of your pocket change into one of those nifty coin sorters at the grocery store, they are charging you a fee in terms of a percent of your money's value, like 7 percent. What does that mean in real terms? It means that for every dollar they count, they are charging you seven cents! That's a huge profit—especially since you're more likely to receive a lesser interest rate on your savings from your own bank!

So I'd like you to consider: If all of these companies and individuals are amassing wealth through their willingness to deal in pennies, why aren't the laws of economics applying to you? Well, the laws of economics are applying to you. You just need to take advantage of all they have to offer. So read on. By mastering a few more strategies, you will be well on your way to securing the future you desire.

Hints for a Healthier Financial Future

As you learned from our penny story, you may not need to increase your salary to increase your standard of living. Even though it may be the fastest way, often times, like winning the lottery, it is not the easiest and not something you can control. After all, it is usually someone else who is making the decision to hire or promote you. However, you can control this: You can work; you can be dependable; and, you can work consistently. By always maintaining a stable and consistent salary of steady wages paid out in regular time periods, you can establish a budget, implement a savings plan, and accomplish more with what you have. Steady and regular pay and effective money management can go a long way to improving your standard of living.

Create a budget! Review your checkbooks, bank statements, and old receipts—any and all of your financial records from the past year or at the very least, the previous several months. Get out a pen and pad or use your computer and begin listing all of your expenditures. Organize them by categories like, Housing, Transportation, Utilities, Medical, Groceries, Enter-

> **"The goal is to find out exactly where your money goes."**

tainment, Restaurants, etc. The goal is to find out exactly where your money goes. Go to the NASD Investor Education Foundation website, www.saveandinvest.org for helpful tools Then, don't make any changes to your spending habits, but monitor yourself for the next month by carrying a diary with you and jotting down even the smallest amount of money you spend—even the $1.29 cup of coffee on the way to work. Write it down!

At the end of this process, you should know exactly where all of your money is going, and you should be able to spot any trouble areas and identify some areas for improvement. Once you have evaluated everything, you should be able come up with a realistic figure of how much it takes for you to live each month. Make sure to separate out your necessary expenses like housing and food from discretionary expenses like entertainment.

Remember, after you have identified areas where you think you might be able to save, implement your changes moderately. Have you been buying your lunch every-day? Perhaps you can modify this by bringing your lunch from home several days a week. Don't penalize yourself by never eating out because you might feel justified in splurging somewhere else. Implement your changes so that you can achieve your financial goals and still feel satisfied by your lifestyle choices. Now that you've gotten into the habit of monitoring your expenses, what should you do with the money you've saved? Professionals typically recommend, "paying yourself first" and usually suggest that 10 percent of your take home pay be put into an emergency funds account. This is excellent advice. And why shouldn't you pay yourself first? Who did all the work? Who put in all the effort? If your employer is going to deduct Social Security and taxes before you receive your check, shouldn't you at least take care to pay yourself next? (And don't get fooled into thinking that you don't earn enough money to do this. Even if you earn a dime, you can still put away a penny!) If you want, just consider yourself another bill, cut the check and deposit it into your savings account.

> **"Even if you earn a dime, you can still put away a penny!"**

Can't wait for that year-end raise or COLA of 1 or 2 percent? Wait until you open your first paycheck of the year, and see that after taxes your long awaited raise isn't enough to pay your cable bill. The money you actually receive does nothing to elevate your standard of living. So why take it? Do something better by investing that money into a savings or retirement account. And, if you take the initiative to invest the additional income before you receive that raise, you will never miss it. After all, haven't you already demonstrated that you could successfully get by on what you earned last year?

Remember your first goal to create an emergency savings account? You need to keep that savings account in cash or "fluid" investments like a money market so that you can access it in the event of an emergency. Visit your local bank or credit union, and open up an interest-bearing savings account or look for a no-load (no fee) money market fund. (Money magazines, like Kiplinger's Personal Finance Magazine, are great places to find competitive funds and ways to save your money that often earn better rates of return than a standard savings account.) But if you only feel safe with a savings account, be sure the bank's fees don't offset any gain you receive from earning interest. Most financial advisors suggest that you should accumulate somewhere in the neighborhood of several thousand dollars or at least three to six months of take home wages—enough to cover an automobile repair, a broken furnace, a leaking roof, or any other unexpected expense. As the account begins to grow (and it will), stay resolved to save. These funds should never be tapped except for an emergency.

Once you have successfully amassed your emergency fund, you have a choice. You can continue to put some savings away for a home, education, or other major life purchase, or you can begin to save for your retirement. (If you are really ambitious, you may be able to do both!) If you decide to save for a major purchase, your next step will be to decide where and how to save for it. Start by deciding when you'll need the money. If you want to make

> **"If you decide to save for a major purchase, your next step will be to decide where and how to save for it."**

your purchase in the near future or at least less than five years away, you really need to look at what the financial industry calls "cash instruments". Like with your emergency fund, this just means that you should be keeping your money in an interest bearing savings or money market account, in certificates of deposit (issued by most banks), or government savings bonds. Most of these are highly liquid (can be turned into cash quickly) and offer a good way to save money for short-term purposes. One word of caution: Make certain that you ask questions and understand any fees or penalties that may occur if you need your money sooner than you planned. Another idea would be to look into mutual funds, but remember to make sure that you review the information and prospectus carefully. Many funds have fees and administrative costs that may offset any true gain you receive—especially if your fund is taxable.

If you want to make a long term investment, then an excellent savings vehicle is typically your federal retirement plan—especially if the retirement plan offers matching dollars. If the government is willing to contribute a dollar for every dollar you contribute to your own retirement, then you have already doubled your money without doing anything! And, if you realize that most dollars contributed to a retirement plan are pre-tax contributions, you've increased your potential savings there, too.

Think about it. If you are in the 20 percent tax bracket and you contribute a dollar to your retirement plan, then you put a full dollar to work for your future! Had you taken that same dollar dispersed in your paycheck, you would have received only eighty cents, because twenty cents would have been used to pay your taxes. The most that you could then save would be eighty cents as compared to a dollar. Add in deferred taxation and compounding growth and it's an investment that is hard to beat! If you aren't already participating in your retirement plan, then schedule an appointment with your service's Retirement Specialist to learn more about the benefits offered to you. Even if you are not currently able to participate, learn about your options so you can include participation as a part of your future financial planning. Learn the dates of the next open enrollment and set a date to get involved in taking charge of your future.

> **"If the government is willing to contribute a dollar for every dollar you contribute ... then you have already doubled your money without doing anything!"**

Watch Out for Financial Pit Falls!

Credit Cards

Beware of credit cards. They are the downfall of many and the companies that offer them are more interested in lining their own pockets than filling yours. First, understand that using a credit card means you are accepting an unsecured loan from a credit card company and paying them a fee (interest) to borrow money. The interest applies if you do not pay off your credit card balance in full by the due date. So, if an item is on sale, and you charge it, and then don't pay the credit card balance and interest accrues, you have just wiped out the savings on that sale item. If this continues, you may very well end up paying more than the item was worth. Also, since most credit card companies charge interest rates that can go up (variable vs. fixed rates), the item that you agreed to buy at 9.5 percent could suddenly cost you 13.5 percent! If you are seriously considering a large purchase where you know in advance that you are going to be making monthly payments, you might do much better ap-

> **"Beware of credit cards. They are the downfall of many good folks and the companies that offer them are more interested in lining their own pockets than filling yours."**

proaching your local bank or credit union for a fixed rate personal loan. Here are some other good rules to guide credit card use:

- Don't keep them in your wallet. Consider keeping them in a safe deposit box where they are accessible, but not readily so. This will help you control impulse buying by forcing you to make planned purchases. Use the cards for planned major purchases, emergencies, or for purchases that you intend to pay for in full upon receipt of the credit card bill.
- Possess only one credit card—two at most. Opening and using too many credit lines can lower your credit score and cause your interest rates to rise on credit cards you already have since credit card companies routinely check the credit histories of their customers for these opportunities. Pay close attention to those confusing little legal notices you receive from your credit card company! You can rest assured that the revisions to your agreement contained within those notices are not in your favor, but they do offer some choices such as declining to use the card or the increased interest rate—if your finances allow you to take advantage of them! Note that you normally need to respond in writing to the company by a certain date to do this.
- Pay the credit cards off in full at the end of each month or before the bill is due to avoid being charged interest on your account. The grace period typically only applies if you pay the balance in its entirety. If you are already carrying balances on your credit cards, select the credit card with the highest interest and pay that one off first. This may mean making the minimum payments on other credit cards for a while. Once you have paid off the entire amount on the highest interest credit card, decide whether or not to cut up the card and throw it away. However, if you want to improve your credit score (which is determined by your credit report), then you may wish to keep that card account open. If, on the other hand, you are trying to manage your current debts by cutting down on the number of credit lines available, then send the company written notice that you are closing the account. Make sure to keep a copy for your records. Proceed to the next credit card with the next highest interest rate and repeat the entire decision-making process.

> **"Read your fine print and use your credit card wisely!"**

- Ask questions about fees before choosing a payment method. Most companies offer multiple ways to pay your monthly bill: mail, phone and online. You don't want to get into the habit of paying fees just to pay your bill—this greatly reduces the amount of money you are using to pay down your debt.

- Select credit cards with the lowest interest rates. Once again, Kiplinger's Personal Finance Magazine is a great source of information for helping you locate the best card for your situation.
- Watch out for tiered interest rates now being offered by some credit cards. They have several different interest rates being applied to different types of transactions all made with the same card. For instance, balance transfers, cash advances and purchases may all be treated differently. In some circumstances, even purchases may be separated into different categories with different interest rates. Read your fine print and use your credit card wisely!
- Don't use those cash advance checks sent to you in the mail (or, use them cautiously if you are transferring a balance from one card to another)! Cash advance interest rates (not promotional interest rates) are always higher than interest rates for purchases, yet credit card companies typically apply your payments to lower interest rate purchases before cash advances in order to increase their profits.
- Keep an eye on the calendar! Many cards have significant penalties for late payments and you may have as little as 25 days to make your payment on time. Credit card companies count this grace period from the date the bill is mailed not when you receive it. Be sure to read the fine print. The penalties can range from significant fees, to an increase in your interest rate, or, if the lateness is reported to the credit reporting agencies, an increase in the rates on other cards you hold. In addition, keep tabs on your credit limit. A purchase you are attempting to make may or may not be turned down at the cash register. This can cause you to go over your available limit and the assessment of another fee. This can also happen automatically. If the interest assessed each month is added to your outstanding balance and you go over your credit limit, you will usually be assessed another fee. In some circumstances, this can go on month-in and month-out. If you fall into the situation, where accumulating interest and fees interfere with your ability to pay down your debt, seek help immediately! You can contact the credit card company directly, your military family support service, a reliable no fee credit counseling agency, or your state representatives—especially if you believe you are being treated unfairly.

> **"Pay close attention to those confusing little legal notices you receive from your credit card company!"**

- If you are a homeowner, you may be offered a home equity loan in order to pay off your credit card debt. Financial professionals have differing opinions about this practice. There are, however, several factors to consider:

- If you do not have your spending under control, do not take out a home equity loan unless you have closed all of your credit card accounts. I repeat: Do not take out a home equity loan unless you have your spending under control. Otherwise, you will run the risk of creating additional debt by using your credit cards all over again. In fact, many individuals who do this, end up having to make payments on both a home equity loan and credit cards, too. Sometimes, the strain is so great that these individuals find themselves in bankruptcy court and at risk of losing their homes.

> **"This only works if you do not replace the consolidated credit card debt with new debt!"**

- This brings up another very important point. Credit card debt is called "unsecured debt." If you don't pay it back, the company can place you in "collections," ruin your credit rating, and even take you to court; but they can't come directly after your home or personal belongings like a collateralized loan. If you take out a home equity loan, you are really collateralizing your loan with your home—basically offering your home as security—until you pay off the loan. This is called a "secured loan." If you don't make your payments, the bank or lender can enter proceedings to take your home. As a rule of thumb, it does not make sense to take "unsecured debt" and convert it into "secured debt."
- So does it ever make sense to convert unsecured debt into secured debt? Well, interest paid on credit card debt is not tax deductible, whereas interest paid on home loans, usually is. If you have a lot of unsecured debt and happen to be in a high income tax bracket, then you may wish to consider converting the debt in order to lower your interest rate and maximize your tax savings. Check with your accountant for advice.

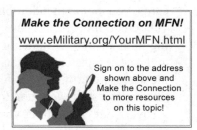

Make the Connection on MFN!
www.eMilitary.org/YourMFN.html

Sign on to the address shown above and Make the Connection to more resources on this topic!

- It also makes sense if you have your financial situation under control so that you will not fall prey to major credit card debt again. Thus, if you consolidate your high interest credit card debt into a home equity loan, you lower your interest, create a possible tax savings, and lower your monthly payment. Once again, at the risk of being repetitive, this only works if you do not replace the consolidated credit card debt with new debt!
- And finally, it may make sense, if you have so much credit card debt that you just can't afford to make all the monthly payments required.

Then, consolidating the debt in order to make one monthly payment, that is usually a lower amount, may make sense. But be careful if you choose this route!

- Another note about credit cards. If you have an excellent credit history and payment record, and have a manageable amount of debt on your credit card that you could pay off if you wanted to, then you should pay attention to actions taken by the FOMC (Federal Open Market Committee)—the government's monetary policy-making group that discusses economic and financial conditions. If they announce that they are lowering the Federal Funds Rate (Fed rate) then interest rates will drop. This is an excellent opportunity for you to contact your credit card company and insist that they lower your interest rate. Many will oblige. If they refuse to negotiate with you, however, then find a new card company.

- Finally, if you think you can't make your credit card payments, don't run and hide. Be proactive. Examine your situation. Decide what you can pay. Can you pay only a lump sum amount? Can you make monthly payments? Then, call the credit card company and ask to speak with someone who can make an immediate decision today about your account. When that person gets on the phone, make your offer and be willing to negotiate. State your terms and ask whether they will accept them. For example, you might offer to pay such and such amount each month until the debt is satisfied, agree not to use the card, and ask that the company work with you by lowering the amount of the monthly payment and freeze all ongoing interest charges. Most credit card companies would prefer not to write off your debt or sell it to a collection agency for fractions on the dollar. As a result, they will often work with you to resolve emergent financial difficulties. So, contact them when the going gets rough. And don't forget to follow up your conversation with a letter outlining in writing the terms that you and the credit card company have agreed upon. Go to The Military Family Network at www.eMilitary.org/YourMFN.html for resources offering sample letters to guide you in this process.

Payday Lenders

They're in every military town. In fact, they seem to be about everywhere you go. And, why wouldn't you see them? These are lucrative businesses – not for you, but for their owners. You see their signs and ads everywhere saying, "I just need enough cash to tide me over until payday" or "Get cash until payday...$100 or more...Fast!" You find these ads on the radio, television, the Internet, even in the mail. They appear to be

Make the Connection on MFN!
www.eMilitary.org/YourMFN.html

Sign on to the address shown above and Make the Connection to more resources on this topic!

the perfect solution. After all, you only need a quick fix till your next pay-check. Well, the Federal Trade Commission (FTC) says that "Payday loans = Costly Cash" so it's important for you to take a moment to understand why there are better alternatives available to you when you are cash-strapped and need a short term loan.

Here's how they work. These ads refer to payday loans—which come at a very high price. Check cashers, finance companies and others are making small, short-term, high-rate loans that go by a variety of names: payday loans, cash advance loans, check advance loans, post-dated check loans or deferred deposit check loans. Usually, a borrower writes a personal check payable to the lender for the amount he or she wishes to borrow plus a fee. The company gives the borrower the amount of the check minus the fee. Fees charged for payday loans are usually a percentage of the face value of the check or a fee charged per amount borrowed—say, for every $50 or $100 loaned. And, if you extend or "roll-over" the loan—say for another two weeks—you will pay the fees for each extension.

Under the Truth in Lending Act, the cost of payday loans—like other types of credit—must be disclosed. Among other information, you must receive, in writing, the finance charge (a dollar amount) and the annual per-centage rate or APR (the cost of credit on a yearly basis).

A cash advance loan secured by a personal check - such as a payday loan - is very expensive credit. Let's say you write a personal check for $115 to borrow $100 for up to 14 days. The check casher or payday lender agrees to hold the check until your next payday. At that time, depending on the particu-lar plan, the lender deposits the check, you redeem the check by paying the $115 in cash, or you roll-over the check by paying a fee to extend the loan for another two weeks. In this example, the cost of the initial loan is a $15 finance charge and 391 percent APR. If you roll-over the loan three times, the finance charge would climb to $60 to borrow $100.

There are alternatives to payday loans. Consider the possibilities before choosing a payday loan:

- When you need credit, shop carefully. Compare offers. Look for the credit offer with the lowest APR - consider a small loan from your credit union or small loan company, an advance on pay from your employer, or a loan from family or friends. A cash advance on a credit card also may be a possibility, but it may have a higher interest rate than your other sources of funds: find out the terms before you decide. Also, a local community-based organization may make small business loans to individuals.
- Compare the APR and the finance charge (which includes loan fees, inter-est and other types of credit costs) of credit offers to get the lowest cost.

- Ask your creditors for more time to pay your bills. Find out what they will charge for that service —as a late charge, an additional finance charge or a higher interest rate.
- Make a realistic budget, and figure your monthly and daily expenditures. Avoid unnecessary purchases—even small daily items. Their costs add up. Also, build some savings—even small deposits can help—to avoid borrowing for emergencies, unexpected expenses or other items. For example, by putting the amount of the fee that would be paid on a typical $300 payday loan in a savings account for six months, you would have extra dollars available. This can give you a buffer against financial emergencies.
- Find out if you have, or can get, overdraft protection on your checking account. If you are regularly using most or all of the funds in your account and if you make a mistake in your checking (or savings) account ledger or records, overdraft protection can help protect you from further credit problems. Find out the terms of overdraft protection.
- If you need help working out a debt repayment plan with creditors or developing a budget, contact your military family support center or local consumer credit counseling service. There are non-profit groups in every state that offer credit guidance to consumers. These services are available at little or no cost. Also, check with your employer, credit union or housing authority for no- or low-cost credit counseling programs.
- If you decide you must use a payday loan, borrow only as much as you can afford to pay with your next paycheck and still have enough to make it to the next payday.

Pawnshops, Title Loans and Rent-to-Own Stores

Pawnshops can be an expensive way to obtain a loan, and a risky one as well. You could just end up losing the item that you pawned. The same could be said for title loan outfits, too. The basic principle here is that you place down an item that you own as collateral for the loan that you receive. Typically, you will receive only a fraction of the item's true value. You are also charged interest on the loan as well as other charges if

Make the Connection on MFN!
www.eMilitary.org/YourMFN.html

Sign on to the address shown above and Make the Connection to more resources on this topic!

you fall behind in your payments. These charges could be late fees, collections fees, repossession fees as well as storage fees—if your automobile is held on the company's property. If you fail to repay the loan, you lose your collateral since the store has the right to sell your pawned items. If you have used your automobile to obtain the loan, you have just lost your car!

Rent-to-Own stores operate a bit differently, but are still just as expensive. Sometimes military families use these stores when they transfer to a new duty station. They may have disposed of some of their belongings to make the weight limit or simply because the item was too old to bother moving. At any rate, Rent-to-Own stores can be an expensive alternative to buying or replacing the item that you need. At first glance, the payments seem small and manageable. But if you look more closely, and do the math, you will see that the weekly rental you are paying multiplied by the number of weeks it will take you to own the item outweighs the true value of the item. Add in any sales taxes and possible delivery fees and you have really over paid for that refrigerator! Had you purchased the refrigerator out right, you would have saved hundreds of dollars. Look around – there are more affordable ways of getting what you need.

MyPay

Recently, two private U.S. industry firms disclosed that overseas hackers broke into myPay user accounts. According to the Chief Information Officer (CIO) at one of these firms, these attacks were carried out by "key logging" software installed on users PC's. This software allowed the thieves to steal the users account information from their home computers, by capturing the user's keystrokes. They were able to detect passwords, IDs and other personal information from a diagnostic used in the software development, which is also known as "keystroke logging." Key logging software is often installed on systems when an individual simply views emails or clicks links that look and seem like reputable sites.

As the Defense Finance and Accounting Service (DFAS) continues to protect information and data on myPay—it's important to remember that you have a responsibility to take measures to protect your personal information from scams and identity theft.

myPay uses a variety of security features to protect data and in its transmission to users' computers. The features include items such as 128 bit encryption, firewalls, Virtual Private Networks (VPN) and other measures. Despite these measures, it is vital that service members do their best to secure their accounts by remaining alert to the potential possibility of online fraud.

For instance, "phishing" attacks trick people into parting with personal information by luring them to false corporate Web sites or by requesting that personal information be sent in a return email. According to the Federal Trade Commission, "phishers" send emails or pop-up messages claiming to be from a business or organization you would routinely deal with—an In-

Make the Connection on MFN!
www.eMilitary.org/YourMFN.html

Sign on to the address shown above and Make the Connection to more resources on this topic!

ternet service provider, bank, online payment service or even a government agency. The message usually says that you need to 'update' or 'validate' your account information and might threaten dire consequences if you don't respond. You are directed to a Web site that mimics a legitimate organization's site. The purpose of the bogus site is to trick you into divulging personal information so the scam operators can steal your identity and make purchases or commit crimes in your name.

Whether it is phishing, identity theft, government email scams, credit card offers or electronic commerce fraud, there are scammers on the Internet who are very creative and constantly coming up with new scams or variations on old scams. The only way to fight back is with knowledge.

Here are several things myPay users should consider to protect data, not only when using myPay, but with any electronic commerce activity (e.g. online banking, credit card purchases, etc.):

- Install operating system and application software (e.g. Internet Explorer) updates regularly. Many of these updates are issued to fix security problems, which have been identified.
- Install and use anti-virus software and personal firewalls. Keep this software updated. The correct use of these programs can help protect your system from being compromised by malicious software (e.g. software which can capture information processed on your computer, etc). The DoD Computer Emergency Readiness Team (CERT) makes this type of software available to most DoD employees (military and civilian). Check with your agency or visit:
  a. https://www.jtfgno.mil/antivirus/home_use.htm
  b. http://www.mcafee.com/dod/
- Do not store your various User-IDs and passwords in files on your computer. If someone gains access to your computer this is the type of information they look for and would aid them in accessing your account.
- After using your browser (e.g. Internet Explorer, etc) to access sites where you process sensitive information (e.g. myPay, your bank account, etc.) close all of your browser windows and restart a new browser session. Sometimes the browser can hold that information in memory (e.g. cache, etc) and some web sites know where to look to find it.
- Be very careful when installing software that gives others access to your computer. Remote service software or peer-to-peer software used for file sharing can create unintended openings into your computer that outsiders can use if the software is not configured correctly.
- Don't email personal or financial information. Email is not a secure method of transmitting personal information. If you initiate a transaction and want to provide your personal and financial information through a Web

site, look for indicators that the site is secure, such as an image of a lock or lock icon on the browser's status bar or a Web site address that begins "https:" (the "s" stands for "secure").

- DFAS does not send email messages asking myPay users to update or validate information. myPay does send email messages that provide important information about a user's pay account, but myPay never asks for users to send passwords, login names, Social Security numbers, or other personal information through e-mail.

Finally, if you identify or suspect malicious activity regarding your account, contact DFAS immediately. You will find important contact information by going to: https://mypay.dfas.mil/FAQ.htm#ABOUT%20myPay and selecting the "Assistance/Customer Support" link.

With all this discussion about financial pitfalls and owing others, you might be asking about now if there is anyone who owes *you*. Well, actually they might! Many states have "Unclaimed Property" departments where they hold millions of dollars of assets for people just like you. As a member of the military community, you've probably lived in more than one state and moved more than once. Each time you've relocated, you've opened a bank account, put a housing or utility deposit down, or had to move without being able to leave a forwarding address. As a result, money—in your name—may have been left behind and sent to the unclaimed property department in the state where you lived. Look for your money today – here's how:

The Military Family Network has consolidated the unclaimed property departments for all 50 states in one simple place on our website at www.eMilitary.org. You can click, visit, and search for free every place you have ever lived for what you may have left behind. And, it may not be chump change. I know someone who collected $1,700 dollars! And keep in mind, if you are ever contacted by a company claiming to have located money for you, but won't tell you where it is until you pay a fee for their services, don't be fooled! The states *never* make you pay for this service!

> **"The states never make you pay for this service!"**

Don't be afraid of your finances. Don't be confused by money jargon. And, don't be afraid of learning - Read, read, read! Pick up the Wall Street Journal. Subscribe to personal investment magazines like Kiplinger's Personal Finance Magazine, and Military Money. Watch the nightly business news. The advice and education you receive will be worth more than the cost of the subscription or the time you sit to watch and listen!

Here's a primer to get you started. No matter how fancy it all sounds, there are really only three basic investment types: cash, bonds and stocks. Pretty much everything else out there is a variety of these fundamental building blocks. So, now want to hear the good part? You already know a lot about these three things.

Make the Connection on MFN!
www.eMilitary.org/YourMFN.html

Sign on to the address shown above and Make the Connection to more resources on this topic!

Cash is, well, the cash in your pocket. Bonds are like an I-Owe-You (IOU). For example, a friend needs money so they borrow it from you and agree to pay you interest until they've repaid it to you. This is similar to how a mortgage works. And then, there are stocks. Let's say that same friend has a lemonade stand and wants to raise money to buy a bigger sign. Instead of borrowing money from you (like with a bond), they agree to share their earnings (and losses) with you by making you a part owner of the lemonade stand. A stock certificate signifies that you are an owner in a company. So, when your company does well, you make money and when your company does poorly, you lose money. Now, this is a very simple and basic explanation of cash, bonds and stocks and you are urged to take the next step to learning more about them; but I wanted you to see that, by breaking down the financial jargon, it's really not so intimidating. You can do it!

And lastly, be prepared. Every one needs estate planning—no matter how much or how little you earn. Take charge of your own financial worth now. Don't let the state make your decisions for you. It matters how you register your home, your car, and your bank accounts. For instance, many advisors recommend that, especially for a deployment, both husband and wife should have access to marital assets and that the couple's financial assets, like their bank account, be registered jointly. For most of us, this is probably the right advice. However, for the very wealthy, this could be a very expensive mistake. It matters how you want your assets distributed to your heirs. It matters how you want your children cared for. Estate planning can be a complex process and is certainly too weighty a subject to be covered here. So, review the legal section of this book and visit an attorney now.

 **FAQs**

Q. I'm working very hard at managing my money. How can I keep credit card and home equity line of credit offers out of my mailbox? I hate junk mail!

A. *Stop annoying solicitations from reaching you by making sure that the credit bureaus are not selling your name and personal information by selling their mailing lists. Recent legislation has given the public more ways of controlling the types of mail that they receive. Visit the Credit Info Center at http://www.creditinfocenter.com/cards/preventSellLists.shtml for a comprehensive list of opt-out resources by both telephone and mail. Keep in mind that in some cases you will need to renew your preferences every two years.*

Q. In your helpful financial tips, you mentioned that the states where I've lived might owe me money. Where did you say I should look for this information? I could use the cash!

A. *Every state in the Union has an official website where they list their Unclaimed Property Departments. If you want, you can look up and visit each state's website separately or, to speed things up, The Military Family Network has done the work for you and placed all of the unclaimed property departments in one place. Visit the following link and have fun on your treasure hunt! http://www.emilitary.org/forums/index.php?showtopic=760*

Q. I don't understand what it means when I'm asked how I feel about my finances. I mean, when I have it, I feel great; when I don't, I don't. It seems pretty straightforward to me. Am I missing something?

A. *Yes—especially if you have a spouse, significant other, or family involved. When you are asked to consider your feelings about money, what you are really being asked is to prioritize your desires versus your needs, establish financial goals, and measure your investment risk. In addition, when others are involved, money management requires a team approach. It is important to have their feedback, too, since they may have different ideas about money. You may have to compromise. Check out this money personality quiz offered by the Myvesta Foundation to briefly size up your approach* *to your finances and then share it with others. Visit www.Myvesta.org, note "resources" in the left hand column of the website, skim down and select "Money Personality Test".*

Q. How can being in debt affect my military career?

A. *Learn about it now! Visit www.Myvesta.org, note "resources" in the left hand column of the website, skim down to "Special Situations" and select "Military Finances." Once the new page loads, scroll down until you see "How Being in Debt Can Affect Your Military Career." There is some other great information here, too.*

 Need to Know

Common Mistakes Young Adults Make with Money

- Buying items you don't need . . . and paying extra for them in interest
- Getting too deeply in debt
- Paying bills late or otherwise tarnishing your credit rating
- Having too many credit cards
- Not watching your expenses
- Not saving for your future
- Paying too much in fees
- Not taking responsibility for your finances

Make the Connection on MFN!
www.eMilitary.org/YourMFN.html

Sign on to the address shown above and Make the Connection to more resources on this topic!

Financial Fraud and Theft

Identity theft is a serious crime. It occurs when your personal information is stolen and used without your knowledge to commit fraud or other crimes. Identity theft can cost you time and money. It can destroy your credit and ruin your good name.

The rigors of military life can compound the problems that identity theft creates.

Deter: Minimize Your Risk

Deter identity thieves by safeguarding your information.
- Shred financial documents and paperwork with personal information before you discard them.

- Protect your Social Security number. Don't carry your Social Security card in your wallet or write your Social Security number on a check. Give it out only if absolutely necessary or ask to use another identifier.
- Don't give out personal information on the phone, through the mail, or over the Internet unless you know whom you are dealing with.
- Never lend your credit cards or account information to anyone else.
- Do not click on links sent in unsolicited e-mails; instead, type in a Web address you know. Use firewalls, anti-spyware, and anti-virus software to protect your home computer, and keep them up-to-date. Visit OnGuardOn-line.gov for more information.
- Don't use an obvious password like your birth date, your mother's maiden name, or the last four digits of your Social Security number.
- Keep your personal information in a secure place, especially if you live in barracks or with roommates.
- Don't let mail pile up unattended if you can't collect it. Use a mail stop or P.O. Box, or have someone you trust hold your mail while you are away.

Detect: Identify Suspicious Activity

Detect suspicious activity by routinely monitoring your financial accounts and billing statements. If you are unable to take these steps while you are deployed, consider placing an active duty alert on your credit report.

- Inspect your credit report. Credit reports contain information about you, including what accounts you have and your bill-paying history. The law requires each of the major nationwide consumer reporting companies — Equifax, Experian, and TransUnion — to give you a free copy of your credit report every year if you ask for it. Visit www.AnnualCreditReport.com or call 1-877-322-8228, a service created by these three companies, to order your free credit reports each year. You also can write: Annual Credit Report Request Service, P.O. Box 105281, Atlanta, GA 30348-5281.
- Inspect your financial statements. Review your financial accounts and read your billing statements regularly, looking for charges you did not make. If you review financial accounts online from a public computer, be sure to log off financial sites before you end your session. **Be alert to signs that require immediate attention:**
  - Bills that do not arrive as expected
  - Unexpected credit cards or account statements

Make the Connection on MFN!
www.eMilitary.org/YourMFN.html

Sign on to the address shown above and Make the Connection to more resources on this topic!

- Denials of credit for no apparent reason
- Calls or letters about purchases you did not make

Defend: Take Action Immediately

Defend against ID theft as soon as you suspect it.

- Place a "Fraud Alert" on your credit reports, and review the reports carefully. The alert tells creditors to follow certain procedures before they open new accounts in your name or make changes to your existing accounts. The three nationwide consumer reporting companies have toll-free numbers for placing an initial 90-day fraud alert; a call to one company is sufficient:
  Equifax: 1-800-525-6285
  Experian: 1-888-EXPERIAN (397-3742)
  TransUnion: 1-800-680-7289
  Placing a fraud alert entitles you to free copies of your credit reports. Look for inquiries from companies you haven't contacted, accounts you didn't open, and debts on your accounts that you can't explain.
- Close accounts. Close any accounts that have been tampered with or established fraudulently. Call the security or fraud departments of each company where an account was opened or changed without your okay. Follow up in writing, with copies of supporting documents.
- Use the "ID Theft Affidavit" located at http://www.ftc.gov/bcp/conline/pubs/credit/affidavit.pdf to support your written statement.
- Ask for verification that the disputed account has been closed and the fraudulent debts discharged.
- Keep copies of documents and records of your conversations about the theft.
- **Explain the situation to your commanding officer.** You don't want your C.O. taken by surprise if contacted by creditors looking to collect on charges made by the identity thief. You also may want a referral to a legal assistance office.
- File a police report. File a report with military law enforcement and the local police (if you are in the United States). Their reports will help you with creditors who may want proof of the crime.
- Report the theft to the Federal Trade Commission. Your report helps law enforcement officials across the United States in their investigations.
  Online: Report ID Theft at https://rn.ftc.gov/pls/dod/widtpubl$.startup?Z_ORG_CODE=PU03

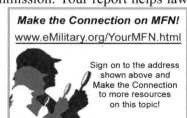

Make the Connection on MFN!
www.eMilitary.org/YourMFN.html

Sign on to the address shown above and Make the Connection to more resources on this topic!

By phone: 1-877-ID-THEFT (438-4338) or TTY, 1-866-653-4261
By mail: Identity Theft Clearinghouse, Federal Trade Commission, Washington, DC 20580

- Make sure to keep copies of all reports that you file.
- Visit www.creditinfocenter.com/ to find a step-by-step guide on what to do if your wallet or purse is stolen. Click on the link in the left hand column that says "Identity". When the page loads, scroll down to the article entitled, "The woeful tale of a waylaid wallet - Things to think about before you lose yours" by Maureen Rooney.
- If you are deployed away from your usual duty station and do not expect to seek new credit while you are deployed, consider placing an "active duty alert" on your credit report. An active duty alert requires creditors to take steps to verify your identity before granting credit in your name. The law allows you to use a personal representative to place or remove an alert. An active duty alert is effective for one year, unless you ask for it to be removed sooner. If your deployment lasts longer than a year, you may place another alert on your report. To place an active duty alert, or to have it removed, call the toll-free fraud number of one of the three nationwide consumer-reporting companies. The company you call is required to contact the other two.

92 Tips for Spending Less
Department of Defense Military Assistance Program

Visit www.dod.mil/mapsite, look to the top of the web page and note the image of a "map"; within the image, you will see a dollar sign ($) and the heading "The Money Station". Click on this link. Once the new web page loads, scroll down to the center of the page to see a link that says "92 tips for Spending Less". Select this topic and learn 92 ways to keep more money in your pocket! (This is also a great resource for financial calculators and other important information.)

When You Need Help:
- Chain of Command
  - Offers advice and support
  - Suggests resources that might help you
  - Help you deal with your creditors
  - Lend a sympathetic ear
- Family Support and/or Readiness Center
  - Can review your situation and help you prepare a debt repayment plan to share with your creditors

- Offer advice on working with creditors and can provide financial counseling to help you change your spending habits and attitude toward debt
- Services are provided free of charge—if you're looking for assistance with your debt, look there first.
- Here's a great resource for helping you to discuss financial issues with your spouse and plan for deployment or relocation. It is offered by NASD Investor Education Foundation and the website is located at www.saveandinvest.org. (Once there, select "Deployment and PCS" from the left side column and then, the "Money and Mobility" link. This is a great tool that should be worked through page-by-page, but you will find the tips for talking with your spouse if you advance about ten pages forward through the document.)
- Your local library contains free information on getting out of financial trouble, managing debt, and dealing with creditors and collection agencies. If you have access to the Internet and online services, you'll find all types of help with managing debt. To start, check out the list of resources located at http://www.emilitary.org/YourMFN.html.

Make the Connection on MFN!
www.eMilitary.org/YourMFN.html

Sign on to the address shown above and Make the Connection to more resources on this topic!

- And, if you want to fix it yourself, try a visit to www.creditinfocenter.com/ and look at the left side column. Notice a link that says "Sample Letters". Click on this link and when the page loads, select the form letter that bests suits your needs. All of the forms are designed to help you with various credit situations. There is a lot of other helpful information located at this web site as well. Just remember, when you are doing things on your own, it is wise to verify your information against several sources before proceeding.

Professional Friends Every Family Needs
- A physician
- An attorney
- An accountant
- An insurance agent
- An investment advisor

Make the Connection on MFN!
www.eMilitary.org/YourMFN.html

Sign on to the address shown above and Make the Connection to more resources on this topic!

Remember to do your due diligence when selecting a professional advisor. Ask friends for referrals, check prospective advisors through their professional association and interview them carefully to determine whether he or she understands your needs and will be attentive to your concerns so that you will have a strong, working relationship that includes trust. Ask for references, check out regulatory agencies like the state attorneys office and licensing boards and don't forget organizations like the Better Business Bureau (BBB). Most importantly, make certain that you are comfortable with the individual. If, at any moment, your gut doesn't agree, find someone else!

Toolkit

Take some time and develop your emergency financial first aid kit. This tool takes you step-by-step in building a comprehensive reference document to keep you and your financial records organized and accessible. This resource will help to prepare and sustain you in the event of an emergency. Do it today!

Emergency Financial First Aid Kit © Operation HOPE, Inc.

National Credit Union Administration.gov

Visit www.ncua.gov, look at the left hand column, scroll down to "General Information" and select "Publications".
Once the new page has loaded, skim down to "Brochures" and select "Emergency Financial First Aid Kit".

Make the Connection on MFN!
www.eMilitary.org/YourMFN.html

Sign on to the address
shown above and
Make the Connection
to more resources
on this topic!

10 Finding Bargains Online

From the Field with Michael Allen

Michael T. Allen is the Founder and President of Shopping-Bargains.com, LLC and moderates an online forum community with the Military Family Network where he works to connect the military community to military deals found on the Internet.

Why shop online? In addition to convenience, Internet shoppers enjoy many advantages, including time and fuel savings by avoiding travel, easy access to brand name stores, products not available locally, and lower costs made possible through intensively competitive pricing and coupons.

This chapter serves as a guide on how to take greater advantage of this incredible money-saving resource. It is based on my personal experience from a decade of shopping online and marketing more than 1,000 online stores featured on Shopping-Bargains.com.

Some Personal Advice Regarding Online Shopping

Today you can buy almost anything online—from engagement rings to truck tires, clothing to pet supplies, groceries to home improvement products, and almost everything in between. Many services are available online as well: you can post your resume online, search for jobs, buy postage, convert your digital photos into artwork, go to school, participate in weight-loss classes, and so much more. And the good news is that it's getting easier to do these things online as more creative Internet tools are developed.

In addition to the convenience advantage, there are tens of thousands of bargains and online coupons available to savvy Internet shoppers. Online coupons work similarly to traditional manufacturer coupons in that they provide a discount for making a purchase. Online coupons, however, are often called coupon codes since they are typically a word or numeric "code" that can be typed into a special box in the shopping cart during checkout to provide free shipping, a dollar value, or percentage price reduction, or some other incentive. Sometimes online coupons are simply made up of a special link that must be clicked to activate a specific discount that is applied during checkout.

Given the vast number of options for shopping and saving money, the best practices for online shopping involve a compromise between time and money. Since we all have limited amounts of both, we have to strike a balance between searching for the best bargain and not spending too much time conducting that search. And, with the high price of fuel, it is wise to factor in your transportation time and costs and compare this to the cost of shipping.

> **"Internet consistently contains the best source of current product reviews, brand comparison tables, and pricing options."**

Financially Savvy Online Shopping Strategies

The online shopping strategy varies depending on whether or not you know the exact product you want to buy. For example, if you are looking for a basic MP3 player, I advise one strategy that varies slightly from what I recommend to those who are looking for a specific Apple iPod model. If you are looking for a product to meet a specific need, such as maternity clothing, then my shopping strategy takes another twist to help you save more money. In general, though, I've found that the Internet consistently contains the best source of current product reviews, brand comparison tables, and pricing options.

If you don't know the specific product or brand you want, then here's my advice. In researching an MP3 player, for example, I suggest two approaches. One involves using a search engine to look for "MP3 player reviews." This approach, however, could be a bit risky because many websites are created specifically to rank well for search terms like this and they might not really contain unbiased reviews. The preferred way is to check out a trusted review website (like www.consumerreports.org, www.epinions.com, or www.cnet.com) or an online store that carries many competing brands. Read their product reviews. Many online stores now post real customer reviews and detailed feature comparisons of specific products to help you get a good idea of the positives and negatives. You can then narrow down your options—features, warranties, accessories, etc.—to find the specific brand and model you wish to purchase.

If you know exactly the product and brand you want, then move directly into the process of finding the best price and shipping combination, based on your timeframe for delivery.

When you are ready to buy the product, you can sometimes save a lot of money by using some basic price comparison tools (some websites like www.epinions.

> **"Read their product reviews."**

com and www.cnet.com offer both price comparison tools and product reviews). These tools help you compare pricing, and sometimes shipping, across many online stores for the specific brand and product model of many items. I recommend narrowing your search down to three or four stores offering the lowest price. Be sure to factor in shipping costs, sales taxes, and the store's reputation, return policies, and customer service options when making your selection. Also, please note that comparison tools are not 100 percent accurate and do not include all online stores.

> **"Read their product reviews."**

After you have selected three or four stores you are willing to buy from, I then suggest that you shop at a "coupon site" (such as www.shopping-bargains. com) and see if there are any coupon codes or special offers that can give you additional savings, free shipping, or some other benefit at one of these stores. Remember, in order to activate an online code you need to click the coupon link and usually type the coupon code into the special coupon or promotion code box during checkout.

Earlier, I mentioned that my suggestions take a bit of a twist for more generic products where brand is not as important. In these cases, to find the best deal, you can often skip all the above and go directly to a coupon and deals-oriented website to see which online store offers the best coupons or bargains at that time. At Shopping-Bargains. com you can browse stores "by department" to compare current offers from similar stores and determine which store offers free shipping or the largest coupon code discount. Some coupon sites also offer a "product search tool" that lets you browse a list of similar products from many stores.

Make the Connection on MFN!
www.eMilitary.org/YourMFN.html

Sign on to the address shown above and Make the Connection to more resources on this topic!

It should be noted that advertisements or commissions fund most information, review, and coupon websites. Advertisers pay the website to display ads—from obvious banners and pop-ups to less noticeable text links embedded in related information and coupons. Other websites earn commission based on sales that originate from shoppers who clicked a store or product link on their website and then bought something from that linked store. This is how these companies stay in business and are able to bring the best deals to consumers. In order for the company where you found the code to get credit for bringing your business to the manufacturer, you must "click thru" their site and redeem the coupon. Think of it this way. You go into a store and a great sales associate finds you the best deal. The nice associate works strictly on commission. If you are happy with their service, the best way to reward them is to make your purchase with them so they earn the commission on your sale. The same is true for most Internet coupon websites. You have to "go to the register" with them by clicking through their website to make your purchase, or they do not get the "commission."

So, reward yourself with the great deal AND the website that brought it to you, by clicking through their doors!

 **FAQs**

Q. I'm afraid to use my credit card online. How can I tell if it is safe?

A. *All reputable online stores use encryption technology to protect your credit card and personal information. One way your web browser will let you know if the web page you are viewing is safe (encrypted) is by displaying a padlock icon in the bottom of the browser window. Double click this icon for specific information on the level and type of security employed. If you don't see the padlock icon, then you should not enter personal or credit card information on that page.*

One more thing to consider: Many people who are afraid to shop online are not concerned about giving out their credit card information over the telephone to an operator. However, a telephone line is rarely encrypted. For this reason a properly secured website is a far safer place for financial transactions than an ordinary telephone line, especially when using a wireless or cell phone.

Q. I've heard the Internet is dangerous. What should I avoid when shopping online?

A. *It can be dangerous to just get in your car and drive without a map or a plan for getting from point A to point B. The same is true for browsing the Internet. There are some dangerous places online—places that entice you to download things that also deliver ads or contain "spyware" or even computer viruses—thus it's wise to establish a general plan for your safety. Make sure you have up-to-date anti-virus software and your internet security settings prompt you about potentially harmful things while downloading.*

> **Check out our Online Security Chapter earlier in the book for more detailed information on keeping safe.**

Q. How can I tell if an online store is reputable?

A. *For clues on the reputation of a specific online store, I recommend looking for one or more reputation or security seals issued by the Better Business Bureau Online (BBBOnline), VeriSign, TRUSTe, and ScanAlert - to name a few. Then, click on the seal to verify that it is legitimate since anyone can place an image of a trusted seal on their website. If they are valid seals, they will go to a page that contains information about the website claiming them. This information will reside on a page issued by the company owning the seal so check your browser's address bar to make sure the address reflects the seal's address for this information page. If the address does not change, then report that site to the company behind the seal they are impersonating. Security seal companies have skilled legal teams to address illicit usage of their trusted symbols. I would not do business with anyone who attempts to forge a trusted symbol in this manner.*

 Need to Know

Three general rules of thumb to help you online:
1. If it sounds too good to be true, then it probably is. For example, the word "free" is much overused, so read the fine print before completing the transaction. The same can be said for many online sweepstakes and "you are a winner," offers.

Make the Connection on MFN!
www.eMilitary.org/YourMFN.html

Sign on to the address shown above and Make the Connection to more resources on this topic!

2. Beware of free downloads—even seemingly harmless things like free ring tones, screen savers, software "tools" to speed up your computer, and spyware removal tools—and only download software from known and reputable sources. Some "free" downloads are only free because they also serve popup advertisements (adware), monitor and report your browsing activities to better target advertisements to you (spyware), or even include malicious features that violate your online privacy and security. The "if you don't know, then don't" principle can avoid many problems later.
3. Non-U.S. websites may not be required to honor the same privacy policies and business practices, as U.S. websites, so know whom you are doing business with before you provide any personal information. (Gambling and "adult" websites are especially risky since many are not governed by U.S. law.)

11 The Military Exchange

From the Field with Jennifer Johnsen

Jennifer Johnsen is a Public Affairs Specialist with the Army & Air Force Exchange Service.

Since the first formal exchanges were established in 1895, an exchange system has served side-by-side with soldiers in tents and trucks, in the field and in permanent facilities, on posts and bases around the world.

The Army & Air Force Exchange Service (AAFES) is defined by its two-fold mission: to provide quality merchandise and services at competitive prices and to generate earnings to augment the Services' Morale, Welfare and Recreation (MWR) programs. AAFES' military service members and their families look primarily to the low prices that have traditionally characterized exchange shopping. To them, AAFES is the BX (Base Exchange) and PX (Post Exchange) they have shopped throughout their careers, and they look upon their Exchange as a major form of non-pay compensation. Each day, AAFES strives to fulfill these expectations and is committed to providing value, service, and support to military members, their families, and retirees.

AAFES has matured into a progressive, global retailer with more than 45,000 employees in more than 30 countries, five U.S. territories, and 49 states. AAFES customers are the 11.6 million active duty, Reserve, National Guard, and retired military members and their families stationed around the world. AAFES also provides service to Marines in Okinawa, Iraq, and Afghanistan. Operating more than 3,100 customer service facilities worldwide, AAFES provides a wide variety of retail, food, and services operations. In addition to its well-known anchor—the BX/PX main stores—AAFES provides the military community a wide range of convenience and specialty stores for things such as DVD/video rental, furniture, military uniforms, and accessories. Our business portfolio also includes car care centers, gas stations, and a variety of vending operations. Additionally, AAFES operates 1,765 food activities providing a combination of name brand fast food including Burger King and Taco Bell, and AAFES proprietary brands like Robin Hood specialty sandwiches and Anthony's Pizza.

AAFES often provides the only source of comfort items and necessities in combat and contingency locations. Service members depend on AAFES for day-to-day health and comfort items, such as soap, shampoo, and toothpaste. Also, AAFES is the primary provider of snacks, beverages, and entertainment items. AAFES even provides Select uniform items and clothing.

> **"Service members depend on AAFES for day-to-day health and comfort items"**

Since the beginning of Operation Enduring Freedom, AAFES has worked to partner with the American public to safely and effectively send support to troops serving far from home. "Gifts from the Homefront" is an innovative initiative that allows any American to make a direct impact on the morale of deployed troops around the world. "Gifts from the Homefront" gift certificates can be purchased 24 hours a day, seven days a week, every day of the year by calling 877-770-4438 or logging on to www.aafes.org. From there, a PX/BX gift certificate is sent to an individual service member (designated by the purchaser) or distributed to "any service member" through the American Red Cross, Air Force Aid Society, Fisher House Foundation, or the USO.

"Gifts from the Homefront" certificates are available in denominations of $5, $10, $20, $25 or $50 and are subject to a $4.95 shipping and handling processing fee. "Gifts from the Homefront" can be purchased by anyone with a U.S. credit card or check, but only authorized AAFES customers can redeem them at PXs and BXs located throughout the world, including Operations Enduring and Iraqi Freedom.

Because they can be used for merchandise already stocked at AAFES locations in OIF/OEF)(Operation Iraqi Freedom/Operation Enduring Freedom), "Gifts from the Homefront" provide safe alternatives to traditional care packages. Furthermore, troops are sure to get exactly what they need with the certificates that can be applied to a wide range of products. Reports from Iraq indicate that the certificates distributed most recently are being used for the

Make the Connection on MFN!
www.eMilitary.org/YourMFN.html

Sign on to the address shown above and Make the Connection to more resources on this topic!

latest CDs and DVDs, comfort items such as snacks and beverages and phone cards for those all-important calls home. In fact, the demand for phone cards alone was so strong that AAFES created an additional program dubbed "Help Our Troops Call Home" in April 2004.

Today, any American can help troops in contingency locations call home with an Exchange Global Prepaid Phone Card purchased from AAFES. Up until the "Help Our Troops Call Home" effort began, those wishing to lend a helping hand had no other alternative but to purchase other retailer's pre-paid cards that, in many cases, were not designed for affordable international calling. Now, anyone (even those not in the military) can help troops in contingency operations call home from one of the many AAFES call centers in Operations Enduring and Iraqi Freedom.

 **FAQs**

Q. Who can shop at AAFES (or any military exchange)?

A. *Under AR 60-20/AFJI 34-210, exchange privileges are authorized for:*
- *Active duty military*
- *Retirees*
- *Reservists*
- *National Guardsmen*
- *Dependent family members of the categories above*
- *Other categories of individuals affiliated with the armed services (which includes 100 percent disabled veterans).*
- *Some government civilian employees have shopping privileges when they are assigned or TDY (Temporary Duty) overseas—or they are "TDY and residing" in government quarters on posts/bases in the United States.*
- *Other exceptions are determined by local command.*

Q. How much do I save by shopping at the exchange?

A. *According to a national independent market basket survey, prices at PXs and BXs are on average 22.09 percent lower than comparable retailers. Depending on where a service member or military retiree lives, shopping the PX or BX can offer an average savings up to 31.44 percent considering AAFES customers don't pay sales tax. National name brand items prices were surveyed. In addition to name brand savings, AAFES' private label merchandise, including Exchange Select, keeps even more money in military customers' pockets.*

Q. What is Exchange Select?

A. *With 489 different items in categories such as health and beauty care, household cleaning, laundry and single-use cameras, Exchange Select products provide a low-cost alternative to national brands and are made by reputable manufacturers. Troops and their families can save an average 50 percent over national brand equivalents.*

> **"The exchange can offer an average savings of up to 31.44 percent."**

Representatives from AAFES Quality Assurance team actively ensure the quality of Exchange Select merchandise by visiting suppliers' plants to verify "Good Manufacturing Practices," as set by the Food and Drug Administration (FDA) and other governing agencies. All over-the-counter medicines, such as ibuprofen and acetaminophen, meet FDA established guidelines, which are the same for Exchange Select and national brand equivalent products. AAFES is no longer just a main store, a shoppette and a gas station. AAFES is now an integrator and provider of goods and services across a broad spectrum of military life.

Q. How can I find an exchange location and other information about a particular exchange?

A. *Log on to www.aafes.com and choose the "Store Locator" link for an alphabetical/geographical list of AAFES locations.*

Q. Why should I shop at the exchange?

A. *Purchases at the exchange not only save authorized customers money, but also help fund military quality of life programs. Roughly 70 percent of AAFES earnings are paid to MWR programs. In the past 10 years, $2.4 billion has been contributed by AAFES to military MWR programs to spend on libraries, sports programs, swimming pools, youth activities, tickets and tour services, bowling centers, hobby shops, music programs, outdoor facilities, and unit functions.*

Q. What should I do if I can't find what I'm looking for at the PX/BX?

A. *AAFES is a multi-channel retailer, offering products to authorized customers via catalog and online at www.aafes.com. The Exchange Catalog and Exchange Online store now offer troops and their families more than 25,000 items via the online site, thousands of items from virtual vendor partners and hundreds of thousands of items from www.CentricMall.com partners. Because*

AAFES supports an extremely mobile customer base, the Internet and catalog offerings provide the ability to extend the exchange benefit to customers worldwide, regardless of where they are located. When items are purchased using the Military STAR Card or if the purchase is greater than 49 dollars, in most cases, shipping is free. Customers may also speak to the store or general manager to request additional items be stocked.

Q. Why should I use my Military STAR Card for purchases?

A. *Every time troops use bank issued cards at their exchange, it costs the military community millions of dollars that could be directed to Morale, Welfare and Recreation (MWR) efforts. One way military families can help reduce costs and ultimately strengthen their exchange benefit is to take advantage of the exchanges' exclusive Military STAR® Card. Unlike bank cards, profits generated from the Military STAR® Card are shared with military communities through contributions to the military service's MWR funds. These funds reduce the tax burden of all U.S. citizens, and are used to build libraries, childcare centers, gymnasiums, bowling alleys, and recreational facilities for service members and their families around the world. The Military STAR® Card is accepted at AAFES, Navy, Marine Corps and Coast Guard Exchange activities, as well as the Exchange Catalog and the Exchange Online store at www.aafes.com.*

For more information on the Military STAR® Card, visit www.aafes.com and click on the Military STAR® Card icon.

 Need to Know

Helping service members stay in touch with friends and family has never been easier. Anyone can log onto www.aafes.org and click the "Help Our Troops Call Home" link. From there, those wishing to pay for troops to call home can send a prepaid phone card to an individual at his or her deployed address or to "any service member" deployed or hospitalized. Like the "Gifts from the Homefront" program, AAFES also coordinates distribution of donated phone cards addressed to "any service member" via the American Red Cross, USO, Air Force Aid Society, or the Fisher House Foundation.

Make the Connection on MFN!
www.eMilitary.org/YourMFN.html

Sign on to the address shown above and Make the Connection to more resources on this topic!

12 Shopping the Commissary A Sure Thing for Your Budget

From the Field with Cherie Huntington and Kay Blakley, DeCA Consumer Advocates

The Defense Commissary Agency (DeCA) operates a worldwide chain of commissaries providing groceries to military personnel, retirees and their families in a safe and secure shopping environment. Authorized patrons purchase items at cost plus a 5-percent surcharge, which covers the costs of building new commissaries and modernizing existing ones. Shoppers save an average of 30 percent or more on their purchases compared to commercial prices - savings worth about $2,700 annually for a family of four. A core military family support element, and a valued part of military pay and benefits, commissaries contribute to family readiness, enhance the quality of life for America's military and their families, and help recruit and retain the best and brightest men and women to serve their country.

American families spent just 9.9 percent of their 2005 disposable household income on food, according to the USDA Economic Research Service's most recent statistical report on food expenditures. Sounds like good news, on the surface, but apply it to your own household income and see if a very different picture emerges. In general, the lower your income, the higher the percentage you're going to spend for food. For a family of four to eat a decent diet, using foods purchased at stores and prepared at home, the USDA estimates total expenditures could run from a low of $103.40 (Thrifty Food Plan) to a high of $232.60 (Liberal Food Plan) per week.

> "We're all guilty of spending more time at the drive-thru window than we should."

How does your food budget compare? Would it surprise you to know that Americans spend about 48 percent of their food budgets on food prepared away from home? Probably not—we're all guilty of spending more time at the drive-thru window than we should. It's just too convenient, and so cheap, we tell ourselves. But, is it really? A quarter-pound hamburger (dressed with mustard, lettuce, tomato, and onion) with French fries and a soda prepared at home, using ingredients from the commissary, costs $1.10. The exact same meal from your favorite fast food drive-thru window costs about $4.30. When you can treat an entire family of four to hamburgers, fries, and soda for ten cents more than the cost of just one drive-thru meal, which should you choose? But it's not just your budget you should be concerned about when you shop at the commissary. The nutritional value of the food you buy is even more important.

Shopping with Ease–The Commissary Glide

Consider the Macarena, the Chicken Dance or the Electric Slide—they may still be around, but they're definitely not cool. When you do the Commissary Glide, however, you're sure to be cool for many years to come.

"Commissary Glide?" Actually, it's not a dance but refers to the Defense Commissary Agency's efforts to help you "glide" through the store as quickly and efficiently as possible. Commissaries offer one or more express lanes to make your checkout smooth and speedy. Also, we're proud that our cashiers may be the fastest and most experienced in the grocery industry; they must scan specified numbers of items per minute in order to meet DeCA standards. With the high patron counts of commissaries, we require the best cashiers!

Many stores post signs indicating that military members in uniform may move to the front of the line during specified hours. Don't hesitate—you earned it! Architects design the entire layout of commissaries with your convenience and shopping habits in mind. Stores regularly undergo "resets" that reorganize store layout based on evolving shopping patterns. In general, the store perimeter offers the "fresh" items on your list: produce, meat, dairy and frozen—think "frozen fresh!" The center of the store carries primarily dry goods, boxed, bottled, and canned. It's those fresh aisles around the perimeters where you should spend most of your budget, stocking up on plenty of fresh fruits and vegetables, before you hit the prepared foods.

Some large stores offer self-checkout service for your speedy convenience, but then if your "cashier" is too slow, you have only yourself to blame! The most fantastic thing about the Commissary Glide has to be that you can be quick on your wheels without sacrificing quality, variety or price. You'll still enjoy those national name-brand products, including the newest items on the market, at savings averaging 30 percent or more on your total purchases compared to commercial prices. Go ahead dance! This one's cool.

 **FAQs**

Q. How does DeCA use all the profit that it makes on commissary sales?

A. *Although the commissary system collects about $5 billion per year, there is no profi t generated on these sales. Groceries are sold "at cost" to authorized shoppers as part of the military benefits package.*

By law, commissaries are required to sell goods at prices that are set at a level to recover the cost of goods, with no profit built into these prices. There are also very stringent legal controls on the ways that DeCA can use taxpayer monies that Congress provides to operate commissaries. Because commissaries are prohibited by law from making profit on goods sold, and because of the stringent controls on use of funds provided for commissary operation, commissaries cannot use a lot of merchandising practices that commercial stores use routinely.

For instance, commissaries cannot "double" (or otherwise increase) the face value of coupons, commissaries cannot sell goods below cost to create a low price "image," commissaries cannot pay a "rebate" to patrons who return bags for reuse, or who use non-disposable cloth bags, and commissaries cannot donate money or products to an individual or organization, however worthy.

Q. Why does DeCA make me pay a surcharge on my commissary purchases?

A. *Surcharge is applied to the total value of each commissary purchase because the Congress has mandated collection of surcharge (currently 5 percent) to pay for commissary construction, equipment, and maintenance. All surcharge dollars collected are returned to commissary patrons in the form of continually improved commissary facilities. The amount of surcharge applied to a commissary sale transaction is shown as "SCG" on your sales receipt.*

Q. Do I have to use bagging/carryout services and tip a bagger for providing these services?

A. *Baggers are not commissary employees and work for tips only. However, you may choose not to use bagger/carryout services at all, or you may choose to use the services of a bagger but not provide a tip.*

Q. Why doesn't the commissary carry "store brand" items?

A. *Commissaries are only permitted to carry "name brand" products. The savings on those items compared to commercial grocery stores and super centers averages 30 percent or more overall. Name brands guarantee that our customers can purchase items that are recognized for consistent quality no matter where they live in the world. For overseas customers, brand names they recognize offer a "touch of home" they can count on.*

 Need to Know

Making Your Food Dollars Stretch

If it's time to take tighter control of the amount your family spends on food, follow these easy tips.

1. **Shop the commissary.** For the first step, last step, and every step in between—shop the commissary! Commissaries may look like retail grocery stores, but in reality, DeCA is a government agency with the mission of delivering a non-pay benefit for military members and their families.

   "Baggers...work for tips only."

   Commissaries make no profit —you pay the same price DeCA pays for products, plus the 5 percent surcharge, mandated by Congress, which funds the construction of new commissaries when you need them. You won't have a splashy grocery circular screaming daily specials at you each time you walk through the door, because DeCA is not allowed to advertise prices. Instead, take note of red, white, and blue "Value Savings," "Every Day Savings," and "Extra Savings" signs attached to the shelves alongside the products on sale. All of these are good deals, but you'll find the deepest discounts (often 50 percent or more) with products sporting the "Extra Savings" signs. Consistently shopping the commissary will provide an overall savings of at least 30 percent over retail grocery store prices. DeCA officials know this from typical market basket comparisons made on a quarterly basis, but do the same comparison and see the proof for yourself.

2. **Plan ahead.** Sound meal planning, and consuming more meals at home will go a long way toward reducing your grocery bill. Don't forget to include leftovers in your plan. A large inexpensive roast served on Sunday

can provide the makings for sandwiches on Monday and a protein source in a chef salad served on Tuesday.

3. **Make a list.** Having a definite list when you shop helps avoid impulse buys. If you find an item on sale that you know you'll use later, feel free to add it to your cart, but beware of pretty displays that don't fit into your plan, and never shop when you're hungry.

4. **Read labels/compare prices.** When comparing prices of competing brands be sure to take into account the number of servings per container. A less expensive price on a larger size is only a savings if you actually use those extra ounces. It's no bargain, if you end up throwing them away. Don't automatically assume that a larger size container is automatically a better buy. Sometime it is, but often it's not. Always check the unit price shelf tag, or do the math yourself.

> "…beware of pretty displays that don't fit into your plan, and never shop when you're hungry."

5. **Do it yourself.** The higher price for "convenience" items reflects the labor required to pre-cook, pre-cut, or pre-measure. Substantial savings can be made if you make the time and learn the skills to perform these preparations yourself. Remember the hamburger and fries comparisons mentioned earlier. Spend $4.40 or $17.20 to feed your family of four—which do you choose? The lower price will cost you about 30 minutes of your time.

6. **Redeem coupons.** Coupons and rebate savings can add up fast. All commissaries honor Internet coupons these days, and most commissaries make paper coupons available near the store entrance or in the checkout area. Keep an eye out for those you use most often. And remember, coupons redeemed in European commissaries are good six months past their stateside expiration date.

Ideas and Resources for Making the Most of Your Commissary Benefit

"Though some customers appreciate a leisurely shopping experience, others want to get in and out in minimum time," says DeCA Director Patrick Nixon. "We offer a number of time-saving tools to speed up or simplify your shopping trip."

One tool sure to appeal to any shopper is the floor plan found on each store's Web page. Enter http://www.commissaries.com then click on "Locations" and find your store. On the home page, you'll see "Floor Plan" listed to the right. You can arrange the floor plan either numerically by aisle or alphabetically. You'll see

> "The commissary website offers timesaving links to tons of coupons, recipes, and contests as well as food safety information."

all the items you're shopping for, from air fresheners to wraps. Just print out the list and check off what you need—sure beats writing it all down!

If you have a little more time to prepare your list, you can click on "Shopping" then "Shopping List" and "Create Shopping List." After you select your store, you'll be able to create a detailed shopping list by perusing your store's entire inventory by category, item, and size.

The commissary website offers timesaving links to tons of coupons, recipes, and contests as well as food safety information.

Calling ahead for special orders also saves time. Your store might require 24 or 48 hours notice for specialty cakes, fruit trays or baskets, party trays from the deli, or special cuts of meat, so be sure to check either by phone or by looking on the store Web page.

Whether you're picking up a special order, running in for milk and bread, or racing in for lunch on-the-go, many stores provide 15-minute parking near the entrance.

To find a case lot sale—visit The Military Family Network's Commissary Page at http://www.emilitary.org/deca.html. Plan your case lot shopping. The Military Family Network also tracks regular sales throughout the year as well - all searchable by your installation.

Make the Connection on MFN!
www.eMilitary.org/YourMFN.html

Sign on to the address
shown above and
Make the Connection
to more resources
on this topic!

Part 3
Military Moving

Photo: Luis Trevino

New Housing on Fort Riley

Introduction

Half a million military families move each year into new communities, making new friends and saying farewell to old ones. One of the most challenging times for military families is transitioning from one community to the next.

It is important that we incorporate these moves into our lives and make a tradition of the process. These chapters provide support for you in your military moving tradition and give you tips on how to make it less stressful. Most importantly, it should help you learn how to take care of yourself and to remember that although it is difficult to build relationships, only to say goodbye after a couple of years, those relationships help us to remain strong. They are fountains in which we may find renewal, strength, understanding, support, and peace.

The Military Family Network is proud to be a part of the relationship building process and we are reaching out to every military family, service member, veteran, and American to help us build community so that all of our families, no matter where they move or where their spouses are deployed, may find friendship, security, and the warmth of caring communities around them.

13   From Sea to Shining Sea

From the Field with Caroline Peabody

Caroline Peabody *is the daughter of a disabled Vietnam era Marine, military spouse, former president of The Military Family Network, lifetime volunteer, and distinguished speaker and lecturer on military life. She holds a B.S. in sociology and M.A. in organizational management with extensive research on communication systems as they relate to military well being and community capacity-building. She is a published writer and columnist on matters relating to military families, military learning models, and military relations..*

So, they told you that you would get to see the world when you or your loved one joined the military, right? What they didn't tell you is that you would see it every two years through an endless sea of inventory sheets, mountains of half-peeled inventory stickers, weight limits, claims papers, and dozens of seemingly insane packers responsible for moving your precious things around the world. Sometimes it may seem that your only hope is that they do it in less than eighty days.

It does not seem very long ago that our things were coming out of boxes, taped shut solidly so that they will make it, when we suddenly find ourselves moving again to our next home, our next decorating adventure, our next community.

When you are sitting in the middle of a room, glancing around at the pieces of furniture stacked around you like a fortress, there are a lot of quiet moments. There, tattooed upon their wood, are many colored moving tags like unwieldy passports testifying to their travels with numbered stickers.

A desk might display a faded yellow sticker numbered "643" which means, "small stained desk with scratches on the side top

> **"...we suddenly find ourselves moving again to our next home, our next decorating adventure, our next community."**

corner, from the upstairs left bedroom." According to the moving manifest, another half-torn blue sticker numbered "154" means "white desk, damaged top, broken drawer, from downstairs den." These rainbow tabs are like a small diary documenting the history of their tired travels and the physical signs of wear that they have undergone.

Military families, however, are not made of wood, steel, or paper— yet they know well the toll relocation takes on the spirit, the body, and the soul.

Moving is a challenging experience—there are many things to consider during a move. Moving is stressful, but there are ways to minimize the stress and maximize the potential success of your move. The goal of this chapter is to talk about some ways to ensure a smooth move for your things and to introduce the concept of making moving a personal family tradition.

Moving as a Family Tradition

Change is a major cause of stress. Moving, by definition, means change. However, we can work to shift the perception of what constitutes change. In the "Moving with Kids" chapter, we talk about normalizing the moving experience. Moving is not an unexpected event in the military community. We can make it less stressful by making it a tradition. Traditions have rituals, a cycle of preparation, experience, and closure. By creating a moving tradition with consistent rituals in the moving process, we have made the unknown, known; the unanticipated, anticipated; and, the unexpected, expected. The stress of moving will likely be reduced, because we are now dealing with the "change" of relocation in ways that "do not change" through family moving traditions that we have created for ourselves.

> **"By creating a moving tradition with consistent rituals in the moving process, we have made the unknown, known...the unexpected, expected."**

Field Trips, Vacations, and Moves, Oh My!

Remember the last time that you traveled for work or vacation? How about when your child went on an overnight field trip? There were probably checklists that you prepared for the vacation or were provided by your child's school or club to help you prepare for the activity.

If there are one- or two-page check lists needed for packing a couple of bags for a successful trip or camp experience, why shouldn't there be check lists for moving your entire house and everyone in it?

Yes, Virginia, there should be checklists. You should create your own Personal Moving Plan and Moving Milestones chart. (See The Military Family Network templates at the end of this section that you can personalize for your family).

We have developed some sure-fire suggestions for preparing a house for your move. The first is to sort and go through each room of your house. Bring a couple of trash bags and one or two plastic bags for clothes or items you may wish to donate. You do not want your weight allowance to be taken up by things you are going to end up throwing away. Treat this time as an opportunity to really "Spring Clean" or declutter your life. Encourage your children to do the same.

> **"You do not want your weight allowance to be taken up by things you are going to end up throwing away."**

As you are going through each of your rooms, sort things into like categories (like pictures/decorations, etc.). Anything that is not in daily use can be prepped for the move. We recommend doing this cleaning/sorting about one month before your move. You may be able to stack winter or summer clothes for packing (depending on your moving season). Think about the climate that you are moving to—you may not need any winter clothing if you are going to Hawaii—or summer clothes if your next assignment is Alaska. Take this time to reorganize your wardrobe for weather, size, and wear.

Remember, while most of the work in the move is in the preparation phase, you must also work during the unpacking process as well.

The movers should employ the same protection to your home (carpet and floor protection, door removal, etc) when they unpack as they did when they came to pack your goods. You also have the option of having them unpack all of your goods and put them away. Many people choose not to have this service—it is up to you. However, this service is something that is paid for by the government. If you choose to have the movers unpack and put away your goods, remember the pace is your pace. You do not have to worry about how long they are there. You can even request that they come back the next day to unpack your shipment. The important thing is that when you check off that you received your goods, you are *sure* that you received your goods. Make sure that you mark and notate any changes to condition on your inventory forms.

Notating change in condition is important. This is the documentation you will need when filing a claim. Taking time now to note the "change" in condition allows you to substantiate a claim that damage occurred during the time your goods were in the custody of the moving company.

FAQs

Q. The last time I moved, the moving company damaged the walls. I ended up having to pay for the repairs. Is the moving company responsible for damages to my property during a move?

A. *The moving company is responsible for taking special precautions to protect your home, as well as its contents. All moving companies can use items such as carpet guard and cardboard to protect your flooring, as well as specially constructed furniture pads to pad banisters to avoid marring the woodwork. In addition they are responsible for removing any and all doors and putting them back up when they are done so that all furniture can be removed as safely as possible from your home. It is up to you to ensure they do the right thing and to supervise them while they are moving. If they damage your home or rental during the move, call your Transportation Management Officer (TMO).*

Q. I am used to packing my own things. I know that they are taken care of that way. Is there anything I can do to make sure that my things won't break during the move?

A. *The moving company is responsible for packing and protecting your furniture and household goods. The individuals hired by the moving company to pack your belongings should be experienced and use only the best boxes and packing supplies. Wardrobe boxes (tall boxes with a metal bar) protect your fine clothing, such as suits or dresses, and save you valuable ironing time later on. Mattress cartons are used to protect your mattresses from dirt, grease, rips, and tears during the moving process. Padded dish boxes with dividers help protect your fine china. You may also request bubble wrap to be used around your expensive wood furniture and saran wrap to go around your couches and upholstered furniture.*

If the packers assigned to your move do not have the necessary supplies to safely pack and protect your household goods, do not allow them to start or continue until they do. Remember, you are the customer. If you have a problem with the movers, contact your TMO and let him know what is happening.

Whether you do it yourself or have the moving company do their job, when all things are said and done, you are responsible for ensuring that your things were packed appropriately.

Q. Is the carrier responsible for marking the inventory sheets with everything? I saw my friend move, and her packers just marked the inventory sheet with the number of items and "bedroom," even though some of the things were expensive collectables. How can I make sure the packers inventory our things correctly and completely?

A. *The moving company is responsible for inventorying your things. They should note the location and condition of all your household goods. However, a proper inventory takes time. It is in the best interest of the moving company to pack your belongings as quickly as possible. Sometimes, this is accomplished by shortcutting the inventory process. Don't let this happen. It is in your best interest to make sure the inventory is accurate so make sure you stay on top of this task to get it done right.*

> "It is in your best interest to make sure the inventory is accurate."

Watch the moving company packer who fills out your inventory sheets to make sure he or she describes the condition of your property correctly. If you disagree, document the specific reason for your disagreement at the bottom of each inventory page. Many times there are multiple packers handling your home. If you cannot arrange help to watch each packer to ensure your inventory is complete and accurate, you have the right to make them pack one room at a time. You are in complete control of the process. If the moving company objects, call your TMO and complain.

> "You are in complete control of the process."

Remember, every single item does not have to be documented—but that is your call. Be sure that you have the company document all the items, locations, condition, and descriptions of things that are important to you or your family members. Again, if you disagree, document why on the bottom of the inventory.

Make sure that like items are packed together and marked appropriately.

The moving company should give you copies of the complete inventory. Remember, you are signing papers stating that you acknowledge the work the movers did, that your property was packed carefully and its condition noted. This is especially important should a later dispute arise between you and the moving company regarding the condition of your household goods. While you may be able to recover some of the value of lost or damaged items, the claims process is much easier when you can demonstrate that you exercised due diligence in the care of your household goods.

Need to Know

You Are the Boss!

The Department of Defense may be paying for your move—but you are the customer. Never forget that you are the one who carries the responsibility for making sure that your move is smooth and that the movers do their job professionally and in a manner that will protect your possessions. Here are some tips to make sure you are protected!

These days most people have a video recorder or digital camera. Record every room in your house, with close-up takes of expensive furniture and other property in each room. As you are recording (if video) verbally describe the condition and location of the property. Be sure to take the disk or tape with you—do not pack it with your goods. This will be important for your claims process and for your personal insurance if you experience a loss.

Items that are of high personal or collectable value should not be shipped. For example, important photo albums, precious art, coins, stamp collections, sports cards collections, crystal animals, Beanie Babies, Barbie dolls, etc., should be personally carried to your new location (if possible). If you decide high value items must be shipped, they ABSOLUTELY must be listed on the pickup inventory.

To protect yourself in any future claims process, you must be able to substantiate what you owned and its value. Before the move, prepare your own personal inventory and gather substantiation of your major items (original purchase receipts, charge card receipts, appraisals, etc., for electronic equipment, art objects, paintings, collections, furniture, grandfather clocks, etc.). Take this information with you when you move, or mail it (insured) to a family friend or your future address.

Congress has mandated that the military work to make relocation a successful activity for military families in TITLE 10, Subtitle A, PART II, CHAPTER 53, 1056. The website http://www4.law.cornell.edu/uscode/html/uscode10/usc_sec_10_00001056----000-.html TITLE 10, Subtitle A, PART II , CHAPTER 53, 1056 declares that the Secretary of Defense "shall carry out a program to provide relocation assistance to members of the armed forces and their families." It also states that it will try to keep reasonable lengths of duty to minimize the adverse effects of relocation.

The Military Family Network is designed to help you "Make the World a Home" for your family. Our network website is the premiere source for information on relocation and community information. Visit us online at www.emilitary.org to connect and grow with your community.

Make the Connection on MFN!
www.eMilitary.org/YourMFN.html

Sign on to the address shown above and Make the Connection to more resources on this topic!

Relocation Entitlements (CONUS)

There are nine separate relocation entitlements for which a service member may qualify. **DO NOT ASSUME** that you will receive any of these allowances; ask your local finance office to get the best information.

Dislocation Allowance (DLA)

DLA is intended to help with all of those miscellaneous costs of moving, such as connecting utilities, paying deposits, and the like. It is available for CONUS and OCONUS moves.

- DLA is **NOT PAID** on the last move. Check your orders to be sure. If the "MDC" code is a 7, you are not authorized DLA.
- DLA is not paid on a local move, unless movement of household goods has been authorized.
- DLA is not paid if the service member is assigned to government quarters at the new duty station and is not accompanied by family members.
- DLA is paid when the travel voucher is filed after the move. An advance of 80 percent of the DLA may be requested.
- DLA is figured at two-and-one-half times the service member's BAH Table II rate. The Table II rate is equivalent to the old BAQ rates.

Monetary Allowance in Lieu of Transportation (MALT)

Also known as "mileage," this is the amount paid when the service member or family drives to the new duty station. It is available for CONUS and OCONUS moves.

- Based on the Official Military Table of Distances
- May be paid for up to two vehicles without special approval.
- Rates vary from 15 cents to 20 cents per mile, depending on the number of people in each vehicle.
- May be advanced at 80 percent before the move, and is paid by travel voucher.

Per Diem Allowance
Per Diem is paid to reimburse the service member and family for meals and lodging en route to the new duty station. Available in CONUS and OCONUS.
- For POV (Privately Owned Vehicle) travel, the government divides the distance between duty stations by 350 to get the allowed number of travel days. If the remainder is over 50 miles, an additional day is authorized.
- Per Diem may be advanced at 80 percent and is claimed on the travel voucher.

Temporary Lodging Expense (TLE)
TLE is only paid within CONUS and is intended to help pay the cost of lodging and meals while the family is staying in temporary housing.
- TLE is paid for a maximum of ten days.
- TLE is computed based on several factors, check with your transportation or finance office for your entitlement.
- TLE is not authorized on the last move.

Advance Pay
Advance pay is simply an interest-free loan using your future military earnings as collateral. Available in CONUS and OCONUS.
- Up to three months' base pay may be authorized with documentation.
- Usually repaid over 12 months.
- **Many service members get into serious financial trouble with advance pay.** Remember that this a loan - not extra cash to use as you wish. Advance pay should only be used to pay extraordinary costs of a PCS move.

Advance Basic Allowance for Housing (BAH)
The unit commander must approve this advance. It is generally limited to 3 months BAH CONUS (Contiguous United States) and 12 months OCONUS (Outside Contiguous United States). Remember that this is not extra money, it is an advance on the normal BAH and will be deducted from monthly pay.

Make the Connection on MFN!
www.eMilitary.org/YourMFN.html

Sign on to the address shown above and Make the Connection to more resources on this topic!

14 Moving Yourself

From the Field with Caroline Peabody

Caroline Peabody *is the daughter of a disabled Vietnam era Marine, military spouse, former president of The Military Family Network, lifetime volunteer, and distinguished speaker and lecturer on military life. She holds a B.S. in sociology and M.A. in organizational management with extensive research on communication systems as they relate to military well being and community capacity-building. She is a published writer and columnist on matters relating to military families, military learning models, and military relations.*

Military families move an average of every two to three years. The military pays everything for your move—from the packing and move out to the move in. If something happens, you can prepare a claim with the government and be reimbursed for your moving losses. The government also pays standard rates to the moving contractors it uses for this service. As a result, military moves are very costly to the government.

Because the military does not have the resources to negotiate with moving contractors for the best rates on a family-by-family basis, it knows, that on average, it is paying more for a move than what it may cost for a family to move themselves. This is how the DITY ("Do IT Yourself") move (now called the "Self-Procured Move" or "Personally Procured Move") came into being. The military is giving families the chance to help the Department of Defense save a little money while at the same time giving families the opportunity to possibly put a few extra dollars into their own pockets.

Why Move Yourself and How It All Works
You agree to move yourself based on the idea that you can get a better deal than the military. The government sets the standard. The Department of Defense requires a savings of five percent. This is built into the process. The government will pay you 95 percent of what it would have cost them for the move, based upon the weight you are moving and the distance you are moving

it. Your "mission" is to try to make the most money by getting the best deal with that 95 percent allowance.

That 95 percent is yours to spend as you please. If it costs you less to do the move, you pocket the difference. If it costs you more to do the move, you pay the difference. You can move your goods in a rental truck, a rental trailer, or in your own private vehicle. It is up to you to take the money and get the best deal for yourself that you can.

> **"Your "mission" is to try to make the most money by getting the best deal with that 95 percent allowance."**

The important thing to realize in a Personally Procured Move is that you are responsible for the entire process. You are responsible for the planning, the packing, and the damage you may cause to your goods. You become the government contractor for your move. You have "won the bid" because you have agreed to be paid five percent less than the government's current provider. As the contractor for your move, the government requires some "process" as they would any other contractor. The following are some examples:

You will have to visit the personal property office and get the authorization paperwork for a Personally Procured Move. You will be given all necessary paperwork and instructions. You will be required to get a certified weight of the household goods you are moving prior to completion of the Personally Procured Move. This is done by taking your vehicle to a weigh station and weighing the vehicle empty and then weighing the vehicle with your household goods loaded into it; the weight difference is the weight of your household goods.

Who Qualifies?

The Personally Procured Move is available to military members and the next of kin of a deceased member. When you select the Personally Procured Move option, it allows you to personally move your own household goods (HHG) and collect an incentive payment (the savings you achieve by moving yourself, up to the 95 percent requirement) from the government when you have orders for Permanent Change of Station (PCS), Temporary Duty (TDY), separation or retirement, or assignment to, from, or between government quarters.

In a Personally Procured Move, you can use approved vehicles to move HHG instead of having the government ship them. You can use this option to move all or a portion of the authorized weight allowance.

The personal property counselors will give you

> **"The personal property office does not advise members to move their property first."**

information on the methods and procedures for making a move and advise you on the methods available to you, either alone or in conjunction with a government-arranged move. (In some cases, you may be able to do a partial move and have the government move the rest of your personal goods. Check with your local transportation office for your options.)

Personal property counselors will also prepare a DD Form 2278 (Application for Move) for you. The personal property office **does not** advise members to move their property first and then complete the required documentation afterwards as this may result in forfeiture of incentive. Members may choose one of the following methods:

- **Privately Owned Vehicle (POV) Personally Procured Transportation Move.** You complete all elements of the move with your vehicle.
- **Personally Procured Transportation Move Using Rental Vehicles.** You rent normal types of rental vehicles, equipment, moving aids, and packing material and the member performs all labor for the move. An advance operating allowance is authorized when using this method.
- **"You-Load They-Drive" Method.** Commercial HHG carriers offer this type of service. You perform all or part of the labor for packing, unpacking, loading, or unloading of the van. The commercial carrier supplies the driver and performs the line-haul movement.
- **Personally Procured Transportation Move in Connection with a Government Arranged Mobile Home Shipment.** Articles of HHG that can otherwise be authorized for shipment at government expense, but must be removed from a mobile home to meet safety requirements, may be moved under this option. Such items include, but are not limited to, heavy appliances and

> **"There may be a way to earn money with a Personally Procured Move."**

furniture, air conditioners, skirts, awning, etc. Check with the transportation office if you own a mobile home and want to move yourself. Once again, you only receive the payment if you stay beneath the 95 percent mark the government mandates.

The Bottom Line

There may be a way to earn money with a Personally Procured Move. The transportation official where you were originally stationed will figure out how much it would have cost to move you under a government contract and will give you the 95 percent figure you need to meet. The computation is based on: actual, constructed, or authorized weight allowances, whichever is less. Mileage is computed based on point-to-point mileage set forth in the Defense Table of Official

Distances. They will give you this figure. You will need to carefully consider the benefits and costs for using the Personally Procured Move Option.

There are also other ways to conduct a Personally Procured Move where you are not moving 100 percent of your household goods. You may also choose a combination move divided between a government arranged HHG, local contracted, non-temporary storage, and Personally Procured Transportation. If you elect a split shipment, the transportation officer bases your incentive

> **"Use great care when selecting this option (split shipment)."**

pay (the 95 percent) on the your weight allowance (if you have made no previous shipments), or the balance of the weight allowance (if you have made additional shipments under the same order). You may end up paying more when service finance centers settle all accounts related to the split/multiple shipments. Use great care when selecting this option.

Upon completion of your move you will be required to submit paperwork, and **certified weight tickets** to gain your final incentive payout (the rest of the 95 percent due you). Your counselor will advise you on what paperwork is required and who to submit it to. At this point the actual payment for the move will be computed and sent to the Accounting and Finance Office; they in turn, will pay you. The financial profit portion of this pay is subject to Federal income tax.

FAQs

Q. Can I get any advance pay for the Personally Procured Move?

A. *You may be entitled to an advance operating allowance to help with your operating cost; this allowance is limited to 60 percent of the government shipping cost. You must check with your counselor to see if you are eligible, as each branch of the Armed Forces varies on the entitlement; for example, the Marines allow for 50 percent.*

If eligible, this allowance helps defray the cost of a rental vehicle, gasoline, oil, tolls, packing material, moving equipment, and other services directly related to the move. Personal Property will give you the advance pay paperwork that you will return to your service branch accounting office to actually receive your payment. Keep in mind that it can take more than 10 working days to process advance payments, so turn your paperwork in early enough to receive your advance on time.

Q. Will I be reimbursed for gas, lodging, tolls, etc.?

A. *You will be paid 95 percent of what it would have cost the government to do the move, regardless of gas, lodging, etc. Per Diem and travel entitlements are handled by your service branch's travel department; please consult them regarding per diem, lodging, etc. However, you should save your receipts for gas, tolls, boxes, tape, rental vehicles and any other purchases directly related to your move. Personally Procured Move pay (that 95 percent figure) is taxed at a rate of 28 percent, but taxes will not be taken out of any amount covered by these receipts.*

Q. Am I entitled to storage at destination for a Personally Procured Move?

A. *For Personally Procured Moves, you will have to procure your own storage, but you can file for reimbursement once you have accumulated paid receipts for the storage at destination. You can be reimbursed up to what it would have cost the government to place these goods in storage for you. Contact the Personal Property Office at your destination to obtain a Reimbursement Packet. The government will not arrange storage for inbound Personally Procured Moves; that is part of the "do it yourself" nature of this type of move.*

Q. Can I have somebody at Personal Property look over my Personally Procured Move paperwork before I mail it in for payment, just to make sure I've done everything correctly?

A. *Yes. You can visit the outbound Personal Property Office at destination to have them check your paperwork for errors and/or omissions.*

Q. What if I've already mailed my Personally Procured Move paperwork in for payment? Is there a phone number I can call to check on the status of my Personally Procured Move claim?

A. *Yes, but keep in mind that it can take 30-90 days to process the claim, depending on whether or not there were problems with your paperwork. It is advisable to give them at least 30 days before you call. Contact phone numbers for claims processing are listed below:*

Navy: NAVTRANS, Norfolk VA, 1-888-742-4467 DSN 567-5677
Marines: MCSC, Albany GA, 912-439-5677 DSN 567-5677
Army and Air Force: See your transportation office (locally processed)
Coast Guard: http://www.fincen.uscg.mil/dity.htm

Q. What do I need to bring to Personal Property to arrange my move?

A. *You MUST have your orders before any move can be arranged. If your orders consist of an endorsement sheet, you will need to bring BOTH the endorsement sheet and the original message that it endorses. If you are vacating government quarters, you MUST bring your vacate notice from the Housing Office before any move can be arranged. If you are moving from or to your home of record, you will need to bring your DD Form 4/1 from your service record. This form specifies what city is your home of record, if it is not already specified on your orders. You MUST have official documentation of your home of record before any home of record move can be arranged. If someone else is coming in to Personal Property to arrange the move on your behalf (i.e., your spouse, etc.), they MUST have a Power Of Attorney to make these arrangements on your behalf. You may be required to fill out the "Personal Property Worksheet" located at http://www.naspensacola.navy.mil/logistics/ppworksh. doc and the "Weight Estimation Worksheet" found at http://www.naspensacola.navy.mil/logistics/weightest.xls.*

Q. My service member is retiring and our family would like to move back home to be near our aging parents. Are we entitled to a government sponsored move?

A. *Yes. In cases of retirement or the loss of a service member, the military will provide and pay for one final relocation. Because the paperwork, processing and details for these types of moves may vary, contact your local Transportation Office for information relating to your circumstance.*

Q. What paperwork do I need to fill out for Personal Property?

A. *You will need to fill out the DITY Worksheet located at http://www.naspensacola.navy.mil/logistics/ditywksh.doc that gives all the relevant shipping information. You will also need to estimate the amount of weight being shipped by filling out the Weight Estimation Worksheet found at http://www.naspensacola.navy.mil/logistics/weightest.xls.*

Q. Why do I need to estimate my weight?

A. *The estimated weight is important in determining how much money the government should pay. Nobody expects you to be "right on the money" in your estimate; it is, after all, just an estimate.*

Do not get too anxious about the weight estimate. Being off by a couple of hundred pounds here or there is not going to make a huge difference. However, do make an effort to give a fairly reliable estimate. Use the following worksheet to help you with your calculations.

Weight Estimator Worksheet: http://pptas.ahf.nmci.navy.mil/pptacalc/weightEstimator.xls

 Need to Know

Remember to get insurance on your items. You are the "contractor" for your move and you will be responsible for any loss. Make sure you are insured appropriately. The most recent guidelines on Personally Procured Moves can be found at http://www.dod.mil/comptroller/fmr/09/09_06.pdf

Getting Paid for your Storage when you Move Yourself

- Copy of actual storage agreement and copies of payment receipts for each month of storage paid for by the service member.
- NOTE: Please keep all receipts for tax purposes. They also may be needed to complete your Personally Procured Move claim if the claim exceeds 100 percent of actual expenses.
- If your claim exceeds 100 percent of the cost of what the government would pay, you MUST submit all receipts along with the Letter of Authorization from the Transportation Officer (TO).
- If your claim is for actual expenses, then all receipts are required. Bottom line for getting claims paid in a timely way
- Ensure your name and social security number (SSN) are on all documents.
- Ensure all documents are properly dated.
- Ensure all documents requiring signature of the service member are signed.
- Make sure to keep a copy of everything turned in for payment

Make the Connection on MFN!
www.eMilitary.org/YourMFN.html

Sign on to the address shown above and Make the Connection to more resources on this topic!

Toolkit

SELF-PROCURED MOVE CHECKLIST & CERTIFICATION OF EXPENSES	
Name: (Last, First, MI)	**SSN:**

3 Copies of orders with endorsements and/or amendments
3 Copies of DD Form 2278 (Application for a SELF-PROCURED MOVE)
3 Copies of DD Form 1351-2 (Travel Voucher). Complete blocks 7a-7d, 8,15a-15b, 20a, and20b
2 Copies of a certified empty weight tickets with service member's name and SSN. Ticket also must be validated with the signature of the weight master of the station.
2 Copies of a certified loaded weight tickets with service member's name and SSN. Ticket also must be validated with the signature of the weight master of the station.
1 Copy of registration for personally owned boat or trailer
1 Copy of rental contract, fuel receipts and POV toll receipts

*** Be sure that the service member's name and SSN are on all documents. Make sure all documents are dated properly and include required signatures. Most importantly, make sure to keep a copy of everything turned in for payment.

NOTE: Nontaxable expenses that can be claimed in your SELF-PROCURED MOVE are: payments to rental agencies for rental vehicles, packing materials, and moving equipment such as hand trucks, furniture pads, tools, oil, and weighing expenses. Expenses that are not claimable include tow dollies, tow bars, auto transporters, insurance, sales tax, meals, and lodging. When filing for the Fiscal Year in which you have moved, check http://www.dod.mil/dfas/ .You may be eligible for a tax refund.

Rental Vehicle Expense	
Gas, Tolls and Weighing Fees	
Moving Equipment	
Other Expenses	
Total Expenses Claimed	
Move Origin (City, State)	Move Destination (City, State)

Privacy Act Statement Authority: 5 USC 5701-5742, USC 404-427, and EO9297
Principal Purpose: Used for reviewing, approving, accounting, and disbursing for office travel; SSN is used to maintain identification for individual claims and to report income to the Internal Revenue Service.
Routine Uses: To substantiate claims for incentive payments for movement of household goods.
Disclosure: Voluntary failure to furnish information requested may result in partial or total denial and/or improper tax application.
Note: Expenses certified on this statement reduce taxable income reported on W-2 Form and may not be claimed again as moving expenses. Tax withholding will be 25 percent of profit (entitlement minus expenses).

I certify the above amounts have been incurred as expenses on my SELF-PROCURED MOVE

Signature:

Date:

15 Moving "Over There"

From the Field with Caroline Peabody

Caroline Peabody *is the daughter of a disabled Vietnam era Marine, military spouse, former president of The Military Family Network, lifetime volunteer, and distinguished speaker and lecturer on military life. She holds a B.S. in sociology and M.A. in organizational management with extensive research on communication systems as they relate to military well being and community capacity-building. She is a published writer and columnist on matters relating to military families, military learning models, and military relations.*

Over here, over there—famous words from a famous service song—but none too comforting when you may be facing the prospect of moving to a foreign land. This is especially true if you have kids.

You will become an expatriate. This is a fancy way of saying that you are living out of the country you call home. When you come back, you will "repatriate" which means coming home to your homeland. How you embrace the "away" time will define your overseas assignment as an adventure or a dark period of isolation.

Moves are not easy for children. However, the younger your children are, they may be more willing to adapt to new situations and make new friends. They may surprise you in the fact that they may integrate into different environments far more easily than adults. If you are planning to move to a country that is not English speaking, you will be surprised at how fast your child will pick up the language. Even if you have

> **"How you embrace the "away" time will define your overseas assignment as an adventure or a dark period of isolation."**

studied the language for a while prior to settling into your new home, your child will overtake you by leaps and bounds in a very short while. Children who learn a language before age ten are also able to speak it without an accent.

You will also have to make decisions regarding your child's schooling. Factors like the child's age, the length of time you will be staying in the country, your child's fluency in the language of instruction, and your child's academic ability should all be taken into consideration. If you are planning to stay in the country long-term and the standard of education is high, then it may be good to place your child in the same school as local children. On the other hand, if the standard of education is poor, your child is not fluent in the language, or they are planning to attend university in the next three or four years, you may find that a school that offers the International Baccalaureate program to be the best choice.

After the Novelty Wears Off—It's Going To Be How Many More Years?

The usual accompanied overseas tour is between two and three years depending on the country. After about two months (when you finally receive all of your household items and you are moved in), culture shock may rear its ugly head.

The thrill of learning a new language has turned into an insurmountable barrier; basic things like banking and transport are endlessly frustrating, and you would give your right arm for a bowl of Frosted Flakes (if you do not live near enough to the commissary).

> **"...friendships established during foreign assignments usually last a lifetime."**

It usually takes about six months to get used to a country. Expect that you will feel homesick, that your children will miss their friends at home, and your family will miss its pets. Many countries require a quarantine period for pets that have moved with you. Keep in mind that pets especially will need some additional time to adjust from this separation and change and may seem a little anxious and nuts.

The good news is that friendships established during foreign assignments usually last a lifetime. They happen fast and deepen quickly. The social support network among military families overseas is about the best it can be. Your job is to get active, be social and tap into it. You may even be able to teach English as a second language in a local school. This opportunity is especially available in places like Japan.

All in all, if you chose to embrace it, being assigned overseas is one of the greatest adventures your family can have. America is only a few hundred years old; Europe is thousands of years old, and the world's Asian lands reach back even further in their culture and history. Imagine the fun you can have delving into these rich pasts!

If having a Personal Moving Plan is important with state-to-state moves, it is critical with overseas moves. Your assignment overseas is an opportunity to learn and grow—perhaps even to better understand the greatness of the freedoms and prosperity our country enjoys. It is an opportunity to experience a foreign land, a foreign culture, and a foreign language. With an open mind and good planning, your overseas move can be the adventure of a lifetime.

 **FAQs**

Q. Does everyone in my family need a passport?

A. *Each family member, regardless of age, must obtain a separate no-fee passport. No fee passports are used by eligible DoD personnel and their family members while on official travel to countries requiring passports. Family members must have no-fee passports in their possession before port call. No-fee passports are issued for a specific purpose and may be used only under the conditions and restrictions specified. Service members should contact the servicing military personnel office for the required passport paperwork. To expedite processing, all applicants should have in their possession a certified copy of their birth certificate with a raised seal or a previously issued passport in good condition.*

An individual may possess a valid tourist passport and an official or no-fee passport simultaneously. Tourist passports may be required for off-duty or non-government sponsored travel. Some countries may also require a visa prior to entry. Military personnel clerks should be able to advise travelers on this subject.

Get a passport for you and your family now! Take advantage of this opportunity since passports can be expensive (up to $100 or more for a new one) if you do not take advantage of this opportunity while in the service.

> **Get a passport for you and your family now!**

Q. Does my state license cover driving overseas?

A. *No. If you intend to drive overseas, you must acquire a special license. For example, in Germany, USAREUR POV (Privately Owned Vehicles) licenses are issued by the military for military personnel, civilian employees, and* *family members. POVs are also registered with the military, and a USAREUR POV license is required to operate any USAREUR-registered POV. In Korea, unaccompanied military personnel are typically not allowed to have POVs. For those who do have a POV or must drive a military vehicle, the military issues a special civilian license with a military stamp.*

Q. What is hold baggage?

A. *Hold baggage is the household goods that a service member and family keep back to use for the last thirty days (when everything else goes on the cargo ship overseas). It is the last to go and the first to receive. When service members are on orders to overseas assignments they have a hold baggage shipment. The weight of this shipment*

> **"Hold baggage has a very serious weight limit."**

depends on the rank of the service member and should include "immediate need" items. Furniture items, including large screen TVs, may be prohibited in this shipment. This shipment is sent in a very thick walled cardboard box and will arrive at the service member's duty station approximately 30 days from the day it is shipped. Hold baggage has a very serious weight limit.

Family members on an accompanied overseas tour are also entitled to hold baggage. The weight is figured according to the age of the family member. Once dependent travel is authorized, family members' baggage and household goods will be shipped. Household goods shipments include everyday living items and the furniture a service member and their family may own.

Q. I can't figure out the storage options . . . what is the difference between temporary and non-temporary storage?

A. *There are two kinds of storage: temporary and non-temporary. Temporary storage is used when the service member is en route or has yet to secure housing. There is a 90-day limit on temporary storage; extensions can be requested through the transportation office at the new duty station. When the service member is ready for delivery, the transportation office must be notified.*

Non-temporary storage includes those items that will not be needed by the service member or their family members for the duration of their overseas tour. It is important for individuals to realize that this is not a shipment you can request things from; the whole lot goes into storage and remains there. Service members may need to request an extension of their non-temporary storage if their rotation date back to the States changes and more time is needed. This request is processed through the transportation office that did the non-temp storage paperwork; failure to do this may result in the service member having to pay storage fees.

Some service members on overseas orders would rather have their extra items shipped to a designated location, rather than have the government store them. In this case the transportation office will schedule another pick up at the service member's home and have the items shipped to the specified location. Service members electing to do this must make sure that the designee stated on the transportation paperwork will be available to take possession of the shipped items. Upon completion of the overseas tour, the service member will again elect an additional shipment if these items are to be returned to their household.

Q. I hear it is very complicated to get my car overseas, but I want to drive my own vehicle. How are Privately Owned Vehicles (POV) shipped?

A. *This shipment applies to overseas tours only; stateside moves require the owner to transport their own vehicles. Storage for your POV is not authorized and will not be provided unless the service member is on a restricted tour and POVs (personal vehicles) are not permitted. In this case, the service member must visit the transportation office to get authorization before putting the POV in storage. The service member must pay for the storage and request reimbursement when they PCS back to the U.S.*

Service members who are entitled to ship a POV must take extra steps to ensure this shipment goes smoothly. The transportation office will advise the service member of the location of the nearest port for shipment. Upon receipt of orders, the service member should call the port to see if the vehicle may be shipped in advance and what other steps they should take to prepare the vehicle for shipment. This may include removing all dirt from on, under, and inside the vehicle, making modifications to the engine or exhaust, and obtaining written permission from the lien holder to ship the vehicle outside the United States. Service members have up to one year from their overseas travel date to ship a vehicle. Owners who ship a vehicle overseas from the US are entitled to a return shipment from overseas.

Vehicles purchased overseas may have to be shipped at owner's expense. Service members desiring to ship more than one vehicle overseas have a few options. They can locate a private shipping company and make arrangements with

> **"Vehicles purchased overseas may have to be shipped at owner's expense."**

them to transport the vehicle, or they may call one of the coastal ports to request information on space available shipment of POVs. Space available shipments are generally on US military supply vessels that may dock at locations a good distance from the service member's duty assignment. For example, the U.S. Navy does space available POV shipments from the East Coast, but all vehicles must disembark in Naples, Italy.

Q. Are boats handled the same way as POVs?

A. *Boats are considered household goods. Their weight counts against the total allowance. Within the U.S., any boat, with or without trailer, shorter than 14 feet will be shipped with the rest of the household goods. Boats, with or without trailers, over 14 feet long will require a special one time only shipping contract; the transportation office will do this. The service member is responsible for any extra expenses incurred for moving the boat, such as lift-on and lift-off services, or any other incidentals not normally involved with moving standard household goods.*

 Need to Know

Relocation Pay Benefits (Outside Continental United States (OCONUS))

Move-In Housing Allowance (MIHA)
This allowance is available only OCONUS. It is intended to pay for one-time rent-related expenses, modification to homes for security reasons, and the initial cost of making a home habitable.
- Only available at certain locations.
- State Department determines whether a location is "high threat."

Temporary Lodging Allowance (TLA)
Not to be confused with Temporary Lodging Expense or TLE (a Continental United States (CONUS) type of pay), TLA is for OCONUS only. It is intended to help pay for the cost of lodging and meals while awaiting permanent lodging.
- TLA is based on a formula that is much too complicated to explain here.
- Usually paid for a maximum of 60 days when arriving OCONUS and 10 days when departing OCONUS.

Advance Overseas Housing Allowance (OHA)

OHA is paid in some OCONUS locations to cover the difference between BAH and the actual cost of off-post rental housing.

- Once housing has been located, take a copy of your lease to the appropriate office and complete a DD Form 2367.
- Advances are usually limited to 12 months of OHA.

Advance Basic Allowance for Housing (BAH)

The unit commander must approve this advance. It is generally limited to 3 months BAH CONUS and 12 months OCONUS. Remember that this is not extra money, it is an advance on the normal BAH and will be deducted from the service member's monthly pay.

Make the Connection on MFN!

www.eMilitary.org/YourMFN.html

Sign on to the address shown above and Make the Connection to more resources on this topic!

16 Rent, Buy or Live in Military Housing?

From the Field with Caroline Peabody

Caroline Peabody *is the daughter of a disabled Vietnam era Marine, military spouse, former president of The Military Family Network, lifetime volunteer, and distinguished speaker and lecturer on military life. She holds a B.S. in sociology and M.A. in organizational management with extensive research on communication systems as they relate to military well being and community capacity-building. She is a published writer and columnist on matters relating to military families, military learning models, and military relations.*

There are many unpredictable things in military life. Change is the only constant. This is certainly true when it comes to moving, and the housing choices you have when relocating (PCSing) during your life with the military.

There are three general housing selections you have available as a member of the military community. Depending on your pay grade and the availability of installation housing options, you may have the choice of installation quarters, renting on the economy (in the civilian community where you are stationed), or buying a home.

Your housing choice is one of the biggest economic decisions that you will make for yourself and your family, so your options should be considered with great care. If you have the benefit of choosing from any of the three options, you should evaluate the pros and cons of each as it relates to your personal financial condition and other individual needs.

> **"Evaluate the pros and cons of each [option]."**

Living on the Installation
Depending on the installation, and on your rank and family size, family housing may or may not be available. Some installations actually have excess

housing, and families can move in almost immediately; at other installations, assignment to family housing may take a year or more. Each installation determines how many housing units will be assigned for each rank category. In some cases, assignment to family housing may be mandatory.

One advantage to living on the installation is not paying rent. However, if your installation has been converted to privatized housing, then you will receive BAH (Basic Allowance for Housing) and a utility allowance. If your installation housing has yet to be privatized, then you will not receive BAH; but you will not be required to pay rent or utilities either. This may allow you to build up more savings.

Other advantages include a short commuting time. Your service member may be living minutes away from his place of employment. Your children will probably be going to an installation school and your commissary and exchange shopping may be only blocks away. The reduced driving time not only saves you in gas, but also in wear and tear on your automobile. You also have the social advantage of living close to other military families and may have more opportunities to learn about military benefits and events as they apply to you and your family.

> **"...installation housing is one of the most secure places to live."**

Finally, installation housing is one of the most secure places to live. Access to the installation is limited, and keeping housing areas safe is mission critical to military police.

A disadvantage to living on the installation is not having choice. You do not get to choose your house or your neighbors. There are rules as to how many rooms you may be allotted, and your children (depending on their ages) may be forced to share a room, regardless of their "personalities."

While most families enjoy their military housing experience, it is possible that you may live very close to individuals who do not share your values or social priorities. You are also required to adhere to regulations regarding keeping your home tidy and well maintained—both inside and out. Although rarely enforced, you may receive citations or even be evicted if you do not adhere to these guidelines.

Overseas housing is another world entirely. Most families have no choice but to live in quarters. With a few exceptions, the process for applying for government quarters overseas is much the same as it is stateside. Only command-sponsored families may be housed in government quarters. Non-command sponsored families may, in some cases, receive assistance from the Housing Referral Office in locating off post, economy housing.

Service members who receive Concurrent Travel Orders will know in advance what type of housing they are being assigned to. It will state on the orders: concurrent travel to government/or economy quarters.

There are three types of housing that come under the umbrella of government quarters:

- On-post government quarters,
- Leased quarters which are housing units, subdivisions or apartment buildings that the U.S. Government has leased for an extended period of time to house U.S. Service Members stationed in a foreign country; and,
- Government Housing Rental Program (GHRP), which is generally single-family housing units, either a single family home or an apartment, rented for the period of a service member's tour.

Leased quarters and GHRP housing may be located within a certain distance from the installation. Off-post housing in overseas locations is also called Economy Housing. The assignment to economy housing may or may not be controlled by the Family Housing Office. For example many senior soldiers on unaccompanied tours in Korea will be referred to housing on the economy to rent. Although the housing office helps in the referral process, the lease is a private lease between the service member and the landlord.

As with any lease, especially in a foreign country, it is very important to seek the assistance of a professional from the legal office to make sure that the lease is appropriate for your needs.

Living Off the Installation

Approximately 65 percent of service members live in housing in the private sector. There are benefits to living off the installation. There may be an economic advantage. If you are able to find a place that suits your family and the cost (including utilities and insurance) is lower than your BAH, you will be able to save the difference.

> "Sometimes it helps not being in an environment that is all military, all the time.

Most of the reason, however, that military families choose to live off the installation is for a higher quality-housing environment. Many families desire more property or more square footage than is allotted in military housing. You may want to settle in the community to separate your "military life" from your "family life." Sometimes it helps not being in an environment that is "all military, all the time." When you live off the installation, you are not woken by the morning bugle call or go to sleep to Taps.

Some families choose to live off the installation because they desire private schooling for their children and want to reduce the commuting time. Or, it may just be that installation housing was not available or the waiting list was too long. Once the choice is made to live off the installation, the next question that usually comes up is whether to rent or buy. This is a very sensitive economic decision since the typical timeframe for a military family tour at any installation is around three years. This usually is not enough time to secure enough equity to break even on the sale of your home when PCS orders come through for the next assignment. Families who find themselves in this position either take a loss on the home or choose to rent.

Often, you have less than a month to find a home once you arrive at your new destination. For this reason, it is critical that you do as much research as possible as soon as you receive orders. It is helpful to find a good real estate agent who is willing to work with you, taking pictures of available homes and sending information about neighborhoods well in advance of your travel. The Internet is also an invaluable tool for casing out available housing and neighborhoods before you get there, and your real estate agent can use it to send you links for previewing prospective houses.

Using services like The Military Family Network (www.emilitary.org) to build relationships in your new community is the best way to find the most up-to-date information from individuals living in the community. It also helps you tap into information that you need while you are in the decision-making process. This way, you don't find out something later that you wish you had known earlier when you moved to the community. In the end, you must make the choice that makes the most sense for you, your family and for your finances.

 **FAQs**

Q. How are privatized housing rents determined? How does the DoD ensure that the privatized housing is affordable for military members?

A. *DoD's policy on housing privatization allows rents to be based on the Basic Allowance for Housing (BAH) with the estimated cost of utilities included. The developer normally includes a reduction of 110 percent of expected utility costs in the rent structure to eliminate the chance of any out-of-pocket expenses by the service member. You can check out Installation Housing (Privatized) from the Department of Defense Website on Housing at http://www.acq.osd.mil/housing/faqs.htm.*

Q. Does a service member have to live in privatized housing if it is available or risk losing his or her housing allowance?

A. *No. As with all military family housing, service members are not required to live in privatized housing. The DoD's goal is to create privatized housing developments that are places where military members will want to live.*

Q. What will happen with my utilities? Will I need to start paying for them?

A. *Yes, service members will now be responsible for paying their own utilities. Service members will receive a utility allowance that will be calculated annually and based on historic information. If a service member conserves utilities, then that service member will pocket the difference. If a service member does not conserve, then that service member will probably pay some out-of-pocket costs.*

Q. Renting off installation: What is a military termination clause?

A. *Transferring Military personnel and their families may consider renting or leasing an apartment or home at the next duty station. Always check with the area military Housing Office before doing so, and obtain a sample "military" termination provision to add to your lease.*

To protect landlords, military clauses ordinarily require that notice to terminate be provided in writing, include a specific proposed ending date, and be accompanied by a copy of the military orders or an official letter from the tenant's commanding officer. The orders must specify when the move is to occur (such as "report no later than 15 July") and how long the period will last. In addition, military clauses often state that the lease will terminate 30 days from the next date that rent is due. For example, if rent is paid on June 1st and the military tenant wants an ending date of June 30, written notice must be received no later than June 1. If notice is provided on June 2, the military tenant will still be liable for rent for the month of July.

However, laws may differ from state to state. If you have a question about the lease laws in your state, contact your legal assistance office.

Source: Staff Judge Advocate

Q. What happens if the landlord won't agree to a military clause?

A. *If the landlord will not agree to include a "military" termination provision, the place to go for help is the local housing office. Most apartments located near military installations offer military clauses as a condition to remaining on the local housing office's apartment list. The next place to go is the local legal assistance office to see if a military clause is required by law. If the state where you will be living does not have such a law, you may wish to consider renting from a different landlord.*

Q. Can I break my lease if I get housing?

A. *A provision allowing for early termination to take on-post housing is not a standard provision in military clauses and may take some negotiating with* *the landlord. Consider offering an amount equal to a half-month's rent or a month's rent for the right to terminate and move on post. Avoid clauses that require 60 days notice to terminate early, since the military Housing Office will rarely give more than 30 days notice that quarters on post are available. Obtain a change in writing before signing the lease.*

Need to Know

- When you are moving on base and going through your in-inspection, considering a rental home, or a home for purchase, do not allow yourself to be rushed; inspect thoroughly and ask plenty of questions. If repairs or alterations to the property are a part of the move-in and lease-signing negotiations, get them in writing including a date when the work is likely to be performed. To protect yourself as well as the landlord, perform a walk-through of the property together, upon move in and again when you move out. This needs to be signed by both parties and each should get a copy.

- When you are making your choice to live on the installation, to rent or to buy, take steps to determine the total amount you will be required to pay for rent and deposits or mortgage, to include deposits on utilities and for security and cleaning. If you are renting, be sure to include the fact that many landlords require a cleaning/damage deposit equal to one month's rent. You will also be required to pay the first month's rent in advance. Clearly determine which types of home repairs are the landlord's responsibilities and whether supplies like smoke alarm batteries, fire extinguishers and furnace air filters are to be provided. Consider how much your utilities will cost.

- If you have or plan to obtain a pet, be sure you will be allowed to keep it at the place you rent. Many landlords do not allow pets. Others will allow you to have a pet, but will require a separate deposit for your pet and/or a nominal monthly pet rent.

- Be sure you read **all** documents very carefully before you sign them. Remember, once you have signed any financing agreement or lease, you have entered into a legal contract. If you are renting, the landlord is the only one who can let you out of the lease, unless the landlord defaults on his part of the contract. Verbal agreements will not stand up in court. All agreements must be written and acknowledged by both parties.

> **"Be sure you read all documents very carefully before you sign them."**

- If the landlord defaults on the contract by not maintaining the property or making repairs, do not withhold the monthly rent. In most cases, you will be in violation of your lease. In some states, placing the disputed rent into an escrow account at a bank is a legal alternative; however, landlord laws differ from state to state and can be very complex. If you have difficulty with your rental property and agreement and have tried in good faith to resolve these differences with the landlord with no satisfaction, visit your legal aid office for advice.
- Make sure you get a copy of all documents you've signed.
- Finally, when renting, insurance should be carefully considered. It is relatively inexpensive and could save you thousands of dollars. Should your household items be damaged or lost due to a fire, burglary, flood, broken pipes, etc. items lost would be replaced at your own expense unless you have renter's insurance. Also, under certain conditions, you might be liable for costs to damaged property belonging to the landlord, including the building and its contents.

Make the Connection on MFN!
www.eMilitary.org/YourMFN.html

Sign on to the address
shown above and
Make the Connection
to more resources
on this topic!

17   Moving with Kids

From the Field with Caroline Peabody

Caroline Peabody *is the daughter of a disabled Vietnam era Marine, military spouse, former president of The Military Family Network, lifetime volunteer, and distinguished speaker and lecturer on military life. She holds a B.S. in sociology and M.A. in organizational management with extensive research on communication systems as they relate to military well being and community capacity-building. She is a published writer and columnist on matters relating to military families, military learning models, and military relations.*

Military life is challenging. Moving is a part of this life and can be stressful. However, with the right attitude and the right plan, moving can be a positive experience for the entire family.

Now, to face the drama of moving. For children, especially younger children, the moving just doesn't make sense. Children live in the now— grasping only the present. In the process of a move, the present is full of loss: the loss of friends, the loss of things (seeing their stuff boxed up and taken away) - the loss of their entire known world.

Apart from living in the now, children are also very self centric. Add moving to the normal mix of rebellion, turmoil, and angst of teenage years, and you have a cauldron of potential trouble. It's not that older children can't understand why (after all, they've done this before), they just don't want to leave their all-important friends at this juncture in their lives. Rationality flies out the door. "Why do I have to move? I'm not in the military. I didn't enlist."

Well, of course they have to move. But statements like these send a message. The child is telling the parent about their feelings of powerlessness.

The key to a successful move with children lies in empowering them as much as we can, and by keeping them connected with us as parents (after all, we are the only people they know that are moving with them), and with the relationships that are important to them.

Keeping Positive–Moving as a Part of Life

The key to empowering children is to set a good example. Children watch their parents. If you are stressed out, crazy, yelling, insane, you are teaching your kids to deal with moves in the same way. Expect tantrums, yelling, and frustration from your children. If you shut down and choose not to engage in planning, do not expect your children to make schedules and cooperate with last minute needs.

> **"...do not expect your children to make schedules and cooperate with last minute needs."**

In my experience as a military spouse and family support leader, the most ideal way to handle military moves is to create a family ritual—a tradition, so to speak, for the process. Moving is not an unexpected event. As a military community member, you will be required to move every few years. It is a "known," even though the exact timing and destination may be "unknown." Schedules and rituals help kids deal with challenging situations and life experiences. Since you cannot avoid the move, help make the move—and all that it entails—an understood reality that your family can create a tradition around.

Now, I am not saying that moving can be like New Years Eve with kids smiling and happy horns blowing. However, by creating a moving tradition for your family, you may see your children engage more in the moving experience. This is turn helps them to better anticipate and process their emotions and feelings about the move.

Creating a Tradition

As with any celebration or rite of passage, a family tradition usually involves activities in preparation of the date, activities on a date, and follow-up (clean up) after the date. The same holds true for making your moving process a family tradition. There are many things to do in preparation of a move. Activities need to happen on

> **"Make moving an art."**

the day (or days) of a move, and things need to occur following a move to help re-establish your family. There is another benefit to creating a personal moving tradition and having your kids involved—the more involved they are in the "tradition" of your family's move, the more helpful they may be (less work for you, perhaps?). Have I mentioned that optimism is also very important in handling a military move?

Here are some ideas:

Make moving an "art" where children either paint pictures of their friends, their room or of the house and you frame the artwork. Hang this artwork in your new home. You can also purchase wooden art and paint the name of the town or installation where you were stationed. This will eventually become a "town" of its own. A growing community showing all the places your family has been.

Hold a family design contest where you give the children an amount of money to buy something new for their rooms or to create a new theme for a bathroom. Have the family "vote" on their favorite designs.

These are just a couple of ideas to make each moving experience an exciting and positive memory. You are the subject matter expert on your family-establish traditions that work with your personality and your family's and you are on your way to a smooth move.

Always remember that children are resilient. They can and will get through the challenges of a move. However, creating a tradition for your family by making moving a "normal" part of life helps children anticipate, understand, and engage in the process. They will still experience loss, feel angry, and be sad. Although this is hard for parents to see, as long as you are there to provide the love and structure they will need during this emotional time, chances are everything will be fine.

 **FAQs**

Q. How do we break the news to our kids about the move?

A. *"The Talk"—you have to tell them some time, right? Well, since we know you have to have "The Talk," make "where" it happens a part of your tradition. You can brainstorm your family's own name for "The Talk." You can plan what to take to take to "The Talk." The key is not to be dramatic or too "serious" about this. The idea of making a military move into a family tradition is to normalize the experience as much as possible.*

Q. There is a lot to do when we move. Won't it be too hard to get the kids involved?

A. Moving requires planning and a schedule. There is a lot to think about: sorting, packing, cleaning, traveling—to name a few. Depending on the needs and interests of your family, you can incorporate parts of these activities into your tradition, too. Remember, the more involved the entire family is in the process, the better the move is for everyone.

Q. We are only moving on post, but my youngest child is totally wigging out, what can I do to help him?

A. *For a family undergoing a local move with young children who are having adjustment problems, following the moving truck to the new location may help with the child's transition. If they can't see their things, they can see the truck that has their things. You should also bring your concerns to the child's Primary Care Provider. There may be tools your PCP can recommend to help ease the adjustment concerns. You may also want to discuss the child's adjustment process with their teacher or childcare provider.*

Q. Is there anything I can do to help my kids appreciate all the places they have been?

A. *You may have to wait for your kids to grow up to hear how much they appreciate all the military moving. Making a tradition of the moving can help. Some activities may also encourage kids to appreciate where they have lived during your family's military life. For example, you may create a personal passport for your child. Make a little book with pictures of each of the states and countries you've visited or been assigned to. Also include a blank map of the United States. Every time you live in a place, write the name of the city where you lived on the state and color in that state on the map. Include pages next to each state (like a diary) for the child to log fun or memorable things he accomplished in that state. In time, this will help your child understand how he has been enriched by the military moving tradition in his life. (You may be able to find a commercial product that comes close to this activity—like Rand McNally's Vacation Passport or the National Park Service Passport—but they are not military specific).*

 Need to Know

Ideas for Making Your Personal Military Moving Tradition Ideas for "The Talk"

Ask kids questions about their concerns. Address their fears, worries, and anger with an open-mind. Make sure you research the location you are going to (especially if it is overseas) so that you are prepared to answer questions like "Where's that?" "Sounds like the middle of nowhere!" "There is nothing I can do there." Here are some suggestions for tools to illustrate the Talk:

- A map of the new area in relationship to where you live now

- A Convention and Visitors Guide or Chamber of Commerce packet of information about local attractions
- A printout of local schools
- Lists of organizations (Girl Scouts, Boy Scouts, dancing studios, sports leagues) and contact information for activities that you children are currently involved in now
- Information about any previous friends (of your family or of your children) that are also stationed in the area.

Ideas for "The Plan"
Kids can be involved in a move—no matter what the age. Here are some ideas to engage your children:
- Make a "Moving Milestones" Calendar outlining your family's moving process with dates, activities, and family members involved.

> **"Kids can be involved in a move—no matter what the age."**

- Bring children along on the house-hunting trip if possible or the "scouting" visit to the new location. This will give them a chance to get excited.
- Allow children to help plan the drive and the stops along the way, if you can.
- Let children help with organizing and packing for the move, especially their "stuff."
- Buy special colored storage bins for each of your children and have them decorate it with permanent markers. Allow them to pack their favorite things. (Try to take these bins with you personally, if you can.)
- Buy address books for each of your children (keep them through moves, if you can). Help them get the contact information for their friends and other important relationships.
- Set up an e-mail account (if you do not have one already) for each of your children. Help them make and deliver cards for their friends with their new address and email account.

Ideas for "The Move"
- If you can, have one parent take the kids out to a special place on moving day. Sometimes it can be traumatic to actually "see" the packing of things on the truck.
- Make a ritual of saying "good-bye" to the house. This can be especially fun and humorous for younger children. "Good-bye weed, next to the door, good-bye fireplace bricks, good-bye cabinet that little Stephen always climbed up on when he thought I wasn't looking". It may also help their sense of closure (but be prepared for tears).

- Create an Explorer Backpack with each of the children. The goal of the backpack is to be a traveling survival kit. Ideas for the backpack might be books, small snacks, travel games, etc. Make creating and packing the backpacks a family occasion. Have fun with it.

Ideas for "The New"
- Encourage children to write or call old friends.
- Schedule family outings around the new town- including the things the children expressed interest in seeing.
- Personally take your children (especially the younger ones) to school until they feel comfortable.
- Let your kids in on decorating fun. Get their ideas for where to put stuff in your new home.
- Some adjustment concerns are a normal part of the process—but if you have any doubts or concerns about the well-being and adjustment of any of your family members, call your Primary Care Physician immediately.

Make the Connection on MFN!
www.eMilitary.org/YourMFN.html

Sign on to the address shown above and Make the Connection to more resources on this topic!

18 Personal Moving Plan &My Military Family Facts Book

Tools from The Military Family Network for Your Move

The Military Family Network recommends that you create a *My Military Family Facts Book (MFFB)* which will play an integral part of your personal moving plan. It can take several forms, but we have found that you can make a very usable one with the following items:

- 3-inch, 3-ringed binder (with a window to place a large, easily readable title)
- A box of sheet protectors
- 10-20 yellow routing envelopes
- A couple of plastic pouches (like the three-ringed pouches you buy for kids in school)
- A permanent marker
- Tabbed dividers

Moving Section

For each move, include your personal moving plan. One of the routing envelopes should be used to hold receipts and inventory pages. Keep a separate envelope with all of the original purchase information for valuables. These receipts are necessary when filing DITY paperwork, doing your taxes, or filing claims for lost or damaged household goods. You would also place any videotapes or CDs containing information about your property in this section. Also include:

- Copies of orders
- Phone numbers of family and friends
- Duplicates of luggage/car/other important keys
- Home inventory of household goods plus pictures, receipts, and videotapes.

Family Inform ation Section

Tab a section for each family member. Using the sheet protectors, file the following information for each of your loved ones:

- Birth certificate (original)

- Immunization record
- Social Security number
- Passport (if needed)
- Naturalization papers (if applicable)
- Child ID file
- Adoption papers (if applicable)
- ID card for everyone 10 years or older
- Health records/ medication profile
- Baptismal/Confirmation records
- Education Profiles/Records (IEP/LD Testing)

General Family Information Section
- Marriage certificate
- Insurance policies, (or list companies, policy number, type of insurance, address, phone number).
- Last leave & earnings statement (LES)
- Power of Attorney (check expiration date) and Medical Power of Attorney
- Original will and living wills
- Bank books
- State and federal tax records (recent three years)
- Car registration and title
- Deeds and mortgages
- Professional licenses
- Divorce papers
- Spouse resume and last pay statement
- List of stocks, bonds, mutual funds, and other investments
- Pet documents (shots, licenses, etc)

Personal Moving Plan & Moving Milestones
Make a calendar checklist. Usually military families get orders between 90 and 120 days out. Here's a sample checklist to get you started.

Visit The Military Family Network www.emilitary.org to get the information you need to help you build excitement about your new community home.

Moving Milestones Checklist

MOVING MILESTONE I: THE DAY YOU GET ORDERS

Personal stuff
- ☐ Schedule "The Talk."
- ☐ Check immunizations for each family member.
- ☐ Prepare house for selling or renting (if applicable).
- ☐ If you are selling your home, shop for a realty company that meets your needs.
- ☐ Contact the Housing Office to list your house for rent and obtain more information.
- ☐ Buy address books for all the kids and have them begin getting contact information for friends. Plan a good-bye party.
- ☐ Start planning to ship auto, household goods, etc., to be available when you arrive.
- ☐ Order a current credit report. Check it for incorrect or outdated items. You may need a clean credit report to get a rental or buy a home in the new location.

Military Stuff
- ☐ Get approval for concurrent travel (overseas only)
- ☐ Check into additional service commitment (when does enlistment end).
- ☐ Visit your transportation office to start the household goods moving process. Be sure to discuss:
  - Dependent travel overseas
  - Shipment and storage of household goods
  - Unaccompanied baggage
  - Privately owned vehicles (POVs)
  - Pet shipment
  - Movement of mobile home (if applicable)
  - Do It Yourself Move (DITY)
- ☐ Get approval for dependents' medical and educational clearance.
- ☐ Request a sponsor at your next installation
- ☐ Check with veterinary services about requirements for moving pets
- ☐ Check DEERS enrollment.
- ☐ If a dependent has special medical /educational needs, they must be enrolled in the Exceptional Family Member Program (EFMP).

MOVING MILESTONE II: 60 Days to PCS

Personal Stuff

☐ Check out your new installation on The Military Family Network at www.emilitary.org. Check into the online forums, ask questions about local community, schools, etc. If possible, make a new friend in the area.

☐ If the sponsor is going on a remote tour, you need to decide where the family will reside until the sponsor returns.

☐ If you are residing off post, give notice to the landlord. Usually a 30-day written notice is required for the return of your security deposit.

☐ Start going room to room with a bag for trash and a bag for clothes that do not fit. Encourage children to go through their toys and games.

☐ Plan a trip (if you can) to scout the new location. Take children along or take lots of pictures of the neighborhoods if they cannot go. Take pictures or get information about things that will be of interest to them. If you know where you will be living, take pictures of the local schools they will be attending.

☐ Complete dental work and exams.

☐ Complete eye care and exams.

☐ Contact legal office to obtain Power of Attorney (POA), if necessary. You may need a POA to:
  • Buy/sell a house
  • Ship household goods
  • Ship/register a vehicle
  • Provide for child care
  • Provide medical care
  • Arrange for termination of quarters

☐ Check your homeowners insurance to determine scope of transit coverage. Some policies will only cover one specified location. In some policies 100 percent coverage expires after 30 days. Some policies only cover major perils and not "rough handling, mysterious disappearance, etc."

☐ Take a narrated video or photographic inventory of each room—including the most valuable items. Locate and place receipts and other information about your valuables in an envelope in your Military Family Fact Book. Obtain appraisals for expensive items like art, antiques, etc.

Military Stuff

☐ Make billeting/temporary-lodging arrangements. Call the guesthouse for reservations. Call Finance for details on temporary lodging expense entitlements.

☐ Call the housing office to give notice of intent to terminate military family housing. Make arrangements for re-inspection and final inspection of quarters. BAH will not start until final termination of quarters.

☐ If you are planning to live on post at your new installation, check with your housing office for an advance application if your new installation will accept it. Your application date will be the first day prior to the month you will be arriving at your new base.

☐ Schedule house-hunting trips. Permissive TDY may be granted for up to 10 days.

☐ Be sure to request your TDY prior to leaving your losing installation.

MILESTONE III: 30 Days to PCS

Personal Stuff

☐ Use up things you can't move, such as food, cleaning supplies, and flammables.

☐ Update driver's licenses.

☐ Update ID cards.

☐ Arrange for absentee voting ballots or obtain address where you can write for ballots.

☐ Make a list of everyone who needs to know your new address:
  • Auto insurance company
  • Friends and family
  • Creditors, including credit cards, mortgage company, auto loans, etc.
  • Subscriptions
  • Doctor and dentist
  • Post office
  • Federal and state income tax
  • Department of motor vehicles/revenue department
  • Banks
  • Investments firms
  • Newspapers
  • Magazines
  • Church, synagogue, etc.
  • Veterinarian
  • Attorney, accountant, and other professionals you may have
  • Insurance companies

☐ Obtain a change of address kit from post office and fill out cards. You may need to do this twice if using temporary quarters at next base. You can now do this online at www.usps.com.

- ☐ Establish bank account at new installation. You may be able do this by mail or by phone.
- ☐ Plan for plants. Plants don't travel well and are not allowed overseas.
- ☐ Notify school of your child's last day and request they have records ready. Discuss educational concerns. If you cannot get the records, get the addresses of the schools so the new school can write for them.
- ☐ Pick up medical records from local (off base) physicians.
- ☐ Renew or fill prescriptions for any necessary medications.
- ☐ Make sure that you have school records for special needs children:
  - Academic achievement records (tests, report cards, transcripts)
  - Psychological evaluations
  - Physical therapy, occupational therapy, speech, language evaluations
  - Current and past individualized educational plans (IEP)
  - Behavioral/social evaluations
  - Vocational evaluations (interest, skills, aptitudes)
  - Medications
- ☐ Cancel or transfer memberships such as health clubs, civic organizations, and volunteer programs.
- ☐ Research new dance or music teachers at the new location or other activities your children enjoy.
- ☐ Notify utilities and home services of disconnect dates. Get letters of credit if available. You may be able to establish your utilities at your new location without a deposit if you have these. Don't forget garbage pickup services, cell phones, and Internet providers. Leave essential utilities on until the day after you leave.
- ☐ Arrange for closing or transfer of charge accounts.
- ☐ Check bank procedures for transferring funds or closing accounts. Get a letter of credit or have enough cash available for the new location in case a deposit is required for utilities.
- ☐ Make your personal travel plan- include children in choosing routes or places to see. Get extra copies of maps and information so that everyone can be included. If you are a member of the auto club, AAA, you should be able to get these for free. (By the way, joining an auto club like AAA or adding a towing rider to your insurance coverage is not a bad idea. Both are relatively inexpensive for the peace of mind and services that they provide. It never hurts to be prepared in the event your car breaks down while traveling.) Have children begin to make their backpacks and sort out favorite things in their special packing box.

Military Stuff

- ☐ Have overseas hold shipment ready to go.
- ☐ Review finances. Advance pay may be authorized.

□ Check with finance concerning details and other benefits for which you may be entitled. Be sure of your mode of travel (car, plane) when discussing travel advances to avoid over/under payment.

MILESTONE IV: 14 Days to PCS

Personal Stuff
□ Pick up items from the cleaners.
□ Return borrowed items. Collect things you have loaned.
□ Take pets to vet for required vaccinations and certificates. Get copies of medical records. Obtain a list of hotels/motels that allow pets or kennels for housing your pet.
□ Check luggage and make necessary repairs. Check the locks and make sure you have more than one key for each piece.
□ Purchase new luggage as needed. Buy lightweight, but durable pieces. REMEMBER: They are probably going halfway around the world and in most cases must make a return trip home.
□ Have car serviced/tuned-up for trip. Check oil, water, battery, belts, hoses, brake and transmission fluids, and tires. Invest in a set of jumper cables; they are well worth their cost. In addition, assemble a small tool kit that you can keep in the car as well as a flashlight, small ground reflectors, a can of "Fix a Flat", a blanket, a lighter or a set of matches, a gallon of water and a quart or two of oil.
□ Make travel arrangements.
□ Empty safe deposit box.
□ If renting your home to someone else during your reassignment, make sure homeowners insurance is adequate and that the new tenants have renter's insurance.

Military Stuff
□ Verify schedules and services with Transportation.
□ Prepare to get the house cleaned for inspection.

MILESTONE V: 7 Days to PCS

Personal Stuff
□ Settle outstanding bills.
□ Drain oil and gas from lawn mower and other power equipment. DISPOSE of all flammables.
□ Obtain travelers checks for trip expenses.
□ Pick up medical and dental records. Unless you have a power of attorney, the sponsor cannot pick up the medical or dental records of the spouse.

- Active duty—take one copy of your orders to medical records. The records will be given to you to hand-carry to your next base.
- Spouse and/or dependents 18 years or older—go to outpatient records and dental clinic to pick up the records.
- Either parent may pick up the records of children under age 18.

☐ Take down curtains, rods, shelves, TV antenna, etc. Remove items from attics, crawl space, or similar storage areas. It is your responsibility to make these items accessible to movers.

☐ Arrange childcare for packing and moving day.

☐ Defrost and clean refrigerator and freezer.

☐ Make sure all library books, rented videos, etc. are returned.

☐ If you will be renting your home, make sure that a responsible party (trusted friend, family member or real estate management agent) is provide with a set of house, garage and/or storage keys for access.

☐ Back up computer files. Pack with the items that you will carry yourself. Before movers arrive to pack your possessions for shipment and/or storage, disconnect all major appliances (stove, refrigerator, washer, dryer, etc.) if living off-post.

☐ Empty the refrigerator so it can dry at least 24 hours before the movers arrive.

☐ Dismantle stereo sets, outdoor play equipment, etc.

☐ Always consult your owner's manual for specific instructions.

☐ Owner-packed cartons—leave open so carriers can view contents and take responsibility for cartons.

☐ Place valuables, cash or jewelry, purses, and family records file in a safe place (inaccessible to movers) such as locked in the trunk of your car or with a trusted friend or family member. Include everything that you don't want packed, such as passports, tickets, etc.

☐ Separate items into categories: "hand carry and luggage," "unaccompanied baggage," "storage," "ship," and "professional."

☐ For overseas moves, ship items that will enable you to immediately set up light housekeeping at your new station by "unaccompanied baggage" since it might be 1-4 months before your surface shipment arrives. Suggested items include: iron, dishes, silverware, linens, bedding materials, clothing appropriate for climate, a few of the kids' favorite toys, etc.

☐ Give copy of travel plans, with date, route, and phone number to supervisor, orderly room, sponsor, relatives, etc.

MILESTONE VI: Packing Day & Moving Day

□ Arrange for childcare if you feel that the children will be more distracting than helpful. Remember, you must control your move! Take pets to a friend's home or kennel them.

□ Watch the packers very carefully to see that they understand and know exactly which items are to be packed. You can indicate this by putting different colored stickers on each item or separate by rooms.

□ You may wish to keep a record of the contents of each carton being packed. This may make it easier to locate specific items upon their arrival at your next installation. If any cartons are missing, it will be possible to determine quickly what is missing.

□ Mirrors, paintings, and other items easily damaged or broken should be packed by moving company personnel.

□ If lift vans (huge crates of wood or metal used for overseas shipments) are loaded at your doorstep, watch the packing of them. Be sure everything is protected against slippage, concussion or friction. The heaviest items should be at the bottom of the van.

□ Remember that these vans will be hoisted by cranes, loaded on ships, and treated roughly. If not packed correctly, your furniture will be suitable for firewood upon unpacking.

□ Pack a "moving day needs" box with cleaning supplies, sponges, paper towels, toilet and facial tissue, bath towels, bath soap, shampoo, can opener, paper plates, napkins, plastic eating utensils, snacks, coffee, tea, soda, light bulbs, scissors, hammer, screwdrivers, tape, markers, and trash bags. Put it in your car or safely away from the packers.

□ Put everything you don't want shipped (purses, wallets, garbage) in a locked, labeled closet to prevent packing.

Moving Day

□ Arrange for childcare. Again, pets should be somewhere else.

□ Be certain that every container or crated item has the moving company's inventory tag or tape on it and that each item is listed on the moving company's inventory.

□ Check to see that the condition of your possessions is correctly reflected on that inventory. The exact location of existing scratches and worn or marred spots should be clearly indicated.

□ Read all packing documents and make notes, if necessary, prior to signing.

□ Be sure your copy of the moving company's inventory is legible. This inventory will not be as detailed as the ones you made earlier.

□ Place a copy of the packer's inventory, stored possessions, and baggage receipts in your Military Family Fact Book and take it with you.

☐	Before leaving the house, check each room and closet and make sure windows are down and locked, lights are out, and exterior doors are locked.

MILESTONE VII: During the Move and When you arrive

☐	Keep a log of all moving expenses incurred. This will be helpful at tax time. Keep all receipts. If not needed, discard later. If you and your family are traveling separately, keep two logs.

WHEN YOU ARRIVE

☐	**Immediately** notify the transportation office. They will need to get in touch with you to have your household goods delivered. If they cannot reach you, your shipment will be put into storage and delivery will be delayed.

Make the Connection on MFN!

www.eMilitary.org/YourMFN.html

Sign on to the address shown above and Make the Connection to more resources on this topic!

☐	During the delivery. Make sure you view and inspect each item as it is delivered. Note any problems or changes in condition on a separate sheet and mark your copy of the inventory sheet.

☐	File your travel voucher. You may need more than one voucher, depending on how you moved.

☐	Put away the receipts and other documents that might be needed for tax time.

☐	File any claims for damage to your household goods.

Part 4
Military Family Fitness

Photo: Luis Trevino

Introduction

E xercise is a good thing. It helps with stress management, physical fitness, and our overall state of health and well-being. Exercise and physical fitness are also a required part of the service member's career. It would seem natural then that this "requirement" would translate into a higher level of fitness for the spouse and children. This is not the case. Studies have shown that the state of fitness for military family members is lower than that of their civilian counterparts.

In 2002, The American Academy of Family Physicians published a study documenting that children of military parents had lower scores on measures of fitness than did children of civilian parents. For military spouses, bariatric surgery (for treatment of obesity) rates are on the rise. In 2006, a $4 million contract was awarded one research group to develop a program for approximately 11,000 military family members in Illinois, Indiana, Michigan, and Ohio. Bernadette Marriott, Ph.D., study director for the group said, "Findings from a separate DoD study of cardiovascular risks in a military health care beneficiary population suggest the need for behavioral weight management interventions for all beneficiaries of the military health care system."

The military lifestyle is a hard and stressful one, and the overall fitness of families is an ongoing concern for the military healthcare system. As a result, there are many fitness centers and programs available on the installation and through the TRICARE system to support families seeking to increase their physical fitness and nutritional well-being. This section discusses some of the resources available to the military community.

19 Getting Fit on the Installation

From the Field with Caroline Peabody

Caroline Peabody *is the daughter of a disabled Vietnam era Marine, military spouse, former president of The Military Family Network, lifetime volunteer, and distinguished speaker and lecturer on military life. She holds a B.S. in sociology and M.A. in organizational management with extensive research on communication systems as they relate to military well being and community capacity-building. She is a published writer and columnist on matters relating to military families, military learning models, and military relations.*

The military has many programs to support family fitness efforts. Most installations offer military members and their families a variety of recreational programs and physical activities through installation fitness centers. These programs fall under the installation Morale, Welfare and Recreation (MWR) service. MWR offers everything from high-end fitness complexes with a full menu of physical training classes and equipment to youth activity centers that focus on sports and other fun physical programs to help military kids keep physically active.

Many facilities and programs on installations are offered free of charge or at a minimum cost to military families. The benefits for building in fitness activities are numerous. The Department of the Navy reports some of these benefits. Sailors and families interviewed worldwide repeatedly said that exercise decreases stress; increases energy levels, helps them feel better, look better, and sleep better; reduces their body fat, and, improves how they feel about themselves.

> **"The benefits for building in fitness activities are numerous."**

So, with all of the benefits, why don't more military family members take advantage of the fitness programs offered on installations?

Awareness and Satisfaction with MWR Fitness Services

In the movie *Field of Dreams*, James Earl Jones' character says, "If you build it, they will come." In Hollywoodland, a baseball field in the middle of a cornfield might hold that promise, but the same does not apply to military fitness facilities.

In the September 2000 edition of *Military Medicine*, Lee Harrison of Marywood University, in Scranton, PA, found that, " . . . military spouses consistently reported being unfamiliar with facilities and programs; and female military spouses reported being the least familiar with military facilities and programs."

The study goes on to report that satisfaction with fitness facilities has long been accepted as a positive contributing factor to physical activity, readiness, and overall quality of life for military families.

Almost half of military members were not satisfied with the condition of MWR fitness facilities. The military has responded by updating and expanding fitness facilities across the US and abroad. Even with some dissatisfaction, almost all of the respondents to the study felt that the fitness facilities were an important part of their well-being.

> "...satisfaction with fitness facilities has long been accepted as a positive contributing factor to physical activity, readiness, and overall quality of life for military families."

The main reasons given for not using existing facilities was lack of awareness of programs and services offered and the need for child care.

The availability of childcare for fitness activities has increased on many installations. As for awareness-building, military spouses should make stopping by the fitness centers and youth facilities on the installation a part of their in-processing approach to their installations. Although installations should do more to promote the programs available to families both on and off the installation, the buck stops with the family member who wants and as studies suggest, needs to get fit.

National Guard and Reserve families can also use these facilities and should check to see what is available at their nearest installation. Retirees are also eligible. The key to fitness is commitment. Part of that commitment process is fact-finding. The military is committed to the health of its people and has made investments and updates to its fitness facilities. Now, military families and retirees have the benefit of free access to some of the world's best fitness centers and programs. It is up to you to take that next step.

 **FAQs**

For Adults

Q. Who is eligible to use MWR fitness facilities and programs?

A. *In accordance with AR 215-1, Chapter 6-2, Table 6-1, page 15, the following personnel are authorized use of the fitness center facilities:*
  a. Active duty military personnel and their families assigned to the installation or directly supported by it.
  b. Active duty personnel and their families not assigned to the installation, including members of the Army National Guard and U. S. Army Reserve (you do not have to be activated to use the facility).
  c. Active duty personnel of other service branches and their family members not assigned to the installation.
  d. Retired military and their family members who retain a DOD ID Card.
  e. Medal of Honor recipients and their widow or widower and other family members. Honorably discharged veterans of the U. S. Armed Services with 100 percent service-connected disability.
  f. Civilian employees working at the installation. Staff may request proper identification.

Q. Are there fees to use these facilities?

A. *Almost all services are offered at no cost. General access to facilities, use of equipment, and some classes are free. Specialized classes and personal trainers may be offered at a minimum cost.*

> **"Almost all services are offered at no cost."**

Q. What kinds of activities are available?

A. *Fitness centers offer an array of cardiovascular equipment, weight training equipment, and an assortment of group exercise classes for every need and interest. Some facilities also have swimming pools.*

Cardiovascular **equipment**. Centers usually offer treadmills, stationary bikes, stair climbers, step mills, elliptical orbiters, free runners, rowers, and ski machines to maximize your cardio workout. A professional staff is available to assist you in the proper use and options of each piece of equipment. Most facilities have a cardio section where you may use personal earphones, choose to watch several television stations, or listen to a selection of radio stations.

Variable weights. The latest in variable weight machines, including Body Masters, Cybex, Paramount, and Nautilus® equipment are available for your use. Each machine has a narrative explaining the proper use of the machine and the muscle group worked.

Free weights. Almost all centers have free dumbbells ranging from 3 to 135 pounds. A power lift platform, squat stations, Smith machines, and cable crossovers are also located in the weight lifting area in many facilities. A large assortment of additional plate-loaded equipment for all muscle groups are available including incline, decline, and supine benches.

Locker rooms. *Both the men and women's locker rooms have clean showers with changing areas to facilitate your visit. Sometimes centers have saunas, steam rooms, and whirlpools as well.*

Q. Do military fitness centers have personal trainers or other personalized services?

A. *Yes, some facilities offer specialized fitness services such as:*

Personal trainers. *In most centers, certified staff personal trainers will help you begin or refresh your cardio or weight training program at no charge. If you would like a regularly scheduled session for extra motivation, the average cost for personal trainers is $25.00 per hour.*

Fitness assessments. *When this service is available, eligible participants may request a complete physical assessment by certified staff. Typically it is a one-hour session and includes measurement of resting blood pressure and body composition measurements. A flexibility test, upper body strength and endurance test, and cardiovascular testing may also be performed. After the tests are completed, a fitness profile is made graphing your fitness level in each category. This allows staff to set a time frame in which to help you reach your new goals*

For Kids

Q. What is the mission of Youth Services Sports and Fitness and are there fees to participate?

A. *The MWR CYS Sports and Fitness program provides a wide range of opportunities for participation in team sports, individual sports, clinics and camps. The program emphasizes play, competition, maximum participation* *and physical conditioning, rather than winning or losing. An annual registration fee is assessed to each participant to help defray program expenses.*

Q. What is the sports physical policy?

A. *Youth participants must provide a medical statement by a licensed health care professional that certifies the individual is physically fit to participate in the chosen sport(s) and addresses any pertinent medical condition(s)constraint (s). The medical statement must be current at the time of actual registration and remain valid through the completion of the chosen sport. These requirements are a condition of participation and no child/youth will be authorized to play (practice or participate in games) until a valid physical is furnished.*

Q. Does CYS Sports and Fitness provide uniforms?

A. *Yes. Parents or coaches will sign a hand receipt for all uniforms issued to youth participants, assuming personal responsibility for the items. The signer of the hand receipt will pay for any uniform or equipment that is lost, stolen, or thrown away.*

 Need to Know

Fitness Center Rules and Courtesies

- Most installation fitness centers have rules about young children. On many installations, children aged eleven and under are not permitted in the fitness room at any time. This includes strollers, baby carriers, and children sitting inside the fitness room area while a parent/guardian is exercising. Check the rules regarding teenagers. Often they may use the fitness room equipment when accompanied by a paying adult who is responsible for their direct supervision. An adult is defined as someone 18 years or older, and direct supervision is defined as being immediately adjacent to the machine that the child is using.
- Check the fitness center rules about wardrobe. Usually, there are a few things required like having rubber-soled shoes that cover the entire foot (for health and safety reasons, sandals, spiked shoes, work boots, and flip flops are not usually permitted). Shirts must be worn at all times. Bathing suits and jeans are normally not permitted in the fitness room.
- Food is usually not permitted in the fitness room. Closed, plastic beverage containers are normally allowed.

- Please be considerate of other fitness center members and wipe down equipment after each use, and return the weight plates and dumbbells to the racks provided.
- Cardiovascular equipment use is limited to 30 minutes when people are waiting.
- Using a spotter when lifting weights is recommended. The fitness room is not always supervised and you are exercising at your own risk.
- Be sure to secure your personal belongings. The fitness center is not responsible for personal belongings lost or stolen in the facility.

Make the Connection on MFN!

www.eMilitary.org/YourMFN.html

Sign on to the address shown above and Make the Connection to more resources on this topic!

20 Meals Ready to Eat

From the Field with Kay Blakley, DeCA Consumer Advocate

The Defense Commissary Agency (DeCA) operates a worldwide chain of commissaries providing groceries to military personnel, retirees and their families in a safe and secure shopping environment. Authorized patrons purchase items at cost plus a 5-percent surcharge, which covers the costs of building new commissaries and modernizing existing ones. Shoppers save an average of 30 percent or more on their purchases compared to commercial prices - savings worth about $2,700 annually for a family of four. A core military family support element, and a valued part of military pay and benefits, commissaries contribute to family readiness, enhance the quality of life for America's military and their families, and help recruit and retain the best and brightest men and women to serve their country.

Healthy choices in foods are tucked into every aisle and alcove of your commissary these days, and because we sell our products at cost, you can always count on at least 30 percent or more savings over retail grocery prices. Commissaries are doing their part to help strengthen military families by joining forces with the National Center on Addiction and Substance Abuse (CASA) at Columbia University to celebrate Family Day–A Day to Eat Dinner with Your Children.™

> "...the more often teens have dinner with their families, the less likely they are to smoke cigarettes, consume alcohol, or use drugs."

Family Day is held on the fourth Monday of September. CASA has been conducting back-to-school surveys of the attitudes of teens, and of those, like parents, who influence them most. This research has consistently shown that the more often teens have dinner with their families, the less likely they are to smoke cigarettes, consume alcohol, or use drugs. Empowering kids to stay drug free is of utmost importance, but according to research from other reliable sources, that one strong advantage is just the tip of the iceberg. Consider these findings:

- A study published in the Archives of Family Medicine concluded that families who ate dinner at home consumed more fruits and vegetables, less fried food and soda, and less saturated and trans fat.
- A Department of Defense child health care survey found that kids ages 6 to 12 who reported eating fast foods three or more times per week are 9 to 13 percent more likely to be obese. For children ages 13 to 17, the likelihood climbs to 16 to 21 percent.
- Results of a study published in the journal Pediatrics found that children who ate fast food, compared to those who did not, consumed more total calories, more calories per gram of food eaten, more total fat, more carbohydrates, more added sugars, more sugar-sweetened beverages, and less fiber, less milk, and fewer fruits and non-starchy vegetables.

And finally, can you guess what characteristics a majority of participants in the National Weight Control Registry (an ongoing study of adults, 18 or older, who have lost at least 30 pounds and have kept it off for at least one year) have in common? They rarely eat fast food, they eat an average of just 2.5 meals per week at restaurants, and they prepare and eat most of their meals at home. By the way, the average participant in the registry has lost about 60 pounds, has maintained the loss for five years, and reports being seriously overweight by 11 years of age.

 **FAQs**

Test your "Healthy Eating Quotient" with the following quiz.

Q. Do fruits and vegetables have to be fresh to be considered healthy?

A. *Fresh fruits and vegetables are great choices, but the nutritional value of frozen, canned, and dried fruits and vegetables are comparable to that of fresh. Plus, they offer the benefit of longer shelf life. Limit added sugar by choosing canned fruits packed in natural juice or water. Limit added sodium by choosing canned vegetables labeled "no-added-salt."*

Q. I'd like to use fat free milk, but my commissary doesn't carry it, so is it OK to use skim milk instead?

A. *If you're a stateside commissary shopper, you're probably saying "Huh?" But, in some overseas commissaries, where fresh milk is produced locally, the carton may simply say "skim milk." Skim milk and fat free milk are interchangeable names for the same product—milk that contains 0 - 0.5 percent butterfat. Check the side panel of the skim milk carton for "MAXIMUM B.F. 0.5 percent."*

Q. Doesn't any dark-colored, dense-textured bread, especially those with lots of seeds and nuts qualify as whole grain and high fiber?

A. *No. Breads with names like "multi-grain, stone-ground, 100 percent wheat, seven-grain, or bran," might sound like they are whole grain, but often are not. Take a look at the ingredients label—one of the first two ingredients listed should be referred to as "whole" —wheat, rye, corn, etc.*

Q. If fresh meats don't have a nutrition facts labels, how do you tell what's fat and what's lean?

A. *Remember the terms "round" and "loin" to help you zero in on the leanest meats. Lean beef cuts include round steaks and roasts, top loin, top sirloin, and even chuck shoulder and arm roasts. The leanest pork choices include pork loin, tenderloin, center loin, and ham. Ground beef labeled at least 90 percent lean is "extra lean." Boneless, skinless chicken breasts and turkey cutlets are the leanest poultry choices.*

 Need to Know

Are you convinced yet that family meals prepared and eaten at home are the way to protect your family's physical and emotional health? Are you stressing out already over one more thing to plan for and get done every day, when your days are already filled to the max? Here are a few ideas that will help.

In a perfect world, every military household would be issued a Martha Stewart clone programmed to have the table set and a nice hot meal ready and waiting each evening as the family arrived home. Hmm, could one of you engineer types out there get cracking on that? Until then, think of ways to make it easy on yourself.

- Use your slow cooker—even in the hot summer—and keep an eye out for recipes you can just dump in, plug in, and come home to. One of my favorites is Fiesta Pot Roast. Place a few small red potatoes, cut in half, in the bottom of the slow cooker, top with a 2 to 3 pound chuck roast, pour a jar of chunky salsa over all, and cook on low for 8 to 10 hours. Add a salad (from a bagged mix, if you like), a little bread (whole grain, of course) and dinner is served!

- Buy cubed ends of low-fat and low-sodium deli meats to use as a quick protein source in salads or soups.

- Save time with pre-cut commercially packaged fruits and vegetables—if you can afford the extra cost. Or better yet, if your commissary offers small containers of freshly cut produce, snap them up. You don't pay for the labor it takes to slice and dice when the commissary staff does it. It's all part of the benefit and one more reason to shop the commissary.

- Convince your family that breakfast is okay for dinner. Eggs keep for a very long time in the refrigerator and are always ready when you are. Whip up an omelet, an egg sandwich with cheese and tomato, even French toast (easy on the syrup) in well under 30 minutes.

- If you have a potato per person in the pantry, bake in the microwave and top with cooked broccoli, low-fat shredded cheese, add a dollop of plain yogurt or sour cream, and you've got a meal.

- Keep fresh fruit on hand for snacks and desserts. Display it on the counter in plain sight, so it gets chosen over less healthy snacks tucked away in the cabinet. Keep a few long-lasting choices like apples, oranges, and pears in the refrigerator, too.

- Keep your kitchen well stocked with staples like flour, sugar, vegetable and olive oil, vinegar, dried herbs and spices, shelf-stable milk, and main ingredient items your family likes. If pasta is among their favorites, always have a package on hand. Dried pasta takes only 10 minutes to cook, and can be paired with any number of ingredients, not counting jarred spaghetti sauce. Just let your imagination be your guide.

> **"Just let your imagination be your guide."**

- Finally, when school is in session and the family calendar is where it belongs on the refrigerator door, be sure to block off the fourth Monday of September each year as a time to observe "Family Day–A Day to Eat Dinner with Your Children."

Make it affordable by purchasing your dinner ingredients at the commissary, make it lower in calories and higher in nutrients by preparing it at home, and make it easy on the cook using simple but delicious Cindy's Pasta recipe below. This recipe is so simple you don't even need a recipe. I use the amount of seasonings my family likes, but feel free to adjust to suit your taste.

> **"This recipe is so simple you don't even need a recipe"**

Cindy's Pasta

2 teaspoons olive oil
2 to 3 large ripe tomatoes, roughly diced (substitute 14-oz. can of diced tomatoes, if desired)
½ medium onion, roughly diced
1 heaping teaspoon minced garlic from a jar
5 to 6 slices pickled jalapeno from a jar, finely diced (substitute one fresh seeded and diced jalapeno, if desired)
1 tablespoon fresh or scant teaspoon dried parsley
¼ teaspoon oregano
basil to taste
salt to taste
1 16-oz. package linguini or fettuccini

Make the Connection on MFN!
www.eMilitary.org/YourMFN.html

Sign on to the address shown above and Make the Connection to more resources on this topic!

Cook pasta according to package directions. In a skillet over medium heat, sauté the onion and garlic in olive oil until the onion is tender, but not brown—about 3 minutes. Stir in tomatoes, with juice, jalapeno, parsley and oregano. Use enough dried basil to completely saturate the top of the tomato mixture. Stir together and simmer on low heat for about 10 minutes. Plate fettuccini into individual servings, top with a portion of tomato mixture, and serve. If using fresh basil (roughly chopped), stir it into the tomato mixture at the last minute, or better yet, just sprinkle it over the top of each individual serving. Fresh basil can develop a bitter taste if exposed to heat too long.

21 Connect-Move-Transform with Friends

From the Field with Kim Murphy and Kris Carpenter

Kim and Kris are co-authors *of* The Best Friends' Guide to Getting Fit *and co-owners of ConnectMoveTransform.com—a health and fitness site dedicated to helping women connect with friends, move their bodies, and transform their lives.*

We have been friends for almost 18 years and workout partners for more than eight. When we first began walking together, we could barely make it up a hill without getting winded. Yet over the course of several years, we managed to maintain a routine, to foster a meaningful friendship, and to continually improve our fitness levels—to the full realization of running the Marine Corps Marathon! In doing so, we transformed our lives.

And we realized that the reason we were able to be consistent for the first time in our lives and to actually enjoy exercising together was because of a single factor: our friendship. As a result, we decided that if it could work for us, it could work for lots of other people as well—particularly women. Moreover, it's a philosophy and approach that's especially beneficial for military spouses who are often in even greater need of a support system, an outlet for stress, and a self-care routine.

So we coined the phrase "friendship-based fitness" and developed some easy steps you can take with a friend to make the concept work for you, too.

What Is a Friendship-based Fitness Routine?
Our philosophy is that if you connect with a friend, while you move your body, you can transform your life. When it comes to exercise, most people struggle to be consistent. We all know exercise is good for us. However, there is often a disconnect between knowing what to do, versus, actually doing it. Especially for military spouses whose responsibilities for the family and whose commitments can be overwhelming, taking time to exercise may seem like one more dreaded

chore or a privilege that they can't afford to take. Partnering with a friend can help close the gap between what you know is good for you and what you do about it.

How Does It Work?

If you're like us, knowing you should "just do it" is not usually enough motivation to head out the door for a workout. Yet with a friend at your side, you'll have someone to hold you accountable, someone who is expecting you. And each day, you'll be able to talk without interruption to a person who genuinely cares about you. You'll quickly get addicted to your time together, long before you begin to crave the exercise. When fitness becomes such an integral part of your days, it can transform your life.

> "If you're like us, knowing you should 'just do it' is not usually enough motivation to head out the door for a workout."

But even before you experience the types of big fitness gains that come over time, there are a host of concrete benefits you can enjoy almost instantly when you kick off a friendship-based fitness routine

Special Benefits for Military Spouses

A friendship-based fitness program can work for anyone, but it's especially valuable to the military spouse. When you get fit with a friend, you will give yourself the gift of:

- **Improved self-care**. As a military spouse, you may find you repeatedly put yourself last on the list. It probably seem as if that's necessary in order for you to be able to accomplish all that you need to do in a day. But in truth, the opposite is true. If you care for yourself regularly, by exercising and perhaps eating more healthfully, you will find that you are actually better able to manage daily challenges.
- **Greater confidence**. Having your spouse deployed or simply working long hours, can take its toll on a woman's self-confidence. You may second-guess your ability to make decisions or question whether you have the resolve to stay strong and focused. Boosting your self-esteem and confidence through an exercise routine can help you rid yourself of those shaky, unsteady feelings. The

> "Serving as a support system for your friend, will also help you nourish your own soul through giving and loving."

sense of pride you'll discover when you follow through on your commitment to care for yourself will also buoy your spirit. Best of all, you can ride that wave of newfound confidence through the transitions you face—whether it is a move, readying for deployment, or simply sending your kindergartner off to school.

- **A built-in support system and stress reliever**. Exercise and time with a friend can dramatically reduce stress, making you feel calmer, more centered, and in control. Having a safe place to vent frustrations can also enable you to cope better with the stress of having your spouse deployed or tackling another move. Serving as a support system for your friend, will also help you nourish your own soul through giving and loving.
- **A comforting routine**. Finding a rhythm to your days and having structure can also help you to cope with stress, loss, and absence. When you exercise regularly, even if it's one or two days each week, especially when you do it with a friend, you will find a deep sense of comfort from that routine and your ability to maintain it.
- **Deeper slumber.** Regular exercise can help you sleep better, so you feel well-rested on an ongoing basis.
- A sense of community. When you establish a routine with a friend or group of friends, especially if they are all military spouses, you'll foster a tremendous sense of community amid a group of like-minded individuals.
- **Affordable fitness.** Walking and running are ideal pursuits that don't require health club costs or an investment in gear (aside from buying a decent pair of shoes.) So, you don't have to worry about stretching a tight budget in order to get started.

> "Enjoy chances each day to laugh and escape your worries.

- **Guilt-free fun.** Because you will likely never take time out for coffee with friends each day, this is a guilt-free approach to getting together and having fun.
- **Laughter**. Enjoy chances each day to laugh and escape your worries, even if only for a little while.
- **Show your support**. Sometimes, as a military spouse, you may feel helpless. With a friendship-based fitness program in place, you and your friend(s) can set goals together to participate in events and races that allow you to show support (and raise funds) for the Armed Forces or other causes that matter to you. Participate by walking or running the Army 10-Miler or the Marine Corps Marathon. Or, select a charity that lets you walk to raise money and show your support.

Now Grab a Friend or Two and Get Going

If you look around, there are women everywhere in search of answers for living healthier and feeling more confident. And there are women everywhere in need of deep, meaningful friendships. When it comes to finding a friend to partner with in order to kick off a fitness routine, there is no single best arrangement. Different approaches work well for different people and for different lifestyles. Ideally, you should strive to:

- Connect with a friend in your neighborhood or on your installation, so you meet face-to-face for some type of activity. You don't need to worry about this person being a "best friend." You'll grow closer over time as you establish your routine.

- Partner with a group of friends, so that you have an even larger support system in place. We have found that often times women are a little nervous to approach another friend or acquaintance and to ask them if they're interested in kicking off a friendship-based fitness routine. But using an e-mail to approach a group of women is a simple way to get the job done. You will be amazed at how many are intrigued by the idea.

- To get started, take a few minutes to think of all the women in your area that you know, from book clubs to playgroups to preschool moms. Then, send a mass e-mail to all of them, letting them know what you're thinking about. Want to start a walking group on Tuesday and Thursday mornings? Let them know the details, including location, days, times, and your goal. Invite them to join you. Encourage everyone to commit to each other and to have fun. Tell them a little bit about our philosophy regarding a friendship-based fitness routine or recommend that they pick up a copy of our book, The Best Friends' Guide to Getting Fit.

> **"Tell them . . . about our philosophy regarding a friendship-based fitness routine or...that they pick up...our book, *The Best Friends' Guide to Getting Fit*"**

Looking to the Future

The life of a military family is fraught with change. If you can establish a friendship-based fitness routine during your steadier, stable times, then you can carry what you have learned and nurtured with you wherever you go.

For example, if you succeed in establishing a routine with friends then you will be able to:

- Remember the benefits you enjoyed when you were in your routine and do all that you can to start a group in your new location, immediately.

- Rely on your "old" friends and the support system you established to help you through the transition. Create an e-mail circle, so you can correspond regularly with the group. Have them hold you accountable and help you stay on track with your exercise routine. Allow them to be your incentive for finding or establishing a new group.
- Use the confidence you fostered to be bold and assertive when it comes to finding new friends. Post notices on bulletin boards on the base. Use the Military Family Network website to post messages to help you find new partners. Be creative and committed.

Take Your First Step Today

This chapter contains much of the advice and tips you'll need to get started. But perhaps the best advice we can give you is this: Don't delay. Take your first step today to create a friendship-based fitness routine. If you do, you may discover that—like us—your life will be transformed forever.

 **FAQs**

Q. What is the best type of friendship-based exercise program?

A. *Choose an exercise program that allows you and your friend time to chat. We have found either walking or beginning running programs are ideal because they permit conversation. The friend or group of friends will not only hold you accountable, but will provide you with a deep sense that someone (or a group of someones) genuinely cares about you. You will become "addicted" to the time together and without even realizing it, become addicted to the exercise. Once you and your friend(s) have been consistent for several months, you will be able to pursue other interests outside of walking or running, if you choose.*

Q. Who is the best person or group to partner with?

A. *When selecting a friend or group of friends make sure you are able to "be yourself," because you will be spending large chucks of your time with this person. Consider a friend or several that share many of your interests or are* *in similar stages of their lives. This will provide common ground in terms of daily experiences and help when it's time to compare schedules and to find a time to get together.*

Q. What if I am not enjoying my partner?

A. *You need to find a new partner, but do not give up on the idea of a friendship-based fitness program. It may take a few tries, but the right partner or group is worth the effort—and may be the one thing that has kept you from living a fit life up until now.*

Q. Will I lose weight if I begin a friendship-based fitness program?

A. *We have seen many women lose weight by following our philosophy and our programs. But the reason they lost weight isn't that they kicked-off a crash diet or burned oodles of calories by exercising fanatically. There is no magic pill. No instant solution. They lost weight because they managed to make a fundamental shift in how they viewed themselves, and ultimately, in how they treated themselves. But again, it didn't happen overnight. Instead, they started on a fitness journey that—over time— enabled them to foster the discipline, skills, and focus they needed to make small, concrete changes in their habits and their eating choices.*

> **"There is no magic pill. No instant solution. They...managed to make a fundamental shift in how they viewed themselves, and ultimately, in how they treated themselves"**

If you take the time to connect with a friend (or group of friends) and you move your body every day, you will develop the discipline, resolve, and confidence it takes to make other major life changes—whether it is losing weight, changing careers, or caring better for yourself.

Q. What if I am too busy to dedicate time to a friendship-based fitness program?

A. *There are 24 hours in each day. You deserve at least one of them.*

Need to Know

1.   Learn to listen to your body. It takes several weeks for your body to adjust to exercise on a regular basis. This means you will likely experience aches, pains, and soreness in the first fe w weeks. Take note of whether these aches and pains diminish during your exercise, once you are warmed up. Try to determine whether the aches and pains lessen as your body begins to adjust to the activity. Sore muscles are common and do not need to be pampered; injuries need to be tended to so they don't worsen. If you ever have a question or concern, seek out the help of a trained professional or your physician.

2.   Set a stretch goal. Stretching becomes more important the more you exercise, because it can help reduce your risk of injury. Stretching is also a great way to combat stress. Set a goal to stretch daily before and after you exercise—or whenever you need to relax and unwind.

3.   Keep an exercise log. Track your workouts in a log. Logs help you document progress and identify any challenges you may have related to various elements of your program. Simply jot down the time, activity. Also make note of how you felt during your workout (Were you tired? Stiff? Or, Strong?) Write down notes about the weather or any particular aches and pains you felt. Because so many elements come together during exercise—from eating and hydration habits to bathroom routines—it's very helpful to track the details so that you can make tweaks and changes in your program and your lifestyle.

4.   Drink more water! Be sure to start drinking plenty of water, before, during, and after your exercise. One quick way to determine whether or not you are properly hydrated is to check the color of your urine: When it's clear and colorless, then you're properly well hydrated!

5.   Buy good shoes. To purchase a quality shoe, from salespeople who understand the sport or activity you are beginning, go to a store that specializes in selling running shoes. They will outfit you correctly.

Some Do's and Don'ts to consider while you're at the store:
- Do not rush.
- Do not be shy.
- Do talk about how many miles you will walk or run in a week; or whether you're training for a race or particular distance; or if you're a beginner.
- Do talk about how you may roll your feet when you run—outward or inward (supination or pronation).
- Do ask them to watch you walk or run if you do not know whether you roll inward or outward.

- Do talk about any feet or leg pains you may be experiencing.
- Do take your old shoes along so they can be examined for signs of supination or pronation.
- Do ask them to make note of the particular model you purchase in their computer system as well as the size, so that you have a record of your shoe (in the future, you may forget which model you bought and yet you may want to buy the very same pair).
- Do consider purchasing a half-size larger, to allow your feet to swell or expand during exercise.
- Do look for models with a roomy-sized toe box, to allow your toes to move.
- Do try the shoe on with the type of sock you intend to wear.

You may want to purchase two pairs of shoes at the same time, even if they are the same model. This can lengthen the life of your shoe, giving you an alternate pair to use. It can also prevent a particular shoe from causing irritations; and, if they are different models, allow you to work slightly different muscle groups.

Make the Connection on MFN!
www.eMilitary.org/YourMFN.html

Sign on to the address
shown above and
Make the Connection
to more resources
on this topic!

Part 5

Military Family Health & Well-Being

Photo: Luis Trevino

Introduction

The military offers a comprehensive health care benefit to its service members and families. In order to make the most of this benefit, it is important to understand how the system works and how to advocate for yourself and your family. Start by educating yourself about the benefits offered by the TRICARE health program and the programs and services available to you and your family's unique health care needs. To ensure your family's well being you should have a firm understanding of the following elements of your healthcare program while you are associated with the military: eligibility for services, program options, coverage and claims processes.

In the environment of multiple deployments and extended tours, many families are encountering issues relating to the combat experienced by their loved ones. Post Traumatic Stress Disorder (PTSD) will affect almost 20 percent of returning service members some time in their lifetime. It is important to become educated on the tools available to you to help with adjustment and understanding if your family should experience PTSD or other combat-related concerns.

Exceptional Family Members in the military require a high level of advocacy so it is important to understand both the health care programs offered by the military and the civilian resources where you are located when your family's need extends beyond the system. The bottom line is this, if you are not receiving the care you feel is appropriate, you are responsible for seeking resolution and ensuring your voice is heard.

This section discusses some sensitive needs many military families have with regard to their family health care. Topics range from the importance of maintaining your personal health care records to issues relating to eldercare. We have also included extended chapters on PTSD and EFMP because of the increasing need among families to know about and gain access to resources about these issues.

Please note that this section is meant to be the beginning, not the end-all, of your access to information about resources available to you in the military health care environment. We encourage you to visit the Military Family Network website at www.eMilitary.org to gain a deeper understanding of the information you will need to make the best decisions for you and your family.

22 TRICARE

From the Field with Linda Nash Foote

Linda Nash Foote is the Director of the Public Affairs Office, TRICARE Management Activity

TRICARE ranks among the very best health care benefits in the nation. Our access is unparalleled with a worldwide network of 70 military hospitals, 411 military health clinics, and the Department's extensive private sector health care partners. In addition, we have a national network of more than 220,000 physicians, hundreds of U.S. hospitals, and 55,000 retail pharmacies to supplement military treatment facilities worldwide.

What Is TRICARE?
TRICARE is the Department of Defense's health care program for eligible active-duty service members, retirees, eligible National Guard and Reserve members, their families and survivors. It's a fully integrated system that unites the Army, Navy, Air Force, and Coast Guard health care resources and supplements them with civilian health care professionals for better access to care and high-quality service, while maintaining health care support for military operations. The military health system delivers the TRICARE benefit to provide a cost effective, quality health benefit for all TRICARE beneficiaries.

Your Health Care Options
TRICARE beneficiaries may get health care services through military treatment facilities or civilian health care providers—and enjoy several health care options both in the United States and overseas. The most common options are TRICARE Prime, TRICARE Extra, and TRICARE Standard. But TRICARE includes a wide range of other benefits and covered services such as a voluntary comprehensive dental benefit, a robust pharmacy program, and TRICARE for Life for Medicare-TRICARE eligible uniformed services retirees, TRICARE Reserve Select for qualified members of the National Guard and

Reserve, the Extended Care Health Option for active duty family members with special needs, and many more.

The TRICARE benefit also extends beyond the continental United States. The TRICARE Overseas Program blends many of the features of the stateside program, while allowing for significant cultural differences unique to foreign countries and their health care practices. The TRICARE Overseas Program consists of three areas: Europe; Pacific; and Latin America and Canada, including the Caribbean Basin, Puerto Rico and the

Virgin Islands. Learning how TRICARE works and proactively engaging in your health care will help service and family members take advantage of this benefit. The military and civilian leadership in the Defense Department and across the military health system honor the great sacrifices our service members and their families make, especially in time of war. Their sacrifices remind us of the valuable contributions made by those who served in years past. We know the health benefits you enjoy are richly deserved, and the military health system is committed to delivering the finest health care for many years to come!

> **"Learning how TRICARE works and proactively engaging in your health care will help service and family members take advantage of this benefit."**

 **FAQs**

Q. Who is eligible to participate in TRICARE?

A. *All active-duty service members, retirees, their spouses, and unmarried children (including stepchildren) under the age of 21 (or 23 if attending school full time, and rely on sponsor for 50 percent of income) may be eligible for TRICARE. In addition, National Guard and Reserve members called to active duty for 30 consecutive days or more are eligible for comprehensive health coverage through TRICARE, which includes coverage for their family members.*

Q. What is DEERS?

A. *The Defense Enrollment Eligibility Reporting System (DEERS) is a worldwide-computerized data repository of uniformed services members (active* *duty, National Guard and Reserve, and retirees), their family members, and others who may be eligible for military medical benefits, including TRICARE. Service members (sponsors) are automatically registered in DEERS, but sponsors must ensure their family members are registered correctly.*

Sponsors must ensure their family members' status (marriage, divorce, new child, etc.) is correct. They should also make sure their residential address, telephone numbers, and e-mail address are correct with DEERS so their families may receive important TRICARE information.

Q. Why is it important to keep DEERS records current?

A. *The key to receiving TRICARE benefits—health care services, prescriptions, claims processing—is proper registration in DEERS. Sponsors and eligible family members must show as eligible for TRICARE in DEERS. Network providers and pharmacies verify TRICARE eligibility in DEERS before rendering services or filling prescriptions.*

Q. What can beneficiaries do to ensure prompt claims payment, if they must file a claim?

A. *Here are some helpful tips to avoid processing delays:*

1. Make sure DEERS information is correct and current.
2. Submit all claims on a DD Form 2642. (Forms are available online or by contacting your regional contractor)
3. Provide accurate information, including sponsor's Social Security number, your home address and phone number, etc.
4. Confirm diagnosis code with the provider who rendered service.
5. Sign the claim form. If you don't sign, TRICARE will deny the claim.
6. Indicate on the claim form if someone else is responsible for your injury and if so, complete a DD Form 2527 to submit with the DD Form 2642.
7. If you have other health insurance, file claims with your other health insurance before filing with TRICARE.
8. Dual eligible beneficiaries (Medicare- and TRICARE-eligible) file claims first with Medicare. Medicare will transmit claims to TRICARE for secondary processing.
9. Keep copies of everything you submit to the claims processors.
10. Send claim forms to the correct address. (Available online under "claims," or by contacting your regional contractor)
11. File claims as soon as possible. You must file within one year of the date-of-service.

12. Submit each claim separately.
13. Regional contractor customer service staff may answer basic claims questions.

Q. What is TRICARE Reserve Select, and how do I know if I'm eligible?

A. *TRICARE Reserve Select (TRS) is a premium-based TRICARE health plan that qualified members of the Selected Reserve may purchase. Your Service/Reserve Component office determines and validates your qualifications to purchase TRS coverage and identifies the appropriate premium tier.*

 Need to Know

Patient Safety Starts With Communication

TRICARE works hard to provide the best possible health care and to keep our beneficiaries safe, but we need your help. Be a proactive part of your health care team.

> **"Be a proactive part of your health care team."**

How Can You Help?

Ask, listen and learn. Talk to your doctor regarding all health care decisions. If you can't speak for yourself, ask a family member or friend to go to the appointment with you and ask questions on your behalf. This person must understand your health care preferences so he or she may speak on your behalf, if needed. Here are some questions to ask:

- What is my illness or condition?
- What is your treatment plan?
- Will I need to take any tests?
- When, where and how will you give me test results?
- If I need surgery, exactly what will be done?

Keep track of your health care information. Write down the following important information and always carry it with you.

- Prescriptions, including doses;
- Over-the-counter medications, including doses;
- Allergies;

> **"Keep track of your health care information."**

- Names and telephone numbers of all of your doctors;
- Name and telephone number of your pharmacy; and,
- Name of individual(s) to contact in case of emergency.

Take simple steps to stay safe. There are easy ways you can protect yourself and be involved with your health care, including the following:
- Write down all medicines, vitamins and herbal supplements you take;
- Throw away all old or expired medicine;
- Tell your doctor what medications you take, any allergies and any adverse reactions you have to medications;
- Ask what your prescribed medicine does and what side effects it may cause; and
- Ask when and how to take your medication.

Check to see if you need prior authorization for care. Before you get specialty health care services or see a specialty provider, call your regional contractor or overseas office to see if you need prior authorization.

Most importantly, be involved in your health care. Take part in every decision about your health—the more involved you are, the better care you will get.

Make the Connection on MFN!
www.eMilitary.org/YourMFN.html

Sign on to the address
shown above and
Make the Connection
to more resources
on this topic!

23 Your Exceptional Military Family

From the Field with Heather Hebdon

Heather Hebdon is the Founder and Director, Specialized Training of Military Parents (STOMP), mother of 3 children, all of whom were enrolled in the Exceptional Family Member Program, during her husband's 22-year military career, she has a strong commitment to working with other military families. Ms. Hebdon's oldest son has Down Syndrome, lives and works in his community, and continues to be a source of inspiration and exasperation to his mother, as do her other two children. Heather is located at the Headquarters office, when she isn't traveling, and welcomes calls from families and providers.

Military families who have children with disabilities face numerous challenges in getting the educational services their children need, especially with their highly mobile lifestyle. During the average military career, a service member can be expected to receive PCS (Permanent Change of Station) orders every eighteen months to three years. The frequency of these PCS orders will depend on a number of factors.

These include:
- Where the service member is located (CONUS–Contiguous United States or OCONUS–Outside the Continental United States);
- Whether the assignment the service member is currently fulfilling is considered command sponsored (where the military provides transportation and services for the family members) or as an unaccompanied tour (where the family is not expected to travel with the sponsor);
- The specific job assignment of the military member;
- If the military member's MOS (Military Occupational Specialty) is required at other assignments.

Additionally, the branch of service the military member is associated with affects the frequency of PCS orders. If, for instance, the military member is in the Navy, and has a family member with a disability enrolled in the Exceptional Family Member Program (EFMP) who is in category 4, the family is located at those duty stations where medical services are readily available.

Because of the family's needs the assignment can be extended for as much as five years. If the family member has a category 5 enrollment, the family is homesteaded (meaning the family will be co-located at one duty station). This does not mean that the military member is only assigned to these locations. It does, however, limit the opportunity for the family to move to other locations, and may require the Navy member to do more sea duty rotations, posing an additional burden on the family, but allowing the military member to remain located at the identified duty station for longer periods of time.

All branches of the service have a mandatory EFMP enrollment. Until June 2003, each branch of service used different criteria and processes for enrollment in the Exceptional Family Member Program (EFMP). While the program has now become a Department of Defense (DOD) initiative, and all branches use the same paperwork, the program services are still different from branch to branch. For instance:

> **"All branches of the service have mandatory EFMP enrollment."**

- The Navy program only provides coding services. There are no advocacy supports available.
- Within the Air Force, the services of coding are done under the auspices of the Family Advocacy Program (FAP). There are limited advocacy services, and these are provided through the Airman and Family Readiness Center's Information and Referral services.
- Within the Army and Marine Corp the program provides both coding and advocacy services. However, while the Marine Corp has fenced monies to support these services, the Army does not. Therefore, many of the advocacy services are done by individuals who hold more than one job and who may have limited knowledge regarding the variety of systems and services available. This can lead to confusion and difficulties for the military member who is enrolling their family member.

In 1994, the Army was the first branch of service to send out a directive stating that consideration of a new duty assignment under EFMP would not be disallowed based on the lack of educational services. The explanation provided was that all states and locales were required to comply with the Individuals with Disabilities Education Act (IDEA). The only reason for denial of an assignment for the family is

> **"...the Army was the first branch of service to send out a directive stating that consideration of a new duty assignment under EFMP would not be disallowed based on the lack of educational services..."**

due to lack of medical related services. The other branches of service have followed suit with this directive.

Previously, families were able to argue that a new duty assignment did not provide effective educational opportunities. This argument is no longer relevant. Due to the directive, families are being reassigned to installations where the services they are accustomed to are not available. All of these factors impact on the military family's ability to effectively advocate on behalf of their child. The stress factors associated with frequent moves and reestablishing links is exacerbated when there is a lack of consistency from place to place or from one branch of service to another.

Families are in need of a clear understanding of what IDEA requires in the way of services and activities. The terms for the name of the team—i.e. Case Study Committee (CSC), Multidisciplinary Team (MDT), Arrival Review and Dismissal (ARD) Committee, IEP (Individual Education Plan) Team, etc.—may be different from one assignment to another, as may the way the team functions. Yet, military families need to understand the basic premise behind the IDEA that ensures effective parent participation in decisions regarding the identification, evaluation, provision of services, and Free Appropriate Public Education (FAPE) for the child.

> **"These families must have the knowledge to make informed decisions and to provide effective input into the development of the IEP."**

These families must have the knowledge to make informed decisions and to provide effective input into the development of the IEP. Transition from birth to three programs (where infants enter toddler aged or daycare schooling) and transition to adult services (high school to adult settings) are also areas that the family, and in the case of transition to adult services, the student and other interested members need to have knowledge of to move with success. Families need the following:

- Knowledge regarding record access and effective communication skills to work with others involved in the development of the child's IEP;
- Understanding the implications of NCLB (No Child Left Behind) on services to students with disabilities and how the state implements NCLB requirements; or in the case of DODEA (Department of Defense Education Administration) systems, what education reform activities they are implementing and to what extent do they or do they not include students with disabilities in their accountability system.

These families require support in accessing services and resources that will benefit them not only in their current duty assignment, but in future duty assignments as well. They also need to become actively involved in their child's care as well as making sure that they stay well informed. Additionally, these military families need to develop and cultivate skills necessary to effectively communicate with others like care providers and educators regarding their child's needs.

Military families may find their child with special education needs served in one of three educational systems. These include:

- U.S. Department of Education (USDOE) Schools located in the state in which they are stationed
- Department of Defense Dependent Schools (DODDS) located at installations in Europe, the Pacific, Cuba and Panama
- Defense Dependent Elementary and Secondary Schools (DDESS) located in the United States (primarily in the South), Guam, and Puerto Rico.

Another issue of importance for military families is access to medical services.

This plays a significant role in the special education planning for some students. For example, TRICARE can pay for durable medical equipment, therapies, and counseling under certain circumstances or programs. However, as this is an entitlement program (not insurance), all other programs pay first, except Medicaid.

With the Reauthorization of IDEA (PL 108-447) TRICARE can now be used to assist in payment for early intervention services (under Part C); yet families are finding significant difficulties in trying to access this system to help pay for the services. These difficulties include lack of appropriate information going out to Part C providers on how to access TRICARE, lack of information on the various programs under TRICARE, and lack of support for families applying for TRICARE benefits. These problems compounded with the low payments allowed under TRICARE and the length of time for receipt of payments, have left many families and providers disenchanted with TRICARE.

These many challenges faced by military families require a multifaceted approach to serving them.

FAQs

Q. Does learning environment mean just classroom activities?

A. *No, a learning environment is any part of the school day, or program, where a student can learn skills. This includes, but is not limited to: social skills such as those needed to participate in extra-curricular activities or learning appropriate lunchroom behavior. It could include turn-taking on the* *playground or attending assemblies. It can also include learning appropriate skills or behaviors on a school bus. The learning environment goes across the student's educational career.*

When considering what is an appropriate learning environment, consider your child and his or her needs both academically and socially. If he or she is of transition age (age 16 on), consider what skills he or she will need in the areas of self-help, decision-making, and social skills as well as job skills. We all continue to gain skills. This is no different if the person has a disability. Looking across the school day and across the school career will open many potential doors to identification of areas that are strengths, as well as areas your son or daughter may need to gain additional skills.

Q. My child's teacher gave him a permission slip to go on a field trip, but on the bottom of his form the teacher wrote red letters "If (child's name) does not have an adult chaperone he will not attend." Can she do this?

A. *Does the child need additional supervision in an outside classroom setting or unfamiliar classroom setting? If this is already documented or observed (like in assemblies), then there is a warrant for concern. However, the parents are not responsible to provide such accommodations without remuneration. It is the responsibility of the school to provide for equal access of all school related activities for the child in question. And to deny access of the activity based on the child's disability is a violation of their IEP and their rights.*

Q. We just found out we are PCSing overseas and we need to go through EFMP screening. What should we expect?

A. *Every military member may face an overseas assignment at some time during his or her military career. When it is expected that the family will accompany the military member, they are required to go through EFMP screening. This screening is required of ALL personnel (including civilian personnel) who are being sent to a duty station outside the Continental United States.*

This process should be completed within 30 days of receipt of orders for the overseas assignment. Delays in getting the screening done can cause delays or denial of family travel to the new duty assignment. If you know you have a family member who would qualify for enrollment in the EFMP, you don't need to wait until you have orders to get the process going and get the family member enrolled. Identification during overseas screening can result in a delay of approval for the family member travel if the family member has a special medical or educational need and has not been enrolled in the EFMP previously.

The steps in the process are:

1. Service member is notified of an assignment outside the continental United States.

2. Losing Military Personnel Division/ personnel service battalion verifies family members' eligibility for accompanied tour.

3. Service member authenticated DA Form 5888 (Family Member Deployment Screening Sheet) for screening and DA Form 4787-R (Reassignment Processing) for reassignment processing.

> **"...you don't need to wait until you have orders to get the process going and get the family member enrolled."**

4. Losing military treatment facility screens family members for medical and/or educational needs.

5. The service member/spouse completes DA Form 7246 (EFMP Screening Questionnaire) and signs and authenticates DA Form 5888.

6. If no medical or developmental problems are identified in the screening process, block 9a is checked to indicate that EFMP enrollment is not warranted. No further EFMP action is necessary.

7. If a family member requires further evaluation, DA Form 5862 (EFMP Medical Summary) and/or DA Form 5291 (EFMP Educational Summary) are completed.

8. If enrollment is warranted, the forms are forwarded to the appropriate regional medical command for coding.

9. The regional medical commands enroll eligible active service members into the program. The date that DA Form 5862 and/or DA Form 5291 is sent for coding is entered into block 9b of DA Form 5888.

10. Military Personnel Division/personnel service battalion coordinates with the gaining command to determine if services are available.

11. Military medical makes recommendations on locations where medical services are available.

12. Department of Defense (DoD) Dependents Schools identifies pinpoint locations where educational needs can be met (if applicable).

13. Housing office indicates availability of housing.

14. When services are not available at the location where service member is to be assigned, personnel agencies consider alternative assignment locations based upon existing assignment priorities or, upon approval of the appropriate authority, send the service member on an unaccompanied tour.

- Deletion from assignment instructions is not granted solely because of a service member's enrollment in the EFMP. The EFMP is designed to be an assignment consideration, if the service member is enrolled, and not an assignment limitation. Service members could be reassigned to an "all others tour" to meet military requirements.
- Deferment for service members with family members enrolled in the EFMP is granted when family travel decisions from the gaining command are not finalized.

Need to Know

How to Advocate for Your Child in the Military

When advocating for a child within the various military systems, families need to stay focused on what is necessary and appropriate for their child. Communication is vital in ensuring that the needs of the child are clear to all involved.

We strongly recommend that families maintain a strong home file of all information, work with the military professionals and community members, and be willing to ask questions and listen to all sides of the issue before making a decision.

Make the Connection on MFN!
www.eMilitary.org/YourMFN.html

Sign on to the address
shown above and
Make the Connection
to more resources
on this topic!

The more families know, work with the resources available to support them, and keep abreast of the services their child is receiving the better they will be at advocating for their child.

Families need to understand that they are the only constant in their child's life. No matter how good the teacher, or doctor, or program is, they cannot pack it up in their whole baggage and ship it or them to the next duty station.

Families need to be knowledgeable and willing to work effectively with the teams they will come into contact with.

24   Your Medical Record

From the Field with Jolene Elliott, RHIT-AHIMA & Megan Turak.

Jolene Elliott, RHIT-AHIMA is the Director of the Health Information Management Department for Wayne Memorial Hospital located in Jessup, Georgia Megan Turak is the daughter of a WWII Army veteran and spouse of a Vietnam era Marine, Executive Vice President and co-owner of The Military Family Network, former Medical Records Manager with the Department of Veteran Affairs, a published writer of informative topics positively impacting the well-being of military families and has over twenty combined years of experience in executive leadership in the financial management and communications industries.

The earliest cave dwellings have shown drawings of medical care that was given to cavemen. Then and now, it is of the utmost importance to record the events surrounding the medical care that is given to each individual. It is really a story of your life, medically speaking. From the time you are born until the end of life, everything that happens to you or is done to your body should be recorded.

These records are referred to as your medical record, your medical chart, or simply, your chart. Your chart and its contents are extremely valuable and vital to your well-being. They will include immunization records, visits to the emergency room or your local doctor, hospital stays, or day surgeries. It also contains dental visits and eye or ear exams as well as birth and death certificates.

Caregivers should be able to review your medical record to get a clear picture of your health history, and what has already happened to you. Armed with this information, they can then make recommendations to help you with decisions for your continued care. Medical records and their contents are extremely important in circumstances where you are unable to speak for yourself and when you need continuity of care across multiple health care providers.

Things such as your allergies or sensitivities to certain medicines, chemicals, plants or foods, should be recorded and available in your chart. Current medications that you might be taking should also be listed. Your life could depend upon information contained in your record; therefore, information in them should be accurate and readily accessible.

There are rules and regulations from various organizations and government agencies that help assure your information is kept accurately and timely. These rules may vary somewhat from state to state, but are basically the same. In 1996, the Health Insurance Portability and Accountability Act (HIPAA) was passed by Congress to help assure your medical information is

> **"You have a right to review or have a copy of your medical information."**

used appropriately. This means that your private information will only be shared with others as provided for by law. Whether your records are a paper copy or are totally computerized (or some form of both), all the laws, rules, and regulations are the same for both kinds of records.

You have a right to review or have a copy of your medical information. The procedure to obtain your medical information may vary, but usually, you need to request the information in writing from the Health Information Management Department (or the Medical Records Department) of a facility where you have received treatment or from your doctor, dentist, etc. Be prepared to pay a nominal fee (although there may not always be a charge). Request your copy well in advance of when you think you will need them to allow adequate time for the provider to prepare your record.

If you are expecting a child, a healthcare provider will be assisting you in the completion of the birth certificate. Though the actual certificate may vary, you should receive some type of record after the baby is born for your own personal safekeeping. You also can obtain a certified birth certificate, which usually involves a charge. The repository for birth and death certificates can differ, but could be the local Probate Judge or Health Departments. Generally, each state has a State Vital Records office as a part of the Department of Human Services.

Another very important part of your medical records is a copy of your Durable Power of Attorney for Healthcare, or Living Will. Seek the assistance of an attorney in making a Living Will or ask your hospital if they have preprinted forms that you can complete. Preparing one of these documents will assure, that should the time ever come when you cannot make decisions for yourself con-

> **"Another very important part of your medical records is a copy of your Durable Power of Attorney for Healthcare, or Living Will."**

cerning your medical treatment, you have already designated another individual of your choice to make those decisions for you. These documents will make a difficult time easier for your loved ones and will make your wishes concerning medical treatments known to your doctors. You should keep the original in a safe place and a copy for yourself in your own personal medical record if you have one. Provide a copy to your physician, and give another copy to your hospital. . Make sure the individual you name, as your agent, is aware you have appointed them and that they know what decisions you have made regarding your end of life care. Appoint a secondary person as well in the event that the primary individual you named is unavailable or unable to carry out your requests. The time to prepare such a document is when you are young and in good health. It will be too late once you are unconscious or incapacitated.

As we travel through our life, one of the most important concerns should be assuring our health care is the best we can obtain. One way to do this is to make sure our medical records are accurate, complete and available to our healthcare providers.

 **FAQs**

Q. What does the HIPAA Privacy Rule do?

A. *Most health plans and healthcare providers covered by the new rule must have complied with the HIPAA requirements by April 14, 2003. The HIPAA Privacy Rule for the first time creates national standards to protect individuals' medical records and other personal health information.*

- It gives patients more control over their health information.
- It sets boundaries on the use and release of health records.
- It establishes appropriate safeguards that health care providers and others must achieve to protect the privacy of health information.
- It holds violators accountable, with civil and criminal penalties that can be imposed if they violate patients' privacy rights.
- It strikes a balance when public responsibility supports disclosure of some forms of data—for example, to protect public health.
- For patients—it means being able to make informed choices when seeking care and reimbursement for care based on how personal health information may be used.

- It enables patients to find out how their information may be used, and about certain disclosures of their information that have been made.
- It generally limits release of information to the minimum reasonably needed for the purpose of the disclosure.
- It generally gives patients the right to examine and obtain a copy of their own health records and request corrections.
- It empowers individuals to control certain uses and disclosures of their health information.

Q. Why is the HIPAA Privacy Rule needed?

A. *In enacting HIPAA, Congress mandated the establishment of federal stand-ards for the privacy of individually identifi-able health information. When it comes to personal information that moves across hos-pitals, doctors' offices, insurers or third par-ty payers, and state lines, our country has relied on a patchwork of federal and state laws. Before HIPAA, personal health infor-mation could be distributed—without either notice or authorization—for reasons that*

Make the Connection on MFN!
www.eMilitary.org/YourMFN.html

Sign on to the address shown above and Make the Connection to more resources on this topic!

had nothing to do with a patient's medical treatment or healthcare reimburse-ment. For example, unless otherwise forbidden by state or local law, without the Privacy Rule patient information held by a health plan could, without the patient's permission, be passed on to a lender who could then deny the pa-tient's application for a home mortgage or a credit card, or to an employer who could use it in personnel decisions. The Privacy Rule establishes a fed-eral floor of safeguards to protect the confidentiality of medical information. State laws, which provide stronger privacy protections, will continue to apply over and above the new federal privacy standards.

Healthcare providers have a strong tradition of safeguarding private health information. However, in today's world, the old system of paper records in locked filing cabinets is not enough. With information broadly held and trans-mitted electronically, the HIPAA Rule provides clear standards for the protec-tion of personal health information.

Q. How can I find more questions and responses about medical records?

A. *For more frequently asked questions about personal medical records, vis-it: http://www.myphr.com/faqs/index.asp#1 AHIMA.org – My Personal Health Records and other FAQs*

Need to Know

Tips for Managing your Personal Medical Record

- **Ask for copies on the same day that you receive services from your provider.** In most cases, like regularly scheduled doctor's visits, this is an easy request to fill. If, however, the care you received is more complex, like a radiological procedure, then you will not be able to receive a copy of the report right then. However, you will at least be able to complete a "Release of Information" form to pick up a copy in the future.

- **Do not let military doctors or hospitals tell you that you are not entitled to a copy of your medical record.** You may not be able to have the original record (since law requires that the institution keep comprehensive documents on each individual it treats); however, they must make you a copy for your own records. There may be a fee for this service. Pay it. You will be glad that you have this information—especially if you find yourself heading overseas.

- **Take a moment to familiarize yourself with the types of documents filed inside your medical record**. These are several of the most common: laboratory reports, consults, operative or surgical reports, progress reports, consent forms, doctor's notes, pathological reports, radiological reports, med sheets, prescription orders, referrals, and nursing evaluations. When you are requesting copies of your records, if you can identify what you want, you will have a better chance of getting what you want as well as saving a few dollars in the process. But don't despair; if this is too much, just request a copy of your entire medical chart.

> **"There may be a fee for this service. Pay it. You will be glad that you have this information—especially if you find yourself heading overseas."**

- **Never, never, never give your personal medical records over to a provider without having another copy on hand**. If you must take your only copy with you, tell the nurse or doctor to make a copy of what they need, right then, right now, and return your record to you. Sometimes, this request is met with a bit of hesitation; don't let this deter you from your mission. It has cost you time and money to assemble your medical record, and it is the story of your health and can mean a matter of life and death. Do not leave your medical record behind!

- **If you think assembling your medical record is too time consuming and that the medical industry, doctor's office, hospital will take care of this for you, they will.** But I assure you, they will not take care of your record the way you would. This is your life. And, if you are a military veteran, then the contents in that medical record can also determine your eligibility for care, entitlements, and monetary awards for, say, a disability. Now, tell me, who has more interest in making sure that this information is kept safe and accurate?

- **Accuracy. Not enough can be said about this.** When you receive the copies of your records that you requested, use them! Look them over, read them, and check for errors. Is there a problem with the medications listed? Are your allergies missing? Are you being billed for services not listed in your chart or are listed but never received? Are you confused about something a provider wrote in your chart? Use this information to ask questions. Get involved in taking control of your health care. And, by the way, if something doesn't seem right, speak up.

- **Don't remain silent.** Serious errors occur all of the time in hospitals. And, any time you are asked to take a medication, ask what you are being given or you are taking. If it doesn't sound correct, don't take it—make the provider double-check the order or consult with your doctor.

- **Don't be a patsy for the work of others**. If your physician is referring you to a specialist, or even if you are choosing to see a specialist on your own, provide a release of information to the referring doctor and request that they fax over your records to the specialist. When copies of medical records transfer from physician office to physician office, there is typically no expense to you.

- **Read your consent forms thoroughly!** And read them before you take any drugs that may alter your ability to understand what you are signing. Any time you undergo a procedure, you are requested to sign a consent form authorizing the procedure. Normally, these consents are designed to cover any

> **"If you don't agree, don't sign! If anything makes you feel uncomfortable, state it."**

and all situations, risks and/or procedures that may be utilized. But they also contain a lot of other things, too. For instance, they may over generalize who will be performing the procedure; they may indicate the use of media such as filming, photographing and computerized images for the sake of science, education or other studies; and, they may outline a procedure for the collection of tissue samples and the release of this information as determined by the medical institution. If you don't agree, don't sign! If anything makes you feel uncomfortable, state it. Just because it is a preprinted consent form, does not mean that you need to agree to all of the terms. Simply strike out what you don't agree with or write-in your own terms. Don't forget to initial the changes and bring them to the attention of your physician. And also, make sure that you request that your doctor will be doing the entire procedure—unless you don't care—since many times procedures are assisted by doctors in training.

- **Every time you visit the doctor's office, you are provided with a HIPAA Privacy Rule form and are asked to sign that you have received it, agree to its terms and understand the rule.** You can sign it, you can amend it, or like a friend of mine, you can create one of your own based on the law and submit it to your provider. For more information on HIPAA, visit http://www.hhs.gov/ocr/hipaa/.

- **Never pack your medical record when you move.** You cannot afford to lose this information. It would be far too difficult and costly to try to rebuild this information from scratch.

- **Always make sure that you have your military identification card with you and that of your child or those of your children when requesting your medical record or their medical record(s).**

- **Keep an ongoing and current file of all of your and your family's healthcare providers including outpatient clinics and hospitals where you may have received care and treatment.** This list should include names, addresses and telephone numbers, fax numbers, physician specialty, notes regarding any care received and contact information for the medical records department or release of information section.

Make the Connection on MFN!
www.eMilitary.org/YourMFN.html

Sign on to the address
shown above and
Make the Connection
to more resources
on this topic!

25 Post Traumatic Stress in the Military

From the Field with Dr. Frank Ochberg by interview; Research by Caroline Peabody, former president, The Military Family Network

Caroline Peabody *is the daughter of a disabled Vietnam era Marine, military spouse, former president of The Military Family Network, lifetime volunteer, and distinguished speaker and lecturer on military life. She holds a B.S. in sociology and M.A. in organizational management with extensive research on communication systems as they relate to military well being and community capacity-building. She is a published writer and columnist on matters relating to military families, military learning models, and military relations.*

"I recovered from PTSD. I served in Vietnam. Now my son is deploying to Iraq. I am afraid it will all come back and when he comes back, I am scared it will be the same for him," said a middle aged Army nurse while browsing through resource tapes from Gift from Within about Post Traumatic Stress Disorder (PTSD) at a recent Military Family Network event.

She is not alone in her experience or her fears. In 2005, almost 216,000 veterans received PTSD benefit payments totaling almost $4.3 billion dollars. A 2006 *Journal of the American Medical Association* study shows that 9.8 percent of service members returning from Iraq have screened positive for PTSD symptoms and 11.9 percent were diagnosed with a mental disorder within the first year home. An additional 50,000 veterans from Iraq and Afghanistan are believed to be suffering from mental health problems—nearly half of them from PTSD.

When 22 soldiers killed themselves—accounting for nearly one in five of all Army non-combat deaths in 2005, Congress mandated a review of how the Department of Defense works to identify and treat members of the Armed Services suffering from PTSD.

PTSD as a Political Issue

The United States is actively engaged in an ongoing war against terrorists. Although deployed to countries like Afghanistan and Iraq, territory or borders do not define the war. The tactics and strategies of the enemy are those of a new age—urban warfare where nontraditional, guerrilla attacks place service members on the frontline wherever they find themselves.

The majority of troops return home and will not experience any long-term psychological concerns from their combat service. However, the extended nature of this war has resulted in multiple redeployments and extensions for many military service members, which has caused increased stress to both them and their families. It is estimated that nearly 20 percent of all returning veterans of this war will develop PTSD in their lifetime. Still more will experience a wider range of psychological effects including depression and anxiety. Service members returning from war also experience higher rates of divorce, anger management, and drug and alcohol issues.

The combat action faced by service members place them in constant and immediate danger of loss of limb and life. As the following chart demonstrates, almost all members of the Army know someone who has been seriously injured or killed in action.

Frequent Combat Experiences Reported by Members of the U.S. Army, 2003		
	Afghanistan	Iraq
Being attacked or ambushed	58%	89%
Receiving incoming fire	84%	86%
Being shot at	66%	93%
Seeing dead bodies or remains	39%	95%
Knowing someone seriously injured or killed	43%	86%

(Source: National Center for PTSD)

Dr. Frank Ochberg, founding board member of the International Society for Traumatic Stress Studies, founder of Gift from Within, and former associate director of the National Institute of Mental Health, has decades of experience with traumatic stress. He is credited with defining the Stockholm Syndrome.

According to Dr. Ochberg, increasing the education, awareness, and availability of treatment for service members experiencing combat stress should be one of the highest priorities of the Armed Services. He recommends that families reach out and work to get their concerns publicly recorded and acknowledged. He says:

If this doesn't come from military families, it's not going to get the attention it deserves. And military families are in a powerful political position. They're not powerful in raising concerns that aren't asked for within the military chain of command. But at the ballot

> **"...increasing the education, awareness, and availability of treatment for service members experiencing combat stress should be one of the highest priorities of the Armed Services ..."**

box, and in writing articles, and in entering into the national conversation, it's terribly, terribly important. People listen to widows. People listen to the parents of military, who have sacrificed. So we are talking about something that is crucial, and it's relevant, and it's timely. We can do what we're attempting to do here, which is to de-stigmatize, and normalize, symptoms of PTSD. If you are having flashbacks, and you know it, and yet, you have a military career, and you want to keep that career, you don't talk about the flashbacks.

Frontline soldiers face extreme violence in Iraq. According to Department of Defense studies, more than 90 percent said they had been shot at. Nearly 20 percent said they saved someone's life. More than 80 percent of Marines said they saw injured women and children they had been unable to help.

Of those Iraq veterans surveyed who reported symptoms of mental distress, 40 percent of Army troops and 29 percent of Marines said they had sought professional help. Those who did not seek assistance reported several reasons mostly related to their military role. The top reasons given for avoiding such help, from a multiple-choice list provided by the researchers from the Army in the field, were, in order: "I would be seen as weak," "My unit leadership might treat me differently," "Members of my unit might have less confidence in me," and, "It would harm my career."

A terrible irony exists for these combat veterans experiencing distress. Reporting has an impact on their careers, but reporting ensures timely help at the earliest point of onset and supports a rapid therapeutic process. Self-reporting is also complicated by the combat veteran's perception of negative peer judgment, his own feelings of weakness for having distress, and his internal struggle with guilt over leaving his unit to receive treatment.

Dr. Ochberg stresses that education is the key to removing the negative perceptions of PTSD:

Once you've got it, it is a medical disorder, and it's best to consider it as such. Helps to get treatment for it. Helps to get information about it. Helps to have [ongoing] discussions so that family members can be up to speed and realize 'there but for the grace of God go I.' There's nothing morally wrong or physically wrong with the person who gets PTSD . . . and with a lot of adults who have served in uniform, branches of government, they manage to do their service, despite their feelings—all while they were on duty. But afterward, when you're safe, when you're in an entirely different environment, your body and your mind start to react.

War changes a person. Service members train every day to serve their country, to fight and win America's wars. Prolonged exposure to hazardous environments, daily exposure to violence and death, have a deep affect.

> **"Prolonged exposure to hazardous environments, daily exposure to violence and death, have a deep affect."**

Dr. Ochberg's lifework has been to help people, who have been exposed to trauma, to heal. His message is one of hope and support to all service members and their families.

I want to thank our men and women in uniform for their service. That service carries risk. That risk is to the body and to the spirit. Some of the wounds to the spirit take the pattern of PTSD or depression. They can be treated and treatment is good, and hopeful. Post traumatic stress, depression; even alcoholism and family discord are all treatable conditions.

> **"So, we may not be 'the same' but not being the same is okay."**

Sometimes, some of us have gone through hell, and we're never going to be exactly the same. We've seen things that we'd rather not admit exist. So, we may not be 'the same' but not being the same is okay.

 **FAQs**

Q. What is PTSD?

A. *PTSD is three different things at once. The first of those three things is "trauma memory." Trauma memory is different from usual memory. It comes back when you don't want it to come back. It can wake you up in the middle of the night. It can be very subtle, so you're not quite sure what it is until you realize, oh, my God, I'm having the feelings that I had when I was raped. That's what's going on. Or it can be very, very specific, like a hallucination. 'I'm smelling what I was smelling when I was raped . . . I hear his voice, I feel his hand on me.' When it is what I just said, so real, like a hallucination, you don't have any time sense. That's very important. You don't realize that it's in the past. And it feels like it's in the present. So it's called "Re-experiencing" rather than remembering.*

One of the things that is most important in working with people who have a "trauma memory" is to help them develop a time sense, so they're not scared out of their wits. And therapy is all about transforming a trauma memory into an autobiographical memory. You don't forget about it, but you know it's in the past.

The second cluster of symptoms is almost the opposite. It's feeling numb. It's like having emotional anesthesia. And you're really not the person you once were, and even though that emotional anesthesia may dampen down feelings of terror, they take away feelings of love, and hope, and connection. And a lot of what a person does, who is numb, is to avoid things. They avoid people, often people who might trigger the reminder of the traumatic event. They move into a shell and they're not the person they once were. It's a very sad part of the disorder.

> **"It's like having emotional anesthesia."**

The last part of the disorder is being a nervous person. You're easily startled, you don't concentrate well, you don't sleep well, and you're irritable

You can think of it as having a lot of adrenaline, although it doesn't necessarily mean you do, it means that your threshold for being made anxious has been lowered a lot. That's why, for a lot of people, PTSD is primarily an anxiety disorder, and they do well when they're treated with a medication that helps with anxiety.

Q. Is PTSD the same as depression?

A. *Because of the second cluster, it feels like depression. It technically is not depression. There's nothing in a PTSD diagnosis that says that you're sad, hopeless, helpless, worthless; and, if you are sad, hopeless, helpless, worthless, you have to call it both PTSD and depression.*

For PTSD, there's a clear precipitating event, and when it happened, you felt very scared, or horrified, or helpless at the time. That's number one. Number two is you have all three clusters of symptoms, and they're all happening within a period of a month. The last part of the diagnosis is that the symptoms have gone on for at least a month after you were traumatized. You don't call it PTSD if you have symptoms on the second day after the traumatic event.

> **"You don't call it PTSD if you have symptoms on the second day after the traumatic event"**

Q. What is Acute Stress Disorder?

A. *Acute Stress Disorder is used to identify the kind of people who are more likely to develop PTSD, based on their behavior, a few days after exposure. It's almost exactly the same as PTSD, except you look for a little more trance-like symptoms early on, and that's called, technically, dissociation.*

When we are very, very shocked, traumatized, nervous, we go into a trance. If you think of the first meaning of shellshock, it is the image of the soldier on the battlefield, in a daze, corpses around, with the smell of cordite in the air. In these battle scenes, people were thrown into an altered state of consciousness.

What Acute Stress Disorder means is that you have a reaction right away, you're in a daze, and if that lasts for a while, there's more of a chance of it becoming PTSD. If it continues for over a month, you no longer call it Acute Stress Disorder, you call it Post Traumatic Stress Disorder.

 Need to Know

Some service members report feeling upset or "keyed up" even after they return home. Some may continue to think about events that occurred in combat, sometimes even acting as if they are back in a combat situation. These are common "combat stress reactions" (also called acute stress reactions) that can last for days or weeks and are a normal reaction to combat experiences. When these reactions continue for over a month, the service member may be experiencing PTSD.

Below is a list of common reactions:

Behavioral Reactions	Physical Reactions	Emotional Reactions
Trouble concentrating	Trouble sleeping, overly tired	Feeling nervous, helpless, or fearful
Jumpy & easily startled	Stomach upset, trouble eating	Sad, guilty, rejected or abandoned
Being on guard, always alert	Headaches and sweating when thinking of the war	Edginess, easily upset or annoyed
Bad dreams or flashbacks	Lack of exercise, poor diet or health care	Experiencing shock, being numb, unable to feel happy
Avoiding people or places related to the trauma	Rapid heartbeat or breathing	Feeling hopeless about the future
Work or school problems	Too much drinking, smoking, or drug use	Irritable or angry
Loss of intimacy or feeling withdrawn, detached and disconnected	Other health problems becoming worse	Not trusting others, being over controlling, having lots of conflicts

For More information about PTSD, sign on to The Military Family Network at www.eMilitary.org or get in touch with Gift From Within at www.giftfromwithin.org

Make the Connection on MFN!
www.eMilitary.org/YourMFN.html

Sign on to the address shown above and Make the Connection to more resources on this topic!

26 Treatment and Considerations for PTSD

From the Field–An Interview with Dr. Frank Ochberg

Dr. Frank Ochberg, founding board member of the International Society for Traumatic Stress Studies, founder of Gift from Within (www.giftfromwithin. org), and former associate director of the National Institute of Mental Health, has decades of experience with traumatic stress. He is credited with defining the Stockholm Syndrome.

Ochberg's Counting Method

PTSD clients may come to therapy soon after a traumatic event or decades late. They may or may not have told details to others. The trauma may have been circumscribed, prolonged, or repetitive. Rapport and trust between client and therapist may develop quickly or slowly. Some clients are reluctant to reveal details; others are grateful for the first chance to vent. For these and other reasons, there are no firm guidelines for deciding when to initiate the first Counting Method session. It allows, metaphorically, elective rather than emergency surgery. It suggests that other dimensions of the therapeutic alliance come before tackling a core problem.

Once therapist and client agree that Post-Traumatic Therapy is underway, that progress is occurring, that the client feels less like a victim and more like a survivor, the Counting Method can be scheduled.

The Counting Method is a newly devised brief treatment approach to the desensitization of PTSD symptoms. Developed by Frank Ochberg, MD, the Counting Method provides a subtle and effective way to help clients to process their traumatic memories without provoking high levels of affect. By overcoming their avoidant responses, clients are able to process the entire memory and thereby reduce their fear response, as in other behavioral treatments for anxiety.

The core of the method consists of a Preparation Phase, the Counting Phase, where the therapist counts out loud from 1 to 100 as the client remembers the traumatic event, followed by a Review Phase. Preliminary research as well as clinical experience indicates significant reductions in arousal to traumatic memories can often be achieved in only a few sessions. Dr. Ochberg explains how the counting method would work with a client:

When a client is ready to try it, we set up a time. I'll have told them about the process. I count out loud, to a hundred. While I'm doing the counting, the patient is letting himself remember the traumatic event, without talking about it.

> **"Once therapist and client agree that Post-Traumatic Therapy is underway, that progress is occurring, that the client feels less like a victim and more like a survivor, the Counting Method can be scheduled."**

I'm sitting in my chair, he's sitting in his, and I can see him. By the time I'm counting to forty, fifty, there can be tears flowing, or his fists are all clenched up.

The instruction is to go through the whole event. I already pretty much know what he is going to be re-living. I tell him, "When I'm counting in the forties and fifties, make sure that you're in the worst of it. And when I'm counting in the nineties, make sure you've reached a point in the memory where you're relatively safe." I time it very carefully. If I have an hour with the person, I do this in the beginning of the hour, so they have plenty of time to recover afterward.

Right after he's done with it, the patient usually comes up as though he's come back from a trip to China. I give the person time, sometimes he talks right away, and sometimes I have to say, "Tell me what you just went through." I have my yellow pad and I start writing down almost verbatim what he says. I try to get it all down.

Then, I go over it with him, and I read it back, and as I'm reading it back, I'll say things that are acknowledging, respecting him for what he has been through. I may say, "Well, it's not easy, and you remembered it all. That's good." It puts me in memory. Too often, people tell the trauma story in a mechanical way. They've told it to police officers, they've told it to another doctor, they're just telling it. They're not really re-living it. This allows them to relive it in a safe environment—retelling it connected to their feelings.

Preliminary Discussions by Dr. Frank Ochberg for Considering the Counting Method

Some clients are willing to plunge into the Counting Method with little preparation; others want to know exactly how and why the method works. Depending upon the needs of the client, the following points can be discussed:

Counting affords the client a relatively short interval (100 sec), with a beginning, middle, and end, in which to deliberately recall an intrusive recollection.

1. Silent recall allows privacy.
2. Hearing the therapist's voice links the painful past to the relatively secure present.
3. Feelings of terror, horror and helplessness may recur during counting, but they will be time limited and, most likely, modulated by connection to the therapist.

> **"...it's high time we paid the proper attention to emotional wounds and we weren't ashamed of them..."**

4. The traumatic memory itself may be modified. That, after all, is the ultimate objective. If and when the memory emerges spontaneously at some future time, it may be attenuated by the experience of the Counting Method. The client will associate the dignity and security of therapy with the intrusive recollection

Dr. Ochberg on Service Members Getting Treatment

Dr. Frank Ochberg feels strongly about the quality of care provided to our service members, especially those experiencing PTSD. His life's work is dedicated to helping individuals recover from trauma and feels strongly that the men and women of our nation's Armed Forces deserve the best care possible:

My goal is to make sure service members know that I respect them, for their service to my country, to our country. I respect them a lot. And as a doctor, who's gone to Johns Hopkins Medical School, I am sure that emotional wounds are as significant as physical wounds.

As a country, as a species, as human beings, it's high time we paid the proper attention to emotional wounds and we weren't ashamed of them, or embarrassed by them; and when they need professional treatment, we get professional treatment.

And there are many doctors out there like me, who have a lot of respect for members of the Armed Forces, and have a lot of respect for PTSD. It's a powerful enemy, in a way. And the way to defeat PTSD is to bring it out into the light.

Post-Traumatic Therapy concludes when survivor status is achieved. Counting Method sessions are scheduled to help reach this overarching goal of therapy and should not unnecessarily prolong the process.

In sum, the Counting Method is one technique that may help service members with PTSD reduce the debilitating effects of traumatic memories. It was developed with outpatients receiving Post-Traumat-

> **"And the way to defeat PTSD is to bring it out into the light."**

ic Therapy from an experienced clinician. Service members interested in finding out more about this method should speak to their health care professional or visit the Gift From Within website at www.giftfromwithin.org.

 **FAQs**

Q. How can I find a good therapist?

A. *A lot of people say, "Trust your gut." I never say trust your gut, because I don't know if the person I'm talking to has the gut that they should trust. Some people don't have very good instincts to help themselves. Good therapists have good reputations. Good therapists usually have no problems telling you about their education, their own life story; you can interview your therapist.*

A good therapist can make you feel comfortable and confident. And it's important to distinguish between (and this is hard to do) what the therapist is saying, or how they look, that makes you feel anxious, or awkward, and what you yourself are now beginning to bring up that makes you feel anxious or awkward.

A good therapist is going to lead you back through difficult experiences, and will try to lead you back in a way that you can tolerate it, grow from it, benefit from it, and you just feel it happening.

Q. Do you know of any way that I can express how I feel about what is going on with me that is positive, hopeful and inspiring?

A. *Yes. Called the "Survivor Psalm", it was written by Frank Ochberg, MD, and Gift From Within.*

Survivor Psalm
I have been victimized.
I was in a fight that was
not a fair fight.
I did not ask for the fight.
I lost.
There is no shame in losing
such fights.
I have reached the stage of
survivor and am no longer a
slave of victim status.

I look back with sadness
rather than hate.
I look forward with hope
rather than despair.
I may never forget, but I need
not constantly remember.
I *was* a victim.
I *am* a survivor.

 Need to Know

Treatment Options for PTSD from the National Center for PTSD

Participating in treatment for PTSD can be challenging, as patients are invited to directly face memories and feelings that they may have avoided for many years. For this reason, individuals should seek to find qualified professionals to guide them in their treatment and recovery. It is unwise to try this alone or with a family member or friend and might actually be harmful to all involved. In addition, patients are much more likely to succeed in treatment if the following prerequisites are in place:

- Patient is not abusing alcohol or using any street drugs. As stated earlier, substance abuse is often an issue for patients with PTSD. Patients need to learn skills (such as through a substance abuse treatment program) to cope with strong emotions so that they can directly face the traumatic memories without numbing themselves with substances.
- Patient has adequate coping skills (not suicidal or homicidal).
- Patient has sufficient social support.
- Patient has a safe living situation (not homeless or in an abusive environment).

Although each patient's individualized treatment plan is unique, the following goals are often important aspects of therapy:

- Examine and learn how to deal with strong feelings (such as anger, shame, depression, fear, or guilt).
- Learn how to cope with memories, reminders, reactions, and feelings without becoming overwhelmed or emotionally numb. Trauma memories usually do not go away entirely as a result of therapy, but become less frequent and less intense.
- Discover ways to relax (possibly including physical exercise).
- Increase the frequency of patient's pleasant activities.

- Re-invest energy in positive relationships with family and/or friends.
- Enhance sense of personal power and control in his/her environment

Components of Treatment for PTSD

Most treatment programs involve a comprehensive approach, including several modalities:

- Psychiatric medications
- Education for client and family
- Group therapy
- Cognitive behavioral therapy
- Writing exercises
- Psychiatric medications

> **Re-invest energy in positive relationships with family and/or friends."**

  o Choice of medication(s) depends on the patient's specific symptoms and any co-morbid difficulties (e.g., depression, panic attacks).
  o In general, medications can decrease the severity of the depression, anxiety, and insomnia. However, there is no "cure" for PTSD.
  o Medications may be prescribed by the patient's primary care provider or psychiatrist.

Education for Family and Client

Education is very important, both for the patient and the family. It typically addresses the nature of PTSD (e.g., symptoms, course, triggers), communication skills, problem-solving skills, and anger management. The education may occur in a variety of modalities, such as couples/family therapy, psycho educational programs, support groups, etc.

Group Therapy. In general, groups "counter the profound sense of isolation, social withdrawal, mistrust, and loss of control. The acknowledgment by victims that they are not alone, can support others, and can safely share their traumatic experiences within a responsive social context provides an opportunity for healing." (Hadar Lubin, MD, 1996). Groups have a variety of formats, including process oriented, trauma oriented (e.g., telling one's story), present-day focused (e.g., coping skills), and/or psycho educational (e.g., anger management)

Cognitive/Behavioral Therapy. Cognitive therapy involves inviting patients to examine their thinking processes and replace irrational thoughts with more realistic thoughts. This form of therapy has received strong research support. Cognitive restructuring is a cognitive therapy approach used with PTSD. Behavioral therapy involves inviting patients to change their behaviors, which results in a shift in their

Make the Connection on MFN!
www.eMilitary.org/YourMFN.html

Sign on to the address shown above and Make the Connection to more resources on this topic!

mood/mental state. Behavioral interventions may include teaching relaxation techniques, imagery, and breathing techniques. Anger management training may involve both cognitive and behavioral skills. Exposure based therapy (e. g., flooding, desensitization) involves helping the patient to repeatedly "re-tell" the traumatic experience in great detail, such that the memory becomes less upsetting. Researchers have found this approach to be very effective in decreasing symptoms of PTSD.

27   PTSD and Military Families

**From the Field with Dr. Frank Ochberg by interview;
with Research by Caroline Peabody, former president, The
Military Family Network**

Caroline Peabody *is the daughter of a disabled Vietnam era Marine, military
spouse, former president of The Military Family Network, lifetime volunteer,
and distinguished speaker and lecturer on military life. She holds a B.S. in
sociology and M.A. in organizational management with extensive research on
communication systems as they relate to military well being and community
capacity-building. She is a published writer and columnist on matters relating
to military families, military learning models, and military relations..*

My name is Stefanie Pelkey and I am a former Captain in the U.S. Army. This testimony is on behalf of my husband, Captain Michael Jon Pelkey, who died on November 5, 2004. Although he was a brave veteran of Operation Iraqi Freedom, he did not die in battle, at least not in Iraq. He died in a battle of his heart and mind. Michael passed away in our home at Ft. Sill, Oklahoma from a self-inflicted gunshot wound to the chest. I feel that my husband is a casualty of this war and to date the Army has not done enough for post-traumatic stress.
—Stephanie Pelkey's Congressional Testimony, 2005

There are thousands of soldiers across the country coming home with minds tortured by what they've experienced in Iraq. An Army study published in *The New England Journal of Medicine* found that approximately19.1 percent of soldiers and Marines who returned from Iraq met risk criteria for a mental health concern, compared with 11.3 percent for those deployed to Afghanistan and 8.5 percent for those sent to other locations. The Army's first study of the mental health of troops who fought in Iraq found that about one in eight reported symptoms of Post Traumatic Stress Disorder. The Walter Reed Army Institute of Research survey also showed that less than half of those with problems sought help, mostly out of fear of being stigmatized or of hurting their careers.

How can couples prepare for the chance that a traumatic combat event may affect the well being of a returning loved one? What happens when dinnertime is quiet or your spouse explodes for no reason? It is a difficult situation. While most service members come home without significant concerns, those who do return home hurt need support from their loved ones and from trained professionals.

Dr. Frank Ochberg, founder of Gift from Within and co-founder of the International Society for Traumatic Stress Studies, suggests that sometimes the service member is not ready to see a professional, but recommends that the spouse can reach out and start the process:

It's usually the wife who wants help and the husband who doesn't. And the husband is either embarrassed or he feels he can't control his temper . . . and he doesn't want to get himself triggered. Because he knows that's going to make it a whole lot worse. Sometimes what I do is more like shuttle diplomacy. I try to get the guy involved, just seeing me. It usually works out pretty well, because a lot of these guys will say, "I've got an anger management problem." And then you can work on it with them.

However, less than 50 percent of affected combat veterans seek help for trauma related distress. Unfortunately, the primary key to the success of a therapeutic option is the acceptance and willingness of the victim to seek help. If the service member is not ready to reach out, the spouse should reach out for professional support. It is the best place to start to help build coping mechanisms and a toolbox to sustain the family through the time of adjustment.

> **"...sometimes the service member is not ready to see a professional, but...the spouse can reach out and start the process."**

According to Dr. Ochberg, the most difficult thing for families is watching their loved ones suffer from PTSD and the time of waiting before the service member is ready to take the first step and reach out for help. Love and communication are two of the most critical tools families must employ during this time. It is also important to realize that family members must reach out and get help if they are feeling overwhelmed by the situation with their loved one.

 **FAQs**

Q. What happens if my spouse acts out in front of the children? How do I talk to them about PTSD?

A. *It may depend on Daddy and on the way it's being manifest. If it's that Daddy is hitting the bottle and behaving in a destructive way, then it could* *be pretty firm, "That's your dad, that's my husband, he did something wrong. Now, we respect him, but we've got to figure out how we're going to help him and it's not going to be easy."*

Q. Should I talk with my husband about what to say to the kids?

A. *Yes. If you're the wife, say, "Charlie, let's face it, you've got PTSD, like a million other people. Now, are you okay with me telling the kids about this? They want to learn about it." And if Charlie says, "Hell, yes, I'd like them to know," then you have no problem. If Charlie says, "Well, I don't think they're ready for it," that's a different conversation. If Charlie says, "No, this is private, I don't want anyone knowing," that's another condition.*

If you can get him to the point where it's okay to tell the kids and to tell family that is good. My message to the family member or the friend is: you want to be the smartest person on your block about PTSD. PTSD is affecting someone you love. Get a crash course and get yourself up to speed.

Q. What should I do if my spouse is having a flashback or night terror? Sometimes it scares me a lot to hear my spouse or see him.

A. *Fear is a fundamental and helpful human emotion. If you are afraid, do what you need to do to protect yourself. Ask him, when he's not having a flashback, what he would like you to do. Some guys might say, "Oh, get out of there." Some of them might say, "Pinch me." Some might say, "If you touch me, you'll make it worse." If you think maybe he's entering a flashback or a nightmare, do what you can to wake him up, bring him back.*

 Need to Know

- Do not push or force your loved one to talk about the details of his/her upsetting memories. Try to avoid feeling jealous if your loved one shares more with other survivors of similar traumas or to his/her therapist than to you. Rather, be pleased for them that they have a confidant with whom they feel comfortable.
- Do not pressure your loved one to talk about what he/she is working on in therapy. Also, avoid trying to be his/her therapist.

- Attempt to identify (with your loved one) and anticipate some of his/her triggers (e.g., helicopters, war movies, thunderstorms, violence). Learn and anticipate some of his/her anniversary dates
- Recognize that the social and/or emotional withdrawal may be due to their own issues and have nothing to do with you or your relationship.
- Do not tolerate abuse of any kind—financial, emotional, physical, or sexual. Individuals with PTSD sometimes try to justify their behavior (e.g., angry outbursts, destroying property, lying) and "blame" their wrongdoing on having this psychiatric disorder. Patients may try to rationalize their behavior by stating that they were "not themselves" or "not in control" or "in another world." However, patients should always be held responsible for their behavior.
- Pay attention to your own needs.
- Take any comments that your loved one makes about suicide very seriously and seek professional help immediately.
- Do not tell your loved one to just "forget about the past" or just "get over it."
- Explore the available treatment options in your community, and encourage your loved one to seek professional help. However, respect that they know if/when they are ready to take this courageous step, and do not pressure them excessively.

Need to Know for Families by Michelle Sherman
Sherman, M.D. (2003). *S.A.F.E. Program: Support and Family Education: Mental Health Facts for Families.* Oklahoma City VA Medical Center. 2nd edition. w3.ouhsc.edu/safeprogram

What we'd like our family members and friends to know about living with PTSD
1. GIVE ME SPACE when I need to be alone—don't overwhelm me with questions. I'll come and talk to you when I'm ready.
2. Get away from me if I am out of control, threatening, or violent.
3. Be patient with me, especially when I'm irritable.
4. Don't personalize my behavior when I explode or get quiet.
5. Learn and rehearse a time out process.
6. Don't patronize me or tell me what to do. Treat me with respect and include me in conversations and decision-making.
7. Don't pity me.
8. Don't say, "I understand" when there are some things that you cannot understand.
9. Realize that I have unpredictable highs and lows—good and bad days.

> "Realize that I have... good and bad days."

10. Anticipate my anniversary dates—recognize that these could be tough times.
11. I'd like to share my traumatic experiences with you, but I fear overwhelming you and losing you.
12. I want to be close to you and share my feelings, but I'm afraid to . . . and sometimes I don't know how to express my emotions.
13. I also fear your judgment.
14. Know that I still love and care about you, even if I act like a jerk sometimes.
15. Don't ask me to go to crowded or noisy places because I'm uncomfortable in those settings.

Social anxiety

- Families may become isolated due to the social anxiety many veterans experience. As veterans often feel very uncomfortable in large groups and crowds, the family may be quite limited in their activities.
- The veteran may pressure the family members (directly and/or indirectly) to stay home with him, thereby narrowing caregivers' social contacts and limiting their ability to obtain support. Family members often feel guilty for pursuing independent activities.

Angry outbursts

- Anger is often a weapon in the veteran's arsenal of protection against painful feelings, memories, and thoughts. Anger can function as a barrier and further isolate the veteran, as other people often pull away from the frightening hostility and rage.
- Due to the veteran's difficulty in managing his anger, the family may live in an atmosphere of constant chaos. This lack of emotional and sometimes physical safety can be damaging to the mental health and development of all family members.

> **"Anger is often a weapon in the veteran's arsenal of protection against painful feelings, memories, and thoughts."**

- Family members may be at greater risk for being exposed to verbal abuse (e.g., yelling, name calling) and physical abuse (e.g., throwing things, aggression). Both veterans with PTSD and their spouses/partners engage in higher levels of physical violence than do comparable family members when the veteran does not have PTSD (Jordan et al., 1992). These repeated negative interactions damage the trust and cohesion within the family.

- Children may acquire maladaptive patterns for the expression of anger. A large nationwide survey revealed that the children of Vietnam veterans with PTSD are more apt to have behavioral problems than children of Vietnam veterans who do not have this disorder (Jordan et al., 1992).
- Wives are often torn between caring for the acting-out veteran and protecting the children from his angry outbursts (Glynn, 1997).
- The rage exhibited publicly may further alienate the family from their social network.

Emotional unavailability

- Patients with PTSD may be emotionally unavailable due to preoccupation with managing mental stress. The emotional distance in the relationship may also stem from the higher levels of fear of intimacy experienced by both veterans with PTSD and their partners (in comparison to couples in which the veteran does not have PTSD) (Riggs, Byrne, Weathers, & Litz, 1998).

> **"The rage exhibited publicly may further alienate the family from their social network."**

- The veteran may be reluctant or unwilling to share his feelings with his wife and children (Matsakis, 1989). Consequently, family members may feel rejected and lonely, and they may blame themselves for their loved one's emotional distance.
- The individual may struggle with experiencing and expressing positive emotions. He may be unavailable to his children and unable to meet their emotional needs (Curran, 1997)

Sleep disturbance

- Given the difficulties many veterans with PTSD have with sleep (including insomnia, frequent waking, nightmares, etc.), many couples choose to sleep in separate beds (and rooms). This physical separation can parallel the emotional distance experienced in the relationship. Physical intimacy can also be adversely affected by this sleeping arrangement.

> **"The veteran may be reluctant or unwilling to share his feelings with his wife and children."**

- In addition, the veteran's behavior during a nightmare can be very frightening for the spouse and family. In the midst of a nightmare or flashback, some patients become physically aggressive, thinking that their wife/partner is the enemy in a combat situation. Wives often report extreme terror and confusion about these experiences, as they do not understand the out-of-control behavior.

Difficulty managing family roles and responsibilities

- Given the veteran's emotional instability, the wife may assume some traditionally male roles, such as primary breadwinner, "head of the household," manager of family finances, and chief disciplinarian. The wives may feel overwhelmed by all of the demands in their lives, and wives may resent the veteran's withdrawal from familial responsibilities (Peterson, 1997).
- Given that the wife has taken over many of the veteran's tasks, she may be unable to pursue her own goals (Matsakis, 1989), which can breed further bitterness.
- Children may acquire adult responsibilities at an earlier age, resulting in their maturing quickly and sometimes taking on the role of a "parentified child" (Catherall, 1997).
- Individuals with PTSD often have difficulty keeping their jobs, thereby creating financial duress on the family.

References

Read articles on this topic by visiting **Gift From Within** – a non-profit organization founded by Dr. Frank Ochberg and located at www.giftfromwithin.org. Find articles such as "Posttraumatic Therapy", "Partners With PTSD", "Reintegration & Readjustment Program for Iraqi Veterans: for officers returning from the war in Iraq" as well as DVDs like "Living with PTSD: Lessons for Partners, Friends and Supporters". This program featuring Dr. Frank Ochberg and Dr. Angie Panos is valuable for those who care about the PTSD sufferer in their life. It explains what PTSD is, why it is important to learn about this medical disorder, what you can do to help, ways to treat it, how to deal with caregiver burden, and how PTSD affects the family and other relationships.

Ancharoff, M. R., Munroe, J. F., & Fisher, L. M. (1998). "The legacy of combat trauma: clinical implications of intergenerational transmission." In Y. Danieli (Ed.), *International handbook of multigenerational legacies of trauma, pp.* 257-275. New York: Plenum Press.

Cosgrove, L., Brady, M. E., & Peck, P. (1995). "PTSD and the family: Secondary traumatization." In D. K. Rhoades, M. R. Leaveck, & J. C. Hudson (Eds.), *The legacy of Vietnam veterans and their families: Survivors of war: catalysts for change, pp.* 38-49. Washington: Agent Orange Class Assistance Program.

Dansby, V. S., & Marinelli, R. P. (1999). "Adolescent children of Vietnam combat veteran fathers: A population at risk." *Journal of Adolescence*, 22, pp. 329-340.

Harkness, L. (1993). "Transgenerational transmission of war-related trauma." In J. P. Wilson & B. Raphael (Eds.), *International handbook of traumatic stress syndromes,* pp. 635-643. New York: Plenum Press.

Harkness, L. (1991). "The effect of combat-related PTSD on children. National Center for PTSD." *Clinical Quarterly,* 2(1).

Jordan, B. K.; Marmar, C. B.; Fairbank, J. A.; Schlenger, W. E.; Kulka, R. A.; Hough, R.L.; et al. (1992). "Problems in families of male Vietnam veterans with posttraumatic stress disorder." *Journal of Consulting and Clinical Psychology, 60,* pp. 916-926.

Make the Connection on MFN!

www.eMilitary.org/YourMFN.html

Sign on to the address shown above and Make the Connection to more resources on this topic!

Kellerman, N. (2001). "Psychopathology in children of Holocaust survivors: A review of the research literature." *Israel Journal of Psychiatry and Related Sciences,* 38, pp. 36-46.

Parsons, J., Kehle, T. J., & Owen, S. V. (1990). "Incidence of behavior problems among children of Vietnam War veterans." *School Psychology International,* 11, pp. 253-259.

Sherman, M.D. (2003). *S.A.F.E. Program: Support and Family Education: Mental Health Facts for Families.* Oklahoma City VA Medical Center. 2nd edition. w3.ouhsc.edu/safeprogram

Rosenheck, R., & Fontana, A. (1998). "Transgenerational effects of abusive violence on the children of Vietnam combat veterans." *Journal of Traumatic Stress,* 11, pp. 731-742.

SPECIAL REFERENCE: An additional resource created by Michelle Sherman for the TEENS whose parents are military—a book called *Finding My Way: A Teen's Guide to Living with a Parent who has Experienced Trauma.* It is the ONLY resource available for teens. Learn more about it at: www.seedsofhopebooks.com

28 PTSD and Youth

From the Field with Dr. Michelle Sherman

Michelle Sherman, Ph.D. is a licensed clinical psychologist. She is the Director of the Family Mental Health Program at the Oklahoma City Veterans Affairs Medical Center and is a clinical associate professor at the University of Oklahoma Health Sciences Center. She created the Support And Family Education (SAFE) Program (w3.ouhsc.edu/safeprogram), the only family education program created for the VA system. Along with her mother, a teacher, she has also written a book for teenagers titled Finding My Way: A Teen's Guide to Living with a Parent Who has Experienced Trauma *(www.seedsofhopebooks.com).*

Very large numbers of men and women serving our country in the Global War on Terror are experiencing traumatic events, ranging from seeing human remains to being shot at or ambushed (Hoge et al., 2004). Furthermore, many service members are experiencing considerable distress upon homecoming, including depression, anxiety and post-traumatic stress disorder (PTSD) (Hoge et al, 2006; Seal et al., 2007).

To date, over 1.5 million military personnel have been deployed in support of this war. Further, at any one time, over half a million children have one or more parents deployed in support of the GWOT. Hence, many families are facing the challenges associated with deployment and subsequent reintegration back into the family and community. Most families are resilient and cope successfully with the myriad of changes associated with each phase of the deployment cycle. Each family's experience is unique, and the support of family and the broader community can be invaluable throughout each stage.

However, this transition often takes time and can be challenging. For example, after returning home from the Global War on Terrorism, LT. Col. Mark Smith said: *"The journey home marks the beginning of an internal war for the Marines. Give them the space they require to slowly turn the switch. The switch from violence to gentle. The switch from tension to relaxation. The switch from suspicion to trust. The switch from anger to peace. The switch from hate to love..."*

(Quoted in *Down Range to Iraq and Back* by Bridget Cantrell & Chuck Dean)

Service members often describe themselves as "not the same person I was before the war," and they may struggle to reconnect with their family members. They may experience a wide range of emotions and changed behavior, such as preoccupation with wartime events, extreme anger, social isolation, insomnia, elevated anxiety, difficulty connecting with other people, and depression. Young people often don't understand why their parent has changed so much, wishing that this "switch" could be turned immediately.

This is a quote from a paratrooper home from Iraq ("Down Range to Iraq and Back") about his interactions with his kids. I think it's very poignant:

"Before I deployed down range I was different about my wife and kids. Now that I'm back, I can only let them get so close before I have to get away from them. I used to have fun letting my boys jump and crawl all over me. We would spend hours playing like that. Now, I can only take a couple of minutes of it before I have to get out. I usually get in my truck and drive back to the base to be with my platoon."

> **"Teenagers may experience a wide variety of emotions, such as confusion, embarrassment, anger, sadness, and fear."**

Impact of Trauma on the Family

Family therapists have long known that when one person in the family is having difficulties, everyone is affected. Everyday life in these families can be confusing and frightening. Nothing feels the same as it was before. Teenagers may experience a wide variety of emotions, such as confusion, embarrassment, anger, sadness, and fear. They may wonder why their parent is so different, asking themselves: *"What is going on with my parent? Why can't he/she just go back to how he/she was before? What do I tell my friends? How can I make my parent better?"*

 **FAQs**

Q: What are common ways that children respond to a parent who has experienced trauma?

A. *Children may respond in a variety of ways to parental trauma. They may distance themselves emotionally and act as if they do not care about the par-*

ent. They may feel abandoned and alienated from the family, sensing that their parent is "there (physically) but not there (emotionally)." They may engage in disruptive behaviors (as negative attention can be perceived as better than no attention at all). They may also experience separation anxiety, clinging even more tightly to the parent.

Q: How can our family grow though this experience?

A. *Despite the challenges involved in dealing with a parent who has experienced trauma, going through difficulties can bring families closer. Both parents and children may discover strengths, and courage in themselves and in each other that never would have surfaced otherwise. Families can grow by talking openly and supporting one another – so that they can get through future difficulties more effectively.*

Additional FAQs from the National Center for PTSD

Q. What are the typical patterns of how children respond to a parent with PTSD?

A. *Researchers have observed a direct relationship between each of the parent's PTSD symptoms and the children's responses. Researchers also have noticed patterns in the ways children respond to the parent's overall presentation of PTSD. Harkness (1991) described three typical ways these children respond:*

The over-identified child: the child experiences secondary traumatization and comes to experience many of the symptoms the parent with PTSD is having;

The rescuer: the child takes on parental roles and responsibilities to compensate for the parent's difficulties; and,

The emotionally uninvolved child: this child receives little emotional support, which results in problems at school, depression and anxiety, and relational problems later in life.

These theories certainly do not represent every possible reaction children may have to parents with combat-related PTSD, but they offer some useful ways of understanding how symptoms might develop for these children.

Q. What are the common problems children of veterans with PTSD face?

A. *Some of the problems include:*

- **Social & behavioral problems.** Research has shown that there is significantly more violence in families of Vietnam veterans with PTSD than in families of veterans without PTSD, including increased violent behavior of the child. Several studies have examined the effect that fathers' combat-related PTSD and violent behaviors have on their children. Results have generally revealed that children of veterans with PTSD are at higher risk for behavioral, academic, and interpersonal problems. Their parents tend to view them as more depressed, anxious, aggressive, hyperactive, and delinquent compared to children of non-combat Vietnam era veterans (who do not have PTSD). In addition, the children are perceived as having difficulty establishing and maintaining friendships. Chaotic family experiences can make it difficult to establish positive attachments to parents, which can make it difficult for children to create healthy relationships outside the family, too. There is also research showing that children may have particular behavioral disturbances if their parent-veteran participated in abusive violence (i.e., atrocities) during combat service.

> **"children of veterans with PTSD are at higher risk for being depressed and anxious"**

- **Emotional problems and secondary traumatization.** Results have also shown that children of veterans with PTSD are at higher risk for being depressed and anxious than non-combat Vietnam era veteran's children. Children may start to experience the parent's PTSD symptoms (e.g., start having nightmares about the parent's trauma) or have PTSD symptoms related to witnessing their parent's symptoms (e.g., having difficulty concentrating at school because they're thinking about the parent's difficulties). Some researchers describe the impact that a parent's PTSD symptoms have on a child as *secondary traumatization*. However, because of the increased likelihood that violence occurs in the home of a veteran with PTSD, it is also possible that children develop PTSD symptoms of their own. Having a seemingly unsupportive parent can compound these symptoms.

Q. Can Children get PTSD from their parents?

A. *It is possible for children to display symptoms of PTSD because they are upset by their parent's symptoms (secondary traumatization). Some researchers have also investigated the notion that trauma and the symptoms associated with it can be passed from one generation to the next. Researchers describe this phenomenon as intergenerational transmission of trauma. Much research has been conducted with victims of the Holocaust and their families, and some studies have expanded on these ideas to include families of combat veterans with PTSD.*

Ancharoff, Munroe, and Fisher described several ways to understand the mechanisms of intergenerational transmission of trauma. These mechanisms are silence, over disclosure, identification, and reenactment. When a family *silences* a child, or teaches him/her to avoid discussions of events, situations, thoughts, or emotions, the child's anxiety tends to increase. He or she may start to worry about provoking the parent's symptoms. Without understanding the reasons for their parent's symptoms, children may create their own ideas about what the parent experienced, which can be even more horrifying than what actually occurred. *Over disclosure* can be just as problematic. When children are exposed to graphic details about their parent's traumatic experiences, they can start to experience their own set of PTSD symptoms in response to the horrific images generated. Similarly, children who live with a traumatized parent may start to *identify* with the parent such that they begin to share in his or her symptoms as a way to connect with the parent. Children may also be pulled to *reenact* some aspect of the traumatic experience because the traumatized parent has difficulty separating past experiences from present.

Q. What should I do if I feel my or my partner's PTSD is affecting my children?

A. *Preventive interventions can be helpful and include explaining to family members the possible impact of intergenerational transmission of trauma, before it happens. Education about the potential impact on children can also be a useful reactive response, when a child is already being affected by his or her parent's trauma history.*

An excellent first step in helping children cope with a parent's PTSD is to explain the reasons for the traumatized parent's difficulties, without burdening the child with graphic details. It is important to help children see that the symptoms are not related to them; children need to know they are not to blame. How much a parent says should be influenced by the child's age and maturity level. Some parents may prefer to have help with what they say to their children, and seeking assistance through therapy or written materials can be helpful. The National Center for PTSD's fact sheet on "Children and Disasters" can help parents talk to children about trauma. This fact sheet also describes how children may react differently, depending on the child's age.

Need to Know

What Do These Youth Need?

How can we support these youth? Consider the following ideas. Youth of parents who have experienced trauma need:

1. **Honest acknowledgement of what's going on in the family.**
   Talk about it! Don't perpetuate secrets that only worsen the situation. Kids need answers to questions like: "What is going on? How can I support my parent? Will my parent ever go back to how he/she was before?" Providing youth with developmentally appropriate books and websites can also be useful. See resource list at the end of this chapter.

2. **To know that they're not alone!**
   Having a parent living with PTSD can be lonely and confusing. Connect the youth with other kids who are dealing with similar situations

3. **Safe people to talk to.**
   When parents are dealing with trauma reactions, they may have less time, energy, and emotion to support their children. Therefore, it can be really helpful to connect these kids with other adults and teens in their extended family, community, school, and church.

4. **To be told that they are not to blame.**
   Remind the kids that they didn't do anything wrong!

5. **To be able to have fun!**
   It's very important for kids to be able to get away from the heavy burdens from home and just have fun.

6. **Hope.**
   It's important for kids to know that things probably won't always feel this tough, and that many effective treatments are available for their parent. Recovery from PTSD is possible!

Make the Connection on MFN!
www.eMilitary.org/YourMFN.html

Sign on to the address shown above and Make the Connection to more resources on this topic!

References

Cantrell, B., & Dean, C. (2005). *Down Range To Iraq And Back.* Pine Hill Graphics.

Hoge, C.W., Castro, C.A., Messer, S.C., Mc-Gurk, D., Cotting, D.I. & Koffman, R.L. (2004). "Combat duty in Iraq and Afghanistan, mental health problems, and barriers to care." *New England Journal of Medicine, 351(1), 13-22.*

Hoge, C., Auchterlonie, J. & Milliken, C. (2006). "Military mental health problems: Use of mental health services, and attrition from military services after returning from deployment to Iraq or Afghanistan." *Journal of the American Medical Association*, 295(9), 1023-1032.

Seal, K.H., Bertenthal, D., Miner, C.R., Sen, S., & Marmar, C. (2007). "Bringing the war back home: Mental health disorders among 103,788 US veterans returning from Iraq and Afghanistan seen at the Department of Veterans Affairs facilities." *Archives of Internal Medicine,* 167, 476-482.

Sherman, M.D., & Sherman, D.M. (2005). *Finding My Way: A Teen's Guide to Living with a Parent Who Has Experienced Trauma*. Edina, MN: Beaver's Pond Press. www.seedsofhopebooks.com

29 This Mother's Life Caught in the Middle of Kids and Aging Parents

From the Field with Mary Beth Sammons

Mary Beth Sammons is the Editorial Director of Carepages.com and Reallifehappens.com. She is a feature writer whose work appears frequently in the Chicago Tribune and Family Circle. She specializes in stories relating to ordinary people doing extraordinary things from a place deep in their hearts. She lives in the suburbs of Chicago with her three children, Caitlin, Thomas, and Emily.

The best thing my mother taught me was that good mothers are supposed to feed sick kids steaming Campbell's chicken noodle soup with crackers spread with peanut butter, read them the works of Louisa May Alcott out loud, coax tea with honey down their throats, and wrap them in cozy blankets. Whenever my siblings or I had a cold, my mother did all of the above. It was only when I found myself hovering over my three children's bedsides armed with Kleenex, Vicks Vaporub and Beatrix Potter, that I fully understood the therapeutic benefits of mothering and nurturing as the center of one's being.

Now that my mother and father are approaching 80, I am summoned—a lot—30 miles away to a now all-too-familiar ER department and the uncertainty that waits at the other end of the middle-of-the-night/mid-hair-appointment or mid-treadmill phone call. I now know several ER docs by first name and an anesthesiologist who waves to me in the hospital cafeteria. I have also mastered the art of struggling to maintain a career via cell phone and laptop, just by stepping outside the electronic hospital doors, and conference calls on the freeway.

As a 49-year-old single mom of three teens and sole sibling living in the same side of the country as my parents, I find myself constantly pulled—racing from the school gym where my eighth grade daughter, Emily, is cheerleading, to the bedsides of my dad and mom. Both have spent most of the last two years tethered to machines, fighting blood clots, pneumonia, broken hips, and tricky cancers at a suburban Chicago hospital.

It's much more difficult to witness my parents bedridden than it was to take care of my son when he was hospitalized as a three-year-old. The reality that they are part of this vulnerable population of the extremely sick and old, teaches me how little I really know about caring for other human beings—especially ones who once cared for me.

Some days I feel like I'm right on the mark when I've cornered a doctor in the hall and pinned down the results of the mammogram, and the graveness of the word "shadow" on my dad's lungs. Or, the days when I can keep my dad laughing, despite the sharp and sudden pains that punctuate his every cough. I need to stay focused to the fact, that despite the traffic and juggling, it was important for me to provide door-to-door service on an especially difficult day in outpatient chemo.

> **"But many times, I feel frustrated that I'm not doing enough, both at home for my three kids, and in the hospital room."**

But many times, I feel frustrated that I'm not doing enough, both at home for my three kids, and in the hospital room. I come home drained as if I am the one who should be sick from the chemotherapy and I feel guilty when I'm dialing for pizza, versus whipping up a "quick and easy" Spring Chicken Scaloppini and spinach salad. Usually, I'm totally at a loss for what to do or say when my dad is calling out in pain for a nurse; or, my mom is lying their paralyzed in fear from what the five different specialists have told her that day, and looking to me for the answers.

"It will be so restful," I lamely told my dad the day they told him he would have to live temporarily in a rehab center (translated in his mind as "nursing home"). It frightened me to see him cry as he begged me not to send him. Taking on the role of the permanent fall guy didn't time out right for me, especially when I had finally decided I could have a life, in a mere five or ten more years when all my kids' teen years were over.

All their lives they sheltered my siblings and me. Now, I had to tell them they had to leave their home. I was trying to be unsentimental and positive when I exclaimed, "This is going to be such an opportunity for you," last Christmas Eve, when my sister flew in from California and we moved our parents to a one-bedroom teeny place at the retirement community.

For a long time, (until I got one of the physician specialists to drive home this point), they insisted they could still drive—until the ugly reality of an accident and the day my father "mistakenly" drove three hours out of the way and got

> **"I've discovered it's easier to take car keys away from a 16-year-old who broke a rule, than it is your parents."**

lost in another state en route from their house to mine. I've discovered it's easier to take car keys away from a 16-year-old who broke a rule, than it is your parents.

I've learned to shift gears—fast. And, I'm not afraid to say that I am part of a trend that I can confidently project will be certain for most of my peers during the next few decades. But it's a trend where the consequences remain uncertain. I'm part of a generation that spent the last 21 years guilt-wracked over how much I worked or didn't work, breast fed or bottle, and suffered free-floating anxiety over fast food as dinner after soccer. I live a life that is a fragile mix of seeming like I have it together, then watching it all fall apart.

The newspaper headlines shout that I am just one of the many family members who are being asked to care for both their younger and elder members over longer periods of time than in the past, and with fewer supports.

It seems the ranks of my parents and the elderly population are expected to grow by 75 percent in the next 30 years. Already one in four people—three times the proportion of a decade ago—are giving 11 hours a week of care to an aging relative. These obligations will only increase with the aging of the population. An estimated 22.4 million U.S. households—nearly one in four—now are providing care to a relative or friend aged 50 or older or have provided care during the previous 12 months.

> **"Already one in four people—three times the proportion of a decade ago—are giving 11 hours a week of care to an aging relative."**

Most of my peers who are 40 and older now are part of this new generation of caregivers, and know firsthand the meaning of the term "Sandwich Generation."

As someone who is usually outspoken on a number of issues, I find my silence around the answers and fragile understanding of how to care for my aging parents confusing and scary. Sometimes, in the hospital elevators I look at the others bearing stacks of crossword puzzle books and flowers to find hints that will explain the ways we're all in this together. I'm hoping that there are some answers on how to do this better so that it feels a little less crazy.

Mostly, I think I'm looking for my mom to show me the recipe for chicken soup for the senior at a time when she sometimes doesn't remember my name

 **FAQs**

The following Frequently Asked Questions and answers are brought to you by the National Family Caregivers Association (NFCA). NFCA is the nation's family

caregivers' organization providing support, education, and a public voice for family caregivers across the lifespan and all diagnoses. More information is available at www.thefamilycaregiver.org. NFCA is an affiliate of CarePages.com.

Q. Are there reputable websites where I can find information and resources, and perhaps even some support?

A. *There is a vast amount of information on the Internet, so finding trusted, credible sources is key. Go to http://www.familycaregiving101.org/help/web_ sites.cfm to view a list of reputable sources for you to find help.*

Q. I know I would feel better about taking care of my spouse if I just had an afternoon each week to myself. How can I find organizations that provide respite care?

A. *You're right—even an hour or two can make a big difference. Lists of some organizations that can help you find respite care in your city is available at www.thefamilycaregiver.org.*

Q. There never seem to be enough hours in the day. The second I get a handle on things, something new crops up and I feel overwhelmed all over again. What can I do to stay ahead of things?

A. *We have a list of suggestions for managing your time, because every caregiver feels like you do. Here are some suggestions on how to better manage your time to make sure you have time for yourself and the many things you need to do each day.*

- **Keep an appointment book or calendar available to schedule your day**. With an appointment book or calendar, you can make "appointments" for all kinds of things ranging from visits to the doctor to doing laundry. You may be surprised how much time you save just by sticking to a schedule.
- **Delegate**. If someone else in your household has the time and ability to take care of a chore that you usually do, why not ask them to do it for you? If no one in your household can take over a chore, there might be a friend or neighbor willing to help. Ask some

> **"You'd be surprised how many people want to help if they understand the scope of your request."**

neighbors for help with a very specific task such as shoveling snow or mowing the lawn. You'd be surprised how many people want to help if they understand the scope of your request.

- **If you can afford it, hire help to take over one or two of your tasks.** Do you do your own housework? Do you live in an area with a grocery delivery service?

These are just a few things you can do, but there are literally thousands of books that provide good advice on time management. Do a search for "household time management" at www.Amazon.com, or ask for books on the topic at your favorite bookstore.

Q. I'm concerned that my husband's health care needs are going to cost us all of our savings and we won't have anything left to live on. Is there any help available for financial planning/support in our situation?

A. *A lot of caregivers find themselves in this situation. It's important to start thinking about your finances before it's too late. The National Family Caregivers Association wrote a comprehensive article on financial planning for family caregivers. It can be found on their web site www.thefamilycaregiver.org in the Fall 2005 issue of their newsletter "Take Care." There is also a list of potential agencies and programs available at http://www.thefamilycaregiver. org/ed/resources.cfm.*

 Need to Know

Caregiver's Survival GuideTips to Fight Stress and Feel Your Best While Caring for Others

The following excerpt is from the Caregiver's Home Companion "Survival Guide for the Caregiver." The full guide is available at www.caregivershome. com. Caregiver's Home Companion is an affiliate of CarePages.com.

- Find a team of medical professionals
- Get legal matters in order
- Take care of yourself, too
- Eat right—a good appetite brings good health
- Beware of weight loss
- Take a break

- Stretch and exercise often
- Don't feel guilty
- Be on the alert for signs of depression
- Keep a journal
- Make your environment attractive
- Let friends and family help
- And remember: When you take care of yourself, everyone benefits.

Make the Connection on MFN!
www.eMilitary.org/YourMFN.html

Sign on to the address
shown above and
Make the Connection
to more resources
on this topic!

Part 6
Military Family Support

Photo: Luis Trevino

Seagulls at rest

Introduction

September 11, 2001 was a day of terrible loss for our nation. The deaths of so many Americans on our own soil was shocking and terrifying. For the military community, this day carries a separate meaning. Since the birth of our nation, military service members and their families have been at the front of our nation's struggle for freedom and democracy. In 1787, Thomas Jefferson aptly described the high price of this great gift: "The tree of liberty must be refreshed from time to time with the blood of patriots and tyrants." Our military communities are these patriots, the torchbearers of freedom, always at the ready, willing, as President John F. Kennedy stated, "to pay any price, and bear any burden."

Our nation is now leading the Global War on Terror. Today, nearly a million military family members (parents, spouses, and children) come home to dinner tables with an empty chair. They carry forward in their daily lives with the knowledge that their loved one is on the front lines, struggling each day to help neighboring countries reach peace in their lands so that we may be more secure in ours. They realize that the doorbell may ring at any moment with news that their loved one may soon be counted among the lost.

This section addresses each member of our military family from the single service member to the military parent. The chapters offer personal experiences and resources to help empower you in your service to our nation.

You will find words of support, tools for readiness, and messages of hope. Most of all, you will discover that you are not alone.

A Special Message on Family Readiness from David White, Chief, Army Well-Being Liaison Office

I don't think you will find a person who has served this great military that will disagree with the notion that our service to the military and this nation is tough and uncompromising. Expectations concerning deployments and the time a unit will be deployed, abound. But the plain and simple truth is—we are a nation at war.

Wars do not operate on personal time lines. They have their own schedule, and we don't always control that schedule. Military leadership does their best to remain within the established deployment time frame, but circumstances on the battlefield are what dictate the time line for deployed units.

Learning to understand this reality is the first step towards being mentally and emotionally prepared to face the challenges of military deployments. We ask our service members everyday to be mentally and emotionally prepared, but it's not an easy request for the families they leave behind. The Department of Defense's operational needs always take precedence. It is always a great day when we can tell a unit to prepare for their trip home, and a bad day when we tell a unit they need to stay a little while longer.

The uncertainty of this war makes our life more challenging than ever and leaves us vulnerable to a dampened spirit or resolve, but our service members and families manage to come through every time. They keep giving, and giving, and our Army families tell me that they will continue to do this until the mission is complete.

It takes a special type of person to be the family of a service member, and to understand the realities of this war. The military is definitely a part of the equation; but the enemy is also a factor that separates what we want to happen from what must happen.

Our families must be mentally tough and resilient. Over the past ten years we have made significant progress in trying to provide a level of stability that is more conducive to a predictable environment. However, it always seems that the only thing that is predictable is the lack of predictability. During times of war, this fact seems even truer. In time, the future military will be more predictable, but operational requirements will always provide a level of the unknown.

Part of the family preparedness mantra must include the reality that our service members don't come home until they get home. In the future, there will be units that come home early, and units that have their redeployment date extended. This is a fact that we must know and understand.

The fact that the military is both tough and uncompromising is what attracted me to the Army. We don't accept being second best, and anything less than winning is not a part of our cultural mindset. I, along with most other members of this Army, live for being a part of an Army that is the best. Being the best means sacrifice, commitment, and focusing all our energy on the task at hand. .

Military families make major sacrifices, and they are committed. The notion of family is deep and ingrained within the Armed Forces. Today, more than ever, the term family doesn't always mean being married, or having the traditional type of family that sits down at dinnertime for a good meal. Our service members make time to share their experiences with their family whenever and wherever they can, and sometimes that means being virtual, or taking advantage of technology to stay in touch with those we love.

There is no simple recipe for making military life easy. I have always seen this as a good thing. Who do I want fighting for my freedom: people who require security and well-being? I want the tough, the courageous, and those who have the strength of character to stick with it until the job is done. I want those who keep their promises and see things through to the end. I want those who understand our values and live by a value system that is just and moral. I see an adaptive service member and an adaptive family as a way of life unlike any other. And it is this way of life that I love the most. Our best efforts as an institution are realized in the qualities of our people.

The beginnings of family readiness in the military occurred as early as the American Revolutionary War. Esther Reed was the first true pioneer as she started what is known now as the first wives club or Family Readiness Group. Her passion for freedom and its cause was her inspiration. In tough times, she had the passion and strength to go beyond surviving to thriving.

Though our military families are strong and resourceful, to thrive they must have the wealth of wisdom collected by those who've gone before them. An old-fashioned healthy mentor is sometimes the best resource. Military families of the past have been there, and done that, and they have the T-shirts to prove it. Those who know our system make the best navigators for those who are just beginning to explore it, because they understand the reality that the military doesn't always have the resources necessary to serve every need.

While military families must be strong, self reliant, and resilient, they too must understand that there is never anything wrong with asking for help. It is also important that they know that the only "stupid questions" are those that remain unasked.

There is no way to properly thank our service members and their families. They are the true backbone of this country. Though we may become disillusioned from time to time, we must continue to excel. Personally, I only know to do my best on a daily basis, and we get this from our soldiers and their families every minute and every hour of every day of the year.

My job is to provide the most up-to-date information to our families and soldiers. Our website, www.ArmyFamiliesOnline.org, is the official website of Army families, and it is the most comprehensive resource of its kind in the Army. Come visit us and say hello, or tell me what's on your mind.

30 Military Life

From the Field with Sylvia Kidd

Sylvia Kidd is the Association of the United States Army (AUSA) Family Programs Director. During her long association with the United States Army, Mrs. Kidd has been active in community and family activities. She is one of the original developers of the Army Family Team Building Program and continues to have an active interest in that program. Mrs. Kidd has served in numerous volunteer positions at installation level as well as at Department of the Army and Department of Defense level. She has accumulated over 8,500 hours of Army Community Service time. Mrs. Kidd is married to former Sergeant Major of the Army Richard A. Kidd. The Kidd's have two children.

I started my married life as a young wife in an Army that rarely even acknowledged the family. I thought that having been the daughter of a career soldier, being a wife wouldn't be that much different. But there was a whole world of difference. I found myself at 17 years old, living 3,000 miles away from my family with a 23-year-old husband who was a "gung ho" 82nd Airborne Division paratrooper. A short time later he went to Special Forces, and then he was really gone a lot. It wasn't an easy life for a 17-year-old. It wouldn't have been easy if I had been 27 or 37 either and I was totally miserable. I was so unhappy that when he was gone, I would literally draw my drapes and sit in the house alone, crying a great deal of the time - just me and my dog.

No one called from the unit. There were no unit family briefings to tell us what our husbands were doing or really even whom we should contact if we had a problem. It was just "call the unit," never mind that you would usually reach someone who either didn't know or didn't care how to answer your questions. There really wasn't much thought at all given to wives or families, and that attitude continued in the military for quite some time.

I was totally miserable every time he left, for whatever reason the Army was sending him away. Finally, one night, after he had been gone for several weeks, I felt so desperate that I picked up the unit alert roster, and decided I would start at the top and call each number until I found the friendly voice of some other wife whose husband was away. Maybe for a short time, we could help each other through the loneliness. After all, misery loves company.

I did find that friendly voice and while I don't remember what I said or even what her name was, I still remember the feeling I had as we talked. This lady was my first experience with family support. We would talk on the phone, share concerns, and even get together once in a while. That contact made it so much easier to get through the separations.

That initial effort to reach out and not sit at home with the drapes drawn was the hardest. From then on, it really wasn't difficult at all, because even making just that much of an effort, started building my confidence and gave me a sense of control.

If I hadn't taken that first step to reach out for the support that I needed, I doubt that my husband and I would have stayed married for the following years of his military career. It probably would have quickly come to the point of "It's either the Army or me." It was a good thing I found friendship and support when I did, because I certainly needed all of the confidence I could find when he left for war. I had a 3-month-old baby to take care of then and I couldn't fall apart any more.

> **"If I hadn't taken that first step to reach out for the support that I needed, I doubt that my husband and I would have stayed married for the following years of his military career."**

I believe very strongly that once we have children in a military marriage, we owe it to them to make them feel safe and secure, even when daddy or mommy is gone. They had no choice about being born into a military family. We have to allow our children their childhood; we can't burden them with unnecessary anxiety, or fear, or responsibility. If they are a little older, we have to make sure that they don't feel as if they have to shoulder all of the household problems, because they are either "the man of the house" or "they have to take care of Daddy, while Mom is gone."

Because I think it is so important, I want to emphasize —what I have learned myself and what studies have also found to be true: that spouses who remain home and carry on the normal routine of the household do better for themselves and, provide environments where their children do well, too. Things are so different

> **"...spouses who remain home and carry on the normal routine of the household do better for themselves..."**

now, but one thing hasn't changed: It is still left to the individual to participate and take advantage of what is available to them, or not. Believe me, I know. I've stayed at home with my drapes drawn and cried, but I've found that being prepared and involved is much more comfortable.

I've also had the opportunity to see how a young spouse can use the time to grow when her soldier is away. Team Building Master Trainer's course, I encouraged the wife of a soldier that was overseas to come help out. At first, she said there wasn't anything she could do, but I felt she was really lonely and didn't know what to do with herself while he was gone and that having her join us would benefit us both.

By the end of just that first week, the difference in her was phenomenal. She became more outgoing and began to contribute her ideas on how thing could be done. She not only helped by giving out training materials, but she also benefited from the classes themselves. She volunteered that entire summer and then became president of the spouses' club. She also decided to take advantage of classes being offered by the Red Cross and became a dental hygienist. She told me much later, after we had connected again, that my encouragement to take that first step had made such a difference in her life; and, she thanked me for taking the time to convince her to do it.

I cannot encourage you strongly enough to gather information about various programs, make contacts, and become informed and involved. Prepare yourself and your children now, so that if a situation arises, you don't have to waste valuable time and energy searching for assistance. Volunteering is a great way of making those

Volunteering with The Military Family Network is a great way to support military families and get connected.

connections, learning about what is available and even getting away from the kids for a while for some adult conversation. Many volunteer programs offer childcare as a free benefit. You will feel much better knowing that you are not facing these separations alone. You have many supporters who want to help, but you have to take the first step. They can't help you if you do not reach out.

The Association of the United States Army (AUSA) will always be a valuable resource for you. We are here to inform and assist you. This is the lifestyle that we have chosen. There is much that we have no choice about; however, how we react is the one element that is totally within our control. You and your soldier often have much to endure to keep our nation strong and free. Thank you for all you have done and continue to do.

 **FAQs**

Q. Why should I make the effort?

A. *Our military lifestyle is often demanding and stressful; but in the past few years, families have faced ever-increasing turmoil. We presently have hundreds of thousands of service members deployed; many other units are either preparing to leave or are leaving almost on a daily basis. Reserve and National Guard soldiers are being sent away for back-to-back tours or being told that they may be gone for up to two years. Families are certainly being asked to cope with a lot, and many feel that they have lost total control over their lives. So how do we regain that control so that we can continue to help our children through these months of separations and support our soldiers while still staying sane ourselves?*

We are not ever going to be able to totally remove stress, and we will probably always have separations of one kind or another as part of being married to the military; but we do have the means to empower ourselves and to take control of certain elements in our lives. The Army, the Department of Defense and even those in the private sector have really worked hard to come up with programs to address the many family issues that have arisen because of the Global War on Terrorism.

> **Take a moment to re-read the chapter on building your personal support network, then sign online at www.eMilitary.org to find a friend and get connected.**

Knowing where to go and what to do before a situation arises can not only give the family a sense of security, but it also helps the deploying soldier so he or she can concentrate on the Army mission and come home safely. Even with repeated deployments, when we ask soldiers what we can do to support them, they tell us, "Take care of my family and you will be taking care of me."

Q. Where do I go?

A. *There are many programs and resources available to military families. Although some are new, many existing programs have been updated so that they will address the most current challenges that families and soldiers are facing. If* *you are living on an installation or near one, go to the local Army Community Service. They are your on-site help for learning what is available to you and are also a good place to go if you want to find a program for which to volunteer.*

For those who do not live near a military installation, there are many online sources that can be contacted. AUSA Family Programs provides information to those who call us (800-336-4570) or e-mail us: familyprograms@ ausa.org. Check out our website: www.ausa.org/family and we will give you information about how we can assist you as well as many links to other online resources. The Military Family Network, www.emilitary.org, provides a portal for national, regional, s and local programs, organizations, and resources. The Department of Defense's Military OneSource, www.militaryonesource.com, is another good online site for information for every military family. You can also call them at (800-342-9647). I've only named a few organizations, but with a little research you can find information on anything you need to know.

Q. What kind of information is available?

A. *There is information about general family readiness, healthcare, helping your child transition easily from one school to another, relocation, and obviously deployment and reunion information. There are really too many topics to list, but you will find something for whatever you need whether it is written information or someone to contact directly.*

With the repeated deployments that are occurring now, there is more of an emphasis on mental health issues for the entire family. There are tips for helping children to cope if they are having difficulties. Researchers have found that even very young children can be affected by having a parent leave for an extended period or by having a parent leave again without having been fully reintegrated into the family unit; and now we have ways to help parents address those concerns as well.

> **Read our chapters about PTSD and the military family in section five of this book.**

Recently, AUSA Family Programs, the Military Education Coalition (www.militarychild.org), advisors from the Department of Defense Education Office and others partnered with Sesame Workshop to gather information to ensure that they addressed the correct issues that young children were experiencing. After holding a number of focus groups with spouses of deployed service members and child development center caregivers, Sesame Workshop developed a tool kit that is available upon request and at no charge through several sources, such as AUSA Family Programs, Military OneSource and the Military Child Education Coalition.

 Need to Know

Attend unit activities and Family Readiness Group meetings. You all have the same concerns. Many even provide childcare on-site. Making contact with other families provides a link for information and also someone who understands, and it helps to diminish loneliness and isolation.

- Become involved in your community, whether it is on the installation or outside the gates.
- Use your time apart to grow. It will help to make time pass faster and you will feel like you are not just sitting and waiting.
- Try as much as possible to maintain your normal household routine for yourself and your children. Reassure them that they are safe and that you are there for them. If you feel like they are changing some how, talk with their teacher or find someone that can evaluate them so that possible problems can be addressed early. Have the Sesame Workshop tool kit on hand. Take care of yourself and make time for yourself. Do

Make the Connection on MFN!
www.eMilitary.org/YourMFN.html

Sign on to the address shown above and Make the Connection to more resources on this topic!

something you enjoy at least once a week to help you unwind. Keep yourself strong and healthy, both physically and emotionally.

31 Keeping your Military Relationship Healthy, Wealthy and Wise

From the Field with Gene Thomas Gomulka

Gene Thomas Gomulka is a retired Navy Chaplain with over 30 years of pastoral and military experience. Having received the Alfred Thayer Mahan Award from the Secretary of the Navy "for literary achievement and inspirational leadership", his goal is to promote better military marriages. He is the author of The Survival Guide for Marriage in the Military, and his Marriage and Military Life inventory for dating and married couples. He is a Military Family Network (www.emilitary.org/forums) forum leader for topics concerning military relationships. His website is located at www.plaintec.net.

If you want to get into great physical shape, a trainer will tell you that the three key elements to being physically fit are exercise, diet, and rest. If you want to have a healthy military relationship, there are eight different areas that will require work: communication, conflict resolution, finances, sexuality, children, family/friends, expectations, and religion.

Effective communication is one of the most important factors of a successful relationship. When partners feel secure enough in their relationship to discuss their feelings honestly, including their past disappointments, present concerns, and future hopes, their chances of a happy life together are significantly enhanced. Because military life often involves being separated for long periods of time, military couples must communicate better than most civilians, particularly if their relationship is to endure multiple deployments. How well do you and your partner communicate?

The second element in having a strong military relationship involves conflict resolution skills. The success or failure of marriages is often determined by the way couples handle differences and conflicts that inevitably arise. Relationship problems are generally compounded when partners try to resolve them by employing destructive techniques (e.g., screaming, physical abuse, threats, name-calling, silent treatment). The ability to negotiate and resolve conflicts through constructive dialogues marked by mutual respect is an art worth perfecting. Do you generally feel satisfied with the outcome of your arguments?

Military chaplains and family support counselors report that financial problems are responsible for the majority of military marriage problems and divorces. Conflicts often arise over how a couple's income is managed. In order to avoid serious problems involving finances, couples are urged to adhere to a budget that reflects their mutually agreed upon priorities. Are you and your partner familiar with your respective incomes and expenses, and committed to maintaining and following a budget?

> **"The ability to negotiate and resolve conflicts through constructive dialogues marked by mutual respect is an art worth perfecting."**

The fourth factor to consider in your relationship, love, can be expressed in a very fulfilling and meaningful way through our sexuality. While partners can experience a deep sense of intimacy from physical expressions of their love, sexuality can also be a source of frustration and anxiety. An honest sharing of one's feelings about sex can enhance a couple's appreciation of how their sexuality complements their love for one another. Are you both satisfied with the degrees and ways you demonstrate your love for one another?

Children can play an important part in helping couples grow in their love for one another. Because people come from many different family backgrounds—large families, small families, healthy families, and even broken families—couples need to discuss their family vision and their respective responsibilities in regard to having and raising children. Are you in agreement about when and how many children you would like to have?

Because military families experience frequent moves from one duty station to another, they do not have the same degree of family support that many civilian couples have whose relatives and friends often live nearby. While husbands and wives need to be best friends, they also need good friends and family members to support them throughout their married lives. Are both of your families and friends supportive of your relationship?

The seventh element to consider in developing a healthy military relationship involves expectations. Past performance is often an indicator of future behavior. Recognizing that people are not changed by a wedding ceremony, partners need to honestly discuss their likes and dislikes in the present, as well as their hopes and dreams for the future. Unrealistic expectations usually lead to unhappiness. Expectations need to be identified and discussed while dating and engaged, as well as at various times throughout the marriage. Are you keenly aware of each other's expectations?

The final element that can impact a couple's relationship is religion. Individual and shared religious views can have a major impact upon marriage and family life. Studies show that shared religious practice contributes to higher degrees of marital happiness and reduces the chances of divorce. A couple's spirituality affects not only their own lives but also the lives of their children and those around them. Are you in agreement about the role religion plays in your relationship?

 **FAQs**

Q. What suggestions can you offer to help us improve our communication?

A. *Effective communication requires both a speaker and a listener. While men have traditionally been portrayed as confrontational warriors and women as less aggressive, the opposite is often true in the realm of human relations. Women tend to be more willing and determined to address an issue, while men tend to withdraw and avoid confrontation by using the "silent treatment." Unfortunately, this can create an unhealthy cycle in which the woman only becomes pushier, causing the man to retreat all the more. While there is a time for speaking and a time for remaining silent, one woman discovered that if she refrained from being "pushy" and gave her partner some "space," her partner was more inclined to discuss an issue with her after having been given some time to reflect upon it. By understanding these differences, women can take steps to become less contentious and men can try to become less withdrawn when faced with a given problem.*

Q. What are some of the major reasons for financial problems among military couples?

A. *The most common sources of financial problems among military couples include mismanagement of credit cards, buying more car than they need to get from point A to B, borrowing advances against their future pay, and making major purchases based solely on the advice of a salesman. Also, military family counselors point out that too many couples fail to understand how "compound interest" charges from borrowing can* *significantly increase the cost of items. For example, a piece of furniture that could have been purchased for $500 in cash may end up costing a couple $2,000 as the result of borrowing money from "loan shark" companies, cash advance and payday lending establishments, or utilizing a firm's financing plan with compound interest charges often written in fine print.*

Q. What can I do to help my partner deal with anger?

A. *Unfortunately, abuse does take place within both military and civilian families. Excessive anger can be manifested in various forms of abuse (e.g., verbal, spousal, child). Anger-management classes and other therapies can help arrest such behavior and reduce the chances of divorce, hospitalization of the victim of abuse or even incarceration of the abuser. For more information about*

> **"...speak with a chaplain or family support counselor. They are trained and ready to help you."**

resolving conflicts in constructive ways, speak with a chaplain or family support counselor. They are trained and ready to help you.

Need to Know

Five Tips To Keep Your Love Alive

1. If you become upset when you are separated, calm down and give more thought to a matter before pushing the "send" button on an e-mail or mailing the letter.
2. When you find yourselves disagreeing over an issue, instead of trying to win the argument, try to find a compromise in which you are both winners.
3. After discussing a particular shortcoming together, avoid ever bringing up this "sin of the past" lest this wound never heal and your partner be discouraged from improving.
4. Be spontaneous in showing affection and realize that flowers and gifts are not only appropriate on birthdays and anniversaries.
5. Hug and kiss each other in front of your children thereby enhancing their own ability to love and be loved.

Make the Connection on MFN!
www.eMilitary.org/YourMFN.html

Sign on to the address shown above and Make the Connection to more resources on this topic!

32 Military Children Serve Too!

From the Field with Dr. Mary M. Keller

Dr. Mary M. Keller is the Founder and Executive Director of the Military Child Education Coalition™. The Military Child Education Coalition (MCEC) is a private, non-profit organization addressing the unique academic needs of military children. Working with all of the armed services, parents, and educators, MCEC develops and provides programs and timely information designed to ease transitions and deployments. For more information about MCEC and its initiatives to help military children, please visit www.militarychild.org.

"Military children serve, too!" has become a common phrase as the impact on being a military family has increased with the War on Terror and the frequent deployments to Iraq and Afghanistan. Now in its eighth year, the Military Child Education Coalition (MCEC)™ has used extensive research to focus on the inherent challenges faced by military children as they transition from one school to another, from one community to another, and, oftentimes, from one culture to another. The military-connected child will make these transitions an average of six to nine times from kindergarten through high school graduation.

Now, there is an added burden with the deployment of one or both parents to hostile areas where there is an ever-present danger. And, with the activation of National Guard and Reserve units, thousands of "suddenly military" children are directly affected.

MCEC™ has used its research into the needs of military-connected children to come up with numerous institutes and special programs to aid these children, believed to number 1.8 million. The organization has developed programs for parents to serve as their children's best advocates in the field of education; it has trained high school and middle school students to assist their peers in the transition process, and it has even created an early literacy program to assist daycare providers in teaching toddlers through pre-kindergarten students to develop literary skills and foster a love for learning.

Institutes are being held to assist families—and especially the children—of National Guard and Reserve personnel.

In an effort to assist parents of transitioning students in the daunting task of selecting a new school for their child, MCEC™ established a program called SchoolQuest™. SchoolQuest™ is a website devoted to helping families learn more about schools in a new area so they can investigate the educational options prior to a move and find a good match for their child's individual needs. The site also includes resources to help families prepare for and successfully navigate a move. The information available on SchoolQuest™ is accessible at no cost to families.

Believing that communications between sending and receiving schools is the key to successful transitions, MCEC™ has established a secure, video-conferencing network along schools throughout the world, making it possible for counselors, students, and parents from a sending school to confer with the receiving school through audio, video, data, and document imaging.

> **"...communications between sending and receiving schools is the key to successful transitions [so] MCEC™ has established a secure, video-conferencing network along schools throughout the world..."**

MCEC™ also makes full use of the Internet, with its website, www.militarychild. org, which is packed with information helpful to military children and families.

To fulfill MCEC's™ mission of establishing a strong network of partnerships, Memorandums of Agreement were signed between military installations and the school districts that serve the installations. This network is now spread around the globe, and expands each year.

The local installations/school districts develop plans of action that result in projects and programs that mirror the MCEC goal of "leveling the educational playing field" for all military-connected children.

 **FAQs**

Ask MCEC's™ Aunt Peggie!

Q. **We are scheduled to transfer to X in January and will be living in the X area. How do we locate the best school for our children?**

A. *You can begin the search for schools through our new Internet tool, SchoolQuest™. Although this is a project in process and not all installations* *are currently available, there is a wealth of knowledge there, including profiles which when completed provide virtual counselor advice and an online library of resources.*

In addition, the MCEC™ Education Resource Library presents links to state-specific information on assessment, curriculum, special education services, home schooling, graduation requirements, and more. Through the state report card link, you can find school district and school accountability information that will assist you in reviewing local school performance.

For local school information, also check with the School Liaison Officer or the Community Service/Fleet and Family Support Center. These resources are available through The Military Family Network (www.eMilitary.org) and the Department of Defense's Military Homefront website.

Q. Our son is a senior in high school, and we will be transferring to X next month. He has completed all of the testing requirements for graduation here in X. Will the new school accept his test results, or will he have to take state tests at his new school? Will he be required to pass these tests in order to graduate?

A. *In 2006, twenty-two states currently require exit exams for graduation, and by 2012, the number will rise to twenty-five. Only a limited number of states accept results from other states' exit test or an alternate test (SAT or ACT). The rules differ from state to state, and you must have current information. Visit the MCEC™ Education Resource Library and select both Graduation/Promotion Requirements and Assessment for your state of interest to learn more about state assessments and your options. It is important to make this a priority question when you speak to a school counselor at the new school prior to the move.*

> **"The rules differ from state to state, and you must have current information."**

Q. I am a senior in high school and plan to attend college next year. Paying for college is difficult enough but now I am told that the state may even charge me out-of-state tuition when my dad transfers to another state. Please help!

A. *As you are learning, qualifying for in-state tuition is just like receiving a scholarship when you are not living in your state of record. This can be very complicated, and you need current, correct information. There are two* *resources that can assist in determining whether or not you qualify for in-state tuition or a waiver from paying out-of-state tuition: the College Board State Residency (look for exceptions to requirements for residency or requirements for residency) and the Army Continuing Education System In-state Tuition site. Both have resources listed for further questions.*

It is imperative that both parents and students clearly understand residency policies including the acceptable time frame for eligibility, the impact of change of major or degree plan, or if a transfer to another state post-secondary institution is permissible. And here's some encouraging news: some states are making changes to existing laws as applied to in-state tuition eligibility for the military community. Make sure to see if yours is one of them.

> **"It is imperative that both parents and students clearly understand residency policies…"**

Q. Our third grade daughter receives special services for X in her current school. What can I do prior to our move to facilitate a smooth transition to her next school?

A. *In addition to preparing for any child to transition, you will also need to locate the special needs/office in the district prior to your move. You will need to have a copy of her current or new Individual Education Plan (IEP), current copies of any school assessment results, her current work portfolio, records from her doctors as well as records from other professionals who have worked with your child, and letters of introduction. You may also want to videotape her in the classroom as the teacher and/or aide works with her. Be sure any specialized equipment required for successful learning is visible while in use.*

A copy of this special education checklist is found in the Online Library on SchoolQuest™.

Q. I am an eighth grade student in X. I heard about your student program that helps new students at a school and would love to start a program like it in our school. How do I do this?

A. *For information on the original research-based high school Student 2 Student program, which address both academics and relationships, please visit the MCEC website under the Students/Parents tab. Note the S2S© links to a brochure on the program and the list of schools. Good news—Junior Student 2 Student©, a middle school program, is now underway as well. For information on the programs and updates, you can also visit with the MCEC™ S2S© coordinator.*

Q. Our son is currently in the GT (Gifted and Talented) program here at X. I have already called his new school, and I was told that I must complete all these forms for screening and that he will have to be tested. The testing is not scheduled until after school begins, and this means he will miss at least two months in the correct classes. What can I do?

A. *It is very difficult to understand how children who qualify for gifted and talented programs in one state may not qualify for programs in another state. The reason, simply stated, is states define their own programs (which differ considerably) and establish different criteria for qualifying for services.*

Inquire as soon as possible about things that you can do prior to leaving the old school that may facilitate qualifying at the new school. Ask if previous assessment results may be substituted for the local requirements and bring copies of those reports. If recommendations will be needed or teachers must complete special forms, ask for them now so teachers who already know your child can complete them. Make sure your child has a current portfolio, especially original work and compositions.

 Need to Know

A Quick Checklist for School Moves From the Parent/ Guardian:
- Student's birth certificate
- Student's social security number
- Student's health record (immunization, etc.)
- Legal documents as needed
- Proof of residency/military orders

School Information:
- Address, phone numbers, other contact information
- Course description book/grading scale (if available for 6th grade and above)
- Copy of the cover of each textbook or the title page
- School profile/handbook
- School webpage (URL)
- Other:

School Records:
- Copy of cumulative folder (only the copy mailed between schools is considered official)
- Current schedule
- Report cards
- Withdrawal grades or progress reports
- Test scores (standardized or special program testing, etc.)
- Other:

Special Programs Records as Appropriate:
- Individual Education Plan (IEP)/Accommodation Plan (504)/gifted program description
- English as a Second Language (ESL) or bilingual education
- At-Risk or other action plans for classroom modifications
- Other:

Make the Connection on MFN!
www.eMilitary.org/YourMFN.html

Sign on to the address
shown above and
Make the Connection
to more resources
on this topic!

Other Documents and Examples:
- Writing samples and other work examples
- Activities records (co/extracurricular)
- Community service or service learning
- Other work or performance examples
- Academic recognitions and competition participation
- Other:

33 Military Moments

From the Field with Laura Lea

*Born and raised in central Georgia, **Laura Lea** learned the value of faith and family from parents who, believe it or not, are still together after all of these years. Her experiences in a small, somewhat rural town shaped her life and her writing. A former Middle School teacher, Laura is now finding her voice as a writer. She is the author of four books, including Moments: A Guided Journal and A Time for Peace. She has written and performed many songs during the last nine years that speak of her need to understand God and his intense love for man. She is the mother of four, ages 3 to 9.*

One day while I was visiting my parents, I came across a lavender fabric-covered book. I opened the book and instantly recognized my mother's beautiful handwriting. Page after page was filled with her unique script and common shorthand symbols.

Seized by a wave of guilt, I hesitated. Wasn't I prying into my mother's personal life by reading her journal? Of course not, I convinced myself. I knew everything there was to know about her. Ignoring the hint of guilt, I read every word on every page.

Until that day, I assumed I knew my mother well, and yet the woman whose words flowed so beautifully across the pages was a stranger.

As I traveled the roads created by her words, the moments she recounted came to life. I cheered as she used a journal entry to confront a co-worker for advancing his cause at her expense. I cried as she whispered the events surrounding the death of her mother, my grandmother, and their final visit together. I smiled as she joyfully recounted the birth of her first grandchildren, twins born near Christmas.

Although my mother's journal contained a wide variety of topics, for the most part she used its pages to sort through troubling situations. In the absence of confrontation, she was free to bear her soul, to write exactly what she felt. With the weight of her words amassed between the covers of her journal, the load she carried was considerably lighter.

It was enlightening to see facets of my mother's personality that I had never before seen. No longer was she the poster child for Southern charm, she was real. For the first time we were more similar than different. I felt camaraderie with her that had nothing to do with DNA . . . I wanted to be her friend.

So you may ask, "What does this have to do with me?"

Here is what this has to do with you.

The fact that you are reading this implies that you have a connection to the United States Military. Regardless of your affiliation, the likelihood that you will be personally affected by global events is great. Not only are you subject to all that civilian life entails, but you must also be prepared for the realities unique to military service. Every situation you face must be filtered through the military sieve, which frequently results in additional pressure for you and your family.

> "Not only are you subject to all that civilian life entails, but you must also be prepared for the realities unique to military service."

With regard to the family, one of the most difficult aspects of military service is deployment. Separation for long periods of time leaves no one unscathed. For the soldier who is away from home, there is an unspoken loneliness, and for the spouse and family left behind a void is created that cannot be filled.

When troops are deployed the stresses of daily life become magnified burdening everyone involved with problems they may or may not be equipped to handle. When military service separates you from your loved ones, the pages of your journal can become a surrogate companion.

Sharing the Load

Last November I traveled to Fort Stewart for a book signing. While I was there, I met a career soldier who had just returned from a rather lengthy stay in the Middle East. We talked about his experiences there and how he coped with being away from his wife and kids. His coping mechanism, not surprisingly, was his journal. Each evening, he would tell his wife everything that happened during his day. He likened these writing sessions to the conversations he and his wife shared each evening after they put their kids to bed. For this soldier, keeping a journal enabled him to feel connected to his family.

Can you imagine what a relief it was for this Sergeant Major to sit down each night and pour his thoughts onto the pages of his spiral bound notebook? Knowing he would face no repercussions or admonitions, he was free to expose his most intimate thoughts and

> "…keeping a journal enabled him to feel connected to his family."

feelings. Like removing his protective outerwear, he shed the burdens his position heaped upon him. Absent the weight of his concerns, rest came easy. By the time the following morning arrived, he was physically, as well as mentally, ready to tackle another day.

Do you find this soldier's story inspiring? I do. I love the fact that he longed for home at the end of each day. I love the notion that he could command troops in a war zone by day and yet still be tender and sentimental when he sat down to spend time with his wife each night. I wonder if his wife has any idea just how essential she was to his success in the field.

Regardless of whether you are shipped off to the Middle East or hold up in post housing with a couple of kids, you are understaffed in the support department. Weighty issues normally handled as a team suddenly fall on a single pair of shoulders. You know you would feel better if you could vent your frustrations; and yet the only person you truly trust is half a world away.

This is when it pays to think like the Sergeant Major. Let your fingers do the talking. Grab a pen and paper and start writing. Whether you write in complete sentences or emotionally charged fragments, use this time to say *everything* you need to say and don't forget there are advantages to having a one-sided conversation. First and foremost, you need not fear criticism or unsolicited advice. Another positive to keep in mind is that it is impossible to hurt a journal's feelings. Best of all, the pages of your journal will listen as long as you need to talk. When you have nothing more to say, put your pen down, close the notebook, and walk away.

Something magical happens when your thoughts find their way onto the pages of a journal. They cease to be emotionally charged notions that consume your every thought and become legitimate expressions of who you are at a given moment.

Revisiting the Response

One of the more beneficial aspects of keeping a journal is the ability to revisit issues from your past. Viewing life retrospectively is healthy. In the absence of heightened emotion, it becomes possible to examine past events with greater objectivity. In many ways revisiting your past is like uttering a huge "Ahh." It is an opportunity to acknowledge your inadequacies confident in the knowledge that they were powerless to defeat you.

> "Viewing life retrospectively is healthy. In the absence of heightened emotion, it becomes possible to examine past events with greater objectivity."

We All Need Each Other

I have often wondered if the Sergeant Major shared his journal with his wife after he returned from the Middle East. Did he trust her with his most intimate thoughts? Could she handle his insecurities and weaknesses? Was she aware that she was essential to his success while he was away? I will never know the answers to these questions. And yet there is a part of me that would treasure the opportunity to read for myself the pages of his journal.

As a wife, I would covet a deeper understanding of the sacrifices both emotional and physical made by my husband while serving his country. As a civilian, I need to be reminded that soldiers and their families give much and receive little in return. Short of enlisting for active duty, there is no way to fully appreciate all that military families come up against.

Now, let me make this clear. I am not advocating that you place your journal on the coffee table for others to peruse. On the contrary, most journals contain thoughts far too personal for that. Instead, I would like to encourage you to share your experiences with others only to the degree that you feel comfortable doing so.

This need not be difficult. It is simply a matter of engagement. Open your eyes and ears to the world around you. Life has taught you lessons that others need to learn. Whether it is the lady struggling with young children in the Post Exchange or the soldier who returns from war knowing he will never walk again, there is someone out there who is desperate for the encouragement only your story can provide. You have the power to positively affect the people with whom you come in contact.

> **"Open your eyes and ears to the world around you. Life has taught you lessons that others need to learn."**

Lesson Learned

I suppose this is a good time to come clean with respect to my mother's journal. Eventually I confessed my indiscretion. Telling my mother that I read her journal was difficult. I fully expected to receive a tongue lashing for my offence, but surprisingly, I did not. Instead my mother looked me in the eye and said, "Didn't I teach you better than that?"

"Yes, Ma'am," I responded knowing what she expected.

"You should have checked with me before you read my journal." She was right. I should have. It was her final comment, however, that seemed to stick with me. Through a sheepish grin she made her point.

"I hope you learned something," she said.

Fortunately for me, I had.

 **FAQs**

Q. Why should I keep a journal?

A. *A journal provides a tangible record of information that can be retrieved at a later date. Journals are used by all sorts of people for all sorts of reasons. For example, your doctor may request that you track your body's response to a new medication or therapy. You may wish to keep a record of all routine maintenance performed on your vehicle or home should you ever decide to resell. Or, more often than not, you may simply need a silent friend whose only job is to listen.*

Q. What do I need to get started?

A. *More than likely you have everything you need to get started. If you use a computer frequently you may wish to type your journal entries into a folder or file using a word processing program. There are also online journal options for those of you who want to use a template. The only concern regarding this method is your ability to safeguard your journal entries. It is imperative that you back up your files regularly.*

Should you decide to keep your journal the old-fashioned way, all you will need is a pen and paper. Journals of all styles and sizes can be purchased from a great number of retailers. If you consider yourself to be a minimalist a spiral bound notebook works great and can be purchased almost anywhere.

Make the Connection on MFN!
www.eMilitary.org/YourMFN.html

Sign on to the address
shown above and
Make the Connection
to more resources
on this topic!

Q. How often should I write in my journal?

A. *Once you have established your reason for keeping the journal, the frequency with which you record new information will establish itself. For example, if you are keeping a journal to track your progress while training for a marathon, you will want to record the number of miles you completed each time you set out to run. If your journal is designed to produce an historical account of your babies first year of life, you will want to identify the milestones* *you deem important in advance and then write about each milestone as it occurs. If your journal is a secret friend with whom you share your most trusted thoughts, you will want to write when you have something to share.*

Q. What should I expect to gain from keeping a journal?

A. *Just for the record, the benefits of journaling vary greatly and are directly related to the reasons for keeping the journal. Listed below you will find just of few of the most common benefits associated with keeping a journal.*

- A permanent record of your experiences and/or thoughts.
- With the passage of time, emotions level out making it possible to critique your reactions to past experiences.
- You discover ways to handle situations should you encounter them in the future.
- Your ability to organize your thoughts is improved.
- You recognize the emotional benefits associated with voicing your frustrations as opposed to holding them inside.
- You have a non-threatening way of sharing your experiences with others.

 Need to Know

Should you experience difficulty getting started with your journal writing, it will help if you follow a few guidelines.

- Always begin your journal entry with the month, date, and year. Be sure to list the day of the week, as well.
- Avoid writing when you are tired.
- Find a comfortable place to do your journal writing.
- Create your own personal writing prompts that can be used each time you sit down to write. This will get your thoughts flowing. Possible journal prompts:
    o Name three people you spoke with today.
    o Describe the weather.
    o Name two things you accomplished today.
    o Describe the happiest moment of your day.
    o Name one thing you admire about a member of your family.
    o Name one thing you hope to accomplish tomorrow.

Online Journal Resources

There are literally thousands of journal-related websites. To find these, you simply choose a search engine and type in related words. I chose to use the terms "journal", "journal writing", "keeping a journal", and "keeping a diary". You could spend all day perusing individual sites, but be aware that few are designed to help you keep a journal for your own sake.

If you prefer to keep your journal using an online journaling site, you must be aware that most of these services require a fee. In addition, there are also issues with privacy you must address prior to signing on.

I did find one site that was especially helpful in identifying techniques commonly used by people to keep a journal: "Keeping a Journal: 10 Techniques," on www.about.com. Look for it at: www.lds.about.com/od/1/a/les_ journal.htm.

Make the Connection on MFN!

www.eMilitary.org/YourMFN.html

Sign on to the address shown above and Make the Connection to more resources on this topic!

34 I Have a Child in the Military, Now What?

From the Field with Vicky Cody

Vicki Cody is the wife of General Richard Cody, Vice Chief of Staff, U.S. Army, and the mother of two Apache helicopter pilots with the 101st Airborne Division (Air Assault). Mrs. Cody turns her own 30-year experience as the wife and mother of Soldiers into advice and consolation for other parents with deploying children. She is the author of Your Soldier, Your Army: A Parents' Guide *published by The Association of the United States Army Institute of Land Warfare (ILW).*

When I think about how things have changed since September 11, 2001, I can't help but think in terms of the military and their families. Most noticeable is the frequency and length of deployments. Because of the large numbers of active duty, National Guard, and Reserve Soldiers deploying, this war more than others, is impacting hundreds of thousands of families and their communities all across America.

These families need information and want to feel connected. That is exactly what the Military Family Network is doing, connecting families of all services with each other, providing much needed information, resources, and a forum for discussion.

I'm thankful to be able to contribute to this book that I believe will help so many family members.

In this chapter, I will share some of my experiences and tell you what helps my husband and I get through deployments. I don't have all the answers, by any means, but I do have thirty years of experience as an Army wife and five years as an Army mom.

I always tell people my defining moment came in February 2002 when our oldest son deployed to Afghanistan for Operation Anaconda (he was twenty-four years old and fresh out of flight school). He was in the same Division his Dad was commanding. Suddenly I found myself in a dual role . . . I was not only an Army spouse, trying to support other spouses, but I was also the mother of a Soldier who was deploying with their spouses. It was the scariest time of my life, sending a son off that first time. That deployment lasted six months and as scary as it was, it was manageable. What a relief when our son came home safely!

He was home (at his duty station) for six months and then we were sending him off again for the beginning of combat operations in Iraq. Once again, my husband and I thought we were in the scariest time of our lives. That deployment would end up being twelve months. If that wasn't stressful enough for us, our younger son finished flight school, and six months into the deployment he joined his brother's brigade over in Iraq. So we had both sons deployed and a new daughter-in-law. Maybe that was the scariest time of my life! But it was also a time in my life when I realized I could either give into my worries and fears and drive myself and everyone around me crazy, or I could do something positive and try to help other parents who were going through what we were going through.

> "I could either give into my worries and fears...or I could do something positive and try to help other parents . . ."

You see it didn't matter who my husband was, what his position at the Pentagon was, because at the end of the day we were just parents like everyone else who were scared and worried about our kids. I knew that I had something that I could offer to other parents of Soldiers. If I could reach out to others, I could also get myself through a very difficult time. I wrote the book Your Soldier, Your Army: A Parents' Guide. It was very therapeutic for me.

Would you believe both our sons are deployed again? They are back in Iraq for their second combat tours, serving in the same battalion. They are flying helicopters in the very battalion that their Dad commanded in Operation Desert Storm, and once again, I'm doing what I can to get through the twelve months. The following is excerpted from *Your Soldier, Your Army: A Parents' Guide:*

I feel like we were just welcoming them home. Yet, here we are again just 18 months later, same Army Post, same gymnasium full of Soldiers and families, same lump in my throat, same knot in my stomach.

This time as I stood in the crowded gym, I found myself watching the faces of the Soldiers' parents. In their faces I saw fear, tears, worries and a lot of love and pride . . . exactly what I was feeling. I love it that many of them drove all night or hopped on a plane just to say good-bye to their Soldier. I love it that they cry like I do. I love it that they hug their Soldier no matter how old he/she is. I love it that they support their Soldier and his/her buddies. I was struck by the fact that no other profession brings parents and their grown kids together and encourages them to show their love for each other so openly. It was comforting for me to be with these families. It was comforting to meet our sons' buddies and commanders.

In many ways, it was just as hard saying good-bye this time as it was that first deployment in February 2002. In other ways, it was easier because I knew what to expect. I've learned that the hardest part is the actual good-bye and letting go. I've learned that I will get back into my normal routine and get through the next 12 months. But I will never stop worrying and missing my sons, no matter how old they are and how often they deploy.

> **"I was struck by the fact that no other profession brings parents and their grown kids together and encourages them to show their love for each other so openly."**

This is a stressful time to have a Soldier in your family. It takes a lot of courage to be a parent of a Soldier and especially to send one off to combat. People ask my husband and me all the time how we can support this war, how we can let our sons go off to combat. Each of us has our own answer––my husband as a military leader and a father, and me as a mother––but our answers are basically the same: we respect what our sons have decided to do with their lives. We want them to do something important and good, something with meaning that will have an impact on this world. They chose it willingly, knowing full well what it means to serve their nation. All of the young men and women, who have enlisted in the military since 11 September 2001, know what they are getting into. If this is what your son or daughter wants to do, how could you not support them? For me, the pride outweighs the fear. I look at the man my husband is and I am so thankful our sons are following in his footsteps.

The best advice I can give you is to embrace your service member's way of life and be as much a part of it as you can. Visit where your service member is stationed. Go to ceremonies and promotions whenever possible. It will give you insight and a glimpse into this very unique way of life. You will learn so much about the military and their career. It

> **"You will learn so much about the military and their career. It will help you be able to support your service member when they need you."**

will help you be able to support your service member when they need you. Being involved will help all of you get through the scary and tough times, and it will make the good times even better. It will bring you closer as a family and give you special moments to remember. I always say, "If life in the military teaches you nothing else, it teaches you to make the most of your time as a family and to appreciate each other and make those memories today, rather than wait for tomorrow."

You should feel so proud. Regardless of where you come from, your race, religion or political views, you need to realize how important your service member is to our military and to our country. You may have mixed feelings about all of this, but above all, you should be bursting with pride. You should be 'lump in your throat, goose bumps on your arms, and tears in your eyes' proud! There is no greater profession, nothing more noble than wearing the uniform of our U.S. Military. Your service member raised their right hand and swore to protect and defend this great country and its Constitution. Wow, that's pretty powerful!

 **FAQs**

Q. Can I be a part of our service member's Family Readiness Group?

A. *Absolutely. Before your service member deploys, make sure they sign you up so that you are linked up with the FRG. Even if you don't live near an FRG location, you can receive newsletters, e-mails, and any other information regarding the unit. Make sure the unit has your current information, telephone number, address, etc. If that changes, notify the unit and/or rear detachment commander immediately.*

Q. What if my service member gets injured while deployed overseas, how will I find out?

A. *If the service member is injured, the primary next of kin will be notified by telephone. If there is a death, the next of kin will be notified in person by a notification officer from that branch of service, i.e., the Department of the Army, Navy, etc.*

Q. What if there is an emergency back home, like a death in the family? How can I get word to my service member?

A. *Contact the American Red Cross and they will relay the message for you.*

Q. If my service member is single do they need a Power of Attorney?

A. *I think it is a good idea for someone in the family to have a Power of Attorney, in case the service member needs something done while deployed, like a car registration renewal or if they own or rent a house. I always have a POA for our single son . . . I don't always need it, but I have used it a few times during various deployments. A lot of things can be taken care of online by the service member, but sometimes they are deployed to a remote site with no Internet service or some issues just can't be taken care of from overseas. I think we have it for peace of mind. More importantly, though, is to make sure your service member has all their affairs in order before they deploy. A Power of Attorney is just one of them.*

 Need to Know

Vicky's Tips and Advice

1. Know the name and phone number of your service member's unit commander, and anyone who is directly in charge of your service member. If the unit deploys, know the name and number of the Rear Detachment Commander; this is your link to the FRG and to the unit.

2. If you don't live near the unit FRG, then try to find a support group in your community, even if it is for a different service. It doesn't matter if it's active duty, National Guard, Reserve or another service. Sometimes it's just nice to be with other family members who are going through what you are going through. If you can't find one to join, then start one. I guarantee there are other

> **"If you can't find [a support group] to join, then start one."**

people in your community who have service members in their family, and they might be looking for a group, too.

3. Send lots of letters, packages, and e-mails. Staying connected to your service member is so important and it's good for morale . . . for the both of you.

4. Have faith and trust in the leadership that is in charge of your service member. I worry about a lot of things, but that is one thing, I don't waste my

time worrying about. The Officers and NCO's in charge of your service member are the best-trained professionals in the military, and are absolutely dedicated to the training, the safety, and the well-being of the men and women under them.

5. Be positive and upbeat, especially when talking on the phone. Your service member may only get a few minutes to call so you don't want to worry or upset them unnecessarily.

6. Be prepared for some reunion "blues." It can be a very emotional time for all of you. Watch for signs of depression and/or PTSD. Every unit has professional counselors, Chaplains, and services to handle this aspect of military life. Encourage your service member to seek help if it is needed.

7. If you can be there when your service member deploys, that's wonderful. But if not, try to be there when they return from the deployment. I know it is not always possible, but if you can be there, you will never regret it. Seeing your service member get off the plane or ship is unforgettable.

Make the Connection on MFN!
www.eMilitary.org/YourMFN.html

Sign on to the address
shown above and
Make the Connection
to more resources
on this topic!

35 A Single Soldier's Story

From the Field with Edward W. Luzadder, Jr.

Edward W. Luzadder, Jr. is a retired United States Army National Guard Captain and an employee of the Department of Veterans Affairs.

As a single soldier serving in the United States Army (and Army National Guard), I have participated in a variety of deployments during my more than twenty years of military service. I consider deployments an "opportunity" and a unique chance to learn and grow from experiences encountered while away from home.

While in the military, I deployed numerous times during the mid-1980s to the East German and Czecho-slovakian border regions of the former West Germany with the 1st Squadron, 2nd Armored Cavalry Regiment (ACR). Later, I was deployed to Saudi Arabia, Iraq, and Kuwait during Operation Desert Storm with the 1st Battalion,

> "I consider deployments an 'opportunity' and a unique chance to learn and grow from experiences encountered while away from home."

201st Field Artillery. Also, I was deployed to Bosnia in 1997 to conduct peace-keeping operations with 3rd Squadron, 2nd ACR. And, finally, I was deployed to Iraq again in 2004 with the 1st Battalion, 201st Field Artillery.

During these deployments, I noticed good and bad things that happen when single soldiers are deployed to faraway places. Here are a few key points:

Pros to Being a Single Soldier

Saving Money

As a single soldier deployed to a combat zone, I managed to save quite a bit of money. I saved because the military paid for my lodging and my meals. The only expenses I had were related to items "back home": rent on my apartment (including utilities), car payments, and credit cards bills.

Although I was saving money, I didn't deprive myself of fun things while I was deployed. I purchased a television (we were allowed one television per tent), a DVD player, and other semi-luxury items to make my stay in Iraq more comfortable. My married friends told me that these luxuries were a major advantage of being a single soldier.

Becoming Debt Free

Going hand in hand with *saving money*, I managed to become debt free while I was deployed. After approximately five months of saving, I realized that I could pay down my debts, one debt at a time. I started with my largest debt and began eliminating debt after debt as the months passed. I felt a sense of pride in myself for managing to become debt free by the time I returned home. When I returned home, I still managed to accumulate money in both my checking and savings accounts.

Cons to Being a Single Soldier

Mail Call

I always hated mail call when I was deployed because many times I would go out for mail call and not receive anything. It wasn't because my parents didn't love me or my friends didn't care, but because they couldn't send me something every day. My recent deployment was a little better because colleagues and friends sent well wishes, plus organizations (such as Operation Troop Appreciation) sent letters and gifts to the troops, which made all of us feel great.

> "Wishes from fellow Americans (some I never knew or met) made life easier during mail call."

Why did it make us feel so good? Well, it was the general good feeling I received knowing that there are other people who care about us and appreciate what we are doing for our country. Wishes from fellow Americans (some I never knew or met) made life easier during mail call.

Protecting Things At Home

One of the major problems faced by the single soldier is: who is going to watch your property while you are away? With my most recent deployment, I had one day to pack and ready my apartment for a sixteen-month to two-year deployment. Also, I had to find somebody who could watch my apartment, and from time-to-time check inside the apartment so I could maintain peace of mind regarding my personal property. I also had to worry about my car.

If you live in the barracks this makes it easier, but if you live on your own or away from post, this is a genuine concern. As is often the case, most of our friends are deployed with us, so there's no one available to watch our homes.

I was fortunate to have someone from my civilian workplace that lived around the corner keep an eye on my apartment (which was greatly appreciated) because my father lived three hours away and was not able to travel regularly to my home to check on my property. During my sixteen months away,

> **"As is often the case, most of our friends are deployed with us, so there's no one available to watch our homes."**

I was fortunate that my apartment and vehicle remained safely undisturbed.

Whether you are leaving for Operation Iraqi Freedom, Operation Enduring Freedom, or just deploying locally to the field for an extended period of time, it is my sincerest hope that these bits of information help you as you prepare for deployment, deploy, and then return home from your specific military mission. Remember the motto of the Second Armored Calvary Regiment, *"Toujours Prêt"* (Always Ready). You know that being ready to deploy at a moments notice will ease the transition when deployment time comes.

 **FAQs**

Q. What should I do prior to deployment?

A. *Before you deploy, you need to identify the person/persons who will take care of your house or apartment and your automobile. Next, prepare your finances so that you can leave at a moment's notice and remain financially stable for thirty to sixty days. If you take time to accomplish these steps prior to your deployment notification, when that notification arrives, you will be ahead of the game.*

Q. What personal items would be nice to have while deployed?

A. *When I deployed, I always managed to have a short wave radio so that I could keep up with the news and current events while away from other sources of media like the Internet or television (be sure to pack some extra batteries too). Other nice items to have that will fit into your cargo pockets are: a deck of cards, a small camera (digital or traditional film), a pad of paper with a pen* *or pencil, and a small flashlight. These items will allow you to have fun with your friends, record moments, and write home from time to time. Also, try to pack a small bag that can be easily carried. In this bag, I took a poncho liner, at least one change of underclothes (including socks), and my shaving kit on the offhand chance I stayed somewhere overnight without access to my basic equipment.*

Q. What items cannot be mailed to me by my family and friends?

A. *Some examples of commonly used items restricted or considered hazardous under USPS regulations include:*
- **Perfumes**
- **Nail polish**
- **Glues**
- **Flea collars or flea sprays**
- **Fireworks**
- **Aerosols**
- **Cleaning supplies**
- **Bleach**
- **Mercury thermometers**
- **Pool chemicals**
- **Dry ice**
- **Paints**
- **Airbags**
- **Matches**
- **Fuels or gasoline**
- **Items previously containing fuel**

Other items, such as alcoholic beverages (beer, wine, liquor), are not considered hazardous but are prohibited, and boxes displaying such markings are also prohibited.

 Need to Know

By remembering some of the items/issues below, you may make your pre-deployment and deployment much easier. The list below is *not* an all-inclusive list, but provides some basic points to consider and remember before you deploy.
- **Standard Operation Procedures** (SOPs) are designed to give you a starting point for packing for deployments or training events. Following the

SOP may mean that you have too much equipment, but not following it may mean that you may not have enough to accomplish your mission. If you are unfamiliar with your unit's SOP, obtain a copy and read/review the information each year. If you change units, remember to request a copy of their SOP when you arrive.

- **"Pack Light, Freeze at Night."** During Operation Desert Storm some members of my unit sent their sleeping bags home, because they were going to the desert, and they assumed that the bulky item would not be necessary. Consequently, they were very cold almost every night just because they didn't want to carry it with them. If you don't pack the cold weather equipment, be-

Make the Connection on MFN!
www.eMilitary.org/YourMFN.html

Sign on to the address shown above and Make the Connection to more resources on this topic!

  cause you're deploying to the desert, you should reconsider now. Even in the desert, temperatures can go as low as 20 to 30 degrees at night during the winter months. In some instances, you can even feel cold when the temperature reads 70 to 80 degrees, because that's a 40 to 50 degree temperature change (dropping from 120 degrees during the day to 70 or 80 degrees at night).
- **Plan for deployments before you know you are going to deploy.** You should have copies of lease agreements, birth certificates, previous discharges (if you had a break in service), marriage certificates, power of attorneys, divorce decrees, and any other legal documentation that may be required by the military to complete or update your personnel/medical records at the time of your deployment. Always keep all of this information in a safe place.
- **A book about leadership** may not sound like the type of book that would help someone preparing to deploy or who has deployed, but if you are a leader or wish to be a leader, this is a must read. I made room in my bag for this book while I was deployed, and although it is written for enlisted leaders, it has a wealth of information for officers to evaluate your leadership style. This book also contains some information for single personnel in the military. The Three Meter Zone: Common Sense Leadership for NCOs, by J. D. Pendry, Command Sergeant Major, United States Army Retired, Presidio Press, 2001.
- **Look for online resources concerning pre- and post-deployment,** deployment, and family resources. There are many other resources online, but use caution when searching the Internet and beware of organizations that require you to be a paying member or ask for other identifying information before providing you with information.

36 Deployment: A National Guard Couple's Success with Separation

From the Field with Judy and John Sexton

Judy and John Sexton are a National Guard couple from Pennsylvania. They share their story, each from their own perspective, and offer guidance and advice to other military couples facing deployment. They have two children.

Judy's Story

"I'm deployed," my fiancé said as he walked through the door after a day at drill. The announcement every loved one dreads hearing.

Words cannot describe the way I felt. I didn't have any of the details yet, but just knowing that he was leaving was traumatic. What do we do now? The question many ask when their loved one is deployed.

There was a lot to get done. We had about three weeks to spend as much time together as we could and get everything in order. We have one son who did not go to day care, but he was in preschool. We were not married at the time, which made it more difficult. Only immediate family can take care of personal issues. The first item on our "to do" list was to get married. We applied for a marriage license and contacted the Justice of the Peace. In three days we were married.

Until this point, we didn't need day care because we worked different schedules and so could care for our son on our own. Now that my husband would be gone, I would need to find a quality day care. Lucky I found one that I came to love. It was clean, and the staff was loving and supportive. The other items, such as his living will, Power of Attorney (POA), and finances, were easy to finalize.

John did the majority of the paperwork during his pre-deployment period. He then trained for six months in Texas before heading to Iraq. At this point, we didn't know when we would see him again. Fortunately, he got to come home three times throughout his deployment. Our son and I flew to Texas and visited him. He was granted a forty-eight-hour pass, which allowed him off base.

I will say that before you decide to visit your loved one, make sure the Commander is not pulling the passes after you get your plans finalized. There

259

are many reasons why a pass may be issued and then pulled. We faced this issue. I had purchased two plane tickets and reserved a hotel room, and then John's Commander decided to pull the pass. If you can, purchase travel arrangements that are refundable or permit changes in your itinerary for a nominal fee.

As I write this, it is after Thanksgiving, and he is on his way back to Iraq. Again, it's a big waiting period for all of us. We communicated a lot during his leave, and this helped me get through a lot of rough times. Many soldiers do not have that privilege. If you do not have a lot of communication with your soldier, try to remember, "no news is good news."

The good news is that when the deployment is over, your main job is to welcome your Hero home. Be sure your loved one doesn't mind a welcome home party. Remember, your Hero has to adjust to "real" life. It may take time for them to adjust to large crowds and loud unidentified noises.

> **"If you do not have a lot of communication with your soldier, try to remember, 'no news is good news.'"**

John's Story

As a member of the Armed Forces, I can say for pretty much everyone that deployment is never easy. Whether you're single or married, your deployment will affect someone in some way. I have to say, in my experience being deployed, the military did a good job in getting us ready.

I suggest that you be up front with your family members, whether it's your girlfriend, wife, or parents. It's much harder on them then on the individual going on the deployment. Having children is even harder. I would suggest being honest with your children, too. Let them know that you will be going to a dangerous place, but that you'll stay in touch with them.

At the time of my deployment, my son was only four years old. How do you explain to a four-year-old that daddy is leaving for a year or more? It was bad enough trying to tell him daddy was leaving, let alone trying to tell him how long a year is.

Support of loved ones, spouses, and family members, is very important. Without question, the strength of your loved one is the saving factor in being deployed. The stronger your loved one is, the easier your deployment will be, not only during deployment, but after the deployment as well.

> **"...the military did a good job in getting us ready."**

Everyone should give themselves time to adjust to coming home. Time cannot pick up where you left off. Everyone goes through changes, and even more so during a deployment. Time and understanding will hopefully make the adjustment easier for everyone.

 **FAQs**

Advice from Judy

Q. How do you raise a four-year old and work full time?

A. *Well, for the first three or four months, I would get up at 0430 to get the day going. This is the time that I would prepare for the day—do laundry and dishes, pay bills, or just go through the mail. I tried to keep our son's life as "normal" as possible.*

What is "normal"? Continue with your child's sports and activities—I continued to take him to soccer and T-ball. We started going to the library. We'd get books that we could read throughout the week. Our son continued with preschool and started day care. Zachary and I would talk about daddy a lot. We picked a day that we called "daddy day." On this day, we would spend the day making crafts and writing and mailing a letter to daddy. This was a very special day for us.

Q. How do you explain this to your four-year-old son?

A. *You cannot explain it to a four year old. He knew that daddy had a second job, and we had always called it "daddy's Army job." When daddy left, I explained to him that daddy had to go away for his "Army job." I work in Emergency Medical Services (EMS), and Zachary is well aware that I help sick and injured people all the time. I would just tell him that daddy had to go help sick and injured people, like mama does. This helped him to know that daddy was needed in another place and that he would return soon. Every night at bedtime we would say our "daddy prayer."*

Q. Is it hard for you and your son to adjust now that your husband is home?

A. *Yes, I got used to doing it all myself. Now that he is home and helping out, I have extra time on my hands. I found myself not letting him do anything around the house without even knowing it. He also did not want to go anywhere at first. He never really talked about what it was like in Iraq, but I came to figure out that he was always on the look out. While driving down the road or when he* *was stopped at a red light and if the person in the car beside him looked over, he would get nervous. Public places such as church, stores, and malls would cause anxiety. There is a lot of adjustment for your soldier and your whole family. Remember, it takes time to readjust. I would try to remember that the FOB (Forward Operating Base) was his secure place, and home is now his secure place.*

 Need to Know

Advice from John
✓ Make sure all paperwork is in order and that you have plenty of copies. You will need at least five copies of the deployment orders.

✓ Make sure you have your military ID photo card. If this is your first time getting one, the soldier has to be present. Then, you will need to get another one when the soldier is on active duty.

✓ Contact all credit card companies if your spouse's name is on the account. Providing them with the deployment order will reduce your interest rate. Also contact your home mortgage and car loan accounts. Keep the myPay website, located at https://mypay.dfas.mil/mypay.aspx, handy in case there are discrepancies or delays in pay or combat pay.

✓ If you have children, keep their life as "normal" as possible. This is hard on them, too.

✓ Read up on the military's procedures.

✓ Have important numbers with you at all times.
- Armory phone number.
- Red Cross phone number.
- The Family Action Center phone number.

✓ Have a letter with you at all times stating that you give medical personnel permission to release medical information to the Red Cross. Make sure your Commander's information is on that letter. Hospitals will not release information about your condition otherwise.

Make the Connection on MFN!
www.eMilitary.org/YourMFN.html

Sign on to the address shown above and Make the Connection to more resources on this topic!

✓ Be patient with your children and spouse when he/she returns.

✓ Obtain passports so you can travel quickly in the event of an emergency. This includes children, even infants.

37 Military Family History & Society

From the Field with Stacey Brown

*Army Family Historian and active duty reserve spouse, **Stacey Brown**, chronicles her family experiences with deployment; reviews the path she walks in the footprints of spouses before her, and offers guideposts to Modern Military Spouses to help them recognize their common journey.*

Who can forget the tearful conversation between United States Army Specialist Shoshana Johnson and her daughter upon Ms. Johnson's release from captivity during Operation Iraqi Freedom? For some, the image revealed the progression of history. For others, the media coverage brought back reminders of time served in past wars, time spent waiting for loved ones to return, the sound of the phone ringing, the knock at the door, the volleys, and the final bugle.

In 2003, Specialist Johnson, a single, African American female soldier left her daughter behind with her parents and deployed to the Persian Gulf. Her daughter remained at home, waiting, like so many other family members, for her mother's safe return. This scenario was not within the realm of possibilities in 1775 when George Washington began assembling the first Continental Army. Women did not enlist during the Revolution; they served in limited capacities as service support personnel. African Americans, although not initially considered for duty, fought for a country that did not even grant their freedom.

Most families remained at home, although as time progressed, the number of camp followers increased. Command responsibility for families was limited. Regulations prohibited marriage for enlisted men unless they received permission, and officers maintained accompanying family members largely at their own expense.

Over time, this meager camp following grew and blossomed into a full-fledged military family community, with many of the members traveling to remote posts and overseas and witnessing some of the most exciting events in the history of the United States. Along the way, they created a common bond that allowed them to endure hardships no matter where they were stationed.

Certain experiences remain consistent throughout the two-hundred-year history of the U.S. military family. But consistency does not imply that the community remained stagnant while the military organization developed around it. In fact, just the opposite is true. Today, members of the military family—through the availability of programs, services, and benefits—enjoy a quality of life greatly improved from the days on the early frontier. Through elevated Command awareness and commitment, and the efforts of liaison and advocacy groups—created and staffed, in large part, by family members—the community embraces the ability to lobby on issues still of concern.

> "Today, members of the military family—through the availability of programs, services, and benefits—enjoy a quality of life greatly improved from the days on the early frontier."

Not only has the community changed, but also the members themselves are different. The deployment of troops to locations away from the continental United States and the broadening of family policy expanded the opportunities for multicultural spouses to join the military family community. On the home front, the official acceptance of African Americans and women into the armed forces and the emergence of dual-service couples and single-parent households further expanded not only the complexity of the community, but also the family awareness required from the Command.

A Proud History and Continuing Challenges
The diaries, letters, and books left by women such as Elizabeth Custer, Eveline Alexander, and Martha Summerhayes provide wonderful information about early life with the army and can assist any member of the military family community in understanding the long heritage of service and sacrifice to which they belong. It is the devotion of these early women and the continuous dedication of current family members that contribute to the overall success of the total community.

Countless men, women, and children have followed their military spouse in order to remain together as a family. Limitations and obstacles never deterred them. They have, in many ways, been the source of strength that holds the greater community together. The consistent presence of spouses and children and their willingness to maintain a home under

> "Such experiences shared by members of the community have transcended time and taken on a ritualistic quality."

any circumstances has done as much for the status of the military family as any piece of policy or legislation. The military would not have provided for a community that did not exist.

The military family community has grown and strengthened through the advent of such policies as the United States Army's Family Well-Being Initiative, the creation of family-driven organizations such as the Military Family Network, and, of course, through the sacrifice and perseverance of military families through the centuries.

 **FAQs**

Q. Is the military family heritage the same for all branches of service?

A. *YES! The heritage shared by military spouses has little to do with branch definitions. Every member of the military family started out with the same roots—continental camp followers and wives and children traveling on the early frontier.*

Q. Do you have to live on the installation to be a part of the heritage?

A. *NO! You only have to be a member of the community. The rest comes as an added bonus. You do not even need to live in the United States; in fact, families who travel overseas may even experience a greater connection to our past.*

Q. The change from military "wives" to military "spouses," is it necessary? Are there that many husbands? Do they really share the same experience and heritage?

A. *This is a YES, NO, and MAYBE SO question! While it is still difficult for some to refer to the dependent spouse group as military spouses and not military wives, it is necessary in order for total inclusion into the military family community. However, dependent wives do outnumber dependent husbands. As for whether or not they share in the same experience and heritage that remains to be seen. They are certainly members of the community, and they do take on* *the duties of the dependent spouse, but there is not enough evidence at this time to determine whether husbands feel the same connection to the military and to the past, as wives do.*

Q. Can I learn more on my own about the heritage of the military family? Where do I look? Can I help preserve military family heritage?

A. *YES! Military family heritage is all around you. You can look into your local installation history, visit the local museum and library (there are many books and articles available), talk with families who have served longer, veterans, retirees, and even some of your own family members. You can help preserve your heritage by being involved in your local military family community, keeping a journal, or joining the Military Family Network.*

Q. I'm new to the military. What should I expect?

A. *ANYTHING and EVERYTHING! Expect the unexpected. Revel in the adventure. Find your installation community service centers, contact your unit family readiness group, get to know those around you, and volunteer. What ever you do—do not let yourself get house-locked; there's plenty to do for every age and ability. Get out and look around. Explore your new world.*

 Need to Know

Get to know your military family history... and walk proud.

We live in a free society that relies upon volunteers to defend it borders. However, during the last two centuries, the quality of life led by the members of this force has been mediocre at best, and close to the depths of poverty at its worst. Service members and their families serve despite the quality of life afforded them either by services in kind or monetary stipends. Nevertheless, future generations of family members will go forward, knowing that those who have gone before found that following the army and supporting the mission was important enough to fight for things such as better housing, programs, and medical benefits.

The growth of programs, benefits, and services during the latter part of the twentieth century, and the improvement in Command attitude towards the family community directly affected the quality of life for the accompanying family members. This progress, however, does not change the stories or the attitudes of the accompanying family. Whether one family traveled thousands of miles to reach a post with no tents and another made the same journey only to find that there was a waiting list for housing and the rental market was flooded, the result is the same—there is no available housing at the end of a long forced move.

For the family experiencing this event, the type of structure is irrelevant. The realization that the institution that forced the family's relocation without considering how to provide for them upon arrival at the destination is the same no matter where or when the move took place. Such experiences shared by members of the community have transcended time and taken on a ritualistic quality.

Through the years, military family members accumulate many hours spent alone, taking care of home and family. This is not, nor has it ever been, an easy task. However, just as our military leaders compile their "lessons learned," so too can the military family learn from past experiences. By looking back at the heritage left by other spouses and children, today's family members can better prepare for the future and understand their role in the military family community, as well as understand the broader history and heritage of the military family. Within this history, current family members will find a bond with others and discover that no matter what the situation, someone else has already walked down that road before, and that others still walk it with them.

The common bond held by members of the military family community is absolute. Anyone who serves will move, pack, unpack, and learn that boxes make great end tables and sheets make great curtains. Members of the military family will commit to memory the numbers to the automated housing waiting list, know the quickest way to the PX, stand retreat at a stop light, endure separation, and come to understand the meaning of mission first. Most importantly, they will participate in a community whose sole purpose is to provide support for the men and women of the armed forces whose primary mission is the maintenance and protection of our freedom.

Make the Connection on MFN!
www.eMilitary.org/YourMFN.html

Sign on to the address shown above and Make the Connection to more resources on this topic!

Part 7
Military Family Fun

Photo: Luis Trevino

Fishing by Fort Monroe

Introduction

Morale Welfare and Recreation (MWR) programs contribute to the over-all readiness of the Armed Forces. They help promote good health for service members (a physically fit force is a ready force). Service members who take advantage of MWR services can meet the needs of the current high op-tempo (service members deploying rapidly and repeatedly) where personal fitness and mental clarity become critical to our military's capability to maintain mission effectiveness.

The services are interested in keeping MWR available because the personal fitness of service members contributes to military readiness since it increases productivity, provides preventative health benefits, and results in medical cost savings.

There isn't a working couple that would want anything less than the nationally accredited child development centers offered on installations to care for their youngsters. Similarly, youth and teen centers overseas are not simply MWR benefits for the families there. Life without them would be unimaginable. The same goes for fitness centers.

It is important for families to become more aware of the MWR benefits available to them on the installations and to use them. Why? Well, the Department of Defense looks at numbers. If families do not see fit to use the facilities, why should they be funded? If you do not want to see these benefits diminish or disappear over time, get informed, see what fits, and make use of what the military is providing as a benefit for your service.

Everything from free to nearly free family movies to state of the art fitness centers are available to military ID card holders. This chapter reviews some of the MWR benefits available to you as a military ID card holder.

38 Morale, Welfare, and Recreation

From the Field with Caroline Peabody

Caroline Peabody *is the daughter of a disabled Vietnam era Marine, military spouse, former president of The Military Family Network, lifetime volunteer, and distinguished speaker and lecturer on military life. She holds a B.S. in sociology and M.A. in organizational management with extensive research on communication systems as they relate to military well being and community capacity-building. She is a published writer and columnist on matters relating to military families, military learning models, and military relations.*

Morale, Welfare, and Recreation (MWR) is a name that covers many different programs—family support centers, youth services, family programs, and outdoor recreation programs, etc. Anything fun, any organized sport, anything you need to participate in your favorite hobby can probably be found under an MWR program.

Do you like to fish, work out, travel, play sports, act in plays, or coach? Or do you like relaxing, watching the big game on TV, hanging out with friends, and eating hot pizza? Or maybe you're a golfer, bowler, swimmer, racquetball player, skier, or snowboarder? Well, you are in luck. MWR caters to all of these interests and more! And, most importantly, MWR is there to take care of your family when you're deployed. Your children will have lots of fun interacting with others, yet be safe and supervised. What better way for them to pass the time until you come home?

Child and Youth Services (CYS) programs reduce the conflict between mission and parental responsibilities. Basic CYS programs are child development centers, family childcare home systems, before- and after-school programs, school liaison and school transition services, youth sports and fitness programs, and partnerships with Boys & Girls Clubs and 4-H Clubs. Services are provided year-round and include full-day, part-day, after school, hourly, special needs, and seasonal supervised programs and care options. Because of the breadth and richness of services provided, Congress and the White House have recognized the military childcare system as a "model for the Nation."

Individual and team sports for men and women include basketball, soccer, volleyball, rugby, softball, and martial arts. At gymnasiums, certified instructors conduct aerobics for cardiovascular fitness and supervise strength training with weights. Recreation centers offer a variety of social activities, games (table tennis, billiards, etc.), classes, and meeting space. Installation libraries provide books, magazines, electronic information resources, and professional reference services for academics and recreational reading. Installation libraries send book kits to remote and isolated sites (geographically separated housing areas, etc) as well as to deployed soldiers.

Outdoor Recreation (OR) opportunities vary by geographic location, climate, and demand. They range from high-challenge activities such as ropes courses, mountain climbing, and rappelling to extreme sports such as snowboarding, paragliding, and windsurfing. Many installations have forests, parks, rivers, and lakes that invite fishing, hunting, hiking, camping, and boating. Need equipment? You may want to beef up your camping experience with grills and other types of things that you may not want to buy. You can rent it from Outdoor Recreation.

> "Arts and crafts centers are outlets for creativity and are money savers, too."

Arts and crafts centers are outlets for creativity and are money savers, too. Trained staff members ensure safe use of tools and equipment. At automotive craft shops, you can change your car's oil or change a motor. The centers offer tools, bays, classes, and assistance available for nominal fees. Outlets for creative expression in the performing arts include music and theater events such as Battle of the Bands, one-act play festivals, community theater, entertainment contests, and chart-topping celebrity performers who stage concerts at installations.

Sports bars, casual dining restaurants, fast food outlets, and community clubs offer ethnic and traditional foods as well as nightlife on post. Military members enjoy significant discounts at many major amusement parks, resorts, and attractions. Expect to pay fees and charges for MWR and family programs; profits are reinvested locally in MWR programs. A percentage of profits from the Army and Air Force Exchange Service (AAFES) and MBX (Marine Base Exchange) and NEX (Navy Exchange) are used to fund MWR programs. When you shop at AAFES, MBX or NEX and patronize MWR, you help sustain these programs for the future. MWR programs are for all service members and families: active duty, reserve components, and retirees, married and single, living on or off the installation.

 **FAQs**

Q. Who is authorized to use MWR facilities and programs?

A. *Personnel authorized to use MWR activities and facilities include active duty members and their families, reserve members, retired military personnel and their dependents, medal of honor recipients and their surviving spouses and family members, un-remarried surviving spouses of retired military personnel and their family members, Academy midshipmen and cadets, ROTC cadets when on active duty during college vacation, drilling member of reserve components and dependents.*

Q. Are there fees involved in MWR programs?

A. *It depends on the program. Many facilities and activities are of no cost, but some require registration fees or usage fees. Check with the program center for more information*

 Need to Know

The major military installations in the CONUS and OCONUS maintain full-service Morale, Welfare & Recreation offices and/or Outdoor Recreation Centers and provide most of the following services for service members, National Guard and Reserve, retirees, and their dependents:

- Recreational Vehicle Parking/Campgrounds
- Recreational Vehicle Storage
- Vehicle Storage upon Mobilization
- Vehicle Resale Lot
- Equipment Rental (camping gear, boating & fishing equipment, sports equipment, lawn & garden equipment, rug cleaners & cleaning supplies)
- Archery and Skeet Ranges
- Swimming Facilities

- Tours (shopping, hiking, horseback riding)
- Ticketing Services (concerts, movie theaters, sports events, performing arts, special events)
- Discount Tickets for Major Tourist Attractions, both local and regional (Disneyland, Sea World, etc.)

In general, to take advantage of these services, show your ID card. Some of these services are provided for free; the rest are offered at a cost that is frequently a lot less than comparable civilian services. In some cases, you may be able to secure tickets at discount prices that are only offered to military personnel and their dependents.

Resorts

AFRC (Armed Forces Recreation Center) resorts are affordable Joint Service facilities operated by the U.S. Army Community and Family Support Center and located at ideal vacation destinations. AFRCs offer a full range of resort hotel opportunities for service members, their families, and other members of the Total Defense Force. AFRCs are self-supporting and funded by nonappropriated fund revenues generated internally from operations. Revenues from AFRCs are continually reinvested to maintain and improve the physical plant while providing the greatest possible value for AFRC guests. Providing high-quality, affordable resort-style facilities at the AFRCs is in accordance with the Department of the Chief of Staff of the Army philosophy that soldiers are entitled to the same quality of life as the citizens they are pledged to defend. The Army continues to promote strong family values by providing the AFRCs - a reflection of their strong commitment to improved quality of life. AFRC room rates are affordable and based on rank, pay grade, duty status, room size, and/or room location

> **"AFRCs offer a full range of resort hotel opportunities for service members, their families, and other members of the Total Defense Force."**

The AFRCs are centrally-managed, U.S. Army Community and Family Support Center-operated facilities with a mission to provide rest, relaxation, recreation, and sustainment for Army personnel, their families, and other members of the total Defense Force.

Facilities include:
- Shades of Green on the grounds of The Walt Disney World Resort, Florida
- Edelweiss Lodge and Resort, Germany
- Hale Koa Hotel, Hawaii
- Dragon Hill Lodge, Korea

Authorized users include active-duty military, retirees, currently employed and retired Department of Defense civilians, reservists, delayed entry recruits, and family members. Reservations are required as these facilities are often full.

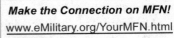

Make the Connection on MFN!
www.eMilitary.org/YourMFN.html

Sign on to the address
shown above and
Make the Connection
to more resources
on this topic!

39 Space Available: Travel for Free

From the Field with John D.

John D. is an active duty service member who has spent years traveling around the world using the benefit of Space-A travel. He is the creator and manager of the information website www.spacea.net where he encourages the military community to find out about and use this valuable service benefit.

Military space available (Space-A) travel is a benefit that allows active duty and retired military members and their dependents to travel for free on U.S. Department of Defense aircraft when space is available. This great opportunity for free travel is probably one of the most mysterious and misunderstood military benefits available.

To most people, Space-A travel ranks right up there with Public Speaking––everyone is afraid of doing it the first time. Much of this fear comes from lack of knowledge and the unpredictability of flights. The more you learn about Space-A travel the less fear you will have. I can't speak for everyone but I learned by reading the regulations and by "Just Doing It." (The Internet, e-mail and the Space-A message boards didn't exist when I started!)

Actually, doing a Space-A trip is the real teacher and don't be surprised if you learn some hard lessons your first time out. On the other hand, your first experience may be a pleasant one where everything goes as planned. In that respect "Space-A is like a box of chocolates – you never know what you're going to get!" I'd recommend taking a "dry-run" trip or if you're near a PAX (passenger) terminal go visit and hang out for a day and talk to some of the folks waiting for flights. Following the tips in this chapter and experiencing the Space-A environment by visiting a PAX terminal will help to reduce some of the apprehension you may have.

> "Space-A is like a box of chocolates – you never know what you're going to get."

A few years ago, I created the Military Space-A FAQ (Frequently Asked Questions) to supplement the information available from the USAF's Air Mobility Command in an attempt to make this benefit less "mysterious." The Space-A FAQ has evolved over the years into my "hobby" and now consists of a set of web-based Space-A resources maintained at www.spacea.net.

The FAQ and other web page resources available at www.spacea.net are the result of inputs from many fellow Space-A travelers who participate in the late Roy Buckman's message board (www.spacea.info) and Dirk Pepperd's Space-A Message Board (www.pepperd.com). In addition, I've included some lessons I've learned over nearly twenty years of using this wonderful benefit.

Military Space-A travel has become more user-friendly over the last few years. In the "old days," one had to physically go to a location to put your name on the Space-A register and get in the "queue." In addition, you used to have to wear your uniform while traveling and pay for the privilege from many of the larger military locations. (It was not always a "free ride".)

> "...uniforms are no longer required and the only Space-A charges are for the contracted 'Patriot Express' flights."

Now, with the advent of the Internet and e-mail, one can sign-up "remotely" using a web form, e-mail, or fax. In addition, uniforms are no longer required and the only Space-A charges are for the contracted "Patriot Express" flights. "Command Sponsored" active duty military dependents stationed OCONUS (Outside the Continental United States) and "non-command sponsored" dependents can now travel to and from OCONUS without their sponsor. A big improvement has been the recent policy change that now allows active duty and dependents of retired service members to accompany their sponsor on flights within the CONUS (Continental United States). Finally, military members now have the advantage of the Internet resources and message boards mentioned above.

Military Space-A travel is not for everyone. If you are flexible, adventurous, and enjoy meeting people, then you'll enjoy planning and executing a trip using Space-A military travel. You may even save some money!! On the other hand, you may not save any money; that's the gamble you take and it ends up being part of the experience and adventure!!

For example, since there are many categories of eligible passengers and you are rated on a priority basis, you may not be able to get a flight back that you thought would be available. Available flights may also be shut down depending on the security level issued by the

> "You must always remember that 'Space Available' means just that...and sometimes space may not be available..."

Department of Defense or the Department of Homeland Security. You must always remember that "Space Available" means just that…and sometimes space may not be available for a variety of reasons. If you need to get back at a specific time, you must plan for a back up means of travel.

I hope the Military Space-A FAQ and other resources will help you to plan your first and subsequent Space-A adventures! Check it out—you may get addicted!

 **FAQs**

Q. Who is eligible for Space A Travel and what are "Categories (Cats)?"

A. *Basically, your travel status "category" is your priority ranking, i.e., who gets first dibs on plane seats. There are six categories (CAT-I thru CAT-VI). CAT-I is highest priority (first to get offered a Space-A seat) and CAT VI is the lowest Category (last to get offered a Space-A seat after CAT I thru CAT V). A GENERIC explanation of each category is:*

> **"…your travel status 'category'…[determines] who gets first dibs on plane seats."**

CAT I: Emergency Leave Unfunded Travel

CAT II: Environmental and Morale Leave (EML): Leave granted at overseas installations where environmental conditions require special arrangement for leave in more desirable locations at periodic intervals.

CAT III: Active Duty Ordinary Leave and accompanied dependents, House Hunting Permissive TDY (Temporary Duty), Medal of Honor Holders

CAT IV: Unaccompanied Dependents on EML or using Deployed Sponsor Upgrade Letter and DoDDS Teachers on EML During Summer

CAT V: Unaccompanied Command Sponsored and Non-Command Sponsored Dependents of Active Duty, Permissive TDY (Non house Hunting), Students

CAT VI: Retired and their accompanied Dependents, Reserve, ROTC, NUPOC, and CEC

If you're not clear what category you are in, you can find a more *complete explanation* of each category in DoD 4515.13-R, Chapter 6, Table 6.1.

Q. How do I get started?

A. *First, determine your eligibility for Space-A travel. Then:*

1. SIGN-UP (Register)

Some terminals have a web form you can fill out to register. You can also sign-up (register) in person, by e-mail, or fax.

Note, you are not "signing-up" for a particular flight, and you do not make flight "reservations!" When you sign-up, you go on "the list," and you compete for flights based on your priority on

> "If something is not correct with your registration, fix it then!"

"the list" within your category. When your "sign-up request" is received, you are assigned a date/time based on the Julian date and Zulu time your sign-up was received. Your sign-up date/time determines your position/priority within each Space-A Category. Passengers are manifested during a Roll Call under a priority system starting with Category-I (CAT-I) through CAT-VI.

2. SHOW UP

Once signed-up, you'll have to decide where you want to depart from (e.g., Dover, Andrews, McGuire, etc.). It helps to phone the terminal you think you want to depart from and monitor their recording of flight departures to get a feel for possible destinations. As soon as you physically arrive at a location, check in with the folks at the passenger service desk to verify you are listed on the Space-A register with the correct date/time/seats. If something is not correct with your registration, fix it then!

3. GIDDY-UP

Now that you're at the terminal, the adventure begins. You're next step is to be physically present at the terminal. You'll need to be "travel-ready" (i.e., luggage, dependents, and proper paperwork in-hand and car parked) for the "show-time" of the particular flight you'd like to be manifested on. If you are selected for the flight at the Space-A Roll Call, you'll be manifested and on your way!

Q. How do I "sign-up?"

A. *At most USAF locations, there are four ways to sign-up for Space-A travel: A completed paper* **AMC Form 140***, online sign-up (including e-mail), fax, or in person. Active duty personnel can sign-up as soon as they begin "leave or pass status."*

Roy Buckman (now deceased) developed a one-stop shopping sign-up site that allowed you to sign-up for multiple destinations at the same time. However, that service is now out of service. Rob G. (another Space-A volunteer) has developed an identical one-stop sign-up site at www.takeahop.com/sign-up/

However you choose to sign-up, an experienced Space-A traveler will print out their e-mail sign-up receipts and bring them along in case you arrive at a departure point and they "lost" your sign-up. The terminal personnel will normally honor your hand-carried sign-up showing your original day/time of sign-up, thus pre-

> **"…print out [your] e-mail sign-up receipts and bring them along in case you arrive at a departure point and they 'lost' your sign-up."**

venting a disaster! Once you are added to the Space Available register, you are eligible for any flights that depart that location for the duration of your sign-up.

Note: On most Navy bases you have to sign-up in person per mission (flight) and e-mail and fax sign-up may not be available. Some Navy locations such as Norfolk, Jacksonville, Naples, Sigonella, and Rota act as AMC terminals so they provide for the "normal" sign-up methods.

 Need to Know

Keep all documentation you need on hand and current throughout your trip including:

- ✓ Military ID card (if eligible to have one- children under 10 are not required)
- ✓ Passport as required for potential OCONUS destinations (Active Duty on leave consult the Foreign Clearance Guide)
- ✓ Active duty must have a copy of their current leave orders
- ✓ Unaccompanied Command Sponsored Dependent: need Command Sponsorship letter (copy is OK) signed by sponsor's commander

Make the Connection on MFN!
www.eMilitary.org/YourMFN.html
Sign on to the address shown above and Make the Connection to more resources on this topic!

- ✓ Unaccompanied Non-Command Sponsored Dependent: Non-Command Sponsorship letter (copy is OK) signed by sponsor's commander
- ✓ Active Reservist/Guardsmen (not on Active Duty over 30 days) must have a DD Form 1853 signed by their commander or First Sergeant

Part 8
Military Education and Employment

Photo: Luis Trevino

Land of Opportunity

A Special Message on Maximizing Your Talents from The Military Family Network

Get Seen, Get Heard, Get Hired!

There is no one quite like you. No one has your exact experiences or the specific skills and talents you have developed through those experiences. You have your own way of seeing the world, and you have built your character through your own successes and failures. You have created your own style and have applied yourself diligently towards showcasing your personal qualifications and achieving your goals. So why have you distanced yourself, hidden your personality and uniqueness from the hiring process by blindly submitting your resumes along with thousands of other applicants to classified ads and to Internet job boards?

Job-hunting is often seen as a daunting and arduous task full of stress and anxiety as countless individuals try to read the minds and needs of potential future employers. Applicants scan the papers, visit libraries, and log online looking for employment openings and position descriptions that they can "fit into" by scaling down their attributes to editorial sound bites. Something like trying to fit a square peg into a round hole.

It is common knowledge that job statistics have proven that this approach yields modest success in securing employment, yet thousands of hours are lost each year by applicants and employers alike engaged in this practice. But job-hunting doesn't have to be this way. It can be exciting, exhilarating—an adventure, a new beginning. And, it can be fun. Yes, a lot of fun, but you must be willing to accept the challenge of stepping up to the plate and thinking outside of the box.

Please don't misunderstand: there is a lot of great advice on the job search process that should be considered. And, most importantly, your job search should consist of multiple approaches. And that is what this section on employment addresses.

Each chapter is dedicated to covering situations, information, and resources inherent to military life. They speak to the particular challenges that face military spouses, transitioning service members and veterans in the employment market and provide guidance and support on how to turn those obstacles into winning strategies for success. So whether you are a military spouse whose career may be interrupted at any time by relocation, a spouse residing overseas or working from home, a retiring service member wondering how to turn those high-level technical skills into civilian qualifications, or a veteran seeking retraining opportunities, this section will talk to each of these experiences with an eye towards making the most of your talents, discovering ways to promote your best qualities, and showing you how to network professionally from the inside-out.

These chapters will argue that you should be doing a little of everything you've ever heard about from assessing your interests and submitting resumes to calling friends and colleagues. But let's not stop there. Accept the challenge to go one step further, and here's just the job search attitude to get you started:

First, consider your product. It's YOU! Who knows you better than yourself? You are the You-EXPERT. This makes you the professional in your field and this knowledge is unquestionable. The interview process becomes less intimidating when you are the onsite genius.

Second, consider your experiences, skills, and talents in the proper scope. Were you born yesterday? Can you read? Can you write? Can you answer a phone? Can you THINK? And, more essentially, can you learn? Most of us have possessed these skills for twenty or thirty years or more. More importantly, every employer must invest in training—whether it is where to locate an in-box or how to present the company's business. Employers want to know that their training efforts and dollars are invested in the right individual.

Third, consider the fact that most of us are not gifted with ESP. How do you know the internal needs of an organization—especially if they haven't encountered YOU? Many times, an organization might not even know they NEED you until they have met you. Often, an employer will have an opening, and in the process of trying to fill that vacancy, will discover a new need and/or create a new position for a talented individual.

Fourth, consider the cliché that "a picture speaks a thousand words." You have got to be seen and heard. Grab your resumes, put on your smile, pound the pavement, and knock, knock, knock. Stop by any establishment that sparks your interest, walk in, and ask for the hiring manager or how to make an application. Don't qualify your target based on your past experience—only on your current interest. If your past experience is your current interest, well then, all the better. You already know that you can think and learn and have the perseverance and discipline to succeed. Communicate and don't forget to share these abilities with your potential employer.

Fifth, don't forget the follow-up. This "thank-you" and reiteration of your strengths and interest as an applicant is an essential part of the whole process. But, of course, you already knew that.

And finally, remember that most applicants are not orchestrating their job search in this fashion, because many are too timid or just don't know how. This gives you front running and allows you to stand out among the pack. In fact, you may even find job opportunities that have not yet been publicized.

Don't forget that you are a winner and that an employer is waiting to meet you!

—Megan Turak, Vice President, The Military Family Network

40 Education: Your Path to Success

From the Field with Megan Turak

Megan Turak is the daughter of a WWII Army veteran and spouse of a Vietnam era Marine, Executive Vice President and co-owner of The Military Family Network, former Medical Records Manager with the Department of Veteran Affairs, a published writer of informative topics positively impacting the well-being of military families and has over twenty combined years of experience in executive leadership in the financial management and communications industries.

There is no better gift than the gift of education. I know that you have heard it said, "Give a man a fish; he eats for a day. Teach a man to fish; he eats for a lifetime." Education will do this for you. It has the power to change your life! And the U.S. Armed Forces, your military, makes this available to you. I will say it loud and I will say it clear and I will make no apology for it: If you are in the military and do not avail yourself of the education-rich environment surrounding you, then you are being foolish and have just squandered the most valuable benefit your career offers you.

Not too long ago, I watched a documentary about a poor, fatherless family of four living in a small mountain mining village in South America. The eldest boy of about fourteen years of age supported his mother, a brother of twelve, and a sister of five by mining in the silver mines of the region. Explosions and lung disease killed many keeping life expectancy to less than forty. Yet despite the long shifts—sometimes a full twenty-four hours with nothing but cocoa leaves for energy—the fourteen-year-old boy struggled to go to school, because he knew that it was the only way to survive and to get out of the mines. School was no easy feat. The boy needed a uniform, shoes, a haircut, books, and supplies. Affording this from his meager salary was a great strain on his family's resources. The distance to the school was another obstacle. Yet, despite these hardships, the boy attended classes and studied whenever he could. This movie was not about 100 years ago. This is happening now, all over the world.

When I finished watching the film, I thought that every school child in America should be required to view it. Our great country offers each of us an education as a birthright, while others, like women and girls in Afghanistan, are shut out of even the most elementary systems due to prejudices and poverty. To treat this opportunity irreverently is not just a shame; it's a tragedy. If you don't feel that education is a privilege to be taken seriously, then consider the children of the world who can't get one.

> **"If you don't feel that education is a privilege to be taken seriously, then consider the children of the world who can't get one."**

Did you happen to know that the World War II generation is one of the wealthiest generations to ever pass on wealth to their heirs? Some of this wealth was accumulated through saving strategies left over from the Depression era, but some came because these World War II veterans took advantage of the then newly created Montgomery G.I. Bill to go to school. From this education, they helped to form what we know now as America's middle class and they propelled our country into today's information era. Now, that's life changing!

So, don't delay. No matter what branch of service you are in, Service Member, there are learning possibilities for you! There are on-the-job training opportunities, technical skills and trade degrees, online and offsite schooling, in class and out of class, scholarships and GI Bill benefits, credit transfers and generous programs offering monetary allowances and course credits for professional experiences.

> **" Now that's life changing!"**

The military knows your career requirements, your available time, your income, and the nature of your mobile lifestyle. They have created programs suited to meet your career requirements and have successfully encouraged private institutions and state affiliated schools to find ways to better serve their people. Say you don't have time? Fixed it. Can't afford it? Fixed it. Don't like classrooms? Fixed it. There is no longer an excuse to stay away. Don't fret, Family Members and Dependants. The military has not overlooked the fact that you serve, too. A lot of these programs are also open and available to you. In fact, the GI Bill has launched a pilot program in the Army that includes some spouses. Contact your branch of service to see if you are eligible and if your GI Bill benefits are transferable to your dependents. In addition, there are many government and independent organizations providing scholarships and grant monies for your education and professional development.

There are plenty of opportunities for children, too. Many private elementary and secondary schools offer full scholarships so that your children can receive a first-rate, private education. Contact the schools, take your child for an interview, complete the application, and send in your child's transcript and recommendations. Usually your child will have to take the Secondary School Admission Test (SSAT). It is all very similar to the college entrance process, but if your child is accepted, it is well worth it! Check out the resources online with The Military Family Network at www.eMilitary.org/YourMFN.html. You'll find educational programs for everyone in your family, including you.

 **FAQs**

Q. Do I need money to get an education? I don't have much money.

A. *Yes, you need money, but not necessarily your own. And, you don't necessarily have to have it on-hand, either. There are many resources available to help individuals fund their education—from federal and state grants and loans to private organizations, businesses, foundations and scholarships. America believes in education. Check out the resources on our network at http://www. emilitary.org/YourMFN.html to find out more.*

Q. What does it take to get a scholarship?

A. *Many individuals assume that they have to be brilliant, or athletically talented, or gifted musically, to earn a scholarship for college. What they don't realize is that sometimes they just need to be persistent!*

Be persistent in getting good grades. Many colleges award scholarships to individuals with significant financial need in the accepted applicant group — a grant that you don't need to repay, just for making the cut and getting admitted!

Good grades won't hurt if you hope to get a scholarship even if your family doesn't demonstrate financial need. When scholarships are awarded on the basis of academic merit, without regard for need, individuals who have worked hard and achieved results in school will be the winners.

You should also be persistent in seeking out other scholarship sources. Sometimes all it takes to get a scholarship is to find out who in your area is offering them: your church, your employer, your parents' employers, veteran service organizations and local civic organizations. You'll just need to fill out any required applications or interviews on time in order to be considered.

Q. I've already had some college courses, but couldn't complete my degree because we moved. Do I have to start all over? I don't know if I could afford that.

A. *No, you don't have to start all over. But what you do need is a visit with the academic counseling center of the school you are considering. You need a helpful, knowledgeable and creative advisor who can guide you through the degree require-ments of your new school. Take this to the top if you have to and ask for the head of the department. Don't accept an advisor who lacks interest in you or is too new to the sys-tem to be of much help. You should also con-tact any prior schools you've attended and obtain your complete transcript as well as a description of the courses you took and the course work. In this way, your advisor will be able to assign your previously earned credits appropri-ately to the new school's requirements. This process may be a bit time consum-ing, but can save you hours in repeated class work as well as a lot of cash.*

Make the Connection on MFN!
www.eMilitary.org/YourMFN.html

Sign on to the address shown above and Make the Connection to more resources on this topic!

Q. It doesn't look like I will be eligible for financial aid. Should I still apply?

A. *Yes. Apply for everything! I recall my father telling my mother that they never realized how poor they were until they applied for financial aid! Many people make the mistake of thinking that this opportunity will not be available to them. Let the school tell you no. By the way, this should apply to everything in your life whether it is financial aid, a scholarship, a grant, loan or allow-ance, a raise, a promotion or just a request for help. Ask. Ask. Ask. The answer just might be yes!*

Q. I have saved money for my retirement, but haven't done as well for my child's education. I don't have enough savings to pay for my child's schooling and I feel bad. Should I use my retirement money to help my child?

A. *No, you should not use your retirement money to pay for education, despite the fact that many laws now make it easier to access your retirement savings to meet this need and some advisors may actually encourage you to do it. There* *are literally thousands of ways to pay for school: financial aid, grants, loans, scholarships, work-study programs, etc. Your child could even help to finance his or her education through employment or an employer's benefit program. (I know, how could I ask the child to pay? Really!) Review the resources at www. eMilitary.org/YourMFN.html with The Military Family Network to see what I mean. Now, take a moment to tell me how many programs, loans, or grants exist for individuals when they retire? Not many and the government is even afraid to promise us that our Social Security will be there. I guarantee you, when you retire, the last thing you're going to want to do with your old, creaky bones, is to get a job or ask your kid for money.*

Q. We have a long and proud tradition in our family of serving our country. Now my children want to follow in their father's footsteps. Are there any military scholarships available for them?

A. *Yes, there are. These scholarships are awarded on the basis of merit rather than financial need:*
- **Army Reserve Officer Training Corps**

Army Reserve Officer Training Corps (ROTC) scholarships are offered at hundreds of colleges. Application packets, information about eligibility, and the telephone number of an ROTC advisor in your area are available from
College Army ROTC
Telephone: **1-800-USA-ROTC (1-800-872-7682)**
Web site: www.goarmy.com/rotc
- **Air Force Reserve Officer Training Corps**

The Air Force Reserve Officer Training Corps (AFROTC) college scholarship program targets students pursuing technical degrees, such as certain engineering and science programs, although students entering a wide variety of majors may be accepted. Information about AFROTC scholarships is available from
College Scholarship Section
Telephone: 1-866-423-7682
Web site: www.afrotc.com
- **Naval Reserve Officers Training Corps**

The Naval Reserve Officers Training Corps (NROTC) offers both two-year and four-year scholarships. For information about the program, contact
Naval Service Training Command
Telephone: 1-800-NAV-ROTC (1-800-628-7682)
Web site: https://www.nrotc.navy.mil
E-mail: pnsc-nrotc.scholarship@navy.mil

Need to Know

Don't get Scammed on Your Way to College!

Financial aid scams are a hot topic these days. Warning! Be wary of organizations that charge a fee to submit your application, or to find you money for school. Some are legitimate and some are scams. Generally, any help that you pay for can be received free from your school or the U.S. Department of Education. The Federal Trade Commission (FTC) cautions students to look and listen for these tell-tale lines:

- "The scholarship is guaranteed or your money back."
- "You can't get this information anywhere else."
- "I just need your credit card or bank account number to hold this scholarship."
- "We'll do all the work."
- "The scholarship will cost some money."
- You've been selected" by a "national foundation" to receive a scholarship - or "You're a finalist" in a contest you never entered.

In addition, if you attend a seminar on financial aid or scholarships, follow these steps:

- Take your time. Don't be rushed into paying at the seminar. Avoid high-pressure sales pitches that require you to buy now or risk losing out on the opportunity. Solid opportunities are not sold through nerve-racking tactics.
- Investigate the organization you're considering paying for help. Talk to a guidance counselor or financial aid advisor before spending your money. You may be able to get the same help for free.
- Be wary of "success stories" or testimonials of extraordinary success - the seminar operation may have paid "shills" to give glowing stories. Instead, ask for a list of at least three local families who've used the services in the last year. Ask each if they're satisfied with the products and services received.
- Be cautious about purchasing from seminar representatives who are reluctant to answer questions or who give evasive answers to your questions. Legitimate business people are more than willing to give you information about their service.
- Ask how much money is charged for the service, the services that will be performed and the company's refund policy. Get this information in writing. Keep in mind that you may never recoup the money you give to an unscrupulous operator, despite stated refund policies.

The FTC says many legitimate companies advertise that they can get students access to lists of scholarships in exchange for an advance fee. Other legitimate services charge an advance fee to compare a student's profile with a database of scholarship opportunities and provide a list of awards for which a student may qualify. And, there are scholarship search engines on the World Wide Web. The difference: Legitimate companies *never* guarantee or promise scholarships or grants.

Choose the Right School!

Going to school is a big investment! You're investing your time. Chances are you'll also have to invest your own money or take out a student loan to go to school. So you need to be sure that you're choosing the right school.

- **Talk to your counselor.** Your school counselor is the first stop for information about the options available to you. Counselors can help you focus on your needs and goals, and they have information about different types of schools. Your counselor also can help you collect or prepare application materials.

- **Shop around.** Contact more than one school. If you're looking for vocational training, check the Yellow Pages under "Schools" for phone numbers. If your area has a community college, call the admissions office and find out what kinds of training the college offers.

- **Visit the school.** Call the school and schedule a visit, preferably while classes are being taught. Get a feel for the school; make sure you're comfortable with the facilities, the equipment, the teachers, and the students.

- **Don't be afraid to ask!** A good school will be happy to answer your questions about its programs. Ask the school about its students: How many graduate? How many get jobs because of the training they received? What kind of job placement services does the school offer students and graduates?

- **Check the cost.** Make sure the school gives you a clear statement of its tuition and fees. Remember that any federal financial aid you get will be applied first to paying the school's tuition and fees. If there's any money left over, the school will give it to you to help you pay for things such as food and rent.

- **Call these numbers.** Call your local Better Business Bureau, state higher education agency, or consumer protection division of your state attorney general's office to find out whether there have been any complaints about the school. Call the toll-free number at the U.S. Department of Education's Federal Student Aid Information Center (1-800-4-FED-AID) if you have any questions about your financial aid at the school.

34 Ways to Reduce College Costs!

1. Most colleges and universities offer merit or non-need-based scholarships to academically talented students. Students should check with each school in which they're interested for the criteria for merit scholarships.

2. The National Merit Scholarship Program awards scholarships to students based upon academic merit. The awards can be applied to any college or university to meet educational expenses at that school.

3. Many states offer scholarship assistance to academically talented students. Students should obtain the eligibility criteria from their state's education office.

4. Many schools offer scholarships to athletically talented students. Parents and students should be careful, however, to weigh the benefits of an athletic scholarship against the demands of this type of award.

5. Some colleges and universities offer special grants or scholarships to students with particular talents. Music, journalism, and drama are a few categories for which these awards are made.

6. A state college or university charges lower fees to state residents. Since public institutions are subsidized by state revenues, their tuition costs are lower than private schools' costs. The college selection process should include consideration of a state school. Although cost should be a consideration, students should not base their choice of a school only on cost.

7. Some students choose to attend a community college for 1 or 2 years, and then transfer to a 4-year school. Tuition costs are substantially lower at community colleges than at 4-year institutions.

8. Some parents may be financially able to purchase a house while their child is in school. If other students rent rooms in the house, the income may offset monthly mortgage payments. Families should make certain, however, that the property they purchase meets all of the requirements of rental property. If you have any questions, consult a tax professional.

9. Commuting is another way for students to reduce college costs. A student living at home can save as much as $6,000 per year.

10. Many schools provide lists of housing opportunities that provide free room and board to students in exchange for a certain number of hours of work each week.

11. Cooperative education programs allow students to alternate between working full time and studying full time. This type of employment program is not based upon financial need, and students can earn as much as $7,000 per year.

12. Another way to reduce college costs is to take fewer credits. Students should find out their school's policy regarding the Advanced Placement Program (APP), the College-Level Examination Program (CLEP), and the Provenience Examination Program (PEP). Under these programs, a student takes an examination in a particular subject and, if the score is high enough, receives college credit.

13. Some colleges give credit for life experiences, thereby reducing the number of credits needed for graduation. Students should check with the college for further information. You can also write to Distance Education and Training Council at 1601 18th(eighteenth) Street, NW, Washington, DC 20009, or call (202) 234-5100.

14. Most schools charge one price for a specific number of credits taken in a semester. If academically possible, students should take the maximum number of credits allowed. This strategy reduces the amount of time needed to graduate.

15. In many cases, summer college courses can be taken at a less expensive school and the credits transferred to the full-time school. Students should check with their academic advisor, however, to be certain that any course taken at another school is transferable.

16. Most schools have placement offices that help students find employment, and all schools have personnel offices that hire students to work on campus. These employment programs are not based upon financial need, and working is an excellent way to meet college expenses.

17. Most colleges and universities offer their employees a tuition reduction plan or tuition waiver program. Under this type of arrangement, the school employee and family members can attend classes at a reduced cost or no cost at all. This type of program is based not upon financial need, but rather on college employment.

18. Most colleges and universities sponsor resident advisor programs that offer financial assistance to students in the form of reduced tuition or reduced room and board costs in exchange for work in resident halls.

19. The Reserve Officers Training Corps (ROTC) Scholarship Program pays all tuition fees, and textbook costs, as well as providing a monthly living stipend. Students should be certain, however, that they want this type of program before signing up because there is a service commitment after graduation.

20. Service Academy Scholarships are offered each year to qualified students to attend the U.S. Military Academy, the U.S. Air Force Academy, the U.S. Naval Academy, the U.S. Merchant Marine Academy, or the U.S. Coast Guard Academy. The scholarships are competitive and are based upon a number of factors, including high school grades, SAT or

ACT scores, leadership qualities, and athletic ability. Students receive their undergraduate education at one of the service academies. They pay no tuition or fees, but there is a service commitment after graduation.

21. One of the most obvious ways of reducing college costs is to attend a low-cost school, either public or private. There are many colleges and universities with affordable tuition and generous financial assistance. Students should investigate all schools that meet their academic and financial needs.

22. Some schools offer combined degree programs or 3-year programs that allow students to take all of the courses needed for graduation in 3 years, instead of 4, thereby eliminating 1 year's educational expenses.

23. Partial tuition remission for the children of alumni is a common practice. Parents and students should investigate their alma mater's tuition discount policy for graduates.

24. Some colleges and universities offer special discounts if more than one child from the same family is enrolled.

25. Some colleges and universities offer discounts to enrolled students if they recruit another student.

26. Some schools offer a tuition discount to student government leaders or to the editors of college newspapers or yearbooks.

27. Some colleges offer bargain tuition rates to older students.

28. Some colleges and universities convert non-federal school loans into non-federal grants if the student remains in school and graduates.

29. Some schools will pay a student's loan origination fees.

30. Some schools offer reduced tuition rates to families if the major wage earner is unemployed.

31. Some colleges and universities have special funds set aside for families who do not qualify for federal or state funding.

32. Some private colleges will match the tuition of out-of-state institutions for certain students. Check with your college to determine whether you qualify for this option.

33. Some companies offer tuition assistance to the children of employees. Parents and students should check with the personnel office for information.

34. Students should try to buy used textbooks.

Repaying Your Student Loan

Federal student loans are real loans, just like car loans or mortgage loans. You can't just get out of repaying a student loan if your financial circumstances become difficult, unless you qualify for bankruptcy. But, it's very difficult to have federal student loans discharged in bankruptcy; this happens only rarely. Also, you can't cancel your student loans if you didn't get the education you expected, didn't get the job you expected, or didn't complete your education, unless you leave school for a reason that qualifies you for a discharge of your loan. Remember, your student loans belong to you; you have to pay them back.

- A loan, unlike a grant, is borrowed money that must be repaid.
- You must repay your loan even if you didn't like the education you received or you can't obtain employment after you graduate.
- You must keep the loan holder informed of a change in your name, address, telephone number, Social Security Number, or enrollment status.
- You must make payments on your loan even if you don't receive a bill or repayment notice. Billing statements are sent to you as a convenience, but you're obligated to make payments even if you don't receive any reminders.
- You can prepay the whole loan or any part of it at any time without penalty. This means you are paying some of the loan before it's due.
- If you apply for deferment, forbearance, or consolidation, you must continue to make payments on your loan until you have been notified that your request has been processed and approved.
- Your student loan account balance and status will be reported to national credit bureaus on a regular basis. Just as failing to repay your loan can damage your credit rating, repaying your loan responsibly can help you establish a good credit rating.
- The consequences of defaulting on a federal student loan are severe and long lasting.
- There are repayment options available to assist you if you're having trouble making payments.

Toolkit

College Preparation Checklist for Your Children

Pre-High School

- ❑ Start saving for college if you haven't already. Look into college savings plans that your state may offer.
- ❑ Take classes that challenge you.
- ❑ Do your best in school. If you are having difficulty, don't give up—get help from a teacher, tutor or mentor.

❑ Investigate which high schools or special programs will most benefit your future interests.

❑ Become involved in school- or community-based extracurricular activities that enable you to explore your interests, meet new people and learn new things.

High School Every Year

❑ Continue to save for college.

❑ Take challenging classes in core academic subjects: most colleges require four years of English, at least three years of social studies (history, civics, geography, economics, etc.), three years of mathematics, and three years of science, and many require two years of a foreign language.

❑ Round out your course load with classes in computer science and the arts. To increase your chances of receiving an Academic Competitiveness Grant in college, follow a "rigorous high school program." For more information, visit www.FederalStudentAid.ed.gov/funding.

Make the Connection on MFN!
www.eMilitary.org/YourMFN.html

Sign on to the address shown above and Make the Connection to more resources on this topic!

❑ Stay involved in school- or community-based extracurricular activities that interest you or enable you to explore career interests. Consider working or volunteering. *Remember—it's quality (not quantity) that counts.*

❑ Save copies of your report cards, awards, honors and best work for your academic portfolio.

❑ Athletes, artists, scholars and others should start collecting items for their portfolios (such as game tapes, newspaper clippings, stats, awards, artwork, photographs, school papers, etc.).

9th Grade

❑ Take challenging core classes. (Core subjects are listed above, under "Every Year.")

❑ Start planning for college and thinking about your career interests. At www.FederalStudentAid.ed.gov you can register with MyFSA and research your career and college options.

10th Grade

❑ Continue to take challenging core classes. (Core subjects are listed above, under "Every Year.")

❑ Meet with your school counselor or mentor to discuss colleges and their requirements.

- ❏ Talk to adults about what they like and dislike in their jobs and about what kind of education is needed for each kind of job.
- ❏ Consider taking a practice Preliminary SAT (PSAT), or the PLAN exam, also known as the "pre-ACT". Remember: Register for all tests in advance and be sure to give yourself time to prepare appropriately! If you have difficulty paying a registration fee, see your school counselor about getting a fee waiver.
- ❏ Plan to use your summer wisely: work, volunteer or take a summer course (away or at a local college).

11th Grade All Year

- ❏ Continue to save money for college.
- ❏ Continue to challenge yourself academically. Most colleges require four years of English, at least three years of social studies (history, civics, geography, economics, etc.), three years of mathematics, and three years of science, and many require two years of a foreign language.

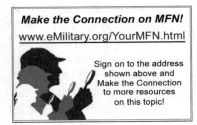

Make the Connection on MFN!
www.eMilitary.org/YourMFN.html

Sign on to the address shown above and Make the Connection to more resources on this topic!

- ❏ Round out your course load with classes in computer science and the arts. To increase your chances of receiving an Academic Competitiveness Grant in college, follow a "rigorous high school program." For more information, visit www.FederalStudentAid.ed.gov/funding.
- ❏ Stay involved in school- or community-based extracurricular activities that interest you or enable you to explore career interests. Consider working or volunteering. *Remember: it's quality (not quantity) that counts.*
- ❏ Update your portfolio. (A portfolio might include awards, game tapes, newspaper clippings, artwork, etc.)
- ❏ Talk to people you know who went to college to learn about what to expect.
- ❏ Research colleges that interest you. Visit them and talk to students. Make lists to help you compare different colleges. Think about things like location, size, special programs and college costs.
- ❏ Go to college fairs and presentations by college representatives.
- ❏ Investigate financial aid, including scholarships. Understand the different types of aid and sources for aid. Check your school's scholarship postings, colleges' financial aid Web pages and your library for directories of special scholarships.

❑ For more information about scholarships and federal student aid opportunities, visit

❑ www.FederalStudentAid.ed.gov.

Fall

❑ Take the Preliminary SAT/National Merit Scholarship Qualifying Test (PSAT/NMSQT). Even if you took it for practice last year, you must take the test in 11th grade to qualify for scholarships and programs associated with the National Merit Program.

❑ Write to your U.S. senator or representative if you would like to attend a U.S. military academy.

❑ See your school counselor if you are interested in participating in an ROTC program.

Spring

❑ Register for and take exams for college admission. When registering for and taking the SAT or ACT, enter "9999" as one of the college choices to have test scores sent to the Clearinghouse. Many colleges accept the SAT I or SAT II: Subject Test, while others accept the ACT. Check with colleges you are interested in to see what tests they require.

❑ Make sure you file with the NCAA (National Collegiate Athletic Association) Clearinghouse if you want to play for a Division I or II team.

Summer Before 12th Grade

❑ Narrow down the list of colleges you are interested in attending. If you can, visit schools that interest you.

❑ Contact colleges to request information and applications for admission. Ask about financial aid, admission requirements and deadlines.

❑ Decide whether you are going to apply under a particular college's early decision or early action program. Be sure to learn about the program deadlines and requirements.

❑ Begin preparing for the application process: draft application essays; collect writing samples; assemble portfolios or audition tapes.

❑ If you are an athlete and plan to play in college, contact the coaches at the schools to which you are applying and ask about intercollegiate and intramural sports programs and athletic scholarships.

❑ Remember: Register for all tests in advance and be sure to give yourself time to prepare appropriately! If you have difficulty paying a registration fee, see your school counselor about getting a fee waiver.

12th Grade All Year

- ❑ Keep taking classes that challenge you. Most colleges require four years of English, at least three years of social studies (history, civics, geography, economics, etc.), three years of mathematics, and three years of science, and many require two years of a foreign language. Round out your course load with classes in computer science and the arts. To increase your chances of receiving an Academic Competitiveness Grant in college, follow a "rigorous high school program." For more information, visit www.FederalStudentAid.ed.gov/funding.
- ❑ Update your portfolio. (A portfolio might include awards, game tapes, newspaper clippings, artwork, etc.)
- ❑ Work hard all year; second-semester grades can affect scholarship eligibility.
- ❑ Stay involved and seek leadership roles in your activities.

Fall

- ❑ Meet with your school counselor: are you on track to graduate and fulfill college admission requirements?
- ❑ If you haven't done so already, register for and take exams such as the SAT I, SAT II: Subject Test, or ACT for college admission. Check with the colleges you are interested in to see what tests they require.
- ❑ Apply to the colleges you have chosen. Prepare your application carefully. Follow the instructions, and *PAY CLOSE ATTENTION TO DEADLINES*!
- ❑ Well before your application deadlines, ask your counselor and teachers to submit required documents (e.g., transcript, letters of recommendation) to the colleges to which you're applying.
- ❑ To prepare to apply for federal student aid, be sure to get a PIN at www.pin.ed.gov so that you can complete your application and access your information online. One of your parents must also get a PIN.

Winter

- ❑ Encourage your parent(s) to complete income tax forms early. If your parent(s) have not completed the tax forms, you can provide estimated information on your federal student aid application, but remember to make any necessary changes later.
- ❑ As soon after Jan. 1 as possible, complete and submit your *Free Application for Federal Student Aid* (FAFSA), along with any other financial aid applications your school(s) of choice may require. You can complete the FAFSA online at www.fafsa.ed.gov or on paper, but completing the application online is faster and easier. You should submit your FAFSA by the earliest financial aid deadline of the schools to which you are applying, usually by early February.

❑ If you have questions about the federal student aid programs or need assistance with the application process, call 1-800-4-FED-AID (1-800-433-3243) or TTY for the hearing impaired, 1-800-730-8913.

❑ After you submit the FAFSA, you should receive your *Student Aid Report* (SAR) within one to three weeks. Quickly make any necessary corrections and submit them to the FAFSA processor.

❑ If the schools you are applying to require it, complete the CSS (College Scholarship Service) Profile. Many private colleges and universities use this information to help them award nonfederal student aid funds.

❑ Complete scholarship applications. Apply for as many as you can—you may be eligible for more than you think.

❑ Parents should check their eligibility for the Hope Credit, Lifetime Learning Credit or other tax benefits.

Spring

❑ Visit colleges that have invited you to enroll.

❑ Review your college acceptances and compare financial aid packages.

❑ When you decide which school you want to attend, notify that school of your commitment and submit any required financial deposit. Many schools require this notification and deposit by May 1.

❑ Remember: Register for all tests in advance and be sure to give yourself time to prepare appropriately! If you have difficulty paying a registration fee, see your school counselor about getting a fee waiver.

Source: www.FederalStudentAid.ed.gov/pubs

41 Getting Hired

From the Field with Megan Turak

Megan Turak is the daughter of a WWII Army veteran and spouse of a Vietnam era Marine, Executive Vice President and co-owner of The Military Family Network, former Medical Records Manager with the Department of Veteran Affairs, a published writer of informative topics positively impacting the well-being of military families and has over twenty combined years of experience in executive leadership in the financial management and communications industries.

Congratulations, military spouses! According to employment figures, you are a workforce that possesses more education, more skill sets, more qualifications, better training with more diversified work experiences, and greater hours of volunteerism than the average American worker. In addition, you are likely to have a strong work ethic, will be more dependable, more reliable, and prompt. You, military spouse, are an employer's dream!

But, before you get too giddy, there's some bad news, too. Unfortunately, you are also one of our nation's best-kept secrets. And, as a result, some employer's, operating from a "penny-wise, pound-foolish" perspective and fearful of losing training dollars when you PCS, will miss out on some of the greatest talent available to them. As a result, you are often underemployed, underpaid, and overqualified for the jobs you perform. And, although you feel its sting in your household income and feel its bite in your daily living, to you, it's a sacrifice you make for the country you love.

Now that you understand how valuable you and your services are to others, let's explore how you can personally reap more of the rewards for yourself and your family!

Start by expanding your job search skills, and then initiate a career plan that incorporates a strategy for optimizing the advantages of your mobile lifestyle.

It will be very important for you to become a super sleuth. Develop the habit of discovering resources that you can tap into that will keep you ahead of the employment curve. These resources might be found through the Internet—the government websites in particular have some amazing tools and features—as well as libraries, state-funded workforce centers, colleges, and universities. Of course, you'll contact your military employment office, too. Almost all Family

> **"..don't underestimate what the local business chamber of commerce has available, and take some time to contact and visit businesses that interest you."**

Support Centers have military spouse employment program managers. These individuals will work with you one-on-one to help you write your resume, develop your interviewing skills, and match you with an employer. Also, don't underestimate what the local business chamber of commerce has available, and take some time to contact and visit businesses that interest you. Individuals in both of these places will have a wealth of knowledge that will help you in securing desired employment.

Practice the art of networking and building relationships. Join professional groups, volunteer, tell everyone you meet what you're doing, want you want, and most importantly, how they can help. If you aren't sure what you want or aren't certain whether a job meets your skills, then talk to people about your skills and abilities! Ask people what they do and how they got started. Get interested! Contact your local veteran service organization—many of them have chapters in hundreds of locations, especially near military installations. Ask them for help—especially if you will be relocating. See if they would be willing to connect you with the veterans in the local chapter where you will be moving. Many of these veterans are also business people as well as being service-oriented and connected with community organizations and local government. If they're willing to share their relationships with you, it can make the employment search process so much warmer and friendlier. Soon you will find opportunities appearing that you could never have imagined!

Become organized. Map out a plan and then, work your plan. It's OK if it changes from time to time: there is no way for you to know all of the opportunities that will present themselves to you. Make changes, modify, but keep moving. Take this seriously especially if you're relocating to another town where you are uncertain of the employment landscape. You will need to spend some time in preparation—before you move—to check out the resources and opportuni-

> **"Make changes, modify, but keep moving."**

ties available. And, it's a good time to do it. You'll be less stressed and better able to focus on one objective as opposed to when you're actively trying to settle in from the moving process. And, you'll feel more confident that you know where to begin and how to manage your time and job-hunting prospects.

Handling Interruptions

So now that you have mastered multiple job seeking skills, what do you do about the interruptions in your career progression and advancement? Many military spouses feel frustrated because this job disruption causes them to move from one entry-level position to another. It wreaks havoc on your retirement plans, too! One way to address this is to seek employment in well-established, national companies that offer the availability of transferring your position with their firm, thereby retaining your seniority, benefits, and tenure with the company. Another avenue for overcoming this challenge is to continue your education. While you may not have years of experience progressing through your industry of choice, you may be able to rise above the entry-level dilemma by securing an advance degree. The federal government often uses education in lieu of experience for promoting their employees.

Speaking about federal employment, make sure to examine your eligibility for spousal preferences. This is an attempt to level the playing field by providing you a minimal advantage to compensate you for your career disruptions. Make sure to look into unemployment compensation as well. Some states, like Texas, now provide benefits to dislocated spouses to overcome the economic impact on the family.

If job transitions stateside are a bother, you can imagine how your counterparts feel when they learn they are moving overseas! Overseas employment opportunities are more difficult to find. You will need to be diligent, persistent, and resourceful. Get your butt in to see that family program manager! They will know how to work the local opportunities and where to uncover employment advantages, as well as connect you to federal job openings.

> "Some states, like Texas, now provide benefits to dislocated spouses to overcome the economic impact on the family."

For example, all of the military families exiting the installations will undoubtedly create vacancies. Since these families are processing out, this information will become readily known. And then, you arrive; ready to snap up the job! Typical overseas jobs include federal employment non-appropriated funds positions on the installations like MWR, teaching English as a second language, DoD schools, and home-based childcare. In addition, larger companies with an overseas presence may offer you the option of Internet-based or telecommuting job positions.

Now, it's up to you. You've got the tools. You can make it happen. Get seen, get heard, get hired!

 **FAQs**

Q. What is military spouse preference?

A. *Military spouse preference provides priority in the employment selection process for military spouses who are relocating as a result of their military spouse's PCS. Spouse preference does not apply to separation or retirement moves. Spouse preference may be used for most vacant positions in DoD and applies only within the commuting area of the permanent duty station of the sponsor. Spouse preference is not limited to the branch of military in which the sponsor is serving, or to only those who have previously worked for the federal government. Spouses must be found best qualified for the position and may exercise preference no more than one time per permanent relocation of the sponsor.*

Preference does not mean that positions will be created or made available, especially for the military spouses, or that spouses will be given any special appointing authority. Preference does not provide any guarantee of employment.

For more information on Military Spouse Preference, visit My Army Life Too at:

http://www.myarmylifetoo.com/ and search for Military Spouse Employment

Q. What is unemployment compensation?

A. *According to the U.S. Department of Labor, unemployment compensation is a benefit paid to individuals who are unemployed and looking for work. Each state administers an unemployment program within minimum guidelines set forth by the federal government.*

Unemployment payments (compensation) are intended to provide the unemployed worker time to find a new job equivalent to the one lost without major financial distress. Payments are intended to meet the basic necessities of life (food, shelter, and clothing) while a search for work takes place. However benefits are paid as a matter of right and are not based on need.

Q. Is unemployment compensation available for relocating military spouses?

A. *A spouse's eligibility is determined by the state in which he or she worked prior to relocating, and eligibility differs from state to state, so it is advisable to contact your unemployment office when in receipt of orders.*

Some states view termination of employment by military spouses as "voluntary," and the spouse is rendered ineligible for benefits. Other states recognize that personnel in the armed forces have no control over reassignments to different geographical locations. Therefore, these states view terminations of employment by military spouses as "involuntary," and the spouses are rendered eligible for the benefit.

Q. How do I apply for compensation?

A. *Your state employment office administers the program. Therefore, requirements and benefits will vary from state to state. Because of this, only the office where you apply will be able to tell you the amount and duration of your entitlement. Employment offices are generally listed in telephone book "blue pages" under the state government's Department of Labor and Unemployment Insurance Compensation Division. You may also wish to try this Cornell Law School website: http://www.law.cornell.edu/topics/unemployment_compensation.html.*

 Need to Know

Around the web for Check Lists

Employment Readiness Checklist:
A great check list for employment and for transition is available at the My Army Life Too website. We recommend that you visit it and check under employment for this information.
http://www.myarmylifetoo.com/

Employment Preference Assessments
This is a questionnaire that assesses your interest in performing certain duties and then matches your interests with various occupations: http://www.usajobs.opm.gov/careers/explor/guideq.asp

Investigate tasks you like to do, and they will be matched to jobs available in the federal government. This list also contains some of the most common occupations in the federal government: http://www.usajobs.opm.gov/careers/explor/jobint1.asp

Comparing opportunities at different locations

Sperling's "Best Places" allows for the comparison of two geographical locations for a number of important categories like salaries, taxes, housing, food, etc.: http://www.bestplaces.net/col/

Salary Calculator and tools for assessing employment opportunities

- ❑ Homefair.com: Salary Calculator and much more: http://www.homefair.com/homefair/calc/salcalc.html
- ❑ America's CareerInfo Net: Evaluating a job offer: http://www.acinet.org/acinet/crl/library.aspx?PostVal=10&CATID=78
- ❑ Salary.com: http://www.salary.com/salary/layoutscripts/sall_display.asp

Make the Connection on MFN!
www.eMilitary.org/YourMFN.html

Sign on to the address shown above and Make the Connection to more resources on this topic!

Avoiding Employment Scams and other Common Sense Tips

- ❑ Overseas Digest: avoiding job scams and other tips: http://www.overseasdigest.com/scams.htm
- ❑ Federal Trade Commission: Work-at-Home warnings: http://www.ftc.gov/bcp/conline/pubs/invest/homewrk.htm
- ❑ Monster.com article on working abroad: http://workabroad.monster.com/articles/tentips/

42   Working from Home

From the Field with Tara Crooks

Tara Crooks is a freelance writer, talk show host, and trainer. She currently owns and operates two websites; www.ArmyWifeTalkRadio.com and www. FieldProblems.com, Tara's journey with the military began in 1998 when she married her husband. Her family, or "Household 6", includes her husband, Kevin (US ARMY) their daughter, Wrena and two dogs and a cat. Tara resides with her family in Richmond Hill, GA.

Less than twenty years ago, large numbers of women slowly began making their way into the workforce, some out of necessity and some out of wanting a career outside of the home. It is getting increasingly harder to make ends meet with just one income. Many women have since bridged the gap in income while simultaneously stressing the importance of staying home with their children by starting their own home-based businesses.

What progress! Owning a home-based business does more than just allow you to earn a living, it gives you the freedom to test your limits and see what you can accomplish. There are many benefits to working from home: low overhead, no need for childcare, tax deductions, flexibility, safety, security, and it's simple to relocate.

However rewarding, working from home is harder than it seems. No matter what your choice for working from home might be, you need to realize a few things before you take the plunge.

Working at home requires discipline. All too often individuals want the money but they do not want the work. Success takes work. Images of watching daytime TV or meeting the girls for lunch everyday must be set aside. Self-employed people must keep focused on setting up the business and sticking to deadlines. Remember, you have not said goodbye to the boss. The boss you have now is you, your customers, and your success.

If you work from home you must expect the unexpected. You must be prepared to adjust your schedule at any given moment for any number of reasons—a sick child, a backed up drain, or an upset client.

You might have to give something up to work at home. Whether you have a full-time job with a steady income or are just starting out and wanting to make some spending money, you will have to invest either your time or your money. Remember millions don't fall off trees so expect to put something toward your business.

You must always be on top of your game. To run a business as well as manage a household takes determination and scheduling. You may not feel like you have a schedule, but take a look at your day/week and see how you are spending your time.

> **"To run a business as well as manage a household takes determination and scheduling."**

The reality is that tomorrow you will not wake up and "sign-up" to work from home. Your paycheck will not be instant. Legitimate employers with home-based jobs hire the same way traditional employers do. There will be an application process and possibly an interview or test. Therefore, it is a good idea to have a resume written that outlines your skills and experiences.

If you choose direct sales, your sign-up might be instant, but the money will not. You will have to work hard to plan parties and online sales. You will also have a lot of networking to do if you plan on making it a long-term success. Plan your work and work your plan.

Lastly, if you choose to develop your own business concept, your work will encompass hours of research and development, marketing and promotion, and business planning.

I'm most certainly not trying to scare you about working from home. It is the most rewarding thing I have ever done. Military life takes us through many twists and turns, and I can always take my business with me.

 **FAQs**

Q. How do I find a genuine telecommuting job?

A. *Legitimate employers with home-based jobs hire the same way traditional employers do. There will be an application process and possibly an interview or test. The key to finding work-at-home jobs is to search where people post jobs. Employers are not looking for home workers. They are looking for qualified people to fill a position, and they advertise on job-related sites. The com-*

petition for a work-at-home job will be fierce. You need to set your submission apart from the rest by having a professional, error-free resume.

Q. How do I keep from getting scammed?

A. *The Better Business Bureau offers these tips (http://www.bbb.org/Alerts/ article.asp?ID=436). Look out for businesses that:*
- "Never offer you regular salaried employment.
- Promise you huge profits and big part-time earnings.
- Use personal testimonials but never identify the person so that you can verify their experience.
- Require money for instructions or merchandise before telling you how the plan operates.
- Assure you of guaranteed markets and a huge demand for your handiwork.
- Tell you that no experience is necessary.
- Take your money and give you little or nothing in return except heartbreak and grief."

Q. What is a direct sales company?

A. *The American Marketing Association defines direct selling as: "a marketing approach that involves direct sales of goods and services to consumers through personal explanation and demonstrations, frequently in their home or place of work.."*

A direct sales company is a company such as Avon, Mary Kay, Discover Toys, Pampered Chef, where the company itself offers a "consultant" opportunity for you to do the direct selling of their product.

The Military Family Network offers a direct sales contracting opportunity to all military spouses and veterans who want to work from home. They help the network expand the Military Family Neighbor of Choice Business Network by signing up businesses for a fee. Spouses get a commission of each sale. More information is available by emailing info@emilitary.org

Q. How do I decide what direct sales company is best for me?

A. *First, take a peek at this website that has a list of over ninety direct sales businesses: http://www.directsellingopportunities.com/search_opportunities Then base your decision on the following:*

- Passion: your interest, excitement, and general feeling about the company and products
- Products: place an order, use the products, and test their worth to you. Do you believe in the product? Would you buy them?
- Investment: most companies will have an initial investment, so check to make sure this is in line with your budget.
- Minimums: do you have to meet a sales quota, party quota, or call quota?
- Compensation: what amount of money are you going to make for the work that you put into this business?
- Control and support: is there a support system and do you have control over your business?
- Advertising: are you in charge of all of your advertising or will the company do it for you? Do they have advertising in place?

Q. Where do I start if I have a business idea of my own?

A. *First ask yourself if there is a market for your product or service, and then research it. Find out for yourself, first-hand, just how many people there are in your area who are interested in your proposed product or service and would be "willing to stand in line and pay money for it." Also, don't forget to ask yourself why others aren't already doing what you are proposing to do. This simple question may help you to think about your idea in a way that exposes prospective problems or obstacles and, in the long run, may save you both time and money.*

Also, find out if your proposed business has any competitors. This is known as defining your market and pinpointing your customers. This will also allow you to find out what others are charging for their product/service. Regardless of what kind of business you start, you must have the capital and the available time to sustain your business.

Create a business plan. Get educated and make a list of what you should do. A good place to start is with the Small Business Administration. They have an abundance of resources and individuals to help you. The Service Corps of Retired Executives (SCORE) is one of them. And, if you are a veteran, they offer some really great programs for you, too. In the age of the Internet, you can find most of this information very simply by searching online using keywords: "small business startup" or "home business startup." Remember, if you fail to plan, you plan to fail.

Need to Know

Whether you choose to work from home by telecommuting, direct sales, or developing your own home business, the following checklist will help you with your start-up.

- ❑ Create your resume.
- ❑ Find a mentor or another businessperson you can go to for advice.
- ❑ Research the product or service.
- ❑ Choose a business.
- ❑ Create a business plan.
- ❑ Create a business identity (name and/or logo and slogan).
- ❑ Determine your niche market and profitability.
- ❑ Decide on funding (grants, loans, credit, etc.).
- ❑ Develop a budget.
- ❑ Research professional and trade associations.
- ❑ Get an education (brush up on techniques or skills needed for your new endeavor).
- ❑ Check with local and state regulations for home-based businesses.
- ❑ Decide on sole proprietorship, LLC, partnership, etc.
- ❑ Get your business license or certificate.
- ❑ Purchase insurance (if needed).
- ❑ Purchase equipment (fax, phone, computer, etc.).
- ❑ Organize your office.
- ❑ Get business cards.
- ❑ Set up your website.
- ❑ Set goals for your productivity.
- ❑ Make your schedule.
- ❑ Organize your inventory and supplies.
- ❑ Develop a marketing plan.
- ❑ Network.
- ❑ Advertise.
- ❑ Endure (don't give up, success takes hard work and time).

Make the Connection on MFN!
www.eMilitary.org/YourMFN.html

Sign on to the address shown above and Make the Connection to more resources on this topic!

43 Volunteer: Make Success Happen

From the Field with Megan Turak

Megan Turak is the daughter of a WWII Army veteran and spouse of a Vietnam era Marine, Executive Vice President and co-owner of The Military Family Network, former Medical Records Manager with the Department of Veteran Affairs, a published writer of informative topics positively impacting the well-being of military families and has over twenty combined years of experience in executive leadership in the financial, management and communication industries.

People hire people, not resumes

If this is true, (and it is), then why spend so much time developing the perfect dossier recording your achievements, documenting your experiences, and highlighting your accomplishments and specializations? Doesn't this effort have some value?

Of course it does—but it only serves as a manner of introduction, a method for gaining the interview. After that, you're on your own. You are responsible for communicating to your future employer that you are the ideal candidate for the job and that, if they don't hire you, they are missing out on a fantastic opportunity not only to know you better, but also to bring a certain measure of success to their company.

The routine of submitting resumes and preparing to showcase yourself for the interview process adds up to one thing: a lot of stress. After all, how do you effectively encapsulate all of your experiences and communicate your potential in fifteen minutes? An hour? There's got to be an easier way. And there is.

Besides worrying about how to find a job to pay the bills, what else are you doing while waiting for opportunity to knock? Many individuals who are between jobs or changing careers employ avoidance tactics or methods of distraction like sleeping late, watching television, surfing the Internet—even researching opportunities they never pursue. These activities may provide temporary relief, but rarely leave you feeling good about yourself or your situation.

So here's something you can try that is guaranteed to work: volunteer.

Yes, volunteerism not only leaves you feeling productive and good about yourself, but also provides you with the opportunity to learn new skills and sharpen old ones. Besides, it helps you to gain a realistic outlook about your situation and keeps you grounded and confident.

In addition, and perhaps most importantly, it provides you with the opportunity to interact with others and to get your name known. As an example, The Military Family Network and all their community partners listed elsewhere in this book, provide professional volunteer opportunities that will expose you to area businesses and civic and military leadership. In other words, volunteering can help introduce you to a wide array of individuals who you can network with for the job you want. Most employers would prefer to hire someone brought to their attention through a personal recommendation. They also like to hire from within, if possible. Who knows? Maybe that volunteer position could become the job you've always wanted.

So, volunteer; in helping others, you may just be helping yourself.

Don't wait for success—make it happen!

 **FAQs**

Q. Are there any volunteer opportunities where I can get experience and get paid, too?

A. *Yes. One example is AmeriCorps, which is like the Peace Corps, but here at home. It offers experience, and depending on the assignment, the potential for a modest stipend and/or housing benefit. It is unlikely that this amount will provide an opportunity to save, but AmeriCorps offers an educational allowance that can be applied to furthering your educational goals. Visit their website for more information. www.americorps.gov*

Q. Is there any recognition or award possibilities out there for community volunteering that would look good on my college application or resume?

A. *Absolutely. The Military Family Network is a certifying organization for the Presidential Volunteer Service Award. You can register as a group or individual for what your do in support of military families and we will give you* *access to tools to track your hours. After a certain amount of hours (50 for youth and 200 for adults) we can certify your time and you can get an award and letter from the President of the United States. More information about this program may be found at www.eMilitary.org/cchome.html.*

Q. I want to help. How can I find a place to volunteer my time and services?

A. *Volunteers are always in short supply. You don't have to look far or wide to find an opportunity that's right for you. Visit the library, newspaper or your military family support service. Call the local hospitals and social service agencies. Check out the nonprofit organizations in your area. Visit some of the resources at the end of this chapter. Ask at your church or temple, school or local veteran service*

Volunteer with The Military Family Network by visiting www.eMilitary.org/cchome.html MFN is an official certifying organization for the Presidential Volunteer Service Award.

organization. Or, visit the community connection section of this book and contact one of the organizations helping service members and their families to see how you can help. You can even find a virtual volunteer opportunity! Check with The Military Family Network if this appeals to you.

Q. What are some common installation volunteer opportunities?

A. *Formal volunteering entails registering with the Family Support/Family Readiness Center on the Installation and having a signed Volunteer Agreement on file with the organization for which you are volunteering. Complete Volunteer Agreement form (DD Form 2793) and have hours tracked on a volunteer time record. Usually volunteers receive paid childcare through the certifying volunteering agency.*

Q. What installation volunteer opportunities will track for award programs?

A. *Here are several of the volunteer opportunities that will track for award programs:*

Family Support/Family Readiness Center Administrative Support: The additional benefit here is that hiring typically comes from those who have a history of volunteering for the center.

Family Readiness and Family Support Groups: Operate like mini-non-profit organizations directly supporting your spouses unit.

American Red Cross: Offers a wide variety of volunteer opportunities at the installation community hospital or in the American Red Cross Station. FREE childcare is available for volunteers.

Cub/Boy Scouts: Volunteer to help boys between the ages of five and eleven in a Cub Scout program or volunteer to help boys between the ages of eleven and eighteen in a Boy Scout program. Adult volunteers are always needed.

Girl Scouts: Volunteer to help girls between the ages of 5-18 in a Girl Scout program.

Installation Schools: "Make a Difference in a Child's Life—Be a Mentor." Volunteer one day a week for thirty minutes for a minimum of six weeks and make a difference in a child's life.

Mayors: Mayors are volunteers that reside in a housing area on post who commit at least ten hours per month to helping their housing community. The Mayors Council is very active in all community events and informs neighbors of opportunities within the community. Adult volunteers are needed.

Thrift Shop: Looking for a volunteer opportunity to meet new people? Volunteer for installation Thrift Shop and have instant relationships develop. You usually have the inside scoop on great deals! FREE childcare is available for volunteers.

Youth Sports: Choose your favorite sport and have fun with your child and others. Adult volunteers are needed as coaches and assistant coaches for all sports, i.e., basketball, football, soccer, baseball, roller hockey, etc.

Q. Can I use volunteer experience the same as paid experience for job applications and resume preparation?

A. *Yes, and volunteering is a great way to obtain more skills and fine-tune those you already have. Experience you gain through volunteer work should be included in resumes and job applications.*

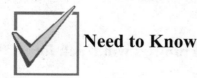 **Need to Know**

Ten Reasons to Volunteer
- Meet new people
- Feel connected, purposeful, and hopeful
- Explore and broaden areas of interest

- Develop experiences in your field of study
- Build new skills
- Network for career positions
- Help others
- Get involved with issues you care about, a mission, and its values
- Provide a way to act upon your faith
- Strengthen your resume

Ten Things to Ask Yourself Before Volunteering

- Do I have time?
- How much time do I have?
- When can I volunteer? What will my schedule permit?
- What kind of commitment can I make? For how long?
- What kind of work can I do or help can I give?
- Do I prefer working alone or with others? Can I work independently?
- Am I willing to contribute personal resources?
- What level of responsibility am I comfortable with?
- Do I have any restrictions on my ability to volunteer or for certain types of work?
- What are my personal goals and what do I hope to achieve through my volunteerism?

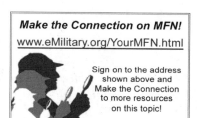

Make the Connection on MFN!
www.eMilitary.org/YourMFN.html

Sign on to the address shown above and Make the Connection to more resources on this topic!

44 Beyond the BDU: Transitioning from the Military

From the Field with Don Mertz

Don Mertz is a retired United States Air Force service member. He lives in Hampton Virginia with his spouse Peggy Mertz and their son.

Transitioning from the military is a time of excitement; you feel a personal sense of accomplishment and, at the same time, apprehension. While one part of your life is coming to a close, another is now beginning. Although this time may occasionally feel distressing because you are replacing the old with the new, remember that the military has prepared you well. You have all you need to thrive; you may only need to apply your talents and skills a little differently. Change doesn't have to be scary; in fact, this change can be a really good thing when you think of it as a natural culmination of all of the training, experiences and successes you have achieved in your military career. The purpose of this chapter, then, is to help you minimize your apprehension, enjoy your accomplishments, while preparing you to move on to the next stage of your life.

If I were limited to giving one bit of advice, it would be that it's never too early to begin planning for life after military retirement. As you progress through your career, keep an eye towards the civilian sector so that you can spot opportunities or places where your skills and job training could easily transfer. Keep informed as well as you can. Also, keep retirement a recurring topic in your home with your spouse and imagine different transition scenarios. Make sure you take the time to understand your spouse's expectations. You will want to consider how your retirement will affect your family, too. But when you submit your retirement papers for approval, it's definitely time to get serious. By now, you and your spouse will have already discussed your future options, but may still be in the decision-making process. In most cases, your spouse will have sacrificed life objectives for your military career. Together, you may decide to follow your spouse's career, or agree that you will continue to be in the breadwinner role.

The challenge is to become motivated to begin your transition planning while still having a full workload at the unit. Given that you'll soon be retired, you should approach your supervisor and discuss his or her expectations regarding your workload.

Most supervisors will understand your need since they too will eventually face the retirement process. You should give up the long-standing desire to take on more duties and begin transitioning your responsibilities to your replacement, or at least someone who will cover for you until your replacement arrives.

> **Most supervisors will understand your need since they too will eventually face the retirement process.**

Traditionally, the replacement rarely arrives before you go on terminal leave. Thus, training someone to cover for you is vital, since you'll be spending increased amounts of time away from the unit as you prepare to transition out.

Remember, the unit still has to get the mission done, with or without you. You will be remembered, in part, by how you left the unit. Did you leave your duties in a shambles for others to clean up? Or, did you leave everything in good shape, documented and easy to find with a well-trained replacement to carry on your duties?

The New Job

When you start your new civilian position, be advised that the first week or more after starting will be filled with briefings, paperwork, human resources presentations, and, ultimately, decisions on your part. During this time, it's a good idea to have with you the same kind of background information and documentation that you took to the interview.

Once you actually begin the work of your new employment, ask more questions as opposed to making lots of statements. Learn the company's internal procedures, take any training courses and orientation lessons they assign, and begin to learn the company's culture.

At this time, it's prudent to volunteer to assist your new co-workers with their tasks even if it's not your project. In this way, you'll learn faster and show that you're a team player, who is not afraid to get his hands dirty.

FAQs

Q. How important are security clearances?

A. *Having a security clearance today is extremely important. An active clearance tells a potential employer that the candidate has been vetted and has been judged to be trustworthy. Time and effort spent on troubled employees drains a company's time, resources, and productivity. Companies in the defense industry are well served by those who already hold a clearance. Active clearances alleviate the need for companies to pay for periodic reinvestigations for a specified period of time.*

Q. When should I start interviewing and how do I go about it?

A. *About two to three months from your terminal leave date; you should start receiving invitations to interview with interested companies. In preparation for these interviews, conduct more research into the company in question. Know who they are, what services they provide, and how you may be able to help them. It may be a good idea to prepare a spreadsheet with information you feel is pertinent about the company and about your experience. My spreadsheet included the following information: company; POC name, e-mail address, and phone number; company website; notes detailing history of contact (when, where, what happened); follow-up action and dates; and a rating as to the desire to work for the company; and a rating as to the probability of getting hired.*

The day before your interview, make sure you have reference material collected and are ready to go. Your reference material should include: extra resumes, your reference list, your last SF86 security clearance form (if applicable), a copy of your spreadsheet, business cards, etc.

On the day of the interview, plan your schedule in reverse to ensure that you have ample time to get dressed, travel to the interview site, and have a few minutes to relax before the event. Be aware that you are technically in the interview from the time you enter the company's

> **"Greet the receptionist and interviewer with confidence."**

property until you leave the property. This includes waiting in your car or sitting in the receptionist's area. Greet the receptionist and interviewer with confidence.

Do not be upset by changes in schedules or in interview forums as previously described to you, etc. As an example, the interviewer may bring in additional people to talk to you—one after another, or together in a panel-like forum. If your resume describes a specific technical skill, be prepared to demonstrate your ability to perform that task.

Upon completion of the interview, thank everyone involved with a handshake. Once back home, write out your impressions of the interview in the spreadsheet with any follow-up actions noted. Normally, the interviewer will tell you they will get back to you in seven to ten days. During this intervening period, write a thank you note to the interviewer and send it either by regular mail or by email. Although e-mail is faster and more time efficient for the receiver, handwriting a personal note is sometimes more effective.

Be prepared for follow-up interviews. During these interviews, the company is more likely to bring in additional people to talk to you, including higher-level staff.

> **"Be prepared for follow-up interviews."**

If the company does not contact you, don't be afraid to contact them to see if you received the job. If you don't receive the offer, take a moment to ask the interviewer why and what you can do in the future to secure a position with the company. Tell them that they were your first choice (if they were) and that you would like them to keep your resume on file should another position become available. You may also want to ask them if they know of any other companies in the industry currently looking to fill similar positions. (This may seem bold; but often, individuals network with their counterparts within an industry and have a lot of transferable job knowledge that they may be willing to share with you.)

Q. I am not sure what the next step is. Do I get another job? Do I try to stay in the same field?

A. *After twenty-plus years in the military, you must decide whether you want to have a career or a job. There is a difference, and your decision may be based on financial necessity rather than your desire. I define a career as a long-term commitment where you are willing to apply yourself fully to the tasks at hand, work whatever hours are required, and meet all necessary responsibilities to reach a certain goal. In many ways, this is not too different from your days in the military. Normally, your pay will reflect this commitment.*

On the other hand, you may decide to step back and focus your work efforts in something less stressful, or you may even pursue a position completely unrelated to your military experiences, knowledge, and training. This may result in reduced income, but it will most likely lead to greater quality of life, i.e., more time off, better hours, more time at home, less stress, etc. Whatever the outcome, all of these factors need to be weighed and a family decision made, allowing enough time for you to prepare.

Whether you decide on a job or a career, you will need to go through the job search adventure. As soon as it is practical, sign up for the Transition Assistance Program (TAP) at your local Family Support Center or equivalent. No program can possibly prepare you with all there is to know about the latest in transition, benefits, interviewing, job trends, and procedures, but TAP is the best overall source for information and does a good job at orienting you to the employment search process. TAP brings in people – experts and speakers - who are current on employment trends and the tools retirees need to successfully transition.

> **"Whether you decide on a job or a career, you will need to go through the job search adventure."**

At a minimum, you'll benefit from networking with those who are in the seminar with you. You'll also learn first hand about job fairs, interviewing, and working through the local veterans' employment commission to get into the "system." The best advice for those going through TAP is: go in with an open mind, ask questions, learn, and build contacts. This is your first opportunity to be a mister or misses (After all, you have been called by your rank for a long time). At the conclusion of TAP, build a schedule that reflects events all the way out to your projected terminal leave. Include job fairs, milestones noted on the TAP checklist you received, out processing tasks, leave, projected TDYs, etc. This schedule is a confidence builder and helps ensure you are ready to move on once terminal leave begins.

Q. How to I go about job hunting? It seems so overwhelming. A lot of companies are asking me if I would relocate. What do I do?

A. *Job hunting is not an easy process. Even if you have a good idea what you want to do, the numerous options can leave you feeling confused and indecisive. A mistake many make is the decision to live in a certain location, and then find a job. On the contrary, you should go where the opportunities are and live there.*

> **"… you should go where the opportunities are and live there."**

Even if you do it the "normal way" and base your search on a given location, build a spreadsheet to track your progress. This administrative tool will keep your job search focused, organized and moving forward. As I mentioned before but it's worth repeating here, my spreadsheet included the following information: company; POC name, e-mail address, and phone number; company website; notes detailing history of contact (when, where, what happened); follow-up action and dates; and a rating as to the desire to work for the company; and a rating as to the probability of getting hired. I found this method to be invaluable, especially if you start your exploratory job search more than three months before your retirement date.

Q. How do I know when to take a job offer?

A. *Once a company is interested in you, they'll make an offer. Do not necessarily take the first offer you receive. Additionally, no company expects you to accept an offer without taking time to think about it. Sometimes, the offer will come in the mail, with a follow-up phone call from the company's human resources person or the interviewer. Normally, you get five to seven days to consider the offer before an answer is expected.*

Offers should not be just a salary figure. Today's competitive environment also leads to benefit packages that include such advantages as medical care, dental care, insurance, retirement and investment plans, paid time off, personal days, etc. Consider these packages with your family's situation in mind. In addition, think about the company culture and work environment. Was it friendly and inviting? Can you see yourself happy working there?

Additionally, it's a good idea to create an estimated budget to ensure that the salary offer will meet your lifestyle expectations. If you believe that the pay offer is too low, don't hesitate to negotiate. The company may be willing to meet your need. Once you accept an offer, the company will discuss your start date. You have a say in this, too. In fact, now is the time to articulate anything about your new job that is important to you: money, work hours, location, start date, etc. One way to think about this is as your 'honeymoon' period. A lot of times, especially if you are a highly desired applicant, a company will consider your proposals seriously. They may not always agree to them, but then again, they may. You won't know unless you ask. Just remember, this is not the time to be demanding or unreasonable; it is, however, a fair time to address any of your job concerns. And finally, as a professional courtesy, you should notify any other company who was interested in you that you have taken another offer.

Need to Know

Job Fairs

You will learn about job fairs in TAP, but some things need to be emphasized.

Research: Conduct preliminary research on the companies that will be present.
Have a good idea what the company does and
where they do it. Rarely are they there to fill
positions in some other geographic location.
In this day of company mergers, ensure you
know what the particular business elements of
the companies are. Namely, large companies
have many divisions with similar names who
do not work together and seek different specialties.

Make the Connection on MFN!
www.eMilitary.org/YourMFN.html

Sign on to the address
shown above and
Make the Connection
to more resources
on this topic!

The First Time: For initial job fairs, take a stack of general resumes with you
that cover your whole career and can go to any company present.

Your Appearance: Your appearance at the job fair is critical. Do not attend in
uniform unless you have to; this shows that you are not ready to transition.
Wear a suit (or equivalent) that is clean, well fitting, and professional. It makes
a great first impression and will show that you are genuinely interested in getting hired.

Talking Job Fair Talk: The next point is to speak to the recruiter in a confident
(but not arrogant) manner. Be articulate in your language and professional in
your demeanor. Tell the recruiter why you're interested in his or her company,
but don't get too detailed in your technical knowledge since the recruiter is
normally a human resource specialist and not a specialist in your career field.

After the Fair: Soon after the job fair, input the results in the spreadsheet
while it is still fresh in your mind. Be sure to add follow-up dates that will
prompt you for further action. Be sure to note the correct instructions for sending electronic resumes to the human resources person to whom you talked.
When e-mailing resumes, tailor the resume a bit to the company in question.
Use a cover letter – even if it is in the body of the email. Modify the file name
to reflect the company receiving the resume and the date sent. This will assist
in tracking if you end up sending a follow-up resume to them.

Interview: Once you get an interview opportunity, you should tailor your resume
to the interviewing company or the specific position you are applying for.

45 Protecting Your Civilian Career

From the Field with Bob Hollingsworth

Bob Hollingsworth is the Executive Director of the National Committee for Employer Support of the Guard and Reserve (ESGR)

With nearly half of our military manpower in the National Guard and Reserve, our national security depends upon a strong and viable Reserve Component. A major characteristic that distinguishes Guardsmen and Reservists from their Active Component counterparts is that the Army, Marine Corps, Navy, Air Force, and Coast Guard share their Reserve Component members with civilian employers.

In 1972, the Department of Defense established Employer Support of the Guard and Reserve (ESGR) to gain and maintain support from civilian employers for this shared resource—the men and women of the National Guard and Reserve. ESGR provides free education, consultation, and if necessary, mediation for civilian employers of National Guard and Reserve employees.

ESGR operates through fifty-six field committees located in each state, the District of Columbia, Puerto Rico, Guam, the Virgin Islands, and Europe. Primarily staffed by dedicated volunteers from diverse backgrounds, ESGR field committees administer ESGR award programs and conduct employer outreach activities such as Bosslifts and "Briefings with the Boss." At the request of an employer or Reserve Component member, ESGR ombudsmen can mediate disputes that arise from an employee's military service obligation.

Congress recognized the importance of a strong Reserve Component and passed the Uniformed Services Employment and Reemployment Rights Act (USERRA) in 1994. USERRA is the federal law that protects the civilian employment of Guardsmen and Reservists. USERRA requires civilian employers to provide Guardsmen and Reservists with leaves of absence for military duty, prompt reinstatement upon return from military duty, reinstatement of employee benefits upon return, training or retraining as needed, and protection against discrimination on the basis of military service. USERRA also outlines the service member's responsibility to provide his or her civilian employer with prior notice to employer, serve under honorable conditions, and to return to work in a timely fashion.

The relationship between the civilian employer and the Guardsman or Reservist works best when both parties mutually respect each other's needs. Guardsmen and Reservists can establish trust with their civilian employer by providing advance notice of upcoming absences due to training or deployment. Employers can establish trust by assuring Guardsmen and Reservists that their service is valued and supported by the company.

> **"Your civilian employer is permitted and encouraged to call your commanding officer with questions about your service.'**

For more information on USERRA and employer support, please visit the ESGR website at www.esgr.mil or call 1-800-336-4590.

 **FAQs**

Q. How much notice am I required to give to my employer, prior to a period of service?

A. *We (ESGR) recommend that Reservists and National Guard members give as much advance notice as possible, but USERRA does not specify any minimum period of notice. Circumstances arise, especially in a mobilization scenario, when the individual has very little advance notice from military authorities. USERRA's legislative history indicates that Congress intended that the lateness of the notice to the civilian employer should not defeat the right to reemployment, especially when the individual had little or no notice from the military.*

Q. Am I required to provide my employer with a copy of my military orders when I give notice of an upcoming period of service?

A. *No. USERRA imposes no such requirement. We (ESGR) recommend that National Guard and Reserve personnel provide to their employers such documentation as is readily available. Your civilian employer is permitted and encouraged to call your commanding officer with questions about your service.*

Q. I take a lot of time off for military training and service. Now, I have been asked to perform service at a time that is particularly inconvenient for my employer. Is my employer permitted to veto my request for military leave?

A. *No. 38 U.S.C. 4312(h). You are only required to give your employer notice, not to obtain your employer's permission. However, as a matter of courtesy, we (ESGR) recommend that you phrase your notice as a request for permission. The employer has no right to veto the timing, frequency, duration, etc., of your military training and service. However, the employer is permitted to contact your commanding officer. It is Department of Defense (DOD) policy that the commanding officer should work with your employer to resolve conflicts of this kind. The commanding officer will accede to your employer's reasonable request to reschedule military training, unless doing so would detract from unit readiness and mission accomplishment.*

If the timing of this training period presents a real problem for your employer, the commanding officer will try to adjust the schedule, but please understand that such rescheduling must be kept to a minimum. National Guard and Reserve units train together, and they must go to war together. The training periods are scheduled so that the unit can be trained together. If you perform training at a different time, you may miss important training that the rest of the unit received. As a result, you may not learn how to perform some critical task, resulting in additional casualties and endangering the accomplishment of the mission. Under the "Total Force Policy," our nation is more dependent than ever before upon the National Guard and Reserve for essential military readiness. The National Guard and Reserve make up almost half of the total pool of available military personnel.

> **"Under the "Total Force Policy," our nation is more dependent than ever before upon the National Guard and Reserve for essential military readiness."**

Q. Is my employer permitted to make me find a replacement for the time that I will be away from work performing service?

A. *No. You are responsible for giving the employer advance notice, if possible, but not for rearranging your schedule or finding a replacement.*

Q. Is my employer permitted to make me use vacation for my military training or service?

A. *No. If you want to use vacation, you have the right to do so, but it is unlawful for your employer to make you use vacation—38 U.S.C. 4316(d).*

Q. Is my employer required to pay me for the period that I am away from work performing military training or service?

> "...it is unlawful for your employer to make you use vacation."

A. *USERRA does not require an employer to pay an individual for time not worked due to service. Another federal law (5 U.S.C. 6323) gives federal civilian employees the right to 120 hours per fiscal year of paid military leave. About forty states have similar laws for state and local government employees. If you are exempt from the Fair Labor Standards Act (FLSA) overtime rules (because you are a manager, for example), the employer is not permitted to make a deduction for a part of a pay period missed because of temporary military leave. See 29 Code of Federal Regulations 541.118(4). This is an FLSA requirement, not a USERRA requirement.*

Q. Is my employer required to provide me other benefits of employment while I am away from work performing service?

A. *If, and to the extent that your employer provides benefits to employees who have been furloughed (laid off) or to employees on some kind of non-military leave (jury leave, educational leave, etc.), your employer must provide similar benefits to employees who are away from work performing service in the uniformed services—38 U.S.C. 4316(b). An employee who is away from work performing service in the uniformed services is entitled to elect continued health plan coverage through the civilian job. If the period of service is less than thirty-one days, the employer is permitted to charge the employee only the employee share (if any) of the cost of the coverage. If the period of service is thirty-one days or more, the employer is permitted (but not required) to charge the employee up to 102 percent of the entire premium, including the part that the employer normally pays in the case of active employees—38 U.S.C. 4317(a).*

Q. Other than status and prompt reinstatement, what are my other entitlements as a returning veteran?

A. *You are entitled to immediate reinstatement of your health plan coverage, through the job, including coverage for family members. There must be no waiting period and no exclusion of "pre-existing conditions" (except conditions that the U.S. Department of Veterans Affairs has determined to be service-connected)—38 U.S.C. 4317(b). You*

> **"You must be treated, for seniority purposes, as if you had been continuously employed."**

must be treated, for seniority purposes, as if you had been continuously employed. You are also entitled to receive missed employer contributions to your pension plan, as if you had been continuously employed.

Q. Does USERRA protect me from discrimination by an employer or prospective employer?

A. *Yes. "A person who is a member of, applies to be a member of, performs, has performed, applies to perform, or has an obligation to perform service in a uniformed service shall not be denied initial employment, reemployment, retention in employment, promotion, or any benefit of employment by an employer on the basis of that membership, application for membership, performance of service, application for service, or obligation." 38 U.S.C. 4311(a).*

Need to Know

As a uniformed service member, you have rights under the Uniformed Services Employment and Reemployment Rights Act (USERRA), Title 38, Chapter 43, United States Code.

Your Rights:
- Military leave of absence (includes weekend drills, required training, all involuntary service, and up to five years of voluntary service)
- Prompt reinstatement back into your job
- Accumulation of seniority, including pension plan benefits
- Reinstatement of health insurance, regardless of pre-existing conditions
- Training or retraining of job skills, including accommodations for disabled
- Protection against discrimination

Your Responsibilities:
- Before reporting for duty: Provide prior notice to employer (preferably in writing)
- While performing duty: Serve under honorable conditions
- After release from duty: Return to work in a timely manner (see timetable)

Reemployment Timetable:
- Less than thirty-one days of service: report next scheduled
- 31-180 days of service: apply for reinstatement within fourteen days of release from active duty
- Over 180 days of service: apply for reinstatement within ninety days of release from active duty

How to Resolve an Employment Issue:
- Inform your unit/military chain of command
- Contact ESGR (1-800-336-4590, option 1)
- If not resolved, contact the Department of Labor (1-866-4-usa-dol or www. dol.gov)
- May consult a private attorney (at own expense, may preclude ESGR assistance)

How to Recognize Your Employer:
- Nominate them for an award from ESGR
- Go to the ESGR web site at: www.esgr. mil
- Click on "Military Members" and then "ESGR Programs" and then "Awards and Recognition"
- Fill out and submit the Patriot award nomination form right on line!

Make the Connection on MFN!
www.eMilitary.org/YourMFN.html

Sign on to the address shown above and Make the Connection to more resources on this topic!

46   Veteran Employment Training Services

US Department of Labor

Over the years, the Department of Labor (DOL) and the Department of Defense (DoD) have worked closely together on issues related to service members' transition to the civilian labor force. Both departments have recognized that while the objective of education, training, and experience obtained during an individual's military service is to provide tangible benefits for the nation's defense, those skills can also contribute significantly to the civilian workforce.

In today's global economy, our nation needs an increasingly skilled workforce. As part of the President's High Growth Job Training Initiative, DOL has been working closely with business and industry to identify those skills and occupations that are in high demand. DOL has also been working with the state and local workforce investment systems, community colleges, economic development agencies, and industry to target job training toward actual employment opportunities. This is all part of DOL's commitment to help American workers obtain good jobs at good wages with solid career paths in order to leave no worker behind. And there is no more deserving or more valuable group of American workers than our nation's service members and veterans.

VETS is the Agency responsible for providing employment, training, educational, and reemployment rights information and assistance to veterans and other military personnel who are preparing to transition from the military.

The mission statement for VETS is to provide veterans and transitioning service members with the resources and services to succeed in the twenty-first century workforce by maximizing their employment opportunities, protecting their employment rights, and meeting labor-market demands with qualified veterans today.

VETS Programs

Transition Services

Recovery & Employment Assistance Lifelines
If you have been injured or wounded while on active duty or a family member needs assistance, contact your REALifelines representative at 1-888-774-1361. Be sure to ask to speak with your REALifelines representative and get the assistance you deserve.

REALifelines Advisor
The Recovery and Employment Assistance Lifelines (REALifelines) Advisor provides veterans and transitioning service members wounded and injured as a result of the War on Terrorism, and their family members, with the resources they need to successfully transition to a rewarding career.

> " While this site, located at http://www.dol.gov/vets/REALifelines/index.htm, is intended for use by wounded and injured transitioning service members, it offers extensive information and resources that can benefit all veterans."

Developed by the U.S. Department of Labor's Veterans' Employment and Training Service (VETS), the REALifelines Advisor provides valuable information and access to contact information for one-on-one employment assistance and online resources to assist wounded and injured transitioning service members and veterans in their reintegration into the civilian workforce.

While this site, located at http://www.dol.gov/vets/REALifelines/index.htm, is intended for use by wounded and injured transitioning service members, it offers extensive information and resources that can benefit all veterans.

Compliance Assistance
- Department of Labor issues comprehensive regulations on USERRA
- Veterans' preference information
- Federal contractor program information

Employment Services

Disabled Veterans' Outreach Program Specialists and Local Veterans' Employment Representatives</c>
This grant provides funds to exclusively serve veterans, other eligible persons, transitioning service members, their spouses, and, indirectly, employers.

The grant also gives states the flexibility to determine the most effective and efficient distribution of their staff resources based upon the distinct roles and responsibilities of the two positions.

Disabled Veterans' Outreach Program Specialists

Disabled Veterans Outreach Program (DVOP) specialists provide intensive services to meet the employment needs of disabled veterans and other eligible veterans, with the maximum emphasis directed toward serving those who are economically or educationally disadvantaged, including homeless veterans, and veterans with barriers to employment.

Local Veterans' Employment Representatives

Local Veterans' Employment Representatives conduct outreach to employers and engage in advocacy efforts with hiring executives to increase employment opportunities for veterans, encourage the hiring of disabled veterans, and generally assist veterans to gain and retain employment.

> **"These centers serve at no cost to employers or job seekers who access the services available."**

State Level Employment Outcomes for Veterans and Disabled Veterans

State Workforce Agencies nationwide operate One-Stop Career Centers that provide employment and workforce information services in local communities. These centers serve at no cost to employers or job seekers who access the services available. State Workforce Agencies also provide priority of service and supplementary assistance to veterans and disabled veteran job seekers.

Contracts and Grants for Veterans

Visit the Department of Labor's site: http://www.dol.gov/vets/grants/main.htm

 **FAQs**

Q. What is "veterans' preference"?

A. *The U.S. government has laws to assist veterans who seek federal employment from being penalized for their time in military service. Veterans who*

are disabled or who served on active duty in the armed forces during certain specified time periods or in military campaigns are entitled to preference over others in hiring from competitive lists of eligibles and also in retention during reductions in force. Preference applies in hiring for virtually all jobs, whether in the competitive or excepted service. The Office of Personnel Management (OPM) administers entitlement to veterans' preference in federal employment under title 5, United States Code, and oversees other statutory employment requirements in title 5 and 38. However, the veterans' preference laws do not guarantee veterans a job, nor do they give veterans preference in internal agency actions such as promotion, transfer, reassignment, and reinstatement.

For more specific information on veterans' preference, OPM has developed the VetsInfo Guide. This guide explains how the federal employment system works and how veterans' preference and the special appointing authorities for veterans operate within the system. It is available on the Internet at: http://www.opm.gov/veterans/html/vetsinfo.htm.

Q. Do I have recourse if I believe my rights under the veterans' preference have been violated?

A. *Yes. The Veterans Employment Opportunities Act (VEOA) of 1998 provides that a veteran or other preference-eligible person who believes that his or her rights under any law or regulation related to veterans' preference have been violated may file a written complaint with the U.S. Department of Labor's Veterans' Employment and Training Service (VETS). If a person believes his or her eligibility for preference in the federal government is not being extended for the purposes of hiring or a*

> **"Information on veterans' preference is available at http://www.dol.gov/elaws/vetspref.htm."**

Reduction in Force (RIF), that person may file a complaint, in writing, to VETS, within sixty days of the alleged violation. If VETS finds the case to have merit, VETS will make every effort to resolve it. If resolution cannot be achieved within sixty days, the claimant may appeal to the Merit Systems Protection Board (MSPB), at which time VETS ceases all investigative activity. However, in cases where VETS is making progress and the claimant does not choose to appeal to the MSPB, investigative and resolution efforts by VETS may be continued indefinitely. If VETS determines the complaint to be without merit, the claimant still retains the right to appeal to the MSPB following receipt of the no-merit determination. If the MSPB has had such an appeal for 120 days and has not issued a judicially reviewable decision, the claimant may file a claim in the U.S. District Court, at which time MSPB will cease all activity on the claim. If the MSPB or the District Court find for the claimant, they may order the agency to comply with the applicable provisions of law and award compensation for any loss of wages or benefits.

A failure by a government official to knowingly fail to comply with veterans' preference requirements is now treated as a prohibited personnel practice (PPP). However, in the case of this particular PPP, the law stipulates that "corrective action" for the claimant (for example, reinstatement, back wages) is not available. Therefore, a claimant should go through the redress process with VETS first, in order to obtain the remedies discussed above. Following the redress process and after the claimant has been "made whole," then the case can go to the Office of Special Counsel (OSC) as a potential PPP. VETS does not investigate PPP cases. Information on OSC procedures and how to file a claim may be found at: http://www.osc.gov.

Information on veterans' preference is available on an interactive veterans' preference advisor program. The Internet site is: http://www.dol.gov/elaws/vetspref.htm.

To file a veterans' federal employment preference claim, contact the VETS' office located in each of the states. They can be located in the "Blue Pages" of your telephone book. In addition, the VETS' homepage website contains a directory of VETS offices as well as information on this and other VETS programs and services:

http://www.dol.gov/vets/aboutvets/contacts/main.htm.

Q. How do I find qualified veterans?

A. *Visit* **Hire Vets First***, a government website dedicated to matching employers with experienced veterans of America's military. http://www.hirevetsfirst.gov/*

Q. What is the Uniformed Services Employment and Reemployment Rights Act of 1994 (USERRA 38 U.S.C. 4301-4334) and how does it apply to me?

A. *The Department of Labor, through the Veterans' Employment and Training Service (VETS), provides assistance to all persons having claims under USERRA.*

The Uniformed Services Employment and Reemployment Rights Act (USERRA) clarifies and strengthens the Veterans' Reemployment Rights (VRR) Statute.

USERRA protects civilian job rights and benefits for veterans and members of Reserve components. USERRA also makes major improvements in protecting service member rights and benefits by clarifying the law, improving enforcement mechanisms, and adding federal government employ-

> **"USERRA protects civilian job rights and benefits for veterans and members of Reserve components."**

ees to those employees already eligible to receive Department of Labor assistance in processing claims.

USERRA establishes the cumulative length of time that an individual may be absent from work for military duty and retain reemployment rights to five years (the previous law provided four years of active duty, plus an additional year if it was for the convenience of the government). There are important exceptions to the five-year limit, including initial enlistments lasting more than five years, periodic National Guard and Reserve training duty, and involuntary active duty extensions and recalls, especially during a time of national emergency. USERRA clearly establishes that reemployment protection does not depend on the timing, frequency, duration, or nature of an individual's service as long as the basic eligibility criteria are met.

USERRA provides protection for disabled veterans, requiring employers to make reasonable efforts to accommodate the disability. Service members convalescing from injuries received during service or training may have up to two years from the date of completion of service to return to their jobs or apply for reemployment.

> **"Service members convalescing from injuries…may have up to two years…to return to their jobs or apply for reemployment."**

USERRA provides that returning service members are reemployed in the job that they would have attained had they not been absent for military service (the long-standing "escalator" principle), with the same seniority, status, and pay, as well as other rights and benefits determined by seniority. USERRA also requires that reasonable efforts (such as training or retraining) be made to enable returning service members to refresh or upgrade their skills to help them qualify for reemployment. The law clearly provides for alternative reemployment positions if the service member cannot qualify for the "escalator" position. USERRA also provides that while an individual is performing military service, he or she is deemed to be on a furlough or leave of absence and is entitled to the non-seniority rights accorded other individuals on non-military leaves of absence.

Health and pension plan coverage for service members is provided for by USERRA. Individuals performing military duty of more than thirty days may elect to continue employer-sponsored health care for up to twenty-four months; however, they may be required to pay *up to* 102 percent of the full premium. For military service of less than thirty-one days, health-care coverage is provided as if the service member had remained employed. USERRA clarifies pension plan coverage by making explicit that all pension plans are protected.

The period an individual has to make application for reemployment or report back to work after military service is based on time spent on military duty. For service of less than thirty-one days, the service member must return at the beginning of the next regularly scheduled work period on the first full day after release from service, taking into account safe travel home plus an eight-hour rest period. For service of more than thirty days but less than 181 days, the service member must submit an application for reemployment within fourteen days of release from service. For service of more than 180 days, an application for reemployment must be submitted within ninety days of release from service.

USERRA also requires that service members provide advance written or verbal notice to their employers for all military duty unless giving notice is impossible, unreasonable, or precluded by military necessity. An employee should provide notice as far in advance as is reasonable under the circumstances. Additionally, service members are able (but are not required) to use accrued vacation or annual leave while performing military duty.

> **"An employee should provide notice as far in advance as is reasonable under the circumstances."**

The Department of Labor, through the Veterans' Employment and Training Service (VETS) provides assistance to all persons having claims under USERRA, including federal and postal service employees.

If resolution is unsuccessful following an investigation, the service member may have his or her claim referred to the Department of Justice for consideration of representation in the appropriate District Court, at no cost to the claimant. Federal and postal service employees may have their claims referred to the Office of Special Counsel for consideration of representation before the Merit Systems Protection Board (MSPB). If violations under USERRA are shown to be willful, the court may award liquidated damages. Individuals who pursue their own claims in court or before the MSPB may be awarded reasonable attorney and expert witness fees if they prevail.

Service member employees of intelligence agencies are provided similar assistance through the agency's inspector general.

For more information about U.S. Department of Labor employment and training programs for veterans, contact the Veterans' Employment and Training Service office nearest you, listed in the phone book in the United States Government section, under the Labor Department, or visit our site:

> **"TAP helps service members and their spouses make the initial transition from military service to the civilian workplace..."**

http://www.dol.gov/vets/aboutvets/contacts/main.htm

Q. What is the Transition Assistance Program?

A. *The Transition Assistance Program (TAP) was established to meet the needs of separating service members during their period of transition into civilian life by offering job-search assistance and related services.*

The law that created TAP established a partnership among the Departments of Defense, Veterans Affairs, Transportation, and the Department of Labor's Veterans' Employment and Training Service (VETS) to give employment and training information to armed forces members within 180 days of separation or retirement.

TAP helps service members and their spouses make the initial transition from military service to the civilian workplace with less difficulty and at less overall cost to the government. An independent national evaluation of the program estimated that service members who had participated in TAP, on average, found their first post-military job three weeks sooner than those who did not participate in TAP.

TAP consists of comprehensive three-day workshops at selected military installations nationwide. Professionally trained workshop facilitators from the state employment services, military family support services, Department of Labor contractors, or VETS' staff present the workshops.

Workshop attendees learn about job searches, career decision-making, current occupational and labor market conditions, resume and cover letter preparation, and interviewing techniques. Participants also are provided with an evaluation of their employability relative to the job market and receive information on the most current veterans' benefits.

Service members leaving the military with a service-connected disability are offered the Disabled Transition Assistance Program (DTAP). DTAP includes the normal three-day TAP workshop plus additional hours of individual instruction to help determine job readiness and address the special needs of disabled veterans.

Although experience shows that veterans generally enjoy a favorable employment rate in the nation's job market, many veterans initially find it difficult to compete successfully in the labor market. The TAP program addresses many barriers to success and alleviates many employment related difficulties. To view the TAP Workshop Participant Manual, visit: http://www.dol.gov/vets/programs/tap/tapmanualmar06.pdf

For more information about the U.S. Department of Labor employment and training programs for veterans, contact the Employment and Training Service office nearest you, listed in the phone book in the United States Government section, under the Labor Department, or visit our site: http://www.dol.gov/vets/aboutvets/contacts/main.htm

Need to Know

Ten Reasons to Hire Vets

- Accelerated learning curve
- Leadership
- Teamwork
- Diversity and inclusion in action
- Efficient performance under pressure
- Respect for procedures
- Technology and globalization
- Integrity
- Conscious of health and safety habits
- Triumph over adversity

Make the Connection on MFN!
www.eMilitary.org/YourMFN.html

Sign on to the address shown above and Make the Connection to more resources on this topic!

Part 9

Military Family Law
& Legislation

Photo: Luis Trevino

Sunset

Introduction

Military family life is unique. Unlike most Americans, military families experience many communities, many states, and in some cases, many countries. Since there are many life matters that are governed by legal or legislative system and how these matters are handled may differ from assignment to assignment based on your location, this section deals with the resources and support you have available to you and how you can get involved.

One of the most basic tools every military family has access to for guidance is the legal assistance attorney. Legal assistance attorneys are civilian or military attorneys in the Army, Air Force, Navy, Marine Corps, or Coast Guard. They may advise you and your spouse on your personal legal affairs. In addition to legal advice and referral, these attorneys and their staffs prepare powers of attorney, bills of sale, and wills; review contracts; notarize documents; advise on family law matters (e.g., adoption, marriage, divorce), leases, immigration, and naturalization; and answer tax questions.

In some unique situations, your legal assistance attorney may be able to help you in civil court. When they cannot represent you in court, they can help you find a local civilian attorney.

Legal assistance is an important quality of life program, and many military families are not aware of the array of services that are available to them. The value of these services can save your family thousands of dollars during your military career.

Given the mobility of the military lifestyle, the Legal Assistance Office can also help you understand the differences in state laws that may apply to you when you move. Questions relating to taxes, divorce, insurance law, etc., may be answered by a simple appointment.

Even in cases where they will not be able to be directly involved, they are able to steer you in the right direction so that your legal need may be satisfied. It is like having a professional legal coach at no cost. One of the most valuable benefits to consulting with a legal assistance officer is that you can be confident that they are offering non-partial advice in your matter. They do not have a monetary incentive to guide you in one way or another.

Not legal advice: *The Military Family Network website (www.eMilitary. org), nor the information presented here, are a substitute for legal advice or a solution to your individual legal problem(s). Consult your attorney for advice.*

47   Your Voice on Capitol Hill

From the Field with Michelle Joyner

Michelle Joyner is the Director of Communications for The National Military Family Association, a national organization focused on the military family and whose goal is to influence the development and implementation of policies that will improve the lives of the families of the Army, Navy, Air Force, Marine Corps, Coast Guard, and the Commissioned Corps of the Public Health Service and the National Oceanic and Atmospheric Administration.

The National Military Family Association (NMFA) is the only national non-profit organization that focuses solely on the families of the Army, Navy, Air Force, Marine Corps, Coast Guard, the Commissioned Corps of the Public Health Service, and the National Oceanic and Atmospheric Administration. For more than thirty-five years, NMFA's staff and volunteers, comprised predominantly of military family members, have built a reputation as the leading experts on military family issues.

NMFA works tirelessly with the Department of Defense, other federal agencies, and federal, state, and local governments to improve the lives of military families. Recently NMFA successfully led the fight to overturn a proposal that would have provided greater benefits for survivors of service members killed in combat than service members who died elsewhere. Now all surviving families of service members who were killed on active duty receive the same benefits.

For military children, NMFA hosts *Operation Purple* Summer Camps, a free summer camp program for military children coping with the deployment of one or both of their parents. In appreciation of the value military families place on education, NMFA's Joanne Holbrook Patton Military Spouse Scholarship Program allows military spouses the opportunity to receive financial assistance to further their educations.

While our servicemen and women serve the nation in foreign and domestic lands, their families also serve. In order for service members to focus effectively on their missions, they must be confident that their families are physically and emotionally secure. There is nothing that can fully prepare the family for the challenges that come when a loved one is called to serve, but Americans can ensure that these families have the tools and resources available to face their challenges head-on and with success. This is a vital role we call on everyone to fulfill by joining NMFA.

Visit the National Military Family Association website, *www.nmfa.org*, for more information on how you can support military families by working with NMFA.

 **FAQs**

Q. Why should I get involved?

A. *Many of the benefits that military families have today did not originate with the Department of the Defense or any of the military service branches. Rather, they are the direct result of organizations such as NMFA pushing for resources and solutions to address military family needs. Additionally, NMFA has started programs to address some specific needs of military families.*

> **"the Survivor Benefit Plan (SBP)... provides ongoing financial support for widows of retirees."**

Q. What does NMFA do in support of security for military widows?

A. *In 1969, a group of uniformed service wives gathered to discuss the abysmal government effort to provide economic security for surviving widows of retired service members. Instead of bemoaning the situation, these wives decided to act. Their efforts resulted in Congress creating the Survivor Benefit Plan (SBP), which today provides ongoing financial support for widows of retirees. In recent years, NMFA worked to expand SBP coverage to the survivors of those killed while on active duty and continually works to ensure all these survivors may receive the benefits owed to them by a grateful nation.*

Q. What about access to quality health care?

A. *Military families tell NMFA that no benefit is more important to their qual-ity of life than quality health care. NMFA has long worked to improve that benefit and families' access to quality care. NMFA was a leader in the creation of the TRICARE den-tal insurance programs and fought for the creation of TRICARE Prime*

> **"...more than 115,000 kids have at least one parent who is deployed to Iraq or Af-ghanistan..."**

Remote. The Association worked to secure expanded benefits, such as TRI-CARE coverage for school-required physicals and enhanced coverage for military family members with special needs. Today, NMFA works to ensure military families are not forced to shoulder the burden of DoD's higher health-care costs and that they can access the full range of health-care services where and when they need them.

Q. Can NMFA make changes to access to our benefits as National Guard families?

A. *Yes, the Commissary is a good example. Military families shopping at the commissary experience a savings of over 30 percent compared to commercial prices. To an average family of four, this is a savings worth $2,700 a year. Originally, National Guard and Reserve service members and their families were prohibited from using the commissaries and later were restricted to only twenty-four visits to a commissary per year. NMFA and other military organi-zations championed the cause to remove these restrictions. Today more than 1.2 million Guard and Reserve personnel and their families can enjoy the sav-ings the commissary benefit provides.*

Q. What about changing things overseas?

A. *The Child Nutrition Act of 1966 included provisions for a supplemental food and nutritional education benefit for women, infants, and children (WIC). Today, approximately one half of all infants born in the United States, including many born to military families, qualify for WIC. Because WIC is administered by individual states, it was originally unavailable to military families living overseas. NMFA campaigned for years for Congress to extend this valuable program to these families. Finally, in 1999, Congress mandated that DoD set up and fund a WIC-like program overseas. Since the program's implementation in 2001, more than 128,000 military service members, DoD civilian employees, contractors, and their families have participated in WIC Overseas.*

Q. Does NMFA do anything to support children?

A. *At any given time, more than 115,000 kids have at least one parent who is deployed to Iraq or Afghanistan; this staggering figure doesn't even include those experiencing routine, but often lengthy, deployments and separations supporting the War on Terror. NMFA created Operation Purple, a free summer camp program specifically for military children coping with the absence of a parent. Operation Purple camps give kids the coping skills and support networks of peers to better handle life's ups and downs.*

Q. Is NMFA able to help families with expenses, especially during deployment?

A. *In 2004, a Congressional staff member contacted NMFA to inquire about ways to aid military families who were suffering hardships due to deployments. From this discussion came the suggestion to increase the Family Separation Allowance from the rate of $100 per month to $250 per month. The idea received much support, and the increase was later made permanent.*

Q. What other programs does NMFA offer families?

A. *NMFA knows that pursuing a higher education is often difficult for a military spouse who moves regularly or whose life is interrupted by deployment schedules. To address this, NMFA developed the Joanne Holbrook Patton Military Spouse Scholarship program in 2004. Since then we have seen the number of applications*

> **"...military spouses need more education resources."**

grow exponentially. This confirms what many of us already knew—military spouses need more education resources. Understanding this, NMFA published the NMFA Military Spouse Education Guide, available at www.nmfa.org, to connect military spouses with resources they could use. NMFA also works to make more funds available to support the schools that educate military children and assists parents in becoming more effective advocates for quality education for their children.

Q. Wounded service members have wounded families, what does NMFA do for us?

A. NMFA recognizes that when a service member is wounded or injured in the line of duty, the entire family—spouse, children, parents, and siblings— experiences a life change. NMFA has successfully advocated for increased family support services at the military medical centers caring for the largest number of wounded service members. Recognizing that the injury of a service member and related disruptions to the life of a family can create financial hardships, NMFA was one of the primary supporters of the new Traumatic Service members' Group Life Insurance (TSGLI). The TSGLI provides payments of up to $100,000 to service members injured in the line of duty, giving the military family a financial cushion until other benefit programs begin.

Need to Know

The United States Congress is continually acting on legislation of vital importance to military families. Do you understand the issues involved? The National Military Family Association's newsletter and fact sheets will keep you informed and assist you in making your views known to government policymakers.

Your Participation Does Make a Difference!

Recent elections have shown the importance of the absentee ballot, especially those cast by military voters. Military voters voiced their concerns about the election process to the press and to their members of Congress. The 107th Congress, responding to these concerns, passed the Help America Vote Act of 2002, which directed the Pentagon to ensure that ballots and other election materials are processed quickly through the military mail system. It also emphasized the need for more education for service members and families concerning registration and applying for absentee ballots. The law also emphasized state responsibilities for ensuring that service members' right to vote is not infringed upon.

Communicating with Members of Congress

- Write to your own senators and representatives. You can contact the representatives or senators from your home of record and from where you are stationed. State early in the letter or e-mail that you vote in the member's district or that you are a uniformed services member or family member on orders in the district. Most congressional offices do not read mail from people not in their districts.

> **"Let the members know what you want them to do..."**

- Use your own words—speak from your own experience.
- Discuss one issue in each letter or e-mail, briefly and to the point. Let the members know what you want them to do: introduce or co-sponsor a bill,

vote in favor of or against a bill, provide information, investigate a problem, change a law.

- Identify legislation by bill number or title, if possible, otherwise by subject.
- NMFA always includes bill numbers when it discusses them in its publications. For information about the bill, try the site: *http://thomas.loc.gov* or contact NMFA at families@nmfa.org.
- Explain how the legislation would affect you and your family.
- State your position clearly—support or protest; summarize your reasons.
- Ask for a reply to your letter or e-mail and acknowledge it with a word of thanks.

How to Contact Your Representative

United States Senate
The Honorable (Full Name)
United States Senate
Washington DC 20510
Dear Senator (Last Name)
To locate individual e-mail addresses:
www.senate.gov/senators

United States House of Representatives
The Honorable (Full Name)
United States House of Representatives
Washington DC 20515
Dear Representative (Last Name)
To locate individual e-mail addresses:
www.house.gov/writerep

Capitol Switchboard
(to reach members of Congress)
(202) 224-3121

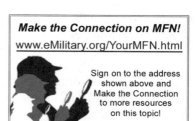

Make the Connection on MFN!
www.eMilitary.org/YourMFN.html

Sign on to the address shown above and Make the Connection to more resources on this topic!

The Chief Executive
The President
The White House
1600 Pennsylvania Ave. NW
Washington DC 20500
Dear Mr. President
To e-mail the White House
www.whitehouse.gov
White House Switchboard
(202) 456-1414
White House Comments Desk

48   Peace with A Living Will

From the Field with The Law Firm of Gold, Khourey & Turak

*Since 1978, the law firm of **Gold, Khourey & Turak** has represented thousands of individuals with their legal concerns. They are licensed to practice in Ohio, West Virginia, and Pennsylvania, but have supported clients from across the country in obtaining the legal services necessary in their time of need. Their website is located at www.gkt.com.*

As personal injury attorneys, we see firsthand the devastating effects that an injury or death can have on a family. Oftentimes the injured person can make a full recovery and maintain a healthy lifestyle, however, this is not always the case. Unfortunately, there are times when the injured person becomes incapacitated with little or no chance to recover, or the family member dies as a result of the accident. While no family is truly ever fully prepared to deal with a serious injury or the loss of a loved one, the challenges they face can be made easier if their loved one has a living will, a medical power of attorney, and a will. It is our experience that most families are ill prepared to make decisions for their loved one.

As a military family, your needs are similar to those of a civilian family. An unexpected tragedy can strike a member of your family at anytime. If a loved one sustains a life-threatening illness or injury while you're overseas, you may not know about decisions made by hospital administrators or doctors. If family members are local, they will be under tremendous stress deciding what is in their loved one's best interest. Parents often hold as much legal standing as a spouse, so conflicts can arise when family members disagree on how to proceed when a dramatic change in the health status of their loved one occurs.

While no one wants to think about an unexpected incapacitating injury, illness, or death occurring to themselves or a loved one, consideration should be given to the benefits of having such documents

> "... preparing these documents forces you to ask yourself difficult questions and provides you, and your loved one, the opportunity to think things through with a clear mind ..."

as a living will, a medical power of attorney, and a will. Having these documents can remove any potential guilt or confusion experienced by your loved ones by letting your family members know your preferences in advance. This also relieves your family of the stress and conflict that often arises with having to make these types of decisions. In addition, preparing these documents forces you to ask yourself difficult questions and provides you, and your loved one, the opportunity to think things through with a clear mind before any significant health changes occur.

The Terri Schiavo case brought national attention to the importance of having an advance health-care directive. Having an advance health-care directive, such as a living will, medical power of attorney, or health-care power of attorney, can help you communicate your wishes regarding medical care if you are unable to speak for yourself. Anyone can create an advance health-care directive, and the process is relatively easy. There is no need to hire an attorney. Check the resources listed on The Military Family Network for websites to forms and information for each of the fifty states and the District of Columbia. These forms are free and can serve as legally binding documents when properly completed. If you do not have access to a computer, your local hospital may have information packets available that include these forms. In addition, the hospital may have a representative on staff that can answer your questions and, if necessary, assist you in completing the forms.

While living wills and power of attorneys can be easy to complete, you should consider contacting an attorney to assist you in preparing your last will and testament. Depending on your circumstances, the issues surrounding wills and trusts can be extremely complex, and an attorney can help make sure your preferences are set forth in your will without any confusion, and in accordance with state law.

 **FAQs**

Q. What is a living will, is it the same as an advance directive?

A. *A Living Will, also known as a health-care directive or health-care declaration, is a legal document that goes into effect while you are still alive. Generally, your condition is such that you have no reasonable chance of recovery* *to what you consider a meaningful life. A living will generally sets out your wishes regarding end-of-life medical treatment, but it may not appoint a decision maker should you become unable to communicate your wishes.*

Q. What is a Medical Power of Attorney?

A. *A Medical Power of Attorney allows you to designate someone to make health-care decisions for you when you are unable to make those decisions for yourself. The person should be knowledgeable of your wishes, values, and beliefs, and be someone who has your trust and confidence to make health-care decisions in your best interests.*

Q. What is a will?

A. *Wills are legal documents, when drafted and executed in accordance with law, that allow you to name your beneficiaries for such items as jewelry, property, money, and other assets in your name at the time of your death. In your will, you may also wish to nominate a person to care for your young child and select an executor of your estate. An executor has the responsibility of distributing your assets in accordance with the provisions of your will.*

 Need to Know

In preparing to meet with your attorney regarding your last will and testament, it is helpful for you and your attorney if you bring the following information with you:

- **Personal information about you and, if married, your spouse:** including full legal names, address, telephone numbers, date and place of births, and information about your children, if applicable.
- **Information about marital status:** date and place of marriage(s), bring any agreements or contracts; list any children from previous marriage.
- **Summary of your assets:** including, but not limited to, cash and bank accounts, life insurance policies, pension plans, property, and personal items that have sentimental value. Where are these items located; list account numbers and designated beneficiaries.
- **Summary of your debts:**

bring a list that includes amounts owed and to whom for loans, mortgages, and any other debt in your name.

- **Outline of your beneficiaries:**
  who will receive your cash distributions and amounts, and whom do you want specific possessions to go to?
- **Determine who will represent your interests:**
  bring full names and addresses of your executor, trustee, and guardian for infant children, if necessary.

Make the Connection on MFN!
www.eMilitary.org/YourMFN.html

Sign on to the address shown above and Make the Connection to more resources on this topic!

49 Legal Assistance

From the Field with Megan Turak

Megan Turak is the daughter of a WWII Army veteran and spouse of a Vietnam era Marine, Executive Vice President and co-owner of The Military Family Network, former Medical Records Manager with the Department of Veteran Affairs, a published writer of informative topics positively impacting the well-being of military families and has over twenty combined years of experience in executive leadership in the financial management and communications industries.

A mother of a sailor called concerned about her son. Although his job was going well, his personal life was a disaster. He was separated from his wife and she was abusive to their children—one, a newborn. She was seeing another man outside of their young marriage and she was addicted to drugs. She had tried rehab before, but had relapsed. The young sailor had very little money and was contacting his mother for help. He told her that he wanted to get sole custody of his children, but didn't know how to do it, and he was very worried.

The woman on the phone, cried. *"I'm not military. I live states away from where my son is stationed. I have very little money and even if I could afford to hire an attorney, I don't know how to find one who can help him. And, I don't know if there are different rules for people in the military and whether an outside attorney would need to have special skills in order to help. Can the military help him?"*

My response provided her with great relief. It wasn't a perfect solution, but it empowered her with the information she needed to guide her son. She found out that the military has many sources of support to help in situations like this. What she also learned was that her son, as the military service member, was the one who needed to approach the services to ask for the help.

Besides informing her about Chaplain services and family support services for her son, she was introduced to the Naval Legal Service Office for legal assistance. Legal Assistance is available for all branches of the service and is often an under utilized benefit.

The Legal Assistance offices are located on almost every base, ship, and installation. At major installations, the Naval Legal Service Office (NLSO) or simply the Legal Assistance Office for other services, is a key source for providing legal assistance. If there are not any of these in the service members' area, contacting the local staff or station judge advocate is the appropriate office for referral.

Some, but not all, of these services are also available for spouses. There are no charges for advice, document preparation, notary service, etc. Many times (like in the case of adoption), the legal assistance office provides advice and counsel—but cannot "represent" the service member. A private attorney is usually necessary in these types of cases.

 **FAQs**

Q. If my spouse and I wish to make an adoption, can I get help through legal assistance?

A. *If you and your spouse want to adopt a baby, a legal assistance attorney can assist you by explaining the appropriate legal procedures. In some areas, a legal assistance attorney can assist you in the preparation of the required paper work. A legal assistance attorney can also provide information about Adoption Expense Reimbursement Programs.*

Q. If my spouse and I are having marital difficulties, can legal assistance help here, too?

A. *If you and your spouse are having marital difficulties and need legal advice, a legal assistance attorney can advise you or your spouse concerning the legal and practical implications of annulment, paternity, legal separation, divorce, and child custody.*

Additionally, if the matter is uncontested (that is, you and your spouse are in total agreement about how to resolve the situation), assistance may be given, by separate legal assistance offices, to each party in preparing the necessary pro se documents, meaning you represent yourself before a court.

One legal assistance office may not represent both parties in legal matters, such as divorce, even if it is uncontested. The amount of assistance available will vary according to local practice.

Q. Can legal assistance help in spousal and child support matters?

A. *If your spouse is not providing sufficient support for you and the children, and you don't know how to enforce the obligation, a legal assistance attorney can assist you in determining whether your spouse is meeting his or her obligation, how you can enforce this obligation and what, if any, legal action you may take in order to ensure that your spouse will continue to meet this obligation in the future.*

Legal assistance may include the legal assistance attorney notifying your spouse in writing that he or she has an obligation to support his or her family members, notifying your spouse's commanding officer of your spouse's non-support, and/or advising you to seek an involuntary allotment from or garnishment of your spouse's military pay.

If you are the non-custodial parent supporting your spouse and children, a legal assistance attorney can advise regarding your support obligations.

Q. Can legal assistance help me in the preparation of important legal documents like wills, trusts, or estates?

A. *If you want to ensure that your worldly possessions go to the individuals you have chosen, then a will is the solution.*

> "A will is a legal document that specifies how you want your property distributed after your death."

A will is a legal document that specifies how you want your property distributed after your death. It may also include other matters such as appointment of your child's guardian. Not every person needs a will, but don't make this decision for yourself. A legal assistance attorney can advise you whether you need one and how it can affect the disposition of your estate. The legal assistance attorney generally can draft a will that fits your particular desires and needs.

If the legal assistance attorney determines that he or she cannot provide adequate advice or assistance regarding your estate, then he or she will assist you in locating a civilian attorney so that your needs can be fulfilled by a specialist in estate planning.

A legal assistance attorney may be able to provide an "advance medical directive" or a "living will," which relates to the use of extraordinary life-sustaining measures if the event you become injured or seriously ill.

Trusts

If you are concerned about how your children will be able to pay for college if you are not around to assist them, or if your family will be taken care of financially in the event of your death, your legal assistance attorney can give you advice on options.

One possible solution may be a trust. A trust is a legal document whereby you place certain properties and assets—perhaps monies, stocks, or real estate under the control of a third party that has an obligation to ensure that those properties and assets are applied toward a certain goal such as your children's educational needs.

> **"Legal assistance attorneys may include trust provisions in a will, but are not permitted to draft so-called 'living trusts.'"**

Because the laws vary among all the states as to trusts and their validity, you must consult an attorney before establishing a trust.

Legal assistance attorneys may include trust provisions in a will, but are not permitted to draft so-called "living trusts."

Q. Can I get help with consumer issues like debts, buying a car that turns out to be a "lemon," or lease issues?

A. *Yes, but the depth of assistance that can be provided varies depending on circumstances. See the following for more information:*

Debts and Bankruptcy

Most service members borrow money at some time during their life. Some service members get into financial difficulties and need help getting out of debt. A legal assistance attorney can advise you on the laws and legal protections as they relate to loans, credit cards, credit bureaus, and bankruptcy.

"Lemon Law"

If you have recently purchased an automobile that doesn't perform well and are unable to get proper service from your dealer, your legal assistance attorney can advise you as to possible remedies, which may include asserting your rights under an applicable "Lemon Law," contacting the manufacturer's area representative, or filing a complaint with the local Better Business Bureau against the dealership.

Leases

If you buy a house, then get permanent change of station orders to a different geographic location, and you don't want to sell the house, you may want to consult your legal assistance attorney. If you decide to rent or lease your house, your legal assistance attorney can assist you by explaining the local laws regarding

> **"In some areas, your legal assistance attorney may draft a lease to fit your needs."**

the rights and duties of a landlord and by explaining the best ways to resolve difficulties with the house or tenants while you are away.

In some areas, your legal assistance attorney may draft a lease to fit your needs. A legal assistance attorney will also provide assistance to tenants by reviewing their lease and advising them of their rights under local law.

Q. What is a "Power of Attorney"? Should I have one?

A. *If you need to give someone permission to release your household goods shipment because you're leaving before your furniture does, your legal assistance attorney can acquaint you with an area of law known as "agency," which allows you to appoint another person to act in your place when you cannot be available. Such an appointment is commonly accomplished by a power of attorney. Your legal assistance attorney will advise you that a power of attorney may be drafted to authorize a person to act on your behalf in most of your affairs through a general power of attorney, or only in specific situations such as obtaining emergency medical care for your children or registering your car through a limited or "special" power of attorney. Your legal assistance attorney will explain the differences, advising which type would best meet your needs, and prepare an appropriate power of attorney.*

Q. What other services can I obtain from Legal Assistance?

Credit laws

If you receive your monthly credit card statements and feel it contains unauthorized charges, your legal assistance attorney can advise you as to your rights under the federal and state laws on credit card billing, can advise you of appropriate action you should take, and prepare or assist you in the preparation of necessary documents and correspondence.

> **"Many legal assistance offices also have civilian notaries."**

Notary public

Legal assistance attorneys are empowered under federal law to act as a notary without the usual five-dollar fee most public notaries charge. Many legal assistance offices also have civilian notaries.

Civil courts

A legal assistance attorney can advise you as to your protection under the Soldiers and Sailors Civil Relief Act. This act provides certain protections to active-duty members who have been sued in a civil court (as distinguished from a criminal proceeding) and who, because of their military duties cannot defend themselves from the lawsuit. This protection may include:

- The civilian court appointing an attorney to represent you.
- The court postponing the proceedings until you are able to reasonably defend yourself.
- The court may allow you to void a default judgment if such was awarded against you.

 Need to Know

Legal assistance available to service members include:
- Drafting powers of attorney
- Drafting wills
- Estate planning advice
- Reviewing contracts and leases (ideally, before you sign)
- Providing notarizations
- Personal finance advice
- Family and domestic relations advice (divorce, separation, family support, adoption, custody, paternity, and name changes)
- Consumer affairs
- Tax advice on real and personal property and income (and in certain locations tax preparation and electronic filing (ELF)
- Answering questions about landlord-tenant issues (including leases, security deposits, and evictions)
- Providing advice on immigration and naturalization issues

In summary, what can and cannot legal assistance do for me?
Legal Assistance CAN:
- Serve as advocate and counsel for an eligible client.
- Prepare and sign correspondence on behalf of an eligible client.
- Negotiate with another party or that party's attorney.
- Prepare legal documents, as permitted by the JAGMAN, other regulations, and local practice.
- When necessary, refer eligible persons to a civilian lawyer.
- Your legal assistance attorney holds all conversations and dealings with you in strict confidence, as required by the rules of professional responsibility.
- Provide legal assistance to those not eligible to receive such assistance

- Provide legal assistance via a third party. The attorney must deal directly with the client, not a friend or relative of the person to be assisted.
- Assist or counsel eligible persons regarding legal problems arising from the client's business or commercial interests.
- Provide in-court representation for an individual (except in limited cases).
- Under normal circumstances, give advice over the telephone.
- Represent both parties in a dispute.

Make the Connection on MFN!
www.eMilitary.org/YourMFN.html

Sign on to the address
shown above and
Make the Connection
to more resources
on this topic!

50   The 411 on Emergencies

From the Field with the Red Cross

Contributed by the American Red Cross, a nonprofit, nongovernmental organization that provides relief to victims of disasters and helps people prevent, prepare for and respond to emergencies.

Today, the American Red Cross provides services to 1.4 million active-duty personnel, more than 1.2 million members of the National Guard and the Reserves and to all their families in communities across America.

We help these personnel and their families: Active-duty personnel, National Guard members, Recruiters, Reservists, ROTC, U.S. Army Corps of Engineers, U.S. Coast Guard, U.S. Public Health Service, Veterans.

All Red Cross services to military members and their families are provided free of charge 365 days a year, 24 hours a day, and 7 days a week. The Red Cross receives no government funding for these services, but relies entirely on the generosity of donors and volunteers.

Red Cross workers in hundreds of chapters and on military installations brief departing service members and their families regarding available support services and explain how the Red Cross may assist them during the deployment. Red Cross Armed Forces Emergency Services (AFES) volunteers and employees work in more than 700 chapters in the United States, on 61 military installations around the world and with our military personnel in Kuwait, Afghanistan and Iraq.

FAQs

Q. Can the Red Cross help me contact my service member in case of emergency?

A. *Yes. Both active-duty and community-based military can rely on the Red Cross to provide emergency communications that link them with their families back home. The AFES Emergency Communication Services program keeps military personnel in touch with their families and loved ones, providing important news on such things as the birth of a child, serious illness of a family member, or death of a loved one. These messages are delivered through a worldwide network of Red Cross volunteers and employees to members of the Armed Forces anywhere in the world, whether they are on ships at sea or at isolated military units and embassies.*

Commanders have come to rely on Red Cross messages when making their decision to grant emergency leave. Red Cross messages are verified and contain the most current information.

Q. If my family needs assistance, how can the Red Cross help?

A. *The Red Cross provides social services, including access to financial assistance, counseling, family support, and assistance with representation at the Board of Veterans Appeals. When an emergency arises that requires the presence of the service member or his or her family, the Red Cross may provide access to an interest-free loan for travel expenses and other emergency situations through a partnership with military aid societies. The Army Emergency Relief, Navy-Marine Corps Relief Society, Air Force Aid Society and Coast Guard Mutual Assistance provide the funds.*

Funds may be authorized for other emergencies as well and are disbursed on the basis of need. Referrals to other organizations in local communities that provide financial aid and/or resources are also available to service members and their families and are made through Red Cross chapters.

Q. Does the Red Cross offer services to Veterans?

A. *The Red Cross provides social services to veterans, widows and dependents from all over the world to include access to counseling and assistance with neutral representation at the Board of Veterans Appeals in Washington, D.C.*

Trained personnel specialize in providing assistance with claims and appeals. The Red Cross does not charge for this service or ask for membership fees.

The Red Cross also provides services to veterans in VA health care facilities across the nation via the Veterans Affairs Volunteers Services (VAVS) program. Through this volunteer program, the VA coordinates volunteer services in its hospitals, outpatient clinics and nursing care facilities. The VAVS provides a broad range of volunteer opportunities including numerous community-based programs that use health care teams to provide compassionate follow-up care in the community.

Q. My family is going overseas, is the Red Cross active internationally, can my service member contact the Red Cross when he is deployed?

A. *American Red Cross workers do not participate in armed conflict; however, AFES staff members are deployed in direct support of troops in conflict areas. In the friendly atmosphere of communication and support centers, soldiers can enjoy coffee and share personal and family concerns in a safe and confidential environment. Talking with Red Cross workers provides an outlet for military personnel who may not be able to voice their concerns elsewhere. Red Cross teams also visit patients in hospitals and clinics.*

Q. I am a military family member, can I volunteer with the Red Cross? What opportunities does the Red Cross offer?

A. *The Red Cross has many opportunities for military family volunteers, including:*

- **Job Skills and Personnel Development.** In addition to the services provided for those in uniform, the American Red Cross also offers many volunteer opportunities to members of the military community. Volunteer programs on military installations and in military hospitals provide opportunities for community service, education, enhancement of job skills, and personal development. Volunteers are important assets to the installation command and to military medical facilities.

Volunteers are placed based on their areas of interest and on need. If they do not have a specific request or area of interest, they may be placed in an area where the need is the greatest. Volunteers may provide services as greeters, hospital guides, wheel chair escorts, patient chaperones and pharmacy aides.

- **Casework.** Volunteer caseworkers provide information, referrals, and access to emergency financial assistance for active-duty members and their families, retired military personnel, their dependents, widows and widowers.

Caseworkers receive extensive training and are critical links in the world-wide emergency communications network, linking soldiers and their families in times of crisis. Additional training in disaster casework is available at Red Cross offices located outside the continental United States.

- **Youth Volunteers**. Many installations offer youth volunteer programs that introduce youth to career possibilities in medical fields. These programs also provide valuable experience and community hours. These are often a requirement for admission into colleges, universities and the workplace.

Q. Does the Red Cross offer services to members of the National Guard, Reserves and their families?

A. *The Red Cross has found that all too often, community-based military personnel have not known about valuable Red Cross services until they were mobilized. Since 2000, the Red Cross has been reaching out to this population through the Get to Know Us Before You Need Us Program.*

Offered in communities across the United States, the program provides National Guard members, Reserve units, military recruiters and members of ROTC units with information relating to Red Cross programs and services. Get to Know Us Before You Need Us briefings to military personnel and their families teach how to use the valuable services offered by the Red Cross. These services include reaching deployed loved ones in case of an emergency, counseling, access to financial assistance and coping with separation issues.

 Need to Know

How to Access Red Cross Assistance

- Active-duty service members stationed in the United States and their immediate family members may call the Red Cross Armed Forces Emergency Service Centers for help 7 days a week, 24 hours a day, 365 days a year by dialing 1-877-272-7337.
- Other family members who do not reside in the service members' household, members of the National Guard and Reserves, retirees and civilians may access Red Cross services through their local Red Cross chapter, which is listed in local telephone books and at www.redcross.org/where/where.html
- Overseas personnel stationed on military installations should call base or installation operators or the on-base Red Cross offices.
- For general information about Red Cross programs and services, please browse our website, www.redcross.org

- If you would like information about Red Cross training classes, volunteer opportunities, military emergency communications or other programs and services available in your area, please call the Red Cross chapter nearest you, or browse your chapter's website. You may locate your local chapter by entering your zip code on the www. redcross.org homepage. If you do not have internet capability, you may call 1-800-RED CROSS and listen to the menu options.

 **Toolkit**

Contacting Your Service Member in an Emergency

To contact a service member regarding an emergency, call the nearest Red Cross office or you may call 1-800-RED CROSS and listen to the menu options. Be ready to give the following information about the service member:

NAME: _____

BRANCH OF SERVICE: _____

RANK: _____

SOCIAL SECURITY NUMBER: _____

COMPLETE MILITARY ADDRESS: _____

DATE OF BIRTH: _____

SERVICE MEMBER'S TELEPHONE NUMBER: _____

SERVICE MEMBER'S CELL PHONE NUMBER: _____

LOCAL RED CROSS PHONE NUMBER: _____

51 Military Family Domestic Abuse

From the Field with Caroline Peabody

Caroline Peabody *is the daughter of a disabled Vietnam era Marine, military spouse, former president of The Military Family Network, lifetime volunteer, and distinguished speaker and lecturer on military life. She holds a B.S. in sociology and M.A. in organizational management with extensive research on communication systems as they relate to military well being and community capacity-building. She is a published writer and columnist on matters relating to military families, military learning models, and military relations.*

In 2002, the murders of four Fort Bragg soldiers' wives in the space of six weeks stunned the Army and sent waves of concern throughout the military community, especially those working with family advocacy programs. Three of the four soldiers had recently returned from Afghanistan, where they served with Special Forces units. Given the prolonged nature of the War on Terror and the multiple deployments, domestic violence rates are on the rise.

Some reports have noted that the stresses of military life (extended and repeated separations from deployments and the exposure to the harsh violence of urban warfare in the nation's war on terror) have resulted in increased incidences of domestic violence.

Domestic violence and child abuse is an ongoing concern for the military community. In 2000, the Department of Defense (DoD) declared domestic violence a new priority and began initiatives across all services to help promote healthy families and prevent abuse.

Family advocacy programs are available on all installations. Military program managers coordinate with communities in order to provide resources, help, and support to military families.

There is support available both on and off military installations. While an investigation is being conducted, battered women's shelters in the community can be a safe haven for families. Counseling and support are available through churches and other civilian organizations.

On base, family advocates serve as prevention specialists, promoting public awareness activities to help people identify family violence and ways to prevent it. They provide information about on and off base resources.

Within the military community, chaplains offer marriage enrichment programs that focus on improving communication and respect for each other in the marriage. Family advocates offer individual counseling, support groups, and classes on anger and conflict management, marital communications, and other subjects.

> "The important part of addressing domestic violence as a part of a military family is to realize that you are not alone."

The important part of addressing domestic violence as a part of a military family is to realize that you are not alone. Family advocacy program specialists will help you understand your rights as a military dependent and guide you through the process of getting help for yourself and your family.

Family advocacy program specialists are also trained to help military dependents in abusive situations understand what economic resources they have or may be available to them. Many times, spouses will not report abuse because they fear what may happen economically. What will happen if the service member (if they are the abuser) loses his job or goes to jail? A spouse may not have assets in their name and feels completely dependent on the abuser for their economic survival.

In 1995, Congress set up a program to help military spouses caught in this bind. The program provides the victim health and dental benefits and compensation based on the service member's pay for up to thirty-six months.

Transitional compensation is awarded when the service member has been administratively separated due to the abuse or has been court-martialed and is getting a less than honorable discharge as a result of the abuse. Transitional compensation ends if the couple reunites.

Because of the nature of the abuse cycle, reconciliation and re-abuse often occur. If the spouse re-separates, the transitional compensation may resume. However, if the spouse decides to separate or divorce, and the service member has not been separated from active duty as a result of the abuse, they are not eligible for transitional compensation. The point is that the service member must be identified as an abuser for transitional pay to occur.

Family advocates help victims of abuse understand their rights, weigh options of pressing charges, and figure out how to move forward with or without their spouse. In some cases, depending on the individual circumstances, family advocates help couples with referrals to marriage counselors or anger management classes. In other words, they work to help victims set realistic expectations in understanding the

> **"Family advocates help victims of abuse understand their rights..."**

chances of reconciliation with the abuser and of the likelihood that the abuser will change. They work to help victims understand that there may not be a high probability of peaceful and meaningful reconciliation.

Victims of domestic abuse can also suffer from serious depression as a result of the abuse cycle and from the process of separation from the abuser. Advocates can help victims find the inner resources and outside assistance to make a new life for themselves.

 **FAQs**

Q. What is domestic violence?

A. *Domestic violence is a pattern of behavior where one person in a relationship tries to gain power and control over his or her partner through fear and intimidation. This can take the form of threatening or actually using physical violence, or the abuse can be emotional, economic, or sexual.*

Q. How big is the problem?

A. *Domestic violence often goes unreported, but an estimated three to four million American women are beaten each year by their spouses or partners. The prevalence rate of spousal abuse in the military has increased steadily since 1990, according to DoD statistics. Officials attribute the higher rate to greater public and command awareness and concern, an increase in the number of reports by victims themselves, and more funding for family advocacy programs.*

A comparison of 1995 domestic violence rates among the services shows the Army and Marine Corps with the highest rate of 24 confirmed reports of abuse per 1,000 spouses. The Navy had a rate of 15 confirmed reports per 1,000, and the Air Force had a rate of 14 confirmed reports per 1,000. In its 2002 report to Congress on reported domestic violence incidents, DoD stated that of the 2,173 Army and Air Force incidents for which sufficient evidence existed to take disciplinary action, 1,027—or 47 percent— had no actions identified,

In 2000, the DoD created a program called "Initiatives" to help. However, six years later, Congress's Government Accountability Office (GAO) says that the DoD is falling far short of fulfilling recommendations to address the problem. The 2006 GAO report, states that out of 194 task-force recommendations, less than half have been implemented, including training military police on proper handling of abuse cases and implementing violence intervention initiatives.

The GAO report underlined the lack of accurate data on rates of domestic violence as a significant barrier to responding to the problem. In addition to failing to collect reports of emotional abuse and off-base incidents, a number of criminal acts of domestic violence have gone unreported.

> **"Domestic violence can flare up with little or no warning and from a spouse who is a loving partner in many other ways."**

Q. Can domestic violence be prevented?

A. *Domestic violence can flare up with little or no warning and from a spouse who is a loving partner in many other ways. The abuse may start as verbal or psychological, and then escalate to physical assault. Therefore, the best time to seek counseling and take other preventive steps is at the first sign of abuse. In order to prevent future abuse, both partners must be committed to making a nonviolent relationship work.*

Q. How are victims protected?

A. *Police can help when physical violence is occurring or seems imminent. The courts can provide special orders to keep abusive partners away from their victims. Counselors and support groups are available for both victims and abusers. Local domestic violence shelters offer safe havens for victims and children as well as counseling and education programs.*

Q. What happens if a domestic or child abuse report is made?

A. *Domestic violence and child abuse reports are serious and involve both military and civilian law enforcement. When a report is made about violence or abuse in a military family home, many agencies become involved. The service member's chain of command is*

> **"The service member's chain of command is informed . . . "**

informed, and there will be two concurrent investigations conducted—one from the military, the other from the civilian authorities.

Once a report occurs, the following individuals will conduct the investigation and/or counseling to ensure the healthiest outcome for the military family:

Case Manager

This Family Advocacy Program staff person is responsible for assessing the report of suspected abuse, determining family strengths and treatment needs, developing a treatment plan, presenting the incident to the Case Review Committee, and coordinating the services provided from military and civilian agencies to meet the requirements of the treatment plan.

Case Review Committee

This multidisciplinary team of service providers and other professionals directly involved with individual incidents of abuse and neglect coordinate installation and civilian resources to:
- Assess the credibility of the reported incident of family violence; and,
- Plan the appropriate treatment for the victim and abuser, based on the severity of the harm and risk of future harm.

If the service member is found guilty of domestic violence charges or of child abuse, there will be punitive action taken. Depending on the outcome of the investigation and the seriousness of the crime, the service member may be sentenced to time in a military prison and dishonorably discharged.

Q. What is a military protective order?

A military protective order (MPO) is issued by the command of a suspected abuser. A MPO may be verbal or written. A MPO may direct service members to stay away from victims or designated places, refrain from doing certain things, require the service member to move into government quarters, and provide support for family members.

> **"If the service member is found guilty of domestic violence charges or of child abuse, there will be punitive action taken."**

Q. What is a disbarment order?

Disbarment orders govern the conduct of suspected civilian abusers. The order denies the civilian access to the military installation. Essentially, the order separates the civilian abuser from the abused by preventing access to the installation where the family resides.

Q. Who is responsible for the enforcement of a MPO or disbarment order?

Enforcement of such orders is the responsibility of the command issuing the order. Apprehension and arrest are not mandated for military police or command. Local law enforcement may respond to an incident and take custody of the service member under a Memorandum of Understanding/Agreement. Local law enforcement does not have the authority to arrest a service member for violation of a MPO.

Q. Are Civilian Protection Orders (CPOs) enforceable on military installations?

The Armed Forces Domestic Security Act (P.L. 107-311) requires the enforcement of CPOs on military installations. The protocols have not been developed and implemented by the Secretary of Defense to date.

Q. Do the firearms restrictions concerning respondents subject to CPOs apply to military personnel?

The official use exemption for law enforcement and military personnel permit a service member to possess firearms and ammunition as required by the terms of service or employment. The exemption does not apply to personal firearms used outside the scope of employment.

Q. Do the provisions concerning persons convicted of misdemeanor domestic violence apply to military personnel?

The Domestic Violence Offender Gun Ban, a.k.a. the Lautenberg Amendment, is applicable to military personnel upon conviction of a misdemeanor crime of domestic violence. The Interim Policy of the Department of Defense does not automatically disqualify or separate military personnel from service.

 Need to Know

(Courtesy of the U.S. Office of Personnel Management handbook on domestic violence.)

Recognizing domestic violence is not always easy, even for the victims. This is because domestic violence is much more than physical abuse. In fact, many women who are controlled by their partners and who live in danger and fear have never been physically assaulted. In the early stages, the pattern of abuse is hard to recognize. People in abusive relationships, however, consistently report that the abuse gets worse over time

The following checklist of behaviors may help you decide if you or someone you know is being abused. Does your partner:

- **Use emotional and psychological control?**
  - o   Call you names, yell, put you down, make racial or other slurs, or constantly criticize or undermine you and your abilities as a wife, partner, or mother?
  - o   Behave in an overprotective way or become extremely jealous?
  - o   Prevent you from going where you want to, when you want to, and with whomever you choose as a companion?
  - o   Humiliate or embarrass you in front of other people?

- **Use economic control?**
  - o   Deny you access to family assets such as bank accounts, credit cards, or a car?
  - o   Control all the finances, force you to account for what you spend, or take your money?
  - o   Prevent or try to prevent you from getting or keeping a job or from going to school?
  - o   Limit your access to health, prescription, or dental insurance?

- **Make threats?**
  - o   Threaten to report you to the authorities (the police or child protective services) for something you didn't do?
  - o   Threaten to harm or kidnap the children?
  - o   Display weapons as a way of making you afraid or directly threaten you with weapons?
  - o   Use his anger or "loss of temper" as a threat to get you to do what he wants?

- **Commit acts of physical violence?**
  - o   Carry out threats to hurt you, your children, pets, family members, friends, or himself?
  - o   Destroy personal property or throw things around?
  - o   Grab, push, hit, punch, slap, kick, choke, or bite you?
  - o   Force you to have sex when you don't want to or to engage in sexual acts that you don't want to do?

These common control tactics used by abusers are certainly not the only ones. If your partner does things that restrict your personal freedom or that make you afraid, you may be in an abusive relationship.

Military Family Advocacy

- http://child.cornell.edu/army/fap.html- Presents World Wide Web resources in support of the U. S. Army Community and Family Support Center. http://child.cornell.edu/army/fap.html.

- **DoD**'s tools and resources available to installations. http://www.dod.mil/fapmip/tools.htm

- **Information about DoD's Family Advocacy Program** can be found on the Internet at www.mfrc.calib.com.

- **Gift from Within** is a non-profit organization dedicated to those who suffer post-traumatic stress disorder (PTSD), those at risk for PTSD, and those who care for traumatized individuals. GFW develops and disseminates educational material, including videotapes, articles, books, and other resources through its website. GFW

Make the Connection on MFN!
www.eMilitary.org/YourMFN.html
Sign on to the address shown above and Make the Connection to more resources on this topic!

also maintains a roster of survivors who are willing to participate in an international network of peer support. www.giftfromwithin.org

- The **Justice Department** also includes information on sexual assault, stalking, and other crimes at www.ojp.usdoj.gov/vawo.

- **The Miles Foundation** is a private, non-profit organization providing comprehensive services to victims of violence associated with the military; furnishing professional education and training to civilian community-based service providers and military personnel; conducting research; serving as a resource center for policymakers, advocates, journalists, scholars, researchers and students; and serving to ensure that public policy is well-informed and constructive.

The Foundation is responsible for the development of a coalition of organizations throughout the country and abroad fostering administrative and legislative initiatives to improve the military response. The foundation and its partners drafted "Improving the U.S. Armed Forces Response to Violence Against Women: Recommendations for Change." A copy of the Recommendations may be obtained at 203-270-7861 or Milesfdn@aol.com.

- The **Federal Office of Personnel Management** provides a wealth of information on domestic violence at www.opm.gov/workplac/html/domestic.html-ssi.

The Justice Department also includes information on sexual assault, stalking and other crimes at www.ojp.usdoj.gov/vawo.

For more OPM information on domestic violence, go to www.opm.gov/workplac/html/domestic.html-ssi.

- **Gift from Within**

Gift from Within is a non-profit organization dedicated to those who suffer post-traumatic stress disorder (PTSD), those at risk for PTSD, and those who care for traumatized individuals. GFW develops and disseminates educational material, including videotapes, articles, books, and other resources through its website. GFW also maintains a roster of survivors who are willing to participate in an international network of peer support. www.giftfromwithin.org

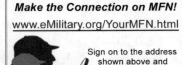

Make the Connection on MFN!
www.eMilitary.org/YourMFN.html

Sign on to the address shown above and Make the Connection to more resources on this topic!

52 Divorce in the Military

From the Field with Gene Thomas Gomulka

Gene Thomas Gomulka is a retired Navy Chaplain with over 30 years of pastoral and military experience. Having received the Alfred Thayer Mahan Award from the Secretary of the Navy "for literary achievement and inspirational leadership," his goal is to promote better military marriages. He is the author of The Survival Guide for Marriage in the Military, and his Marriage and Military Life inventory for dating and married couples. He is a Military Family Network (www.eMilitary.org/forums) forum leader for topics concerning military relationships. His website is located at www.plaintec.net.

More than half the people who serve in the armed services today are married. Unfortunately, more than half of those who marry while on active duty will divorce, many even before they complete their first term. This does not have to happen to you.

Why do so many military marriages fail? There are a number of reasons including financial insecurity, particularly among junior enlisted personnel; loneliness and stress caused by frequent deployments and separations; immaturity on the part of service men and women who tend to marry much younger than their civilian counterparts; and the challenge of raising children from a previous relationship that predispose some families toward divorce. While some of these factors are not unique to couples in the armed services, the more of them that are present in a particular relationship, the harder it may be for that couple to achieve lifelong marital happiness.

In an effort to help couples remain strong in their love for one another, many counselors will employ inventories to assess couples' strengths and weaknesses. However, because many military personnel are often hesitant to seek professional help from a counselor or chaplain, these diagnostic tools are rarely utilized. It was for this reason that I developed *Marriage and Military Life* and the self-grading inventory that, in addition to being a marriage preparation tool, can also help married military couples identify problematic aspects of their relationship.

Once problems are identified with the help of an inventory, the next step is to determine how serious they are (e.g., problems involving long-term infidelity in which there is emotional involvement is more serious than being dissatisfied with a spouse's culinary shortcomings). If it is discovered that the problems are quite serious and cannot be resolved by the spouses themselves, then the couples will ordinarily need to seek professional help if the relationship is to be saved and renewed.

> **"About half the military marriages that end in divorce today could have been saved with professional help."**

About half the military marriages that end in divorce today could have been saved with professional help. Unfortunately, many people will go to a lawyer to file for a divorce before first attempting reconciliation with the help of a counselor, chaplain, or member of the clergy.

While a number of couples can achieve reconciliation and renew their love for one another, others may have problems that are so serious and deep-rooted that divorce is the only option to avoid abuse, continued infidelity, or other truly "irreconcilable differences." In such cases, it is important to work to reduce any long-term negative affects that can harm future relationships and any children involved.

Couples with children often recognize how their marital relationship impacts the lives of their children. Even if a couple does not divorce, a problematic marital relationship still can prove psychologically and emotionally harmful to children. While a divorce can be a relief for children in some families, particularly if abuse was involved, children will react in different ways. Their reactions will depend upon such factors as: the quality of their relationship with their parents, the past and present relationship between their parents, the age and gender of the children, how their parents helped the children handle the situation, and remarriage.

Like most forms of cancer that have higher remission rates if treated early, so too can early detection and professional treatment of serious marital problems result in higher reconciliation rates leading to stronger and more fulfilling relationships. If a person is smart enough to go to a doctor when certain symptoms become more problematic, why wouldn't a couple seek professional help when they are incapable of resolving their relationship problems? If your partner were ever to raise the issue of divorce, would you both be willing to seek professional help in an effort to save the relationship? Chaplains and family support counselors are readily available to help military couples that wish to resolve relationship problems and deepen their love for one another. In most cases, they are no more than a phone call away.

 **FAQs**

Q. Will military lawyers help couples obtain a divorce?

A. *Military lawyers offer very little help when it comes to divorce proceedings. While they can provide general advice, and in some cases a referral to a civilian attorney, they cannot become involved in the actual divorce process. For matters involving divorce, separation, or child support, military personnel and their spouses should consult with a civilian attorney who is not only knowledgeable of the laws of a particular state, but has experience with military-related family law. Such an attorney will have knowledge of the provisions of the Servicemembers Civil Relief Act (SSCRA) and the Uniform Services Former Spouse Protection Act (USFSPA), as well as specific provisions required for garnishment of military pay.*

Q. What are some of the harmful effects of divorce upon children?

A. *Children who have experienced the divorce of their parents often score worse on measures of self-esteem and psychological adjustment. They exhibit more health, behavioral, and emotional problems than do children living with intact families or children living with single mothers who have never been married. Children whose parents have divorced are increasingly the victims of abuse and have higher rates of suicide. They are also involved more frequently in crime and drug abuse than adolescents from families in which their parents remained married. Children from disrupted families are also more likely to repeat a grade or drop out of high school than those from intact families. Those who do graduate from high school are less likely to go on to college. This lack of educational achievement may predispose them to long-term underemployment and even, unemployment.*

> **"Children from disrupted families are also more likely to repeat a grade or drop out of high school than those from intact families."**

Q. How can divorced parents reduce the harmful effects of divorce on their children?

A. *While a divorce can be a relief for children in some families, particularly if abuse was involved, children will react in different ways, depending on such factors as the quality of their relationship with their parents, the age and gender of the children, and remarriage.*

Children perceive post-divorce conflict as continued divisiveness, thus extending the divorce trauma. Parents should avoid saying inappropriate things to their children about their ex-spouse or attempt revenge by finding ways to spoil visitations that can only further traumatize their children.

Need to Know

Tips for your Marriage

1. One of the major causes of divorces in the military is financial mismanagement. If you find that you are spending more money than you are making, get budgeting help immediately before financial problems become the least of your worries.

2. Multiple back-to-back deployments have also weakened the love of many military couples. Following a deployment, go on a marriage enrichment retreat together or use a book like *The Survival Guide for Marriage in the Military* designed to strengthen marriage relationships despite the challengers posed by military life.

3. The effects of infidelity can destroy most marriages unless both partners want to try to save the marriage. If it becomes known that a partner was unfaithful, don't try to resolve the problem on your own. Seek professional help to help reconciliation and healing occur.

> **"Seek professional help to help reconciliation and healing occur."**

4. Couples who pray together not only have lower divorce rates, but also are happier and more sexually fulfilled than non-religious couples. Reduce your chances of becoming a divorce statistic and increase the quality of your love for one another by experiencing the encouragement and support that comes from involvement in a faith community.

5. Most divorces can be prevented by early detection of problems and treatment by a counselor or clergy person. If you are having problems in your marriage that you are incapable of resolving on your own, seek professional help before little problems become big problems that can destroy your marriage and family life.

In an effort to promote strong marriages and lower high military divorce rates, the various branches of the military offer a variety of programs and services. In addition to counseling services offered by chaplains and family support counselors, a number of programs have been developed to help offset the consequences of multiple long-term deployments to war torn areas like Iraq and Afghanistan.

 o After recording a significant increase in divorces in the aftermath of 9/11, the Army has implemented new programs, including the Deployment Cycle Support Program, the Building Strong and Ready Families Program, the Strong Bonds marriage education program, and the P.I.C.K. (Premarital Interpersonal Choices and Knowledge) program, which helps single soldiers make wise decisions when they choose mates.

 o Many active duty and reserve Marine Corps, Navy, and Air Force commands have ordered and use the *Marriage and Military Life* inventory (particularly with dating military couples) and *The Survival Guide for Marriage in the Military* (geared toward engaged and married couples). Both of these publications are available on line at www.plaintec.net.

 o Chaplains from all branches of the military also sponsor or join family support counselors in offering, marriage enrichment retreats. Many of them take place over weekends in scenic, comfortable, and relaxed hotel settings.

 o In addition to counseling services offered on most bases, Military One Source at 800-342-9647 offers five free counseling sessions that are provided by local licensed civilian counselors.

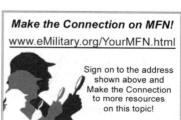

Make the Connection on MFN!

www.eMilitary.org/YourMFN.html

Sign on to the address shown above and Make the Connection to more resources on this topic!

53 Adoption: A Journey of Love

From the Field with Dan and Andrea Turak

Dan Turak is the son of a WWII veteran and an executive with XM Satellite Radio. Dan and his wife Andrea live in the DC Metropolitan area and work to share their adoption journey with other families. Recently, they have welcomed a new addition to their family, a baby daughter, Jillian Marie. Dreams do come true.

O ur story is about hope. It's actually about a dream that we both share and our hope of making that dream come true. Our dream is to become parents. Maybe it's your dream, too. It sounds simple enough, doesn't it? But we know that this dream comes very easily to some, but not to all.

We never imagined how difficult it would be to fulfill this dream. It became an emotionally and physically taxing roller coaster ride. This path was, and still is, filled with hope and excitement but has its disappointments, too. Our journey began over three years ago, and it's still not over; however, we are finally seeing the light at the end of the tunnel.

We're actually pretty typical. There's nothing unusual about our lives. Like many Americans, or maybe even you, we were married later in life. We knew we wanted a family and that we didn't have a lot of time to waste. After having difficulty conceiving naturally, we sought assistance with medical professionals through a fertility center. There, while we saw countless others meet with success, we experienced repeated failed infertility treatments.

We heard our friends and the fertility center talking about adoption. We attended a few adoption seminars to start educating ourselves, but we weren't ready to take that step—until last year. You have to be ready! We started to do some research, talked to adoptive families, and read some books. The more we talked about it, the more we believed that adoption was the chosen path for us.

The process can be daunting and overwhelming, but together we talked and made a plan to take one step at a time. Don't be frightened! The adoption process is just that: a guided, systematic process where someone is helping you each step of the way. Now don't misunderstand us. You will have to do the work of meeting the established requirements just like we did. This can be tedious, time consuming, and frustrating, so we suggest that you break down the process into steps and complete one step at a time. When we did this, we felt

> **"A home study requires you to share, well, everything about you and your life, and the successful completion of this study is required just to get in the door of the adoption agencies."**

more confident that it would soon be over, that we were accomplishing something, and that we were successfully moving closer to achieving our goal.

To give you an idea of what you will need to do, we'll share a glimpse of what it takes to complete a home study. A home study requires you to share, well, everything about you and your life, and the successful completion of this study is required just to get in the door of the adoption agencies. When we went through the process, we had to provide information and documents on our health and well-being, our criminal background, our financial and employment status, our environment and where we lived, and, our relationships with others including family and friends.

This required providing references, written autobiographies, completing questionnaires, and contacting numerous agencies and organizations from multiple levels of government, including federal, state and local offices. If we hadn't already agreed, as a team, to take it one step at a time, we could have lost ourselves in mountains of details!

After completing a stack of paperwork, collecting all of our "very important" documents, passing a home inspection by an environmental agency and the fire department, we were interviewed by a home study counselor in our home. The next part was hard. We waited. There wasn't anything else we could do, but let the process move on. Finally, a few weeks later, we received our certified Home Study Document. We can't describe how good it felt to receive that letter! It meant that we were officially on our way to becoming parents.

In addition to the paperwork, there are applications and registrations with each agency you select to use. There are so many decisions to make. What kind of agency should we use? Should it be a private agency or a public agency, domestic or international? Or,

> **"…we believed that it demonstrated our strong faith in family and our commitment to adoption."**

should we consider a private and independent adoption? What can we afford? Would a newborn or an older child be more appropriate for us? What level of openness with the birth mother do we think is appropriate for us and for our new child? Is the timing right? Are we prepared? What level of risk are we willing to consider? What are the pros and cons of using the home study counselor, attorney, etc? For instance, when an agency makes a match for you, it is automatic, whereas in a private adoption, you have more decision-making authority to complete the adoption.

We have to tell you, it's a bit overwhelming at times. If every biological parent had to go through all of these hoops, we wondered if there would be as many children in this world as there currently are. However, we believed that it demonstrated our strong faith in family and our commitment to adoption.

We decided to explore as many avenues as possible by keeping a few balls in the air at the same time to enhance our chances of a successful adoption. You might want to do the same thing. We decided to open the door for a private, domestic adoption as well as sign up with an agency that specializes in domestic adoptions. Pursuing a private adoption, we started to get the word out that we were ready to adopt. All of our friends, family, and acquaintances learned of our dream. Somewhere, someone might know of a woman (birthmother) who we could help, and in return, she could help us. Adoption attorneys will legalize the adoption.

As far as agencies are concerned, after researching a list of adoption agencies in the U.S., we finally decided on one. This is not an easy decision. You need to find the right fit. We applied, completed more paperwork, talked to the agency staff, and created our adoption profile. We were finally approved and "activated" last month.

Now, again, for the second time, we wait. This is the hard part. Sit and wait for the phone to ring. The bad news is that we don't know when it will ring. The good news is . . . it will ring. On that day, we will learn all about our birthmother and will be able to start planning for our family.

> **"Hope is a powerful experience."**

Hope is a powerful experience. It is one that gives us the strength and confidence to know that there is a child that needs us, and we in return, need him or her. We hope that our dream comes true. We are excited about how far we have come and what lies ahead.

And we share this hope with you, too. We have learned a lot from research and our own unique adoption experience. You will, too. Every adoption process is different and will present different challenges and different benefits. We have hope, though, that our effort and yours, will result in the pitter-patter of two more feet in your home and ours.

 **FAQs**

Q. Should I adopt internationally or domestically?

A. *This is a personal decision that only you (and your spouse) can make. We were told very early in the adoption process, that adoption comes with risk. There are different risk factors as well as different benefits with international vs. domestic adoption. You need to educate yourself on both options and make a decision that works for you.*

Q. How do I start the adoption process?

A. *It's always hard getting started. Think about the different avenues of adoption: a private or public agency or a private adoption. Start by doing some research on the Internet and by reading a few books. There are a lot of resources available to you. It's also important to know the adoption laws in your state. We joined a national organization, RESOLVE, which offers educational materials, seminars, and support groups. Build a network. The seminars connected us to our attorney and home study counselor.*

Q. How long will it take?

A. *This is the most difficult part. Timing is different for everyone depending on your adoption path. The home study takes approximately two months, but can happen faster if necessary. Some adoption agencies claim shorter time frames than others once you are "activated." The agency we chose told us that our match can happen at any time with in the next year. Privately, the timing is dependent on your advertising commitment. As soon as you find a birth mother and everyone agrees to the adoption plan, it will happen faster.*

Q. Who can adopt?

A. *There are plenty of children that need a home. Every agency will summarize their criteria for adoptive parents. If you pursue private adoption and find a birth mother who meets your criteria and she meets yours, you can adopt. Basically, if you have a safe, stable home and a big heart, you can adopt (assuming no criminal record). Some agencies work with single parents and some* *do not. If you are concerned about your financial situation, you can still adopt as long as you can demonstrate financial stability. As a matter of fact, there are several programs that assist families financially. Look online to find out what is available. Don't give up hope.*

Q. What is the basic adoption process if you decide to use an agency?

A. *There are several steps in the process:*
1. Application (birth, marriage, and divorce certificates, medical statement, financial statements, verification of employment, letters of reference, criminal background checks, child abuse checks, etc.)
2. Home Study (autobiography, reason for adopting, your strengths and weaknesses, personality, strength of marriage, health, work, family plans, religion, family life, expectations of adoption)
3. Write a birth-parent letter and create a profile. This becomes your resume for the birth mother to review. It should be an honest and sincere snapshot of you.
4. Call notifying you that the birth mother has chosen you.
5. Meet with birth mother (depends on birth mother)
6. Birth and relinquishing the birth mother's rights dependent on the state laws
7. Placement Day—Yippie!!! You are finally a parent!!
8. Post Placement visits—your home study counselor visits again!
9. Finalization—approximately six months later

Military Families and Adoption: A Fact Sheet for Families
Courtesy of the Child Welfare Information Gateway: http://www.childwelfare.gov/

Adoption is a realistic option for military personnel who want to expand their families. This fact sheet answers the most common questions asked by military families.

Q. How do I get started?

A. Adoption: Where Do I Start? *A fact sheet by Child Welfare Information Gateway, answers many of the questions families have when considering adoption. Visit your Family Service Center and see if they are aware of an adoptive parent support group on or near your installation. If you live overseas, talk with your installation's school or medical clinic personnel, who are often familiar with local resources and services.*

Q. Where can I learn about adoption laws?

A. *State law governs U.S. adoptions. The State Statutes Search, compiled by Child Welfare Information Gateway, provides information on the adoption laws in each State. Your Judge Advocate General (JAG) officer may be able to point you to applicable laws and policies as well as applicable agreements between the United States and other countries where military personnel are stationed.*

Q. Does the home study process differ for military families?

A. *The home study process will generally be the same for military families. The Adoption Home Study Process, a Child Welfare Information Gateway factsheet, provides information regarding what is generally included in a home study and topics discussed in this process. The process may differ slightly for military families in the following ways:*

- ✓ More criminal background checks may be requested because agencies often require background checks for every State in which you have lived.
- ✓ Overseas families will need to have a home study completed by a social worker licensed in the United States to do adoption home studies.
- ✓ Adoption of a child born in the United States requires checking with the State adoption specialist in the **State where the child resides** to verify that State's requirements **before** completing the home study.
- ✓ Adoption of a child born outside the United States requires families to comply with the laws of their State of record, United States immigration law, and the laws of the foreign country where the child resides.
- ✓ The National Adoption Directory contains a State-by-State listing of adoption specialists and adoptive parent support groups.

Q. How will deployment impact my home study?

A. *You may be able to have some of your home study documents transferred to an agency near your installation; however, many agencies require their own forms and protocols for the home study. The International Social Services—phone: (410) 230-2734—has social workers in 140 countries where the United States has military installations.*

Q. How long will this process take?

A. *While each family's situation is different, it usually takes at least 2 to 10 months (depending on agency waiting lists and training requirements) to com-*

plete the home study. After that, it may take as many as 6 to 12 months for a child to be placed. It is not unusual to wait up to 2 years to find an appropriate adoptive child. Older children may require more pre-placement visits to ease their transition into a new family. Overseas families may need to travel back to the United States to meet and visit with their child. Realistic expectations about the waiting period, and making use of that time to prepare for the child you would like to parent, can help ease the frustration of the wait.

Q. How long will I have to stay in the state?

A. *Families are able to move to different States after a child has been placed in their home; however, the Interstate Compact on the Placement of Children needs to grant prior approval any time a child moves to another State for the purposes of adoptive placement.* Military Families and Adoption: A Bulletin for Professionals *has more information on the Interstate Compact.*

Q. What if I am deployed?

A. *Deployment Deferment or Extension of Assignment are options military families may request if they need to remain in one State to finalize an adoption.*

Q. How much leave can I get?

A. *Military families are not eligible for leave under the Family Medical Leave Act (FMLA); however, according to U.S. Department of Defense (DoD) Instruction 1341.9, commanders are encouraged to approve requests for ordinary leave once a child is placed in the home of a service member. Check with your JAG if there is a question about this instruction, as interpretation varies from installation to installation.*

The instruction states that single members or one member of a military couple shall receive a 4-month assignment and deployment deferment immediately following the date a child is placed. A child is considered a dependent in determining travel and transportation allowances (Public Law No. 102-190, section 621, reference (d)).

Q. How much will adoption cost?

A. *The costs of adoption can range from nothing (if you adopt from the foster care system and use a public agency), to more than $30,000 (if you adopt independently).* Cost of Adopting, *a Child Welfare Information Gateway publication, has more information. There are several resources to help defray the cost of adoption:*

Adoption Reimbursement. According to DoD Instruction 1341.9, up to $2,000 per child (or up to $5,000 per year) for qualifying expenses is available to military families whose adoptions were arranged by a qualified adoption agency. Benefits are paid after the adoption is complete. The National Military Family Association has a factsheet, *DoD Adoption Reimbursement Program* (PDF - 35 KB), with further information on allowable expenses.

Adoption Assistance (sometimes called Adoption Subsidies) is available for some children with special needs. A Child Welfare Information Gateway factsheet, *Adoption Assistance for Children Adopted From Foster Care: A Factsheet for Families*, is another resource. Not all children will qualify for adoption subsidies, and the subsidies will vary depending on the needs of the child.

The military defines special needs more narrowly to mean "persons with physical or mental disabilities or severe illness." This differs from what adoption professionals often refer to as children with special needs—more broadly defined to include children who may be healthy but are older, in sibling groups, or members of a minority group.

Q. What services are available after adoption?

A. **Child Development Programs** *are available at approximately 300 DoD locations, including 800 childcare centers and approximately 9,000 family childcare homes. The services may include full day, part-day, and hourly (drop-in) childcare; part-day preschool programs; before- and after-school programs for school-aged children; and extended hours care, including nights and weekends. Not all services are available at all installations.*

The **Exceptional Family Member Program** within the military provides many services including assisting families who need to be stationed in areas that provide for specific medical or other services that might not be available in remote locations.

Family Service Centers located on every major military installation can provide military families with information regarding adoption reimbursement and other familial benefits.

Post Adoption Services are provided by many public child welfare agencies. Child Welfare Information Gateway factsheet, *After Adoption: The Need for Services*, has more information. If you are stationed in the United States, your adoption caseworker or State Adoption Specialist can help you find the services available in your State. Adoptive parent support groups are also a great source of information about the services in your area. Some military installations have active adoptive parent support groups.

The Value of Adoptive Parent Groups and Tips on Selecting an Adoption Therapist factsheets from Child Welfare Information Gateway may be helpful.

Q. What about medical coverage for my child?

A. *An adopted child, including a child placed in the home of a service member by a placement agency, is eligible for benefits after the child is enrolled in the* **Defense Enrollment Eligibility Reporting System (DEERS)—phone: 800.538.9552.** *The patient affairs personnel at a specific medical treatment facility may have information. Specific information on access and eligibility is available on the TRICARE Web site or by calling the DoD Worldwide* **TRICARE Information Center at 888.363.2273**.

 Need to Know

- Are you ready? (emotionally, financially, time wise)
- Why do you want to adopt? It has to be for the right reason. It's a challenging path.
- Are you interested in domestic vs. international adoption? There are pros and cons to both.
- What are your state laws? Every state is different.
- Learn about the different types of adoption:
  o Agency (private vs. public)
  o Independent/private adoption
- Education. Research everything!! Know the risks and benefits. Tap into the Internet, books, and talk to adoptive families. Join associations, attend seminars, and sign up for adoption newsletters.
- Home Study. This is a requirement, no matter which path you choose. Be prepared for a mountain of paperwork. Take it one step at a time.
- What type of adoption are you comfortable with? Open, semi-open or closed? This is a personal decision.
- Design an adoption plan that fits your personality and weighs your risk tolerance.
- Let go of control. It's hard. Control what you can and make educated decisions that you and your spouse are comfortable with.

Reference Books, Magazines and Newsletters

The Complete Adoption Book, by Laura Beauvais-Godwin and Raymond Godwin, Esq.

Adopting in America by Randall B. Hicks
The Essential Adoption Handbook, by Colleen Alexander-Roberts
The Penguin Adoption Handbook: A Guide to Creating Your Own Family, by Edmund Blair Bolles
Raising Adoptive Children: A Practical Reassuring Advice for Every Adoptive Parent by Lois Ruskai Melina

Roots and Wings Adoption Magazine
www.adoption.org
Adoptive Families of America Newsletter
800-888-7828

Make the Connection on MFN!
www.eMilitary.org/YourMFN.html

Sign on to the address shown above and Make the Connection to more resources on this topic!

54   Citizenship

From the Field with Caroline Peabody

Caroline Peabody *is the daughter of a disabled Vietnam era Marine, military spouse, former president of The Military Family Network, lifetime volunteer, and distinguished speaker and lecturer on military life. She holds a B.S. in sociology and M.A. in organizational management with extensive research on communication systems as they relate to military well being and community capacity-building. She is a published writer and columnist on matters relating to military families, military learning models, and military relations.*

According to a report on "Naturalization and Citizenship in the Military," since the events of September 11, 2001, and the war against terrorism started with Operation Enduring Freedom and Operation Noble Eagle, there has been interest in legislation to expand the citizenship benefits for aliens serving in the military. Legislative interest supporting citizenship for foreign-born military service members has increased considerably since the beginning of Operation Iraqi Freedom in March 2003.

The reported deaths in action of noncitizen soldiers has drawn attention to provisions of the Immigration and Nationality Act (INA) that grant posthumous citizenship for those who die as a result of active-duty service during a period of hostilities. The INA also provides for expedited naturalization for noncitizens serving in the United States military.

During peacetime, noncitizens in the military may petition to naturalize after three years aggregate military service rather than the requisite five years of legal permanent residence. During periods of military hostilities, noncitizens serving in the armed forces can naturalize immediately. On July 3, 2002, President George W. Bush designated the period beginning on September 11, 2001, as a "period of hostilities," which triggered immediate naturalization eligibility for active-duty U.S. military service members, whereupon the Department of Defense and the former Immigration and Naturalization Service announced that they would work together to ensure that military naturalization applications were processed expeditiously. This has sparked interest in legislation to further expedite the naturalization process for military service members. As of February 2003, there were 37,000 noncitizens serving in active duty in the U.S. armed forces, almost 12,000 foreign nationals serving in the selected reserves, and another 8,000 serving in the inactive National Guard and ready reserves.

 **FAQs**

Q. How can I qualify for citizenship as a service member?

A. *There are general requirements and qualifications that must be met in order for you to become a U.S. citizen. These include:*

- Demonstrating that you have good moral character
- Demonstrating knowledge of the English language
- Demonstrating knowledge of U.S. government and history ("civics")
- Demonstrating attachment to the United States by taking an oath of allegiance to the U.S. Constitution.

Q. What requirements am I exempted from as a military member?

A. *As a member of the military there are other naturalization requirements that you may be exempted from, including the required residency and physical presence in the United States. These exceptions are outlined in Sections 328 and 329 of the INA.*

Section 328, INA:

This section applies to all members currently serving in the U.S. Armed Forces or those who have already been discharged from service

- Have you served honorably for a total of one or more years?
- Are you a lawful permanent resident?
- Will you be filing your application for naturalization while still in service or within six months of being discharged?

> **"...applies to members of the U.S. Armed Forces who currently serve or have served in active-duty status during authorized periods of conflict..."**

Section 329, INA:

This section applies to members of the U.S. Armed Forces who currently serve or have served in active-duty status during authorized periods of conflict as outlined in the INA (WWI; September 1, 1939-December 31, 1946; June 25, 1950-July1, 1955; and February 28, 1961-October 5, 1978) or any additional period designated by the President in an Executive Order.[1]

- Have you served honorably in the U.S. Armed Forces during an authorized period of conflict?
- After enlistment, were you lawfully admitted as a permanent resident of the United States, OR at the time of enlistment, reenlistment, or induction were you physically present in the United States or qualifying territory?

Q. What changes went into effect in 2004?

A. *Recent legislation has called for additional benefits to members of the military. These benefits will go into effect on October 1, 2004.*

- **No fees** will be charged when you file for naturalization.
- The naturalization process will be made available overseas to members of the Armed Forces at U.S. embassies, consulates, and where practical, military installations abroad.

Q. What do I do if I qualify?

A. *Every military installation should have a designated point-of-contact to handle your application and certify your* Request for Certification of Military or Naval Service (N-426). *You should inquire through your chain of command to find out who this person is, so they can help you with your application packet.*

Your point-of-contact will send your N-400, G325B, and certified N-426 to:

The Nebraska Service Center, PO Box 87426, Lincoln, NE 68501-7426.

The Service Center will review your application and perform the necessary security checks. Then, they will send it to the district office closest to your location. If you have a preference as to where you would like to be interviewed, you can provide that information in a cover letter attached to your naturalization packet. The district office will set a date to interview you and test your knowledge of English and civics. If granted, USCIS will inform you of the date you can take your oath of allegiance.

> **"The Service Center will review your application and perform the necessary security checks."**

1 Recently, the President signed an Executive Order identifying September 11, 2001, and after as an authorized period of conflict.

Need to Know

Applying for Citizenship

If you are a member of the U.S. Armed Forces and are interested in becoming a U.S. citizen, you may be eligible to apply for citizenship under special provisions provided for in the Immigration and Nationality Act (INA). Generally, service in the U.S. Armed Forces means service in one of the following branches: Army, Navy, Marine Corps, Air Force, Coast Guard, Certain Reserve components of the National Guard, and Selected Reserve of the Ready Reserve

Recent changes in the relevant sections of the INA (Sections 328 and 329) make it easier for qualified military personnel to become U.S. citizens if they choose to file a naturalization application. U.S. Citizenship and Immigration Services (USCIS) has created a streamlined process specifically for military personnel serving in active-duty status or who have recently been discharged.

> "Recent changes in the relevant sections of the INA (Sections 328 and 329) make it easier for qualified military personnel to become U.S. citizens if they choose to file a naturalization application."

Spouses of U.S. Citizens Deployed Abroad

If you are married to a U.S. citizen who is a member of the U.S. Armed Forces and your citizen spouse is or will be deployed abroad by the Armed Forces for one year, you may be eligible for expedited naturalization under section 319(b) of the INA. For more information, please refer to the USCIS handbook, "A Guide to Naturalization" (page 22) at http://uscis.gov/graphics/services/natz/English.pdf.

Posthumous Benefits

The INA allows for the awarding of posthumous citizenship to active-duty military personnel who die while serving in the Armed Forces. In addition, surviving family members seeking immigration benefits are given special consideration. To learn more, contact your military point-of-contact or the local district USCIS office.

Veterans of U.S. Armed Forces

Certain applicants who have served in the U.S. Armed Forces are eligible to file for naturalization based on current or prior U.S. military service. Such applicants should file the N-400 Military Naturalization Packet.

> **"Certain applicants who have served in the U.S. Armed Forces are eligible to file for naturalization based on current or prior U.S. military service."**

Lawful Permanent Residents with Three Years U.S. Military Service

An applicant who has served for three years in the U.S. military and who is a lawful permanent resident is excused from any specific period of required residence, period of residence in any specific place, or physical presence within the United States if an application for naturalization is filed while the applicant is still serving or within six months of an honorable discharge.

To be eligible for these exemptions, an applicant must: have served honorably or separated under honorable conditions; completed three years or more of military service; be a legal permanent resident at the time of his or her examination on the application; or establish good moral character if service was discontinuous or not honorable.

Applicants who file for naturalization more than six months after termination of three years of service in the U.S. military may count any periods of honorable service as residence and physical presence in the United States.

Naturalization Applicants Who Have Served Honorably in Any Specified Period of Armed Conflict with Hostile Foreign Forces

This is the only section of the Immigration and Naturalization Act that allows persons who have not been lawfully admitted for permanent residence to file their own application for naturalization. Any person who has served honorably during a qualifying time may file an application at any time in his or her life if, at the time of enlistment, reenlistment, extension of enlistment or induction, such person shall have been in the United States, the Canal Zone, American Samoa, or Swains Island, or on board a public vessel owned or operated by the United States for noncommercial service, whether or not he has been lawfully admitted to the United States for permanent residence.

An applicant who has served honorably during any of the following periods of conflict is entitled to certain considerations: World War I, 4/16/17 to 11/11/18; World War II, 9/1/39 to 12/31/46; Korean Conflict, 6/25/50 to 7/1/55; Vietnam Conflict, 2/28/61 to 10/15/78; Operation Desert Shield/Desert Storm, 8/29/90 to 4/11/91; Operation Enduring Freedom, 9/11/01 to (open); or any other period which the President, by Executive Order, has designated as a period in which the Armed Forces of the United States are or were engaged in military operations involving armed conflict with hostile foreign forces.

Applicants who have served honorably during any of the aforementioned conflicts may apply for naturalization based on military service and no period of residence or specified period of physical presence within the United States or any State shall be required.

Forms you will need to complete and submit:

- N-400, Application for Naturalization http://www.uscis.gov/graphics/formsfee/forms/n-400.htm
- N-426, Request for Certification of Military or Naval Service (*This form requires certification by the military prior to submission to USCIS*) http://www.uscis.gov/graphics/formsfee/forms/n-426.htm
- G-325B, Biographic Information http://www.uscis.gov/graphics/formsfee/forms/g-325b.htm

Forms and Handbooks

To get these forms, you can call the USCIS Form Line at: **1-800-870-3676** to request the "Military Packet" and obtain a copy of the handbook, "A Guide to Naturalization," or visit the website http://www.uscis.gov/graphics/index.htm.

Make the Connection on MFN!
www.eMilitary.org/YourMFN.html

Sign on to the address shown above and Make the Connection to more resources on this topic!

55   Military Law in Review

From the Field with Luis Trevino

Luis Trevino is a Vietnam era Marine, co-owner and Vice President of Media and Communications for The Military Family Network. Trevino has over thirty years of experience in owning and operating successful small businesses and entrepreneurial ventures. He is a published author and photographer on matters relating to military family life.

We know that laws exist to protect us. It doesn't mean we always understand them or the consequences that can happen if we break them. In fact, we probably know even less about the process of the law, how it works and our rights. Think about a time where you encountered the law. Like most of us, it was probably some minor traffic violation. Did you fully understand what was happening and the briefing you received from the officer? Did the idea of appearing in traffic court scare you because you had no idea of what to expect? Or maybe it was a family member who was in trouble. You felt concern, but you just didn't know how to help or what to do.

This chapter covers a small segment of the massive Military Law library to give you an overview of what can happen to a service member who has broken a law under the Uniform Code of Military Justice (UCMJ) on or off a military installation. You will get a glimpse of the Office of General Counsel and its areas of responsibility. Then, you will learn about how the military deals with someone who has committed a minor offense to someone who has severely taken liberties with a military code of ethics, and how punishment is handed down by a Commanding Officer. You will also gain a fuller understanding of a service member's rights while serving in the military.

When it comes to breaking the law, everyone who joins the military quickly learns that "the military takes care of its own."

When in the protection of military jurisdiction, service men and women are under a military umbrella that protects them from the outside world as they serve their country. In most

> **"…when a fellow service member violates a military code, it is understood that they are breeching a standard of excellence, honor and integrity."**

cases, the military is the officiating authority over legal violations made by its service members. This is one of the ways that the military judicial system differs from the civilian world. In addition, military service men and women are expected to represent the best citizens our country has to offer. They are taught to lead by example. It is an honor bestowed upon them, and for the most part, a duty that most service members take to heart. It is not surprising then, that when a fellow service member violates a military code, it is understood that they are breeching a standard of excellence, honor and integrity. When punishments are meted out in the military, this factor is taken into consideration. This is another way the military is different. Service members are reminded often not to embarrass their branch of service.

Their service is their family. It provides protection, it supplies discipline and it also, dispenses punishment. The following information will guide you in understanding the formal process for military disciplinary proceedings.

The Office of the General Counsel, headed by the General Counsel of the Department of Defense (DoD), is responsible for a multitude of high-level functional areas including the provision of advice on standards of conduct involving personnel of OSD and the oversight of the performance of legal services within the DoD. It is highly unlikely that you will ever be involved with this regulating authority; however, judicial authority and the official powers to enforce that authority are granted by the Office of the General Counsel to the leadership of your service branch including you local command.

Commanding Officers Convening Authority

A commanding officer (CO) has the authority to impose non-judicial punishment. The CO also has many other responsibilities, including authorizing searches and seizures of property; making the initial determination to confine an accused; and exercising prosecutorial discretion.

In exercising discretion, a CO may dismiss charges; effect non-punitive measures; impose non-judicial punishment; or refer a matter to court-martial. In referring a matter to court-martial, the CO becomes the convening authority. As such, the CO decides what charges to refer to the court-martial; what type of courts-martial; and selects the court-martial members (jury).

Additionally, the convening authority may negotiate

> **In exercising discretion, a CO may dismiss charges; effect non-punitive measures; impose non-judicial punishment; or refer a matter to court-martial. In referring a matter to court-martial, the CO becomes the convening authority.**

and bind the particular branch of military service to pretrial agreements; grant immunity to witnesses; disapprove findings; and grant clemency on the sentence. These powers are not absolute. The Uniform Code of Military Justice (UCMJ), the Manual for Courts-Martial (MCM), and the Manual of the Judge Advocate General (JAGMAN) govern commanding officers and convening authorities in their actions.

 **FAQs**

Q. What is a Court-Martial?

A. *The Uniform Code of Military Justice (UCMJ) provides* for three different types of court-martial: summary, special, and general. These forms of courts-martial differ in their make-up and the punishments that may be imposed. The Military Rules of Evidence apply to all classifications of courts-martial. Moreover, an accused must be proven guilty beyond a reasonable doubt.

Q. What is a Summary Court-Martial?

A. *A summary court-martial consists of one commissioned officer and may try only enlisted personnel for non-capital offenses. The punishment that may be imposed depends on the grade of the accused. In the case of enlisted members above the fourth pay grade, a summary court-martial may impose restriction for no more than two months, forfeiture of two-thirds of one month's pay, and reduction to the next inferior pay grade.*

In the case of all other enlisted members, the court-martial may also impose confinement for not more than one month and may reduce the accused to the lowest pay grade, E-1. The accused has the absolute right to refuse trial by summary court-martial. The accused does not have the right to representation by an attorney. The accused does have the right to cross-examine witnesses, to call witnesses and produce evidence, and to testify or remain silent.

Q. What is a Special Court-Martial?

A. *A special court-martial consists of not less than three members and a military judge, or an accused may be tried by military judge alone upon request of the accused. A special court-martial is often characterized as a mis-*

demeanor court and may try all persons subject to the UCMJ, including officers and midshipmen. A special court-martial may impose admonition, reprimand, restriction, extra duty, confinement for no more than six months, and forfeiture of two-

> "A special court-martial is often characterized as a misdemeanor court and may try all persons subject to the UCMJ."

thirds of a month's pay for six months in all cases. In addition, enlisted members may be reduced to the lowest pay grade and receive a bad-conduct discharge.

Q. What is a General Court-Martial?

A. *A general court-martial consists of not less than five members and a military judge, or an accused may be tried by military judge alone upon request of the accused. A general court-martial is often characterized as a felony court and may try all persons subject to the UCMJ, including officers and midshipmen. A general court-martial may adjudge any punishment not prohibited by the UCMJ, including death when specifically authorized.*

Q. What is Non-Judicial Punishment?

A. *Non-Judicial Punishment (NJP) is known by different terms among the services, such as "Article 15," "Office Hours," or "Captain's Mast," but the purpose of NJP is to discipline service members for minor offenses such as reporting late for duty, petty theft, destroying government property, sleeping on watch, providing false information, and disobeying standing orders.*

Note: Determining if an offense is "minor" is a matter of discretion for the commander imposing punishment, but the imposition of punishment for an offense other than a minor

> "The extent of these punishments depends on the grade of the officer imposing punishment, the grade of the accused, and whether the accused is attached to or embarked on a vessel."

offense does not rule out a court-martial for the same offense. Although the actual punishments under an NJP offense are limited to confinement on diminished rations, restriction to certain specified limits, arrest in quarters, correctional custody, extra duties, forfeiture of pay, detention of pay, and reduction in grade. The extent of these punishments depends on the grade of the officer imposing punishment, the grade of the accused, and whether the accused is attached to or embarked on a vessel.

Prior to the imposition of non-judicial punishment, an accused is entitled to notification:

- that the imposition of non-judicial punishment is being considered
- a description of the alleged offenses
- a summary of the evidence upon which the allegations are based
- notification that the accused has the right to refuse the imposition of punishment
- and any rights the accused has if NJP is accepted.

Except for individuals attached to or embarked on a vessel, service members have the right to refuse the imposition of non-judicial punishment. However, refusal of NJP will normally not result in the dismissal of charges. A commanding officer can still refer the charges to court-martial. An accused has the right to a personal appearance before the officer imposing punishment. During this appearance, the accused has the right against self-incrimination, the right to be accompanied by a spokesperson, the right to be informed of the evidence against him or her, the right to examine the evidence against him or her, the right to present matters on his or her own behalf, and to have the proceedings open to the public.

An accused may waive a personal appearance, if agreeable to the officer imposing punishment, and submit written matters for consideration by the imposition authority. The Military Rules of Evidence, other than rules concerning privileges, do not apply to the imposition of non-judicial punishment. The officer imposing punishment may consider all relevant matters so long as the accused has been given proper notice and the opportunity to respond. The officer must be convinced of the accused's guilt by a preponderance of the evidence. The accused may appeal the imposition of non-judicial punishment on the grounds that it is unjust or disproportionate to the offense. The appeal must be in writing and forwarded to the next superior authority via the officer who imposed punishment. The appeal must be referred to a judge advocate (JAG) for consideration and advice before the authority who is to act on it may make any decision.

> **"The accused may appeal the imposition of non-judicial punishment on the grounds that it is unjust or disproportionate to the offense."**

Need to Know

Location of Uniform Code of Military Justice:
http://www.loc.gov/rr/frd/Military_
Law/Military-Law-Review-home.
html
United States Code, Title 10, Subtitle
A, Part II, chapter 47

Part 10

Veteran Support
Caring: It Starts at Home

Caroline Peabody, Megan Turak, and Luis Trevino representing MFN's sponsorship of the dedication of Virginia's first Korean War Memorial located in downtown Hampton.

Photo: John Peabody

Introduction

My father was a veteran of WWII. During his tour of duty, he had surgery on his neck to remove a tumor in his salivary gland. It left a significant scar. He told me that he was slashed by a bayonet while fighting the enemy and showed me his battle souvenir to prove it. Like most school-age children, wide-eyed, naive, and full of wonder—fed on weekly doses of Walt Disney and Tinkerbell—I swallowed the whole story. He was my hero. I knew nothing then of men and their fish tales or war stories. But I was a quick study. One day, while bragging to my friend about my father's glorious triumph, my world came crashing down: my brother appeared, heard my version of my father's heroism, and quickly laid the matter to rest. Apparently, I was a silly little girl who would believe anything.

I guess I took the news pretty hard. After that, I can't say that I was terribly thrilled to hear many more military stories. In fact, as my father grew older, I would tease him: "Dad, a lot of times, older people will get stuck and tell the same stories, over and over, to their family. If you ever get stuck, here are five stories from your life that I could listen to over and over again. Now, if you begin repeating your Army stories like how you typed up the General's speech on note cards and inserted spaces for vocal pauses, we might have a bit of a problem on our hands." He just laughed, and then, would tell me about another experience he had in the Army.

Eventually, I learned to love those stories, or maybe it was just the time I shared with my Dad. Then, as a young adult attending college, I accepted a job with the Department of Veterans Affairs. I worked in the medical hospital. They stuck me on a night shift and put me in the basement filing medical charts. Except for being the only person on my shift, it wasn't so bad. I was able to go to school full time during the day, and I made enough money working to pay for it.

But it would get quiet and still. I would work for hours without a peep, except for my thoughts and the rustle of papers. And then, it happened. I don't recall where I was or what I was doing, but the change was precise and immediate. I wasn't just a clerk with an administrative task anymore. I was a custodian entrusted with the care of countless individuals who had bravely and courageously served our nation. As I saw it, they fought so I could be free.

All of a sudden, I wasn't alone. I was surrounded by thousands of military service members from every branch of service and they, who had sacrificed and cared for me, now depended on me to care for them. I stood up to the call of duty—I filed medical documents like a crazy woman because each of those medical reports now represented some test, some procedure, some needle stuck in the arm of one of my charges. I needed to make sure that they received the care that they deserved.

And, I would pray. As some of the patients passed on and their charts were removed from the active shelves, I would say a silent prayer—a prayer of comfort and gratitude for the gift that they had given me. I don't need to tell you that I saw my dad differently, too. He was my hero again, and this time, my brother wouldn't shake my faith.

This section, then, is about our nation's heroes, like my father, who answered our nation's call when we needed them. It is about our gratitude, and about giving back by caring. It is about providing support.

This section is especially about taking care of our service members and service members who have made the greatest sacrifices: our first chapter begins with the story of Vicky Field's son who survived being shot in the head while serving in Iraq.. It is about how to get the care you and your family need and how to take care of yourself. It is about how to transition from military service to civilian life and how to navigate the system to determine your eligibility and access your benefits.

This section is about those dedicated organizations that won't let us forget that it is our American duty, our responsibility to remember—to remember who our service members are and what they have done for us. It is about how these organizations work every day to help our veterans and the types of services and programs they offer.

And, finally, this section is a call to action, a reminder for all of us that there is more to be done on behalf of these great men and women.

—Megan Turak

56   A Triumph over Tragedy: A Wounded Warrior Story

From the Field with Vicky Fields and Thom Wilborn

Vicky Fields is a mother of a wounded warrior who suffered a severe brain injury as a result of a gunshot to the head while serving in Iraq. She currently serves as the Texas State Representative for the Severely Wounded.
Thom Wilborn *is the Assistant National Director of Communications, Disabled American Veterans.*

My story is a miracle story.

I am the mother of a wounded soldier. My son was shot in the head in Iraq in November of 2004. He was not supposed to live. When he had his surgery in Iraq, I was told that his condition remained critical. As the days passed, to his doctor's surprise, his bleeding stopped and he began to stabilize. They decided to fly him to Landstuhl where he continued to improve. Two days later, his physicians decided to transport him stateside to Walter Reed. Through the prayer and support of countless individuals and through my son's courageous spirit and will to live, my son regained his health. This is not to say that he is problem-free. What it does say is that, recently, my son played eighteen holes of golf with me and is doing well.

My story has a happy ending; but there were a lot of challenges along the way and my experience was not an effortless journey. For this reason, I continue to advocate for others who may be faced with similar situations, and it is why I am the Texas State Representative for the Severely Wounded. There are some very important points to understand when you have a wounded service member recovering in the hospital. You need to understand what will happen to all of you, to develop a support group, and to gain knowledge of how the system works.

Also, you should not ignore the severity of the injury and the effect it has on the injured soldier's life. I have seen many military men and women try to act tough as though their injury were nothing only to have problems stemming from this injury occur later. Your service member needs to be truthful about any pains or lack of mobility that he or she is experiencing so that this can be addressed upfront.

REMEMBER TO ASK QUESTIONS. THIS IS NOT A TIME TO BE BASHFUL. Call upon the Military Severely Injured Joint Support Ops Center because this will be your most useful tool and support group: 1-800-774-1361.

If you feel that your concerns are not being addressed, contact your state representative for assistance. Call and ask for the state representative for the severely wounded and ombudsman for your area. If you are in Texas and have questions, you may contact me at agentvf@gmail.com. May God Bless and keep you.

> **"If you feel that your concerns are not being addressed, contact your state representative for assistance."**

Guidance Along a Difficult Path

As Vicky related, responding to the experience of a wounded service member is a difficult path for a family member or loved one to travel: concern for care and rehabilitation for the wounded coupled with trying to fathom the military's complex language, rules, and forms for benefits and access to care makes it all that much harder. Help is certainly needed by everyone who has a loved one injured, and a caring and compassionate advocate, the Disabled American Veterans (DAV), is providing this help.

Recognizing the needs of newly injured service members, the Disabled American Veterans was quick to provide our expert assistance at Walter Reed Army Medical Center, Brooke Army Medical Center, and Bethesda National Naval Medical Center—the three giant medical centers where returning wounded initially recuperate. Today, a DAV National Service Officer has an office in both Walter Reed and Bethesda, and at Brooke medical facilities. Our NSOs are there to talk to the veterans and their family members, to provide comfort and information, to assist in ensuring that paperwork is accurate and complete, and to help guide the way through the military medical review process and the VA's medical claims process.

> **"Our NSOs are there to talk to the veterans and their family members, to provide comfort and information, to assist in ensuring that paperwork is accurate and complete, and to help guide the way through the military medical review process and the VA's medical claims process"**

Each of our NSOs is an expert in the complex and sometimes difficult processes faced by veterans and their families. Sadly, most returning wounded know little of their rightfully earned benefits, and their families know even less. It is a difficult and confusing time, but our NSOs are in the corner of the veterans and their families, providing advice, foreseeing needs, and working as a trusted advocate.

Any veteran seeking help can contact our National Service Offices located in nearly every VA regional office in the nation. They provide our free expert services to those who have served and sacrificed for the cause of liberty. For additional information and assistance, visit our website at www.DAV.org or call 1-877-426-2838, or 888-872-3289.

 **FAQs**

Q. What is TSGLI?

A. *Traumatic Servicemembers' Group Life Insurance (TSGLI) provides monetary assistance to Soldiers and their families who have suffered an injury resulting in a traumatic loss (i.e. loss of limbs, sight, hearing, traumatic brain injury, etc.). This assistance is vital and enables family members to be with them during their recovery time from such an injury. TSGLI payments range from $25,000 to $100,000 depending on the injury.*

> **Service members may obtain a at the TSGLI web site or by calling 1-800-237-1336, option "2".**

*Service members may obtain a at the TSGLI web site or by calling 1-800-237-1336, option "2". Once they have the claim form, they need to complete the claim form and obtain certification from a health care provider. It is important for health care providers to completely fill in Part B of the TSGLI application. Once the service member has completed Part A, and the healthcare provider has completed Part B, the application can be submitted for an award decision. It is important for service members to understand that they do not have to complete Part C, which will be completed by the TSGLI office. Completed forms can be sent via fax to **1-866-275-0684**. Additional information on the traumatic injury protection benefit, as well as a listing on qualifying injuries, can be obtained by visiting https://www.hrc.army.mil/site/crsc/tsgli/faqs.htm or by calling 1-800-237-1336.*

Q. What is the process that happens when I am injured or have a disability?

A. *When a military member has a medical condition (including mental health conditions) which renders them unfit to perform their required duties, they may be separated (or retired) from the military for medical reasons. The process to determine medical fitness for continued duty involves two boards. One is called the Medical Evaluation Board (MEB), and the other is called the Physical Evaluation Board (PEB).*

Title 10, U.S.C., chapter 61, provides the Secretaries of the Military Departments with authority to retire or separate members when the Secretary finds that they are unfit to perform their military duties because of physical disability. Injuries in the field, physical or mental health problems that are incompatible with military duty or that result in disqualification from worldwide deployment for more than 12 months precipitate a Medical Evaluation Board (MEB).

Medical boards are initiated by the Medical Treatment Facility (base medical facility), not the individual or the command. The medical board consists of active duty physicians (not involved in the care of the military member) who review the clinical case file and decide whether the individual should be returned to duty, or should be separated, using the published medical standards for continued military service.

If the MEB determines that the member has a medical condition that is incompatible with continued military service, they refer the case to a Physical Evaluation Board (PEB). The PEB is a formal fitness-for-duty and disability determination that may recommend one of the following:

- Return the member to duty (with or without assignment limitations, and or medical re-training)
- Place the member on the temporary disabled/retired list (TDRL)
- Separate the member from active duty, or
- Medically retire the member

The standard used by the PEB for determining fitness is whether the medical condition precludes the member from reasonably performing the duties of his or her office, grade, rank, or rating. Per DoD Instruction 1332.38, inability to perform the duties of office, grade, rank or rating in every geographic location and under every conceivable circumstance will not be the sole

> **"Veteran service organizations like the Disabled American Veterans, AMVETS, the American Legion and the Veterans of Foreign Wars all have service representatives to help you understand and, if necessary, appeal any determination."**

basis for a finding of unfitness. The ability to be deployed, however, may be used as a consideration in determining fitness.

These recommendations are forwarded to a central medical board and can be appealed by the member, who is permitted to have legal counsel at these hearings. It is very important that you have an advocate for this process. Veteran service organizations like the Disabled American Veterans, AMVETS, the American Legion and the Veterans of Foreign Wars all have service representatives to help you understand and, if necessary, appeal any determination.

Disposition

Four factors determine whether disposition is fit for duty, separation, permanent retirement, or temporary retirement: whether the member can perform in their MOS/AFSC/Rating (job); the rating percentage; the stability of the disabling condition; and years of Active Service (active duty days) in the case of pre-existing conditions.

Fit for Duty:

The member is judged to be fit when he can reasonably perform the duties of his grade and military job. If the member is medically unfit to perform the duties of his/her current job, the PEB can recommend medical retraining into a job he/she will be medically qualified to perform.

> **Once a determination of physical unfitness is made, the PEB is required by law to rate the disability using the Department of Veterans Affairs Schedule for Rating Disabilities.**

Disability Rating Percentage

Once a determination of physical unfitness is made, the PEB is required by law to rate the disability using the Department of Veterans Affairs Schedule for Rating Disabilities. DoD Instruction 1332.39 modifies those provisions of the rating schedule inapplicable to the military and clarifies rating guidance for specific conditions. Ratings can range from 0 to 100 percent rising in increments of 10.

 Need to Know with Vicky

Here are a few things that you can do to make things a bit easier:

- Make sure someone is with your injured service member at all times—preferably someone who will be able to understand and ask questions of the residing physician.
- Ask questions constantly about the injury and seek out other patients with similar situations and injuries, because each family will get different knowledge from other resources.
- Make sure you fully understand what is going to happen when your service member has to be moved and what kind of therapy he or she will undergo. Ask questions as to who will be involved in this care and who can you contact if he or she is not progressing in their therapy and if you have other concerns about his or her welfare. Be proactive!
- Get the names of the persons in charge of his or her unit so you can contact them if there is trouble with paperwork that should have come from them. A lot of paperwork gets lost in the mail from Iraq or someone didn't do their job and write the right report about the injury. This can be difficult to correct and can interfere with your service member's access and eligibility for benefits.
- Make sure that if he or she is due a combat ribbon and Purple Heart that this is addressed immediately. You might not think this is important, but it plays an important role for their service or veteran benefits in the future.

> **"Make sure your service member does not leave the hospital until you know exactly what happens next."**

- Make sure your service member does not leave the hospital until you know exactly what happens next. Make certain that the Social Security paperwork is filled out. Make certain that you understand what happens with his or her retirement from the military, and what happens after that, as they transition into the VA system and out of military care.
- Make sure you understand what TDRL means. TDRL stands for Temporary Disabled Retired List. It's important to know this and other military acronyms to be able to navigate the system in order to best care for your service member.
- Find out if they are eligible for the Traumatic Servicemembers' Group Life Insurance (TSGLI). This is the insurance that they will get for being injured at war. You can find more information on this benefit by visiting http://www.insurance.va.gov/sgliSite/TSGLI/TSGLI.htm. This amount depends on the type of injury they may have and what they were retired as.

- Find a list of support groups out there that you can call on when the need for assistance comes along—because it will. It doesn't matter about the type of injury. You will need support and knowledge and advice from others for all kinds of reasons such as financial help, VA assistance or just a moment to rest yourself. Make sure you find local community support or groups of physicians or therapists to call upon when the need arises.

Make the Connection on MFN!
www.eMilitary.org/YourMFN.html

Sign on to the address shown above and Make the Connection to more resources on this topic!

57   VA For Returning Combat Veterans

From the Field with Phil Budahn

Phil Budahn is with Public Affairs from Department of Veteran Affairs

The Department of Veterans Affairs (VA) has developed special programs to serve the nation's newest veterans—the men and women who served in Iraq and Afghanistan—by assisting them with a smooth transition from active duty to civilian life. VA's goal is to ensure that every seriously injured or ill serviceman and woman returning from combat receives easy access to benefits and world-class service. Combat veterans have special health-care eligibility. Their contact with VA often begins with priority scheduling for care, and for the most seriously wounded, VA counselors visit their bedside in military wards before separation to ensure their VA disability payment coverage will be ready the moment they leave active duty. Through enhanced programs and new policies, VA is striving to ensure it holds open the doors to a seamless transition from soldier to citizen.

Benefits and Services

For two years after discharge, these veterans have special access to VA health care, even those who have no service-connected illness. Veterans can become "grandfathered" for future access by enrolling with VA during this period. This covers not only regular active-duty personnel who served in Iraq or Afghanistan, but also Reserve or National Guard members serving in the combat theaters. Veterans with service-related injuries or illnesses always have access to VA care for the treatment of their disabilities without any time limit, as do lower-income veterans. Hospital care, outpatient treatment, and nursing home services are offered at 1,400 locations. Additional information about VA medical eligibility is available at http://www.va.gov/healtheligibility.

VA's broad range of benefits includes disability compensation and pension; vocational rehabilitation and employment, education, and training; home loan guarantees; automobile and specially adaptive equipment grants; home modification programs for the disabled; life insurance and traumatic injury protection; and survivor benefits. Information on these programs is available at http://www.vba.va.gov/benefit_facts/index.htm.

> **VA launched an ambitious outreach initiative to ensure separating combat veterans know about VA benefits**

VA launched an ambitious outreach initiative to ensure separating combat veterans know about VA benefits. Programs available to them, including compensation for service-related disabilities, are described at http://www1.va.gov/health/index.asp

Each veteran with service in Iraq or Afghanistan receives a letter from the Secretary of Veterans Affairs introducing the veteran to VA and its benefits and providing phone numbers and websites for more information.

Seamless Transition

As with all military members, transition briefings prior to discharge also acquaint them with benefits, as do additional pamphlet mailings following separation. Brochures, wallet cards, and videos have been produced, and briefings are being conducted at town hall meetings and family readiness groups and during unit drills near the homes of returning Guard members and reservists. Because of the large number of reservists and Guard members mobilized in this conflict, VA has made a special effort to work with their units to reach transitioning service members at demobilization sites. In addition, VA has trained recently returned veterans to serve as National Guard Bureau liaisons in every state to assist their fellow combat veterans.

Seamless Transition Liaisons for the Severely Wounded

In an effort to assist wounded military members and their families, VA has placed workers at key military hospitals where severely injured service members from Iraq and Afghanistan are frequently sent. These include benefit counselors who help the

> **"In an effort to assist wounded military members and their families, VA has placed workers at key military hospitals where severely injured service members from Iraq and Afghanistan are frequently sent."**

service member obtain VA services, as well as social workers who facilitate health-care coordination and discharge planning as service members transition from military to VA care. Under this program, VA staff members serve at Walter Reed Army Medical Center in Washington, D.C.; National Naval Medical Center in Bethesda, Maryland.; Eisenhower Army Medical Center at Fort Gordon, Georgia.; Brooke Army Medical Center at Fort Sam Houston, Texas; Madigan Army Medical Center at Tacoma, Washington; Darnall Army Medical Center at Fort Hood, Texas; Evans Army Hospital at Fort Carson, Colorado; and Camp Pendleton Naval Medical Center in San Diego, California.

VA and the Department of Defense have improved collaboration and communication. VA employees based at military treatment facilities brief service members about VA health benefits, disability compensation, vocational rehabilitation, and employment. Coordinators at each VA benefits regional office and VA medical center work both with the out-based VA counselors and with military discharge staff to ensure a smooth transition to VA services at locations nearest to the veteran's residence after discharge. At the VA facilities serving the veteran's hometown, the hospital is alerted when the seriously wounded service member is being discharged so that the continuity of his or her medications and therapy is ensured when they arrive home.

Medical Conditions of Combat Veterans

Patterns of disease shown in diagnoses of recent combat veterans who have come to VA for care have not suggested significant differences from the types of primary care, chronic conditions, or mental health issues seen in earlier combat veterans. However, careful studies will be required to draw appropriate comparisons using control groups of similar veterans, representative samplings, and other scientific methods. An early neurological study tested 654 Army veterans before deployment to Iraq in 2003 and again after returning in 2005, finding mild impairments in memory and attention lapses, but significantly faster reaction times when compared to other veterans not deployed to the theater. These warrant further investigation. VA also will analyze combat veterans' deaths from diseases in hopes of publishing mortality studies in the future.

> **"Nationally automated data from VA's payment system for service-connected diseases and disabilities does not distinguish between combat-related injuries and those incurred or worsened while the service member was in non-hostile locations."**

Nationally automated data from VA's payment system for service-connected diseases and disabilities does not distinguish between combat-related injuries and those incurred or worsened while the service member was in non-hostile locations. Some of the most common service-connected conditions among those who served at some point in the Iraq and Afghanistan theaters include musculoskeletal conditions and hearing disorders.

Polytrauma Centers Provide Specialized Care

Improvised explosive devices and rocket-propelled grenades often result in devastating injuries, including amputations, sensory loss, and brain injury. Modern body armor and advances in front-line trauma care have enabled combat veterans to survive severe attacks that in prior wars were fatal. In response to the demand for specialized services, VA expanded its four traumatic brain injury centers in Minneapolis, Minn., Palo Alto, Calif., Richmond, Va., and Tampa, Fla., to become polytrauma centers encompassing additional specialties to treat patients for multiple complex injuries. This is being expanded into a network of twenty-one polytrauma network sites and polytrauma clinic support teams around the country providing state-of-the-art treatment closer to injured veterans' homes.

> **In response to the demand for specialized services, VA expanded its four traumatic brain injury centers in Minneapolis, Minn., Palo Alto, Ca., Richmond, Va., and Tampa, Fla., to become polytrauma centers encompassing additional specialties to treat patients for multiple complex injuries.**

These centers treat traumatic brain injury alone or in combination with amputation, blindness, or other visual impairment, complex orthopedic injuries, auditory and vestibular disorders, and mental health concerns. VA has added clinical expertise to address the special problems that the multi-trauma combat injured patient may face. This can include intensive psychological support treatment for both patient and family, intensive case management, improvements in the treatment of vision problems, and rehabilitation using the latest high-tech specialty prostheses. Polytrauma teams bring together experts to provide innovative, personalized treatment to help the injured service member or veteran achieve optimal function and independence.

Because brain injury is being recognized as the signature injury of the current conflict, VA launched an educational initiative to provide its clinicians a broad base of knowledge with which to identify potential traumatic brain injury patients, mechanisms for effective care, and a better understanding of patients who experience this condition. VA has made training mandatory for physicians and other key staff in primary care, mental health, and rehabilitation programs.

Mental Health Care and Post-Traumatic Stress Disorder

About one-third of these combat veterans who seek care from VA have a possible diagnosis of a mental disorder, and VA has significantly expanded its counseling and mental-health services. VA has launched new programs, including dozens of new mental-health teams based in VA medical centers focused on early identification and management of stress-related disorders, as well as the recruitment of about 100 combat veterans in its Readjustment Counseling Service to provide briefings to transitioning servicemen and women regarding military-related readjustment needs.

> VA has launched new programs, including dozens of new mental-health teams based in VA medical centers focused on early identification and management of stress-related disorders, as well as the recruitment of about 100 combat veterans in its Readjustment Counseling Service to provide briefings to transitioning servicemen and women regarding military-related readjustment needs.

Many of the challenges facing the soldiers returning from Afghanistan and Iraq are stressors that have been identified and studied in veterans of previous wars. VA has developed world-class expertise in treating chronic mental health problems, including post-traumatic stress disorder (PTSD).

Post-traumatic stress involves a normal set of reactions to a trauma such as war. Sometimes it becomes a disorder with the passage of time when feelings or issues related to the trauma are not dealt with and are suppressed by the individual. This can result in problems readjusting to community life following the trauma. Since the war began, VA has activated dozens of new PTSD programs around the country to assist veterans in dealing with the emotional toll of combat. In addition, 207 readjustment counseling "vet centers" provide easy access in consumer-friendly facilities apart from traditional VA medical centers.

One early scientific study indicated the estimated risk for PTSD from service in the Iraq war was 18 percent, while the estimated risk for PTSD from the Afghanistan mission was 11 percent. Data from multiple sources now indicate that approximately 10 to 15 percent of soldiers develop PTSD after deployment to Iraq, and another 10 percent have significant symptoms of PTSD, depression, or anxiety and may benefit from care. Alcohol misuse and relationship problems add to these rates. Combat veterans are at higher risk for psychiatric problems than military personnel serving in noncombat locations, and more frequent and more intensive combat is associated with higher risk. With military pre- and post-deployment health-assessment programs seeking to destigmatize mental-health treatment, coupled with simplified access to VA care for combat veterans after discharge, experts believe initial high rates likely will decrease.

> **"Combat veterans are at higher risk for psychiatric problems than military personnel serving in noncombat locations . . ."**

Studies of PTSD patients in general have suggested as many as half may enjoy complete remission, and the majority of the remainder will improve. Research has led to scientifically developed treatment guidelines covering a variety of modern therapies with which clinicians have had success. Treatments range from psychological first aid to cognitive behavioral therapy. Psychopharmacology may include drugs such as Zoloft or Paxil—with newer drugs under studies now in progress. More information about VA's PTSD programs is available at http://www.va.gov/opa/fact/docs/ptsd.doc and http://www.ncptsd.va.gov.

VA Benefits for Survivors of Military Personnel Involved in Operations Iraqi Freedom and Enduring Freedom

The Department of Veterans Affairs (VA) has a variety of programs to assist the survivors of military personnel who die on active duty. These provisions also apply to those serving on active duty outside of the combat theater.

Survivors receive certain payments or benefits regardless of whether the in-service death is due to combat, accident, or disease, including:

- Burial benefits for the deceased service member, which include a gravesite in any VA national cemetery with available space, perpetual care of the grave at no cost to the family, a government headstone or marker, and a Presidential Memorial Certificate.
- Dependency and Indemnity Compensation for a surviving spouse and more if there are dependent children. Visit www.vba.va.gov/benefit_facts/index.htm for current values.
- Life insurance, which most military members carry at the highest level, $400,000.

More information about how VA services apply in individual cases is available from veterans' services representatives at 800-827-1000.

 **FAQs**

Q. What is the Casualty Assistance Program?

A. *VA has a Casualty Assistance Program to give personal attention to surviving family members after in-service deaths and to help them with benefit information and applications. A casualty assistance officer is designated at each of VA's fifty-seven regional offices. These VA officers work closely with military casualty officers to ensure timely assistance is available to beneficiaries.*

Q. Are Reservists and National Guard eligible?

A. *When a member of the Reserves or National Guard dies while federally activated or on inactive duty for training, the death is considered service-connected for VA death benefits. Activation of a National Guard unit by a governor alone in support of current security operations does not qualify unit members for these VA benefits, except life insurance.*

Q. What are the monthly payments for spouse and children?

A. *When a service member dies while on active duty, the death is considered service-connected unless it was due to willful misconduct. VA pays Dependency and Indemnity Compensation (DIC) to surviving spouses. In most cases, survivors' claims are processed within forty-eight hours.*

In some cases, VA can pay an additional Dependency and Indemnity Compensation (DIC) benefit for each dependent child who is unmarried and under age eighteen, or up to age twenty-three if studying at a VA-approved school. Also, for a surviving spouse who has one or more dependent children below

> **"The basic rate for survivors is adjusted annually, and payments continue generally until the death or remarriage of the spouse before age fifty-seven."**

age eighteen, an additional value is added to the monthly DIC from the date DIC entitlement begins. This additional amount is removed at the end of two years following the date DIC entitlement began or earlier if all the dependent children attain age eighteen. Visit www.vba.va.gov/benefit_facts/index.htm for current amounts.

Payments are increased if the surviving spouse is housebound or needs a home aide. The basic rate for survivors is adjusted annually, and payments continue generally until the death or remarriage of the spouse before age fifty-seven. Remarriage after age fifty-seven does not affect benefits. Additional information about benefits for family members, to include low-income parents of the veteran, is available at www.vba.va.gov/bln/dependents/.

As of January 2005, VA has provided DIC benefits to 865 surviving family members of those killed in Operation Iraqi Freedom and 108 family members where the service member was killed in Operation Enduring Freedom. Benefit recipients include spouses, children, and in some cases, parents of the service member.

Q. What about life insurance?

A. *Most service members and reservists take VA's life insurance coverage, Servicemembers' Group Life Insurance, though a few decline coverage. Coverage is very inexpensive and offers a very good benefit if something were to happen. Most choose coverage at the highest levels and their designated beneficiary receives a payment of $400,000. VA has paid every claim related to Operations Iraqi Freedom and Enduring Freedom within forty-eight hours of receiving the necessary paperwork. VA also offers beneficiaries free, personalized financial planning through a financial services company.*

VA also offers beneficiaries free, personalized financial planning through a financial services company.

As of February 2005, VA had received from the service branches notice of 1,409 Operation Iraqi Freedom casualties who had life-insurance coverage. Insurance payments have been made to 1,772 survivors, as a service member may designate more than one beneficiary. Some additional payments were awaiting beneficiaries' completion of their claims. Of some 155 casualties of Operation Enduring Freedom, 210 beneficiaries have been paid life insurance benefits.

VA's experience with these casualties shows that only 10 (less than one percent) had no coverage. While thirty-one service members had opted for less than the maximum coverage amount, twenty-three of those were for $100,000 or more.

More information about insurance benefits is available at www.insurance.va.gov.

Q. What burial or funeral benefits are there for service members?

A. *Burial in a VA National Cemetery*

Members of the armed forces and veterans, their spouses, and dependent children may be buried in any of VA's national cemeteries with available space. There currently are 120 national cemeteries across the nation and eighty-three have available grave space. More information is available at www.cem.va.gov.

Burial in a Non-VA Cemetery

Deaths of active-duty members are not covered by VA's financial burial allowance benefits, since the military services assist survivors with funeral expenses and the cost of burial in private cemeteries. If a family wishes to arrange burial in a non-VA cemetery, VA will provide a headstone or marker for the grave.

Burial in a State Veterans Cemetery

Although not a benefit provided by VA, burial in a state veterans cemetery is an option available in many states for those who die on active duty. Some states have residency requirements and may impose additional limitations.

Military Funeral Honors

Upon request, the Department of Defense will provide military funeral honors. The funeral director typically makes this arrangement. At least two uniformed service members fold and present the flag and play "Taps" by a recording or a bugler. Additional information about funeral honors is available at www.militaryfuneralhonors.osd.mil.

> **"If a family wishes to arrange burial in a non-VA cemetery, VA will provide a headstone or marker for the grave."**

Military Burial Flags

In the case of in-service deaths, the Defense Department provides a U.S. flag to drape the casket or to be presented at a memorial service. After the service, the flag is given to the next of kin.

Q. What are the health care benefits for survivors of military service members killed in action?

A. *Health-care benefits for the survivors of service members killed in action in Operations Iraqi Freedom or Enduring Freedom are provided by the military. For more information, see http://www.tricare.osd.mil.*

Q. Are there any Educational Assistance Programs available to survivors of military service members killed in action?

A. *When an active-duty service member dies in service, VA's Survivors' and Dependents' Educational Assistance Program generally provides up to forty-five months of education benefits to the un-remarried surviving spouse for twenty years, or for children aged eighteen to twenty-six. Visit www.gibill.va.gov/pamphlets/CH35/CH35_Pamphlet. pdf for information on rates for full-time attendance, with lesser amounts for part-time education. This benefit may be used to pursue secondary school programs; associate, bachelor, or graduate degrees; technical or vocational training; apprenticeships; and other types of training, including work-study programs. More information is available at www.gibill.va.gov/pamphlets/CH35/CH35_Pamphlet_General.htm.*

> **When an active-duty service member dies in service, VA's Survivors' and Dependents' Educational Assistance Program generally provides up to forty-five months of education benefits to the un-remarried surviving spouse for twenty years, or for children aged eighteen to twenty-six.**

Q. Is there a refund of Service Member's unused GI Bill contribution?

A. *If the deceased service member had contributed to the Montgomery GI Bill education program, the designated life-insurance beneficiary or surviving spouse is entitled to a refund of the money that was collected through payroll deduction but was not awarded in education benefits during the service member's lifetime. Most active-duty military members participate in this educational benefit program, which deducts $1,200 from their pay at $100 monthly during their first year of service.*

Q. Do surviving spouses qualify for the home loan program?

A. *Surviving spouses of military members may be eligible for a VA-guaranteed home loan from a private lender. The loan may be used to purchase, construct, or improve a home; to refinance an existing mortgage; or for certain other purposes. As with the program for veterans, VA guarantees part of the total loan, permitting the purchaser to obtain a mortgage with a competitive interest rate. Except for manufactured homes and other select cases, the surviving spouse may obtain a no-down-payment loan if the lender agrees.*

Need to Know

Combat Veteran Information. http://www.va.gov/Environagents/page.cfm?pg=16
PTSD and Combat Veterans. http://www.ncptsd.va.gov/ncmain/index.jsp
Survivors Benefits. http://www.vba.va.gov/survivors/index.htm
Transition Assistance Program. http://www.va.gov/opa/fact/tranasst.asp
Women Veterans Information. http://www.vba.va.gov/bln/21/Topics/Women/
Federal Benefits for Veterans and Dependents
This booklet lists the variety of federal benefits available to veterans and their dependents. http://www1.va.gov/opa/vadocs/current_benefits.asp

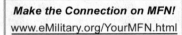
Make the Connection on MFN!
www.eMilitary.org/YourMFN.html

Sign on to the address
shown above and
Make the Connection
to more resources
on this topic!

58   Wounded Warrior Benefits

From the Field with Carla Webb

Carla Webb is a National Service Officer with AMVETS and is their National Guard Liaison Officer

A MVETS (American Veterans) is a Veterans Service Organization (VSO) and was established in 1947 to serve all veterans and their family members in developing and filing claims for benefits from the Department of Veterans Affairs (VA). Becoming a member of AMVETS is not required to receive this service.

Eligibility for VA benefits extends to veterans with a discharge or release under conditions other than dishonorable. Eligibility may also extend to a veteran's dependent, a surviving spouse, child, a parent of a deceased veteran, an active duty service member, and members of the Guard and Reserve.

AMVETS service department is comprised of National Service Officers (NSOs), who are trained to assist veterans or their dependents in obtaining benefits from the VA.

Most often AMVETS service officers' primary function is to help the veteran apply for compensation benefits for disabilities incurred in service. The first step in this process is a personal interview with the veteran or dependents. At this time, the claimant has the opportunity to ask questions, express their concerns, and get information. The service officer usually takes this time to review service medical records and any private treatment records that are available. A VA claims form can be completed during this interview if the claimant so desires. The service officer will guide the claimant through the process of properly completing this form. Other benefits such as health care, home loans, insurance, education benefits, vocational rehabilitation, and dependents' benefits may be discussed. The claimant will receive the VA Benefits Manual and is encouraged to call the service officer (if necessary) on letters received from VA concerning the claim.

Claimants have basic responsibility for their claim and are expected to do what they can for themselves to initiate action and comply with requirements of the VA. The service officer is responsible for service, advice, and counsel rendered to claimants who have designated AMVETS as their representative. When a veteran has requested service from a VSO like AMVETS, the VSO must submit the VA provided form, *VA Form 21-22* (Appointment of Veterans Service Organization as Claimant's Representative). This power of attorney is not binding and can be revoked at any time.

> **"Claimants have basic responsibility for their claim and are expected to do what they can for themselves to initiate action and comply with requirements of the VA."**

Navigating through the VA can be an intimidating undertaking and having a "guide" can relieve uncertainty, reassure the claimant, and aid in getting the maximum benefits. Often the information received from an interview with the veteran can lead to opportunities for additional benefits. The veteran many times is not aware of benefits such as Special Monthly Compensation, Vocational Rehabilitation, or educational benefits for spouses/children, which are in addition to the service-connected disability.

Transition Assistance

AMVETS is also involved in Transition Assistance/Disabled Transition Assistance Programs (TAP) for service members. The TAP generally involves a three-day employment assistance workshop, which will provide sufficient employment information and vocational guidance to allow separating or retiring service members to make informed career choices. An integral portion of these workshops is a briefing on the wide array of VA benefits and services for which these service members may be eligible.

This transition time is the optimum time to file a claim with the VA. You may file a claim for benefits at any time, but there are many reasons to file as soon as possible after the completion of military service. Often, you can "protect" the claim for benefits by ensuring the requirement for continuity is not compromised. The VA has many requirements for awarding service connection

> **"The VA has many requirements for awarding service connection for disabilities; and as a rule, the process is more advantageous to the veteran if this is done in a timely fashion."**

for disabilities; and as a rule, the process is more advantageous to the veteran if this is done in a timely fashion.

For more than sixty years, AMVETS has taken to heart the credo of service set forth by the organization's founding fathers. In so doing, this service-oriented organization endeavors to provide veterans with the type of support they truly deserve. This outreach effort takes many forms, from the professional advice service officers provide concerning earned veterans' benefits, to the legislative efforts on Capitol Hill, to the work done by hospital volunteers. Other AMVETS members involve themselves in a range of initiatives aimed at contributing to the quality of life in their local communities. These two areas—veterans' service and community service—drive AMVETS commitment to making a difference in the lives of others.

 **FAQs**

Q. How long will it take to get a decision on my claim?

A. *The adjudication process varies in the different VA Regional offices (VARO). You may have the rating decision back in two to three months, but in some VAROs the process may take up to a year.*

Q. How does a Reserve or Guard member qualify for VA benefits?

A. *Reservists and Guard members who served on active duty establish veteran status and may therefore be eligible for VA benefits, depending on the length of active military service and the character of discharge or release. In addition, reservists and Guard members who are never called to active duty may qualify for some VA benefits.*

Q. What is VA "compensation"?

A. *A monthly payment made to the veteran because of a service-connected disability that is at least 10 percent disabling.*

Q. How does receiving VA disability pay affect the military retiree?

A. *Currently, military retired pay is offset by the amount of VA disability received. Under the Concurrent Retire-ment and Disability Payment (CRDP) if the combined disability rating is 50 per-cent or greater the retiree is qualified to receive additional payment. Members who retired under disability provisions must have twenty years of qualifying service. There is no application required, and DFAS will determine these ben-efits automatically.*

> **Currently, military retired pay is offset by the amount of VA dis-ability received.**

Q. What is necessary to obtain a favorable decision on the claim for disability?

A. **Evidence** that an injury, illness, or disease occurred in service, **evidence** of a current medical condition, and a **nexus** or link between the two. (Source: *More FAQs from the National Military Family Association, "Wounded War-rior FACT Sheet."* This information is current as of October 2006. Please visit www.nmfa.org for updates and to download printable copies.)

Q. What is a casualty?

A. *The word casualty can be a very frightening term for families to hear. It is good to know that the term actually has several meanings. A casualty is any person who is lost to the organization by reason of having been declared beleaguered, besieged, captured, dead, diseased, detained, duty status whereabouts unknown, injured, ill, interned, missing, missing in action, or wounded. (Source: DoD Joint Publication 1-02 http://www.dtic.mil/doctrine/jppersonelseriespubs.htm and Department of Defense Instruction (DoDI) 1300.18 http://www.dtic.mil/whs/directives/corres/html/130018.htm).*

When a service member is killed, injured, gets sick, or is hospitalized, he or she becomes a "casualty." The service member is then further categorized by and reported according to his/her *casualty type* and the *casualty status*. *Casualty type* is the term used to identify a casualty as either a hostile casualty or a non-hostile casualty.

Casualty status is the term used to classify a casualty for reporting purposes. According to DoD Joint Publication 1-02, there are seven casualty statuses:

Casualty type is the term used to identify a casualty as either a hostile casualty or a non-hostile casualty.

1. Deceased
2. Duty status-whereabouts unknown (DUSTWUN)
3. Missing
4. Very seriously ill or injured (VSI)
5. Seriously ill or injured (SI)
6. Incapacitating illness or injury (III)
7. Not seriously injured (NSI)

Q. What is the process for notifying families of casualties?

A. *Remember to keep in mind that each Service is responsible for notification of next of kin and has its own specific procedures for ensuring expeditious and personal notification. In the event of a service member injury or illness, only the primary next of kin (PNOK) will be notified and may be notified telephonically.* All notified families will have ready access to information as it becomes available. In all death and missing cases, the PNOK and secondary next of kin (SNOK), and any other person listed on the DD Form 93 (Record of Emergency Data), will be notified in person. The notification will be made as a matter of highest priority, taking precedence over

In the event of a service member injury or illness, only the primary next of kin (PNOK) will be notified and may be notified telephonically.

all other responsibilities the notifier has. Whenever possible, the notifier's grade is equal to or higher than the grade of the casualty. When the PNOK is also a service member, the notifier's grade will be equal to or higher than the grade of the PNOK. Personal notification will generally be made between 0600 and 2200 hours local time. The PNOK is always notified first.

Although each Service's notification process is slightly different, in general the process works as follows:

- The Service will notify all PNOK and SNOK as soon as possible, generally within 24-48 hours.
- In injury cases deemed to be VSI or SI, the PNOK is normally telephonically notified. For minor injuries, notification generally comes through other channels (i.e., the hospital or directly from the service member).

Q. How is the primary next of kin (PNOK) determined?

A. *The person most closely related to the casualty is considered the PNOK for notification and assistance purposes. This is normally the spouse for married persons and the parents for unmarried service members/individuals. The precedence of NOK with equal relationships to the casu-*

> **The person most closely related to the casualty is considered the PNOK for notification and assistance purposes**

alty is governed by seniority (age). Equal relationship situations include divorced parents, children, and siblings. Minor children's rights are exercised by their parents or legal guardian. The adult NOK is usually the first person highest in the line of succession who has reached the age of eighteen. Even if a minor, the spouse is always considered the PNOK. The following order of precedence is used to identify the PNOK:

- Spouse
- Natural, adopted, step and illegitimate children
- Parents
- Persons standing *in loco parentis* (*In loco parentis* means a person who is charged with a parent's duties and responsibilities in the place of a parent, normally someone who stood in the relationship of a parent to the deceased for a period of at least 5 years prior to the service member reaching 18 years of age.)
- Persons granted legal custody of the individual by a court decree of statutory provision
- Brothers or sisters, to include half-blood and those acquired through adoption
- Grandparents
- Other relatives in order of relationship to the individual according to civil laws
- If no other persons are available, the Secretary of the Military Department may be deemed to act on behalf of the individual
- SNOK is any other next of kin other than the PNOK.

Q. What causes delays in notification of family members?

A. *The number one reason causing a delay in notification to families that the service member has been wounded/injured is incorrect phone numbers provided on the emergency information data card. It is IMPERATIVE the service member keeps this information up-*

> **The number one reason causing a delay in notification to families that the service member has been wounded/injured is incorrect phone numbers provided on the emergency information data card.**

dated. *Precious time is wasted when military officials have to track down correct notification numbers for family members. Delays are also common when the family member leaves the area without notifying the unit Rear Detachment Commander or Family Readiness Point of Contact. The number one rule of thumb is to let someone in the unit know that you are leaving the area and to provide them with a working phone number where you can be reached should they need to contact you.*

Q. How often will families be provided updates on their Service member?

A. *The Service will pass information to PNOK as it becomes available. Since the PNOK will be notified of updates, families/friends should use the PNOK as a focal point for sharing information internally. In the first hours after the incident, information may be limited. If there is no solid evidence a particular service member was involved in the incident, but military officials have reason to believe the service member was involved, families will be given a "believed to be" notification. This simply tells the family that the military has good reason to believe their loved one was involved and that they will be provided updates as they become available. This type of notification will be delivered only when there is overwhelming reason to believe their service member was involved. If it is "believed to be killed" or "believed to be missing," PNOK and SNOK will be notified in person. If it is "believed to be injured," only the primary next of kin will be notified telephonically. All family members who have been notified originally will be kept informed of developments in their cases.*

Q. How do I get to my wounded service member? Who funds my travel?

A. *For very seriously injured/ill (VSI) or seriously injured/ill (SI) patients, the primary next of kin (PNOK) can be issued Invitational Travel Orders (ITOs) if the attending physician determines it is essential to the recovery of the patient and it is verified by the hospital commander. The Services can provide transportation for up to three family members when a service member is classified as Very Seriously Ill/Injured (VSI) or Seriously Ill/Injured (SI), as determined by the attending physician and hospital commander upon injury. ITOs will be offered to immediate family members (spouse, children, mother, father, siblings (including step) OR those acting in loco parentis. The*

Service point of contact/notifier or hospital will provide information concerning travel regulations. Transportation and lodging are provided for up to three family members in two week increments. Wounded service members cases are evaluated every two weeks and at the discretion of the attending physician, family members are authorized additional time at the bedside.

Q. Where will I stay while I am visiting my wounded service member?

A. *If the family members are traveling on ITOs, the Services arrange for family member's lodging before traveling to be with the wounded service member. Families are housed in local hotels, guest lodging at a military installation, or, if available, a Fisher House, which is "a home away from home" for families of patients receiving medical care at major military and VA medical centers. The homes*

> **"Families are housed in local hotels, guest lodging at a military installation, or, if available, a Fisher House, which is "a home away from home" for families of patients receiving medical care at major military and VA medical centers"**

provide comfortable, temporary housing for families of service members recovering from serious medical conditions. Families pay $10.00 per night to stay in a Fisher House; however, this fee is waived for families of wounded service members. The homes are normally located within walking distance of the treatment facility or have transportation available. For more information on the Fisher Houses, go to: www.fisherhouse.org.

Q. Is child care available for my children while I am with my wounded service member?

A. *Hourly childcare slots are often hard to access on military installations and so families should not assume there is childcare available. Childcare is an added expense for families and is not covered in the ITO reimbursement. The individual who notifies you about your service member's injury can direct you to the installation child develop-*

> **Do not forget to bring a copy of the child's shot record as you will need this to register your child at any childcare facility."**

ment center to help you determine if you can make child care arrangements. There may be community resources available to assist with childcare. Do not forget to bring a copy of the child's shot record as you will need this to register your child at any childcare facility. Some medical facilities have Family Assistance Centers (FACs) that provide assistance to the families of wounded service members once they arrive at the MTF. The FACs should be able to provide childcare information.

Q. Who will work with our family during the service member's recovery period?

A. *Wounded service members have case managers assigned to work with them during their recovery period. The job of these individuals is to provide information and help assist the service member and family during the recovery period and the Physical Evaluation Board (PEB) and Medical Evaluation Board (MEB) process. These individuals also provide information on Veteran Service Organizations (VSOs). As stated above, many military hospitals serving wounded or injured service members also have Family Assistance Centers. Families can also seek assistance from the installation chaplains, social workers, and family center: Army Community Services, Marine Corps Community Services, Air Force Family Support Center, Navy Fleet and Family Support Center, and Coast Guard Work Life Offices.*

Q. What is the transition process for my service member?

A. *The shift of a service member to medical retirement, transit on to the Department of Veterans Affairs, or separation from the military is known as Transition. DoD has a mandatory Transition Assistance Program (TAP) for all transitioning and/or separating service members. You can read more about transition at http://www1.va.gov/opa/fact/docs/tranasst.pdf.*

Q. What employment opportunities are there for spouses/family members of wounded service members?

A. *Spouses often ask how they can find work after their service member is injured. Military OneSource offers practical tips and includes information on "Entering the Work Force When Your Spouse Has Been Severely Injured" in the "Special Needs" section at www.militaryonesource.com.*

Q. What legal resources are available?

A. *Families ask where to go for legal support for such things as Power of Attorney, Wills, Advance Directives and other legal affairs affecting a wounded* *service member and their family. Information from the American Bar Association's working group Legal Assistance for Military Personnel (LAMP) is available at: http://www.abanet.org/legalservices/lamp/home.html. Additionally, the U.S. Army Judge Advocate General's Corp (JAG) provides an information portal at http://www.jagcnet.army.mil/legal. Both of these are valuable legal resources.*

Q. What is the Traumatic Injury Protection Insurance (TSGLI) Benefit?

A. *The Traumatic SGLI (TSGLI) benefit is designed to provide financial assistance to service members during their recovery period from a serious traumatic injury. The program is not disability compensation and has no effect on entitlement for compensation and pension benefits provided by the Department of Veterans Affairs or disability benefits provided by the Department of Defense. It is an insurance product similar to commercial dismemberment policies. On December 1, 2005, all members eligible for SGLI automatically became insured for traumatic injury protection of up to $100,000 unless they decline SGLI coverage. The benefit provides payouts of a tax-free lump sum payment ranging from $25,000 to $100,000, depending on the extent of a service member's injury including service members who have lost limbs, eyesight, or speech or received other traumatic injuries as a direct result of injuries received during operations Iraqi Freedom or Enduring Freedom. Coverage is retroactive to October 7, 2001. The retroactive provision of PL 109-13 provides that any service member who suffers a qualifying loss between October 7, 2001, and December 1, 2005, will receive a payment under the TSGLI program if the loss was a direct result of injuries incurred in Operation Enduring Freedom or Operation Iraqi Freedom. The benefit does not apply to service members suffering from disease. For more information about the program, service members should contact their Service TSGLI Representative. The Air Force POC for TSGLI is the Casualty Assistance Representative (CAR). For the other Services, contact the Service Injured Support Program (Army AW2, Marine M4L, and Navy Safe Harbor). See the following section for information about these programs. To*

> **The Traumatic SGLI (TSGLI) benefit is designed to provide financial assistance to service members during their recovery period from a serious traumatic injury.**

read about the TSGLI program, go to: http://www.insurance.va.gov/sgliSite/legislation/TSGLIFacts.htm.

Need to Know with AMVETS

Critical—Key Factors Everyone Should Know about Disability Compensation

1. You may be eligible for disability compensation if you have a service-related disability and you were discharged under other than dishonorable conditions.

Make the Connection on MFN!
www.eMilitary.org/YourMFN.html

Sign on to the address shown above and Make the Connection to more resources on this topic!

2. VA benefits can be awarded for direct service connection, aggravation of a pre-service disability, presumptive conditions as determined by VA law, secondary service connection, and injury due to hospital treatment.
3. VA Form 21-526, Application for Compensation or Pension is the form used to apply for disability benefits. Veterans Service Organizations have service officers who can assist with the application.
4. VA benefits are tax-exempt.
5. You must attend scheduled VA examinations (emergencies excluded). If there is a conflict in scheduling, you should notify the VA.
6. The VA will consider private treatment records along with VA examinations and VHA treatment records.
7. Most states offer additional State/Local Veterans benefits for veterans receiving disability compensation.
8. You may be eligible to receive priority medical care based on the percent of the disability. You will receive free medical care for any service-connected disability.
9. You may be paid additional benefits if you have very severe disabilities.
10. There is no time limit for filing a claim for disability compensation benefits.

Need to Know with the National Military Family Association

Wounded Warrior FACT SHEET

(This information is current as of October 2006. Please visit www.nmfa.org for updates and to download printable copies.)

Basic definitions you should know:

A service member who has incurred an injury due to an external agent or cause, other than the victim of a terrorist activity, is classified as **Wounded in Action (WIA)**. This term encompasses all kinds of wounds and other injuries incurred in action, to include penetrating wounds, injuries caused by biological or chemical warfare agents, or the effects of exposure to ionizing radiation or any other destructive weapon or agent. A person who is not a battle casualty, but who is lost to the organization by reason of disease or injury, is classified as **Disease and Non-Battle Injury (DNBI)**. This category also includes service members who are missing when the absence does not appear to be voluntary or who are missing due to enemy action or internment. When someone is wounded in action or has an illness or disease, they will be further categorized in one of the following statuses:

- **Very Seriously Injured (VSI)**: the casualty status of a person whose injury/illness is classified by medical authorities to be of such severity that life is imminently endangered.
- **Seriously Ill or Injured (SI)**: the casualty status of a person whose illness or injury is classified by medical authorities to be of such severity that there is cause for immediate concern, but there is no imminent danger to life.
- **Incapacitating Illness or Injury (III)**: the casualty status of a person whose illness or injury requires hospitalization, but medical authority does not classify as very seriously ill or injured or seriously ill or injured; the illness or injury makes the person physically or mentally unable to communicate with the next of kin.
- **Not Seriously Injured (NSI)**: the casualty status of a person whose injury or illness may or may not require hospitalization but not classified by a medical authority as very seriously injured (VSI), seriously injured (SI), or incapacitating illness or injury (III); the person is able communicate with the Next of Kin (NOK).
- **Duty Status-Whereabouts Unknown (DUSTWUN)**: A transitory casualty status, applicable only to military personnel, that is used when the responsible commander suspects the member may be a casualty whose

absence is involuntary, but does not feel sufficient evidence currently exists to make a definite determination of missing or deceased.

Air Force Palace HART

The Air Force Palace HART (Helping Airmen Recover Together) program follows Air Force wounded in action until they return to active duty, or are medically retired. It then provides follow up assistance for 5-7 years post injury. The Air Force works to retain injured service members on active duty, if at all possible; however, if unable to return an Airman to active duty, the Air Force works to get them civilian employment within the service. The Air Force also ensures counseling is provided on all of the benefits to which an individual service member may be entitled within the Department of Defense, Department of Veterans Affairs, and Department of Labor. For immediate, 24-hour response, the Military Severely Injured Center can direct you to an Air Force point of contact. It can be reached toll free at 1-888-774-1361 or you can e-mail severelyinjured@militaryonesource.com.

> **"The Air Force Palace HART (Helping Airmen Recover Together) program follows Air Force wounded in action until they return to active duty, or are medically retired."**

U.S. Army Wounded Warrior (AW2) Program (formerly the Army Disabled Soldiers Support System (DS3)

Through the U.S. Army Wounded Warrior Program (AW2), the Army provides its most severely disabled Soldiers and their families with a holistic system of advocacy and follow-up with personal support and liaison to resources, to assist them in their transition from military service to civilian life. AW2 links the Army and other organizations that stand ready to assist these Soldiers and families, such as the Department of Veterans' Affairs and the many Veterans' Service Organizations, to the Soldier. One key goal of AW2 is to provide a network of resources to severely disabled Soldiers, no matter where they relocate and regardless of their component: active, Reserve or National Guard. The goal is to ensure Soldiers, families, and communities receive responsive support services that meet their needs. The AW2 toll free number is: 1-800-833-6622. To read more, go to the current Army website: www.armyds3.org.

Navy Safe Harbor Program

The Navy Safe Harbor Program has a coordinated and tailored response for its men and women returning from Iraq, Afghanistan and other areas of conflict with severe debilitating injuries. Information can be

Make the Connection on MFN!
www.eMilitary.org/YourMFN.html

Sign on to the address
shown above and
Make the Connection
to more resources
on this topic!

found at http://www.npc.navy.mil/CommandSupport/SafeHarbor. For immediate, 24-hour response you can call 1-877-746-8563 or e-mail safeharbor@
navy.mil. Additionally, families can read up to date information on the DoD
Military Homefront website. Go to http://www.militaryhomefront.dod.mil,
and click on the Troops and Families link and then Military Severely Injured
Center in the left column.

Marine for Life Injured Support Program (M4L)

The Marine For Life Injured Support program provides information, advocacy
and assistance from the time of injury through return to full duty or transition
to the Veterans Administration, up to one year after separation. The program is
currently being introduced by Marine for Life staffers to Marines, Sailors, and
their families at National Naval Medical Center at Bethesda and Walter Reed
Army Medical Center in Washington, D.C., with a plan to expand to all major
Naval hospitals as soon as possible.

Marines who have already been medically discharged are being contacted
telephonically. Injured Marines, Sailors or family members needing assistance
can call toll-free: 866-645-8762 or e-mail: injuredsupport@M4L.usmc.mil.
For more information about the Marine for Life Injured Support Program, go
to: https://www.m4l.usmc.mil.

Military Severely Injured Center (MSIC)

The Center is a central Department of Defense (DoD) resource available to
offer support services to seriously in-
jured service members and their families. The Center works with and complements existing Service programs
such as the U.S. Army's Wounded
Warrior (AW2) Program, the Marine
for Life Injured Support System, and
Military OneSource. Support services
are provided as long as seriously injured service members and their fami-
lies require quality of life support. Services are tailored to meet individual's unique needs during recovery and rehabilitation. The Center offers
counseling and resource referral in such areas as financial support, education, and employment assistance, information on VA benefits, family counseling, resources in local communities, and child care support. For immediate, 24-hour response, the Military Severely Injured Center can be
reached toll free at 1-888-774-1361, or you can contact severelyinjured@
militaryonesource.com

> **"Support services are provided as long as seriously injured service members and their families require quality of life support"**

Additionally, families can read up to date information on the DoD Military Homefront website. Go to http://www.militaryhomefront.dod.mil, and click on the "Troops and Families" link.

Deployment Health Support Directorate

DoD established the Deployment Health Support Directorate to see that the medical lessons learned from previous conflicts and deployments are integrated into current policy, doctrine and practice. The Directorate addresses deployment-related health threats to service members. Part of the Deployment Health focus is on outreach. Current information on deployment-related health issues is published on an interactive web site, Deployment LINK: http://deploy-

Make the Connection on MFN!
www.eMilitary.org/YourMFN.html

Sign on to the address shown above and Make the Connection to more resources on this topic!

mentlink.osd.mil. The Directorate operates a toll free, direct hotline number where staff members assist callers in finding the answers they seek in relation to current and past deployments, helping them locate lost medical records, and providing contact information in the Department of Veteran Affairs. That number is 1-800-497-6261.

Toolkit

- AMVETS Service Offices: National Headquarters, 4647 Forbes Blvd., Lanham, MD 20706-4380; PH: (301) 459-9600; FAX: (301) 459-7924; Toll-Free: 1-877-726-8387; www.amvets.org
- Department of Veterans Affairs. www.va.gov
- Veterans Benefit Administration 1-800-827-1000
- Veterans Health Administration 1-877-222-8387

59 Cutting through the Red Tape

From the Field with Joe Moran

Joe Moran is the graphic designer of the Veterans of Foreign Wars (VFW) Publications

Imagine spending years wading through the bureaucratic red tape offered up by VA only to find you've been denied a disability claim. Where would you turn? Maybe you'd just throw up your hands and walk away in defeat. VFW understands the frustration associated with claims, and that's why its National Veterans Service (NVS) program was formed.

With a nationwide network of service officers, both on the Department (state) level (full-time, professional advocates) and Post level (volunteer advocates), NVS assists more than 120,000 veterans and their families each year. Service officers also are VFW members, making them well-versed in the organization's goals.

Specifically, service officers assist in filing the entitlement claims for veterans and will present veterans appeals before the VA Board of Veterans' Appeals and the Court of Appeals for Veterans Claims, if need be.

Furthermore, field representatives operating out of the Washington, DC office evaluate VA operations and services—health-care facilities, regional offices, cemeteries, and vet centers.

Another facet of NVS is the hospital volunteer program, which includes the Veterans Affairs Voluntary Service (VAVS). VFW was one of five groups comprising the original National Advisory Committee in 1946 that formed VAVS.

More than 6,000 regularly scheduled VFW volunteers provide more than one million hours of service annually to our nation's veterans in federal, state, and community hospitals and nursing homes through VAVS.

Volunteer opportunities vary by VA location. Here are just a few experiences offered by some VA facilities:

- reading to patients
- transporting patients to appointments
- manning clothes closets, and
- providing camaraderie

Expediting Claims for Departing Service Members

In 2001, VFW launched its Benefits Delivery at Discharge (BDD) program at military installations across the country. A cooperative initiative with VA and the Pentagon, BDD was established to assist GIs departing from the military.

> "In 2001, VFW launched its Benefits Delivery at Discharge (BDD) program at military installations across the country. A cooperative initiative with VA and the Pentagon, BDD was established to assist GIs departing from the military."

Pre-discharge claims representatives at each BDD site help wade through all the paperwork for vets seeking VA entitlements. These reps also discuss education and medical benefits, VA home loans, as well as different types of prosthetic equipment, when necessary.

In many cases, the pre-discharge claims reps are the service members' first exposure to VFW. That's why each maintains a certain level of professionalism at all times.

Currently, there are nine BDD sites from San Diego to Ft. Bragg, N.C., with more to come.

We want to help you with your earned entitlements. But if you don't contact us, we won't know, and you'll be missing out on a valuable service. To this end, VFW established the Tactical Assessment Center (TAC), a 24-hour help-line for veterans with questions or concerns about VA entitlements.

TAC collects the facts necessary to create a national database—tracking the timeliness, accessibility, and quality of VA medical and benefit services to veterans—and, in many instances, to directly intervene with VA. Since its inception, the TAC has assisted more than 70,000 veterans.

To reach TAC, call 1-800-VFW-1899 or visit www.vfwdc.org. /index. cfm?fa=vets.levelc&cid=3574.

 **FAQs**

Q. What is the Home Loan Guaranty program?

A. *The U. S. Department of Veterans Affairs (VA) operates a home loan guaranty program. Applicants must have a good credit rating, have an income sufficient to support mortgage payments, and agree to live in the property.*

Visit the VA Home Loan Guaranty website for more information, including eligibility and forms. You may also write or call: Department of Veterans Affairs, Cleveland Regional Loan Center, 1240 East Ninth Street, Cleveland, OH 44199; 1-800-729-5772

Q. What health care is available from the Veterans Administration?

A. *The U.S. Veterans' Administration Health Care System provides a standard health plan for most enrolled veterans. The Medical Benefits Package is geared to providing the appropriate care in the appropriate health-care setting. The program includes no-fee and fee-based services, depending on the veteran's condition and status. If you have questions about veteran health benefits, you can call the VA's Health Benefits Service Center at 1-877-222-8387 (1-877-222-VETS).*

Q. Who is eligible for VA health-care benefits?

A. *In general, to be eligible for enrollment for VA health-care benefits, you must have:*

- Been discharged from active military service under honorable conditions
- Served a minimum of two years if discharged after September 7, 1980 (prior to this date there is no time limit)
- If a National Guardsman or reservist, served the entire period for which you were called to active duty other than for training purposes only

Q. How can I enroll for VA health-care benefits?

A. *You may enroll in the VA Health Care System by completing VA Form 10-10EZ and returning it to the nearest VA Medical Center or Community Based Outpatient Clinic. You can also enroll on-line https://www.1010ez.med.va.gov/sec/vha/1010ez.*

 Need to Know

Veteran Benefit Summary from VA publication 21-00-1

The U.S. Department of Veterans Affairs, "VA" for short, offers a wide range of benefits for our nation's veterans, service members, and their families.

VA benefits and services are in these major categories: Compensation, Pension, Health Care, Vocational Rehabilitation & Employment, Education & Training, Home Loans, Life Insurance, Dependents and Survivors, Burial.

Q. Who is eligible?

A. *You may be eligible for VA benefits if you are: a veteran, a veteran's dependent—a surviving spouse, child, or parent of a deceased veteran—an active duty military service member or a member of the Reserve or National Guard.*

> **VA can pay you monthly compensation if you are at least 10 percent disabled as a result of your military service.**

Benefits

Compensation : VA can pay you monthly compensation if you are at least 10 percent disabled as a result of your military service.

Pension: You can receive a monthly pension if you are a wartime veteran with limited income, and you are permanently and totally disabled OR at least sixty-five-years old.

Time Limits: There is no time limit to apply for compensation and pension benefits.

Health Care: VA provides a number of health-care services:
- Hospital, outpatient medical, dental, pharmacy, and prosthetic services
- Domiciliary, nursing home, and community-based residential care
- Sexual trauma counseling
- Specialized health care for women veterans
- Health and rehabilitation programs for homeless veterans
- Readjustment counseling
- Alcohol and drug dependency treatment
- Medical evaluation for disorders associated with military service in the Gulf War, or exposure to Agent Orange, radiation, and other environmental hazards

Combat Veterans: VA will provide combat veterans free medical care for any illness possibly associated with service during a period of hostility for two years from the veteran's release from active duty.

Vocational Rehabilitation & Employment: VA can help veterans with service-connected disabilities prepare for, find, and keep suitable employment. For veterans with serious service-connected disabilities, VA also offers services to improve their ability to live as independently as possible. Some of the services VA provides are:
- Job Search: Assistance in finding and maintaining suitable employment
- Vocational Evaluation: An evaluation of abilities, skills, interests, and needs
- Career Exploration: Vocational counseling and planning
- Vocational Training: If needed, training such as on-the-job and non-paid work experience

> **For veterans with serious service-connected disabilities, VA also offers services to improve their ability to live as independently as possible.**

- Education Training: If needed, education training to accomplish the rehabilitation goal
- Rehabilitation Service: Supportive rehabilitation and counseling services
- *Time Limits:* You generally have twelve years from the date VA informs you in writing that you have at least a 10 percent rating for a service-connected disability.

Education & Training: VA pays benefits to eligible veterans, reservists, and active- duty service members while they are in an approved education or training program. Based on the type of military service, benefit programs are:

- **Active Duty Service:** Persons who first entered active duty after June 30, 1985, are generally eligible under the Montgomery GI Bill (Chapter 30). Those who entered active duty for the first time after December 31, 1976, and before July 1, 1985, are generally eligible under the Veterans Educational Assistance Program (VEAP).
- **Reserve/Guard Service**: Benefits are available to Reserve and National Guard members under [a] the Montgomery GI Bill (Chapter 1606) who signed a six-year commitment with a reserve unit after June 30, 1985, and remain actively drilling and in good standing with their unit, and [b] the Reserve Education Assistance Program (Chapter 1607) who were activated under Federal authority for a contingency operation and served ninety continuous days or more after September 11, 2001.

> **"...veterans have ten years from the date they were last released from active duty to use their education and training benefits, and Reserve and National Guard members have fourteen years from the date they became eligible for the program unless they leave the Selected Reserves before completing their obligation."**

- *Time Limits*: Generally, *veterans* have ten years from the date they were last released from active duty to use their education and training benefits, and *Reserve and National Guard members* have fourteen years from the date they became eligible for the program unless they leave the Selected Reserves before completing their obligation.

Home Loans: VA offers a number of home loan services to eligible veterans, some military personnel, and certain surviving spouses.

- **Guaranteed Loans:** VA can guarantee part of a loan from a private lender to help you buy a home, a manufactured home, a lot for a manufactured home, or certain types of condominiums. VA also guarantees loans for building, repairing, and improving homes.

- **Refinancing Loans:** If you have a VA mortgage, VA can help you refinance your loan at a lower interest rate. You may also refinance a non-VA loan.
- **Special Grants:** Certain disabled veterans and military personnel can receive grants to adapt or acquire housing suitable for their needs.
- *Time Limits*: There is no time limit for a VA home loan.

Life Insurance

- **Service members' Group Life Insurance (SGLI)** is low-cost term life insurance for service members and reservists. Coverage of up to $400,000 begins when you enter the service. Generally, it expires 120 days after you leave the service.
- **Traumatic SGLI** is automatically included in SGLI and provides for payment up to $100,000 for service members who lose limbs or incur other serious injuries.
- **Veterans Group Life Insurance (VGLI)** is renewable term life insurance for veterans who want to convert their SGLI up to an amount not to exceed the coverage you had when you separated from service. You must apply within one year from separation from service.
- **Service-Disabled Veterans Insurance**, also called "RH" Insurance, is for service-connected veterans. Coverage is $10,000. You may be eligible for a $20,000 supplemental policy if you are totally disabled. You must apply for RH within two years of being rated service connected by VA.

Dependents & Survivors

- **Dependency and Indemnity Compensation (DIC)** is payable to certain survivors of:
  o   Service members who died on active duty
  o   Veterans who died from service-related disabilities
  o   Certain veterans who were being paid 100 percent VA disability compensation at time of death.
- **Death Pension** is payable to some surviving spouses and children of deceased wartime veterans. The benefit is based on financial need.
- **Parents' DIC** is payable to some surviving parents. The benefit is based on financial need.
- **VA Civilian Health and Medical Program (CHAMPVA)** shares the cost of medical services for eligible dependents and survivors of certain veterans.
- **Dependents & Survivors Education & Training:** Some family members of disabled or deceased veterans are eligible for education and training benefits.

- **Home Loans:** Certain surviving spouses may be eligible for this benefit.
- *Time Limits*: For education and training benefits, spouses and surviving spouses have ten years from the date VA first finds them eligible. Surviving spouses of service members who died while on active duty have twenty years. Children are eligible from age eighteen to twenty-six. These time limits can sometimes be extended. There are no time limits to apply for the other benefits described above.
- **Burial:** VA offers certain benefits and services to honor our Nation's deceased veterans.
  - o **Headstones and Markers:** VA can furnish a monument to mark the unmarked grave of an eligible veteran.
  - o **Presidential Memorial Certificate (PMC):** VA can provide a PMC for eligible recipients.
  - o **Burial Flag:** VA can provide an American flag to drape an eligible veteran's casket.
  - o **Reimbursement of Burial Expenses:** Generally, VA can pay a burial allowance of $2,000 for veterans who die of service-related causes. For certain other veterans, VA can pay $300 for burial and funeral expenses and $300 for a burial plot.
  - o **Burial in a VA National Cemetery:** Most veterans and some dependents can be buried in a VA national cemetery.
  - o *Time Limits*: There is no time limit to claim reimbursement of burial expenses for a service-related death. In other cases, claims must be filed within two years of the veteran's burial.

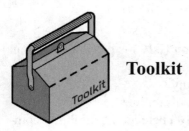 **Toolkit**

Department of Veterans Affairs. For detailed information about all VA benefits and services, visit www.va.gov.

Toll-Free Service Benefits Information & Assistance. For more information about specific benefits, visit the nearest VA regional office or call 1-800-827-1000.

Federal Benefits for Veterans and Dependents (2007 Edition). This booklet lists the variety of federal benefits available to veterans and their dependents. http://www1.va.gov/opa/vadocs/current_benefits.asp

Information on obtaining education forms. http://www.va.gov/vaforms gov/opa/feature/index.asp.

Special Toll-Free VA Numbers and websites:

- CHAMPVA 800-733-8387
- Direct Deposit 877-838-2778
- Education & Training 888-442-4551
- Headstones *(status of claims only)* 800-697-6947
- Health Care 877-222-8387
- Helpline (Agent Orange & Gulf War) 800-749-8387
- Office of SGLI 800-419-1473
- Telecommunication Device for Deaf *(TDD)* 800-829-4833
- VA Life Insurance 800-669-8477
- Department of Defense Voluntary Education Homepage . http://www.voled.doded.mil/
- St. Louis Regional Processing Office. http://www.gibill.va.gov/contact/RPO_Sites/stlouis/stlouis_index.htm
- U.S. Navy SMART transcripts. https://smart.cnet.navy.mil
- WAVE- Web Automated Verification of Enrollment. http://www.gibill.va.gov/wave1.cfm

Make the Connection on MFN!
www.eMilitary.org/YourMFN.html

Sign on to the address shown above and Make the Connection to more resources on this topic!

Part 11

Death of a Family Member

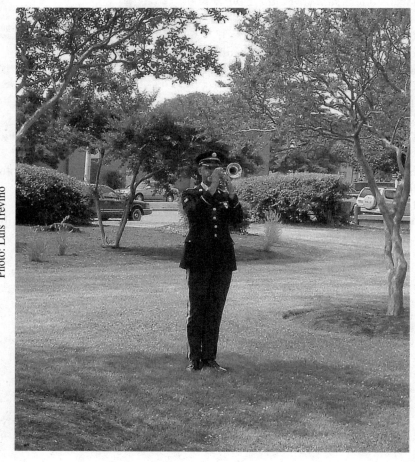

Photo: Luis Trevino

Introduction

The loss of a loved one is tragic, especially a sudden loss. No matter how many discussions you may have had with your service member or how many preparations you may have made together, you are never ready. Losing your service member during a deployment is especially hard because of the separation. You may not have spoken with your loved one soon before their death, or perhaps you may have been going through a tough time together and your last words were not as loving as you would have liked them to be. Or, your last visit was just fine. The point is that you still have things you want to say and share with your service member, but you can't. This will be a very difficult time for you and your family.

Immediately after your notification, you will have many days where it will seem as if you do not have time to grieve for your loved one. You will need to handle your loved ones arrangements, deal with benefit questions, and media inquiries—all on top of everyday life and (if you have children) parental duties.

There is nothing that you can do to bring your service member back. During this time, your only goal may be a very simple one: coping – just simply allowing yourself time to take in the loss. But there are things that you can do to help you through this difficult time. One is to understand now what to expect should the unthinkable occur. Another is for you to know that there are many loving people and organizations out there to help support and comfort you in this time of need.

In the next several pages, we hope that the information being provided will serve this important purpose.

60 When the Unthinkable Happens

From the Field with Caroline Peabody

Caroline Peabody *is the daughter of a disabled Vietnam era Marine, military spouse, former president of The Military Family Network, lifetime volunteer, and distinguished speaker and lecturer on military life. She holds a B.S. in sociology and M.A. in organizational management with extensive research on communication systems as they relate to military well being and community capacity-building. She is a published writer and columnist on matters relating to military families, military learning models, and military relations.*

Losing a family member is a tragedy. In the military, there will always be the possibility that your loved one will be lost while serving our nation. In the Global War on Terror, as with all wars, this country has seen the loss of many brave service members. Our nation has also witnessed countless wounded passing through the doors of Walter Reed and other critical-care military hospitals.

If your loved one loses his or her life while serving our country, it will be devastating to your family, and the effects will extend beyond your home. The whirlwind that follows the death of a loved one can leave family members in such a state of shock and numbness that support from family and friends may be lost in a haze of sorrow.

There is absolutely nothing that can be said or done that will ever replace your loved one. Your family has paid the highest price that can ever be paid for defending a country. You have a right to expect that your loss will be treated with the highest degree of respect and courtesy.

A nation at war has a duty to honor, respect, and support all sacrifices made during these times of conflict. Each service has a process for supporting the family of the fallen service member to ensure that your privacy as well as your rights and benefits are handled with the greatest of care. It is important to know what to expect if the unthinkable should happen. Although difficult to deal with, being familiar with process that will happen in the event of the death of your loved one will be a small source of comfort in this time of need.

The first thing that happens is notification. This is accomplished with a visit where the casualty assistance officer (CAO) will briefly tell you what happened. At the meeting, you will be asked for information about your family. You will also be informed of the circumstances surrounding the loss of your loved one. It may seem like a lot of information happening at one time. Part of this information process is verification of the information provided to the military from your service member about your family. The military has to know about any marriages, children, custody matters, etc. There may also be a follow-up meeting where you may need to provide copies of court orders (adoption, divorce, custody). The purpose of this information gathering is to ensure that all eligible family members receive the benefits entitled to them. If the military does not have accurate information, processing of benefits may be delayed or turned down entirely.

> **"The purpose of this information gathering is to ensure that all eligible family members receive the benefits entitled to them."**

There is an immediate benefit that you are entitled to receive to help in the continuation of your household and to handle necessary arrangements. This benefit is called a Death Gratuity. The primary next of kin (PNOK) is entitled to receive this compensation. The amount set and changed from time to time by Congress. The Gratuity is lump sum payment is intended to help you with immediate living expenses until other benefits begin. It is normally paid within seventy-two hours after notification of death.

By law, only certain persons are eligible to receive these payments, and an order of precedence has been established. Those eligible to receive payment and their order of precedence are:
- The surviving spouse
- The children (if no surviving spouse) in equal shares (without regard to age or marital status)

- If designated by the Soldier, any one or more of the following persons: parents or persons *in loco parentis* (in place of natural parents), brothers, or sisters. Please consult with the Legal Assistance Office for a more detailed discussion of the order of precedence.

Release of Information

Part of the meeting you have with the casualty officer will include a release of information request. This will permit the military to release information about your service member's death. There are many organizations, leaders, and media that desire to know about those lost during their service. There are many organizations that have been founded to support families like yours through this time. They may have fellowship, grants, educational scholarships, and other benefits to help support your family through your loss. Leadership, local and national, may desire to offer condolences to you and your family, as well as appreciation for your spouse's service and sacrifice.

> **"Organizations may have fellowship, grants, educational scholarships, and other benefits to help support your family through your loss. Leadership, local and national, may desire to offer condolences to you and your family, as well as appreciation for your spouse's service and sacrifice."**

The media may want to interview you about your circumstance. This can be a very emotional and sensitive event. You always have the option to decline or stop an interview at any point. If you need help, you can request a Public Affairs representative from your service to help you navigate media requests.

The most important thing is your family's well being. You are not obligated to anyone else except yourself and your loved ones.

An Emotional Time

Losing your loved one is a traumatic experience. You will experience many different emotions. Some feelings you may have include disbelief, numbness, denial, anger, extreme fatigue, or grief. These are all normal. It is an enormous loss and although many people talk about steps in the grieving process, know that everyone has a unique way of dealing with death, and the process may be different for you than for someone else. Be kind to yourself and give yourself time. When others offer to help, let them. If you have a specific need, tell them. Be specific. Sometimes people are uncomfortable about loss and don't know what to do with their desire to help. You may need to show them how to be there for you. The important thing is to accept as much support as you can during this time.

 **FAQs**

Q. Who is the Primary Next of Kin?

A. *The person most closely related to the service member is considered Primary Next of Kin (PNOK). Federal statutes provide certain benefits to a service member's relatives and, in some cases, to non-family members. Some benefits are based upon a person's relationship to the service member and the role he or she played in the service member's life. Other benefits are based on choices made by the service member.*

Q. What are the casualty assistance officers called in each of the services?

A. *The Military Services have different titles for their casualty assistance officers:*
- **Army**—Casualty Assistance Officer (CAO)
- **Marine Corps**—Casualty Assistance Calls Officer (CACO)
- **Navy**—Casualty Assistance Calls Officer (CACO)
- **Air Force**—Casualty Assistance Representative (CAR)

Q. Who can accompany a service member?

A. *There are two types of escorts authorized to accompany the remains of active-duty service members: a military member selected by the deceased member's command, or a close relative of the deceased. A family escort requires official approval. Obtaining this approval can be a lengthy process, which may cause a delay in moving the remains. If the service member died overseas and burial will be in the United States, the remains will be returned to the United States as soon as possible, usually within a few days depending on the circumstances and location of loss.*

Q. Can someone other than PNOK decide where my service member is buried?

A. *Yes. The Person Authorized to Direct Disposition (PADD) will determine where the burial will take place. The Military Service will provide all necessary assistance to satisfy the PADD's decision on burial location to include burial in a national, state, private, or public cemetery. All active-duty service* *members are eligible for burial in Arlington National Cemetery or any national cemetery that has available space. Information on burial in a national cemetery is available from any local office of the Department of Veterans Affairs (DVA). Spouses and children under eighteen may be buried with their loved ones in DVA national cemeteries.*

Your funeral director will assist you with burial arrangements for any cemetery in the National Cemetery System, including Arlington National Cemetery.

Q. Who is eligible for Military Funeral Honors?

A. *The following service members are eligible:*
- Military members on active duty or in the Selected Reserve
- Former military members who served on active duty and departed under conditions other than dishonorable
- Former military members who completed at least one term of enlistment or period of initial obligated service in the Selected Reserve and departed under conditions other than dishonorable
- Former military members discharged from the Selected Reserve due to a disability incurred or aggravated in the line of duty

 Need to Know

Funeral Honors

The arrangements and discussion of military funeral honors for your loved one usually occur on the installation level of your service members command or, in the case of a veteran, the designated local official in charge of these affairs. The funeral director should have a contact for requesting appropriate funeral honors. In addition, you will be able to include your service member's service insignia in their obituary if you desire. You have the right to select all or some of the following depending on status of deceased (active, retired, veteran, rank/occupation) in honoring your loved one:
- The coffin is draped in a U.S. flag as a pall.
- The flag is folded and presented to next of kin, "on behalf of a grateful nation." (Generally, the flag is given to the next-of-kin as a keepsake after its use during the funeral service. When there is no next-of-kin, the flag is presented to a friend making a request for it.)
- The flag for someone who dies during active duty is provided by that individual's branch of service. The U.S. Veterans Benefits Administration

(VBA) provides a U.S. flag at no cost, to drape the casket or accompany the urn of a deceased veteran who served honorably in the U.S. armed forces.

- The coffin is sometimes transported by way of a horse-drawn caisson.
- A three-volley salute is fired for most branches of the military. For the Navy, a cannon will be fired, a practice that originated in the British Navy. When a cannon was fired, it partially disarmed the ship, therefore firing the cannon represents trust and respect.
- Gun salute for those eligible (e.g., general officers, presidents, other high-ranking officials).
- "Taps" is played on the bugle, or "Amazing Grace" is played on the bag-pipes, at a distance (thirty to fifty yards) from the gravesite.
- A fly-by by military jets in a missing man formation is performed when request-ed at funerals for flyers and general officers of the United States Air Force.

Presidential Memorial Certificates

A Presidential Memorial Certificate (PMC) is an engraved paper certificate, signed by the current president; to honor the memory of honorably discharged deceased veterans. This program was initiated in March 1962 by President John F. Kennedy and has been continued by all subsequent presidents. Statu-tory authority for the program is Section 112, Title 38, of the United States Code. Eligible recipients include the deceased veteran's next of kin and loved ones. More than one certificate may be provided.

The Department of Veterans Affairs (VA) administers the PMC program by preparing the certificates, which bear the current president's signature expressing the country's grateful recognition of the veteran's service in the United States Armed Forces. Eligible recipients, or someone acting on their behalf, may apply for a PMC in person at any VA regional office or by U.S. mail only. Requests cannot be sent via e-mail. There is no form to use when requesting a PMC. Please be sure to enclose a copy of the veteran's discharge and death certificate. Please submit copies only, as original documents cannot be returned. If you would like to request a Presidential Memorial Certificate:

1. **Fax** your request and all supporting documents (copy of discharge and death certificate) to: (202) 565-8054, or
2. **Mail** your request and all supporting documents using either the U.S. Postal Service or a commercial mail service, such as one of the overnight or express mail delivery services, to: Presidential Memorial Certifi-cates (41A1C), Department of Vet-erans Affairs, 5109 Russell Road, Quantico, VA 22134-3903

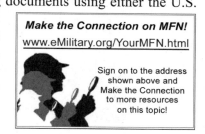

Make the Connection on MFN!
www.eMilitary.org/YourMFN.html
Sign on to the address shown above and Make the Connection to more resources on this topic!

Appendix 1:

Service-by-Service Guide to Family Support Systems

ARMY

Army Well-Being Program

The Army Well-Being Program takes care of all members of the Army community before, during, and after deployments. The Army Well-Being website (www.Ar-myWell-Being.org) is a one-stop resource-driven site that features direct access to Well-Being programs through links. The site also features a forum that enables constituents to share their opinions and issues. The site includes a section entitled "Focus On . . ." to provide constituents with important facts and information on an important Well-Being topic each month, and more importantly, provides them with an opportunity to express their opinion through participating in a related poll.

The Army's Well-Being Liaison Office (WBLO) assists the Army Leadership with its constituent communities—Soldiers (Active-Duty, National Guard, and Army Reserve), Civilians, Retirees, Veterans and Army Families—to ensure the effective delivery of Well-Being programs to the Army by providing focused representation of constituent interests and attitudes as they relate to Well-Being. The WBLO accomplishes this through its Integrated Service Delivery System (ISDS) that incorporates the organization's core functions — advisory, liaison, outreach, feedback, and evaluation. The WBLO has been tasked to provide accountability assistance to the Army G-1 and the Army's Office of Civilian Personnel. They are chartered to provide Well-Being support to the Army's constituent communities in the event of a natural disaster. This mission is largely accomplished through the WBLO's Army Information Line (1-800-833-6622).

The WBLO's mission is composed of five Core Functions:

- Advisory–Provide informed recommendations to Army leadership regarding the impact of policies, programs and practices on the Well-Being of the force based on constituent perspectives.
- Liaison–Establish and maintain two-way communication networks between constituencies and the Army leadership.
- Outreach–Improve constituent understanding of the Well-Being initiative by using existing Communication tools: World Wide Web; publications, e-mail; conferences/councils.

451

- Feedback–Obtain verifiable and non-verifiable constituent feedback on applicable Well-Being functions.
- Evaluation–Compile and evaluate the full spectrum of data reflecting the constituent point of view regarding the effectiveness of Well-Being programs.

The WBLO's Integrated Service Delivery System (ISDS) incorporates a variety of tools and resources:

- **Army Families Online (www.ArmyFamiliesOnline.org)**– Army Families Online is the cornerstone of the WBLO ISDS. The site improves constituent understanding of Well-Being initiatives and obtains constituent feedback. The site offers valuable news and information relevant to Army Life, a "Resources A-Z" section that offers one-stop access to information through Web links and phone numbers, access to online Well-Being Polls and electronic versions of Well-Being publications such as "FLO Notes" monthly newsletter and "Army Well-Being" quarterly magazine.
- **The Army Information Line (1-800-833-6622)**–The Army Information Line is a toll-free telephone resource to provide accurate information, useful resources and helpful referral services to those with issues or concerns pertaining to Army Life (deployment, child support, family readiness, etc.). It serves as a safety net for those who have exhausted all other resources. WBLO constituent liaisons are available from 8 a.m. to 4:30 p.m. EST, Monday through Friday to assist members of the Army's constituent communities.
- **FLO Notes newsletter**–FLO Notes newsletter is the Army's premier Family Readiness information resource, and is produced on a monthly basis. The newsletter is sent via direct mail to senior Army spouses each month. This publication is intended to assist in the dissemination of information that is useful to Army Family Readiness Group leaders in keeping members of their group informed about items of interest to Army families. FLO Notes is also available in electronic form via Army Families Online.

Deployment Cycle Support (DCS)

The Army's Deployment Cycle Support Program is a comprehensive process that ensures Soldiers, DA civilians and family members are better prepared and sustained throughout the deployment cycle. DCS provides the means to identify Soldiers, DA civilians, and families who may need assistance with the challenges inherent to extended deployments. As of Sept. 30, 2006, some 435,890 Soldiers have completed DCS tasks in theater since the program's data collection began on May 3, 2003. A summary of the phases related to redeployment is included below.

DCS Redeployment Phase begins in the Redeployment Assembly Area (RAA) in theater and concludes upon departure. This phase includes safety and medical requirements, which must be certified by the Soldier's chain of command, for returning Soldiers. It includes the following: Commander's Risk Assessment; Suicide Awareness and Prevention Training; documentation of exposures in-theater using the DD Form 2796. In addition, medical personnel assist the Soldier in identifying any recently acquired health problems, refer Soldiers with deployment related medical problems to appropriate local agencies for assistance before redeployment, and treat and document any adverse or potentially adverse exposures or negative health-related behaviors that occurred during deployment/mobilization and ensure the availability of behavioral health assets for Soldier's in the RAA.

The next DCS Phase begins upon arrival at the Demobilization Station for the Reserve Component (RC) and Home Station for the Active Component (AC) and concludes upon departure from the Demobilization Station for the RC or when the AC is released for their unit's block leave. This phase includes the following safety and medical requirements for each returning soldier which also must be certified as completed by the chain of command: Briefings on Post-Deployment Stress, Normalization of Experiences, Changes in Relationships, Communication with Spouse, and Children (where applicable), and Driver and Safety Training (autos, drinking, water sports, sexually transmitted disease, etc.). Redeploying married Soldiers take a marital enrichment assessment instrument and must complete any Phase I tasks not completed by Soldiers or DA civilians in-theater/AOR. In addition, before Soldiers depart the Home Station or Demobilization Station, medical personnel complete the following: medical record review; screen behavioral health records (where existing); update individual's permanent health record with deployment health records; ensure that DD 3349 (Medical Profile) is completed prior to release; perform initial TB tests and schedule the 90-day follow-up TB tests; continue to identify any recently acquired health related problems; and finally provide mandatory medical assessments and treatments to include laboratory work-ups.

A third DCS Phase begins at Home Station for both AC and RC. The gaining command is responsible for any DCS tasks not completed in the previous phases. The following are required during this phase: married Soldiers complete marital assessment instrument; commanders provide time for Soldier readjustment (i.e. half day work schedule for AC, no drill for 60 days for RC); conduct leader counseling after block leave; RC units conduct command climate survey; complete outstanding medical board actions (i.e. Military Medical Review Board, Medical Evaluation Board, Physical Evaluation Board); conduct family day activities; reintegrate RC Soldiers back into civilian workplace; complete 90-day TB testing and serum specimen requirements; complete update of Soldier individual health record with deployment health record; Employer Assistance Program (EAP) counselors continue to provide support to AC/RC Soldiers and family members referring serious cases for medical treatment; provide AC spouses opportunity to take marital assessment instrument: provide AC with voluntary marriage education/enrichment workshops; continue TRICARE benefits briefings; provide legal assistance to RC members on issues arising from mobilization; and finally conduct Suicide Intervention Skills Training for all units.

More information on Deployment Cycle Support, visit the DCS Web site at http://www.armyg1.army.mil/hr/dcs.asp.

— **Colonel Dennis Dingle**
Chief, Army Well Being Division

Army Family Programs

The Department of the Army position is the following with regard to military family support. Services delivered through Army Family Programs are critical to the well-being of Soldiers and families, and directly influence the Army's ability to sustain mission readiness during times of peace, war, and national crisis. The most significant family challenges are meeting needs relating to deployment, improving the Army's response to family distress, and relocation issues such as spouse employment.

The U.S. Army Family, Morale, Welfare, and Recreation Command's (FMWRC) Army Community Service (ACS) take care of Soldiers' families. These programs ease tension and enhance retention. Services range from financial readiness, spouse employment, mobilization/deployment support, training for Rear Detachment Commanders and Family Readiness Groups, Army Family Team Building, Army Family Action Plan, exceptional family member services, and Volunteer Management.

The following are brief descriptions of some of these family support programs in place:

- **Military One Source**: Provides 24-hour, seven-day a week toll-free information, referral telephone line and internet/web based service to Active Duty, National Guard, Reserve Soldiers, deployed civilians, and their families. 1-800-464-8107, or www.militaryonesource.com .

- **MyArmyLifeToo.com**: Serves as the "single gateway for Army information" www.MyArmyLifeToo.com.

- **Virtual Family Readiness Groups**: A web-based system that provides all the functionality of a traditional FRG in an online setting providing separated families a "sense of community." www.armyfrg.org

- **Multi-Component Family Support Network**: A cohesive support system with alternative delivery options to meet the diverse needs of Active, mobilized Guard and Reserves regardless of where they reside.

- **Army Sexual Assault Prevention & Response** provides a framework for the Army to integrate and coordinate medical, legal, advocacy, and support services for victims in both the garrison and operational environment.

- **Rear Detachment Commander (RDC)/Family Readiness Group (FRG) Leader Online Training Courses** will ensure the RDC and FRG leaders have the guidance and support needed to be effective in their positions by providing them with the most relevant information and training.

- **Military Family Life Consultants** are professionals who work directly with ACS to provide reunion and reintegration support to Soldiers and their families in a variety of formats reducing the stress affecting families. The goal is to prevent family distress by providing education and information on family dynamics, parent education, available support services, and the effects of stress and positive coping mechanisms

- **OP READY** a comprehensive training program to assist commanders in meeting family readiness objectives and prepares Army families, Soldiers and key unit personnel (RDC and FRG leaders) for deployments and reunions.

- **Family Readiness**: As the Army has increased its reliance on the total force, ACS has stressed the importance of family preparedness of both the active and Reserve component families. Global War on Terrorism resources are funding the Military One Source 1-800 number that provides pertinent information/referral and counseling services 24/7. Military One Source provides information ranging from every day concerns to deployment/reintegration issues. The Army Guide to Family Readiness Group (FRG) Operations (AR 608- 1, Appendix J) provides interim guidance until inclusion in new Army regulations. The guide provides easy to understand guidelines and examples for: FRG Roles and Functions, Authorized

Support, FRG Informal Funds, FRG Fund-raising, Solicitations and Donations, and Commercial Sponsorship. The guide recommends a $5,000 annual cap for FRG funds, restricts FRGs to internal fund-raising only, and prohibits FRGs from soliciting donations and gifts.

- **Virtual Family Readiness Group (vFRG).** The vFRG supports the creation of on-line FRGs at the brigade, battalion and company levels. The vFRG corresponds to an existing traditional FRG, but also supports the creation of ad hoc FRGs due to the dispersion of family members and volunteer FRG leaders without geographical or unit integrity of those families. The vFRG program is available to units in all Army components who are deployed or preparing for deployment. The vFRG links the deployed Soldier, their family, the FRG Leader, the unit commander, and other unit family readiness personnel on their own secure web page to facilitate the exchange of information and provide a sense of community. www.armyfrg.org
- **The Army Family Team Building Program** builds stronger, more self-reliant families by providing education and readiness training that is particularly targeted to family members at every level, to include junior enlisted spouses who are new to the Army and its ways. Demand for classes increases during deployment and times of crisis when families need current information and strengthened coping skills.
- **The Army Family Action Plan Program** provides a "grassroots" mechanism to raise well-being issues of concern to senior leaders and establishes a protocol to work the issues through resolution. Issues historically reflect the concerns arising from changes that have a direct effect on the force and its families. The issues result in changes to legislation, Department of Defense and Army policies, and improved programs and services.
- **New Parent Support**: The program is congressionally mandated to prevent child maltreatment and/or family violence. It supports the screening, assessment, and provision of home visitation services to families with children from birth to five years of age who may be at risk for abuse and or neglect.
- **Transitional Compensation** provides support to victims of abuse during their transition from military to civilian life when the sponsor is separated from active duty as a result of a dependent-abuse offense. Payments are for a minimum of 12 months or until what would have been the Soldiers' end of obligated service, whichever is greater, but may not exceed 36 months. The current monthly rate is $1,033.00 for the spouse and $257.00 for each eligible child residing with the spouse, and $438.00 for the child only.
- **Victim Advocacy.** The Defense Task Force on Domestic Violence and DoD Task Force on Sexual Assault recognized the critical need to increase services to victims at all installations. Victim Advocacy is an integral part of the Army's Family Advocacy Program. Victim Advocates ensure victim safety, provides crisis support, and information and referral to victims of domestic violence and sexual assault. The Army also establishes Memorandum of Agreements with community based victim centered programs to provide services at installations that do not have contract or GS advocates.
- **Sexual Assault Prevention and Response Action Plan (SAPRP).** The Army implemented a comprehensive program that focuses on prevention, training, and

victim support to victims of sexual assault. A commander's program on the installation ensures that Soldiers are trained to provide services to victims in deployed
environments. .

- **Spouse Employment Partnerships**. The 2002 National Defense Authorization
Act directed the Secretary of Defense to examine existing Defense and other federal, state, and non-governmental spouse employment programs. In Oct 2003,
the Army formally signed a Statement of Support with 13 Fortune 100 and 500
companies and 2 military agencies who pledged their best effort to increase employment and career opportunities for Army spouses. At present ASEP has 21
corporate and military partners. As of August 2005, there have been over 11,000
spouses hired through ASEP. In July 2005, the military job search website, www.
msjs.org hosted by ASEP was launched. This site is an association page with
the Department of Labor's America's Job Bank that provides military spouses a
portal for their resumes and allows ASEP partners the opportunity to post jobs on
site. To date, there are over 53,000 military spouse-friendly jobs posted on the
site. Currently 21 civilian and military organizations belong to the partnership.

- **Multi-Component Family Support Network**. The Integrated Multi-Component
Family Support Network is a seamless array of family support services that can be
easily accessed by the Soldier and family – Active, Guard, and Reserve, regardless of their geographical location. MCFSN links existing community support services enabling the Army to embrace every family equally regardless of component
or physical location and draw upon resources in local communities. To integrate
Family Programs, the MCFSN successfully piloted three different models within
the Army components and a joint service model, all of which focused on working
with families, working with units, and working with communities.

- **Relocation Readiness Program (RRP)**: Customized services at individual locations
provide information and referral assistance, classes, counseling and use of web-based
programs. Key RRP components include: an established Relocation Assistance Coordinating Committee (RAAC) to ensure cooperative coordination among the varied installation relocation services and Standard Installation Topic Exchange Service
(SITES) on-line information on worldwide military installations (e.g. Housing, Education, Family Centers). Relocation counseling (individual or group) is available to
both inbound and outbound transferees with extensive preparation and planning before the move, during the actual transfer and while settling in. Education and training
provides mandatory overseas orientations, re-entry workshops, pre-arrival information, destination services, lending closet loan of household items for a limited period,
post-move newcomers orientations, services to multicultural families, outreach services (identification, counseling, advocacy) for waiting families and sponsor training
of unit sponsorship trainers and/or sponsors and youth sponsorship.

Army Basics (facts on Army Programs for spouse education, outreach and support)

- **Army Family Team Building** – trains active, Guard and Reserve volunteers to
be Master Trainers, Core Volunteer Instructors and installation volunteers to be
self-reliant.

- ✓ Additional courses for spouse attendees at the AWC and USASGM Academy.
- ✓ AFTB Net-trainer provides on line access to training. (FY05: 8,395 enrollments)
- **MyArmyLifeToo.com** – website, www.myArmyLifeToo.com provides single portal access to accurate, up-to-date information on a variety of topics for active, Army National Guard, and Reserve. Contains spouse portfolio component and volunteer database.
  - ✓ 28 million hits from the official launch in Feb 05 through FY06.
  - ✓ Spouse Mentoring Module available in E-learning Center at MyArmyLife too.com
- **Enlisted Spouse Outreach Plan** – MACOM senior enlisted spouses and SMA spouse developed action plan to increase outreach to junior enlisted spouses.
  - ✓ Working with the Sergeants Major Academy, Accessions and TRADOC to complete actions.
- Army Family Readiness Advisory Council (AFRAC) and Executive Council (AFREC) (previously AFWBAC/AFWBEC)
  - ✓ AFRAC – Reviews and determines action plan for resolution of issues from the field. The AFRAC provides input to family programs. Attendees are 2 and 3-star command and CSM spouses and a selected volunteer representative. The most recent meeting was 14-15 Sep 06.
  - ✓ AFREC – Evaluates and discusses issues/action plans from AFRAC; refers appropriate issues to MWR EXCOM and BOD for resolution. Members are spouses of 4-star commanders and CSMs.
- **Family Program List Serve**–a monthly update of topics related to family readiness emailed to subscribers through MyArmyLifeToo.com website. More than 45,000 registered users!!

Getting Involved
- **Army Family Action Plan (AFAP)**–local, mid-level and HQDA conferences; two General Officer Steering Committees (GOSC) annually chaired by VCSA. Next Conference scheduled for 13-17 Nov 06.
  - ✓ 99 Legislative changes; 145 DoD/Army policy changes; 164 improved programs/services.
- **Army Volunteer Corps**–Volunteer emblem, Code of Ethics, AVC pins, and posters; standardizes recruitment, training and recognition of all Army volunteers for Active, Guard, Reserve. (FY05: ACS volunteers contributed 632, 897 hours of service)
  - ✓ DA level Working Group meets quarterly at CFSC.

Home & Family Life
- **Military One Source**–24/7 telephone, web-based and counseling service for all components (transition to MOS is transparent to user).
- **Family Advocacy**–programs to prevent and treat child and spouse abuse.

- **Victim Advocates**–provide advocacy services for both domestic violence and sexual assault victims.
- **New Parent Support Program**–includes support for new parents; targets new fathers.
- **Exceptional Family Member Program (EFMP)**–helps families with special needs find and use community resources; respite care is not adequate to meet the need.
  - ✓ MCEC completed exploratory study to include recommendations to improve services.
- **Transitional Compensation**–temporary payments to victims of abuse when the Soldier is administratively discharged or court-martialed for dependent abuse.
- **Army Sexual Assault Prevention and Response Program**–CFSC provides sexual assault response coordinators (SARCS) and victim advocates; also trains unit Victim Advocates and deployable SARCS.

Making a Move
- **Pre and Post Relocation Planning and Assistance**– available Army-wide.
- **SITES**–No longer available. Have made the transition to providing relocation information at www.militaryonesource.com and relocation tools at www.Military-HOMEFRONT.dod.mil/moving.
- **Services for Multi-Cultural Families and Waiting Families (Hearts Apart)**–installation services target support for families separated from the Soldier (e.g., 2ID Korea).

Managing Deployment
- **OP Ready Updates**–standardized training materials being updated based on GWOT lessons learned—revisions expected to be completed for FRG Leader and Rear Detachment Commander handbooks and training modules in Oct 06. Trauma in the Unit, Children and Deployment and Family Assistance Center handbooks and training modules expected first quarter, FY07.
- **Military Family Life Consultants**–OSD via central contract provides "life coaches" and counseling to active, Army National Guard and Reserve Components.
- **FRG Deployment Assistants**–Selected Army commands (FORSCOM, USAREUR, USARPAC, and USASOC) and the Army National Guard and Army Reserve have paid personnel to assist FRG volunteer leaders with administrative and logistical support.
- **FRG/Rear Detachment Training**–CFSC has developed on-line FRG Leader and RDC training programs for Army-wide implementation. Located on www.myarmylifetoo.com.
- **Virtual FRG (vFRG)**–provides all the functionality of an FRG in an ad-hoc and online secure setting to meet the needs of geographically dispersed units and families. Funded with Congressional insert in DoD appropriation. Full implementation of vFRG across the Army began Feb 06.
- **Partnership with the Veterans of Foreign Wars (VFW)**–expands service capacity by using VFW Emergency Assistance and VFW Family Assistance Centers (FACs) (60 in the US).
- **FACs**-Both the active Army and the Army National Guard operate Family Assistance Centers.

- **Army Guide to FRG Operations**–established FRGs as official Army programs, provides updated guidance on fund-raising, and sets $5,000 limit cap for the FRG informal fund. Published as Appendix J to AR 608-1, 21 Jul 06. (www. usapa.army.mil)

Money Matters

- Financial counseling services and consumer advocacy–available at every installation; financial counseling for deployed and mandatory for first-term Soldiers. Soldiers receive promotion points for taking classes.
- Council of Better Business Bureaus Partnership–expands the Army capability to track and handle consumer complaints
- Financial Readiness tools–calculators for investments, net worth, budget management, links to Retirement site.
- Life Long Learning *"e*Learning Center"–contains free Financial Readiness and AFTB classes online. Rear Detachment Commander added in Mar 06, Introduction to Computers added in May 06, Family Readiness Group Leader launched in June 06. Promotion points for certain ACS courses: AFTB Level I, NPSP, Introduction to Family Financial Readiness and OP Ready.

Work and Careers

- Employment counseling, assessment, and training available Army-wide.
- **Spouse Employment Partnership** – partnership with Fortune 500 companies and Military Agencies to increase jobs and career opportunities for military spouses. Current partners include AAFES; Adecco USA; ACAP; BellSouth; Boys & Girls Clubs of America; Army Civilian Personnel; Computer Sciences Corporation; Concentra, Inc.; CVS/pharmacy; DeCA; Dell, Inc.; EURPAC Service, Inc.; Hospital Corporation of America; Home Depot; Lockheed Martin; Manpower Inc.; Sabre Holdings/Travelocity; Sears Holdings Corporation; Sprint; SunTrust Bank; and USAA.

General Information

- 90/95 ACS centers accredited (95%) - ensures centers meet standards.
- **Common Output Level Standards (COLS)** is the OSD initiative to develop a common language and toolset for the common delivery of installation support applicable across all installations in a host-tenant relationship (Joint Basing). The DoD Service Standards Teams (SSTs) is in the process of developing the common delivery metrics and standards that will make up the COLS framework for use initially at Joint Basing locations.
- **Integrated Multi-Component Family Support Network (IMCFSN)**–addresses the needs of geographically dispersed families by synchronizing resources of active, Guard, and Reserve family programs. Families can access services where they live regardless of component.

—**Delores Johnson, Director, Family Programs,**
FMWRC, Family Programs, ACS

Marine Corps Community Services

Marine Corps Community Services (MCCS) programs are vital to mission accomplishment and form an integral part of the non-pay compensation system. MCCS programs provide for the physical, cultural, service and social needs of Marines and other members of the Marine Corps family.

There are four basic components of MCCS: Marine Corps Family Team Building, Marine and Family Services, Semper Fit, and Business Operations. These programs provide community support systems that make Marine Corps bases/stations temporary hometowns for our Marines and their families.

The Marine Corps Family Team Building Program synchronizes family readiness programs and provides educational resources, services, and a roadmap to Marine Corps living that fosters personal growth and enhances family readiness. The Key Volunteer Network is the backbone of family team building programs and is an integral part of the Commander's official family readiness program. Key Volunteers provide information, referral, and support to families within the unit and serve as the primary communications link between the commanding officer and unit families. The Lifestyle Insights, Networking, Knowledge, and Skills (L.I.N.K.S.) program offers an orientation to the Marine Corps lifestyle for spouses. The program includes spouse-to-spouse mentoring and small group discussions on real life tips, information on Marine Corps culture, and resources to help manage the demands of Marine Corps life.

MCCS's commitment to assisting Marine families goes beyond spouses; we also offer many children's programs. The Children, Youth and Teen Program provides affordable, accessible care and support of children, youth and teens. Services include parent information, education, in-home and center based childcare, before and after school programs, and youth/teen services for children ages 6 weeks to 18 years of age. Our Child Development Centers are nationally accredited and provide high quality care. The Exceptional Family Member Program (EFMP) is also available to provide assistance to active duty personnel with family members who have special needs.

The Marine and Family Services program continues the tradition of "taking care of our own" by providing programs that teach Marines and their families how to make sound life skills decisions; assistance to parents in balancing the competing needs of parenting and mission accomplishment; educational opportunities through lifelong learning and voluntary education; preventive education on unhealthy lifestyles; and assistance through intervention/treatment. Additionally, these services assist with the mobile military lifestyle by providing assistance during relocation, transition to civilian life, career decision-making, job seeking, and adjustments of service members and their families to life in the military.

The Semper Fit Program encompasses Fitness and Health Promotion, Sports and Athletics, Recreational Aquatics, Outdoor Recreation, Parks and Recreation, and the Single Marine Program (SMP). Semper Fit, through its various program elements, provides the necessary tools to keep Marines in peak physical and mental condition. For the Corps, these benefits translate into increased productivity, enhanced performance, lower attrition and health costs, and an overall increase in mission readiness and quality of life. Sports and athletics have always been an integral component of the support provided to Marines. Participation in organized sports and athletics is a tool in the development of a "fighting spirit" which contributes to fostering esprit-de-corps. Physical fitness is a major force multiplier; however, Semper Fit must be looked at in a holistic manner. Rest and relaxation play a vital part of the readiness equation.

SMP is a conduit to address QOL issues and initiatives, plan recreational activities for their peer groups, and assist MCCS in promoting existing events and activities for single Marines and geographic bachelors. SMP supports the Command by providing the forum through which single Marine QOL concerns are identified and recommendations for improvement are made. Additionally, this forum is the means to assess the interest and needs of single Marines.

Our Business Operations and other revenue producing programs are crucial to our ability to generate the funds necessary to support QOL programs. MCCS operates about 170 resale facilities—from retail and convenience stores; to gas stations, auto service and repair stations, and car washes. MCCS also offer a host of services, such as barbershops, dry cleaning, vending machines, and truck rentals. To ensure that our customers know they are getting a fair deal at our Exchanges, we offer a Price Match Guarantee. On top of that guarantee, our customers do not have to pay sales taxes, so their savings are even greater when they shop their Marine Corps Exchange. Moreover, the quality of our name brands stands-up to products provided at the best department stores. Our Exchange Select product line offers generic household cleaning and health and beauty aids comparable to national brands, but for much less. Our "Another Core Value" items offer name-brand electronics, small electrics, and house wares at great savings. We are particularly pleased with the success of our private label clothing line, "1775." The line offers high-quality in-style clothing and accessories at unmistakable values. 1775 plays to our strengths: value, quality, and the pride of the Marine Corps. Our customers recognize these strengths and our sales reflect it. Of the customers who have purchased a 1775 item, 96 percent said they would do so again.

MCCS is a transformational organization not seen in any other Service with one overriding purpose, to provide the best possible programs and services to support the personal and family readiness of the Marine Corps family.

FAQs

Q. Where can I find information about MCCS programs?

A. *You can find information about MCCS programs on the web by going to www. usmc-mccs.org, or if you are on the East Coast call* (800) 336-4663 *and on the West Coast call* (800) 253-1624.

Q. How can I shop the Marine Corps Exchange online?

A. *You can shop the Marine Corps Exchange online by going to thor.milexch.com.*

Q. Where can I purchase Marine Corps Uniform items online?

A. *The online Marine Corps Uniform store (mcuniforms.nexnet.navy.mil) offers a complete selection of uniform items. Orders can also be placed over the phone by calling the Uniform Support Center at 1-800-368-4088.*

Q. Where can I find information about MCCS sports and recreation programs?

A. *To find information about MCCS sports and recreation programs you should try the Recreation and Fitness Section of the MCCS website or contact your installation Semper Fit office.*

Q. Where can I find information about quality of life programs and services if I'm not located near a Marine Corps installation?

A. *Military One Souce is a great place to start if you have questions about quality of life programs or benefits. Military One Source is available by phone at 1-800-342-9647 or online at www.militaryonesource.com. Highly qualified consultants are available to provide resource and referral services, personalized consultations on specific issues such as education, special needs, and finances, or customized research detailing community resources and appropriate military referrals. Clients can even get help with simultaneous language interpretation and document translation.*

Resources
Web Links
Marine Corps Homepage - www.usmc.mil
MCCS Homepage - www.usmc-mccs.org
Exchange Online - thor.milexch.com
Military OneSource – www.militaryonesource.com

MCCS Installation Web Sites
Marine Forces Reserve - www.mfr.usmc.mil/hq/mccs
MAGTFTC 29 Palms, CA - www.29palms.usmc-mccs.org
MCB Hawaii www.mccshawaii.com
MCLB Albany, GA - www.ala.usmc.mil/mccs
MCLB Barstow, CA - www.bam.usmc.mil/mccs.htm
MCB Camp Allen, VA - www.mccscampallen.com
MCAS Miramar, CA - www.mccsmiramar.com
HQBN Camp Fuji, Japan www.mccsfuji.com
MCAS New River, NC - www.newriver.usmc-mccs.org
MCAS Cherry Point, NC - www.mccscherrypoint.com
MCB Camp Butler, Okinawa - www.mccsokinawa.com
MCB Camp Lejeune, NC-www.mccslejeune.com
MCB Quantico, VA - www.quantico.usmc-mccs.org
MCB Camp Pendleton, CA - www.mccscamppendleton.com
MCRD San Diego, CA - www.mccsmcrd.com
HQBN Henderson Hall, VA - hqinet001.hqmc.usmc.mil/hh/HQBN1.htm
MCCS South Carolina - www.mccssc.com
(MCRD Parris Island and MCAS Beaufort)

MCAS Iwakuni, Japan - www.mccsiwakuni.com
MCAS Yuma, AZ - www.yuma.usmc-mccs.org

**—Bryan Driver, Public Affairs Specialist, Personal
and Family Readiness Division, HQMC**

NAVY

Fleet and Family Support Center Core Programs

The Fleet and Family Support Center is a direct result of the Chief of Naval Operations' commitment to supporting Navy and Marine Corps personnel and their families beginning in 1979. CNIC's Fleet and Family Support Center's are staffed with trained, professional, dedicated people, often military spouses, who provide information and assistance. Core services are geared toward developing or increasing skills to help individuals and families be more self-reliant and adjust to the challenges of military life, while at the same time, providing a safety net of programs and services to assist them when they need help.

All single and married active duty personnel and their family members, reservists (on extended active duty), and their families, may request assistance. Retired members and DoD civilians and their families may receive assistance on a case by case, or space available basis. FFSC welcomes questions and requests from members of all branches of service.

Deployment Programs

Maybe you're new to the Navy. Maybe you've been around awhile. Either way, deployments are easier to get through if you're armed with information and knowledge. Your FFSC offers training for individual family members, Navy members (including reserve and individual augmentees), family readiness groups, and ombudsmen. If you want a deployment presentation or workshop; if you need pamphlets and brochures; if you need anything to help you prepare for a deployment, have questions during a deployment, or are preparing for a homecoming your FFSC is here to help.

Information and Referral (I&R)

Information and Referral are a part of each FFSC program. The purpose is to provide the active linkage of individuals with unresolved information needs with the sources or resources which are best capable of addressing those specific needs. Subject areas include social services, Ombudsman, schools, child care, and community resources. The Fleet and Family Support Center is an efficient way to find information or services that are right for you. If you have a question, are curious about a class that may be available, or have a problem you need to solve, our staff can tell you about a wide variety of military and civilian activities, organizations, and services available on and off base, such as monthly calendars of events, local child care, support groups, shopping in the local area, local and military/civilian resources

Relocation Assistance Program (RAP)

RAP provides support, information, preparation, and education for managing the demands of the mobile military lifestyle. Essential components include briefings;

sponsorship support; counseling before, during, and after moving; settling-in services; and emergency services. The Relocation Resource Library contains a myriad of printed materials on military moves and access to the Standard Installation Topic Exchange Service (SITES), a database that enhances relocation services by offering current information on Installations worldwide.

Transition Assistance Management Program (TAMP)
TAMP was established for personnel and family members who are separating or retiring from military service. TAMP consists of the TAP classes and seminars on SF-171 and resume writing, one-on-one counseling, job banks, interview techniques, and job search strategies. TAP, is a comprehensive, five-day workshop on skills assessment, job search methods, skills for creating an effective resume, effective interviewing skills, employment opportunities nationwide, civil service employment, and veterans' benefits. Computers and printers are available for client use in creating an effective resume or SF-171 application.

Family Employment Readiness Program (FERP)
One of the biggest challenges facing a Navy spouse is having to search for a new job every two or three years. FERP provides a variety of services to enhance career planning and continuity. Frequent relocation due to the mobile military lifestyle often creates career challenges for military spouses. This program offers information on local job and volunteer opportunities, career counseling, and referral, in addition to seminars and workshops, and one-on-one employment counseling services for family members, including educational opportunities, individual counseling, interviewing techniques, job search planning, listing of job openings, resume writing, and volunteer opportunities.

The Fleet and Family Support Center is a great place to start and/or organize your job hunting efforts. The FFSC maintains a full-featured Career Development Resource Program to help provide assistance to active duty military and family members in all aspects of their job search activities. Listings of private-sector and civil service vacancies, including full- and part-time jobs are maintained. A library of reference materials and a suite of computers including internet access are available for your use

Family Advocacy Program (FAP)
The Family Advocacy Program (FAP) is a Department of Defense line-managed, multi-disciplinary program which addresses the prevention, education, intervention, assessment, and treatment of spouse abuse, child physical and emotional abuse, child neglect, and child sexual abuse. The five primary goals of FAP are prevention, victim safety and protection, offender accountability, rehabilitative education and counseling, and community accountability/responsibility for a consistent, appropriate response.

This proactive program provides for the education, prevention, and treatment of family violence. Trained FFSC staff seeks to prevent violence, abuse, and neglect in families, and provide safety planning and intervention if it does occur. Resource materials are available on subjects to promote wellness within the family.

Personal Financial Management Program (PFMP)
The United States Navy is interested in Personal Financial Management Education (PFMP) in order to support mission readiness. The Navy's PFMP is designed to

prevent potential personal problems that can cost valuable time and money that may detract from mission readiness. PFMP provides comprehensive emphasis on personal financial responsibility and accountability through sound money management, consumer education, counseling tools, referral service, and, provides guidance on financial and consumer issues. The FFSC trains Command Financial Specialist for active duty members who go back to the Command to educate and counsel their peers.

Education and Training Program (E&T)

Prevention and enrichment programs provide knowledge, social relationship skills, and support throughout the family life cycle. The program enhances self-esteem, strengthens interpersonal competencies, and offers educational opportunities to individuals and families. Topics vary: parenting, couples communication, anger and stress management.

Counseling Services

Licensed, credentialed clinical counseling professionals provide services for individual, marital, family, and parent-child counseling. Counseling services encompass a wide scope of developmental, preventive, and therapeutic services designed to address the stressors facing today's active duty and their families. Counselors are knowledgeable and sensitive to the Navy mission, culture and lifestyle.

Sexual Assault Intervention Program (SAVI)

Installation FFSP Sexual Assault Response Coordinators provide specialized training for Victim Advocates and serve as a resource for Command awareness and prevention training. Anyone can become a victim of sexual assault, but there are ways that people can reduce their risk of becoming victims. The Navy's Sexual Assault Victim Intervention (SAVI) program provides sexual assault awareness and prevention education and victim support.

New Parent Support Program (NPSP)

The New Parent Support Program utilizes a team of professionals providing supportive and caring services to military families with new babies. New Moms and Dads can be referred to community new baby programs and are eligible to participate in a voluntary home visitation program, free of charge. The New Parent Support Home Visitation Program was developed to assist military families in ways that friends and family would do if you were back home. This program offers expectant parents and parents of newborn and young children the opportunity to learn new skills as parents and to improve existing parenting skills, in the privacy of their own home.

FAQs

Q. What is the Fleet and Family Support Center?

A. *The Navy FFSC exists to provide services which facilitate personal and family readiness and adaptation to life in the naval services. Navy Commands and FFSCs share the common goals of keeping healthy individual families, strong, and facilitating overall self-sufficiency and personal, family and community wellness.*

Fleet and Family Support Center programs offer support in the readiness categories: operational, mobility, and counseling/advocacy. It includes such programs as Information and Referral, New Parent Support, Personal Financial Management, Deployment Support, Relocation Assistance Program, Sexual Assault Intervention, Spouse Employment Assistance Program, and Transition Assistance Management, as well as Individual, Marital and Family Counseling.

Q. What role does the Fleet and Family Support Center play in recruitment, readiness and retention?

A. **Recruitment**: *Fleet and Family Support Centers are a benefit unmatched in the private sector. Unlike the civilian support services, Fleet and Family Support Center programs are specifically designed to meet the demands of military life. No civilian employer in the country can match the quantity, quality or cost. The Fleet and Family Support Center programs are free to service members and their families. Consider them one of your benefits as a military service member or family members.*

Readiness: Fleet and Family Support Center programs are designed to ensure that service members and their families are properly prepared for the mental and emotional demands of military life and to meet surge requirements. Military life is transient, fast paced, and charged with responsibilities that affect the security of our nation. In short, it's challenging. Fleet and Family Support Center programs help service members and their families meet those challenges. With support for families available, our men and women in uniform can perform their duties with fewer worries and distractions.

Retention: Fleet and Family Support Center programs help service members maximize their military experience by giving them the support they need to perform at optimal levels, thereby ensuring a longer and more successful Navy career. Compared to private sector services, military benefits, including Fleet and Family Support Centers, are another good reason to stay in the Navy.

Q. Can you describe the range of services offered?

A. *Fleet and Family Support Center programs offer readiness support in three categories: operational, mobility, and counseling/advocacy. Within these categories, the Center offers various programs. These range from crisis and information, to stress management and parenting workshops, to welcome aboard and overseas transfer seminars. The Center has professional counselors and financial planners available for individual, family, and group consultations.*

Core programs like Deployment Programs, Information and Referral, Transition Assistance Management Program, Family Employment Assistance Program, Relocation Assistance Program, Family Advocacy Program, Sexual Assault Intervention Program, New Parent Support, Personal Financial Management and Individual, Marital and Family Counseling.

Fleet and Family Support Center programs are delivered in many forms, from one-on-one sessions to workshops and classes at the Center, to group presentations aboard ships.

Q. How do services specifically benefit leadership?

A. **Sets a good example**. *Commanders have many of the same mobile lifestyle issues that service members have. The programs are available to leadership for use just as they are to other service members. Whether it's preparing for separation or transition, relocation or deployment, managing finances, or enhancing family relationships, leaders who take advantage of the programs set a good example for their units.*

Helps create a more focused and productive unit. By encouraging service members to seek services from the FFSC, leaders are helping restore focus on work and preventing situations that could negatively impact the service member's career. Problems at home, whether personal or financial, often become problems at work and negatively impact productivity. Happy Sailors are better workers.

Keeps Command mission focused. Leaders who encourage service members to take advantage of Fleet and Family Support Center services will likely have to spend less time on service members' personal issues, allowing more time to concentrate on ensuring that the unit is prepared for its mission.

Q. How do the services specifically benefit family members?

A. *Military life is a challenge, not just for the service member, but for the spouses and children as well. They are also affected, directly or indirectly, by constant relocation, high responsibility, threats of war and terrorism, and the general stress that comes with the job of defending our nation. It is part of the Fleet and Family Support Center's mission to ensure that families have the support they need to deal with these issues.*

All Fleet and Family Support Center programs are available to family members. The Centers provide assistance with everything from finding a job and good schools for the children to deployment support and professional counseling. Service members are more focused on their mission when they are confident that their families are well adjusted to military life.

Q. How does one tap into the services?

A. *Center services are available and free to all service members and their families, including activated Reserves, retirees and Department of Defense civilians on a space available basis. Installations can be located on the website www.ffsp.navy.mil*

Q. What about confidentiality?

A. *All contact with the Fleet and Family Support Center is kept confidential* **except** *when laws have been broken or a life is in danger, which is the same standard in the civilian arena. All clients sign a Privacy Act statement, which explains that counseling services are confidential and that the Command must be notified if there are reports of suicidal or homicidal tendencies, family violence or substance abuse.*

If service members do not feel comfortable walking in the Center during normal business hours, the Center will export classes, i.e., take the services to the service member, or provide services during off hours.

Q. Will using the service have a negative impact on my career?

A. *Not if the service member is proactive. Commanding Officers encourage you to visit the Center if you need help or information. It's part of self-improvement and makes you a better Sailor. If the Commanding Officer sees your name in the local police report blotter and then has to order you to see a Fleet and Family Support Center counselor, that's another story. Take care of issues before they become problems, and you've no worries.*

Q. If a family member or I use the Fleet and Family Support Center, will my Commander be notified?

A. *All contact with the Fleet and Family Support Center is kept confidential **except** when laws have been broken or there is threat of life, which is the same standard in the civilian arena. All clients sign a Privacy Act statement, which explains that counseling services are confidential and that Command must be notified if there are reports of suicidal or homicidal tendencies, family violence or substance abuse. On Command referrals, Command will be notified if the service member kept the appointment and whether continuing services will be provided by the FFSC. Details about the service member's problem and counseling will not be provided to the Command except in the case of Family Advocacy investigations and services.*

Q. I don't have problems. Why should I use the Fleet and Family Support Center?

A. *The Fleet and Family Support Center is not just for crisis and problem solving. Ideally, it should be used for prevention-tackling issues before they become problems, and life and career enhancement. For example, it is much better to attend a personal financial management session before you experience a budget crunch. By doing so, you're more likely to avoid a financial crisis. The same is true with relationship issue or job-related stress.*

FFSC programs are all about self-improvement, providing service members and their families with resources they can use to help themselves. Take advantage of these services. You've earned them through your service.

Q. How can these services help further my military career?

A. *Using the Center's services demonstrates a desire to grow personally and professionally, a good indicator of success oriented individuals who make strong candidates for leadership roles.*

Q. Is the staff professionally trained to address the specific needs of military personnel and family?

A. *Yes. All Fleet and Family Support Center counselors are licensed and credentialed mental healtsh professionals whose qualifications are equal to those in the civilian arena, and are enhanced by the ability to mobilize military and community* resources to support the needs of military personnel. Due to their caseload, training and common client base, the Center's counselors understand military stressors and issues better than their civilian counterparts do.

Q. Compare the Fleet and Family Support Center services to private sector offerings.

A. *Same qualifications, except the FFSC staff know a lot more about military issues and support than civilian counterparts do. Familiarity breeds expertise, and the FFSC serves only one client base. The FFSC is a good place to begin with your questions.*

Resources

1. **LifeLines Service** Network–http://www.lifelines.navy.mil/
2. **Answers for Sailors, Marines and their Families**–Navy-Marine Corps Relief Society http://www.nmcrs.org/. The mission of the Navy-Marine Corps Relief Society is to provide, in partnership with the Navy and Marine Corps, financial, educational, and other assistance to members of the Naval Services of the United States, eligible family members, and survivors when in need; and to receive and manage funds to administer these programs.
3. **Fleet and Family** Support Program http://ffsp.navy.mil–The Fleet and Family Support Program provides support to Sailors, families and communities by providing policy guidance, field support, resources, and information services to people in need, their business partners, the Chain of Command and their field activities. They accomplish this through planning, oversight, advocacy, and research.
4. **Navy Legal Assistance** http://www.jag.navy.mil/–Navy Legal Assistance provides help to Navy personnel and authorized family members on personal legal matters. This site provides general information on services available and state-specific legal information.
5. **Benefits** http://www.govbenefits.gov. GovBenefits.gov helps citizens access government benefit eligibility information through a free, confidential, and easy-to-use online screening tool. After answering some basic questions, the user receives a customized report listing the benefit programs for which the user, or person for whom he or she is entering information, may be eligible.
6. **Pay and Benefits** https://ca.dtic.mil/dfas/s-retired/mil1-pay.htmmyPay allows military personnel financial management of pay information, leave and earnings statements, W-2's and more.
7. **Navy Active Pay Inquiries** https://ca.dtic.mil/dfas/s-retired/mil1-pay.htm Customer Inquiry Request Form for Military Pay - Navy Active Duty
8. **Recreation/Travel–Morale, Welfare, and Recreation Headquarters.** www.mwr.navy.mil/ The Navy MWR administers a varied program of recreation, social and community support activities on U.S. Navy facilities worldwide. Their mission is to provide quality support and recreational services that contribute to the retention, readiness and mental, physical, and emotional well-being of sailors and their families.
9. **Relocation**
   o Surface Spouses http://www.surfacespouses.navy.mil

The Navy Surface Spouses provide a comprehensive resource for sailors and their families enabling them to access information about the Navy communities in which they reside or to which they may be relocating.

o **FFSC**: Relocation Assistance http://www.ffsp.navy.mil/rap/rap.htm FFSC has provided a collection of information and links to take you through the moving process.

o **SmartWeb Move https**://www.smartwebmove.navsup.navy.mil/swm/ Official website of the US Navy for information on relocation and moving personal property.

o **Standard Installation** Topic Exchange —The Office of the Secretary of Defense, sponsors of the SITES website, have made the transition to providing relocation information at www.militaryonesource.com and relocation tools at www.MilitaryHOMEFRONT.dod.mil/moving.

- **Students-Education**
o Dolphin Scholarship Foundation http://www.dolphinscholarship.org/dolsch-his.html. The Dolphin Scholarship Foundation was established in 1961 by the Submarine Officers' Wives' Organizations throughout the United States.
o Seabee Memorial Scholarship Association http://www.seabee.org–The Seabee Memorial Scholarship Association is a non-profit organization established to provide educational assistance to children and grandchildren of Seabees.
o SEAL-Naval Special Warfare Foundation http://www.nswfoundation.org

—**Catherine Stokoe**
Director, Navy Fleet and Family Support

THE UNITED STATES AIR FORCE FAMILY SUPPORT CENTER

Airman & Family Readiness Center
"Personal and Family Readiness is our business!"

Airman and Family Readiness Centers (A&FRC) enhance the quality of life for all DoD military and civilian personnel and their families, single Airmen, Reservists, and retirees. Airman and Family Readiness Centers support the military community by providing programs and training that promote mission readiness through personal and family readiness.

The Center has gone through tremendous changes in the past few years, moving from a stovepipe delivery system to a community readiness model. The Community Readiness delivery of service enables consultants and technicians to more effectively assist customers with individualized needs. The Center delivers services impacting family and work life concerns through center-based and unit based activities.

As part of its center-based activities, professional consultants and technicians provide individualized consultations; offering customers opportunity to develop their own customized service plan. Monthly workshops are conducted to target factors that influence airmen and families throughout a military career—spouse employment, relationship enhancement, financial education, deployment and reunion support, sponsorship and adaptation to new community, separation/retirement from the military, crisis assistance/disaster response, and much more. These workshops are designed to ensure airmen and their families are prepared and ready to meet the demands created by mission readiness.

The Discovery Center, a high tech Information and Referral source, is the central hub of the center and allows customers self-service. Customers have ready access to multi-media resources to research topics relating to family life enrichment, employment, financial education, relocation assistance, volunteer resources, family readiness, transition assistance and much more. Resources are updated continuously and are available for check-out. The Center also serves as a hub for those new to the community, providing a place to check emails and initiate job searches. To enhance the quality of services, a Community Readiness Consultant/Technician and/or the Discovery Resource Manager is always available to provide personalized attention.

Airman and Family Readiness' unit based service delivery system embeds consultants with individual units. These skilled consultants partner and work closely with unit leadership and become acquainted with their personnel. Working together, the unit leader and consultant may identify factors that impact unit's mission capability. A comprehensive service plan may be produced to address these factors and identify strategies to maximize strengths and minimize challenges. The visibility of A&FRC in the units is making a difference!

The core service areas in Airman and Family Readiness Center are still part of our tradition, and are still offered as follows:

- Families in need of financial assistance can visit the **Personal Financial Management** team at the Airman and Family Readiness Center. This team helps both military and civilian personnel with all facets of personal finances, offering information, education and individual counseling. Counselors are available to assist in budget preparation, debt management, and financial concerns of divorce, consumer protection, or investing. PFMP works hand-in-hand with the Air Force Aid Society (AFAS) to restore financial stability to AF members who experience unexpected financial emergencies. No interest loans are available to eligible personnel and families. AFAS also sponsors a wealth of community enhancement programs: Give Parents a Break, Bundles for Babies, Nursing Moms Program, Educational Grants, Car Care Because We Care, Volunteer Child Care, and more!

- The Air Force boasts an extensive **Spouse Employment Resource** program. Spouses can attend monthly employment skills workshops that enhance their marketability in the work place. Job fairs are offered several times each year to support spouse employment. Job referrals, resume reviews, and employment skills workshops, and a state of the art resource center are available to assist job seekers. **NEXStep**, a spouse training program, is available to military spouses in the area and offers a tremendous opportunity to complete job skills training programs.

- Moving is a way of life in the Air Force. The **Relocation Assistance Program** in FSC helps single and married military members (all services) and their families as well as DoD civilians and their families through the moving experience.

  For those who are unable to set up permanent housekeeping immediately because their household goods have not arrived, the **Loan Locker** can offer temporary respite. Dishes, pots, pans, kitchen utensils, small appliances such as toasters and irons, cots are available without charge. The Loan Locker is collocated and operated with Outdoor Recreation. A copy of PCS orders is required when requesting items from the Loan Closet.

- The **Transition Assistance Program TAP** was developed and designed to provide the separating and retiring service member the tools, skills, and know how to market themselves in the private sector job market while also transitioning back into the civilian community. TAP prepares participants to analyze their skills; identify job goals; write a resume and cover letter; prepare for a job interview; evaluate and respond to job offers.
- **Individual and Family Readiness** services are educational and support programs which assist deploying personnel and affected family members successfully manage separation / reunion cycles associated with deployments, remote tours, and extended TDYs. In order to reduce personal and family emergencies, stress of separation, and assist active duty service members and families in preparing for deployment, services are provided before, during, and after deployments. For children, FSC hosts an annual Operation Hero event to familiarize children with deployment and the process their military sponsors' experience.
- **Family Life Skills** education classes are designed for individuals, couples, and families. Life Skills topics are primarily preventive and proactive in nature, and aim to prevent or alleviate difficulties before they seriously affect the AF member and family. Classes provide knowledge, skills, and support to guide personnel and family members to a healthier lifestyle by enhancing self-esteem, strengthening communication skills, family separations, marriage preparation, marriage enrichment, and separation anxiety, and increasing awareness about anger and stress management.
- For new AF spouses, **Heart Link** Spouses Orientation offers indoctrination to Air Force lifestyle and culture.
- Military Family Members who need answers to any questions can contact the Airman and Family Readiness Center.

We are an **Information and Referral** source and we can find the answers. We help with general information, phone numbers, and points-of-contact for civilian and military resources such as child care, employment, housing, schools, DMV policies, food resources, and financial planning, and more.

We are Air Force family members connection to information in their community! There is a team of professional staff and volunteers who are ready to help you and/or your family. Come in and get to know us! Additional information on the programs described is available at your AFRC.

FAQs

Q. Why is Airman and Family Readiness important?

A. *The Air Force realizes there is a direct relationship between a member's ability to successfully accomplish a mission, and the quality of life which his or her family experiences. Because of this relationship, many programs and policies are available to promote a positive family environment. The AFRC helps enhance quality of life for military members and/or family members. The AFRC also helps commanders meet their responsibilities for the health and welfare of every member of the Air Force family.*

Q. Who is eligible?

A. *Active duty military members and their families, Guard and Reserve and their family members, Retired military personnel and their families, DOD civilians and their families*
ATTENTION SINGLES: You do not have to be married or have a family to use the AFRC.

Q. What do Airman and Family Readiness Centers do?

A. *To enhance quality of life, the AFRC serves as the command's service organization for families! To accomplish this, the AFRC:*
- Works with commanders and units to enhance family well-being.
- Is the primary resource for coordinating family programs on and off base.
- Acts as an information and referral resource.
- Provides family education and life skills programs.
- Point of Contact for Air Force Aid services and programs

Air Force Resources Online
- **Air Force CrossRoads**
  http://www.afcrossroads.com/home.cfm
  The Official Community Website for the U.S. Air Force
- **Air Force Aid Society http://www.afas.org**
  The Air Force Aid Society (AFAS) is the official charity of the United States Air Force incorporated in 1942 as a non-profit organization whose mission is to help relieve financial distress of Air Force members and their families and to assist them in financing their higher education goals.
- **USAF Combat Support and Community Services**
  http://www-p.afsv.af.mil/default.htm
  Air Force Services exists to provide combat support to commanders directly in support of the Air Force mission. They also provide community service programs that enhance the quality of life for Air Force members and their families. These programs indirectly support the mission by improving morale, productivity, and retention. They offer a full range of military and community support programs at most major Air Force installations.
- **USAF Judge Advocate General's Corps (AF Legal Assistance)**
  http://legalassistance.law.af.mil/index.php?tabid=1
  Legal offices provide legal assistance in connection with personal civil legal matters to support and sustain command effectiveness and readiness. Legal assistance establishes an attorney-client relationship and consists of Air Force attorneys providing advice on personal, civil legal matters to eligible beneficiaries.

— **Carla E. Diamond**
Chief, Airman and Family Readiness Center, LAFB
Air Combat Command (ACC)

NATIONAL GUARD FAMILY PROGRAM

The Joint National Guard Family Program is a key program for supporting the families of our Army and Air National Guard members as they face a steep increase in military activity, to include involvement in the War on Terrorism, major military operations, Homeland Defense, and responding to natural disasters.

The tragedies of September 11, 2001 and the full-out participation of the military in Operations Noble Eagle, Enduring Freedom, and Iraqi Freedom have brought a heightened focus on the military family and specifically on Guard families. Never before have so many of our Guard members and families participated in all three stages of deployment at the same time (pre-deployment, sustainment, and post deployment). Extended deployments have increased the need for 100 percent outreach and personal contact with all deployed Guard member families. In every state, the State Family Program Directors, Wing Family Program Coordinators and volunteers have been asked to go beyond the call of duty and have stretched to meet the on-going challenges of continuous deployments with skill, dedication and pride.

There is a vital need to assure that all units and states can readily communicate with each other and that all military families have the resources they need to thrive. This is possible through a strong joint-service family support network organized in each state and territory by the **State Family Program Director (SFPD)** at each Joint Force Headquarters (JFHQ). The family support work at the JFHQs is reinforced by the efforts of **Wing Family Program Coordinators (WFPC)** who are at each Air National Guard Wing nationwide. The 54 SFPDs and 88 WFPCs are the primary information resources which provide family readiness support to commanders, soldiers, airmen, and families. Unit level Family Readiness Group Volunteers provide "heart" and vitality to the program, and Family Readiness Networks made up of Family Program Staff, Family Assistance Centers and a range of highly effective programs supply continuity and on-going program stability. Family readiness supports mission readiness!

Volunteers

On a state level, Family Readiness Groups are supported by Family Readiness Assistants who provide training, management support, volunteer recruitment, and assistance to the State and Wing Family Program in order to maintain stability on the home front and ensure mission success. At the national level, a Volunteer Coordinator is responsible for creating and maintaining a recognition system to reward volunteers for supporting the family readiness effort. With their natural connection to others in the unit, volunteers help create a climate of mutual support, understanding and help to spread information that measurably increases unit and family readiness.

Child and Youth Program

The Child and Youth Program mission is to "support the social, emotional, and academic needs of National Guard children and youth." This mission is guided by seventeen program goals that include: awards and recognition, child care, command support, curriculum, initiatives, educational support, faith-based initiatives, marketing, partnerships, research, resources, retention, service learning, state support, technology, training, and youth camps. Personnel implementing these goals include one national level program manager, seven regional youth coordinators, and 54 state/territory youth coordinators.

Training for children, youth, and adults is ongoing and tied directly to the goals of the program. Current initiatives involve expansion of child and youth programs within units to provide community-based support for National Guard children and youth.

Family Assistance Centers (FACs)

FACs are operating throughout the 54 States and Territories and are the primary entry point for any military family member needing assistance during the deployment process. Currently there are over 350 National Guard FACs operating nationwide. These are located in and near communities where military deployments affect significant numbers of the community and the need for military information and services is in high demand. The maximum number of FACs at any one point in time has reached as high as 439. DoD has validated that during a time of reduced military mobilization and deployment, 162 FACs will be maintained throughout the 54 States and Territories.

Family Assistance Centers in any state can be located by going to www.guardfamily.org and clicking on the box labeled "Local Community Resource Finder" and then by using the Advanced Search method, select the state and the category "Family Assistance Center (FAC)."

Family Assistance Centers provide information, services, and referrals intended to encourage self-sufficiency, and offer short-term support and assistance when necessary. FORSCOM REG 500-3-1 (*FORSCOM Mobilization and Deployment Planning System*) and the DoDI 1342.22 (*Department of Defense Initiative on Family Centers*) both require that all military members and their families have access to Family Center services regardless of Service affiliation. Through these directives FACs serve the needs of all geographically dispersed service members and their families.

Services available at FACs include the following areas:

- Mobility and/or Deployment Assistance
- Information and referral
- Relocation Assistance
- Employment Assistance
- Connection to community partners
- Family Life Education
- Crisis Assistance and Referral
- Volunteer Coordination
- Legal and Financial Resources/Referral
- Identification Cards, DEERs and Tricare information

Reaching out to Families and Service Members

Wide geographic dispersion is one of the greatest challenges in meeting the needs of Guard families. Some of the ways to connect with these families include the worldwide web, publications, volunteer Family Readiness Groups, outreach efforts and training.

Online National Guard Family Program

National Guard Family Program www.guardfamily.org is the main Family Program website. This site is a key portal of entry for visitors to navigate to the other sites. This site contains information regarding all of the programs the National Guard Bureau Family Program covers. The Local Community Resource Finder that is on the website has a rich array of resources listed to help individuals find the help they need. The site is recommended for all those connected to or interested in the Guard. Within the site there are links designed specifically for the Service Member, the Family Member, Youth, the Volunteer Corps, School Educators and Administration. These links provide information pertaining to the Family Readiness Program and Program Services.

National Guard Child and Youth Program

One popular link on guardfamily.org website is the youth link that facilitates communication among National Guard youth. This special youth website was launched and is kept up-to-date with current age-appropriate information. The site provides Guard youth with resources on topics related to deployment and resources for dealing with the challenges military children face.

Many family needs relate to quality of life for service members and their families. These needs are met through a combination of web access, training opportunities, and panel group efforts in the Guard Family Action Plan process, the development of volunteer groups, and the development of community outreach and partnerships.

Guard Family Action Plan

National Guard Well Being and Quality of Life issues are captured through the Guard Family Action Plan (GFAP) process and include a published "Family Action Plan" that identifies and addresses issues from the field. Every year, issues are compiled and sent though a review process from the state to the major commands and sent to the national level for review. Volunteers are nominated and selected to participate in panels to review potential solutions to selected issues for submission for General officer review. The AF Community Action and Information Board along with the AF Integrated Delivery System is becoming a vital key in the ANG to contribute issues to the GFAP process.

Training

In order to meet the increased challenges of more frequent and lengthy deployments, National Guard Bureau Family Program staff and in turn, each State Joint Force Headquarters is keenly focused on building individual, family, and unit self-reliance and readiness, regardless of geographic location. The training approach used is a standardized, yet customizable training and development program designed to enhance, educate and train volunteers, staff, family members, anyone in the Guard community.

There are three ways to participate in formalized Family Program training:

- Online: Online courses are a convenient option for anyone whose schedule prohibits on-site training, requires on-demand training or does not live near a military installation.
- On-site: Courses are taught on-site by a Training Program Specialist or Instructor Trainer graduate. The advantage of on-site instruction is the opportunity to customize and develop targeted topics that address the particular needs of an area.
- Centralized location: "Train the Trainer" empowers the Guard community to teach others using the standardized course materials, by completing the Instructor Trainer

Course. Skilled instructors are encouraged to become advanced instructors, enabling them to train trainers within the National Guard. Building a network of local instructors encourages participation, local knowledge and experience, increases volunteer retention and provides local trainers to an area unable to bring in trainers.

The Family Program not only looks within the organization for resources but also goes in search of resources externally. NGB has created partnerships with organizations like the American Red Cross, American Legion, American Veterans (AMVETS), Disabled American Veterans (DAV), Veterans of Foreign Wars (VFW), and the United Service Organization (USO). These organizations are committed to assisting families to cope with unusual and difficult circumstances through requesting support and resources they lack at a given point in time. Requests for this assistance should be channeled through the State Family Program Director or Wing Family Program Coordinator.

There are other resources available to all members of the military and their families to support them through all phases of military deployment and operations. For example, these include Military OneSource, Military Family Life Consultants, and America Supports You. These along with other services and resources are continually being developed for the good of our service members and their families.

Military OneSource

Department of Defense (DoD) resources are also used and disseminated to assist SFPDs and WFPCs, one service is Military OneSource. Military OneSource supplements existing family programs with a 24-hour, seven days a week toll free information and confidential referral telephone line and internet/Web based service. It is available at no cost to active, mobilized Guard and Reserves, deployed civilians and their families worldwide. It provides information ranging from everyday practical advice to deployments/reintegration issues and will provide referrals to professional civilian counselors for assistance.

Phone Numbers for Military OneSource:
- Stateside: CONUS: 1-800-342-9647
- Overseas: *OCONUS Universal Free Phone: 800-3429-6477
- Collect from Overseas: OCONUS Collect: 484-530-5908
- En español llame al: 1-877-888-0727
- TTY/TDD: 1-800-346-9188
- Korea DSN: 550-ARMY (2769)

Military and Family Life Consultants

In order to more effectively assist families who have dedicated service and loved ones to the United States, the Office of the Secretary of Defense (OSD) recognized an emerging need to provide informal support to Soldiers and families in addition to resident counseling within States and Territories. OSD has funded this program to provide support to military families and service members worldwide. The tremendous success of the program in the United States Europe (USAREUR) has resulted in a Department of the Army (DA) initiative to replicate the program.

The goal of the Family Consultants is to prevent family distress by providing education and information on family dynamics, parent education, available support services, and the effects of stress and positive coping mechanisms. Since the introduction of the MFLC's program in March 2006, National Guard service members and their families have been provided assistance upon State request.

The point of contact for the MFLC program is the State Family Program Director in each state. Individual MFLCs are placed on or near military communities. MFLCs will provide a range of services to include educational classes, support groups, presentations and briefings. In addition, they will provide educational presentations for adults, youth, and adolescents on topics such as, but not limited to the following:

- Reunion and Reintegration Training
- Mental Health Screenings
- Pre-Deployment activities
- Grief
- Crisis intervention
- Stress management
- Natural or man made disasters
- Post Deployment Activities
- Marriage Enrichment Seminars

Over an 8-month period from the inception of the MFLC program, 223 Consultants served 11, 940 Army Guard members and their families, while 9 MFLC's served 210 members of the Air National Guard. In total, 232 MFLC's served 12,150 Guard members.

America Supports You

This is a DoD initiative that connects profit, non-profit, and grass roots organizations with service members. This group provides support, services, financial support, entertainment, care packages, tragedy assistance, employment assistance and Veteran services. Many links to information and assistance are available on the Internet at www. americasupportsyou.mil. The National Guard Family Program is a robust and always growing collection of resources to support the families of our many dedicated Army and Air National Guard members serving around the world. Whatever the need, requirement or request, Family Program personnel and volunteers are equipped with resources, ideas and desire to address any issue confronting military members and their families.

—**COL Anthony E. Baker, Sr., US Army**
Chief, National Guard Bureau Family Program

COAST GUARD

Work-Life Programs in the United States Coast Guard

Our central focus is to improve the quality of life of Coast Guard personnel and their families. We also contribute to organizational effectiveness and mission readiness by helping to resolve personal and organizational issues that distract members from their mission focus.

Family Advocacy

The Program Goal is to reduce and prevent family violence through the case management process and prevention initiatives. The following services and resources are available within the Family Advocacy Program

- Victim safety planning
- Domestic Violence Assessment and Rehabilitation
- Referrals to Mental Health Providers for diagnostic assessments
- Referrals to Anger Management, Parenting Classes, Couples Communications, and Substance Abuse Programs
- Ongoing case management by the FAS until successful resolution
- Referrals for financial assistance for victims
- Any other services/resource required toaddress the abusive situation.

If you are unable to contact the Family Advocacy Specialist at your Regional Work-Life Staff, or need additional assistance beyond the information provided here, please contact the Headquarters Family Advocacy Program Manager at (202) 267-6730

Special Needs

The Program Goal is to identify and assist family members with special needs to ensure Coast Guard missions are fully supported. The following services and resources are available within the Special Needs Program:

- Assistance with enrollment in the program
- Resources and referrals
- Advocacy on behalf of families with the Coast Guard and with civilian agencies
- Assurance that appropriate resources are available in areas of proposed relocation by working closely with assignment officers and other Work-Life Staffs.

Employee Assistance

The Program Goal is to provide Critical Incident Stress Management (CISM) interventions and prevention training for suicide, sexual assault/rape, and work place violence. The following services and resources are available within the Employee Assistance Program:

- Counseling and guidance on troubled relationships, parenting, stress, and financial management
- Critical Incident Stress Management counseling
- Drug and alcohol counseling
- Supervisory consultations regarding troubled employees

The following web sites provide information related to the Employee Assistance Program:

- http://www.foh4you.com–Federal Occupational Health EAP. Contains helpful information on a wide range of subjects
- http://www.opm.gov/ehs/Eappage.htm–Office of Personnel Management EAP Homepage
- http://www.mentalhealth.com–Internet Mental Health Website "Free Encyclopedia" of Mental Health Information

The Program Goal is to provide retiring and separating active duty members with information about the available benefits and entitlements upon separating and offer techniques to help them make informed decisions about life after serving the Coast Guard. The following web sites provide information related to the Transition Assistance Program:

- Federal jobs–http://www.fedworld.gov/jobs/jobsearch.html

- Official Federal Government job listings by the Office of Personnel Management –http://www.jsajobs.opm.gov.
- Federal benefits for veterans and dependents–http://www.va.gov/pubaff/fedben/Fedben.pdf

Each Transition/Relocation Manager can assist active duty members in scheduling a Transition Assistance Seminar. This seminar is intended to assist transitioning active duty members in preparing for the civilian job market. Spouses of active duty members are highly encouraged to attend; however, travel funding is not provided. These seminars cover such topics as resume writing, interviewing techniques, salary negotiations, and successful attire strategies. Each seminar will also familiarize the member with the benefits they may be entitled to as a separatee or retiree.

Health Promotion

Program Goal: Optimize CG mission performance through enhanced physical, social, and psychological well being of our people by increasing awareness, education, and intervention programs. The following services and resources are available within the Health Promotions Program:

- PWPs
- Formal Class "C" training: Unit Health Promotion Coordinator course
- Cholesterol Screenings
- Lectures and training sessions on the following: Nutrition, Weight Management, Physical Fitness, Tobacco Cessation and Avoidance, Avoidance of Alcohol Abuse and Drug Abuse, Control of Coronary Heart Disease Risk Factors, Prevention of Chronic Disease, Women's Health Issues, Men's Health Issues, Stress Management, Sexually Transmitted Diseases, Occupational and Environmental Health Injury and Control, and Health Risk Appraisal.

These services or resources can be obtained by contacting the Health Promotions Manager at your Regional Work-Life Staff. Work-Life Staffs are located at Integrated Support Commands CG-wide.

Substance Abuse Treatment and Prevention

Program Goal: Provide resources regarding training, education, treatment, and administrative processing to support CG policy governing substance use, abuse, and chemical dependency for active duty members. Access to resources regarding the Substance Abuse Program, governing policy and guidance related to substance abuse case management is available to Coast Guard Commands and unit CDAR's by contacting the:

- SAPM: (202) 267-6658
- SAPR MLC LANT: (757) 628-4370
- SAPR MLC PAC: (510) 637-1223
- Substance Abuse Prevention Teams (SAPT)
- SAPT LANT (757) 856-2087
- SAPT PAC (707) 765-7081

CAUTION: Obtaining services/care relating to substance use, abuse and chemical dependency outside of the Coast Guard or other DOD Military Treatment Facilities (MTFs) must be pre-authorized. Members obtaining related care without pre-authorization from a TRICARE Health Care Finder or the AREA Service Point of Contact (SPOC) can be held personally responsible for all costs incurred associated with obtaining said care.

Food Services
Program Goal: Recruit and retain food service personnel to build a healthier workforce by providing nutritiously balanced meals. The following web sites provide information related to the Food Service Program:
- http://www.uscg.mil/hq/tcpet/fssch/ Food Service Force Manager Notes
- http://www.uscg.mil/mlclant/KDiv/kseFSAT.htm MLC Atlantic Food Service Assistance and Training (FSAT) TEAM
- http://www.uscg.mil/hq/tcpet/tpf/fssms/fssms.htm FS SMS Petaluma Web Site

Child Development Services
Program Goal: Provide quality and affordable child care center services for CG families. Desired Program Outcomes: Increase the number of eligible children enrolled in CG child care services from 3 percent to 6 percent through our new MOA with GSA. This MOA will allow CG families to use GSA CDCs and also locate & subsidize other center and home-based childcare services nationwide. The following services and resources are available within the Child Development Centers Program:
- Quality child care services for children six weeks through five years old, with summer programs available where there is space
- Parenting information
- Referrals to special services

Ombudsman
Program Goal: To have an individual at the unit level serves as a liaison between a CG command and their families to facilitate communication. An **Ombudsman** is a volunteer (who may be a Spouse, Reservist, or Auxiliarist) **who** is designated by a Command to serve as a link between the command and families, assisting the command in its functions of providing information and related services to families regarding sources of assistance available to them, Coast Guard and command policies, and activities of interest to family members. The following web sites provide information related to the Ombudsman Program:
- http://www.lifelines2000.org/services/fam_support/index.asp?AttribID=527 Ombudsmen site from the Navy's LIFELines Services Network–Contains a myriad of information on DoD Ombudsman programs, including on Ombudsman training module under "Orientation" on "The Reserve Ombudsman Program."
- http://www.lifelines2000.org Ombudsman Journal is available to download online.
- http://www.cgspouses.net Information for spouses including discussion forums, favorite web sites, Ombudsman Directory, relocation tips, and more.

Other Programs
For information on the following subjects, contact Chief of Work-Life (202) 475-5140:
- Adoption

- Scholarships
- Dependent scholarships from the CG Foundation
- Elder Care
- Information and counseling

—Commandant, U. S. Coast Guard, Office of Work-Life (CG-111)
2100 Second St. SW, Washington, DC 20593-0001
Chief of Work-Life (202) 475-5140

Appendix 2

Military Family Network Community Connections & America Supports You

(Left to right) America Supports You Director Allison Barber, Caroline Peabody, Becky Gates, wife of Secretary of Defense Robert M. Gates

The Military Family Network Community Connections Program

The Military Family Network Community Connections Program gives people and community groups a chance to connect and build relationships with military families.

Most military friendly individuals and organizations are looking for ways that military families will get to know them. The Military Family Network gives them the opportunity to talk about their programs through our innovative program and platform

As an "America Supports You" Team Member, the Military Family Network helps America show their support and build awareness of their services and programs, and connect with service members, veterans and their families.

The network is a Google news provider and serves communities and military families across the world by ensuring that information about local, regional and national programs and activities is delivered to military families and the communities that serve them.

The Military Family Network is an official certifying organization for the President's Volunteer Service Award Program and groups and individuals registered with the Military Family Network Community Connections Program can can be recognized for this Presidential award.

Non-profits also benefit with the Military Family Network. By connecting them with other organizations and funding sources, non-profits can grow and expand.

The Military Family Network Community Connections Program also operates as a centralized communication and information portal for military families to receive information from and communicate with organizations and program providers that serve them. Registered organizations receive access to the website to provide information about their organization, can set up a page to interact with the military community, and reach out for support for their mission. MFN helps with press releases and network members are highlighted in The Military Family Networks e-Newsletter.

How It Works

Interested individuals and organizations register FREE on emilitary.org by going to www.eMilitary.org/cchome.html.

- MFN asks organizations to provide ambassadors for their program who will post regularly , so that military families can interact with them. MFN supports events, information and connections for each of the registered programs.
- Individual volunteers with the Community Connection Program provide information about their communities for military families.
- Groups and individual volunteers register with MFN and keep track of their hours online.
- This is how MFN establishes "virtual military friendly community neighborhoods" online and networks on the ground.

Why and Why Now?

Studies conducted by all branches of the military and notable academics such as Dr. James Martin, Dr. Gary Bowen and the RAND corporation indicate that many military members and their families are not aware of what is available to them in their communities—on and off the installation—and community connectivity is key to increasing the well-being of the modern military family.

The bottom line is that our nation is at war. Military families need community, not just a phone book. They need to connect now—to know what is out there, and to be able to learn from each other and build on that knowledge. The Military Family Network is the only interactive network that supports community and military family connections both online and in person in their neighborhoods.

The Military Family Network chose a select few America Supports You and Military Family Network Community Connections for their outstanding work in support of our military community. We encourage you to read about them, join them and support them in their missions.

Together, we all help "Make the World a Home for Military Families"

OFFICE OF THE ASSISTANT SECRETARY OF DEFENSE
1400 DEFENSE PENTAGON
WASHINGTON, DC 20301-1400

PUBLIC AFFAIRS

You sacrifice so much for your country. You leave the safety and security of civilian life for the uncertainty and danger of life in the field. You leave your families and friends for months at a time to take up the cause of defending freedom around the world. For these reasons and so many more, it is the mission of *America Supports You* to make sure that you, all your fellow military members and your families know that the thanks of a grateful nation are with you. We carry this simple message from coast to coast and around the world: for your service and your sacrifice, your patriotism and devotion, America supports you!

We started *America Supports You* in 2004 after hearing concerns from service members in Iraq who were not sure the public was still behind them. At the same time, we recognized a phenomenon of communities, dedicated military-support organizations and corporations nationwide spontaneously stepping up to fill the needs of service members and their families around the world, but their message of support was not getting through. *America Supports You* was conceived to help communicate and connect those displays of patriotism and appreciation to the troops and their families. Since then, our organization has grown to encompass almost 250 homefront organizations working to provide for the every need of service members and their families, more than 35 corporations helping spread the message of *America Supports You* and thousands of individuals across the country looking to do their part.

We are especially proud of our homefront groups, each of them an *America Supports You* ambassador, carrying their own unique message of thanks and appreciation to America's armed services with each care package sent, letter written, home built, veteran comforted, wounded tended and through countless other expressions of support. *America Supports You* thanks all of them for their tireless efforts on your behalf. It is truly amazing what a dedicated group of people can accomplish working together towards a worthy goal.

And most importantly, thank you for your uncompromising dedication to your country and fellow service members. You are our heroes, and we are forever in your debt. Never again will any of our military men, women or families doubt this simple truth: America supports you!

Allison Barber
Deputy Assistant Secretary of Defense for
Public Affairs for Internal Communication
and Public Liaison

The Military Family Network Community Connections National Award Winner

The Military Family Network selected The Association of the US Army (AUSA) Family Programs as the 1st Military Family Network Community Connections National Award Winner for Support of Military Families and for the director's contributions to the success of military support organizations and resources supporting the military community.

Association of the United States Army (AUSA) Family Programs
Director: Sylvia Kidd
www.ausa.org/webpub/DeptFamilyPrograms.nsf/byid/DeptFamilyPrograms.nsfhome

Mission
To support the needs and interests of Army families

Passion: How We Started
Our military lifestyle is often demanding and stressful; but in the past few years families have faced ever increasing turmoil. We presently have hundreds of thousands of service members deployed; many other units are either preparing to leave or are leaving almost on a daily basis. Reserve and National Guard soldiers are being sent away for back-to-back tours or being told that they may be gone for up to two years. Families are certainly being asked to cope with a lot and many feel that they have lost total control over their lives.

We are not ever going to be able to totally remove stress; however, we do have the means to empower families and help them gain some semblance of control. There are many programs and resources available to military families. Knowing where to go and what to do before a situation arises can not only give the family a sense of security but it also helps the deploying soldier so he or she can concentrate on the Army mission and come home safely. I cannot encourage you strongly enough to gather that information, make those contacts and inform yourselves. Prepare yourselves and your children before anything happens so that if a situation arises you don't have to waste valuable time and energy searching for assistance. Believe me, I've been both places and prepared is much more comfortable.

Attend unit activities and Family Readiness Group meetings. You all have the same concerns. Making contact with other families provides a link for information and someone who understands and helps diminish that loneliness.

The Association of the United States Army is a valuable resource. We are here to assist and inform you. This is the lifestyle that we have chosen. How we react to it is the one element that is totally within our control.

Thank you for all you have done and continue to do,

—Sylvia E.J. Kidd, Director, Family Programs
Association of the U.S. Army

Services: How Do We Help
Since 1999, AUSA's Family Programs Directorate has worked to support the needs and interests of Army families by:

- Traveling to installations around the world to make presentations, host focus groups and receive briefings on housing, TRICARE, family readiness programs, Army Community Service programs and children's education issues.
- Gathering information from Army families to use in AUSA legislative and advocacy efforts.
- Representing AUSA on various Departments of the Army and Department of Defense councils and task forces such as the Army's Well-Being Consortium, the Youth Education Advisory Working Group, the AAFES and DeCA Advisory Councils, the In-State Tuition Working Group and the Spouse Employment Summit.
- Supporting the Army Family Action Plan, the Military Child Education Coalition, as well as numerous family readiness activities including active duty, reserve and National Guard family training events
- Administering the annual AUSA Rubbermaid Volunteer Family of the Year Award, which recognizes the importance of families and volunteers to the success of the Army mission.
- Working with AUSA Chapters to support Army family events and programs at local installations.
- Hosting Military Family Forums dealing with Army well-being and family support issues at the AUSA Annual Meeting.

Newsletter
AUSA Family Programs publishes a monthly newsletter with information about Family Programs, activities, and news for Army families.For information, e-mail familyprograms@ausa.org

AUSA Additional Member Benefit ID Card for Spouses
Spouses of AUSA members may obtain this card in their own name. It entitles them to all the benefits and privileges of a regular membership in the Association of the United States Army. To obtain a card, call Valerie Holman at 1-800-336-4570, ext. 191 or e-mail vholman@ausa.org.

Family Programs Will Come to You
To ensure that AUSA Family Programs truly represents Army families, it is very important that we visit installations and units and meet with family members to understand their needs and concerns. To schedule a Family Programs speaker, please contact us at 800-336-4570 x150 or x151 or e-mail familyprograms@ausa.org.

Contact:
Sylvia Kidd
800-336-4570 x150
703-841-4300 x150
skidd@ausa.org

Honored Members of The Military Family Network's Community Connection Program and America Supports You Programs.
The Military Family Network honors these additional Team Members for their outstanding service to the military community.

American Red Cross

www.redcross.org
P.O. Box 37243
Washington, D.C. 20013

The American Red Cross

The American Red Cross is a humanitarian organization dedicated to providing relief to victims of disasters and helping people prevent, prepare for and respond to emergencies. It has more than 700 chapters and blood centers across the U.S., as well as stations at U.S. military installations around the world, and over 90 percent of its work force is made up of volunteers. The Red Cross isn't a government agency; it relies on everyone to come forward with the gifts of time, money, and blood it needs to help.

Services: How Do We Help

Today, the Red Cross provides disaster preparedness and relief assistance; personal and family assistance to members of the armed forces; assistance to the most vulnerable overseas; blood/blood product collection; and training in CPR, AED (automated external defibrillator) use and first aid. Approximately one million volunteers across the country take the lead in teaching preparedness, CPR and first aid classes, respond to local and national disasters, coordinate armed forces emergency messages and assist with local blood drives.

Local Red Cross disaster relief also focuses on meeting people's immediate emergency disaster-caused needs. When a disaster threatens or strikes, the Red Cross provides shelter, food, health and mental health services and more to address basic human needs. In addition to these services, the core of Red Cross disaster relief is the assistance given to individuals and families affected by disaster to enable them to resume their normal daily activities independently.

In your community, the Red Cross also feeds emergency workers, handles inquiries from concerned family members outside the disaster area, provides blood and blood products to those in need and helps those affected by disaster to access other available resources.

Every day, your local Red Cross focuses on other initiatives as well. It provides CPR/AED and first aid training for individuals, parents, teachers and coaches, employees and others; disaster relief training for volunteers who want to respond to local or national disasters by helping feed, handle casework or provide health services to victims across the street and around the country; local blood drives and community disaster education presentations to schools, organizations or concerned citizens who want to help get their neighborhoods prepared. For additional information, visit www.redcross.org or contact your local chapter today.

How You Can Help

There are many ways that you can help. The American Red Cross is a lifeline for deployed military members, allowing them to communicate to loved ones back home during emergencies. Find out about how you can receive training to become an Armed Forces Emergency Services caseworker and help keep military personnel in touch with their families during times of crisis.

The Red Cross also provides services to veterans in VA health care facilities across the nation via the Veterans Affairs Volunteers Services (VAVS) program. Through the VAVS, you can volunteer in hospitals, outpatient clinics and nursing care facilities.

The American Red Cross prepares people to save lives through health and safety education and training such as first aid, CPR/AED, lifeguarding, and babysitter's training. Become a health and safety instructor or authorized provider, or take a course from your local chapter or Red Cross office on a military installation.

You can help ensure that the Red Cross can continue to provide these lifesaving services and has the resources, talent and ability to continue to deliver them by making a donation to support all of its core services today.

Financial Donations

The American Red Cross honors donor intent. You can help the Red Cross keep military families connected with a gift to Red Cross Armed Forces Emergency Services. If you wish to designate a donation for a specific disaster, please do so at the time of donation. To make a financial donation: Call 1-800-REDCROSS (1-800-733-2767) or 1-800-257-7575 (Español). Make a secure, online donation: http://www.redcross.org/donate/donatemail.html

Contact

Find and contact your local Red Cross chapter at http://www.redcross.org/where/chapts.asp
Mail a Donation to:
American Red Cross
P.O. Box 37243
Washington, D.C. 20013
www.redcross.org/donatemail.html

American Legion Auxiliary

www. legion-aux.org
"Empowering Women, Inspiring Communities"

Passion: Who We Are

The American Legion Auxiliary, more than 80 years old and nearly 900,000 members strong, is the largest patriotic women's organization in the world. Affiliated with the American Legion, the Auxiliary is a leading veteran's service organization with members in almost 10,000 communities. Founded in 1919 to respond to the horrific human and social cost of World War I, Auxiliary members are wives, mothers, sisters, daughters, granddaughters and great-granddaughters of these courageous veterans. Some members are veterans themselves.

Its eligible members are exclusively wives, mothers, sisters, daughters, granddaughters and great-granddaughters of those men who served or are serving during designated periods of armed conflict. The Auxiliary has conceived and implemented hundreds of programs centered on helping veterans, their families, young people and communities.

Members believe deeply in the ideals and principles upon which our great country was founded. With the philosophy of "Service, Not Self", the American Legion Auxiliary touches the lives of all Americans, and especially those that have carried the burden directly in defending our country.

The Auxiliary embodies the spirit of America that has prevailed through war and peace and continues to stand firmly behind America today, promoting the ideals and principles of American patriotism, defending the Constitution, promoting allegiance to God and Country and upholding the basic principles of freedom of religion, freedom of expression and freedom of choice. Auxiliary members are patriots in every sense of the word. Their primary goals are to service our veterans, nurture our children, and educate all citizens about the privileges and responsibilities of one of the world's most prized possessions – American citizenship.

The American Legion Auxiliary sponsors programs to support three main audiences: veterans, children – especially those of veterans – and the local communities where our members live. Many programs complement the service activities of The American Legion. Local Auxiliary units are usually affiliated with an American Legion post, although many of the Auxiliary's programs have a more expanded scope to focus on the special needs of women and their families.

Services: How We Help

The services of the American Legion Auxiliary directly and indirectly touch the lives of all Americans. These nearly 900,000 service-oriented women come from all walks of life and are active in virtually every American community. Long imbued with the philosophy of "service, not self," the American Legion Auxiliary develops a strong spirit of volunteerism in its members, who have joined together in the fellowship of giving to others.

Veteran's Affairs and Rehabilitation

The Auxiliary raises more than $18 million every year and reinvests these funds in a variety of programs, some of which include VA medical centers, scholarships and support for other nonprofit organizations serving the audiences of the Auxiliary. Many of the funds used to support veterans are raised through the Auxiliary's longtime Poppy program. Hundreds of thousands of these crepe-paper flowers made by veterans are sold around Memorial Day every year.

Auxiliary volunteers are the backbone of assistance in 171 VA Medical Centers. These volunteers not only provide diversion and entertainment for patients, they assist the hospital staff with numerous administrative and operational duties. In a single year, veterans' programs benefited from the services of more than 100,000 hospital field and home service volunteers who donated millions of dollars and millions of hours to assist veterans.

Since 1989, the Auxiliary has been a proud, national co-sponsor of the annual National Veterans Creative Arts Festival, raising more than $100,000 annually and providing volunteer support for local VA festivals and the National festival. This traveling event brings together and celebrates more than 130 regional medal winners in virtually all disciplines in the creative arts.

Auxiliary Emergency Fund

The fund provides temporary emergency financial assistance to Auxiliary members who have exhausted all other personal and community resources. For members who are suddenly single, deserted, divorced, or widowed, with no skills to support themselves or their families. The fund provides immediate aide to help the member acquire new job skills through schooling or job training. Established in 1969, the Auxiliary Emergency Fund is supported by memorial contributions from Auxiliary Units and members. In the Auxiliary's 2005-06 service year, the AEF donated more than $700,000 in assistance, with much of that figure going to Katrina victims.

Girls State, Girls Nation

Girls State and Girls Nation are two of the Auxiliary's well known and showcase programs. Both are intended for young women entering their senior year in high school with an interest in local, state and federal government. Since the inception of the Girls State program in 1937, nearly one million young people have had the opportunity to learn first-hand how their state and local governments work. Typically, capping off the week of Girls Nation is a meeting with the President of the United States at The White House.

Children and Youth

The Auxiliary supports programs for drug and alcohol abuse, missing children, teen suicide and teen pregnancy while working with organizations like the Children's Miracle Network and Red Cross. Thousands of hours are devoted to crime prevention, instructing children, elderly and the general public on safety and protection within the community. In some cases, the program offers direct financial assistance and services to individual children or to the families of veterans.

The program works to preserve the integrity of the family unit and takes a realistic approach to the needs of children by considering the physical and spiritual, as well as the emotional and educational aspects, of each situation. The Children and Youth program cooperates with many other public and private community agencies and organizations and supports essential legislation for children at the national, state, and local levels. In some cases, the program offers direct financial assistance and services to individual children or to the families of our active military and veterans. Auxiliary members also contribute to The American Legion Child Welfare Foundation, which was established in 1954 to fund special programs and projects that emphasize preventative solutions to difficult children's issues. In the 2005-06 program year, Auxiliary units and departments (states) donated more than $2.3 million to support youth programs in their local communities.

Educating members and the general public about these issues is a primary goal of the Auxiliary's Children and Youth program.

Americanism

The Auxiliary's Americanism program promotes patriotism and responsible citizenship and strives to uphold and promote American ideals and the principles of democracy. The goal of the Auxiliary's Americanism program is to educate every citizen on the fundamentals of American government, the Bill of Rights and the value of active, informed involvement in the home, in the Auxiliary organization and in the community. Contributions donated to the Spirit of Youth Foundation benefit young people through such programs as the Americanism Youth Conference at Freedom's Foundation, the Americanism Essay Contest and the National President's Scholarship program. More than 22,000 students participated in the Essay Contest and more than 75,000 pocket flags were folded and mailed to our military members in Iraq.

Community Service

Auxiliary members study community needs, recommend projects, raise funds and donate their time to accomplish their specific objectives. Special attention is given to the selection of each project to ensure that the work of other organizations is not duplicated. Auxiliary Units also provide assistance on Community Service projects sponsored by American Legion Posts and work with other organizations to implement practical, worthwhile projects for the benefit of the community. Some examples include, blood drives, first aid and CPR training, child safety programs, support for women in shelters, donations to shelters for the homeless, tree plantings, recycling programs, and disaster and emergency preparedness programs. Auxiliary Units contributed $950,000 to community-based programs and logged 250,000 hours on *Make a Difference Day.*

Education

Auxiliary members believe that a solid educational foundation is a cornerstone of American freedom. The Auxiliary's Education program promotes quality education and works actively with educators and local schools to develop and maintain an educational system that serves the needs of all children at every level. Auxiliary volunteers sponsor and support state and national education legislation; establish new scholarship opportunities for students; alert eligible students to existing scholarship resources; help students identify career opportunities and professional job requirements; and encourage students to plan early for college and apply for scholarship opportunities. Auxiliary members in 2005-06 funded $1.1 million in college scholarships, volunteered 60,000 hours in local schools and with literacy programs, contributing another $235,000 at this grassroots level.

Junior Auxiliary Membership

Junior Auxiliary membership for girls under the age of 18 is a training ground that prepares young women for active adult membership. Junior activities and programs reflect and support the work of the Auxiliary and instill the ideals of the organization. The Junior program is an important step in the transition from childhood to responsible adulthood. At age 18, Junior members automatically are eligible for full, active membership. Auxiliary Junior members volunteered 75,000 hours annually in their communities.

National Security

The Auxiliary believes in maintaining a strong national defense and endeavors to educate its members on all vital national security issues. In cooperation with The American Legion, Auxiliary members are briefed on a wide range of topics at local and national meetings and through publications and bulletins. Topics include national and civil defense, crime prevention, emergency and disaster preparedness, and environmental protection. The member's clear understanding of the issues helps to lay the groundwork for community-wide mobilization and support of various national security activities. National activities include the annual Awareness Assembly, a legislative forum in Washington, D.C.; POW/MIA Awareness; crime prevention; and local and worldwide support of USO activities.

Poppy

The Poppy Program is the oldest and most widely recognized Auxiliary program. It is symbolic of the flower that bloomed on the devastated French and Belgian battlefields during World War I. Each year around Memorial Day, Auxiliary volunteers distribute millions of bright red crepe paper poppies in exchange for contributions to assist disabled and hospitalized veterans. The hospitalized veterans who make the flowers are able to earn a small wage that helps to supplement their incomes and increase their self-sufficiency. Members distributed 5.6 million poppies and collected $2.3 million in donations in 2005-2006. The poppy also reminds the community of the past sacrifices and continuing needs of our veterans. The poppy has become a nationally known and recognized symbol of sacrifice and is worn and used by Auxiliary members to honor the men and women who served and died for their country in all wars.

How You Can Help

American Legion Auxiliary is a remarkable organization with dedicated women across the country, devoted to America's veterans, young people and communities. Visit our website www.legion-aux.org/ to learn how you can become a member or lend your support.

Contacts

Indianapolis headquarters: 317-955-3845
Pam Gilley, National Secretary & Chief Operating Officer
Marta Hedding, National Treasurer & Chief Financial Officer
Scott Friend, Development Director (donations)
Christopher Brooks, APR, Marketing & Communications Director
Washington, D.C. office: 202-861-1365
Joanna Truitt, Washington, D.C. Director

AMVETS

American Legion Auxiliary
www.amvets.org
Lanham, Md

Passion: Who We Are

Since 1944, AMVETS has been a leader in preserving the freedoms secured by America's armed forces, providing not only support for veterans and the active military in procuring their earned entitlements, but also community services that enhance the quality of life for this nation's citizens.

AMVETS has earned a reputation as one of the most respected, volunteer-led veterans' service organizations in the country. Headquartered in Lanham, Md., AMVETS and its subordinate organizations number more than 220,000 members with 40 state departments and more than 1,300 posts nationwide. Subordinate national organizations are the AMVETS Ladies Auxiliary, AMVETS National Service Foundation, AMVETS (motorcycle) Riders, Sons of AMVETS, Junior AMVETS, and Sad Sacks and Sackettes.

Services: How We Help

The tenets of AMVETS have always been to enhance the quality of life for all Americans through community services, to support strong national defense, and to guarantee the fulfillment of America's promises to its brave men and women in uniform. The latter has become central to AMVETS' focus during the Global War on Terrorism as the needs of our young veterans grow in direct proportion to our troops' increasing role in combat operations overseas. Now, more than ever, AMVETS urges guaranteed adequate funding for the Department of Veterans Affairs, benefits for all veterans including National Guard and Reserve forces, better housing and pay for active duty service members, and post-service benefits including healthcare, employment and job training, and services for homeless veterans.

To this end, AMVETS hosted the Symposium for the Needs of Young Veterans in October of 2006. AMVETS was the first Veterans Service Organization to take the initiative to focus the attention on the unique needs of our young veterans and attempt to find meaningful solutions. The breakthrough event brought together a diverse and representative group of veterans to discuss how to ensure a system of earned benefits that is both adequate and relevant to the needs of younger veterans including National Guard and Reserve members. The results were then shared in a national venue with all appropriate agencies, including the Department of Veterans Affairs.

First and foremost, AMVETS continues to provide services to veterans. From January through June 2006, AMVETS members provided 292,911 hours of community services ranging from support for National Guard Family Assistance Centers to projects on behalf of young people, such as Americanism and Drug Awareness programs. According to the Independent Sector, a consortium of over 550 non-profit organizations, these services totaled over $9,400,000 in value. During the same period, AMVETS volunteers at 150 VA medical centers provided in excess of 160,000 hours of service totaling $2,883,477 in value as uncompensated employees. Through a memorandum of understanding with the National Guard Bureau, local AMVETS posts and individual members have become additional volunteer manpower for National Guard Family Assistance Centers. Since March 2005, AMVETS national service officers have also increased their operational tempo in providing mobilization and demobilization briefings for our troops and their families.

Key to enacting meaningful, lasting changes in the veterans community has been AMVETS ongoing involvement in the legislative process. Veterans and their families can count on AMVETS to keep close tabs on congressional proposals that affect them, whether retired, or on active or reserve status. In each Congressional cycle, AMVETS' legislative staff deliver crucial testimony on measures to improve veterans' job placement and training, expand education, housing, burial and disability benefits as well as boost compensation.

How You Can Help

To join AMVETS is to commit to serving all veterans as well as to build a better America. By joining AMVETS, you will share a commitment with others who reflect your values and beliefs. As a member, you also share with other veterans the pride that comes from being a member of an organization dedicated to serving all veterans and improving the quality of life for this nation's citizens.

AMVETS membership is open to anyone who has honorably served in any branch of the military from World War II to the present. It remains the only veterans' organization with open membership for National Guard and Reserve members regardless of their deployment status.

Contact

To learn more about AMVETS, call toll free (877) 726-8387, or visit www.amvets.org Average annual membership dues are $20.00 or $150.00 for Life Membership.

For more information about AMVETS or if you have questions, you may contact:
Beryl W. Love
AMVETS National Programs Director
Toll Free: 877-726-8387

Disabled American Veterans (DAV)

www.dav.org

Passion: Who We Are

The Disabled American Veterans (DAV) is a nonprofit association of over 1.2 million U.S. military veterans who suffered some degree of disability while serving in time of war or armed conflict. Founded in 1920 and chartered by Congress, the DAV is dedicated to a single purpose: building better lives for disabled veterans and their families.

With headquarter offices in Cincinnati and Washington, the DAV focuses strictly on serving veterans and their families. A nonpartisan organization, it has no political action committees (PACs) and neither endorses nor opposes candidates for political office. The DAV is totally funded by dues and contributions and receives no federal funding.

The DAV continually fills openings on its professional and management staff with veterans disabled during recent armed conflicts, so we'll be around as long as you and other veterans need our free services.

Services: How We Help

To help you and your family get all the benefits you earned, the DAV maintains a corps of approximately 270 National Service Officers (NSOs) in 72 offices across the United States and in Puerto Rico. There's never any charge for the assistance these veterans' benefits experts provide to you and your family. You don't have to be a DAV member to receive these free services, either.

DAV NSOs are all service-connected disabled veterans themselves, so they understand where you're coming from. They offer counseling on veterans benefits administered by the United States Department of Veterans Affairs (VA), including disability compensation, health care, pension, survivors' benefits, employment rights, education and more. These highly trained professionals help folks like you assemble evidence needed to support claims for benefits, building their cases and preparing claim forms and briefs. They also present claims before government agencies, boards and appellate bodies. The DAV also provides disaster relief to disabled veterans affected by catastrophes such as tornadoes, hurricanes or floods.

The DAV national magazine, local chapter meetings and other functions keep members up to date on issues affecting their rights. There's also a comprehensive package of member benefits, including price discounts and exclusive bargains. On the local level, DAV volunteers transport sick and disabled veterans to and from VA medical facilities for treatment.

In addition, our volunteers annually contribute 2.5 million hours to veterans at VA hospitals. Through a variety of other local programs, these dedicated volunteers reach into their communities to help disabled veterans and their families.

As a nonpartisan organization, it is the DAV's policy to seek only reasonable, responsible legislation to assist disabled veterans and their families. Concentrating on issues such as disability compensation, pension, medical care, job and training programs, burial benefits, education and survivors' benefits, the DAV's legislative goals are set by the organization's members in a process that begins in local DAV chapters.

These legislative goals guide the organization's advocacy for disabled veterans – to help them gain and keep the benefits they have earned by spilled blood, prolonged illness and lost mental well-being as a result of military service.

In addition to services, and programs, DAV membership entitles you to savings on products and services such as new automobiles, hotels, computers, long distance service and many more items. The DAV's Member Benefits Package is an incredible bonus that adds value to being a member in the country's greatest veterans' support organization.

The benefits package enhances the lives of our members and their families, increases the ties between the DAV and the most generous, well-respected corporations in America, and allows DAV Members to enjoy reduced goods and services while supporting DAV programs.

How You Can Help

Join today.
Support the organization that does all this for you!

Contact

Disabled American Veterans
PO BOX 145550
Cincinnati, OH 45250
888-236-8313
www.dav.org

National Next of Kin Registry

http://nokr.org/nok/restricted/home.htm
http://nokr.org/nok/restricted/military.htm

Passion: Who We Are

The National Next of Kin Registry came about because of a personal tragedy in the life
of Mark Cerney, the founder of the organization.

Mark Cerney founded the National Next of Kin Registry (NOKR) because of a
devastating and personal experience. An extended family member of Mark's known as
"MiMi," was the nanny to Mark and his sisters for over two decades.

Mimi eventually became a resident of a convalescent care facility in San Diego,
California due to multiple strokes and had been there nearly a decade. Over the years,
Mark had informed staff that if Mimi were near death or suddenly passed on, he was
to be notified *immediately.* In late May 1990, Mimi passed on. Neither Mark nor his
family members had been notified of her death or burial. The pain of knowing Mimi
had died alone was Mark's grief for many years. The frustration of what took place, the
lack of communication, and out of his love for Mimi, NOKR was born.

Services: How We Help

The mission of NOKR is simple. We are dedicated to making it possible for people to
register their next of kin and others for everyday emergency situations, in natural catastrophes, or man made disasters. We will respond to these events by providing registered information to public trust agencies and coordinate real time information exchange between
government entities, private sector non-profit agencies, and faith based organizations.

We strive to proactively and through preventive measures, help make a painful
or tragic situation less painful for individuals and families. We will help facilitate the
next of kin notification process for families by providing Local and State Agencies
with secured access to online information provided by individuals. This service is free
to the public and to the registered agencies using the search service.

Each day in cities all across America and throughout the rest of the world, people
die alone. This includes people who are traveling and are in cities where no one knows
them, people who are in assisted living facilities, people in the military and people
who are homeless, just to name a few. Most people carry a driver's license or some
kind of identification put these types of ID don't tell the emergency personnel who you
wish to have contacted in case of an emergency. Even worse is when we do not keep
our identification up to date. We move and fail to notify DMV of our new address.

In the cases of homeless people and people in assisted living facilities, it sometimes takes weeks and even months for the authorities to locate a next of kin. In some
cases they never do. Our Goal is to see that this does not happen. We wish to see that
every person has the ability to register their next of kin information so that if something every does happen to them, their designated next of kin can be located and notified in a timely manner. Each person deserves to have a loved one notified in times
of crisis and in cases of death, each person deserves the dignity of having loved ones
close by to say "Good Bye".

At NOKR, our core values are Privacy, Trust, Accountability, Partnerships. While
you have the peace of mind of knowing your next of kin will be notified in case you
can not speak for yourself, you should also have the peace of mind of knowing that
the information you provide is private. We base our organization on trust and accountability and we partner only with organizations that share our values.

How You Can Help

Our services are free to all who choose to use them. We are free to any citizen who wishes to register and we are free to the agencies that are responsible for notifying a person's next of kin. We provide a "Safe Kids" registration for children. We suggest that parents keep current photographs of their children, have their children fingerprinted and add a current photograph of their child to the registration. We believe that keeping our children safe is our highest priority. Should something happen to your child you can have all of their information, including medical information and a photo, archived on our website.

To register yourself or another family member, simply log onto http://nokr.org. Click on "Register Your Emergency Contact" and fill out the form. You may re-register as many times as you wish. Each registration is dated so if you move and wish to update your registration, you may do say. Or you may call 1-800-915-5413 for an emergency phone registration.

The National Next Of Kin Registry is dedicated to protecting your privacy. Your information will not be sold or shared. For privacy reasons we do not list where this information is located. This information is safe guarded to protect our registrant's privacy. This information is only available to Local and State Agencies working in an official capacity, attempting to locate a next of kin or emergency point of contact. The NOKR will NEVER ask for any intrusive information like your social security number or date of birth. NOKR does ask for age optionally which is used as a chronological identifier. Information collected at the Next Of Kin Registry is stored and kept private. We understand many people have worries about providing such information. It should be understood that the information we collect that is required to register is very minimal. NOKR actually collects less information than what is currently available in any household phonebook, which is published and given for free. Your information is stored with the National Next Of Kin Registry for <u>emergencies only</u>. Your information is only accessible to agencies that have registered and must find a family member or next of kin.

To prevent unauthorized access, maintain data accuracy, and ensure the correct use of information, we have put in place, appropriate physical, electronic, and managerial procedures to safeguard and secure the information we collect online.

Your Next Of Kin information is collected inside a SSL (Secure Socket Layer), and then it is transferred encrypted into a secure archiving area. SSL is a protocol that allows for secure online transactions. SSL uses the public-and-private key encryption system from RSA, which also includes the use of a digital certificate. If you have any questions, concerns, or comments about our privacy policies or practices. Please contact us at privacy@pleasenotifyme.org.

Our organization is both volunteer and donation driven. We are a non-profit organization and all donations are tax deductible. We welcome help from other organizations and businesses in the form of both monetary and "In Kind" donations. Visit our website at http://nokr.org and scroll to the bottom left under "Help Now". There are links for donations, volunteers, and other ways to help further out goal.

Contact

If you have any questions about the organization or how you can help, feel free to contact the following:

Mark Cerney
President
admin@pleasenotifyme.org
or
Johnny Keene
Executive Vice President
johnny.keene@pleasenotifyme.org

MilitaryPetsFOSTER Project

Steve Albin, NetPets.Org
http://www.netpets.org/

Passion: Who We Are

NetPets.org's founder and president Steve Albin has created the first ever nationwide and global network of individual foster homes that will house, nurture and care for the dogs, cats, birds and all other types of pets for all the military personnel while they are deployed or mobilized.

N. Myrtle Beach, September 19, 2001 -The NetPets.org's MilitaryPetsFOSTER Project was created to be the liaison and overseer between those in the military who have to place their Pets and the Foster Homes all over this country, Asia, Europe, Canada and Cuba. This is a a free service, as is the actual fostering of the Pets. This Project was born out of the desire to be both patriotic and a deep humanitarian concern for the Pets.

Services: How We Help

The Project brings a much needed and viable alternative from what happened during Desert Storm and Desert Shield. At that time the Armed Forces personnel, who had nowhere to place their Pets, were left with no other option except to put them in the animal shelters. A good percentage of these pets were put to sleep, while the others were adopted out. Either way, the military personnel had to lose their Pets, forever! Now with the creation of the *MilitaryPets*FOSTER Project the military's personnel not only have an option, but they also have the peace of mind in knowing that they will be reunited with their beloved Pet(s) upon their return from their tour of duty.

To date we have fostered well over 8,600 pets for those servicemen and women in the Air Force, Army, Coast Guard, Marines, Navy and all of these branches Reserves as well as the National Guard, AAFES (Army and Air Force Exchange Service, NCIS (Navy Criminal Investigative Service) and the Military Severely Injured Joint Support Operations (at the request of the Deputy Under Secretary of Defense).

*The MilitaryPets*FOSTER Project is listed with ALL the Military branches, their Reserve units, the National Guard, the Coast Guard as well as the Red Cross Armed Forces Emergency Services units and the United Way chapters. Mr. Albin has been interviewed by the DoD's PA office, the Navy News Service, mentioned in the ROA's (Reserve Officers Association) newsletter, the ESGR's (Employer Support Of The Guard & Reserve) newsletter and it will be listed and recommended in all the branches of the Armed Forces magazines, beginning with their next issues.

This Project has been in newspapers, the AP, UPI, NPI and Reuters wire services and on numerous radio and TV shows. The Project has also been written about in the AKC website and in *DogWorld, Dog Fancy, PetLife, Animal Watch, Mary Engelbreit's Home Companion, Readers Digest, Time, Newsweek, USA Weekend, Fine Living, Prevention, Womans World* and hundreds of other pet and non pet related magazines.

How You Can Help

With thousands of volunteer Foster Homes that have already pledged their support to this project, many more are still needed. We are actively publicizing this need on the Internet and all other available media. Currently, NetPets.Org is actively seeking much-needed corporate sponsors and private donations for the *MilitaryPets*FOSTER Project and the public charity.

NetPets, Inc. (an all volunteer non profit organization) was established in 1996 and the NetPets.Org site was created to be the premiere Internet portal for the global pet community.

The mission and goals of our public charity include:

* Free listing for all pet related "non profits" and free hosting of all pet related "non profit's" websites inside our site and dedicated server.
* Assist in improving the relationships that we have with our Pets through educational and informative articles and books in our chartered libraries.
* Through revenues received through membership donations and grants, be able to provide funding to the individual; shelters, rescues, service, therapy and assistance animal groups.
* Promote research to identify the markers of the genetic defects and inherited diseases in our pets.

NetPets.Org is one of the most heavily trafficked pet related websites on the Internet. With over 3 million listings and links inside the website, it has become the primary pet related resource for; Prudential Realty's Relocation Centers, newspapers, journalists, magazines, authors, schools, colleges, websites and numerous other users.

For those of you who are in or involved with the Military please help spread the word about us, what we are doing and what our needs are to continue to serve our brave servicemen and women. For those who are on PCS, please let the relevant base offices know that we need foster homes for the arriving personnel who may have pets in need of assistance until there new residence is ready. Also be aware that the common fees for "boarding" a military pet starts at $300.00 per month (per pet). Since we are the liaison between the Foster Home and the Military Pet owner we have provided emergency medical and other funding while the pets are being fostered. The only way we are able to continue to do this, is through charitable donations.

Contact

NetPets®, Inc.
PO Box 563
904 Baron Lane
N. Myrtle Beach, SC 29597
843-249-5262

nonprofit 501©3 corp. 58-2307874
http://www.netpets.org

The United Service Organizations
Proudly Serving Those Who Serve
http://www.uso.org/

Passion: Who We Are

For more than 65 years, the United Service Organizations (USO) has been a steadfast supporter of military personnel around the world. While times have changed, the USO mission has remained the same: to boost the morale of service members and serve as the link between them and the American people.

The USO was created in 1941 in response to President Franklin D. Roosevelt's challenge for private organizations to handle the on-leave recreation needs of the U.S. armed forces. Since then, the USO has served to improve the lives of those who serve, as well as their families. A nonprofit organization, the USO operates 132 centers worldwide and supports service members with the help of a cadre of 26,000 volunteers, dedicated employees, and donations from individuals, corporations and organizations.

Services: How We Help

Programs and services include:
- free Internet and e-mail access,
- libraries and reading rooms,
- housing and travel assistance,
- support groups,
- game rooms,
- nursery facilities,
- prepaid international and domestic phone cards and
- celebrity entertainment.

In addition to its clear sense of mission, what keeps the USO going is its ability to adapt to the changing needs of the people it serves. To meet the increasing demand for services within the last few years, new centers were opened in Afghanistan, Kuwait and Qatar to support service members participating in Operations Enduring and Iraqi Freedom. Other centers were opened recently on Guam; at the Denver and Charlotte (N.C.) International Airports; at Fort Bliss in El Paso, Texas; and at Incheon International Airport in Seoul, Korea.

The USO initiated two special programs in the last few years for troops deployed to Afghanistan and Iraq: Operation USO Care Package and USO Operation Phone Home. The Care Packages contain items requested by service members, including toiletries, lip balm, sun screen and snacks. Under the Operation Phone Home program, the USO buys bulk quantities of prepaid international phone cards, which are distributed to deployed service members to reach out to their loved ones. The USO will soon distribute more than one million Care Packages and has distributed nearly two million prepaid phone cards.

The USO reaches out to troops through airport centers, welcoming battle-weary and battle-ready military travelers with a place to rest. Family and community centers promote intercultural understanding and orientation to unfamiliar locations. Mobile canteens reach out to troops in remote and sometimes unstable locations around the world.

Celebrities volunteer their time to visit and entertain service members through the USO's Celebrity Entertainment Program. In 2005, the USO produced more than 50 tours, treating nearly 200,000 service members to celebrity visits. Recent tour participants include Toby Keith, Gary Sinise, Jessica Simpson, Montgomery Gentry, John Elway, Drew Carey and Willie Nelson.

The USO's tradition is to be there for our armed forces, wherever they may be sent, and the USO will also be there for the families they leave behind *until every one comes home*. USO centers are open to service members and their families around the world. To locate a USO center, visit the locations directory on the USO World Headquarters' Web site: www.uso.org.

How You Can Help

The USO accepts monetary donations from the general public. Individuals can donate by calling 800-USO-7469 or visiting www.uso.org.

The USO also accepts monetary donations and in-kind donations from companies and corporations. Contact the Development Department at USO World Headquarters: (703) 908-6400.

To volunteer at a USO center, visit the USO World Headquarters' Web site at www.uso.org and identify the nearest USO center in the locations directory. Contact: You can contact the USO by phone, at 703-908-6400. If you wish to make a donation, please call 1-800-876-7469 directly. Or you can reach us online at: www.uso.org/contacttheuso/

Veterans of Foreign Wars (VFW)
http://www.unmetneeds.com/

Passion: Who We Are

VFW takes pride in its commitment to veterans and today's military. Our programs ensure no one is forgotten.

You've most likely heard of the Veterans of Foreign Wars. Our initials "VFW" are emblazoned on many of our 8,500 Posts worldwide. We are the nation's oldest major veterans group, and we've been a part of the country's social fabric for more than 100 years. We are an organization of more than 1.7 million veterans who have served overseas in war zones or areas demanding arduous duty, including those in Afghanistan and Iraq.

VFW traces its origins to 1899 when 13 Spanish-American War veterans convened in Columbus, Ohio. By 1914, this group had merged with two other Spanish-American/Philippines War veterans' organizations to become known collectively as the Veterans of Foreign Wars. VFW's supreme governing body is the national convention. Each August, thousands of VFW members vote as registered delegates, determining policy by adopting resolutions and making important business decisions.

VFW's National Headquarters is located in Kansas City, Mo., where the organization's administration and programs-related efforts are coordinated. Issue-oriented activities are developed and implemented in VFW's Washington Office in the nation's capital

Joining VFW to accomplish its mission are the Ladies Auxiliary (with its headquarters co-located at VFW National Headquarters); the Men's Auxiliary, of which there are 797 units; the VFW Foundation in Kansas City, Mo. and the Military Order of the Cootie, composed of VFW members dedicated to assisting hospitalized veterans.

VFW is a tax-exempt organization under section 501(c)(19) of the Internal Revenue Service Code and contributions are deductible under section 170(c).

Services: How We Help

What you may not know about us is our continuing commitment to country and community. Our mission extends to those troops serving overseas today and their families waiting back home. VFW's four main objectives — preserving and extending veterans rights, advocating a strong national defense, promoting patriotism and serving local communities — are the core of our existence.

These four goals are best illustrated by:

- Lobbying Congress on behalf of veterans through VFW's National Legislative Service, and monitoring care and seeking assistance through VFW's National Veterans Service. Both functions are especially critical as the number of wounded from the Iraq War continues to grow.
- Keeping a close eye on overseas troop deployments and the Pentagon's budget through VFW's National Security and Foreign Affairs section.
- Educating schoolchildren with the help of VFW members through VFW's Citizenship Education, Publications and Youth Development, Scholarship & Recognition departments.
- Serving communities at the local level, such as VFW Post (chapter) members assisting the families of deployed troops, as well as maintaining Post relief funds to help the needy.

To file a claim, please contact the nearest VFW representative or call our toll-free HelpLine at 1-800-VFW-1899. Also, a list of VFW service officers is available on the Internet at www.vfwdc.org. Click on "National Veterans Service" then click on "Directory." Or e-mail us at vfw@vfwdc.org.

How You Can Help

Join Today!

How do you know if you're eligible for VFW membership? Just look at our color-coded map. Service in the countries colored yellow may make you eligible.

If you are a U.S. citizen and have served honorably as a member of the Armed Forces of the United States in a foreign war, insurrection, or expedition which has been recognized with a campaign medal, ribbon or badge (or) served on the Korean peninsula or its territorial waters for not less than 30 consecutive days, or a total of 60 days (or) while a member of the armed forces served in an area that entitled you to receive special pay for hostile fire or imminent danger, you qualify.

Contact

Visit www.vfw.org or call the VFW Membership Department at (816) 756-3390.

Homes for Our Troops

http://www.homesforourtroops.org/site/PageServer?pagename=homepage

Passion: Who We Are

Homes for Our Troops (HFOT) builds new handicap accessible homes and adapts existing homes for handicap accessibility for severely injured and disabled veterans. Along with providing for the physical necessities of living with disabilities, providing these homes at no cost to the veteran gives him/her a solid foundation and safe haven to an otherwise fragile and uncertain future that they and their families face. Providing a home to a veteran and his/her family at this disruptive point in their lives helps to promote a more stable future and a better chance for recovery.

Homes for Our Troops is a non-profit, non-partisan 501©(3) organization helping Servicemen and Women who have selflessly given to their country and have returned home with serious disabilities and injuries. We assist injured servicemen and women by raising donations of money, building materials and professional labor and coordinating the process of building a new home or adapting an existing home for handicapped accessibility. These services are provided at no cost to the veteran.

Services: How We Help

Our first and foremost goal is to provide homes that allow the veteran and his/her family to live in a home suited for the physical requirements of the veteran's disabilities. The handicap modifications depend on the type of injury, but they can include wide doorways, roll-in showers and baths, grab bars and railings, motion-activated lights and security systems, wheelchair-level countertops and appliances and specialized toilets. There are also many, many items that are needed to address day-to-day issues that you never think about until you are injured – like a TDD phone with a blinking light so a deaf person knows if the phone is ringing, or a keyless entry system so a veteran with a paralyzed upper body can lock and unlock their front door.

Along with the emotional strain of a loved one being seriously injured, there is a great financial strain on the family as well. A spouse or parent often has to quit their job in order to be with the veteran during their recovery and rehabilitation, which can often take over a year. Other costs like frequent travel needed to maintain a household is a further rain on the family. By providing a handicap accessible home at no cost to the veteran, this allows the veteran and his/her family to get back on their feet and be able to plan for a future that was put on hold due to their injuries.

The veteran and his/her family have many stresses in their lives due to the veteran's injuries and the difficult and painful recovery that follows. We believe that undertaking the building or modification of a home is an added stress that they do not need. That is why HFOT manages the home building process, including identifying vendors, managing the work, coordinating materials deliveries and labor services, obtaining permits and paying the bills. We involve the family in the major decisions, but they do not need to worry about dealing with the many stresses that come with the home building process.

HFOT provides handicap accessible homes for severely disabled veterans. Our projects vary from building a new home, to purchasing and adapting an existing home, to making handicap adaptations to a home already owned by a veteran. HFOT raises donations of money, building materials and professional labor and coordinates the process of building a new home or adapting an existing home for handicapped accessibility. Our services are provided at no cost to the veteran or his/her family.

How You Can Help
* Home Projects

When we undertake a project, we reach out to the local community to request donations of home construction materials and labor as well as monetary donations. We work in the veteran to determine the scope of the work based on the needs of their disability, family size and other similar considerations. We then manage the construction process from start to finish.
* Community and Business Support

Individuals and local businesses willing to donate home construction materials or labor can register on our web site—www.homesforourtroops.org - to let us know what materials or services they can provide if we were to take on a project in their area. Go to the Donate page, click on Donate Supplies or Labor, and fill in the requested information.

We also are seeking relationships with regional and national businesses. We currently have sponsorships from Simonton Windows, Hy-Lite, Fypon and Moen. Along with the knowledge that your company is assisting the most seriously wounded of our veterans, you will also be able to promote your relationship with our organization with your own business partners. Please call Kirt Rebello at 508-823-3300 if your company is interested in providing home construction materials or labor on a regional or national basis.

Finally, there are always costs that we must pay – especially the purchase of land – that require us to use monetary donations. A donation of any amount helps us to have the funds needed to undertake and complete these home projects.

Contact
In order to qualify for our services, the veteran must be eligible under the guidelines for the VA's Specially Adapting Housing Grant. Our application can be downloaded from our web site or can be mailed by calling our office, and it details the specific requirements to qualify for our assistance. If you have questions about the application or eligibility, call our office at 508-823-3300 and ask for Kirt Rebello, our Director of Projects and Veterans Affairs.

Sew Much Comfort
http://www.sewmuchcomfort.org/index.html

Passion: Who We Are
At *Sew Much Comfort*, we are inspired when the service members, family members, staff and hospital volunteers comment on the difference the clothing makes in the lives

of the troops. They are able to get out of their bed, their room and even the hospital and resume life again! A hospital volunteer at Walter Reed Army Medical Center told us, "I didn't realize how much help your clothing is to these guys – they absolutely love it! From now on Sew Much Comfort is going to be one of the first things I mention when I meet the soldiers!"

American military personnel are serving their country in a variety of dangerous situations and locations across the globe. As a result of discharging their duties, a number of them are seriously wounded. While the medical community is doing a phenomenal job of addressing their medical situations, they don't address issues such as clothing that will accommodate medical devises and situations, like braces, casts, prosthetics, neurological issues and burns.

Have you ever seen an external fixator attached to the injured leg of an American Service Member? *Sew Much Comfort's* purpose is to provide wounded military members with adaptive clothing that fits over and makes allowances for their appliances. With suggestions and requests from staff and service members, hundreds of volunteer seamstresses across the country have joined forces to produce clothing that addresses the needs of wounded military members.

How We Help

Sew Much Comfort's goal is to provide custom-made "adaptive" clothing, which isn't available from commercial clothiers or medical suppliers, for service members to wear during their recuperation process, at no cost to the service member. Adaptive clothing accommodates their medical devises and situations, provides for ease of use, personal independence and minimizes the visual impact of their medical condition. The objective is to provide each service member with a complete wardrobe of adaptive clothing in order to give them comfort and maintain their dignity. *Sew Much Comfort* is providing an average of 1,000 clothing items each month to over 30 medical centers, wounded warrior barracks, VA hospitals, Landstuhl and Combat Surgical Hospitals.

The majority of our clothing items have been developed from staff requests. Their response is as enthusiastic as the troops! One staff member said that, when he came back from vacation, he thought he was on the wrong floor because the burn patients were up and walking around! Recently, a young medic injured in a helicopter crash sent a thank you note to the ladies who sewed his clothing saying the clothing was "the bomb". A Colonel, who had recently returned from Iraq, wrote, "Thank you for helping the wounded troops. I was assigned to the 332nd Expeditionary Medical Group at Balad AB, Iraq from August 2005 to January 2006. Since our unit was a combat trauma hospital, we saw it all. We had many congressional delegations, distinguished visitors, and entertainers visit us, but what you do makes more of a difference than all the efforts of those other people combined. May God bless you and your work." What a powerful message to our seamstresses about the importance of their work!

How You Can Help

Sew Much Comfort has volunteers in almost every state. They come from across the social and political spectra. Every one of them appreciates the courage and sacrifice of the men and women on the front lines. To date, they have made over 15,000 adaptive items. With this large corps of volunteers and the scope of the need, there's a niche for everyone. A group of California women, the "Sunset Beach Sweatshop", coordinate seamstresses throughout their state, including volunteers from a nearby women's prison. Members of another group, the "Monday Night Football Ladies", sew and socialize while their husbands watch the game! Girl Scouts and Boy Scouts have run clothing drives, church groups cut out patterns and NFL/MLB organizations donate team clothing to be adapted for wounded soldiers who, as fans, have been supporting these teams all their lives and are now feeling the support from their hometown teams! In order to volunteer, go to the website and contact the Regional Coordinator in your area!

Contact

Obtaining the clothing is as easy as having Internet access or a cell phone! Service members who are wounded or their families, can order the clothing online through the website (www.sewmuchcomfort.org). If you don't have Internet access, please feel free to call (703) 798-0127 and leave a message! It's Ginger's cell phone. She'll get back to you as soon as possible! If we know your waist measurement, t-shirt size, injuries and your mailing address, we can get your clothing directly out to you! If you are in a hospital – ask the personnel to see if the clothing is stocked in your hospital! We are more than willing to work with any hospital, clinic or ward to make the clothing available to wounded service members. If you have a special request, or a favorite sports team – please let us know. We will do our best to get your clothing out in a timely manner!

- Ginger Dosedel, co-founder and CEO, can be reached regarding issues related to distribution and media– ginger@sewmuchcomfort.org.
- Michele Cuppy, co-founder and CFO, can be reached regarding donations (personal and corporate) and website issues– Michele@sewmuchcomfort.org
- Debra Galligan, co-founder and COO, can be reached regarding volunteer opportunities– debra@sewmuchcomfort.org.

Regional Coordinator information is also available on the website, so you can obtain information about volunteering in your state!

Project Prayer Flag

http://www.projectprayerflag.org/

Passion: Who We Are

Project Prayer Flag first realized its beginning shortly after the events of September 11th, 2001. During this time of Military deployments and sacrifices, millions of prayers of support went out to our Military Service members and their families.

Project Prayer Flag began as a way of giving comfort and a piece of America, to the troops who Defend and instill Freedom. We began the Project by sending a thank you card, a small American "cloth" pocket flag and a humble gift to a U.S. Service member who had deployed overseas.

Today, over 190,000 U.S. Soldiers have received the small American flag and hope that they carry with them in their pocket. They are reminded of the prayers of millions and the hope of Freedom that they inspire. We continue the Project today, with a fervent belief in the power of Freedom and dedication to those who wear the Uniform and serve our Country.

Services: How We Help

The mission of Project Prayer Flag is to support, boost morale and improve the quality of life of U.S. Armed Forces personnel and their families within The United States and International deployment areas. Project Prayer Flag believes, contributes and enhances a cooperative relationship between U.S. Military communities and the supporting civilian organizations, Faith Institutions and Business communities.

Project Prayer Flag continues to enhance morale and support programs affecting Regular, Active, Reserve and National Guard Military members, their families and respective Government support organizations.

We believe by supporting our Military Personnel through various outreach and support programs, we will enable them to better perform their mission of Protecting and Instilling Freedom not only in America, but throughout the world. Project Prayer Flag believes in ensuring a sure foundation through Faith and support of an American and International community that cares.

The Department of Defense has approved Project Prayer Flag to be a Military support organization through the America Supports You program; and we remain focused to supporting those who remain committed to ensuring the Freedoms that we all enjoy.

Locations Served: United States, International and Worldwide Programs /Services
Patriot Packs™- Project Prayer Flag packets.
Military Units, Commanders, Chaplains and Solders, each receive a personal cloth American Pocket Flag, an encouraging bookmark with a Bible verse & a thank you card with a morale boosting message printed on them. Over 190,000 have been shipped to Iraq and Afghanistan.

Operation Christmas Care™

Project Prayer Flag receives thousands of requests from soldiers who wish to have an American Family send them a Christmas package during the Holidays. American Families send the soldier a Christmas box with goodies and gratitude for the solider! The American family "Adopts the Soldier" for their duration of Military Service.

Freedom Families™

Project Prayer Flag volunteers answer the requests for help and support from those Military Family members at home and abroad. Volunteers conduct Hospital Visitations; Faith based family outreaches and related Military support events.

Any deployed active duty or reserve service member, their families and Unit Liaisons (Chaplains / Commanders / NCO'S), may review our web site and contact us requesting support. We will ensure a timely response and make every effort to respond to the request.

Project Prayer Flag supports Active duty, Reserve and National Guard members and their families. In addition, we support and help those organizations who perform similar support and Government related U.S. contractors.

How You Can Help

Many of our support programs are dependant on the generosity and help of many business and volunteers. The best way to help is through monetary donations. These gifts allow us to be flexible and mobile with our support services. Many companies and individuals have donated and have allowed us to reach thousands with hope and the love of fellow Americans who care.

Contact
For information on how you can help and the programs available for service members and their families, please review our website at www.ProjectPrayerFlag.Org.You may also reach us at:
Project Prayer Flag, c/o Shawn or Angelica Black
108 Clearbrook,
Irvine, Ca 92614
Or our new satellite office at
Project Prayer Flag , C/O Shawn or Angelica Black
P.O. Box 907
Big Bear Lake Ca, 92315

Operation Ensuring Christmas
Robert McDowell - Founder/President
www.OpChristmas.org

Passion: Who We Are
My love for our Armed Forces came from growing up in a Hero's home. Although I never served in the military, my father, Robert L. Z. McDowell, was severely wounded in WWII on Letye Islands in the Philippines. Because of his bravery and sacrifice, as a child, I remember thinking that my father singlehandedly won the war with Japan. As my father told me his stories, his experience became my experience and his love of service became my love of service. I owe my love for children to my parents, too. They cared very deeply for the health and happiness of children and it showed in all they said and did. It was only natural that this passed on to me. So, after the start of Operation Enduring Freedom as we began to lose another generation of heroes, I began hearing stories of military children being left behind and my two passions united as one and Operation Ensuring Christmas (OEC) was born.

In the summer of 2006, I was at Disney enjoying an afternoon getting to know the family of SFC David Salie who was killed in Baqubah, Iraq. We brought the family in for their Operation Ensuring Children Christmas in July VIP vacation. His mother and grandmother told me that Hunter, who was four years old, ". . . for the most part, had shut people out, been quiet and introverted since losing his father. Since being at Disney, he has opened up, talking to people, maybe this really is a magical place." This is one of many examples of why helping these children be kids again is my passion and my purpose.

Services: How We Help
Operation Ensuring Christmas provides financial, moral and rehabilitative support to the Children of Fallen American Troops by providing them Christmas Gift Cards at Christmas and a 'Christmas in July', VIP theme park trip to Orlando, Florida. This support is to help them recover from the grief and trauma caused by the ultimate sacrifice a child can make for their country...the loss of a parent serving our nation in a time of war.

Operation Ensuring Christmas was founded for the purpose of bringing a little extra Christmas, cheer to children who have lost a parent in Iraq and Afghanistan after 9/11. For some this will be the first Christmas without their parent. While we may not be able to make this a *merry* Christmas we all know and love the look of a child's face when they open a Christmas gift. Any problems or heartache seem to fade away even if only for a while as they excitedly open their presents.

The grief and trauma they suffer is often compounded by the tragic way their parents have died in combat. They are constantly reminded in graphic ways through the intense media coverage of the war in pictures and graphic detail of how their parents may have suffered. Through our 'Christmas in July' program we try to make a difference in the lives of these children by helping them escape for a while and just be *kids again*. Many of these children have fallen through the cracks and did not receive substantial benefits following their loss. This may be the only way they ever get to experience a Theme Park vacation that so many of us take for granted. Their parents gave their lives for our "pursuit of happiness". We simply want to be sure that *their* children have the same opportunity.

We hope to provide our programs to all of the children of the fallen as soon as we have sufficient funds available. Beyond that our ultimate goal would be to go out of business by having no more children in need of our programs. Until that day comes we will strive to be a respected, viable organization able to handle any number of children who need us in the foreseeable future.

We should all honor the loss of our very brave military men and women who have made the Ultimate Sacrifice for our country. One way to honor them is to take care of the children they left behind who have made the Ultimate Sacrifice that a *child* can make. They are this nations VIP's, Very Important *'Precious lil heroes'*.

The Operation Ensuring Christmas Gift Card Program sends the children of Fallen Troops Christmas Gift Cards during the Christmas Holiday season. The Christmas Gift Cards are put in a Christmas card with a copy of several donor sentiments to the children, placed in an envelope and sent by Ground Carrier to the children. The donor sentiments are messages of condolences and hope provided by donors when making their gift to OEC. Those cards that are sent just prior to Christmas Day are sent 1 or 2 day air to be sure the children get them before *Santa* arrives. Sending the children a Christmas Gift Card is the most efficient and cost effective way for these children to get a few more of the presents they have asked Santa to bring them for Christmas.

On OEC's web site, www.opchristmas.org, there are pictures of children with their Christmas Gift Cards or with presents purchased with the cards. When you see the smiles on their faces, you get a sense that we have brought a little extra Christmas cheer to the children. It also let's these children know that the American people care and have not forgotten them, especially at Christmas time.

OEC's Christmas in July program sends the Children to Orlando, Florida for a VIP Theme Park vacation. The children pick the park they wish to visit. The vacation plans are then made through AAA Travel, a well respected national travel agency. At www.opchristmas.org, you can see pictures of the children as they spin, splash and ride their way to being kid's again.

We have received numerous letters from surviving parents who tell us the parent who was lost promised their children a Theme Park trip to Orlando when they came home only to be lost before their return. We help to keep the promise made by these American Heroes to Americas *'precious lil heroes'*.

To be eligible for the programs provided by Operation Ensuring Christmas, the surviving parents of children who have lost a parent in Iraq or Afghanistan since 9/11, need only to go to our web site www.opchristmas.org and fill out a simple application. Once the information provided is verified, the children are placed in our files in the order the application was received. Christmas Gift Cards are sent to the Children the first Christmas after the applications are received and the families are notified when funds are available to send their children on their Christmas in July VIP vacations.

How You Can Help

Operation Ensuring Christmas needs your financial support to continue providing our programs to these *'precious lil heroes'*. To make a donation online or get a mail in donation form, please visit www.opchristmas.org. If you or your company would like to become an OEC sponsor or put on a fund raiser to benefit OEC please visit www.opchristmas.org or call 321-251-7850.

If you are the surviving parent of children of a Fallen Hero lost in Afghanistan or Iraq and would like to apply for our programs for your children, please visit www.opchristmas.org for a simple application form or call 321-251-7850.

Contact
Robert McDowell–Founder/President
www.OpChristmas.org
e-mail: oechristmas@aol.com
Phone: (321) 251-7850
Cell: (407) 702-7943

Mothers of Military Support
www.mothersofmilitarysupport.org

Passion: Who We Are

Mothers Of Military Support is a tax-exempt, 501(c)3 organization founded by Mrs. Elizabeth Johnston in 2003. Our mission is to provide positive support of our service members, family and community by providing services that are consistently available, accessible, and responsive to the needs of individual service members, families, and groups seeking assistance; to work with the community to contribute, facilitate, and promote awareness of the needs of our men and women in the armed service to the enrichment of all.

Our goals are to provide high-quality, compassionate and comprehensive services to as many military personnel and their family's as possible by offering a wide range of services such as sending soldiers needed item (Comfort kits) in order to boost moral. We also are hosts to a talk show called "Military Soup" that provides helpful information for soldiers and their families as well as other topics concerning our military, past and present.

We are expanding our online internet presence that will provide service members and their families with access to our online community in order to corresponds with each other as well as purchase products that help support Mothers Of Military Support. Mothers Of Military Support (MOMS) was founded by Elizabeth Johnston, after learning her son was being deployed to war. Struggling to stay strong, Elizabeth listened intently to what her son had to say. As he sat next to her, he explained that he and his fellow Marines were not afraid to fight for this country nor were they afraid to die for this country. Their true concerns were that when they returned, an angry nation of people would be waiting for them, repeating history of the Vietnam War era. Elizabeth then vowed to support our service members unconditionally.

Services: How We Help

- Our first program was sending large shipments of Comfort Kits to the troops that didn't have items readily available to them. In our research, we found that some items might be needed by special request so we will be putting on line a simple request form for families and friends to access to submit requested items. Comfort Kits are one gallon size zip lock bags filled with comfort items with the donors name and address packed with it.

- Project "Stateside" A multi-service mission that reaches out to deployed families, nationally, with assistance and is also pro-active and instrumental in providing guidance to those returning stateside and also those adjusting to a new civilian role.

- Wives of Military In most communities of base, there is little support for military wives for lack of identifiable resources. Our vision is to provide support information and resources to those wives in need. In addition, provide on line access between service member and spouse. We also encourage them to come together with our program Truffle Tuesdays. This program promotes the networking of family to share experiences concerning deployments in a comfortable surrounding. MOMS purchases Coffee Gift cards to be given to these individual groups.

- Kewl Troops
  This is a program where we take in the donations for neck coolers (a piece of cloth you soak for 15 minutes, it swells with water retention and is used to cool the body's core temperature. parenthesis We pack them HD Ziploc bags so the soldier can just pour a small amount of water in for the reaction. We then place the name and address of the donor in with it.

- Glory Boots
  We purchase Danner Desert Acadia boots (top of the line) for our Military. Command notifies us of who in the unit should receive them. We are currently a distributor for Danner, Inc.

- Pay It Forward
  We purchase gift cards from various variety stores and give to the wives and families of the deployed. This is NOT a hand out...this is an opportunity for American Citizens to say thank you for the great support of military families while their soldier is at war.

How You Can Help
In addition, we will be implementing a membership program that will allow the community, organizations, and businesses to help support our organization. For those that would just like to contribute please visit our web site.

Contact
If you would like to apply for information regarding Comfort kits for our service members please contact Mrs. Elizabeth Johnston at MOMSEvent@aol.com Listed above are just a few of the programs we will implementing. For further information on how M.O.M.S. began, please visit Mothers of Military Support at www.mothersofmilitarysupport.org or email them at MOMSEvent@aol.com

Flags Across the Nation
http://www.flagsacrossthenation.org/

Passion: Who We Are
Flags Across The Nation promotes patriotism through the arts. We create opportunities for children and adults to demonstrate love for America. We are an exciting and uplifting organization that provides fun events and activities that show respect for the American flag and pride in the American fundamentals of freedom and democracy.

How do we manage to bring together kids and families of all ages with veterans, military, and seniors? It's simple, "LOVE FOR AMERICA." Our unique 501(c) (3) organization is grounded with the spirit of creativity and the theme of national patriotism. This allows us to have a wonderful platform to reach out and touch the hearts and souls of our troops and veterans.

We partner with many veteran organizations, such as the VFW, American Legion, The Military Family Network as well as businesses, such as Aspen RMG Group, KidzArt, Faces Photo T-Shirts, My Studio Space, and Waxhaw Family Counseling. Scouts, libraries, public, private and home schools and youth organizations get involved with us to wave patriotism through art and letters.

We are a proud member of the Department of Defense's America Supports You team where Flags Across The Nation's love for the United States of America allows us to make a patriotic difference. This love for America acts as the foundation for the myriad of creative patriotic programs that we offer the youth of America and all civilians, veterans and deployed military.

One of our goals is to reach the entire nation with art exhibits and visual demonstration of patriotism. We have established 3 traveling patriotic exhibits that regularly move to various venues. Our creative patriotism can be seen in museums, public walls, veterans' homes and VA medical centers, and on t- shirts and quilts and in letters to the troops.

We welcome volunteers of all ages. As a grass roots organization, we depend on 1,000's of volunteers from across the nation to step forward to help with promoting patriotism through the arts. Everyone is important and welcome to join with us. This organization is making history, so that 5, 10, 20, 50 years from now, the new youth of our nation will show pride in America as well as understanding the uniqueness and responsibility of freedom.

Life in this nation is rapidly changing as new immigrants arrive to experience a land of the free. We, at Flags Across The Nation, open our patriotic arms and hearts to the new immigrants and wish to give them opportunities to participate side by side with citizens, as we creatively demonstrate patriotism.

Services: How We Help

Flags Across The Nation welcomes you to jump in and participate with us. Our love for country and support for our troops is seen across the nation in our annual art contest, "Flags of Freedom," Letters to the Troops, Blankets 4 Recovery, Robes for Troops, Caps for Troops, Pocket Patriotism, Operation Snail Mail, Tiles of Freedom, Chalk it Up for the Troops, Patriotic Note Cards, Snacks and Stuff for the Troops, Freedom Flags, Messages of Freedom Traveling Exhibit, Quilts of Freedom Traveling Exhibit, the Red White & You traveling patriotic art exhibit and so many other creative and visual projects and events seen by millions in public spaces, government buildings, veterans' homes, military facilities and more.

We recognize the importance of educating kids about flag etiquette and the importance of learning to give to those who serve. We support our deployed troops and wounded veterans through the myriad of creative programs that demonstrate patriotic love for America.

How You Can Help

We have established an annual art contest for kids, and two annual celebrations; I Love America Day on March 19 and Waving Patriotism around September 11 to remember 9/11/01 and to Support our Troops.

You are important in the success of Flags Across The Nation. Stand up, call us, email, and shout, "Hey, I want to help." Each and every one of you is valuable to the continuation of our organization.

Volunteers are loved for taking responsibility for a project. Just let us know that you want to do one of our projects and we will support you and your ideas with press releases and over-all enthusiasm. Let's think about the financial end of running a national organization: Money! Your pennies and dollars help us do what we are doing. If you love and believe in the arts and love and believe in our country, then don't wait. Support Flags Across the Nation today! Individuals, businesses, corporations, schools; take the lead and promote patriotism with us. Your donations, in kind services and pro bono help works for us.

Contact

Can you share? We're a growing organization with a need for more space and operational support. We are based in Charlotte, North Carolina. Contact us and find out how you can make a patriotic difference. You may contact us by calling (704) 654-8529 or email us at info@flagsacrossthenation.org or by mail, P.O. Box 78995 Charlotte, NC 28271-7045. Be sure you visit our web site to see what we are all about. www.flagsacrossthenation.org
Eileen Schwartz, Founder

Military Mom in Action

Kathy and Ken Buckley
www.militarymominaction.org

Passion: Who We Are

Military Mom in Action started in 2003 when our two oldest sons were deployed to Kuwait and then into Iraq as part of Operation Iraqi Freedom. We started sending snack items to them to encourage them and help keep our minds busy. They started sharing them with their friends and the requests to be added to our mailing list grew.

As things were growing, one of our local television stations found out about our two sons being in harms way and started airing stories about what we were doing. Local people who watched asked if their friend or family member could be included on our mailing list.

This list grew to well over 450 names in 14 countries around the world. Our goal has grown with this increase from our two sons to the many we now support even after our sons returned home.

Services: How We Help

Military Mom in Action sends boxes of prepackaged snack items and toiletry items, as needed, to deployed men and women in our armed forces. We also send special boxes to a medical unit in Balad, Iraq for injured personnel. These items are meant to bring a "touch of home" to those who are away from family and friends while defending our freedom and liberty. We have received many letters and e-mails (from officers and enlisted alike) telling about increased morale and encouragement knowing someone cares about them. The following are a few examples:

"I must say they are some of the most <u>outstanding</u> care packages I have received in my almost 30 years of service. The letter you included was very heart felt, a great motivator and spiritual pickup for my men. It is Americans like you 'Mom' that keep us motivated and proud to serve and protect our great country."

"Thanks again for everything. You are all true patriots and my men and I are thankful and grateful."

"I received your box of girl scout cookies, beef jerky and assorted snacks today. The vultures on the wards have already devoured them. They are now happy vultures. Thanks. You are the best."

To this day we continue to provide support and encouragement to our men and women in the armed forces both at home and abroad. As they are away from family and friends, we want to make sure they do not feel forgotten but are encouraged and supported through their deployment.

Our primary outreach is to those who are not receiving anything from home but we are always honored to accept names from anyone who would like the support. We also work with unit Chaplains as they get out to remote areas where normal mail delivery is slow or non-existent. They are then able to reach out to those who need a special touch.

We also work with medical units treating seriously injured and sick personnel. These people usually have only the clothes on their backs and have need of special encouragement. It is our goal to continue to remind the general public not to forget our brave men and women who stand in the gap protecting out freedom and liberty. As several Vietnam era veterans reminded us of how they were treated upon their return home, we do not want that to happen again.

Military Mom in Action sends snack boxes out to those on our mailing list. These boxes contain prepackaged snack items like Damn Good Beef Jerky, cookies, hard candies, cereal bars, fruit snacks, nuts, toaster pastries, gum, etc. We also include a letter of support and encouragement. This letter also shares updates on several different sports like baseball, football, and NASCAR. We include wild life stories, weather updates (sometimes including pictures), encouraging Scripture verses and the ever popular letters from school students, Girl Scouts, Boy Scouts and church youth groups.

We have a few chaplains on our list who get several boxes to hand out as they go into some remote areas where mail is slow or non-existent. These boxes provide a morale boost and are appreciated by all who receive them. They also help enhance their ministry to individuals.

How You Can Help

We gladly accept names on our web site: www.militarymominaction.org or by mail at: PO Box 153 Melrose, NY 12121. We can be reached by e-mail at: milmom@nycap.rr.com. Our phone number is 518-235-0365. All names and addresses are kept strictly confidential and are not given to any person or group for any reason for security reasons.

Contact

Military Mom in Action is a registered 501 © 3 charitable organization.
Questions or comments about Military Mom in Action?
Kathy and Ken Buckley
Email milmom@nycap.rr.com
Call us: 518-235-0365
Or write to us at:
Military Mom in Action
P. O. Box 153
Melrose, NY 12121-0153

Children of Fallen Soldiers Relief Fund

Rebecca Campbell, Founder
http://www.childrenoffallensoldiersrelieffund.org/

Passion: Who We Are

I am a mother of three grown sons, a grandmother with a young grandson and now a granddaughter. My father, grandparents and uncles had all served in our Armed Forces when I was a child and although I was too young to understand the ramifications of the Vietnam War, I began feeling it now as a mother. My youngest son, enlisted in the armed forces, and was deployed to Kuwait on his father's birthday, February 14, 2003; my nephew was in the USMC and had already been deployed to Afghanistan.

I cannot begin to explain the fearful and sleepless nights during my youngest son's year of deployment. You wait for months to hear from him, not knowing where he and his comrades are and wondering if the car that is driving down your street will park in your driveway only to see military officials at your door.

How do you protect your child who is away in another land protecting our freedom and helping to protect the rights of others? You can't, you watch the events as they unfold on television, you lay awake in your bed asking the lord to protect him and all the other troops, and you keep faith that all will be well. However, you imagine and envision horrendous thoughts of your son coming home in a body bag, while you desperately and silently pray for his return.

My son did come home as well as other comrades, many who had lost their limbs and many more who are in Medical Hospitals, such as Walter Reed and Bethesda Naval. Lives are change forever with memories of horrendous sights that many of these troops will have to deal with for the rest of their lives.

I began sending care packages and making baskets filled with holiday items overseas after September 11th and entertained injured soldiers who were receiving care at Walter Reed by taking them out to watch football on big screen televisions and treating them to meals. The courage and honor they displayed despite their loss of limbs was admirable and I am honored to have known them. That was not enough though.

During my son's deployment I decided to raise funds for one or two children that had lost their parent overseas and founded The Children of Fallen Soldiers Relief Fund. Initially the thought was to have friends and family participate in a local walk and collect pledges to help with college financing. Within two weeks we held our first walkathon and raised $3,700.00. I could not find it in my heart to stop and my dream is to provide as much financial and emotional support to the families affected as possible.

Services: How We Help

Our Mission is to help support surviving U.S. Military children and spouses who have lost a loved one during their service in the Afghanistan or Iraq wars by providing them with assistance with College Grants and financial assistance for those in need. Our program was expanded to include children and spouses who have a severely disabled parent or spouse that was injured during their deployment to either war.

Our goal is to make awards to applicants in need, some whose funds were raised or donated from others within their particular State that have children under the age of 18, and who are in need of assistance with housing, repairs, utilities, medical expenses, groceries, clothing, school supplies and other expenses deemed necessary in order to help alleviate their need.

Our grant committee meets quarterly to review applicants that have applied for financial assistance and semi-annually for college applicants. Those in need of assistance can apply through our website at: www.childrenoffallensoldiersrelieffund.org or www.cfsrf.org. In cases where the internet may not be available they may contact us at (301) 865-6327 to request an application packet that will be mailed to their current address. All of our members are volunteers and have full-time employment elsewhere so we ask that all submissions be complete and all required documentation be enclosed in order to be considered.

Our first application was received in January 2005 and since then we have provided $40,500.00 in College Grant Awards that have assisted six spouses and two children of our fallen. Some of these awards are recurring awards as our grant committee has pledged to continue to help some of the recipients until they graduate. The financial awards made to date totals $39,250.00 and have provided assistance to families with eleven children of our fallen.

Many people are not aware of the hardships that these families have had to withstand like children who were left without savings, life insurance proceeds or did not benefit from proceeds from the death gratuity. Or, others whose military parent had requested trust funds be set up by grandparents (or others) and whose wishes were not kept. And still more who were left with minimal funds or who can no longer survive financially on one income. Some of our families have to care for other children who are disabled and the caregivers are no longer able to work or have had to take leave in order to care for their families; others cannot afford to attend their spouses funeral or they live without proper heat, damaged roofs, or leaking basements. Although the needs of these families may vary, one thing they share in common is their broken homes and heavy hearts full of grief.

I maintain a full-time job and neither I nor any of the Officers, Board members or volunteers receive funds for our involvement. All website design, printing, advertising, mailings, etc., are done by myself in my home during off work hours in an effort to keep expenses to a minimum. In order to continue providing them with the necessary support, both emotional and financial, we must now find a way to be there for them during the day the only way we can do this is to raise funds through grant making or receive donations specifically for administration and management expenses.

We do our best to keep expenses low in an effort to provide the help that is necessary to our military families; however, we cannot continue our mission on a 100% volunteer basis and are asking for help with donations that can used for our administrative costs and/or a professional volunteer grant writer that can assist us with our goals.

How You Can Help

The generosity of the public has been overwhelming; many who hold their own charity or fundraiser events to help those in need, children whose parents have opted to forgo presents during birthdays and baptisms, older children who have asked others to send donations to help other children in lieu of birthday presents and many others who honor the memory of their lost service member by having their family and friends donate to our organization in their loved ones name.

Volunteers are needed in all States that can represent the CFSRF and assist others during their fundraising events. We are happy to report that our 2005 financial review indicates that 3% of our revenues received were used for management and administrative expenses. This is the least we can do for those who have guaranteed the continual freedom of our families and children. There is no substitute for a parent, but we are determined to ease their pain and suffering their to children's.

Contact

Rebecca Campbell, Founder
P.O. Box 3968
Gaithersburg, MD 20885-3968
(301) 865-6327
http://www.childrenoffallensoldiersrelieffund.org/

Operation Remembrance

Julie A. Pierce and Kristen T. Pirog
www.operationremembrance.org

Passion: Who We Are

Operation Remembrance is a non-profit organization that provides memory boxes to the families of fallen Soldiers. Created and run by an all volunteer staff of Army spouses, Operation Remembrance allows Army spouses to reach out to fellow spouses during a time of great loss and sorrow. It is our small way of saying we are sorry and their loved ones will not be forgotten. Many say that blood is thicker than water, but anyone who has ever been a part of an Army family knows that camouflage comes close.

How We Help
Our Mission

- To provide memory boxes to the families of fallen Soldiers
- To work in unison with Army organizations to provide support from Army families to Army families
- To research and develop programs that help Army families through their grieving process
- To honor the memory of our fallen Soldiers

Our memory boxes are crafted from cherry wood with a velvet-lined interior. The hinged lid has a glass front opening large enough to display a 4" x 6" photograph. The exterior dimensions of the boxes are 7" x 11" x 3" and the interior dimensions are 9" x 6" x 2". Each memory box is presented with a personalized letter from the volunteers at Operation Remembrance and is tied with a symbolic yellow ribbon.

How You Can Help

For more information on our organization, to make a donation or become a volunteer, please go to: www.operationremembrance.org

Contact:

Currently Operation Remembrance provides memory boxes to the spouse or parents(s) (if the Soldier was single) of Soldiers killed in action while serving in Afghanistan and Iraq and those who die tragically while on active duty. :www.operationremembrance.org

Julie A. Pierce and Kristen T. Pirog
Operation Remembrance
548-A Dickman Rd
Fort Bliss, TX 79906

Specialized Training of Military Parents (STOMP)
STOMP Headquarters Office
6316 S 12th St
Tacoma WA 98465

http://www.stompproject.org/

Passion: Who We Are

STOMP (Specialized Training of Military Parents) is a federally funded Parent Training and Information (PTI) Center established to *assist military families who have children with special education or health needs.* STOMP began in 1985, it is a project of Washington PAVE, and is funded through a grant from the U.S. Department of Education.

The staff of the STOMP Project is comprised of parents of children who have disabilities and have experience in raising their children in military communities and traveling with their spouses to different locations.

STOMP Philosophy We believe that parents should be the primary spokesperson for their child until the child is confident and able to share that responsibility.

We believe that a child with special educational needs has the right to an education developed to address his or her unique needs and abilities whether they are academic, social, vocational or behavioral.

We believe that the STOMP staff and volunteers should never take the role of the parent, but instead should provide information, assistance and training to enable the parent to feel confident in their role as their child's best advocate.

This combination allows STOMP to deliver training information and to facilitate empowerment beyond o ur resources. The STOMP Project provides *information about parent rights and responsibilities* in achieving special education services for military children whether located in the United States or overseas. The Project also *assists military families in accessing resources* for their children by enabling them to navigate a variety of educational and medical systems/programs, both military and civilian, regardless of their current duty station/location.

Services: How We Help

STOMP serves families in four main ways:

1. By providing information and training about Laws, regulations and resources for military families of children with disabilities
2. By connecting families to other families
3. By assisting parents and professionals in developing their own community parent education/support group
4. By providing a voice to raise awareness of issues faced by military families of children with disabilities.

For military families of children with disabilities, *STOMP is a one-stop shop for information and training regarding special education and other resources.* STOMP is proud to be a Project of Washington PAVE, a grass roots parent-directed organization. This is a powerful combination that brings together:

Expert, comprehensive knowledge on disability/ special education laws, rights, regulations and responsibilities as they pertain to military families

A wealth of personal experience, network of personal contacts

A parent driven approach

STOMP is a parent-directed project exists to empower military parents, individuals with disabilities, and service providers with knowledge, skills, and resources so that they might access services to create a collaborative environment for family and professional partnerships without regard to geographic location.

The STOMP Project *provides workshops and presentations* on a variety of subjects. In the last two years, STOMP has provided workshops all over the world. From Aviano AFB, Italy to Fort Stewart Georgia, to the Marine Corps EFMP STOMP Training held here in Washington state, parents and professionals alike from all branches of service have benefited from STOMP trainings and will continue to benefit for years to come. Each workshop is planned and carefully tailored to best meet the needs and concerns of families at the specific installation/location, taking into account the unique strengths and challenges of the community. Workshop topics typically include (but are not limited to):

- Working with the educational or early intervention planning teams to get services for their child who has a disability.
- Accessing educational and medical records and developing a comprehensive home file.
- Accessing resources in both current duty stations and future duty assignments so that the child can begin receiving services quickly when the family transfers.
- Making informed decisions with respect to overseas assignments and/or services within DoDDS (Department of Defense Dependent Schools) overseas and DDESS (Domestic Dependent Elementary & Secondary Schools).
- Working effectively with military systems such as Tri-Care, and the EFMP (Exceptional Family Member Program) for their branch of service.

For more information regarding trainings, please contact the STOMP HQ office directly and as much in advance as possible of your projected workshop date. Due to high demand, bookings for workshops can be made 9-12 months in advance.

How You Can Help
In addition to the 2 STOMP offices, STOMP has a network of volunteers who have attended one of the annual STOMP Parent Professional Teams Workshops. This network has been in existence for over ten years but has recently been revitalized! Find more about PPTW (Parent Professional Teams Workshops)
STOMP Headquarters Office

Contact
6316 S 12th St
Tacoma WA 98465
Phone: 253-565-2266 v/tty 1-800-5PARENT v/tty
Fax: 253-566-8052
Contact :stomp@washingtonpave.com
STOMP Central Regional Office
3910 Via Del Trinidad
Sierra Vista AZ 85650
Ph/Fax: 520-458-7911
Contact: amartinez@washingtonpave.com
STOMP East Coast Office
115 Mazak Court
Ft. Bragg, NC 28307
Ph/Fax: (910) 864-9165
Contact: vpatterson@washingtonpave.com

National Military Family Association
http://www.nmfa.org

Passion: Who We Are

The National Military Family Association (NMFA) is the only national nonprofit organization that focuses solely on the families of the Army, Navy, Air Force, Marine Corps, Coast Guard, the Commissioned Corps of the Public Health Service, and the National Oceanic and Atmospheric Administration. For more than 35 years, NMFA's staff and volunteers, comprised predominantly of military family members, have built a reputation as the leading experts on military family issues.

Services: How We Help

NMFA works tirelessly with the Department of Defense, other federal agencies and federal, state, and local governments to improve the lives of military families. Recently NMFA successfully led the fight to overturn a proposal that would have provided greater benefits for survivors of service members killed in combat than service members who died elsewhere. Now, all surviving families of service members who were killed on active duty receive the same benefits. For military children, NMFA hosts *Operation Purple* Summer Camps, a free summer camp program for military children coping with the deployment of one or both of their parents. In appreciation of the value military families place on education, NMFA's Joanne Holbrook Patton Military Spouse Scholarship Program allows military spouses the opportunity to receive financial assistance to further their educations.

While our servicemen and women serve the nation in foreign and domestic lands, their families also serve. In order for service members to focus effectively on their missions, they must be confident that their families are physically and emotionally secure. There is nothing that can fully prepare the family for the challenges that come when a loved one is called to serve, but Americans can ensure that these families have the tools and resources available to face their challenges head-on and with success. This is a vital role we call on everyone to fulfill by joining NMFA.

How You Can Help.

Visit the National Military Family Association website, www.nmfa.org, for more information on how you can support military families by working with NMFA.

Military Money

http://www.militarymoney.com/

Contact

www.nmfa.org

Passion: Who We Are

The lifestyle of the military family can prove both challenging and rewarding – especially to the family finances. Saving, investing and budgeting on a military income can require special considerations, skills and planning. Frequent moves... career changes for the spouse... new schools for the kids... Let's face it: Simply raising a family within the ranks of the military can pose unique obstacles.

InCharge® Education Foundation believes that a military family's commitment to serve must not inhibit its ability to save – and build for a brighter future. InCharge developed *Military Money*® to provide an authoritative financial resource for military families and help ensure the fighting readiness of America's armed forces by enhancing their financial readiness to make informed decisions in their everyday lives.

The magazine and its companion website, www.militarymoney.com, explore such personal finance issues as money management, home and family life for military families, education and career advice, deployment and relocation, and transitioning to the civilian world.

Created as part of the U.S. Department of Defense's "Financial Readiness Campaign" with the support of the Office of the Under Secretary of Defense for Military Community and Family Policy, *Military Money* magazine reaches an estimated 500,000 readers each quarter through distribution at military bases around the world. Additionally, "Military Money Minute" radio broadcasts are heard daily on American Forces Radio Network and the U.S. Army's Soldiers Radio and Television Network.

Military Money received the 2004 Consumer Financial Information Award from the Association of Financial Counseling and Planning Education (AFCPE) and the 2005 Dr. Lowell G. Daun Award from the National Military Family Association.

Services: How We Help
InCharge Education Foundation, the national non-profit organization that publishes *Military Money*, develops a variety of innovative personal finance tools ranging from content-rich magazines, workbooks and websites to print-, CD- and web-based educational programs to meet the needs of unique groups of consumers – such as America's military families – that are underserved by traditional media.

Contact
Military personal finance managers (PFMs) and military family support personnel may be eligible for free personal finance education materials. To order the tools that best meet your needs, browse the InCharge product catalog at www.militarymoney. com/financial_readiness. To discuss corporate sponsorship and support, call 407-532-5616. And please visit www.militarymoney.com.
Military Money and InCharge Education Foundation
Carl Surran
Editor, Military Money
InCharge Education Foundation
2101 Park Center Dr., #310
Orlando, FL 32835

Operation Troop Appreciation

Kristen Holloway
http://www.operationtroopappreciation.org

Passion: Who We Are
Upon learning of a friend's deployment, OTA President & Founder, Kristen Holloway embarked on what she thought was a single gesture of support for a friend. At the

same time, (future) OTA Vice President, Monica Orluk was looking for a way to do more to support the troops than sending letters and care packages to a deployed loved one. These are only two of the many individual volunteers who came together to form Operation Troop Appreciation. Two years and over 10,000 soldiers later, OTA has grown into a team of Americans who demonstrate every day the spirit of volunteerism that can only be found in America. The desire to help deployed soldiers would catapult into the creation of a national non-profit organization benefiting deployed American troops fighting the War on Terror.

In March 2006, President Bush personally awarded OTA President Kristen Holloway the Presidential Volunteer Service for her work with OTA. His award and recognition of OTA's important work is the highest honor a volunteer or non-profit organization can receive. In October 2005, President and Founder Kristen Holloway was featured and awarded one of eight "Mothers and Shakers" awards from Redbook Magazine. This annual award recognizes women who make a real difference in their community via volunteer work and grass roots efforts. Previous winners of this award include: First Lady Laura Bush, crusader Erin Brokovich, Duchess of York Sarah Ferguson and journalist Katie Couric.

Operation Troop Appreciation puts the soldier serving and sacrificing for our country on a pedestal. We want to present a united front to our deployed military by supporting them as individuals, for every one of them memorializes our nation's past, sacrifices to maintain our nation's culture and freedoms, and ensures the safety and freedom of our nation's future generations.

A non-political, non-partisan organization, we believe that America's support of our deployed troops should extend beyond political alignment or personal feelings of our military involvement. Working with all branches of the military, active duty, National Guard and Reserves, we strive to reach out to as many troops as we can.

Services: How We Help

Since July 2004, OTA [a 501 ©(3) non-profit organization] has provided more than 10,000 deployed troops "wish list" items that are carefully tailored to meet their unique wants and needs. We've worked with dozens of deployed units (a central point-of-contact within each unit helps us determine what those needs are) in Iraq, Afghanistan, Kuwait and Africa. We even provided badly needed Under Armour® t-shirts for a battalion of 750 Louisiana National Guard troops deployed to New Orleans to help in the aftermath of Hurricane Katrina.

In addition to helping our soldiers on the ground, we have also provided gifts such as DVDs, video games, CDs, board games and phone cards to hundreds of wounded heroes recovering in military hospitals in Iraq, Germany and the United States.

How You Can Help

As all non-profits require, OTA also relies solely on private and corporate donations to do its work. OTA's specialty is providing little luxuries and "wish list" items that extend beyond the basic care package. OTA strives to provide Under Armour ® clothing, musical instruments, phone cards, and other relatively more expensive items that our troops cannot otherwise obtain for themselves. As such, financial contributions are always welcome!

For those who would prefer to donate "things" instead of money, we have four items we continuously collect: New or gently DVDs, CDs, video games (PS2 or Xbox) and unused phone cards. Civic, religious, school and other groups have completed collection drives for these types of things that are ALWAYS in high demand by our troops. We invite individuals or groups to continue this trend and help collect these things for OTA to send to those deployed units who request such items.

Also, in the spirit of grass-roots efforts and word-of-mouth that gave OTA its start, the organization is always looking for passionate, committed volunteers who can continue to carry the torch and spread the word of the organization to friends, family, employers, religious groups, etc. Because OTA does not use and donated funds to purchase advertising or marketing services, it relies solely on its volunteer base to bring exposure to OTA.

We would also love those with creative ideas for planning and executing fundraising activities to contact us. We have done concerts, golf outing, a "Soldier's Christmas in August" vendor sale, and other community projects and fundraisers. We'd love to your ideas and your help to continue in this vein.

We are also looking for individuals, small-business and corporations to "sponsor" a unit of deployed troops. Sponsorship opportunities are available for any donation level.

We often get offers from people to help us pack boxes, stuff envelopes, or other "traditional" care package activities. OTA is unique in that we rely on the manufacturers of the products we buy to ship these things directly to the troops. This keeps our costs low and subsequently, OTA does not have to perform on these types of traditional activities.

Contact

For more information on OTA, our projects, news and update, please go to our website at www.OperationTroopAppreciation.org
All donations are tax-deductible (as allowed by law), and can be sent to:
Operation Troop Appreciation
PO Box 14550
Pittsburgh, PA 15234
Or made securely on-line on our website.
www.OperationTroopAppreciation.org
Visit our forum on Military Family network: www.eMilitary.org/forums
Community Connections Forums > MFN Programs and Community Connections > Operation Troop Appreciation

Operation Gratitude

Carolyn Blashek
www.operationgratitude.com

Passion: Who We Are

The benefits of the Operation Gratitude program can be found in the Mail Call section of the Operation Gratitude website, www.operationgratitude.com which displays thousands of letters from troops that have received the care packages. One theme that runs through the letters is how surprised and appreciative the troops are that total strangers have taken the time to show they care. Perhaps the impact is best described by Major General Mark Hertling, then Assistant Division Commander, 1st Armored Division, Baghdad Iraq:

"What kind of difference has it made? Our Commanders made it a point to visit every single battalion and brigade during the three days surrounding Christmas. In every location, I saw numerous Operation Gratitude packages. Every soldier received a personalized note, some holiday cheer, and some treats. And you know what? It wasn't the gifts or the cards or the notes that made such an impression...it was the realization that someone cared about our soldiers as individuals, understood the importance of their mission and appreciated their sacrifice."

Services: How We Help

Operation Gratitude, www.operationgratitude.com, is the nonprofit, all-volunteer organization that sends care packages and letters of support to troops deployed overseas. Its mission is to lift morale, put a smile on a service member's face and express the appreciation of the American people for the sacrifices of the men and women defending our freedom. To date, Operation Gratitude has sent over 153,000 care packages to individual Soldiers, Marines, Airmen and Sailors in Iraq, Afghanistan, Kuwait, Bosnia, Korea, Kosovo, Guantanamo Bay, Africa and onto ships all over the world.

After 9-11, founder Carolyn Blashek felt a passionate desire to help fight the war on terrorism. Although then a 46-year-old mother of two living in Encino, Calif., her first thought was to join the Military. She quickly found out she was too old for duty and started volunteering at the military lounge in the Los Angeles airport. One day in March 2003, a soldier came into the office and broke down at her desk. He was on leave from a war zone for his mother's funeral, his wife had left him and his only child died as an infant—he had no one else in his life. "I'm going back over there; I don't think I'll make it back this time, but it really doesn't matter because no one would even care" he told her. Right then Blashek realized that when bullets are flying, it's critical for troops to know that someone cares about them as an individual. That's when Operation Gratitude was born.

While most organizations ask people to support the troops by writing a check, Blashek wanted to provide a more personal and hands-on connection with our troops overseas. She started asking everyone she met if they knew a deployed service member needing extra TLC so she could send them care packages of snacks and entertainment items. Most importantly, each package would include letters of encouragement from appreciative citizens. Now, Blashek is contacted by leaders and commanders in the field who see the positive impact the Operation Gratitude care packages have on their troops in combat.

This grassroots organization started at Blashek's dining room table but now encompasses churches, schools, businesses and service groups all over the country donating items and writing letters to troops through Operation Gratitude. Since November 2003, Operation Gratitude has conducted its packing Drives in the California Army National Guard Armory in Van Nuys, Calif. Operation Gratitude plans to move into its own facility in 2007. All staffing remains on a volunteer basis and Blashek is committed to keeping it that way.

Operation Gratitude is a 501©(3) organization. All financial donations are tax-deductible and are used entirely to pay the costs of communications and shipping, which average $10-15 per care package. All items included in the packages are donated.

Operation Gratitude is an original member of America Supports You, a nationwide program launched by the Defense Department that recognizes and communicates citizens' support to our military.

President and Mrs. Bush invited Operation Gratitude founder, Carolyn Blashek, to the White House on March 10, 2006 to thank her and the entire organization for their invaluable support of the United States Military.

The organization, now with 2000+ local volunteers and tens of thousands of supporters across the country, holds both a Holiday Drive (that kicks off over the Veteran' Weekend in November) and a Patriotic Drive (which starts during the Armed Forces and Memorial Weekends in May) each year.

How You Can Help

Operation Gratitude welcomes volunteers as well as donations of funds and products for the packages.
Wish List Items include (but are not limited to):
• DVDs and CDs
• International Phone cards
• Computer Flash Drives
• Batteries
• Personal Cooling Products: Bandana Cool-Ties, Battery Operated Mini-fans
• Boxes of Girl Scout or other Cookies (non-chocolate preferred)
• Individual Packets of Trail Mix, Dried Fruit or Nuts, Snack Foods, Beef Jerky, Energy/Power bars, Candy, Gum
• Ready to Eat Food Kits (Tuna, Chicken Salad); other Non-Perishable Food Products
• Packets of Powdered Hot or Cold Beverages
• Disposable Cameras; Handheld Electronic Games
• Novelties (promotional items)
• Mini Stuffed Animals, Small Toys
• Baseball Caps, Knit Hats and Gloves, Neck Warmers, Decorated T-shirts
• Toiletries: Sunscreen, Foot Products, Lip Balm, Body Lotion, Toothpaste, Razors
• Unsealed Personal Letters and Cards
• Used Cell Phones and Ink Jet Cartridges (for recycling)

In just over a year, Operation Gratitude grew from Blashek sending 10 or 15 packages a week from her home to an organization sending tens of thousands of care packages during the year. Blashek's goal is that Operation Gratitude will continue for as long as the United States Military has a service person deployed anywhere in the world. She envisions Operation Gratitude as a permanent means for civilians to show their support and respect for the military in a direct, personal and hands-on manner. Each year, Operation Gratitude will hold both the Patriotic and Holiday Drives, and send packages in between when notified by commanders of urgent situations.

Contact
For more information, please contact:
Carolyn Blashek
16444 Refugio Road

Encino, California 91436
www.operationgratitude.com
cblashek@aol.com

The National Defense University Foundation
www.nduf.org
"The National Defense University has served as one of our country's premier centers for learning and thinking about America's national security."
—President George W. Bush

Passion: Who We Are
The National Defense University looks to the NDU Foundation for financial and program support beyond what is available through government funding. Federal appropriations can not possibly cover the multitude of valuable NDU programs, activities and capital needs. For instance, federal regulations preclude the use of appropriated funds for endowments, honorariums, student awards, and other university activities.

In addition, the NDU military staff and faculty, including the University President, are prohibited by law from any form of fundraising—primary advocates at comparable Universities.

Finally, and perhaps most importantly, the NDU Foundation provides a special opportunity for all America to directly invest in our national security and to help protect our cherished democratic freedoms. The National Defense University Foundation was established in 1982 to support and enhance the mission and goals of the National Defense University (NDU). NDU is America's preeminent institution for military, civilian, and diplomatic national security education, research, outreach, and strategic studies. The main campus is located at Fort McNair in Washington D.C.

How We Help
The NDU Foundation promotes excellence and innovation in education by nurturing high standards of scholarship, leadership, and professionalism. It brings together dedicated individuals, corporations, organizations, and groups that are committed to advancing America's national security and defense capabilities through NDU.

The Foundation provides privately funded resources for:
- Education, Research, Library, and Teaching Activities
- Academic Chairs, Faculty Fellowships, and Student Awards
- Endowments, Honorariums, Seminars, and Conferences
- Multicultural, International, and Interagency Programs
- National Security and Homeland Defense Outreach

What we support:
The NDU Foundation supports the following NDU colleges and programs:
- Industrial College of the Armed Forces (ICAF)
- National War College (NWC)

- Joint Forces Staff College (JFSC)
- Information Resources Management College
- Institute for National Strategic Studies (INSS)
- Center for Hemispheric Defense Studies
- Near East South Asia Center (NESA)
- Africa Center for Strategic Studies (ACSS)
- Center for Technology and National Security Policy (CTNSP)
...And more than 17 other National Security Programs

International Fellows Program

NDU offers one-year fellowships to select senior officers from 44 countries to study and conduct research at either ICAF or NWC. Fellows come to NDU from every continent and have demonstrated exceptional leadership ability within their own military.

The American Patriot Award

Each year the American Patriot Award recognizes an exceptional American who has demonstrated a profound and abiding love of country and whose inspirational leadership and selfless dedication to American national security have significantly advanced our Nation's ideals, values and democratic principles.

The American Patriot Award Gala, hosted by the National Defense University Foundation, is an annual signature event that honors exceptional Americans and showcases the importance of patriotism as an admirable quality of American citizenship.

The event gathers Administration officials, Members of Congress, senior military leaders, and corporate executives from across the Nation to celebrate the unique American spirit of patriotism.

Held at the Ronald Reagan Building and International Trade Center in Washington D.C., the American Patriot Award Gala hosts more than 700 guests who gather to pay tribute to America's greatest patriots.

The evening includes an exclusive reception, a formal dinner, and an inspirational program for the selected honoree. Special remarks are made by prominent individuals who have been particularly touched by the honoree's life and career.

On November 16, 2006 John Glenn will become the eighth honoree of the American Patriot Award following General Colin Powell, The Honorable Caspar Weinberger, former President George H.W. Bush, The Men and Women of our Nation's Defense Team, The Honorable Bob Dole, The Honorable Daniel K Inouye and The Honorable Ted Stevens.

The American Patriot Award's "Sponsor a Patriot" Program

The "Sponsor a Patriot" Program provides the opportunity for exceptional U.S. Service Men and Women to attend the American Patriot Award Gala, NDUF's annual celebration of patriotism.

One of the most stirring moments of the evening occurs as U.S. Service Members, hosted by NDUF through the "Sponsor a Patriot" Program, are thanked by tribute speakers and the other nearly 700 guests in attendance. Last year, those who stood to honor the attending "Patriots" included such notables as General Richard B. Myers, USAF (Ret), Former Chairman of the Joint Chiefs of Staff, and Senators Daniel K. Inouye and Ted Stevens, the 2005 honorees.

The gala's patriots are chosen by senior enlisted officers and many of these young men and women will have recently returned from Iraq, Afghanistan or other overseas deployments. Some may be recovering from injury sustained while deployed. Others will be actively serving their country on military installations and in communities across America. "The opportunity to give these young men and women a special night on the town is wonderful. However, the greatest part of the "Sponsor a Patriot" Program is when, during the ceremony, the patriots are thanked and recognized by tribute speakers, such as Chairman of the Joint Chiefs of Staff Peter Pace in 2005. The grand atrium space in the Ronald Reagan Building and International Trade Center fills with humility and gratefulness. It's overwhelming," says Pam Shilling, NDUF Program and Development Associate and coordinator of the 2006 "Sponsor a Patriot" Program.

Visit us a www.nduf.org or www.americanpatriotaward.org for more information on activities surrounding this great program.

How You Can Help

Support the University that Shapes the National Security Decision Makers of the Future!

You can help support the National Defense University Foundation by making an unrestricted gift or pledge to the Foundation, which can be applied to any program or funding requirement where the need is greatest.

Make a restricted gift or pledge to a special project, program, endowment or activity.

Contact

Consider the wide range of giving options: stocks, cash, real estate, in-kind service or goods, life insurance, bequests, and many other planned giving opportunities.
251 3rd Avenue, Building 20
Fort McNair, DC 20319-5066
202-685-3797
Visit www.nduf.org for more information

Freedom Team Salute
www.freedomteamsalute.com
"The challenges we face together are what make the Army a big family."
• LTC Leon Wiggins (Retired), Freedom Team Salute Recipient

Passion: Who We Are

Freedom Team Salute is a unique Army program that provides a way for Active Duty Soldiers to recognize their team of supporters back home, including spouses, parents, and employers, and for any American to thank Army Veterans for their service and legacy.

Services: How We Help

Active, Guard and Reserve Soldiers can nominate their supporters online at the Freedom Team Salute website at www.freedomteamsalute.com Active Duty Soldiers may nominate their spouses and parents; Reserve and Guard Soldiers may nominate their spouse, parents and employers. Anyone can nominate an Army veteran.

Recipients of a Freedom Team Salute will receive a Commendation package that includes an Army lapel pin, an Army decal, a certificate and a letter signed by the Secretary of the Army and the Army Chief of Staff thanking them for their loyal support of the Army family.

Freedom Team Salute can assist with hosting a public Recognition Ceremony for groups of nominees. The program is supported by a network of Ambassadors who help Freedom Team Salute reach out to the Army support community.

Contact

For more information on the program or to become an Ambassador, please contact Freedom Team Salute at freedomteamsalute@hqda.army.mil

---

Gift From Within
Joyce Boaz, Director
www.giftfromwithin.org

Passion: Who We Are

I've been asked to give an example of how this organization helps trauma survivors, and one particular member's experience with domestic violence comes to mind. She expressed the value of Gift From Within when she said: "GFW changed my life by explaining my symptoms and giving a name to what I suffer. Additionally it grouped me with other women who understood me and validated me."

Mission Statement: Gift From Within (GFW) is a non-profit organization dedicated to those who suffer post-traumatic stress disorder (PTSD), those at risk for PTSD, and those who care for traumatized individuals. GFW develops and disseminates educational material, including videotapes, DVDs, articles, books, and other resources through its website. GFW maintains a roster of survivors who are willing to participate in an international network of peer support. GFW is designated by the Internal Revenue Service as a 501©(3) public charity, eligible to receive tax-exempt grants, gifts, and donations.

Gift From Within was started in 1993 under the direction and guidance of Dr. Frank Ochberg. Dr. Ochberg is a psychiatrist and the former Associate Director of the National Institute of Mental Health, and a member of the team that wrote the medical definition for Post Traumatic Stress Disorder (PTSD). He is the editor of America's first treatment text on PTSD. Dr. Ochberg is more than a trauma specialist; he is one of the pioneers who created the International Society For Traumatic Stress Studies and served on the founding board. He is the 2003 recipient of the Society's Lifetime Achievement Award.

Services: How We Help

Gift From Within has created a credible online environment where trauma survivors, their loved ones, and other supporters find materials that are educational, friendly and supportive. PTSD is real and to those who do not understand it, it can seem mysterious. We offer resources to help explain the condition without being too technical or too superficial. We also offer A-V materials for mental health practitioners, including pastoral counselors, instructors, and trainers. Our programs are being used by the United States Army's and Air Force's Sexual Assault Recovery & Prevention Program Coordinators and in VAs and Bases around the USA and abroad.

In our goal to support trauma survivors, GFW provides a unique matching service. The purpose of GFW's peer support is to give survivors the opportunity to connect emotionally with others about what they are feeling and experiencing. This support system also gives survivors the unique opportunity to help others in need. This service is not meant to be a substitute for any kind of professional help. Participants are screened, required to sign a form and must agree to certain conditions. This network is only open to women at this time. The URL is http://www.giftfromwithin.org/html/penpal.html.

Here are just a few of our resources:

GFW members contribute their art and poetry to our online survivor poetry & art gallery, our personal book reviews section, inspirational stories, finding a therapist, and ideas for coping and living with PTSD. We also provide a list of retreats and respites that tell survivors about comfortable (not hospitals or inpatient facilities) places they can visit to get away from life's stresses for a while. The retreats are located at this link: http://www.giftfromwithin.org/html/retreats.html.

In addition, we have articles and essays written for trauma survivors and professional helpers, a monthly Q&A on PTSD with Frank Ochberg and guest clinicians, and links to other helpful websites including the Military Family Network Forum in which GFW is a contributing member at http://www.emilitary.org. Another excellent resource is The Gateway To PTSD Information at http:// www.ptsdinfo.org. Four national and international organizations are here to help, with articles, references, web-links, mini-courses, 800 phone access and e-mail pen-pal resources. Our Public Service Announcements which aired nationwide on PTSD are included on this Gateway website.

Our educational A-V programs can be found at this link: http://www.giftfromwithin.org/html/video.html.

A few worth mentioning for the audiences reading this book include:

- "Living With PTSD: Lessons for Partners, Friends and Supporters," is valuable to those who care about the PTSD sufferer in their life. It explains what PTSD is and why it is important to learn about the medical disorder, what you can do to help, how to deal with caregiver burden, and how it affects the family and other relationships.
- "Explaining PTSD Is Part of Treating PTSD: Lessons For Mental Health Professionals." Two experts, Dr. Frank Ochberg and Dr. Angie Panos give new therapists, and therapists new to PTSD insightful and thoughtful suggestions about explaining the condition. Dr. Ochberg models describing PTSD to a patient and GFW board member, Dr. Angie Panos, an expert in traumatic stress treatment shows how to explain the causes of PTSD to a general audience.
- "When Helping Hurts: Sustaining Trauma Workers," was produced for trauma workers, relief workers and those exposed to trauma due to their professions or work as volunteers. This program outlines the symptoms of Secondary Traumatization and Compassion Fatigue. It also discusses what organizations and supervisors can do to prevent or reduce the effects of Compassion Fatigue in trauma workers. A shortened version excellent for individuals, training and/or the classroom is available.

- "Recovering From Traumatic Events: The Healing Process," presents recovered survivors and therapists discussing their experiences with the healing process after traumatic events. This film sensitively presents insight into the impact of trauma in the survivor's life, however, the main focus of the film is on what helped or did not help during the healing process. Family members and community will also learn how they can assist in the recovery of their friends, loved ones and neighbors.

Contact

For more information you may contact Director Joyce Boaz at her email address: JoyceB3955@aol.com, by calling (207) 236-8858 or by writing to Gift From Within, 16 Cobb Hill Road, Camden, ME 04843 USA. Please visit the Web site at http://www.giftfromwithin.org.

Twin Towers Orphan Fund
www.TTOF.org

Passion: Who We Are

Created just one day after the attacks of September 11, 2001, the Twin Towers Orphan Fund (TTOF) began its mission to mitigate the damage caused to our nation by ensuring the young sons and daughters of those who perished on 9/11 receive a good education and quality mental and physical healthcare.

Though it is difficult for any child to experience the loss of a parent – consider adding to the mix elements of national shock, fear, anger and disbelief at the public murder of so many innocents, non-stop footage of the collapsing buildings forcing the children to relive their parent's death over and over, the country pulling at them, watching them, putting them under a spotlight (and then abruptly turning it off) - and you soon realize there are many more issues to learn to cope with and understand in order to get past the grief and move on with life.

In addition, the majority of these children experienced some degree of PTSD. Evidence suggests PTSD causes biological changes in the brain chemistry of children and adolescents, affecting them at important stages in their lives. Children appear to be getting better, only to begin experiencing difficulties again as they enter puberty and high school or step into the world and go to college. Even very young children, who did not experience problems at first, begin to struggle as they become more aware of the world around them.

We understand the uniqueness of these very special children. By providing long-term assistance we ensure that when the need arises, they have the resources to begin and/or continue the healing process. With our assistance, these victimized children have the opportunity to lead as normal a life as possible and become responsible, contributing members of society.

We rebuild futures, one child at a time.
Michele Weaver
Co-Founder, Twin Towers Orphan Fund

Services: How We Help

The Twin Towers Orphan Fund was founded on September 12, 2001 for the sole purpose of providing educational and welfare assistance to the children who were orphaned (who lost one or both parents) by the terrorist attacks on September 11, 2001. The mission of the Twin Towers Orphan Fund is to provide long-term higher educational assistance and mental and physical healthcare assistance for (a) children who lost parents in the World Trade Center, at the Pentagon, or onboard the four downed airliners, and (b) children of victims of future terrorist attacks.

Via individual Sec. 529 Higher Educational Saving Accounts funded in the names of the child beneficiaries, as well as general program funds, the TTOF helps to provide: tuition assistance, room and board support, books and supplies and other educational expenses to enrolled students at accredited two- and four-year colleges and universities and recognized trade schools. We provide reimbursements for approved and nationally recognized health care insurance programs, including premiums, co-pays and deductibles, where applicable, for children under the age of 18, or to age 22 if continually enrolled in institutions of higher learning. We also offer supplemental long-term mental heath care assistance by providing reimbursements for individual and group counseling and other means available and approved by the TTOF. Finally, we have funding for other charitable organizations that offer direct services benefiting mental and physical health care, scholastic tutoring for college bound children and other activities deemed beneficial for the long-term well being of enrolled children.

How You Can Help

Operating at under 10 percent administrative overhead, our beneficiaries include more than 1,100 children in 26 states and territories. Nearly 65 percent of the children are 10 years or younger - including 32 babies born after 9/11/01. We continue to receive child registrations.

For additional information visit the Twin Towers Orphan Fund website at
    www.TTOF.org
    4800 Easton Drive
    Suite 109 Suite 109
    Bakersfield CA 93309
    e-mail: info@ttof.org
    Phone: (661) 633-9076.

Beirut Remembrance Walk

Passion: Who We Are

"At approximately 0622 on Sunday, 23 Oct. 1983, the Battalion Landing Team headquarters building in the Marine Amphibious Unit compound at Beirut International Airport was destroyed by a terrorist bomb. The catastrophic attack took the lives of 241 Marines, sailors and soldiers and wounded more than 100 others. The bombing was carried out by one lone terrorist driving a yellow Mercedes Benz stake-bed truck that accelerated through the public parking lot south of the BLT headquarters building, where it exploded. The truck drove over the barbed and concertina wire obstacle, passed between two Marine guard posts without being engaged by fire, entered an open gate, passed around one sewer pipe barrier and between two others, flattened the Sergeant of the Guard's sandbagged booth at the building's entrance, penetrated the lobby of the building and detonated while the majority of the occupants slept. The force of the explosion [12,000 pounds] ripped the building from its foundation. The building then imploded upon itself. Almost all the occupants were crushed or trapped inside the wreckage." —DoD Commission Report

Services: How We Help

The Beirut Remembrance group encourages others to join the procession and walk a lap or three, 50 or even all. Each lap is approximately ½ mile around the pond/gardens and takes under 10 minutes to complete. Those not walking the full distance will be given an index card before each lap with a Marine, Sailor, or Soldier's name/information killed while serving as a Peacekeeper. After completion of the lap, participants are asked to sign the card on the back, and return it so someone else can walk in memory of that soldier. Those 'going the distance' will receive a roster with all the names/information accordingly, checking a name after each lap completed.

The walk is free and open to Beirut Veterans, Family Members, Veterans, Active Duty Military and the general public (Anyone affected by terrorism).

From a Blog online

I am a veteran of the 1983 Beirut Bombing that many people have never even heard of. For the past 22 years I have held back the anger that day has caused me. The fury that only a terrorist attack of that magnitude could possibly cause. I am here today, but 241 of this United States best are gone. I am hoping and praying that I will be able to educate the people of this nation about this attack on our troops so that one day, they will be remembered, as it should be

Contact

For more information on how to support this effort and participate in the annual event, contact:
Bill Kibler   (USMC Beirut Veteran)
2005 Columbia Pike #624
Arlington, VA 22204
bill@beirutveterans.info

Virginia Air & Space Center

www.vasc.org
Visitor Center for NASA Langley Research Center and Langley Air Force Base

Passion: Who We are

From historic air and space craft suspended from the Center's 94-foot ceiling, to giant IMAX films, imaginations will soar with a visit to the award-winning Virginia Air & Space Center, the visitor center for NASA Langley Research Center and Langley Air Force Base.

Located in Hampton, Virginia, the birthplace of America's space program, the Virginia Air & Space Center features dozens of hands-on air and space exhibits that are kid friendly and family approved. Among these are a premiere interactive aviation gallery, *Adventures in Flight*, and more than 30 historic aircraft, including a replica *1903 Wright Flyer* and an actual *DC-9* passenger jet. Visitors can marvel at unique NASA space flight artifacts like the Apollo 12 Command Module, a three-billion-year-old moon rock, a Mars meteorite, and the *Mercury 14*. A variety of interactive exhibits, including state-of-the-art flight simulators, allow guests to launch a rocket, pilot a space shuttle, become an air traffic controller, fly an airplane, and ride in a WWII bomber!

These interactive exhibits provide an engaging environment for learning about Hampton Roads' role in aerospace research, aviation, space exploration and technology. In addition, the Virginia Air & Space Center highlights the wonderful world of science with several blockbuster-traveling exhibits each year.

Guests can also enjoy the ultimate movie experience with a giant-screen IMAX film in the Riverside IMAX Theater...you have to see it to believe it! With crystal clear images projected on screens five-stories-high and wrap-around digital surround sound, IMAX takes you to places only imagined. Guests can even experience 3D films or some of their favorite Hollywood movies currently being released in the extraordinary IMAX format.

Services: How We Help

As the visitor center for NASA Langley Research Center and Langley Air Force Base, the Virginia Air & Space Center supports the military through discount admission and special events. Each year the Center presents FREEdom Days in partnership with The Military Family Network. FREE-dom days are a series of Military Appreciation events that allow military personnel and their families to visit the museum and other local attractions for FREE. The Military Family Network helps us promote this special program to our military community. Military guests enjoy the museum and can also participate in children's make-n-take activities, science demonstrations and more. FREEdom Days are held throughout the spring for each military branch. For information on upcoming FREEdom Days visit www.vasc.org or call (757) 727-0900.

Since it's opening in 1992, the Virginia Air & Space Center has served more than four million visitors. Each year attendance continues to grow. The key elements to this growth have been the continuing upgrading of exhibits, and the addition of interactive and state-of-the-art technologies. The Virginia Air & Space Center is the top attraction in Hampton, and the second-most visited science museum in Virginia.

How You Can Help

As a private, non-profit organization, we depend on our faithful supporters to help us fulfill our mission of inspiring the next generation of explorers. From annual giving and corporate sponsorship to family memberships and engraved stars, there are numerous ways to support the Center's mission to " . . .*educate, entertain, and inspire explorers of all ages."*

Contact

To learn how you can make a difference contact the Center's development office at 727-0900, ext. 741or visit www.vasc.org.

Army Wife Talk Radio
Tara Crooks, Owner
www.ArmyWifeTalkRadio.com

Passion: Who We Are
Thousands of military families are dealing with the anxiety of being separated from their loved ones. It helps to have someone to talk to.

Tara Crooks, whose own husband serves our great nation, is not only providing a much-needed service for Army spouses, she's turned it nto a career as an internet talk show host.

Every week, Crooks reaches out to military wives and families all over the world with her Internet talk show, Army Wife Talk Radio (www.ArmyWifeTalkRadio.com), discussing topics like deployment, military moving and finding things to do with your kids over the summer. With the help of her computer and phone line, she records the show right from her home.

"My husband was deployed and I was looking for a way to reach out to other spouses," Crooks said. "Army Wife Talk Radio was born on a whim."

For Crooks, recording the show is therapy. She hopes it means that much to others. "My first show, we had just over 30 listeners. Now we have 800 to 1,000 a week."

While her husband is away, she admits to having her ups and downs, but says she's determined to hold things together. Phone calls, pictures and emails and even web cams help to ease the separation. "During deployment, Mom is not just Mom. She's Mom. She's Dad. She's the lawn maintenance worker. She's so many different things and I'll tell you what, I miss him when I'm out there and I'm pushing my lawnmower and I'm thinking, 'I've got so many other things to do. Why am I mowing the lawn?'"

Crooks works full time from home, and couldn't be happier. "It fits my personality. It's a great place for me to be. I feel at home here, but I never thought this is what I was going to do. It wasn't like this was my ambition growing up but I'm really happy to say this is what I do and I'm proud." She feels the reason for her success is simple. "I really am what everybody else is. I am what they are. I'm a military spouse. I go through the same problems, the same issues, I see the same things."

Army Wife Talk Radio is *the* Internet talk radio show designed specifically for army wives *by army wives*. Our Life. Our Family. Our Soldier. We feature information, special reports, empowerment, inspiration, stories and interviews that affect *YOU*!

Services: How We Help
Army Wife Talk Radio is a weekly 45 min show that is available every Monday via the website. You can download the audio or stream it and listen through your computer. The show includes information relative to military spouses and families; many different topics are covered each week.

Our purpose is to motivate, inspire, and empower Army wives worldwide to make the most of their lifestyle choice. We strive to do this by providing helpful information, interviews, and tips that take the guesswork out of Army life. We also provide forums & conferences, in which relationships can be formed and people can "grow".

Contact

To listen to the talk show, sign up for the mailing list, and receive information on new shows visit http://www.ArmyWifeTalkRadio.com.

If you or your business are interested in sponsorship of Army Wife Talk Radio or would like to advertise visit http://www.armywifetalkradio.com/advertise,shtml.

To visit the Army Wife Talk Radio Message Boards go to: http://www.armywife-talkradio.com/community/

To visit the Army Wife Talk Radio Blog go to: http://awtr.blogspot.com/

To leave feedback via the AWTR listener's line call 1-888-364-0210, enter extension 1275, and leave your message.

To submit a show topic for Army Wife Talk Radio visit: http://www.armywife-talkradio.com/showtopics.shtml

To be a guest on Army Wife Talk Radio visit: http://www.armywifetalkradio.com/beaguest.shtml

General contact information for Army Wife Talk Radio:

Phone: 1-888-866-5041

Fax: 320-514-4582

Mailing Address:

Army Wife Talk Radio

211 Lancaster Way

Richmond Hill, GA 31324

Blue Stars for a Safe Return

Jimm and Shellie Mooney, Founders

www.bluestarsforsafereturn.com

Passion: Who We Are

When our oldest son was training to deploy to Iraq for his second tour, Jimm Mooney created a graphic, now our signature design, "Praying for Their Safe Return" for our own use. We were encouraged to put it on a website and our passion began to burn deep inside us. We love this country and all that it represents; freedom, democracy and so much more.

Our military members, past and present, have stood in the gap for all of us defending and maintaining our freedoms. Our Passion is to thank them for serving and shake their hands in person, from deep within our hearts.

Services: How We Help

Since the beginning our mission has been to provide an alternative method for people to show their pride in this country, our troops and to honor the Veterans. We still pursue that mission with our own custom designed shirts and caps on our website, but it has grown to so much more. Our mission now includes playing an active role in reminding communities that there are service members and Veterans in their own communities that we need to say thanks to. We also want to remind those serving, veterans, and their families that there really is someone out there that really does truly appreciate them, even they are perfect strangers. And yes, we actually do reach out our hand and say "Thanks for serving" to every Veteran or military member we meet, every single day. Another part of our mission is to provide organizations an alternative to their current fundraising options.

We accomplish our mission as vendors in a wide variety of events such as fairs, community events, car shows, fundraisers and others. One of our goals is to be a different kind of participant, or vendor, at the events we are invited to attend. Our booth is known to be a rather emotional place, and a safe haven to show those emotions. We talk to family members of those serving, families of Fallen Heroes, and many Veterans. We have shared many tears and hugs, and even listened with lumps in our throats while visitors shared with us. Not all end up as customers, but all walk away knowing that someone really does care. And, more often than not, we are thanked for being there for them. We ride this emotional rollercoaster, almost every weekend from early spring until late in the fall; we go where we are led to go. Always, we go with an open heart, knowing that we are there for a reason, to touch the lives of someone we haven't even met yet.

Our main goal is to go where God leads us to go, to be where we need to be to touch the lives that need to be touched. And at the end of the day, our success is not measured by the amount of dollars in the register, but in how many lives we have touched. And we always seem to wonder, isn't there more we can do? We know that we have only begun this journey, and we walk in Faith knowing that the good Lord will provide us with the directions we are to pursue as we grow. As a family, and as a business, our daily prayers, and our mealtime prayers, include prayers for our military and their families.Additional goals include:

To continue to have names added to our international virtual Walls on our website; Wall of Heroes; Veterans Wall of Honor, Fallen Heroes Wall and the POW/MIA Wall, to further honor those who serve or have served us in the military, not only from our own country but also our allies.

How You Can Help

Our first project, "Prayers for Water in the Desert" is a specially labeled bottled water project. Initially, we wanted to have this water shipped to the troops in Iraq and Afghanistan.

Initially we wanted to have that shipped to the troops in Iraq and Afghanistan. But, as of the writing of this we have not been able to get that done. So we have shifted gears a bit, and are trying a different approach. Now, we are working to put it into the hands of troops leaving for Iraq, and Afghanistan, or as part of welcome home celebrations in communities across the country. This can be done through small to medium businesses, individuals or groups within the community. Military hospitals are also a place we can send them to for our wounded soldiers. Our name doesn't appear on the label, and we do not make a dime on any water shipped to communities for this purpose. The bottling company has graciously given us a special price for the bottled water and the labels, so that we can make it available to communities for their military members going to or returning from Iraq.

Our second project is working with organizations in their fundraising efforts. We offer a wide range of products and designs. We also can help organizations create special designs for their own group, for fundraising. Our design assistance is provided at a discount flat rate, and very affordable for any organization. With no minimum purchase (ever), a wide assortment of existing designs, a variety of media imprinted with our designs, and a reasonable graphics charge to help you create your own, it's a win-win opportunity. Our fundraising is geared towards military family support groups or FRG's and veteran's organizations, but we also work with a variety of civic groups as well.

Our third project is providing families of Fallen Heroes with one of our Framed Personalized "Lost But Not Forgotten" Gold Star Displays, at no charge. This is something we now do as we personally meet those families, and want to extend that out across the country. This can possibly be done through veterans' organizations such as the VFW or American Legion or a host of other groups. We want this done in good taste without adding further trauma to the families. Many families of Fallen Heroes who have received these Gold Star Displays have expressed gratitude all the Fallen Heroes families we have presented these to have been very grateful.

Contact

Anyone who wants to help organize these efforts in your communities or for more fundraising information contact: Jimm or Shellie Mooney 541-523-9804, or email at safereturn@msn.com .

Anyone wanting to donate to either the "Prayers for Water in the Desert", or Gold Star projects, can donate on our website www.bluestarsforsafereturn.com (under our memorial project link), or they can send checks or money orders to: Blue Stars for a Safe Return 2010 15th St Baker City, OR 97814

Appendix 3

State Resources for the Military

The States Resources Appendix offers statements of support from our nation's Governors as well as contact information for the states' veteran services and a few of the largest national veteran service organizations.

Each State and Territory offers programs, services, and benefits for the military community. These benefits vary by location, length and type of service, residency, and other eligibility criteria but cover such areas as finances, health, education, employment and protection of rights, to name a few. Recently, states have also been expanding, revising and updating existing programs as well as creating new programs to support their military citizens.

To guide you, The Military Family Network has taken the liberty of compiling a comprehensive list of federal, military, state and local programs, services and benefits for which you may be eligible. Because these programs are subject to change, The Military Family Network is providing these resources at www.emilitary.org to ensure that the information provided to you is current and accurate. We invite you to visit www.emilitary.org to see what benefits may be available to you.

Alabama

OFFICE OF THE GOVERNOR

STATE CAPITOL
MONTGOMERY, ALABAMA 36130

BOB RILEY
GOVERNOR

(334) 242-7100
FAX: (334) 242-0937

STATE OF ALABAMA

Greetings:

As Governor of the State of Alabama, I would like to recognize and say thank you to all of our men and women serving in the armed forces, veterans, and their families for the sacrifices that you have made to protect the freedom of our nation. On behalf of all Alabamians, we are forever grateful for your selfless service and unyielding dedication.

I also want to commend the efforts of The Military Family Network to support our military families and increase community awareness of their needs. The programs and services provided by this organization are a great resource of information and aid to military citizens and their loved ones. Today more than ever, our servicemen and women are facing the overwhelming demands placed upon them with courage and fortitude, and we Alabamians are caring people eager to do all we can to support our troops and assist their families.

To express our gratitude, Alabama's state agencies, community leaders, and volunteer organizations have teamed together forming a program called Operation Grateful Heart (OGH). OGH is Alabama's program to ensure that all military personnel and their families receive appropriate recognition, tangible support, and neighborly care.

Again, thank you for answering the call to service. Your actions have helped to preserve the freedom and liberties secured by previous generations of brave Americans, and we appreciate the sacrifices you and your family have made. If I may be of any assistance, please feel free to contact my office.

Sincerely,

BR/ps/rs

State and VSO Points of Contact

Alabama Department of Veteran Affairs RSA Plaza Building, Suite 530, 770 Washington Avenue Montgomery, AL Telephone: 334-242-5077 Website:http://www.va.state.al.us/	AMVETS Kevin Ross Marc Courreges VA Regional Office, Room 1-122 345 Perry Hill Road Montgomery, AL 36109 Phone: (334) 213-3442 E-mail for Kevin: kevin.ross@vba.a.gov E-mail for Marc: marc.courreges@vba.va.gov
VFW Department Service Officer 334 213-3439 ,334 213-3689	**American Legion State Service Officer** 334-213-3320
DAV Department Service Director 256-352-4630 775-249-9164	**The Military Family Network** 866-205-2850 connections@eMilitary.org

Alaska

Alaska Governor Statement of Support

"Alaska is blessed with a highly skilled and motivated military. These men and women are proud to do their part in the global fight against terrorism. They have endured many heart-breaking losses this past year, but have also played key roles in numerous successes.

While the politics of war create headlines here at home, our troops are walking through foreign neighborhoods every day trying to foster peace and a sense of security that only freedom can bring. I continue to pray for our military and express my deepest condolences to the family, friends and fellow service members of those who have fallen."

Governor Sarah Palin
Remembering the Military Casualties
January 5, 2007
From Governor's press address honoring Alaska's fallen heroes.

State and VSO Points of Contact

Alaska Department of Military and Veterans Affairs Mailing Address: P.O. Box 5800 Fort Richardson, AK 99505-5800 Telephone: (907) 428-6016 Fax: (907) 428-6019 Website:http://www.ak-prepared.com/vetaffairs/	**AMVETS** 855 E. 38th Avenue Anchorage, AK 99503 (907) 561-VETS
VFW Department Service Officer 907 276-8213 907 278-6780	**American Legion State Service Officer** 1550 Charter Cir Anchorage, AK 99508 (907) 278-8598
DAV Department Service Director Toll Free 1-888-353-7574 Ex. #4803 Local (907) 257-4803 Fax (907) 257-7427	**The Military Family Network** 866-205-2850 connections@eMilitary.org

Arizona

STATE OF ARIZONA

JANET NAPOLITANO   OFFICE OF THE GOVERNOR   MAIN PHONE: 602-542-4331
GOVERNOR   1700 WEST WASHINGTON STREET, PHOENIX, AZ 85007   FACSIMILE: 602-542-7601

November 30, 2006

Dear Military Community:

On behalf of the state of Arizona, I want to extend our gratitude to The Military Family Network.

I commend The Military Family Network for their service. The network provides a venue for military families to connect with their local community and communities throughout our nation. The network also works diligently to make sure that military families know about the programs and services that they are entitled to. These efforts go along way to making sure that the men and women who serve in uniform will not have to worry about their loved ones at home being taken care of.

Here in Arizona we have five active duty military bases and several guard bases. We also have the distinction of having more than 600,000 veterans residing in our state. The veterans in our community are good and honorable people who have served our country. We need to make sure that we are serving them and their families while they are deployed. The Military Family Network does this on a daily basis and we praise them for their work.

Best wishes on your continuing success

Yours very truly,

Janet Napolitano

Janet Napolitano
Governor

State and VSO Points of Contact

Arizona Veteran Services Division	AMVETS
Mailing Address: 3333 NORTH CENTRAL AVENUE, SUITE 1052 PHOENIX AZ, 85012 Telephone: 602-627-3261 Website http://www.azdvs.gov/	5608 West Bar X Street Tucson, AZ 85713-6407 (520) 578-5712 Fax: (520) 578-5713 rvamvets@qwest.net
VFW Department Service Officer 3333 North Central Avenue, Room 1049 Phoenix, AZ 85304 Phone: 602 627-3316 Fax: 602 627-3320	**American Legion State Service Officer** 4701 N. 19th Ave Suite 200 Phoenix, AZ. 85015 Call: 602-264-7706 Fax: 602-264-0029
DAV Department Service Director 38 West Dunlap Avenue Phoenix, AZ 85021 Phone: 602-678-0333 Fax: 602-371-0275	**The Military Family Network** 866-205-2850 connections@eMilitary.org

Arkansas

Arkansas Governor Statement of Support

"As we salute the bravery of our soldiers and pray for their safety, even as we mourn those who have made the ultimate sacrifice, let all Arkansans step forward and declare their intentions to work to make our public life and political goals ones we will be proud of for our state and nation. And let us all embrace a new patriotism, in which each of us is able to lend our energy, talents, and abilities to ensure a brighter future for our world."

Governor Mike Beebe
From Governor's Weekly Column
March 8, 2007
http://www.arkansas.gov/governor/newsroom/index.php?
do:newsDetail=1&news_id=68

State and VSO Points of Contact

Arkansas Department of Military and Veterans Affairs Mailing Address: 2200 FORT ROOTS DR BLDG 65., ROOM 119 NORTH LITTLE ROCK, AR 72114 Telephone: (501) 370-3820 Fax: (501) 370-3829 Website : http://www.nasdva.com/arkansas.html	AMVETS 122 Lacey Street Melbourne, AR 72556 (870) 368-7451 Fax: (870) 368-9451 maclee@century.tel
VFW Department Service Officer 2200 Fort Roots Drive Building 65, Room 119 North Little Rock, AR 72114 Phone: 501 370-3820 Fax: 501 370-3829	American Legion State Service Officer 702 S. Victory St. - P.O. Box 3280 Little Rock, Arkansas 72203-3280 1-877-243-9799 (toll free) - 501-375-1104 Fax: 501-375-4236 e-mail: alegion@swbell.net
DAV Department Service Director P.O. Box 1620 North Little Rock, AR 72115 Fax: (501) 257-1897 National Service Office: (501) 370-3838	The Military Family Network 866-205-2850 connections@eMilitary.org

California

GOVERNOR ARNOLD SCHWARZENEGGER

November 2006

The Military Family Network

Maria and I are delighted to extend our heartfelt gratitude to all the military families who have made tremendous sacrifices so that their loved ones can defend our nation.

America is a beacon of hope and opportunity for people everywhere, thanks to the strength and courage of the men and women of our armed forces. As you may know, California is home to some of the largest and most strategically important military bases in the country. When we meet with services members and their families stationed at these bases, we are humbled and inspired by their stories of strength and sacrifice. To that end, we have made every effort to care for them and their families through Maria's Military Family Initiative and through the signing of bipartisan legislation to protect them from financial hardships.

We thank the Military Family Network and Capitol Books for publishing *Your Military Family Network*. This valuable guide encourages families to build crucial community relationships and reach out to their neighbors and fellow military families. A strong sense of community helps all of us cope with our hopes and fears, so we want to encourage all military families to make full use of this resource.

Please know that California welcomes and supports all veterans, active military personnel and their families. May you experience the best in the months and years ahead.

With warmest regards,

Arnold Schwarzenegger   Maria Shriver

State and VSO Points of Contact

California Department of Veterans Affairs Mailing Address: 1227 O Street Sacramento, CA 95814 Telephone: 1 (800) 952-5626 Website : http://www.cdva.ca.gov/	AMVETS AMVETS Department of California 240 East King Avenue Tulare, California 93274 559.688.3407
VFW Department Service Officer Supervisor, VFW Service Office Oakland Federal Building 1301 Clay Street, Room 1140N Oakland, CA 94612 Phone: 510 835-1246 Fax: 510 835-8029	American Legion State Service Officer 401 Van Ness Ave., Rm 117 San Francisco, CA 94102 Phone 415-431-2400 Fax 415-255-1571
DAV - Department of California 13733 E. Rosecrans Ave. Santa Fe Springs, CA 90670 Phone: (562) 404-1266 Fax: (562) 404-8044 Email: davca@davca.org	The Military Family Network 866-205-2850 connections@eMilitary.org

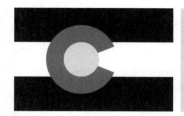

Colorado

STATE OF COLORADO

EXECUTIVE CHAMBERS

136 State Capitol
Denver, Colorado 80203-1792
Phone (303) 866-2471

Bill Owens
Governor

June 15, 2006

Greetings:

On behalf of the State of Colorado, it is my pleasure to endorse the Military Family
Network in its mission to connect military families.

The Military Family Network, with its community-based philosophy and far-reaching
care, has helped our National Guard, veterans, active duty, and reserve soldiers keep in
touch with their loved ones. Their hard work has enabled many of our heroes at home and
abroad to maintain their task of ensuring our freedom and prosperity. The Military
Family Networks tireless efforts on soldiers' behalf continue to help our nation's armed
forces stay connected and prepared.

I heartily support the work of the Military Family Network. Please continue the good
work in serving our nation's military branches. You have my best wishes, now and in the
years to come.

Sincerely,

Bill Owens

Bill Owens
Governor

State and VSO Points of Contact

Colorado Military and Veteran Affairs Mailing Address: 7465 E. 1st Ave, Suite "C" Denver, CO 80230 Telephone: 303-343-1268 Fax: 303-343-7238	AMVETS AMVETS Post CO-0003 456 Verdos Drive Elizabeth, CO 80107 (303) 646-4689
VFW Department Service Officer VA Regional Office 155 Van Gordon Street - Room #360 Box 25126 Denver, CO 80225 Phone: 303 914-5595/96/97	American Legion State Service Officer 7465 E. First St., Suite D Denver, CO 80230 303–477–1655 (fax)303–477–2950
DAV Department Service Director 155 Van Gordon St., VARO Denver, CO 80225 303–914–5570 Fax 303–914–5584	The Military Family Network 866-205-2850 connections@eMilitary.org

Connecticut

STATE OF CONNECTICUT
EXECUTIVE CHAMBERS
HARTFORD, CONNECTICUT
06106

M. JODI RELL
GOVERNOR

August 10, 2006

The Military Family Network
100 Bridge Street #D
Second Floor
Hampton, Virginia 23669

Dear Friends:

On behalf of the State of Connecticut, it is a great pleasure to extend greetings and congratulations to The Military Family Network.

I commend The Military Family Network for their dedication and commitment to connecting military families and their communities throughout the State of Connecticut and our Nation. By creating awareness about programs and services available to military service members and their families, you make life easier for the men and women who selflessly serve and defend our country.

The citizens of Connecticut appreciate the outstanding work and services that The Military Family Network provides. In addition, the State of Connecticut is grateful for the sacrifices that military service members and their families have made on our behalf. The State of Connecticut has much to be proud of in its servicemen and women. I salute your dedication, devotion to duty and loyal service.

It is a privilege to extend my words of tribute to all. Please know that you have my best wishes for a continued success in the future.

Sincerely,

M. Jodi Rell

State and VSO Points of Contact

Connecticut Department of Veterans' Affairs Mailing Address: 287 West Street Rocky Hill, CT 06067 Telephone: 860-529-2571 or 1-800-550-0000 Fax: 860-721-5919 Website : http://www.state.de.us/veteran/	**AMVETS** 70 McKinley Avenue Norwich, CT 06360 (860) 887-6065
VFW Department Service Officer **PO Box 310909** Room 3133 555 Willard Avenue Newington, CT 06131-0909 Phone: 860 594-6610 Fax: 860 667-1214	**American Legion State Service Officer** Department Headquarters, The American Legion 287 West Street Rocky Hill, CT 06067 (860) 721-5942
DAV Department Service Director VA Regional Office 555 Willard Avenue P.O. Box 310909 Newington, CT 06131-0909 (860) 594-6611 (860) 594-6612 FAX (860) 667-1238	**The Military Family Network** 866-205-2850 connections@eMilitary.org

Delaware

State of Delaware
Office of the Governor

Ruth Ann Minner
Governor

August 18, 2006

As Governor of Delaware, I know firsthand how important the members of our armed forces are to the security and safety of the First State. It is my pleasure to provide assistance and guidance through this publication to the men and women who have devoted their time and energy to serving our nation and this great state.

Delaware continually provides valuable services and resources that benefit members of the military and their families. Our servicemen and women are routinely called on to make sacrifices in order to serve and protect, so it is my goal to help make these transitions as easy as possible for soldiers and their families.

Throughout my administration, I have signed legislation to provide additional resources for members of our armed forces and veterans. These bills are designed to protect service member benefits and job security during deployment. In the First State, it is our top priority to serve those who risk their lives every day to protect this nation and state.

I applaud The Military Family Network and its efforts to inform and assist servicemen and women across the country. This resource is sure to provide valuable information to all military members and their families.

Sincerely,

Ruth Ann Minner

Ruth Ann Minner
Governor

State and VSO Points of Contact

Delaware Commission of Veterans Affairs Mailing Address: Telephone: (302) 739-2792 In State Toll Free (800) 344-9900 Fax: (302) 739-2794 Email: mailto:antonio.davila@state.de.us Website : http://www.state.de. us/veteran/	AMVETS E508 Gunnel Road Millsboro, DE 19966 (302) 945-0406
VFW Department Service Officer VA Medical & Regional Office Center 1601 Kirkwood Highway, Room 21 Wilmington, DE 19805 Phone: 302 633-5326 Fax: 302 633-5507	American Legion State Service Officer Regional Office 1601 Kirkwood Highway, Wilmington, DE 19805 Mailing address: PO Box 5696, Wilmington, DE 19808-5696 Phone: 302.998.9448 or 302.633.5323 FAX: 302.633.5388
DAV Department Service Director Department of Delaware Disabled American Veterans P.O. Box 407 Camden De 19934 Phone No. 302-697-9061 FAX: 697-9041	The Military Family Network 866-205-2850 connections@eMilitary.org

Florida

Governor Statement of Support

"I had the opportunity to sit down with some of these courageous men and women at the People's House. I was moved by their patriotism and dedication. These citizen soldiers and airmen are ready to leave their civilian lives and answer the call of duty at a moment's notice. Florida's National Guard is the best combat trained state guard in the United States. They defend our nation overseas and help the people of Florida and others states during natural disasters here at home. I am so grateful to these heroic men and women who protect the freedoms we all take for granted."

Governor Charlie Crist
Notes from the Capital
From Governor's Weekly Column
March 23, 2007
http://www.flgov.com/capitol_notes

State and VSO Points of Contact

Florida Department of Veterans Affairs Mailing Address: 4040 Esplanade Way Suite 152 Tallahassee, FL 32399-0950 Telephone: (850) 487-1533 Website: http://www.floridavets.org/	**AMVETS** 1545 Warmwood Drive Grand Island, FL 32735 (352) 669-8490 Fax: (352) 669-8392
VFW Department Service Officer VFW Department of Florida VA Regional Office, Room 217 (Mail: P.O. Box 1437) St. Petersburg, FL 33731 Phone: 727 319-7483 Fax: 727 319-7776	**The American Legion** Department of Florida P.O. Box 547859 Orlando, FL 32854-7859 407.295.2631 407.299.0901 fax
DAV Department of Florida 2015 SW 75th Street Gainesville, FL 32607	**The Military Family Network** 866-205-2850 connections@eMilitary.org

Georgia

STATE OF GEORGIA
OFFICE OF THE GOVERNOR
ATLANTA 30334-0900

Sonny Perdue
GOVERNOR

November 1, 2006

GREETINGS:

The state of Georgia is home to military service members and families representing every branch of the armed forces. Our active duty service members and our citizen-soldiers in the Georgia National Guard and Reserves continually make tremendous sacrifices in service to the state and the nation.

I commend The Military Family Network for their dedication and commitment to connecting military families and their communities throughout Georgia and across the country. By creating awareness about programs and services available to the military community and their family members you make life easier for the men and women who selflessly serve and defend our country.

The state of Georgia shares in this effort to support our active-duty, guard and reserve service members with the information and resources they need to make the best possible choices for themselves and their families. The sacrifices these military service members make on our behalf deserve our gratitude, and they merit our continued support. I am proud of the Military Family Network's numerous accomplishments and their commitment to those who defend our nation.

Sincerely,

Sonny Perdue

Sonny Perdue

State and VSO Points of Contact

Georgia Department of Veteran Service Mailing Address: Floyd Veterans Memorial Building Suite E-970 Atlanta, Georgia 30334-4800 Telephone: 404-656-2300 Fax: 404-657-9738	AMVETS P.O. Box 1822 Valdosta, GA 31603 (229) 251-7558
VFW Department Service Officer 1700 Clairmont Road - Room 1.318 Decatur, GA 30033-4032 Rm. 1.306 Phone: 404 929-5345 Fax: 404 929-5347	The American Legion Department of Florida 3035 Mt. Zion Road Stockbridge, Georgia 30281 Phone (678) 289-8883
DAV Department 4462 Houston Avenue Macon, GA 31206 Phone: 478-781-7336 Fax: 478-788-2934	The Military Family Network 866-205-2850 connections@eMilitary.org

Hawaii

Hawaii Governor Statement of Support

"We would like to pay tribute to our men and women in the armed forces, National Guard and Reserves, who have served their country both at home and abroad.

The price of liberty has been paid by the sacrifices of those who have fought and died for the freedoms we enjoy today. The veterans who served on the battlefield and those who protected our country at home are true heroes."

Governor Linda Lingle
http://gov.state.hi.us/

State and VSO Points of Contact

Office of Veteran Services: State of Hawaii Tripler Army Medical Center Ward Road VAMROC, E-Wing, Room 1-A103 Honolulu HI 96819 Mailing Address: Office of Veterans Services 459 Patterson Road E-Wing, Room 1-A103 Honolulu HI 96819 Telephone: (808) 433-0420 Fax: Fax: (808) 433-0385 Email: OVS@ovs.hawaii.gov Website:http://www.ovs.Hawaii.gov	**AMVETS** JOHNSTON ISLAND Post 1 Bldg #704, Johnston Island APO AP 96558 (808) 421-0011
VFW Department Service Officer Tripler Army Medical Center 459 Patterson Road, E-Wing Room 1-C104 Honolulu, HI 96819-1522 Phone: 808 433-0494/0495 Fax: 808 433-0388 E-Mail: VFCASTW@vba.va.gov	**The American Legion** 612 MCCULLY ST HONOLULU, HI 96826-3935 PHONE: 808-946-6383 FAX: 808-947-3957 EMAIL:aldepthi@hawaii.rr.com
DAV Department VAMROC, E-Wing 459 Patterson Road, Room 1-C103 Honolulu, HI 96819-1522 (808) 433-0490	**The Military Family Network** 866-205-2850 connections@eMilitary.org

Idaho

JAMES E. RISCH
GOVERNOR

October 30, 2006

The Military Family Network

On behalf of the Great State of Idaho, it is an honor to extend a heartfelt "Thank You" for the support offered by the Military Family Network. It gives me a great deal of pleasure to endorse this valuable resource. I commend the Military Family Network, and all the agencies supporting our service members and their families. They provide an important connection between military families and their communities across the nation.

The State of Idaho salutes the sacrifices made by our service members and their families who serve selflessly around the world. Their dedication to our freedom and security cannot be easily measured. It is a call they have answered, and the State of Idaho recognizes and appreciates the dedication to this higher calling for their strength and perseverance in the defense of our nation.

I wish you all the very best in the services and resources you provide for the supportive families and those who serve. Thank you!

Very Truly Yours,

James E. Risch
Governor

STATE CAPITOL • BOISE, IDAHO 83720 • (208) 334-2100

State and VSO Points of Contact

Idaho Division of Veterans Services	AMVETS
Mailing Address: 320 Collins Road Boise, Idaho, 83702 Telephone: 208-334-3513 Fax: 208-334-2627 Email: info@veterans.idaho.gov Website: www.veterans.idaho.gov	
VFW Department Service Officer 805 W. Franklin Street Boise, ID 83702-5560 Phone: 208 334-1245 Fax: 208 334-3549 E-Mail: resslert@veterans.idaho.gov	**The American Legion** 901 WARREN ST BOISE, ID 83706-1964 PHONE: 208-342-7061 FAX: 208-342-1964 EMAIL: idlegion@mindspring.com WEB:http://idlegion.home.mindspring.com
DAV Department Disabled American Veterans VA Regional Office 805 W. Franklin St., Rm 205 Boise, ID 85702 (208) 334-1956	**The Military Family Network** 866-205-2850 connections@eMilitary.org

Illinois

OFFICE OF THE GOVERNOR
JRTC, 100 West Randolph, Suite 16
Chicago, Illinois 60601

ROD R. BLAGOJEVICH
GOVERNOR

June 2006

G R E E T I N G S

As Governor of the State of Illinois, I am pleased to be a part of the **Military Family Network's** book, *Your Military Family Network.*

This publication will serve as a wonderful source for military families to build relationships with one another. It will also help the military community find valuable resources and information in their respective states. With that said, I would like to express my deep appreciation to each of you for the sacrifices that you made on behalf of all the citizens of this great land. The courage and commitment that each of you exemplified in the United States Military was instrumental in ensuring that our country's liberty and democracy was upheld.

On behalf of the citizens of Illinois, I offer each of you my best wishes for continued health, happiness and success in the years to come.

Sincerely,

Rod R. Blagojevich
Governor

State and VSO Points of Contact

Illinois Department of Veterans Affairs	AMVETS
Mailing Address: 833 South Spring Street P.O. Box 19432 Springfield, IL 62794-9432 Telephone: 217/782-6641 Fax: 217/524-0344 Website: http://www.state.il.us/agency/dva/	2200 South Sixth Street Springfield, IL 62703 (217) 528-4713 Fax: (217) 528-9896 Website: www.ilamvets.org
VFW Department Service Officer 2122 West Taylor Street, Room 127 Chicago, IL 60612 Phone: 312 980-4284 Fax: 312 706-6680	**The American Legion** PO BOX 2910 BLOOMINGTON, IL 61702 PHONE: 309-663-0361 FAX: 309-663-5783 EMAIL: hdqs@illegion.org WEB: http://www.illegion.org
DAV Department VA Regional Office 2122 W Taylor Street, Ste. 104 Chicago, IL 60612 (312) 980-4242	**The Military Family Network** 866-205-2850 connections@eMilitary.org

Indiana

Governor Statement of Support

"Indiana is a state of patriots. One sees it not just on Independence Day, Memorial Day or Veterans Day, but every day. When you hold my job, you see it most unforgettably at the funerals of the fallen.

But our treatment of those who serve in uniform does not fully reflect the love and gratitude we feel for them. It does not match that of other states. Patriotism knows no party label; please join me in upgrading the way we support our soldiers, veterans, and the families who have sacrificed with them to protect the freedoms we all enjoy".

State of the State Address
Governor Mitchell E. Daniels, Jr.
January 16, 2007

State and VSO Points of Contact

Indiana Department of Veterans Affairs Mailing Address: 302 W. Washington Street, Room E120 Indianapolis, IN 46204-2738 Telephone: 317-232-3910 Fax: 317-232-7721 Website: http://www.ai.org/veteran/in-dex.html	**AMVETS** 2840 N. Lafayette Rd. Suite 'A' Indianapolis, IN 46222 317-923-4325
VFW Department Service Officer 575 N. Pennsylvania Street, RM 374 Indianapolis, IN 46204 Phone: 317 226-7932/7936 Fax: 317 226-5412	**The American Legion** 777 N MERIDIAN ST INDIANAPOLIS, IN 46204 PHONE: 317-630-1300 FAX: 317-237-9891 EMAIL: members@indlegion.org WEB: http://www.indlegion.org
DAV Department VARO Federal Building 575 N. Penn. St., Rm. 320 Indianapolis, IN 46204 (317) 226-7928	**The Military Family Network** 866-205-2850 connections@eMilitary.org

Iowa

THOMAS J. VILSACK	**OFFICE OF THE GOVERNOR**	SALLY J. PEDERSON
GOVERNOR		LT. GOVERNOR

July 12, 2006

Dear Military Community,

On behalf of the State of Iowa, I want to extend our deepest gratitude to you. You all make sacrifices for our people to remain safe and free. In appreciation of the immeasurable sacrifice you make for us, the people of Iowa honor and support you.

The greatest asset of this state lies in our sense of community that runs from border to border. Working families join together to ensure that our children receive a quality education, access to affordable health care, a clean environment, and safe streets. Iowa is the heartland of the country, and we take pride in these values.

The Military Family Network supports this community spirit by strengthening the interaction of different groups and organizations and improving the connection between our military and our communities. Through this more effective method of communication, we hope we are better able to honor and support our military community.

I want to again extend my personal thanks to you for everything that you all do. And on behalf of Iowa, I want to invite you into our community of Iowa.

Sincerely,

Thomas J. Vilsack
Governor of Iowa

STATE CAPITOL   DES MOINES, IOWA 50319   515 281-5211   FAX 515-281-6611

State and VSO Points of Contact

Iowa Department of Veterans Affairs	AMVETS
Mailing Address: Camp Dodge, Bldg. A6A 7105 NW 70th Ave. Johnston, IA 50131-1824 Telephone: (515) 242-5331 Fax: (515) 242-5659 Email: info@icva.state.ia.us Website:www.icva.state.ia.us	P.O. Box 77 Des Moines, IA 50309 (515) 323-7538 Fax: (515) 323-7402 www.amvetsia.org
VFW Department Service Officer	**The American Legion**
Federal Building, Room 1033-C Des Moines, IA 50309 Phone: 515-323-7546 Fax: 515 323-7405 E-Mail: terry.lipovac@vba.va.gov	720 LYON ST DES MOINES, IA 50309-5468 PHONE: 515-282-5068 PHONE: 800-365-8387 FAX: 515-282-7583 EMAIL: info@ialegion.org WEB: http://www.ialegion.org
DAV Department	**The Military Family Network**
VA Regional Ofc., 1033 B Federal Bldg. 2nd & Walnut Streets Des Moines, IA 50309 (515) 323-7539	866-205-2850 connections@eMilitary.org

K A N S A S

OFFICE OF THE GOVERNOR   KATHLEEN SEBELIUS, GOVERNOR

July, 2006

Thank you to Military Family Network for providing this service of sharing the resources our state has available to support our military personnel and their families. Whether they are deployed throughout the world or serving on the home front, Kansas has a reputation as being a very military friendly state and our recent enactment of the Kansas Military Bill of Rights goes even further to ensure we take care of our soldiers, sailors, airmen, Marines, National Guard, and Coast Guard personnel in the manner in which they deserve.

I want to express my deep pride and my thanks to soldiers like you who are answering the call of your nation during the Global War on Terrorism.

As Governor, I have been impressed with the total commitment of both the soldiers and families of the Armed Forces of the United States to do what must be done to protect this state and our nation. This is a task that many would not be able to handle. Our fighting men and women's commitment to protecting this country, its values and its people earn them the utmost level of respect. The strength and resolve they must possess as they leave their families, their jobs, and their commitments is mighty.

On behalf of the citizens of Kansas, I wish to thank our service men and women for their many sacrifices on behalf of their fellow Americans. Military personnel stationed in Kansas should rest assured that we will do all we can to support you and your families.

Very Respectfully,

Kathleen Sebelius
Governor of the State of Kansas

CAPITOL BUILDING, ROOM 212S, TOPEKA, KS 66612-1590
Voice 785-296-3232   Fax 785-296-7973   http://www.ksgovernor.org

State and VSO Points of Contact

Kansas Commission on Veterans Affairs	AMVETS
Mailing Address: Jayhawk Towers 700 SW Jackson, Suite 701 Topeka, KS 66603-3743 Telephone: (785) 296-3976 Fax: (785) 296-1462 Email: KCVA007@ink.org Website: http://www.kcva.org/ http://www.ksgovernor.org/ltgov/rights.html	101 East Third Street South Hutchinson, KS 67505 (316) 662-8297 Fax: (316) 668-6866
VFW Department Service Officer 5500 East Kellogg Wichita, KS 67218 Phone: 316 688-6801/6802 Toll-Free: 1-888-878-6881, x. 56801 Fax: 316 688-6777 E-Mail: kcvrhayw@va.gov	**The American Legion** 1314 SW TOPEKA BLVD TOPEKA, KS 66612 PHONE: 785-232-9315 FAX: 785-232-1399 EMAIL: yunker@ksamlegion.org WEB: http://www.ksamlegion.org
DAV Department VA Medical & Regional Office Ctr. 5500 East Kellogg, Rm. 112 Wichita, KS 67218 (316) 688-6722 Disabled American Veterans VA Medical Center 4201 S. Fourth Street Traffic Way Leavenworth, KS 66048 (913) 651-2402	**The Military Family Network** 866-205-2850 connections@eMilitary.org

Kentucky

COMMONWEALTH OF KENTUCKY
OFFICE OF THE GOVERNOR

ERNIE FLETCHER
GOVERNOR

700 CAPITAL AVENUE
SUITE 100
FRANKFORT, KY 40601
(502) 564-2611
FAX: (502) 564-2517

On behalf of the Commonwealth of Kentucky, Glenna and I extend sincere gratitude for your service to our country. We can never adequately say thank you. All Americans should be humbled by the realization of what your commitment, courage and sacrifices contribute to the cause of freedom.

Without the brave men and women who devote their lives to serving this country, our great nation's history would be quite different. The discipline, dedication and determination required to serve in the military command our appreciation and respect. In recent years, this truth has been tragically reinforced to us and we are reminded daily that freedom is not free.

I wish you the very best in all future endeavors. As a proud veteran, Kentuckian and American, I thank you for your life of service.

Sincerely,

Ernie Fletcher

KentuckyUnbridledSpirit.com

An Equal Opportunity Employer M/F/D

State and VSO Points of Contact

Kentucky Department of Veteran Affairs Mailing Address: 1111 Louisville Road Frankfort, KY 40601 Telephone: (502) 564-9203 / (800) 572-6245 Fax: (502) 564-9240 Email: melissa.hall@ky.gov Website: http://www.kdva.net/benefits.htm	AMVETS 1330 Ellison Avenue Louisville, KY 40204-1657 (502) 459-5144 Fax: (502) 459-8642 www.amvetsofky.org
VFW Department Service Officer P.O. Box 2105 Louisville, KY 40201-2105 Phone: 502 566-4422 Fax: 502 566-4425 E-Mail: vavbalou/ro/vfw@vba.va.gov	The American Legion PO BOX 2123 LOUISVILLE, KY 40201 PHONE: 502-587-1414 FAX: 502-587-6356 EMAIL: kylegion@bellsouth.net WEB: http://www.kylegion.org
DAV Department VA Regional Office 545 S. 3rd Street, Rm. 115 Louisville, KY 40202-1838 (502) 582-5849	The Military Family Network 866-205-2850 connections@eMilitary.org

Louisiana

State of Louisiana
OFFICE OF THE GOVERNOR
Baton Rouge
70804-9004

KATHLEEN BABINEAUX BLANCO
GOVERNOR

POST OFFICE BOX 94004
(225) 342-7015

October 20, 2006

Greetings,

I am honored to participate in *Your Military Family Network* and pleased to provide information about special resources available to military men and women as well as their families who live and work in our great state!

On behalf of all our citizens, thank you for being here to carry out your duties of military service. We have an historic and strong tradition that supports your efforts, and we know how important it is to communicate our appreciation, our care and concern. We also want you to know about our state government – particularly, the Louisiana Department of Veterans Affairs – and some of the support programs we've developed and undertaken over the years.

Our heartfelt obligation is to keep faith with all military members and their families – active duty, guard and reserve, veterans, family members alike. Our efforts are genuine acts of compassion as well as smart investments in our future.

During this time, it is especially important to assist our military families, not only while a member is deployed, but after military service is complete. With so many large military installations located here in our state, we respect that military families comprise an important demographic, and we've learned over the years that they become some of our most treasured and valuable retirees.

We believe Louisiana and its people will charm and capture the hearts of military men and women stationed here. Our great joy is having those same men and women adopt Louisiana as their own and settle down here for good.

I encourage you to make your individual and family *Community Connection* in order to feel right at home in a state that has always held you in high regard, welcomed you with utmost respect, and received you with hearts wide open.

Sincerely,

Kathleen Babineaux Blanco
Governor

State and VSO Points of Contact

Louisiana Department of Veteran Affairs P.O. Box 94095 Capitol Station Baton Rouge, LA 70804-9095 Telephone: (225) 922-0500 Fax: (225) 922-0511 Email: jstrickland@vetaffairs.com Website: http://www.vetaffairs.com/index.asp	AMVETS Department of Louisiana 5421 Lapalco Boulevard, Suite A Marrero, LA 70072 (504) 347-0067 Fax: (504) 347-0068
VFW Department Service Officer PO Box 94095, CAP. STA. Baton Rouge, LA 70804-9095 Phone: 225 922-0500 ext. 201 Fax: 225 922-0511	The American Legion 1885 WOODDALE BLVD STE 1110 BATON ROUGE, LA 70806 PHONE: 225-923-1945 FAX: 225-923-3980 EMAIL:adjutant@americanlegion.ntc-mail.net WEB: http://www.lalegion.org
DAV Department VA Regional Office 671A Whitney Avenue Gretna, LA 70046	The Military Family Network 866-205-2850 connections@eMilitary.org

Maine

STATE OF MAINE
OFFICE OF THE GOVERNOR
1 STATE HOUSE STATION
AUGUSTA, MAINE
04333-0001

JOHN ELIAS BALDACCI
GOVERNOR

Greetings:

I am truly honored to represent the entire State of Maine with this sincere expression of appreciation for the countless personal and professional sacrifices that our military members and their families have made in order to protect our many freedoms.

As a nation woven in democracy, we continuously witness the battles between freedom and tyranny. It's the dedication and the perseverance of those wearing America's uniforms that allows freedom to ultimately prevail.

All throughout history Mainers have faithfully answered the call to duty. Today they defend freedom and democracy around the globe, including Iraq and Afghanistan. Their efforts are helping to improve the lives of many people in the countries they have been deployed to and they truly play a vital role in protecting the safety and security of all Americans.

I thank all of our military citizens and veterans for your service to our state and nation. I thank you for your courage and your dedication, the sacrifices you and your families have made to serve our country.

The people of Maine have the utmost respect for its military members and their families. Your contributions have forged a better world. We are very much in your debt and once again on behalf of the entire State of Maine, I'd like to express my sincere appreciation.

Sincerely,

John E. Baldacci
Governor

PRINTED ON RECYCLED PAPER

PHONE: (207) 287-3531 (Voice)   (207) 287-6548 (TTY)   FAX: (207) 287-1034
                                        www.maine.gov

State and VSO Points of Contact

Maine Bureau of Veterans Services	AMVETS
Mailing Address: 117 State House Station Augusta, ME 04333-0117 Telephone: 207-626-4464 Fax: 207-626-4471 Website: http://www.mainebvs.org/	918 Broadway South Portland, ME 04106 (207) 767-5464
VFW Department Service Officer Department of VA Togus Box 3311 Augusta, ME 04330-3311 Phone: 207 623-5723 Fax: 207 626-4732	**The American Legion** PO BOX 900 WATERVILLE, ME 04903-0900 PHONE: 207-873-3229 FAX: 207-872-0501 EMAIL: legionme@me.acadia.net WEB: http://www.mainelegion.org
DAV Department DVARO--Medical Center Bldg. 248, Rm. 113, Route 17 East Togus, ME 04330-3151 Mailing Address: P.O. Box 3151 Augusta, ME 04330-3151 (207) 623-5725	**The Military Family Network** 866-205-2850 connections@eMilitary.org

Maryland

STATE OF MARYLAND
OFFICE OF THE GOVERNOR

ROBERT L. EHRLICH, JR.
GOVERNOR

June 13, 2006

Dear Friends:

As Governor of Maryland, allow me to extend special greetings to the active military personnel and families stationed across the State of Maryland.

Freedom is the basic tenets our which our nation was founded. As a former U. S. Congressman and the son of a Korean War veteran, I understand and appreciate how important a professional and vigilant military is to preserving our nation's freedom. Through the dedicated service of military personnel and the support of their families, our nation's spirit of promise continues to be strong during these challenging times. I'm proud of your noble contributions.

Further, let me extend best wishes to the members of the Military Family Network for publishing this resource. By providing this list of community resources, the Military Family Network is helping military families forge stronger ties with the state and local community.

Thanks again for your contributions to our State and nation.

Very truly yours,

Robert L. Ehrlich, Jr.
Governor

STATE HOUSE, ANNAPOLIS, MARYLAND 21401
(410) 974-3901   1-800-811-8336
TTY USERS CALL VIA MD RELAY

State and VSO Points of Contact

Maryland Department of Veterans Affairs	AMVETS
Mailing Address: The Jeffrey Bldg., 4th Floor 16 Francis St. Annapolis, MD 21401 Telephone: 410-260-3838 Toll Free: 866-793-1577 Fax: 410-216-7928 Email:mdveteransinfo@mdva.state.md.us Website: http://www.mdva.state.md.us/	2626 Felter Lane Bowie, MD 20715 (301) 262-4194
VFW Department Service Officer Fallon Federal Building 31 Hopkins Plaza, Room 114E Baltimore, MD 21201-2823 Phone: 410 230-4480 Fax: 410 230-4481	**The American Legion** WAR MEMORIAL BLDG RM E 101 N GAY ST BALTIMORE, MD 21202 PHONE: 410-752-1405 FAX: 410-752-3822 EMAIL: hdqtrs@mdlegion.org WEB: http://www.mdlegion.org
DAV Department VA Regional Office Federal Bldg. Rm. 111, 31 Hopkins Plaza Baltimore, MD 21201 (410) 230-4440	**The Military Family Network** 866-205-2850 connections@eMilitary.org

Massachusetts

Massachusetts Governor Statement of Support

"The citizens of Massachusetts were among the first to take up arms in defense of our liberty and the Commonwealth today remains extremely proud of our men and women who continue to answer the nation's call to arms. We recognize that our veterans, particularly those with service-related disabilities, have particular needs as a result of the sacrifices of military service…"

Governor Deval Patrick
April 15, 2007
Creation of the Advisory Council to advise Governor and Secretaries
of Health and Human Services and Veterans' Services

State and VSO Points of Contact

Massachusetts Department of Veteran Services Mailing Address: 600 Washington St., Suite 1100 Boston, MA 02111 Telephone: 617-210-5480 or (800) 827-1000 Fax: 617-210-5755 Email: MDVS@vet.state.ma.us Website: http://www.mass.gov/veterans	**AMVETS** State House Room 546-3 Boston, MA 02133 (617) 727-2972 Fax: (617) 727-2973
VFW Department Service Officer John F. Kennedy Federal Building Government Center - Room 1500-C Boston, MA 02203 Phone: 617 303-5688 Fax: 617 227-2024	**The American Legion** STATE HOUSE STE 546-2 BOSTON, MA 02133-1044 PHONE: 617-727-2966 FAX: 617-727-2969 EMAIL: masslegion@verizon.net WEB: http://www.MassLegion.org
DAV Department JFK Fed Bldg. Government Ctr. Kin. 1575B Boston, MA 02203 (617) 303 5675	**The Military Family Network** 866-205-2850 connections@eMilitary.org

Michigan

Governor Statement of Support

"I ask you to take prompt action to protect those who every day put their lives on the line to protect us – the men and women who serve in our National Guard and military Reserves.

I strongly support new legislation that would increase penalties on businesses that refuse to give our service members their old jobs when they return from duty.

It may be impossible to calculate the debt we owe to those who risk their lives for their country, but this we do know. We owe them the right to return to their lives and their jobs in Michigan."

Governor Jennifer M. Granholm
Working Our Plan, Securing Our Future
State of the Sstate Address

State and VSO Points of Contact

Michigan Department of Military and Veterans Affairs Mailing Address: Joint Public Affairs Office 3411 Martin Luther King Jr. Blvd. Lansing, MI 48906 Telephone: (517) 481-8000 Website:http://www.michigan.gov/dmva	**AMVETS** 1249 Washington Boulevard, Suite 2901 Detroit, MI 48226 (313) 965-3002 Fax: (313) 965-3007
VFW Department Service Officer State Service Director VFW Department of Michigan Patrick V. McNamara Federal Building 477 Michigan Avenue, Room 1215 Detroit, MI 48226 Phone: 313 964-6510 Fax: 313 964-6545	**The American Legion** 212 N VERLINDEN AVE LANSING, MI 48915 PHONE: 517-371-4720 FAX: 517-371-2401 EMAIL: info@michiganlegion.org WEB: http://www.michiganlegion.org
DAV Department VA Regional Office McNamara Fed. Bldg. 477 Michigan Ave. Rm. 1200 Detroit, MI 48226 (313) 964 6595	**The Military Family Network** 866-205-2850 connections@eMilitary.org

Minnesota

Governor Statement of Support

"As governor, I've been to a lot of different events, met a lot of different people, been to a lot of different places, and I have never, ever, been associated with a finer group of people than the men and women of the Minnesota National Guard and our United States military. It is my hope and prayer that every Minnesotan will join me in showing their respect and appreciation for these heroes as they continued to serve us at home and around the world."

Governor Tim Pawlenty
Governor Pawlenty meets troops in Afghanistan
March 9, 2007

State and VSO Points of Contact

Minnesota Department of Veterans Affairs Mailing Address: 20 West 12th Street, Room 206C St. Paul, Minnesota 55155-2006 Telephone: (651) 296-2562 Fax: (651) 296-3954 Email: clark.dyrud@state.mn.us Website: http://mdva.state.mn.us/	**AMVETS** 20 West 12th Street, Room 302 St. Paul, MN 55155 (651) 293-1212
VFW Department Service Officer VFW Claims Division Veterans of Foreign Wars of the U.S. Bishop Henry Whipple Federal Building 1 Federal Drive - Room 184 Fort Snelling, MN 55111-4007 Phone: 612 970-5669 Fax: 612 970-5404	**The American Legion** 20 W 12TH ST RM 300-A ST PAUL, MN 55155-2000 PHONE: 651-291-1800 PHONE: 866-259-9163 FAX: 651-291-1057 EMAIL: department@mnlegion.org WEB: http://www.mnlegion.org
DAV Department VARO & Insurance Center 1 Federal Dr., Rm. 192, Federal Bldg. Fort Snelling, MN 55111-4007 (612) 970-5665	**The Military Family Network** 866-205-2850 connections@eMilitary.org

Mississippi

Governor Statement of Support

"One of the most important industries in Mississippi produces only one product: freedom. I want to thank the thousands of National Guardsmen and other Mississippians on active duty overseas who pay for that freedom every day."

State of the State Address
Governor Haley Barbour

State and VSO Points of Contact

Mississippi State Veterans Affairs Board Mailing Address: P.O. Box 5947 Pearl, MS 39288-5947 Telephone: (601) 576-4850 Fax: (601) 576-4868 Email: grice@vab.state.ms.us Website:http://www.vab.state.ms.us/	**AMVETS** P.O. Box 7192 Jackson, MS 39282 (601) 355-6625 Fax: (601) 968-0056
VFW Department Service Officer 1600 East Woodrow Wilson Blvd. Jackson, MS 39216 Phone: 601 364-7180 Fax: 601 364-7226	**The American Legion** PO BOX 688 JACKSON, MS 39205 PHONE: 601-352-4986 FAX: 601-352-7181 EMAIL: legion27@aol.com
DAV Department VA Regional Office 1600 E. Woodrow Wilson Ave. Rm. 113 Jackson, MS 39216 (601) 364-7178	**The Military Family Network** 866-205-2850 connections@eMilitary.org

Missouri

OFFICE OF THE GOVERNOR
STATE OF MISSOURI
JEFFERSON CITY
65101

MATT BLUNT
GOVERNOR

STATE CAPITOL
ROOM 216
(573) 751-3222

To Active Duty Service Members and Families:

Having served on active duty I am aware of some of the sacrifices that those who serve in the Armed Forces make every day to protect our freedom and our nation. Thank you for agreeing to serve in the United States Armed Forces in order to keep our nation secure.

Please know how much your service and commitment to our nation is appreciated and revered by your fellow Missourians. Without the sacrifice and commitment of service men and women, Americans would neither enjoy the freedom nor the privileges that we do today.

I am proud to join with the Military Family Network in providing support for you and your families as you serve your fellow citizens. On behalf of all Missourians, please accept my gratitude and commitment to ensuring your needs are met while in Missouri.

Sincerely,

Matt Blunt

Missouri Veterans Commission	AMVETS
Mailing Address: 205 Jefferson Street 12th Floor Jefferson Building P.O. Drawer 147 Jefferson City, MO 65102 Telephone: 573-751-3779 and 1-866-VET-INFO Email: movets@mvc.dps.mo.gov Website:http://www.mvc.dps.mo.gov/ State_Ben.ht	7707 Lindbergh Drive Apt F St. Louis, MO 63143 (314) 645-4707
VFW Department Service Officer	The American Legion
400 S. 18th Street - Room 105 St. Louis, MO 63103 Phone: 314 552-9886 Fax: 314 231-2957	PO BOX 179 JEFFERSON CITY, MO 65102 PHONE: 573-893-2353 FAX: 573-893-2980 EMAIL: info@missourilegion.org WEB: http://www.missourilegion.org
DAV Department	The Military Family Network
VA Regional Office 400 South 18th Street St. Louis, MO 63103-2271 (314) 552-9883	866-205-2850 connections@eMilitary.org

Montana

OFFICE OF THE GOVERNOR
STATE OF MONTANA

BRIAN SCHWEITZER
GOVERNOR

JOHN BOHLINGER
LT. GOVERNOR

October 23, 2006

Luis Trevino
Military Family Network
100 Bridge Street #D
Second Floor
Hampton, Virginia 23669

Dear Luis,

Thank you very much for contacting me with information on the Military Family
Network. I commend you and your organization's efforts for taking such an
active role in supporting the troops of our country.

Although I have decided not to issue proclamations outside of unique or
extraordinary circumstances, I would like to take this opportunity to offer this
letter of support to help create awareness about programs and services available
to military service members and their families.

We are fortunate to live in a country of men and women who selflessly serve and
defend our country, and the State of Montana is proud of them. I appreciate the
services the Military Family Network provides and wish you continued success. I
am also very proud of Montana's Supporting Troops, a local organization of
volunteers whose founder was honored at the White House last week.

Please do not hesitate to contact me at anytime with updates, and your ideas for
the leadership of Montana. I look forward to hearing more from you.

Sincerely,

BRIAN SCHWEITZER
Governor

STATE CAPITOL • P.O. BOX 200801 • HELENA, MONTANA 59620-0801
TELEPHONE: 406-444-3111 • FAX: 406-444-5529 • WEBSITE: WWW.MT.GOV

State and VSO Points of Contact

Montana Division of Veteran Affairs Mailing Address: P.O. Box 4789 Fort Harrison, MT 59636-4789 Telephone: 324-3740 E-mail: lehall@mt.gov Website: http://dma.mt.gov/mvad/	**AMVETS** Post 3 225 Ryman Missoula, MT 59802 (406) 549-8907
VFW Department Service Officer VA Medical & Regional Office Center Box 52 Fort Harrison, MT 59636 Phone: 406 443-8757 Fax: 406 495-2009 2nd Fax: 406 495-2002	**The American Legion** PO BOX 6075 HELENA, MT 59604 PHONE: 406-324-3989 FAX: 406-324-3991 EMAIL: amlegmt@in-tch.com WEB: http://www.mtlegion.org
DAV Department VA Montana Healthcare System and Regional Office 1892 Williams Street, Bldg. 141, Rm. 109 P.O. Box 189 Fort Harrison, MT 59636-0189 (406) 443-8754	**The Military Family Network** 866-205-2850 connections@eMilitary.org

Nebraska

Nebraska Governor Statement of Support

"In times of war, we are easily reminded of the sacrifices individuals and their loved ones make in the name of freedom. Yet we rarely take the time to consider what those sacrifices mean to our communities, neighborhoods, friends and families. Regardless of where you live in our great state, a law enforcement agency, school, farm, ranch, fire department or business has been affected by our nation's military needs.

Many have lost friends, neighbors, employees or loved ones as part of Operation Enduring Freedom in Afghanistan and Operation Iraqi Freedom. Lt. Governor Rick Sheehy and I have attended the funerals of many Nebraskans who died for the American ideal. As a veteran myself, I care deeply about honoring our soldiers' commitments. They deserve our utmost respect.

We are at a point as a nation where we can honor several generations of heroes at once – from those who served in World War II, Korea or Vietnam through those who have served in Desert Storm, the Balkans and the war on terror. Each performed a service that we can never repay. However, it is also important to remember the friends and loved ones who did not go to war. Their sacrifices have been every bit as real as the soldiers, airmen and marines they love who were called to fight. They have held the home front together while fathers and mothers went to war. They, too, deserve our admiration.

If you know the family of a veteran, take a few moments to thank them for what their loved one is doing. If you know a neighbor who lost a loved one at war, make sure they know their loss meant something to you.

It is the knowledge of those lost friends, relatives and classmates that should remind us all of how blessed we are as a state and as a nation. That is why as neighbors, Nebraskans and Americans, we owe it to the generations to honor our fallen heroes and the heroes who made it home."

Veterans Day Message

State and VSO Points of Contact

Nebraska Department of Veterans Affairs	AMVETS
Mailing Address: 5631 S. 48 St. Lincoln, NE 68516-4103 Telephone: (402) 420-4021 Fax: (402) 471-7070 Website: http://www.vets.state.ne.us/	P.O. Box 4263 Lincoln, NE 68504 (402) 464-6591 or (402) 464-0674 Fax: (402) 464-0675
VFW Department Service Officer 5631 South 48th Street Lincoln, NE 68516 Phone: 402 420-4021/4023 Fax: 402 471-7070	**The American Legion** PO BOX 5205 LINCOLN, NE 68505 PHONE: 402-464-6338 FAX: 402-464-6330 EMAIL: nebraska@legion.org WEB: http://www.ne.legion.org
DAV Department VA Regional Office 5631 South 48th Street Lincoln, NE 68516 (402) 420-4025	**The Military Family Network** 866-205-2850 connections@eMilitary.org

Nevada

OFFICE OF THE GOVERNOR

KENNY C. GUINN
Governor

June 12, 2006

Dear Nevada Service Members and Families:

It is with great pleasure that I forward the thanks and respect of a grateful state and nation for the sacrifices you make every day in helping to make the United States and the world a safer place for our families. As Governor and as Commander-in-Chief of Nevada's National Guard, it is a privilege to share with our regular and National Guard troops from the Silver State the support and pride we have for your efforts to make the world more secure.

In a life full of diverse experiences, a trip I made in to the Middle East in March 2006 to visit our troops in Afghanistan, Iraq, and Kuwait is one of the greatest experiences on my life. I will never forget the opportunity to see firsthand your efforts to bring democracy to a people starving for freedom. It was truly an honor to meet our brave men and women serving in the military.

I also want to commend the families of our brave military personnel serving around the world, whose loved ones represent the best America has to offer. I know you are proud of their efforts, and I want to assure you we are all grateful for their and your many sacrifices as well.

Our sincere hope is that the *Your Military Family Network* publication will serve as a useful tool in determining State of Nevada resources available to assist you in determining the best course of action for you as a valued service member.

Again, thank you for your many sacrifices in protecting our freedoms at home. Your courage and devotion to duty are very much appreciated.

Sincerely,

KENNY C. GUINN
Governor

101 N. CARSON STREET • CARSON CITY, NEVADA 89701 • TELEPHONE: (775) 684-5670 • FAX: (775) 684-5683
555 E. WASHINGTON AVENUE, SUITE 5100 • LAS VEGAS, NEVADA 89101 • TELEPHONE: (702) 486-2500 • FAX: (702) 486-2505

State and VSO Points of Contact

Nevada Office of Veteran Services Mailing Address: 1201 Terminal Way, Room 215 Reno, NV 89502 Telephone: (775) 688-1653 Fax: (775) 688-1656 Website: http://veterans.nv.gov/	**AMVETS** Post 2 (775) 727-7045
VFW Department Service Officer 1201 Terminal Way, Room 106 Reno, NV 89502 Phone: 775 322-1117 Fax: 775 322-4042	**The American Legion** 737 VETERANS MEMORIAL DR LAS VEGAS, NV 89101 PHONE: 702-382-2353 FAX: 702-598-4941 EMAIL: taldon737@aol.com WEB: http://www.taldon.org
DAV Department VA Regional Office 1201 Terminal Way Reno, NV 89502 (775) 784-5239	**The Military Family Network** 866-205-2850 connections@eMilitary.org

New Hampshire

STATE OF NEW HAMPSHIRE
OFFICE OF THE GOVERNOR

June 2, 2006

Dear service members and families,

On behalf of the people of New Hampshire, I want to say thank you – for your service, your courage and your sacrifice. I also want to thank the families who have sacrificed so that you could serve. We all owe you a large debt of gratitude.

You have been there for us, and it is our responsibility to be there for you. In New Hampshire, we are working hard to honor our military community and to ensure that the members of our military receive the support they and their families need.

By providing this list of resources, the Military Family Network helps military families build relationships with the state and local community. New Hampshire is home to many organizations and businesses that reach out to the military community, and these ties help strengthen our state and our nation.

Thank you again for all that you are doing to protect your homes, your communities and our nation.

Sincerely,

John H. Lynch

State and VSO Points of Contact

New Hampshire State Veterans Council Mailing Address: 275 Chestnut Street Room 517 Manchester, NH 03103-2411 Telephone: (603) 624-9230 NH Toll Free 1-800-622-9230 Fax: (603) 624-9236 Email: mailto:mary.morin@vba.va.gov Website: http://www.nh.gov/nhveterans/ bene.html	AMVETS Post 12 (207) 934-7086
VFW Department Service Officer Norris Cotton Federal Building 275 Chestnut Street Manchester, NH 03101 Phone: 603 222-5780 Fax: 603 222-5783	The American Legion STATE HOUSE ANNEX 25 CAPITOL ST RM 431 CONCORD, NH 03301-6312 PHONE: 603-271-2211 FAX: 603-271-5352 EMAIL:adjutantnh@amlegion.state. nh.us WEB: http://www.nhlegion.org
DAV Department Disabled American Veterans VARO-Norris Cotton Fed. Bldg. 275 Chestnut St., Rm. 319 Manchester, NH 03101 (603) 222-5788	The Military Family Network 866-205-2850 connections@eMilitary.org

New Jersey

STATE OF NEW JERSEY
OFFICE OF THE GOVERNOR
P.O. BOX 001
TRENTON
08625
(609) 292-6000

JON S. CORZINE
GOVERNOR

October 27, 2006

Dear Friends,

It is my pleasure to extend warm greetings to The Military Family Network and express
the deepest gratitude to you for all the sacrifices you make to ensure the safety and
freedom of people throughout the nation.

I commend The Military Family Network for their hard work and dedication to
connecting our military families with the best in their communities. By creating a greater
sense of community for our military families you provide better access to programs and
services that make the lives of these selfless individuals easier. Through this more
effective method of communication, we are better able to honor and support our military
community.

Best wishes for continued success in the future. It is only through the concern and
commitment of individuals such as yourselves that we may hope to build a new and
brighter future for all residents of New Jersey.

Sincerely,

JON S. CORZINE

State and VSO Points of Contact

New Jersey Department of Military and Veteran Affairs Mailing Address: P.O. Box 340 Trenton, NJ 08625-0340 Telephone: 1-888-8NJ-VETS Website: http://www.nj.gov/military/	AMVETS 459 Ridge Road Lyndhurst, NJ 90701 (201) 460-8564 or (201) 933-0400 Fax: (201) 933-9234
VFW Department Service Officer 20 Washington Place Newark, NJ 07102 Phone: 973 297-3226 Fax: 973 623-1244	The American Legion 135 W HANOVER ST TRENTON, NJ 08618 PHONE: 609-695-5418 FAX: 609-394-1532 EMAIL: adjutant@njamericanlegion.org WEB: http://www.njamericanlegion.org
DAV Department VA Regional Office 20 Washington Place Newark, NJ 07102 (973) 297-3378	The Military Family Network 866-205-2850 connections@eMilitary.org

New Mexico

State of New Mexico
Office of the Governor

Bill Richardson
Governor

A Message from Governor Bill Richardson

As Governor of New Mexico, it is my privilege to extend to all our service members the greetings and deep appreciation of a grateful state. We honor your commitment, your sacrifice and your courageous service to our nation. We also recognize the sacrifices of your devoted families, whose steadfast support allows you to serve.

When it comes to our military members and their families, words are not enough; we must act. I am proud of the actions New Mexico has taken to honor our military community and ensure that they receive the support they deserve. The Military Family Network provides an excellent resource for military families to get in touch with the New Mexico businesses and organizations that contribute to these efforts.

On behalf of all New Mexicans, welcome and please accept my heartfelt thanks for all that you do to protect our nation and preserve our freedom.

With warmest regards,

Bill Richardson

Bill Richardson
Governor of New Mexico

State Capitol • Room 400 • Santa Fe, New Mexico 87501 • 505-476-2200 • www.governor.state.nm.us

State and VSO Points of Contact

New Mexico Dept. of Veterans Services	AMVETS
Mailing Address:P.O. Box 2324 Santa Fe, NM 87504-2324 Telephone: (505) 827-6300 1-866 433-VETS (8387) Fax: (505) 827-6372 Email: joe.lucero@state.nm.us Website:http://www.dvs.state.nm.us/ben-efits.html	P.O. Box 259 Los Ojos, NM 87551 (505) 588-7414 Email: acasias@wildblue.com www.amvets-newmexico.org
VFW Department Service Officer	The American Legion
500 Gold Avenue, S.W., Suite 3009 Albuquerque, NM 87102 Phone: 505 346-4881 Fax: 505 346-4880	1215 MOUNTAIN RD NE ALBUQUERQUE, NM 87102-2716 PHONE: 505-247-0400 FAX: 505-247-0478 EMAIL: legionnm@osogrande.com
DAV Department	The Military Family Network
VA Regional Office 500 Gold Avenue, SW, Rm. 3508 Albuquerque, NM 87102 (505) 346-4864	866-205-2850 connections@eMilitary.org

New York

Governor Statement of Support

"Let us begin by recognizing all of the soldiers from New York who are serving in the U.S. armed forces around the world...We must also acknowledge those who protect us here at home...our husbands and the soldiers next to you represent the very best New York has to offer. On behalf of all New Yorkers, thank you for your sacrifice and your service."

New York
State of the State Address 2007
Governor Eliot Spitzer

State and VSO Points of Contact

New York Division of Veterans Affairs	AMVETS
Mailing Address: #5 Empire State Plaza, Suite 2836 Albany, NY 12223-1551 Telephone: (518) 474-7606 Email: info@veterans.state.ny.us Website:http://www.veterans.state.ny.us/	43 Mona Court Depew, NY 14043 (716) 684-3031 Fax: (716) 684-3211 amnyed@localnet.com www.amvets-ny.us
VFW Department Service Officer 245 West Houston Street - Room 207 New York, NY 10014-4805 Phone: 212 807-3164 Fax: 212 807-4023	**The American Legion** 112 STATE ST STE 1300 ALBANY, NY 12207-2015 PHONE: 518-463-2215 FAX: 518-427-8443 EMAIL: info@nylegion.org WEB: http://www.ny.legion.org
DAV Department VA Regional Office 245 West Houston St., Rm. 204 New York, NY 10014 (212) 807-3157	**The Military Family Network** 866-205-2850 connections@eMilitary.org

North Carolina

Governor Statement of Support

"As brave men and women depart over seas, risking their lives for American freedom, we here at home must do our part to support them and the families they are leaving behind. We remember that we live in freedom because of the contributions and sacrifices made by those who serve in the Armed Forces of the United States. Many of you have asked how you can help support for our troops and the families they have left behind. This website will give you that opportunity. I am proud that North Carolina is the most military-friendly state in America."

Governor Mike Easley
Statement of Support for Military Families

State and VSO Points of Contact

North Carolina Division of Veterans Affairs Mailing Address: 1315 Mail Service Raleigh, NC 27699-1315; Telephone: (336) 725-8781 Email:charlie.smith@ncmail.net Website: http://www.doa.state.nc.us/vets/va.htm	**AMVETS** 1993 Welcome-Bethesda Rd Lexington, NC 27295 (336) 731-4359 www.amvetsnc.org
VFW Department Service Officer VA Regional Office 251 North Main Street Winston-Salem, NC 27155 Phone: 336 631-5457 Fax: 336 714-0901	**The American Legion** PO BOX 26657 RALEIGH, NC 27611-6657 PHONE: 919-832-7506 FAX: 919-832-6428 EMAIL: nclegion@nc.rr.com WEB: http://nclegion.org/index.html
DAV Department VA Regional Ofc. Federal Bldg 251 North Main St., Rm. 115 Winston-Salem, NC 27102 (336) 631-5481	**The Military Family Network** 866-205-2850 connections@eMilitary.org

North Dakota

Governor Statement of Suport

"…I would like to take a moment to recognize and honor the brave men and women serving in Afghanistan, Iraq and around the world, and all the veterans who have served throughout the history of this great country. Due to their sacrifice, we enjoy unmatched freedom and opportunity. So many have left loved ones, jobs, and school to protect our way of life. Some have come home wounded, showing great courage and dignity. Others have made the ultimate sacrifice, and we will never forget their valor and their service."

Governor John Hoeven
Governor of the State of North Dakota
January 3, 2007
State of the State Address

State and VSO Points of Contact

North Dakota Office of Veteran Affairs	AMVETS
Mailing Address: 1411 32nd Street S P. O. Box 9003 Fargo, ND 58106-9003 Telephone:701.239.7165 or 866.634.8387 toll-free Fax: 701.239.7166 Website: http://www.nd.gov/veterans/	3253 17th Avenue Southwest #202 Fargo, ND 58103 (701) 293-0901 www.tristateveterans.com/ndamvets/
VFW Department Service Officer VAM&ROC 2101 North Elm Street - Suite 205 Fargo, ND 58102 Phone: 701 451-4635 Fax: 701 451-4670	**The American Legion** PO BOX 2666 FARGO, ND 58108-2666 PHONE: 701-293-3120 FAX: 701-293-9951 EMAIL: adjutant@ndlegion.org WEB: http://www.ndlegion.org
DAV Department Disabled American Veterans VA Regional Office 2101 North Elm, Rm. 206 Fargo, ND 58102 (701) 451-4636	**The Military Family Network** 866-205-2850 connections@eMilitary.org

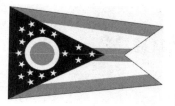

Ohio

Governor Statement of Support

"Ohio has a proud history of its sons and daughters serving in our nation's armed forces. In fact, Ohio is home to over 1 million veterans and tens of thousands more who are serving today. Over 50% of Ohio's National Guard members have answered the call to serve in Iraq and Afghanistan, as well as recent national disasters such as Hurricane Katrina. It is these men and women that have sacrificed for us all. And it is these men and women who deserve a Governor to stand with them and stand for them, recognizing their service and fulfilling the promises made by a grateful nation and a grateful state.

I am proud of my record in support of those who have worn the uniform and those who wear the uniform on our behalf today. As Governor one of my highest priorities will be to make Ohio known for its commitment to its past and present military community."

Governor Ted Strickland

Making Ohio a Place that Our Past and Present Military Want to Call Home

State and VSO Points of Contact

Ohio Office of Veterans' Affairs Mailing Address: 77 South High Street Columbus, OH 43215 Telephone: 614-644-0898 Website: URL: http://www.veteransaffairs.ohio.gov	**AMVETS** 1395 East Dublin Grandville Road Suite 222 Columbus, OH 43229 (614) 431-6990 or (800) 642-6838 Fax: (614) 431-6991
VFW Department Service Officer Federal Building 1240 East 9th Street, Room 1043 Cleveland, OH 44199 Phone: 216 522-3510/3511 Fax: 216 522-7335	**The American Legion** PO BOX 8007 DELAWARE, OH 43015-8007 PHONE: 740-362-7478 FAX: 740-362-1429 EMAIL: legion@ohiolegion.com WEB: http://www.ohiolegion.com
DAV Department Disabled American Veterans VA Regional Office 1240 E. 9th St., Rm. 1015 Cleveland, OH 44199 (216) 5224507	**The Military Family Network** 866-205-2850 connections@eMilitary.org

Oklahoma

Governor Statement of Support

"In the past, Oklahoma's men and women have served with honor, valor and distinction when called to their country's service. Some 370,000 from across our state have earned this badge of courage by serving our nation in times of conflict. Perhaps more than any other state, Oklahoma has the reputation of caring well for our veterans. We are proud of our veterans centers, including the newest – a world-class facility under construction in Lawton which I toured last week. We will open that center as planned this summer.

Let's also take a moment to salute our men and women serving their country today. As they serve, we will support them and their families, and we'll renew our promise of care in the future. Nothing we can say will offer more assurance of keeping that pledge than our actions toward those who have already made that sacrifice. As Governor, I intend to make sure we do not break that promise."

Governor Brad Henry
Oklahoma State of the State Address

State and VSO Points of Contact

Oklahoma Department of Veterans Affairs Mailing Address: 2311 N. Central Oklahoma City, OK 73105 P.O. Box 53067 Oklahoma City, OK 73152 Telephone: 405-521-3684 Fax: 405-521-6533 Email sclymer@odva.state.ok.us Website: http://www.odva.state.ok.us/	**AMVETS** 4704 Motif Manor, Suite 4 Lawton, OK 73505-4800 (580) 695-4695 or (580) 357-3312
VFW Department Service Officer VA Regional Office 125 South Main Street Muskogee, OK 74401 Phone: 918 781-7769 Fax: 918 686-6604	**The American Legion** PO BOX 53037 OKLAHOMA CITY, OK 73152 PHONE: 405-525-3511 FAX: 405-521-0178 EMAIL: oklalegion@sbcglobal.net WEB: http://www.oklegion.com
DAV Department VA Regional Office 125 S. Main St., Rm. 1B30 Muskogee, OK 74401 (918) 781-7764	**The Military Family Network** 866-205-2850 connections@eMilitary.org

Oregon

Theodore R. Kulongoski
Governor

July 18, 2006

Dear Military Family:

As a former Marine, I am dedicated to ensuring that our servicemen and women and their families are given the support they need before, during and after their service. My time in the military during the 1960s changed my life in more ways than I could have imagined. Through the military, I was able to attend college on the GI Bill, visit other parts of the world and experience things that have shaped my perspective on life. And most important, the Marines taught me the importance of duty, honor and courage.

I take great interest in the military and in their families because today there are thousands of young Americans serving in overseas, often in dangerous places. Daily, I meet and hear from families of Oregon service members. And to each one of them my message is the same: I believe in a clear mission, a winning strategy, shared sacrifice, an unchanging definition of victory – and above all – a very warm welcome home.

In my eyes, all veterans and men and women serving in the military are heroes. Each one deserves every laurel, honor, tribute and word of praise that this nation can give. It is our duty as Americans, and my duty as Governor of the great state of Oregon, to make sure that every soldier receives the medical care, education, job training and economic opportunity that they deserve and have earned.

I know that without the strong network of loving and supportive families, many of today's young servicemembers would not be the same people. Our troops need their families now more than every before and the families need the support of the American people now more than ever before.

Sincerely,

THEODORE R. KULONGOSKI
Governor

State and VSO Points of Contact

Oregon Department of Veterans' Affairs	AMVETS
Mailing Address: 700 Summer St. NE Salem, Oregon 97301-1285 Telephone: 503-373-2000 or 800-828-8801 Fax: 503-373-2362 Email: odva@odva.state.or.us Website: http://www.oregon.gov/ODVA/index.shtml	8944 North Clarendon Avenue Portland, Oregon 97203 (503) 777-6677 Fax: (503) 777-4107 garycarver@comcast.net
VFW Department Service Officer VA Regional Office 1220 Southwest 3rd Avenue – Room 1690 Portland, OR 97204 Phone: 503 412-4757 Fax: 503 412-4758	**The American Legion** PO BOX 1730 WILSONVILLE, OR 97070-1730 PHONE: 503-685-5006 FAX: 503-685-5008 EMAIL: orlegion@aol.com
DAV Department VA Regional Ofc. Federal Bldg 1220 SW Third Avenue Portland, OR 97204 (503) 412-4750	**The Military Family Network** 866-205-2850 connections@eMilitary.org

Pennsylvania

COMMONWEALTH OF PENNSYLVANIA
OFFICE OF THE GOVERNOR
HARRISBURG

THE GOVERNOR

GREETINGS:

It is my pleasure to join with the Military Family Network in honoring the selfless, courageous service your loved ones in the Armed Forces are providing to the people of Pennsylvania and the United States.

The history of our nation reflects the contributions and memories of brave men and women who, in both peace and war, have endeavored to preserve our freedom and the freedom of others. These heroes are willing to give their lives in defense of freedom, acting with honor and selflessness to protect the right of all people to live in a free and just world. Their struggles and loyalty have built our nation, and their sacrifice for liberty speaks volumes about who we are as Americans.

Those who have served in the Armed Forces uphold the same traditions and are inspired by the same sense of duty that has distinguished our commonwealth for centuries. We owe an immeasurable debt to these men and women, both past and present, who have sacrificed their safety and their lives in the protection of their fellow citizens and represented the nation with distinction.

On behalf of all 12.4 million Pennsylvanians, it is my honor to recognize the work your family members are doing to protect us and bring peace and freedom to others. May peace be with you as you await their safe return.

Edward G. Rendell

EDWARD G. RENDELL
Governor
July 2006

State and VSO Points of Contact

Pennsylvania Department of Military and Veterans Affairs Mailing Address Annville, PA 17003 Telephone 1-800-54 PA VET phone Email: bfoster@state.pa.us Website:http://sites.state.pa.us/PA_ Exec/Military_Affairs /va/benefits.htm	**AMVETS** Building 3-97 Fort Indiantown Gap Annville, PA 17003 (717) 865-9982 Fax: (717) 865-9440
VFW Department Service Officer 5000 Wissahickon Avenue (MAIL: VARO & Insurance Center) ATTN: VFW, P.O. Box 42938 Philadelphia, PA 19101-2938 Phone: 215 842-2000, Ext. 4213 215 381-3123 Fax: 215 381-3491	**The American Legion** PO BOX 2324 HARRISBURG, PA 17105 PHONE: 717-730-9100 FAX: 717-975-2836 EMAIL: hq@pa-legion.com WEB: http://www.pa-legion.com
DAV Department VAROIC, P.O. Box 42938 Wissahickon & Manheim Sts. Philadelphia, PA 19101-2938 (215) 381-3065	**The Military Family Network** 866-205-2850 connections@eMilitary.org

Rhode Island

On behalf of the State of Rhode Island, I extend my congratulations to the Military Family Network for its work on behalf of our men and women in the military. There is tremendous honor in serving our country, but such service also brings about great burdens to our soldiers and their families.

The Military Family Network helps to build bridges between the military and community services, private employers, government agencies, religious institutions, and schools. For military families that feel overwhelmed, the Military Family Network is there, providing an array of resources and support.

Here in Rhode Island, we are proud of our citizens who have volunteered to enlist in the military. As a state, we continue to do all that we can to support those Rhode Islanders who are serving our country.

In 2005, I signed two Executive Orders to ease the burdens for those members of the Rhode Island National Guard who have been mobilized for duty. With these orders, we are now providing support for Guard members, whether they want to start their own businesses or receive additional job training. We have also extended the deadlines for mobilized Guard members for filing their state income taxes and renewing their driver's licenses. I also introduced and signed legislation to reimburse mobilized Guard members for their life insurance premiums.

The brave men and women who serve in the military make great sacrifices to protect us. Organizations like the Military Family Network are ensuring that the soldiers and their families have the tools they need to balance their military and civilian lives. We must continue to do all that we can for them.

Sincerely,

Donald L. Carcieri
Governor

State and VSO Points of Contact

The Rhode Island Veterans Affairs Office Mailing Address: 480 Metacom Avenue Bristol, RI 02809 Telephone: (401) 253-8000 ext. 695 Website: http://www.dhs.state.ri.us/dhs/dvaoffic.htm	AMVETS 264 Parkview Drive Pawtucket, RI 02861 (401) 724-6181
VFW Department Service Officer 380 Westminster Street Providence, RI 02903 Phone: 401 223-3689/3690 Fax: 401 272-2580	The American Legion 1005 CHARLES ST NORTH PROVIDENCE, RI 02904 PHONE: 401-726-2126 FAX: 401-726-2464 EMAIL: tdequattro@aol.com WEB: http://www.ri.legion.org
DAV Department VA Regional Office 380 Westminster Mall Providence, RI 02903 (401) 223-3695	The Military Family Network 866-205-2850 connections@eMilitary.org

South Carolina

Governor Statement of Support

"The service and sacrifice of men and women in uniform should serve as a constant reminder to all of us that freedom is not free. Military families bear this cost, and know the price"

Governor Mark Sanford
South Carolina
State of the State Address

State and VSO Points of Contact

South Carolina Office of Veterans' Affairs Mailing Address: 1205 Pendleton Street, Suite 369 Columbia, South Carolina 29201 Telephone: (803) 734-0200 Fax :(803) 734-0197 Email: va@oepp.sc.gov Website: http://www.govoepp.state.sc.us/va/	**AMVETS** AMVETS Department of SC Post Office Box 2027 Walterboro, SC 29488-2027 (843) 542-2717 AMVETSDEPTOFSC@comcast.net
VFW Department Service Officer 1801 Assembly Street, Room 119 Columbia, SC 29201 Phone: 803 255-4304 Fax: 803 255-4303	**The American Legion** PO BOX 3309 IRMO, SC 29063 PHONE: 803-612-1171 FAX: 803-213-9902 EMAIL: dept@aldsc.org WEB: http://www.scarolinalegion.org
DAV Department VARO, Suite 129 1801 Assembly St. Columbia, SC 29201 (803) 255-4238	**The Military Family Network** 866-205-2850 connections@eMilitary.org

South Dakota

STATE OF SOUTH DAKOTA
M. MICHAEL ROUNDS, GOVERNOR

November 13, 2006

Luis Trevino, V.P. Media and Communications
The Military Family Network
100 Bridge Street, Suite D, 2nd Floor
Hampton, VA 23669

Dear Luis:

It is with great pride, admiration and respect that I write this letter to say thank you to all the
dedicated men and women serving in our armed forces, to our veterans and to families for their
sacrifices in serving this great state and nation.

The importance of our Armed Forces has never been more apparent, and I commend The
Military Family Network for providing a comprehensive guide to benefits and resources for our
military members and their families.

On behalf of a grateful state, please accept our heartfelt thanks for dedicated service that allows
us to enjoy the freedoms we have today.

Sincerely,

M. Michael Rounds

MMR:ls

STATE CAPITOL • 500 EAST CAPITOL • PIERRE, SOUTH DAKOTA 57501-5070 • 605-773-3212

State and VSO Points of Contact

South Dakota Division of Military and Veteran Affairs Mailing Address: 425 East Capitol Avenue c/o 500 East Capitol Avenue Pierre, SD 57501 Telephone: (605) 773-4981 Fax: (605) 773-5380 Email: andy.gerlach@state.sd.us Website: http://www.state.sd.us/applications/ MV91MVAInternetRewrite /default.asp	AMVETS Post 1 904 Edmunds St. Belle Fourche, SD 57717 (605) 723-2302
VFW Department Service Officer 2501 West 22nd Street P.O. Box 5046 Sioux Falls, SD 57117-5046 Phone: 605 333-6869 Fax: 605 333-5386	**The American Legion** PO BOX 67 WATERTOWN, SD 57201 PHONE: 605-886-3604 FAX: 605-886-2870 EMAIL: sdlegion@dailypost.com
DAV Department VA Regional Office P.O. Box 5046, 2501 W 22nd St. Sioux Falls, SD 57117 (605) 333-6896	**The Military Family Network** 866-205-2850 connections@eMilitary.org

Tennessee

STATE OF TENNESSEE

PHIL BREDESEN
GOVERNOR

October 25, 2006

The Military Family Network
100 Bridge Street
Hampton, Virginia 23669

Dear Friends:

As Governor of the State of Tennessee, it is my honor to thank the Military Family Network for their dedicated service to the men and women in our armed forces and to our country.

The Military Family Network is to be commended for their honorable efforts to enable the members of the United States Military to stay connected with their families. The network provides priceless services to our nation's troops that allow for an easier transition to civilian life.

Again, I wish the very best to all involved with this great organization and hope that all of you continue to find challenge and reward in the future.

Warmest regards,

Phil Bredesen

PB:wh

State Capitol, Nashville, Tennessee 37243-0001
Telephone No. (615) 741-2001

State and VSO Points of Contact

Tennessee Department of Veterans Affairs Mailing Address: 215 Eighth Avenue North Nashville, Tennessee 37243-1010 Telephone: 615-741-6663 Email: John.Keys@state.tn.us Website: http://state.tn.us/veteran/	AMVETS 844 South Germantown Road, Suite E Chattanooga, TN 37412 (423) 624-9835 Fax: (423) 624-9190
VFW Department Service Officer VA Regional Office 110 9th Avenue South, Room 310-A Nashville, TN 37203-3820 Phone: 615 741-1863 Fax: 615 741-6231 E-Mail: william.crawford@vba.va.gov	The American Legion 215 8TH AVE N NASHVILLE, TN 37203-3501 PHONE: 615-254-0568 FAX: 615-255-1551 EMAIL: tnamerle@bellsouth.net WEB: http://www.tennesseelegion.org
DAV Department VA Regional Office U.S. Court House, 110 9th Ave. S. Nashville, TN 37203 (615) 695-6384	The Military Family Network 866-205-2850 connections@eMilitary.org

Texas

Governor Statement of Support

"I want you to know that I support you 100 percent, as I do our commander in chief, our friend and our Texan George W. Bush. When it comes to the execution of the war on terror, I think it needs to be known that Texas stands fully behind ... the men and women in uniform who are day in and day out protecting my freedom and my children's freedom and the freedom of all Texans and Americans."

Texas Governor Rick Perry
Fort Hood Address

State and VSO Points of Contact

Texas Veterans Commission Mailing Address : PO Box 12277 Austin, TX 78711-2277 Phone: 1-800-252-VETS (8387) Fax: 512-475-2395 Email: info@tvc.state.tx.us Website: http://www.veterans.texason-line.com/	**AMVETS** 8008 Elam Road Dallas, TX 75217-4740 (214) 309-1980 (214) 309-0333 (Fax) amvetsdept@sbcglobal.net
VFW Department Service Officer One Veterans Plaza 701 Clay Street Waco, TX 76799 Phone: 254 299-9959 Fax: 254 299-9970	**The American Legion** 3401 ED BLUESTEIN BLVD AUSTIN, TX 78721 PHONE: 512-472-4138 FAX: 512-472-0603 EMAIL: txlegion@txlegion.org WEB: http://www.txlegion.org
DAV Department VA Regional Office One Veterans Plaza, 701 Clay St. Waco, TX 76799 (254) 299-9932	**The Military Family Network** 866-205-2850 connections@eMilitary.org

Utah

Office of the Governor

State of Utah

JON M. HUNTSMAN, JR.
Governor

GARY R. HERBERT
Lieutenant Governor

July 2006

Greetings!

It is my honor to provide a letter of support for the *Military Family Network*. The *Military Family Network* provides a list of resources and services to help families of our military personnel and devoted veterans make the best decisions possible. The program provides the most up-to-date information about deployment, education, community and civic programs, health care, tax services and much more. Results of these actions will help produce a more well-informed and empowered military community.

Thank you for your tremendous service.

Sincerely,

Jon M. Huntsman, Jr.
Governor

East Capitol Complex Building, Suite E220, Salt Lake City, Utah 84114

State and VSO Points of Contact

Utah Office of Veterans Affairs	The American Legion
Mailing Address: 550 Foothill Blvd. #206 Salt Lake City, UT 84108 Telephone: In-State (Toll Free- 800 894-9497) or -(801) 326-2372 Fax: (801) 326-2369 Email: tschow@utah.gov Website:http://www.ut.ngb.army.mil/veterans/	455 E 400 S STE 50 SALT LAKE CITY, UT 84111 PHONE: 801-539-1013 FAX: 801-521-9191 EMAIL: growley@utlegion.org WEB: http://www.utlegion.org
VFW Department Service Officer 550 Foothill Drive, Suite 203 PO Box 581900 Salt Lake City, UT 84158-1900 Phone: 801 326-2385 Fax: 801 326-2388	**The Military Family Network** 866-205-2850 connections@eMilitary.org
DAV Department VA Regional Office 550 Foothill Drive, Rm. G-3 Salt Lake City, UT 84113 (801) 326-2375	

Vermont

Governor Statement of Support

"It is perhaps the men and women of the Vermont National Guard who today best illustrate the strength and resilience of Vermont. We've been fortunate in the last few weeks to welcome home hundreds of our loved ones, our friends and our neighbors who have returned from their deployments—but there are still many for whom we pray, including a member of this General Assembly, Representative Doran Metzger.

We support our troops unconditionally; their personal courage and conviction inspire every Vermonter and strengthen our call to serve the greater good."

Vermont Governor James H. Douglas
State of the State Address

State and VSO Points of Contact

Vermont Office of Veterans Affairs Mailing Address: 118 State St., Montpelier, Vermont, 05620 Telephone: (802) 828-3379 Fax: (802) 828-5932 Email : laura.curtiss@state.vt.us Website: http://www.va.state.vt.us/	**The American Legion** PO BOX 396 MONTPELIER, VT 05601-0396 PHONE: 802-223-7131 FAX: 802-223-0318 EMAIL: alvthq@verizon.net
VFW Department Service Officer VA Medical & Regional Office Center 215 North Main Street White River Junction, VT 05009 Phone: 802 296-5168 Fax: 802 296-5198 E-Mail: leonard.doscinski@vba.va.gov	**The Military Family Network** 866-205-2850 connections@eMilitary.org
DAV Department VA Medical Center 215 North Main Street White River Junction., VT 05009 (802) 296-5167	

Virginia

COMMONWEALTH *of* VIRGINIA
Office of the Governor

Timothy M. Kaine
Governor

August 16, 2006

Dear Military Family Member:

The Commonwealth of Virginia has a long, diverse and proud military tradition. Virginia is home to military service members and families representing every branch of the armed forces. Our active duty service members and our citizen-soldiers in the Virginia National Guard and in the Reserves continually make tremendous sacrifices in service to the Commonwealth and nation. I fully support our military personnel and their families, and I fully support the dedicated individuals and organizations across the Commonwealth that work so diligently to provide them with benefits and resources. The Military Family Network is a valued partner in these efforts.

The Military Family Network helps bridge the gap between military and community life and we're better prepared today for the challenges that face the Commonwealth of Virginia because of the work provided by private organizations like this. With the continued deployment of our active and reserve forces in support of the Global War on Terrorism, the military community is increasingly aware of the support channels and resources available to them due in great part to the collaborative work and ability to deliver on needed services of groups like MFN. The efforts of these organizations aids in the readiness of our troops, families, and commonwealth as a whole.

MFN has partnered with local and state organizations to establish and promote unique information, resource, and referral services to the military community, thereby capturing the military family experience and allowing military families to share community knowledge with each other. We have a shared goal to create awareness about programs and services available to help support our active duty, guard, and, reserve service members and their families so that they are empowered with the information and resources they need to make the best possible choices for themselves and their families. These joint efforts have also helped our community partners and civic leaderships to better understand the needs and concerns of the members of the military community

The efforts of MFN complement those of the Virginia Citizen-Soldier Support Council, which was created to help the state address the needs of Virginian's Guard and Reserve members and their families.

Patrick Henry Building • 1111 East Broad Street • Richmond, Virginia 23219
(804) 786-2211 • TTY (800) 828-1120
www.governor.virginia.gov

State and VSO Points of Contact

Department of Veterans Services Office of the Commissioner Mailing Address 900 E. Main St. Richmond VA 23219 Telephone (804) 786-0286 Website: http://www.dvs.virginia.gov/statebenefits.htm	**AMVETS** 1621 Sheppard Avenue Norfolk, VA 23518 (757) 587-4818 Fax: (757) 451-2491 www.amvets-va.org
VFW Department Service Officer Poff Federal Building 270 Franklin Road, S.W., Room 503 Roanoke, VA 24011-2215 Phone: 540 857-7101 Fax: 540 857-6437 or 540 857-7573 E-Mail: fred.fralin@dvs.virginia.gov	**The American Legion** PO BOX 11025 RICHMOND, VA 23230 PHONE: 804-353-6606 FAX: 804-358-1940 EMAIL: eeccleston@valegion.org WEB: http://www.valegion.org
DAV Department VA Regional Office Federal Bldg. 210 Franklin Road SW, Rm. 505 Roanoke, VA 24011 (540) 857-2373	**The Military Family Network** 866-205-2850 connections@eMilitary.org

Washington

CHRISTINE O. GREGOIRE
Governor

STATE OF WASHINGTON
OFFICE OF THE GOVERNOR
P.O. Box 40002 • Olympia, Washington 98504-0002 • (360) 753-6780 • www.governor.wa.gov

Message from the Governor
of the state of Washington

Washington State has a long and proud tradition of supporting military personnel and their loved ones. Our communities are deeply appreciative of, and humbled by, the sacrifices our brave men and women in uniform willingly make to protect our country's cherished freedoms. We also are gratified that so many of those who have retired from active service choose to make Washington State their home.

Given its strategic location on the Pacific Rim and its reputation as a leader in aerospace, information technology, and other cutting edge fields, it is fitting that our state is the site of nine major military bases and over 100 smaller, related facilities. These installations make essential contributions to our national defense and are critically important to our state's economy. As governor and as the wife of a Vietnam veteran, I will do all that I can to further strengthen this positive relationship.

I commend The Military Family Network for their mission to support military personnel and their families by connecting them with their communities. Their efforts to compile a comprehensive guide to community resources and services that covers all 50 states is a wonderful way to help orient families who are new to an area, in the process of transitioning, or just in search of military-friendly businesses and organizations. I hope you will find Washington State's directory to be useful in meeting your needs.

Once again, I want to acknowledge members of the Armed Forces for their service and dedication. No one performs a higher or more important public service than those who protect freedom and democracy. Thank you for your selfless and courageous devotion to duty.

Sincerely,

Christine O. Gregoire

Christine O. Gregoire
Governor

State and VSO Points of Contact

WDVA, Service Center Mailing Address 1102 Quince Street SE PO Box 41155 Olympia, WA 98504-1155 Telephone 1-800-562-2308 or 360-725-2200 Email : richards@dva.wa.gov Website: http://www.dva.wa.gov/	AMVETS 5717 South Tyler Tacoma, WA 98409 (253) 471-0407 Fax: (253) 475-6715
VFW Department Service Officer 915 Second Avenue, Room 1040 Seattle, WA 98174 Phone: 206 220-6191 Fax: 206 220-6241 E-mail: vfwcfral@vba.va.gov	The American Legion PO BOX 3917 LACEY, WA 98509-3917 PHONE: 360-491-4373 FAX: 360-491-7442 EMAIL: americanlegion@wale-gion.org WEB: http://www.walegion.org
DAV Department Federal Bldg. 915 2nd Ave., Rm. 1040 Seattle, WA 98174 (206) 220-6225	The Military Family Network 866-205-2850 connections@eMilitary.org

West Virginia

State of West Virginia
Joe Manchin III
Governor

Office of the Governor
State Capitol
1900 Kanawha Blvd., East
Charleston, WV 25305

Telephone: (304) 558-2000
Toll Free: 1-888-438-2731
FAX: (304) 342-7025
www.wvgov.org

GREETINGS FROM THE GOVERNOR

As the Governor of West Virginia, the state with the fourth highest per capita population of military volunteers in the nation, I think that this book, *Your Military Family Network*, is a wonderful idea, because it lists all of the resources available in each state to the military community and their families.

I know in the Mountain State, we not only provide numerous resources and services to active military members and their families, but also to the over 184,000 veterans who reside here.

West Virginians are extremely patriotic citizens, who deeply appreciate the sacrifices made by our veterans and active military community to protect our freedom and way of life. For this reason, in our state we feel it is important to give back to these brave citizens by providing numerous resources that help bridge the gap between installation and community life.

Once again, this book, *Your Military Family Network*, has valuable information for the military community and their families. I hope you will find this publication helpful.

With warmest regards,

Joe Manchin III
Governor

State and VSO Points of Contact

Department of Veterans Affairs	AMVETS
MAILING ADDRESS:1321 PLAZA EAST, SUITE 101 CHARLESTON, WV 25301-1400 TELEPHONE:(304) 558-3661 FAX:(304) 558-3662 (call first) EMAIL: wvdva@state.wv.us WEBSITE: http://www.wvs.state.wv.us/va/programs.htm	Post 14 Disabled American Veterans Boulevard 1425 Chestnut Street Kenova, WV 25530 304-453-3086
VFW Department Service Officer 1321 Plaza East Suite 109 Charleston, WV 25301 Phone: 304 558-3661 Fax: 304 558-3662 E-Mail: vaochief@aol.com	**The American Legion** PO BOX 3191 CHARLESTON, WV 25332-3191 PHONE: 304-343-7591 FAX: 304-343-7592 EMAIL: wvlegion@suddenlinkmail.com WEB: http://wvlegion.org
DAV Department VA Regional Office 640 4th Avenue, Rm. 117 Huntington, WV 25701 (304) 399-9350	**The Military Family Network** 866-205-2850 connections@eMilitary.org

Wisconsin

Governor Statement of Support

"Wisconsin is a state with a proud military history and a tradition of honoring the remarkable men and women who have made great sacrifices to serve their country. On behalf of the people of Wisconsin, I want to thank you for your service.

Nearly 500,000 Wisconsin veterans have served our great country, and thousands more are proudly serving our nation in foreign lands today. We owe all of them a debt of gratitude that cannot be repaid. But what we can do is keep the promises we made and always honor their service and sacrifice.

Our veterans have earned our greatest respect and admiration, and deserve the best services and benefits that our nation and state can offer. Every day that we wake up in a free country is a day we must thank our veterans. It is important to remember those who sacrificed so much to ensure our freedoms. As Governor, I am committed to working every day to make sure the service of Wisconsin's veterans is not forgotten, and part of that that means making sure that our veterans program remains the very best in America. I am honored and proud to serve you as your Governor. Through your continued contributions, we can and will make Wisconsin an even better place to live, work, and raise a family."

Wisconsin Governor Jim Doyle
Letter to Veterans of Wisconsin

State and VSO Points of Contact

Wisconsin Department of Veterans Affairs Mailing Address: 30 W. Mifflin Street Madison, WI 53703 Telephone (608) 266-1311 or toll-free 1-800-WIS-VETS (947-8387) Email : wdvaweb@dva.state.wi.us Website: http://dva.state.wi.us/default.asp	**AMVETS** 750 North Lincoln Memorial Drive Milwaukee, WI 53202 (414) 273-5288 Fax: (414) 273-1270
VFW Department Service Officer VFW Department Service Officer VA Regional Office 5400 W National Ave., Rm. 166 WI 53214-3416 Phone: 414 902-5748 Fax: 414 902-9412	**The American Legion** 2930 AMERICAN LEGION DR PO BOX 388 PORTAGE, WI 53901-0388 PHONE: 608-745-1090 FAX: 608-745-0179 EMAIL: info@wilegion.org WEB: http://www.wilegion.org
DAV Department VARO, Room 162 5400 West National Avenue Milwaukee, WI 53214-3461 (414) 902-5736	**The Military Family Network** 866-205-2850 connections@eMilitary.org

Wyoming

Governor's Statement of Support

"Wyoming has extended the Military Members Compensation Committee; provided for the retention of wages, group health insurance, deferred compensation and accrued annual leave for soldiers placed on active duty; and worked on the Wyoming Military Assistance Trust Fund, which assists families of military families in times of need. It's important for the state of Wyoming to lead by example in terms of employer support for the Guard.

These are people who leave behind their families, their work and their normal lives in service to their country. "It's both a remarkable honor and responsibility to take them the message that Wyoming appreciates them and supports what they are doing."

Governor Dave Freudenthal
Freudenthal visits troops in Iraq
January 24, 2006

State and VSO Points of Contact

Wyoming Veterans Commission 5905 CY Ave Casper, WY 82604 Telephone: (307) 265-7372 Office 800-833-5987 Office (307)265-7392 Fax EMAIL: wvac@bresnan.net Website: http://www.wy.ngb.army.mil/ veterans.asp	**The Military Family Network** 866-205-2850 connections@eMilitary.org
VFW Department Service Officer VA Medical & Regional Office Center 2360 East Pershing Boulevard Cheyenne, WY 82001 Phone: 307 778-7340 Fax: 307 778-7549	**The American Legion** 1320 HUGUR AVE CHEYENNE, WY 82001 PHONE: 307-634-3035 FAX: 307-635-7093 EMAIL: wylegion@qwest.net
DAV Department Disabled American Veterans VA Medical Regional Ofc Ctr. 2360 E. Pershing Blvd. Cheyenne, WY 82001 (307) 433-2752	

Puerto Rico

State and VSO Points of Contact

MAILING ADDRESS: APARTADO 11737 FERNANDEZ JUNCOS STATION SAN JUAN, PR 00910-1737 MERCANTIL PLAZA BLDG FOURTH FLOOR, SUITE 4021 HATO REY, PR 00918-1625 TELEPHONE:(787) 758-5760 FAX:(787) 758-5788 EMAIL: luisramos@opv.gobierno.pr WEBSITE: http://www.nasdva.com/ puertorico.html	**DAV:** Chapter CSM J. Rodriquez #16, Baya-mon, PR PO Box 363604 San Juan, PR 00936 Ph: 787-749-9644 Fax: 787-781-0950
VFW Department Service Officer VFW Service Officer P.O. Box 33131 Veterans Plaza Station San Juan, PR 00933-3131 Phone: 787 772-7456 Fax: 787 772-7474 E-Mail: Jaime.domenech@va.gov	**The Military Family Network** 866-205-2850 connections@eMilitary.org

Virgin Islands

MAILING ADDRESS OFFICE OF VETERANS AFFAIRS 1013 ESTATE RICHMOND CHRISTIANSTED, ST CROIX VI 00820-4349 TELEPHONE:(340) 773-6663 FAX:(340) 692-9563 Email: mailto:justinova46@yahoo.com Website http://www.nasdva.com/usvir-ginislands.html	The Military Family Network 866-205-2850 connections@eMilitary.org

Education Benefits

G. I. Loans up to $95,000 at a low interest rate (6%).

Tuition free education at public schools and the University of the Virgin Islands for veterans who entered the armed forces while residing in the Virgin Islands.

Employment Benefits

Veterans 10-point preference (added to score) on local civil service careers examinations.
Administrative leave for Reserve Military Service.
Administrative leave for veterans for burial attendance.

Tax Benefits

Homestead Tax Exemption of $20,000 of the valuation of real property.

Other Benefits

Free out-patient medical care for service connected veterans at the Veterans Administration Community Base Clinic.

Rights of spouse and children

Decedent's estates and fiduciary relations (Veterans Guardianship).
Free burial plot in local cemeteries to veterans who are residents and entered the armed forces while residing in the Virgin Islands.
Up to $2,000 reimbursement to next of kin for burial expenses of local veterans who entered the armed forces while residing in the Virgin Islands.

Appendix 4

The Military Family Network's Neighbor of Choice Business Network

As you saw throughout these chapters, The Military Family Network raises awareness about valuable community resources. that are in the best interest of the military community. We firmly believe that everyone has something to offer and something to receive by connecting with one another through our network.

In the following section, you will meet some of the businesses and organizations in our Network. They want to meet you, too. As proud members of The Military Family Network's Neighbor of Choice Business Network—America's First Business Network for the Military Community—they support your mission, value your service to our country, and are committed to your success. They have pledged to put you first and have agreed to military friendly business practices including, in many cases, special product and service discounts for you and your family. By being there, when you need them most, and by delivering the quality you expect, these businesses and organizations want to earn your respect and trust.

The MFN Neighbor of Choice Business Network is for businesses that are military and family friendly, have quality products and services, and have demonstrated a sincere interest in having a reputable relationship with military families

The Military Family Network receives inquiries all of the time from military service members, veterans and their families asking for information that they can rely on to help them navigate their communities. We, in the military community, understand the power of experience; we survive on word-of-mouth referrals, resources and advice. And, we share that information and community knowledge between ourselves as members of our collective military family.

The businesses and organizations of the Neighbor of Choice Business Network have demonstrated loyalty and support.

So join us in welcoming them to our military family! Please take a moment to familiarize yourself with the following businesses and organizations. Perhaps you have a need right now that they can fill. If not, we trust that you will note their names and patronize them at a future date when it's appropriate for you and your family. We believe that these companies have tremendous value for you and we invite you to visit The Military Family Network Neighbor of Choice Business online at www.emilitary.org where you can find reliable, trustworthy businesses and great savings every day.

Spotlight on the Neighbor of Choice Business Network

Military community entertained from coast to coast with XM

XM Satellite Radio
1500 Eckington Place, NE
Washington DC 20002
202-380-4000
www.xmradio.com
XM Satellite Radio is America's #1 Satellite Radio service.

Message to the Military
Our military family listeners are some of our most ardent and passionate fans. We hear from them every day. They remind us that wherever they are stationed in the country and no matter how often they're required to move, XM is always available coast to coast with the music, sports, news, talk and comedy they've come to depend upon. Last year, XM was pleased to host some of the military bands and orchestras in our studios and HQ in Washington, DC. We were pleased to broadcast their performances across the country. They sounded great...everyone at the performances really enjoyed them...those guys and gals can play!

XM is very pleased to be a Military Family Neighbor of Choice Business. The Military Family Network provides XM with a unique opportunity to communicate directly with military families.

Minnesota Company helps military community with "Life Skills"

Life Skills Education
314 Washington Street
Northfield, MN 55057
507-645-2994
http://www.lifeskillsed.com

Message to the Military
Life Skills Education understands and respects the hard work all members of the military community do for our country every day. We consider it an honor to be a part of that mission support and we will do everything we can to help you help others.

GameZnFlix honored for its low prices and military friendly program

GameZnFlix Inc
PO Box 860209
Wahiawa, HI 96786
808-217-6822

Message to the Military

The GameZnFlix Military Appreciation Membership Offer is located online at www. gameznflix.com/military. Military community members may sign up immediately for their free 30-day movie offer. Special Military Membership packages start at 7.99/ month a full 20% less than other industry providers. GameZnFlix Salutes and thanks all of you that have and continue to serve this Nation's Calling!

GameZnFlix is proud to be a part of a network of businesses that pride themselves on giving back to those that have and continue to serve our great Nation. We will continue to reach out an establish partnerships with those organizations that possess the same values and standards we believe in. We are honored to be and member of the "Military Family Neighbor of Choice Businesses" and we are committed to providing America's Best with the very Best Service possible.

Military Travelers are appreciated at the Victory Inn

Victory Inn Bed and Breakfast
710 8th Street
Wamego, KS 66547
785-456-1393
785-456-1394 (fax)
www.victoryinnbb.com

Our message to the Military

Active duty military personnel enjoy a 50% discount on regular room rates. Just show us your military ID card and current duty station to receive this awesome discount as our way of saying thank you for your service to our country.

Jumpin' Joe's is proud of military families

Jumpin' Joe's Family Fun Center
1634 Sunflower On
Salina, KS 67401
785-827-9090
785-827-4272 (fax)
www.jumpinjoes.com

Message to the Military

Jumpin' Joe's is proud of our service men and woman, the sacrifices they make for our country and their families.

Arts Center thanks military for their service

The Charles H. Taylor Arts Center
4205 Victoria Blvd
Hampton, VA 23669
757-727-1490

757-727-1167 (fax)
www.HamptonArts.net
artscom@hampton.gov
Admission is Free

Message to the Military

Thank you for your service! We couldn't be such a great country without you! Being a member of The Military Family Network is important to us. The Military makes up a large part of the Hampton Roads population and it is important to recognize and reward them for their service.

Historic Theatre invites military community to explore the arts

The American Theatre

125 East Mellen St
Hampton, VA 23661
757.722.ARTS
www.HamptonArts.net
americantheatre@hampton.gov
Admission for performances varies

Message to the Military

Thank you for your service! We couldn't be such a great country without you!

Kansas Arts Center welcomes military families

Manhattan Arts Center

1520 Poyntz Ave
Manhattan, KS 66502
785-537-4420
www.manhattanarts.org

Message to the Military

We welcome newcomers to the Manhattan Community as participants, audience members and volunteers. We offer military discounts to make our programs more affordable and as a way of expressing our appreciation for those who serve in the military.

Ice Cream shop showcases appreciation for those who serve

Baskin Robbins

319 Southwind, Seth Child Commons
Manhattan, KS 66503
785-537-3136
785-537-0102 (fax)
www.baskinrobbins.com

Message to the Military

As a show of support, we offer a 10% discount on our products to military personnel and their families (just show us your id!). We would like to take this opportunity to let you know that we appreciate all that you do for our country and the sacrifices that you make in doing so. Being a family business in a very mobile community, we realize that word of mouth advertising is very important to all our businesses. New members of our community might not know what places are reputable, and we realize this is a great opportunity to showcase our businesses to the service personnel and their families.

Cinema Café treats military families to discounted family fun in Hampton Roads

Cinema Cafe
1220 Forham Drive
Hampton, VA 23464
757-578-3436
http://www.cinema-cafe.com/index.html

Message to the Military

We appreciate your service. We are proud to offer your family discounted admission and special military appreciation nights.

Military Friendly Realtors ensuring smooth moves for families coming to Kansas!
Barbara Torrey assists military families with relocation needs

Barbara Torrey Real Estate Co., Inc.
406 Lincoln
Wamego, KS 66547
785-456-6777
http://www.barbaratorreyrealestate.com/

Message to the Military

We want to help you and assist your military family with all your relocation needs.

Real Estate agent reaches out to help military families make Kansas home

Blanton Realty
Dick Walsh
200 Southwind Pl. Suite 120
Manhattan, KS 66503
785-532-8853
785-537-4027 (fax)
www.dickwalsh.com

Message to the Military

It's been my pleasure to serve those at Ft. Riley, and in particular the members of the 1st Infantry Division, for thirty years. I recognize that the Military Family Network is an important extension of that service, and I'm proud of my partnership with MFN. There is no greater good than the devotion and sacrifice of those who serve and protect the rights of others. Never forget.

Etherington and Co Realtors appreciates military families by finding great homes

Etherington & Co. Realtors
115 NW 3rd St.
Abilene, KS 67410
785 263 1216
785 263 1215 (fax)
etheringtonrealtors.com

Message to the Military
We welcome the opportunity to help anyone in the military with relocation needs, or general questions and concerns they might have after moving into the Abilene area. The Military Family Network gives us a meaningful way to assist military families with their housing needs--a small payback for their service to our Country.

Wamego Realty Team values soldiers and families

McPeak & Pugh Real Estate
411 Lincoln Avenue
Wamego, KS 66547
785-456-899
785-456-1877 (fax)
www.mcpeakpughrealestate.com

Message to the Military
We value the soldiers and families who are working hard for our security and we want to return service to them. Our agents all have military connections within our families and friends. We are excited about the opportunity to help get people and families into local housing as quickly and easily as possible.

Military Friendly car dealership helps families "get around"

Little Apple Toyota/Honda
2828 Amherst Ave.
Manhattan, KS 66502
785-539-7441
785-539-2161 (fax)
www.littleapplecars.com

Message to the Military
We appreciate our association with Fort Riley service members and look forward to serving the military community and their families for years to come. Our entire staff is proud to serve the Fort Riley military community. Several of our employees have served proudly in the Armed Forces.

Great Mileage Rides helps military families have fun

Great Mileage Rides, Inc.
2017 Ft. Riley Blvd.
Manhattan, KS 66502
785-539-1122
785-539-1998 (fax)

Message to our Military
Thanks for what you do for our country. We encourage our military men and women
to WORK HARD & PLAY HARD!!!

U-Pack delivers the best in moving to the military community

ABF U-Pack Moving
3801 Old Greenwood Rd
Fort Smith, AR 72903
800-355-1696
479-494-6925 (fax)
www.upack.com

Message to the Military
Thank you for serving and giving of yourself. We look forward to serving you, as well.
ABF U-Pack Moving takes pride in the fact that we stand among other respected businesses to provide products and services to the faithful men and women who protect
and serve our country.

Carepages keeps Military Community connected through the Military Family Network

TLContact, Inc.
4043 North Ravenswood Ave.
Suite 301
Chicago, IL 60613
866-981-4900
773-348-4964 (fax)
www.tlcontactinc.com or www.carepages.com

Message to the Military
When a loved one is deployed or wounded it can be difficult to stay in touch, keep others
informed and to maintain a central place of support and communication. MFN CarePages are an excellent way to keep your loved ones AND your community up-to-date!

Being a member of the Military Family Network means all branches of the military and the communities they serve can have access to the CarePages service, the
most trusted online community resource. TLContact, Inc. is proud to offer our CarePages service to the military community. CarePages are private, fully secure, personalized Web pages provided to you as a free service at the Military Family Network

Online Magazine keeps Military Families 'Budget Savvy'

Budget Savvy Magazine
516 Cleveland Street
Redwood City, CA 94062
650-299-1500
http://www.budgetsavvymag.com

Message to the Military
Since the inception of the war in Iraq, I have read too many sad stories of families who struggle to make ends meet as they are torn apart by spouses heading overseas. We approached The Military Family Network because we believe that Budget Savvy can help these families to manage their finances and get the most out of the money they have. Through both our online magazine and the targeted forums on the MFN website, we can address many of the service members concerns, while at the same time educating our other readers about the military family experience.

Local Cleaning Service helps Kansas military families pass inspection

Allstar Services Inc
2017 Fort Riley Blvd.
P.O. Box 1647
Manhattan, KS 66505
785-565-8735
785-539-1998 (fax)

Message to the Military
We appreciate all you do for us. Thank-you. LIVE-LOVE-ENJOY LIFE!!! We'll clean it up.

Author brings Life Stories from the Homefront to Encourage the Hearts of Every Woman
Patti Correa, Author
912 Moyer Road
Newport News, VA 23608
757-887-8495
www.patticorrea.com

Message to the Military
As a neighbor and military spouse I am able to jump right in and connect with other military families offering my experiences and words of encouragement to those experiencing the hardship of separation or deployment to war. Military Spouse, military mom and Author bringing military spouses and families together by sharing stories of strength and success, triumph and tribulation. Spotlighting the nobility and true strength of the military family. Together we achieve more and through sharing our stories and encouragement we grow in our ability to cope.

Downtown Dentist celebrated for keeping families in tip top condition

Downtown Dental Group
428 Houston Street
Manhattan, KS 66502
785-776-0097
785-776-0760 (fax)

Message to the Military
Being recognized as a Military Family Neighbor of Choice Business indicates our dental practice has the privilege of providing health care to the families of our fighting forces. As a civilian, it means we can do our part to support the military that serves the greatest country in the world.
Thank you for your service. We are proud.

Nichols Chiropractic thanks service members and families

Nichols Chiropractic
709 Commons Place
Manhattan, KS 66503
785-537-2211
785-537-2211 (fax)
www.nicholschiropractic.com

Message to the Military
Nichols Chiropractic is excited and honored to be part of the Military Family Neighbor of Choice Network and serve members of the United States Military and their families. We are proud to serve the service members and families that protect the freedoms we enjoy everyday.

New church welcomes families home

Bluemont Church
1021 Denison Ave.
Manhattan, KS 66502
785-537-8222
785-537-8222 (fax)
www.bluemontchurch.org

Message to the Military
We're so glad you're serving our country with the level of commitment, sacrifice, and service that you demonstrate every day. Thank you for being willing to move, to inconvenience your families, and to risk your lives for all of us. We're praying for you. We have a great deal of respect and appreciation for those who serve in the military, and for their families. It is our desire to do whatever we can to serve those who make such great and real sacrifices every day.

Business organization celebrates the military

Coliseum Central Business District

2021 Cunningham Drive, Suite 101
Hampton, VA 23666
757-826-6351
757-826-2784 (fax)
www.coliseumcentral.com

Message to the Military

Coliseum Central supports our armed service members and their families. Coliseum Central Business District is proud to be a member of the Military Family Network.

Online Shopping site helps military families find the best deals on the Internet

Shopping-Bargains.com

1004 N Jackson Street
Starkville, MS 39759
622-320-2028
http://www.shopping-bargains.com/

Message to the Military

We appreciate your service to our country! We feel that our free shipping and coupons savings are perfect for military families who want brand name savings and online shopping convenience. Stop by us first when you do your shopping and see if we have a coupon that will help you save at your favorite store! Stop by our military deals forum on MFN to check in for additional money saving deals just for you.
http://www.emilitary.org/forums/index.php?showforum=128

Arizona company celebrated for bringing "DollarDays" to military friendly businesses and non-profit organizations

Dollardays International

7575 E. Redfield Rd., Suite 129
Scottsdale, AZ 85260
877-837-9569
480-922-8155 (fax)
www.dollardays.com

Message to the Military

Our company appreciates your service and those organizations supporting the military community. Our partnership with The Military Family Network in the Charity Wish List Program helps all organizations supporting military families to find items for care packages at bulk rates and support donors with in-kind contributions shipped directly to your charities. Visit www.emilitary.dollardays.com for more information.

For Military Family Network supporters only, we are offering free distributorships. Please see our site at www.dollardays.com and contact Marc Joseph directly at 877-837-9569 ext 103 to set up your free distributorship. www.dollardays.com is proud to be part of The Military Family Network who support our brave military members and their families.

Pingo leads the way in great international calling card rates for military families

Pingo International Prepaid Calling Cards - iBasis, Inc.
20 Second Ave
Burlington, MA 01803
781-505-7500
http://www.pingo.com

Message to the Military
Being a Military Family Neighbor of Choice Business means that we can provide ongoing support to our troops, with a unique service that helps military families stay in touch with their soldiers, at a very low cost. Keep up the good work!

Wireless Phone Company keeps Kansas Military Families Connected

Westlink Communications
1106 East 27th. St., Suite 10
Hays, KS 67601
785-365-5004
785-365-5017 (fax)
www.westlinkcom.com

Message to the Military
Westlink Communications would like to sincerely thank all of our service members and their families for making our world a safer place and preserving our freedom that the men and women before them sacrificed their lives for. God Bless you all and may he hold you in his arm and protect and guide you, and God Bless America. We feel that it is another way to show our appreciation to the families as well as the service members for the sacrifices they make to preserve our freedom.

Terminex serves the military community in the Southeast with pride

Terminix
P.O.Box 2587
Fayetteville, NC 28302
1-800-753-2847 x 5507

Message to the Military
We cannot thank you enough for your sacrifices. Our debt of gratitude is beyond words. Be safe.

Baby retail store appreciates new military parents

Hey Baby!
322-C Southwind Rd
Manhattan, KS 66503
785-539-7000
www.heybabystore.com

Message to the Military
At Hey Baby, we appreciate all Military servicemen, women and their families. Thank you for your dedication and hard work. To make it easier on soldiers and families that are living away from their immediate family, we offer a gift registry that can be given to families across the country. We will soon have the ability to order products online which will better service our customers with family not in the area.

Kansas Beauty College helps military spouses with their careers

Crum's Beauty College
512 Poyntz Avenue
Manhattan, Kansas 66502
Karla Givens
Director of Admissions
785-776-4794
785-776-4482 (fax)
http://www.crumsbeautycollege.com

Message to the Military
Crum's Beauty College would like to extend a warm welcome to the military. Crum's Beauty College is a military friendly business that is devoted to the servicemen and their families. The college offers military discounts on services that are preformed by students under the supervision of licensed instructors. The staff at Crum's Beauty College appreciates the courage and determination of the military. Crum's Beauty College is celebrating 50 years of excellence in education. Come celebrate with us. Call today for additional information (785) 776-4794 or visit us at http://www.crumsbeautycollege.com.

Military Friendly Photography in the South East United States

Glamour Shots SE
Jacksonville, FL-Avenues Mall
10300 Southside Blvd, #1310
Jacksonville, FL 32256
904-519-0995
http://www.glamourshotsse.com

Message to the Military

As a retired member of our armed forces, I know how important it is to have high quality portraits of our loved ones, for those families who are at home and for our service men and women serving away from home.

To honor our Military forces in a difficult time in history, that shows our men and women to be the best trained, the best dedicated and in full support of our American tradition, and willing to sacrifice in order that our freedom and liberties stay protected. We offer all our military families the opportunity to have portraits taken at any of my Glamour Shots locations and take 10% off any purchase you make.

-Al Sciarrino, owner Glamour Shots SE

Glamour Shots Location: Regency Square Mall 1420 North Parham Road, #S140B Richmond, VA 23229 804-740-5470	Oglethorpe Mall 7804 Abercorn St. Savannah, GA 31406 912 -353-8585
Patrick Henry Mall 12300 Jefferson Avenue, #704A Newport News, VA 23666 757-249-0192	3254 Colonial Bel Air Mall Mobile, AL 36606 251-471-1160
Augusta Mall 3450 Wrightsboro Road, Suite #2201 Augusta, GA 30909 706-733-4000	

Military Friendly Employers

Many of the businesses in the Military Family Network have joined because they desire to be known as Preferred Employers for the military community. Membership allows these employers to recruit dedicated and highly trained transitioning and retired military members and highly qualified spouses. It is our duty to support these fine citizens who have dedicated their lives to serving our country. Companies in our Network go above and beyond. They are set apart from the rest because of their practice of hiring and supporting our nation's military and their family members.

The Military Family Network helps these employers market their opportunities both online and by referral during events and relationships with military employment managers on the installation. To learn more about becoming a part of the network and becoming known as a Preferred Employer by the military community, contact us at *info@eMilitary.org* or by calling 866-205-2850.

National
AFLA C

Aflac actively recruits transitioning service members from coast to coast. The following offices are committed to recruiting from our military community.

Aflac 11503 Jones Maltsberger Suite 184 San Antonio, TX 78216 210- 342-0297 210-342-0566 (fax **Aflac** 3738 S. 149th St. #109 Omaha, NE 68144 402-932-7255 402-932-7383 (fax) **Aflac** 3111 Harahay Ridge Manhattan, KS 66502 785-537-9123 **Aflac** 4310 6th Ave SE Lacey, WA 98503 360-705-8885 **Aflac** 4351 Jager Dr. NE Rio Rancho, NM 87144 505-867-3045 **Aflac** 341 West Tudor, Suite 209 Anchorage, AK 99503 907-563-8244	**Aflac** 4950 Brambleton Ave, Suite B Roanoke, VA 24018 540-725-8484 **Aflac** One Commerce Square Philadelphia, PA 19103 215-832-0090 **Aflac** 116 Meadow View Dr. Oxford, PA 19363 610-932-5598 **Aflac** 1600 Heritage Landing Saint Charles, MO 63303 636-939-9764 **Aflac** 22115 NW Imbrie Dr #155 Hillsboro, OR 97124 503-642-7648 **Aflac** 222 Us Hwy One, Suite 213 Tequesta, FL 33469 561-747-8793

Northrop Grumman
1 Hornet Way M/S K09760-N1
El Segundo, CA 90245
Phone: 310-335-3039
Website: http://www.careers.northropgrumman.com
For more information about career opportunities with Northrop Grumman visit us online at www.careers.northropgrumman.com
An equal opportunity employer M/F/D/V.
2006 Northrop Grumman Corporation.

| Grumman Northrop
4400 Sen. J Bennett Johnston Ave
Lake Charles, LA 70615

Northrop Grumman
600 Grumman Rd. West
Bethpage, NY 11714
516- 575-4690

Northrop Grumman
5000 US North #1, St
Augustine, FL 32085 | Northrop Grumman
2000 W Nasa Blvd
Melbourne, FL 32937
321-726-7845

Northrop Grumman
5100 River Rd.
Avondale, LA 70094
800-690-4862, ext. 5568 |

Local Employers set a shining example to military community

APAC Customer Services, Inc

11008 Warwick Blvd.

Newport News, VA 23601

1-800-407-4473

www.apaccustomerservices.greatjob.net of APAC enjoy competitive pay rates, excellent benefits and great career opportunities.

Glossary

This glossary provides useful terms and acronyms to assist you in understanding military language. These are routinely used in written and verbal communication and on The Military Family Network at www.emilitary.org. Some terms are specific to individual branches of service.

Term or Acronym	Definition
AAFES	Army & Air Force Exchange Service – the military agency that operates Army Post Exchanges (PX) and Air Force Base Exchanges (BX). PX and BX are "department store" like activities that can be used by eligible military personnel and their families.
AC	Active Component–active duty forces of the military.
ACS	Army Community Services–provides a range of services to military families.
AD	Active Duty–a period of time when a service member is working for and paid by the military on a full-time basis. Active duty may be for the purpose of training or mission tasks.
ADSW	Active Duty for Special Work.

ADT	Active Duty for Training.
AER	Army Emergency Relief–each service has a relief society. A private non-profit organization funded by donations providing emergency assistance to Army military members and families in need.
AFB	Air Force Base
AFN	American Forces Network–Network of TV and radio stations operated by AFRTS.
AFRTS	Armed Forces Radio and Television Service–A military activity that provides radio and television services to overseas commands.
AG	Adjutant General–a senior military official. The State Adjutant General is the most senior office in a state's National Guard. The Adjutant General of the Army is the Army's senior official for administrative activities.
AGR	Active Guard Reserve–National Guard and Reserve members who are on voluntary active duty providing full time support to National Guard, Reserve, and Active Component organizations for the purpose of organizing, administering, recruiting, instructing or training the Reserve Components.
AIT	Advanced Individual Training; in which soldiers learn a particular skill after they complete basic training.
Air Force Aid Society	A private non-profit organization funded by donations providing emergency assistance to military families in need.
Allotment	A specified amount of money the member designates to be paid to a particular place or person each month directly from his/her pay.
ANG	Air National Guard–State National Guard units supported by the Air Force who may be called to active duty to contribute to the mission of the US Air Force.
ARC	American Red Cross
Armory	A building serves as the headquarters for military reserve personnel; used for storing arms and military equipment.
ARNG	Army National Guard–State National Guard units supported by the Army who may be called to active duty to contribute to the mission of the US Army.
AT	Annual Training–A period of active duty attended by members of the Guard and Reserve for the purpose of training.

BAH	Basic Allowance for Housing–a financial allowance given to individuals on active duty when government quarters are not provided.
BAS	Basic Allowance for Subsistence–monthly food assistance provided to members who do not eat a military facilities.
BDU	Battle Dress Uniform–the camouflaged field uniform.
BT	Basic Training–initial entry military training also known as IET.
BX	Base Exchange–a "department store" like activity on an Air Force base that can be used by eligible military members and their dependents.
CACO	Casualty Assistance Calls Officer–also knows and CAO. This officer provides assistance to family members in case of the death of a military member.
Chain of Command	A military structure that defines responsibility for units. Every unit has a chain of command. Units on active duty have a chain of command that extends from their immediate commander to the President (Commander in Chief). National Guard units not on federal service, have a chain of command through the State Adjutant General to the Governor.
Change of Command	The Change of Command ceremony is a clear, legal and symbolic passing of the authority and responsibility from one commander to the next.
Chaplain	Amilitary member of the clergy.
Classified Information	Information or material that cannot be divulged to others without express permission and/or consent of competent authority.
CO	Commanding Officer–and officer officially appointed to command a unit.
COB	Close of Business–end of the official business day.
COLA	Cost of Living allowance–the amount of money paid monthly to compensate for the high cost of living. The amount authorized, if any, varies depending on the location.
Commander-in-Chief	The President of the United States–Commander in Chief of al military activities under federal control.

Commissary	The store where members and their families can purchase food products.
CONUS	Continental United States
DEERS	Defense Enrollment Eligibility Reporting System–the automated system that lists those enrolled and indicates their eligibility for military benefits.
DFAS	Defense Finance and Accounting Service–the federal military activity responsible for all civilian and military pay processing.
Dependent	A person for whom a member is legally and financially responsible—usually a spouse or child (also called family member)
Deployment	Temporary relocation of a military unit.
DOB	Date of Birth
DOR	Date of Rank–the date on which an individual was officially promoted to a specific grade
DSN	Defense Switched Network–the military telephone service.
EFMP	Exceptional Family Member Program–a program designed to provide support to military families who have members with handicaps or other special needs.
EM	Enlisted Member–a member of the military who is not an officer, warrant officer, or cadet.
Emergency Data Card	A form kept with official records that lists important information for quick reference in case of emergency. It includes names of relatives, addresses, and telephone numbers.
EO	Equal Opportunity
ESGR	Employer Support Guard and Reserve–a program designed to educate employers and encourage them to support their employees' service in the Guard and Reserve.
ETS	Expiration of Term of Service
Exchange	Military Department Store
FAC	Established in times of contingency call-up, mobilization and large scaled deployment to provide support and assistance to Guard and Reserve Members and their families.
FCP	Family Care Plan–soldiers provide written instructions and notarized documents for the care of their family members during separation (can include provisions for finances, wills, and guardianship).

FLO	Family Liaison Office.
FPD	Family Program Director for the Guard and Reserve
FRC	Family Readiness Center–similar to FAC. It's a family service program.
FRG	Family Readiness Group–an officially sanctioned organization of officer and enlisted personnel and their family members. This group provides information and acts as a support network for families and guard members during their association with the unit, especially during periods of separation, e.g., weekend drills, annual training, deployments, and/or mobilization.
FRO	Family Readiness Officer–the commander's staff officer assigned to work family related matters.
FY	Fiscal Year–a year running from 1 October to through the end of September of the following year. Fiscal years are used by congress and the military to budget and control funding for military activities.
GFAP	A standardized management tool that is used to create an information loop between the National Guard community and leadership, which provides a means of monitoring the process of issue gathering, submission, dispersion, and resolution.
GFTB	Education and training program for and about the National Guard Community. Program modules cover a wide variety of topics most often requested by families and National Guard leadership.
ID	Uniformed Services Identification Card–a distinct ID card identifying individuals as active duty, Reserve, Guard, or retired members authorizing them to receive uniformed services. ID cards are also issued to eligible dependents and other eligible individuals authorizing them to receive uniformed services benefits and privileges.
I&R	Information and Referral
ITO	Invitational Travel Order–a document authorizing travel by someone not under military authority. Often used to provide government-funded travel to family members.
JAG	Judge Advocate General–a military lawyer. Often used to identify the senior military legal advisor to a commander.
KIA	Killed in Action
Leave	Paid vacation days. A period of time when a service member is on paid vacation and not performing military duties.

LES	Leave and Earning Statement–a service member's pay slip for military pay. It includes information on gross pay, taxes and other deductions as well as leave earned and taken during a month.
MIA	Missing in Action–a term applied to individuals who cannot be located and whose status in unknown.
MGIB, MGI	Montgomery G.I. Bill–tuition assistance for service members
Mission	The primary task of the military organization.
Mobilization	The assembling of forces in preparation for deployment. The act of the President of the United States to bring members/units of the Guard ad Reserve to active duty for national emergencies.
MRE	Meals Ready to Eat–food packets that do not require refrigeration and can be used by service members who do not have access to prepared hot food.
MTF	Military Treatment Facility–A medical facility operated by military that may provide inpatient and/or ambulatory care to eligible TRICARE beneficiaries.
MWR	Morale, Welfare, and Recreation
NAF	Noncommissioned Officer–senior enlisted service members commonly referred to as sergeants.
NG	National Guard
NGB	National Guard Bureau–a joint bureau of the Department of the Army and Department of Air Force to serve as the channel of communication for the National Guard, Army National Guard, and Air National Guard between the Department of the Army, Department of Air Force, and the several states.
NMFA	National Military Family Association–a not-for-profit private association dedicated to improving the quality of life for military families.
OCONUS	Outside the Continental United States. The continental United States include all states except Hawaii and Alaska.
OIC	Officer in Charge–the individual managing or supervising an activity.
OSD	Office of Secretary of Defense–the office of the cabinet official responsible for national defense.
PAO	Public Affairs Officer–military officer responsible for responding to inquiries from the Press.
POA	Power of Attorney–a legal document that enables one person to sign documents or take actions on behalf of another person.

POC	Point of Contact–a person responsible for a program. The person you call when you need information or assistance.
POV	Privately Owned Vehicle–your family's car or truck.
Promotion	The advancement in grade and pay of members in recognition of their ability to perform at a higher level. The basic ceremony includes the reading of the official orders.
PT	Physical training–Army exercise program
PX	Post Exchange–a "department state" like activity on Army installations.
Quarters	Government–owned housing assigned to personnel or living spaces.
RC	Reserve Components—Reserve Components of the Armed Forces of the United States are: (a). the Army National Guard of the United States; (b). the Army Reserve; (c). the Naval Reserve; (d). the Marine Corps Reserve; (e). the Air National Guard of the United States; (f). the Air Force Reserve; (g). the Coast Guard Reserve
RDC	Rear Detachment Commander–an individual, typically an officer, designated to remain behind after a unit's departure and deployment and other unit members who did not move with unit.
Readiness	A measure of a unit's ability to accomplish its assigned mission. Factors that contribute to readiness are manning, training and equipment.
Reunion	A period of readjustment that follows a member's return from mobilization or training.
R&R	Rest & Relaxation or Return & Reunion.
SBP	Survivor Benefit Plan–a federal program designed to provide annuity to the spouse and/or dependents after a retired service member dies.
SGLI	Service Member's Group Life Insurance–an optional federal program designed to provide insurance coverage to eligible military service members.
SOP	Standard Operating Procedure–a set of fixed instructions for routine operations.
Sponsorship program	Military program in which volunteers greet and help members who have been assigned to a new duty station or unit.
SRP	Soldier Readiness Processing
SSN	Social Security Number

TAG	The Adjutant General
TDY/TAD	Temporary Duty–military duty or active duty away from the unit of assignment normally for a period of 139 days or less.
Telephone Tree	Also known as a telephone roster. It is a way of transmitting information to a larger group of people.
TRICARE	A health insurance program for eligible military members and their eligible dependents.
TSP	Thrift Saving Plan–It offers participants the same type of savings and tax benefits that many private corporations offer their employees under so-called "401(k) plans." Beginning on October 9, 2001, members of the uniformed services will be able to enroll in the TSP during a special 60-day enrollment period.
VA	Department of Veterans Affairs–the federal agency responsible for administering veterans' benefits and providing services to veteran.
WIC	Women, Infants, Children–a program of the Department of Agriculture providing nutrition and education.

About the Authors

Megan Turak is a founding member of The Military Family Network and its Executive Vice President. She is the daughter of a WWII veteran and her experience includes five years with the Department of Veterans Affairs where she received numerous awards for outstanding service. Turak has previously worked as a financial consultant in the world headquarters of Merrill Lynch in New York, Hilliard Lyons and PNC Financial Services. She received her Bachelor of Arts

degree from the University of Pittsburgh where she graduated with honors and is the author of several published articles providing instruction and guidance on life issues for the military community.

Darrell Shue is an Army veteran and founding member of The Military Family Network. He serves as Vice President of Web Administration, Development and Design. As founder and business owner of The Scribe Digital Design, Inc., Darrell has over ten years of experience running a successful web development and graphic design business. He has over twenty-years experience as a computer programming professional and "guru" for local and national organizations, as well as many years in health care and management. He resides in Savannah, Georgia, and is the proud father of a teenage daughter and a son currently serving in Iraq.